REBELS

Also by Peter de Rosa
Vicars of Christ: The Dark Side of the Papacy

REBELS

THE
IRISH RISING
OF
1916

PETER DE ROSA

DOUBLEDAY

NEW YORK   LONDON   TORONTO   SYDNEY   AUCKLAND

PUBLISHED BY DOUBLEDAY
a division of Bantam Doubleday Dell Publishing Group, Inc.
666 Fifth Avenue, New York, New York 10103

DOUBLEDAY and the portrayal of an anchor with a dolphin
are trademarks of Doubleday, a division of
Bantam Doubleday Dell Publishing Group, Inc.

Originally published in Great Britain by Bantam Press,
a division of Transworld Publishers Ltd.

Library of Congress Cataloging-in-Publication Data
de Rosa, Peter.
    Rebels: the Irish rising of 1916 / Peter de Rosa.
    1st ed.
        p.   cm.
    Includes index.
    1. Ireland—History—Sinn Fein Rebellion, 1916—
    Fiction.   I. Title.
PR6054.E754R4   1991   90-42607
823'.914—dc20   CIP
ISBN 0-385-26752-5

TO IRISH PEOPLE

EVERYWHERE

WITH PROFOUND RESPECT

NOTE TO THE READER

REBELS is not faction, still less is
it fiction. This is a true story, but so
extraordinary that it is only believable
because it happened.
With Talleyrand, I say, 'Je ne
blâme, ni n'approuve: je raconte,'
'I blame not, I approve not:
I merely tell a tale.'

'Why is the Rebellion so perennially fascinating? . . . There is nothing to equal it as a drama, except the first months of the Spanish Civil War. The spectacle of the genial Birrell (the Chief Secretary) and Sir Matthew Nathan, the hard-working, dedicated Jewish civil servant, in their fool's paradise, hamleted in Dublin Castle by their consciences and respect for legal procedure, pondering on their list of "suspects", is pure theatre.

'And then the tragic figures come on: Pearse, steeped in Celtic mythology, longing for martyrdom, dangerous as a one-man submarine; Connolly, the militant spokesman for international Marxism; Tom Clarke, the ex-prisoner; Plunkett, the dying strategist; the complicated Casement and his last ineffectual journey by submarine and rubber boat to the Tower – there is scope here for one more masterpiece.'
Cyril Connolly
'A Terrible Shambles',
The Sunday Times,
24 April 1966

'What in the world's history was ever more romantic than the gesture of a few young men who challenged England when she had a million of men in arms, and died, and won by dying?'
Stephen Gwynn
Dublin, Old and New

CONTENTS

LIST OF ILLUSTRATIONS

Eamonn Kent (*Private Collection*)
Cornelius Colbert (*Private Collection*)
Sean McDermott (*National Library of Ireland*)
James Connolly (*Private Collection*)

CHIEF CHARACTERS
(in alphabetical order)

ASQUITH, H. H., British Prime Minister.

BERNSTORFF, Count von, German Ambassador in Washington D.C.

BIRRELL, Augustine, Chief Secretary of Ireland.

BRUGHA, Cathal, second in command to Eamonn Kent.

CAPUCHIN FATHERS who attended the rebels in jail: Albert, Aloysius, Augustine, Columbus.

CARSON, Sir Edward, Dublin barrister and MP, leader of Loyalists in Ulster.

CASEMENT, Sir Roger, former British consular official.

CHILDERS, Erskine, yachtsman, supporter of Home Rule.

CHRISTENSEN, Adler, Norwegian sailor, friend to Casement.

CLARKE, Kattie, wife of Tom Clarke.

CLARKE, Tom, tobacconist, brains of the Irish Republican Brotherhood.

COLBERT, Cornelius, unit commander of Irish Volunteers.

CONNOLLY, James, Union boss, first in Belfast, then Dublin.

CRAIG, James, MP, chief organizer of Loyalists in Ulster.

DE VALERA, Eamon, maths teacher, Commandant of Irish Volunteers.

DALY, Edward (Ned), Commandant of Irish Volunteers.

DALY, John, Ned's uncle and former prison companion of Tom Clarke.

DEVOY, John, Head of Clan na Gael, the Irish-American Revolutionary Organization, in New York.

DILLON, John, Irish Nationalist MP.

FRENCH, General Sir John, British GOC Home Forces.

FRIEND, General L. B., British GOC in Ireland.

GRIFFITH, Arthur, journalist and founder of Sinn Fein.

HALL, Captain (later Admiral) Reginald, Chief of Admiralty Intelligence.

HEUSTON, Sean, unit commander of Irish Volunteers.

HOBSON, Bulmer, Irish Republican Brotherhood, secretary of Irish Volunteers.

KENT, Eamonn, Commandant of Irish Volunteers.

LOWE, General W. N. C., British Army Commander in Dublin.

MacBRIDE, John (Sean), fought as Major in Irish Brigade against British in Boer War.

McDERMOTT, Sean, former barman, chief organizer of Irish Republican Brotherhood.

MacDONAGH, Thomas, academic, Brigadier of Irish Volunteers.

MacNEILL, John (Eoin), academic, Chief of Staff of Irish Volunteers.

McGARRITY, Joseph, Irish-American from Philadelphia.

MALLIN, Michael, silk-weaver, Chief of Staff of Citizen Army.

MARKIEVICZ, Constance Countess, on staff of the Citizen Army.

MAXWELL, General Sir John Grenfell, sent to put down the rebellion.

MONTEITH, Robert, Irish Volunteer, sent to Berlin to assist Roger Casement.

NADOLNY, Captain on German General Staff.

NATHAN, Sir Matthew, Under-Secretary of Ireland.

NORWAY, Hamilton, Secretary of the Post Office in Dublin.

O'FARRELL, Elizabeth, chosen to hand over rebel surrender.

O'FLANAGAN, Father John, Curate of Pro-Cathedral, Dublin.

O'RAHILLY, Michael Joseph, a co-founder of Irish Volunteers.

PEARSE, Patrick, Headmaster of St Enda's, an Irish school.

PEARSE, Willie, Patrick's younger brother.

PLUNKETT, Joseph, strategist of Irish Volunteers.

PRICE, Major Ivor, Chief Intelligence Officer in the Castle.

REDMOND, John, Chairman of Irish Nationalists at Westminster.

SHEEHY-SKEFFINGTON, Francis, (alias Skeffy), pacifist.

SHEEHY-SKEFFINGTON, Hanna, Skeffy's wife, suffragette.

SPINDLER, Lieutenant Karl, skipper of the German arms boat.

STACK, Austin, leader of Irish Volunteers in Tralee.

THOMSON, Basil, Head of CID at Scotland Yard.

VANE, Major Sir Francis Fletcher, British officer sympathetic to Home Rule.

WIMBORNE, Lord Ivor, British Viceroy in Ireland.

ZIMMERMANN, Artur, German Under-Secretary at Foreign Office.

POBLACHT NA H EIREANN.
THE PROVISIONAL GOVERNMENT
OF THE
IRISH REPUBLIC
TO THE PEOPLE OF IRELAND.

IRISHMEN AND IRISHWOMEN : In the name of God and of the dead generations from which she receives her old tradition of nationhood, Ireland, through us, summons her children to her flag and strikes for her freedom.

Having organised and trained her manhood through her secret revolutionary organisation, the Irish Republican Brotherhood, and through her open military organisations, the Irish Volunteers and the Irish Citizen Army, having patiently perfected her discipline, having resolutely waited for the right moment to reveal itself, she now seizes that moment, and, supported by her exiled children in America and by gallant allies in Europe, but relying in the first on her own strength, she strikes in full confidence of victory.

We declare the right of the people of Ireland to the ownership of Ireland, and to the unfettered control of Irish destinies, to be sovereign and indefeasible. The long usurpation of that right by a foreign people and government has not extinguished the right, nor can it ever be extinguished except by the destruction of the Irish people. In every generation the Irish people have asserted their right to national freedom and sovereignty ; six times during the past three hundred years they have asserted it in arms. Standing on that fundamental right and again asserting it in arms in the face of the world, we hereby proclaim the Irish Republic as a Sovereign Independent State, and we pledge our lives and the lives of our comrades-in-arms to the cause of its freedom, of its welfare, and of its exaltation among the nations.

The Irish Republic is entitled to, and hereby claims, the allegiance of every Irishman and Irishwoman. The Republic guarantees religious and civil liberty, equal rights and equal opportunities to all its citizens, and declares its resolve to pursue the happiness and prosperity of the whole nation and of all its parts, cherishing all the children of the nation equally, and oblivious of the differences carefully fostered by an alien government, which have divided a minority from the majority in the past.

Until our arms have brought the opportune moment for the establishment of a permanent National Government, representative of the whole people of Ireland and elected by the suffrages of all her men and women, the Provisional Government, hereby constituted, will administer the civil and military affairs of the Republic in trust for the people.

We place the cause of the Irish Republic under the protection of the Most High God, Whose blessing we invoke upon our arms, and we pray that no one who serves that cause will dishonour it by cowardice, inhumanity, or rapine. In this supreme hour the Irish nation must, by its valour and discipline and by the readiness of its children to sacrifice themselves for the common good, prove itself worthy of the august destiny to which it is called.

Signed on Behalf of the Provisional Government,

THOMAS J. CLARKE,

SEAN Mac DIARMADA, THOMAS MacDONAGH,
P. H. PEARSE, EAMONN CEANNT,
JAMES CONNOLLY. JOSEPH PLUNKETT.

REBELS

MAY-DAY 1916:
'Shoot 'Em'

*'Ireland's history is something the
English should remember and the Irish
should forget.'*

Old Irish saying

At Kilmainham, in a palatial building on the western edge of Dublin, fifty-six-year-old General Sir John Grenfell Maxwell, Knight of the Order of the Bath, Companion of the Order of St Michael and St George, Commander of the Victorian Order and Distinguished Service Order, the new General Officer Commanding His Majesty's armed forces in Ireland, was coughing like a donkey on his first cigarette of the day.

In between respiratory explosions, he was feeling mighty pleased with himself. The rebellion was over.

As he shaved and dressed, still with his comforter in his mouth, he was relieved to have put a stop to this Irish nonsense in no time. That should do his career a power of good. Better still, the politicians had for once had the sense to give a soldier, namely himself, plenary powers to clean Ireland up.

With his newspaper under his arm, he went for breakfast to a room with arched windows that let in the mute gold of a May morning, a ceiling 30 feet high and panelled walls lined with life-sized portraits of former viceroys. Dead centre, on a long polished table, apart from his coffee pot, was only a silver salver with a preliminary report: 450 dead and 2,614 wounded. A sniff of contentment from his enormous nose rose with a muffled ripple-effect to the rafters. In London, Prime Minister Asquith and the Cabinet would think those casualties piffling compared with the massacres in Flanders and Gallipoli.

Military statistics? He ran a yellow finger down the list. Officers: 17 killed and 46 wounded. Other ranks: 99 killed, 322 wounded, and 9 missing. 'Poor buggers, brave chaps.'

Those responsible would be punished; by God, there would be more deaths in Dublin before he was finished.

One welcome sign of normality was the reappearance of the *Irish Times*, a three-day edition. The editorial read: 'The State has struck ... The surgeon's knife has been put to the corruption in the body of Ireland and its course must not be stayed until the whole malignant growth has been removed. The rapine and bloodshed of the past week must be punished with a severity which will make any repetition of them impossible for generations to come.'

A bit rhetorical for his taste but true, for all that. After pushing two cups of black coffee through his yellow hedge-like moustache, he lit up again before summoning his aides to his office. He wanted all potential trouble-makers rounded up.

3

'So get to it, gentlemen,' he whooped. 'If you need names, information, the Royal Irish Constabulary will provide it. They have a list of thousands.'

Slowly, Dublin was returning to normal. The main artery, Sackville (O'Connell) Street, with most of the buildings reduced to a heap of smouldering rubble, was thronged with sightseers, their handkerchiefs pressed to their mouths. Putrefying horses were being lifted and carted away. Shopkeepers were sweeping up debris from looted shops. A coal lorry was picking up the dead. Ambulances were threading their way through the wreckage. Cars carrying priests were going in all directions to minister to the sick and injured. Official cars went by with white-jacketed doctors in the passenger seats. Red Cross nurses in long white dresses and white caps were scurrying on foot or on bicycles.

A few older people were weeping under Nelson's Pillar. Outside the gutted General Post Office, the rebel HQ, some women, whose men were fighting in the British army, were wailing, 'How can we get our allowances now, after what them fecking rebels have done?' So far they had had a reasonably good war, chiefly in the pubs.

Down the street marched a company of British soldiers, commanded by Major Sir Francis Vane, a blimpish-looking officer in a battered peaked cap, with an eye for every pretty girl. Crowds rushed to the side of the road to cheer. But for these boys, all Irish, all loyal to the British Empire, the blood-letting would still be going on. 'Good old Munsters,' they called out.

No one doubted the rebels had lost and lost badly. On street corners, in public houses and the work-place, everyone felt they had humiliated the whole country. They had allied themselves with the Germans by asking them for arms, knowing Germans were slaughtering the Irish in khaki in trenches on the continent of Europe and treading under foot a gallant little Catholic country like Belgium. They had left children hungry, homeless and orphaned, and made the city centre a wasteland worse than France, God forgive them!

Women were bitterest. 'Them bastards,' they shrieked, tightening their black shawls around them, 'should be put up against a wall and shot.'

In a cell in Arbour Hill Detention Centre was Patrick Pearse, the tall Commander-in-Chief of the rebel army with the face of an altar boy. Confident he would be shot very soon, he began writing in a rush.

4

A letter to his mother gave his version of the rising.

> We are ready to die and we shall die cheerfully *and proudly*
> .... You must not grieve for all this. We have preserved
> Ireland's honour and our own. *Our deeds of last week are
> the most splendid things in Ireland's history.* People will
> say hard things of us now, *but we shall be remembered
> by posterity and blessed by unborn generations.* You too
> will be blessed because you were my mother.

In a postscript he added, 'I understand that the German expedition
which I was counting on actually set sail but was defeated by the
British.'

He sent a message to Connolly, the Union leader who had
commanded the Dublin forces in the rebellion, praying that, at
this supreme moment and in expectation of death, the glorious and
wounded leader might make his peace with God.

James Connolly was even then wondering why, when he had been
born in an Edinburgh slum, he was now lying under a splendid
chandelier in a State Room in Dublin Castle.

He had been wounded in the rising. Gangrene had set in from a
bullet wound in his left leg. In spite of morphine, pain made sleep
impossible.

He sent for a priest. Thin as a whip, benign beyond his years,
Father Aloysius, a Capuchin with twinkling eyes, strode through
the Gate of the Castle, now a Red Cross Hospital, up the Great
Staircase lined with armed men, into the room where the prisoner
was lying with his foot in a cradle.

Connolly, bluff and moustachioed, was never happy except when
arguing. He immediately launched into why he could not retract any
of his political beliefs.

'I tell you, Father, not only *can* a Catholic be a Marxist, he *ought*
to be. Did you ever read *The Didache*, one of the earliest Christian
tracts? "Share everything with your brother," it says. "Do not say,
'It is private property.' If you share everlasting things, you should
be even more willing to share things that do not last." '

The friar tugged his beard, trying to keep a straight face.

'Did I say something funny?'

'I am so sorry,' Father Aloysius smiled. 'It's just that I'm a son of
St Francis who never had a bean.' He paused before saying, without

5

a trace of mirth, 'Like St Francis, you have part of Our Blessed Lord's stigmata already. I've heard of your charity towards Christ's poor. So I have no problems sharing everlasting things with you.'

'You mean,' Connolly gasped, 'you will hear the confession of a Marxist?'

'I mean, my son, I will hear the confession of anyone who acknowledges he is a sinner. Besides,' – he patted him on the head – 'I think our Founder would have approved of you.'

At Kilmainham, Maxwell called in General Hutchinson, his Chief of Staff, and Prince Alexander of Battenberg, his ADC.

'I aim, gentlemen, to make sure that no word of rebellion is whispered in this queer country ever again. As to the ring-leaders,' a prodigious sniff, 'they have broken English law, English law will now break them.'

His ADC smirked at the witticism.

'The question of punishment,' Maxwell said.

'I'd like to see them hang,' his Chief of Staff said.

'Mustn't let sentimental considerations influence your judgement, Hutch.' Maxwell exhaled a pillar of cloud. 'That would create problems. In the first place, we'd have to bring a hangman over from England.'

'Odd that,' the ADC said.

'It is, Alex,' Maxwell returned, with a cough like a rifle report. 'Plenty of hangmen around here, I'm sure, but none with professional qualifications.'

'And I suppose, sir, bringing a hangman over,' Hutchinson said, 'would confuse the issue.'

'Correct. Bloody press would poke their noses in, buttonhole him before he gets here. Then there'd be the sickening paraphernalia of civilian lawyers spouting about due process.'

'When,' Hutchinson said, 'we have the names of the ring-leaders on that Proclamation thing—'

'Proclamation of a *Republic*,' Prince Alexander put in, with a boyish laugh.

'Right,' Hutchinson went on, 'we have that and the evidence of our officers who accepted the surrender.'

'Why risk world-wide publicity,' Maxwell said, 'and tedious court cases when the whole damn thing's cut and dried? It'd be like calling in an Oxford Mathematics professor to confirm that two and two make four.'

'Well, sir,' Hutchinson said, 'you have the powers to court-martial them.'

Maxwell nodded. 'That way, we avoid any blarney about a Republic, as if this were a political matter instead of a straightforward alliance of a bunch of crooks with the Huns.' He snapped his nicotined fingers. 'So much *easier* treating them as simple collaborators. Brief trial, swift verdict and' – he pointed a finger like a gun – 'bang!'

Prince Alexander said, 'Pity Roger Casement's in the Tower of London.'

'Yes,' wheezed Maxwell. 'Imagine. He came ashore in Tralee from a U-boat on Good Friday. An open and shut case of treachery. And what did that boneheaded Under-Secretary, Nathan, do but send him out of the country?'

'And now,' the Prince said, 'there'll be a big trial and money spent—'

'And a rope at the end of it,' Hutchinson said, unable to hide his glee.

'Yes,' Maxwell affirmed. 'If Casement had been left over here, I'd have dealt with him. No noise, no mess, just a nice clean finish in the dawn.'

Roger Casement, holder of the South African Medal, Commander of the Order of St Michael and St George, Knight of the Realm, was sitting slumped on the floor in a corner of his cell. Well over six feet tall, he seemed to have shrivelled. Unshaven, without a belt or tie or shoe-laces, he was still in the salt-stained suit in which he had been washed up on the shore of Tralee ten days before and it stank. Once as dark and handsome as any sitter for Van Dyke, he now had a gaunt face, black horseshoe eyes, and lips puckered like a withered flower.

A compassionate man, he had won world fame as a British consul. At the start of the century, he had investigated the Belgian King Leopold's Congo Free State. He found that natives who failed to bring in their rubber quota were killed or had their ears cut off or were driven into the forests to starve. Women and children were beaten with hippopotamus hide. He met Epondo, a fifteen-year-old whose left arm had been hacked off, and many other natives minus arms and legs.

His report changed things.

A few years later, he investigated the British-owned Amazon

Rubber Company. It was a repeat of his Congo experience. He came across an Indian girl, the mistress of an agent, who, when he found she had venereal disease, had flogged her. Then he had a native boy insert firebrands into the openings of her body.

Blazing with indignation, Casement wrote up his report which, after frustrating Foreign Office delays, the British published in 1912. His work earned him a knighthood.

Having defended distant races, Casement, his health broken, dedicated himself to the oppressed natives of his own country, Ireland. It was this that had led him to Germany to seek arms for a rebellion and, now, to imprisonment in the Tower of London.

He pulled a bent nail from firewood in the grate and tried to swallow it, but the nail was big and his throat dry. It fell out of his lacerated mouth like a tooth.

He pushed a lens out of his glasses, broke it on the flagstone and with a jagged piece sawed the veins in his left wrist. Into the running wound he rubbed a poisonous powder he had concealed in his jacket. He would not give the British the pleasure of hanging him.

In Kilmainham, Maxwell was having a final whiskey with his staff when an aide brought him in a file. 'Letters written by prisoner P. H. Pearse, sir.'

Maxwell skimmed through them and snorted, 'The sneaky bastard expects to become famous for murdering my boys in cold blood.' Then the postscript to Pearse's mother caught his eye. He read it out. 'Christ, gentlemen, he admits to treachery in a letter to his *mater*. Let's hope the other rebels are as stupid as this.'

Not far away, in Richmond Barracks, the rebel prisoners in A. Cell were settling down for the night.

Joe Plunkett, who had drawn up the strategy for the battle, was lying in a corner shivering, a frayed quilt under his head. He had not received a wound but he was, nonetheless, dying.

Sean McDermott was asleep on Tom Clarke's lap, sometimes crying, 'Fire, fire,' as he remembered the roof caving in on the GPO. These two, the first young, the other a sparrow-like patriarch, had planned the rebellion from the beginning.

In a neighbouring cell, curly-haired Thomas MacDonagh, Brigadier of the rebel army, was looking nostalgically at pictures of his beautiful wife, Muriel, and his little boy and girl.

*

Next day, Maxwell took a call from the President of the Court Martial.

General Blackadder reported their judgement on Pearse, Clarke and MacDonagh. Guilty. He had not liked doing that, they were fine chaps, but there was no doubt about their guilt. All the same, he wanted to shake their hands, especially Pearse's. He had made a damn fine speech before the Court.

Anticipating the usual week's delay before confirmation and sentencing, Blackadder said, 'We await your decision, sir.'

'Shoot 'em,' Maxwell said smoothly, putting the telephone down.

PART ONE

PREPARING FOR BATTLE
12 July 1914–20 March 1916

'Give us war in our time, O Lord.'
John Mitchel

On Sunday 12 July 1914, on a morning heavy with a golden-ochre mist, the *Gladiator*, a tug from Hamburg, headed for the Roetigen Lightship, at the mouth of the River Scheldt. On the bridge, the skipper, a burly, bearded and unblinking German, glanced at his watch. Ten o'clock. In a couple of hours, two yachts should arrive and rid him of his accursed cargo.

With Dover, England, twenty-five miles to the west, the tug hove to off the Belgian coast, using the mist to keep out of sight as it rocked in a gentle North Sea swell. At the rail stood an anxious young Irishman. His high forehead half-hidden by a tweed bucket-type hat, he kept peering ahead and telling the crew, mainly through gestures, that there would be no delay.

Minute succeeded minute and midday came. Neither of the expected yachts had engines; maybe they were far away, becalmed on that uncannily still sea. The Irishman, Darrell Figgis, was beginning to peck at his chiselled chestnut beard. From time to time, he smiled soothingly at the skipper.

In the afternoon, the clouds cleared and the mist turned silver. Figgis's apprehension grew. So far fortune had favoured him. The day before on the Elbe, he had even managed to bribe the pilot-cum-customs officer with cigars and a few big English notes to turn a blind eye to what was in the hold. Surely things were not going to turn sour now.

'Where,' Figgis muttered to himself, 'are those bloody yachts?'

In Belfast, in the north of Ireland, Protestants were on the streets for the anniversary of the Battle of the Boyne. On 12 July in 1690, King Billy, William III, the Sovereign imported from Holland, had defeated the Catholic King James II. That famous victory had guaranteed the supremacy of Orange over Green in Ulster.

The Twelfth was, by custom, the day when Protestants throughout the province remembered their heritage. It was a colourful day of drum-banging and fifing, of sticks twirled and tossed, of bright Orange Lodge banners held aloft, of bowler-hatted Lodge members with rolled-umbrellas and decorated sashes marching proudly through streets draped in Union Jacks and flags of the Red Hand of Ulster.

But for three years Protestant supremacy had been under threat. The British government was intent on giving Ireland, the whole of Ireland, Home Rule. If that happened, Dublin, by sheer force of numbers, would have the whip-hand. And Dublin was dominated

13

by a Catholic hierarchy. That, Ulster Protestants thought, would demolish their three-centuries-old tradition. But if it was to be war, they were armed, they were ready.

This was why sixty-year-old Sir Edward Carson, the most brilliant and best-paid lawyer of the day, a healthy hypochondriac, lean, with sleek black hair and Punch-like profile, was in Belfast. He had achieved fame through cases that made legal history. Most renowned was his cross-questioning of Oscar Wilde, his contemporary at Trinity College, the ancient university of Dublin. At first Wilde had run rings round him; it led him to underestimate his foe. Then Carson enquired, drily, whether Wilde had kissed a servant boy at Oxford. 'Oh, dear no,' Wilde had replied, 'he was, unfortunately, extremely ugly.' After a telling pause that had the whole courtroom on the edge of their seats, Carson demanded to know why Wilde had said that. Why? Why? *Why?* Was not the implication that had he been handsome, Wilde *would* have wanted to kiss him? That one point pressed ruthlessly home again and again turned the trial and led ultimately to Wilde's disgrace and imprisonment.

The same formidable Carson now wanted to demolish something far more threatening than Oscar Wilde. In the dock now was Rome Rule in Ulster. As an Irishman, he could not bear the thought of any division of his country; and Home Rule would certainly dismember it in a way that, to Protestant loyalists like himself, was intolerable.

Next to Carson stood James Craig, his junior by seventeen years, the big bucolic-looking MP for East Down. With a pugilist's nose and pendulous ears, Craig was first and foremost an Ulsterman, then British, but in no way Irish.

On this sombre Sunday 12 July 1914, rifles that had been smuggled into Larne on the east coast of Ulster in a marvellous gun-running exploit ten weeks earlier were on show for the first time, on the shoulders of thousands of marching Ulster Volunteers.

The celebration was climaxed by Carson's speech.

'I see no hopes of peace,' he roared, in a southern brogue that contrasted with the northern accents around him.

No one doubted that tragedy was soon to burst on their quiet, prosperous community. No simple boundaries could be drawn. In the other three provinces of Munster, Leinster and Connaught, there were as many Unionists as in Ulster, though they were scattered over a large area. In Ulster, Home Rulers made up 40 per cent of the population; in five of the nine counties they were in the majority.

Civil war was bound to be long and bloody.

Carson clenched his fist and thrust it out like a lance. 'I see nothing at present but darkness and shadows.'

When the fiery address was over, the great civilian army, waving Union Jacks and lustily singing 'God Save the King', broke up and went sadly to their homes.

By the Roetigen Lightship, it was 5 in the evening, with a swirling mist returning, when, to Figgis's relief, a battered black-hulled yacht appeared from the west. On its side it bore the name, *Kelpie*. From its deck, a strong Irish voice called out over the eerie silence of the sea, 'Is that the boat with the rifles for the Irish Volunteers?'

'Jesus Christ!' Figgis hissed. He called back warningly, in bad Gaelic, that it was.

The skipper of the *Gladiator* muttered, 'You are speaking the Mexican, *ja*?'

Figgis nodded. It was imperative for the German at least to pretend that the cargo they were about to transfer to the yachts was destined for a rebellion in Central America.

For a couple of hours, Conor O'Brien, a Dublin journalist whose chief hobby after sailing was climbing mountains in his bare feet, directed his small crew with unflagging energy. Great bundles wrapped in canvas and heavy wooden boxes were lowered from the tug. All the while O'Brien hummed rebel songs, happy in the knowledge that soon the Irish Volunteers who wanted Home Rule would start to match the Ulster Volunteers in weaponry.

At 7 o'clock, as the *Kelpie* was casting off, a second shape loomed out of the fog, a smart white yacht with white sails. The 28-ton, 49-foot ketch bore the legend, *Asgard*, an old Norse word meaning, 'Home of the Gods'. Its skipper was Erskine Childers, aged forty-four, Irish-born, trim and handsome. A former clerk of the House of Commons in London, he had made a name for himself in 1903 with his brilliant sea-novel, *The Riddle of the Sands*. His crew consisted of twenty-nine-year-old Gordon Shephard, a British airman, two Donegal fishermen, and two women.

Mary Spring-Rice was in her early thirties. She had a sparkling personality and a waspish nose. Her father was an Anglo-Irish peer and her cousin the British Ambassador in Washington.

The second woman was Childers's wife Molly, an American beauty with thick hair pinned in a bun and soft languid eyes. As a child, she had fractured both hips; she had, as a result, lain for twelve years on her back and walking was never easy. It was love at first sight when Childers met Mary Alden Osgood, whose family went back to the *Mayflower*, at a party in her home-town of Boston. That was ten years before and the *Asgard* had been her parents' wedding gift. Molly had insisted on coming on this trip, leaving their sons, Erskine aged eight and Robert aged three, in the care of her husband's maiden aunts.

'Sorry,' Figgis called down to Childers, 'the *Kelpie* has left you 900 rifles and 29,000 rounds.'

The *Gladiator*'s crew jabbered unceasingly as they handed the cargo down to the *Asgard*. The Donegal fishermen lowered it through the main hatch. It was a sultry night. Soon their muscles ached and sweat poured off them.

Shephard and Mary Spring-Rice stored bundles of twenty rifles in the saloon with the barrels towards the centre. The men had chopped up the bunks to increase storage space but the rifles were soon at table-level. The cabins were next filled, then the passage way, then the foot of the companion hatch. Childers had the rifles taken out of the canvas and the straw wrapping removed so they could be tucked away in drawers and cupboards. Soon everyone was coated with thick black grease.

Before leaving Belfast that night, Carson presided over a secret meeting in Craig's family home, Craigavon. Present was a large group that called itself the Ulster Provisional Government. To each of them, Home Rule meant Rome Rule.

In 1908, Pope Pius X had passed a decree, the *Ne temere*, making mixed marriages between Catholics and Protestants invalid unless in a Catholic Church and with a joint promise to bring all the children up as papists. Protestants saw this as an infringement of their basic rights as parents. Worse still, pope after pope had said that when Catholics were in a majority, they were forbidden to tolerate 'heretical' errors. Northern Protestants could not stomach the idea of becoming a minority in a Catholic state.

'By God,' Carson kept repeating, 'I'd prefer to be governed by the Kaiser than the Pope.'

The Provisional Government made plans to take over every civic post 'in trust for His Majesty the King in every Court and office of the Crown in Northern Ireland'.

As the meeting ended, Craig handed his Chief a piece of paper with a code-word on it. Carson had only to send a telegram containing that word and the Ulster rising would begin. They would be facing not merely the Irish Volunteers; easy meat. No, their main foe would be the British army itself.

Carson looked through the tall west-facing window over the lake that mirrored many orange-flamed bonfires and winced. That telegram would bring rebellion in fire and blood to the streets of Ulster.

By the lightship, the work went on hour after hour into a night lit only by the boats' riding lights. Molly Childers did her bit by putting food straight in the crew's mouths.

It was well after midnight before they started taking the ammunition boxes on board. A German sailor, stripped to the waist, called down, 'Achtung. Careful, bitte, if you knock zem or drop zem, bang!' He lifted both sweaty arms in the air to indicate an almighty explosion.

Three boxes were below when one of the Gladiator's riding lights came loose and dropped straight through the Asgard's hatch. A sailor, bowing over the rail, swore heroically as the lamp bounced off Molly's shoulder, covering her with paraffin before landing upside-down in a heap of straw. The straw flared up in an instant. Molly snatched it away from the ammunition with her bare hands and stamped on it. To everyone's relief the lamp spluttered out.

By 2 in the morning, the cargo was aboard. However well trimmed, it was unevenly distributed and the yacht was dangerously low in the water should they run into a storm.

The German skipper came aboard for a farewell drink. Stepping gingerly on top of rifles piled three feet high, he turned a blind eye to the Irish label on the whiskey bottle.

'If you vish,' he growled good-naturedly, sitting cross-legged, 'I tow you to nearly Dover.'

The crew of the Asgard spread their mattresses over the guns to get some shut-eye as dawn broke and the boat cut the sea at an unusual ten knots. Near the Sussex coast, with the grass- and rose-smells of an English summer wafted over chalk cliffs sweetening the brine, the tow-ropes were cast off.

Figgis stayed on board the Gladiator for Dover where he had business to attend to. He slipped Childers a final note. 'I'll be waiting for you when you land. All the best.'

The skipper of the Gladiator called out, 'Good luck in Mexico,' before his boat disappeared in the mists.

The crew hoisted the sails and Childers set a leisurely course westwards along England's southern coast towards his forbidden destination.

Childers dropped Shephard off at Milford Haven in Wales so that he could rejoin his flying unit.

At 1.20 in the afternoon of 24 July, the *Asgard* began the last stage of her journey across the Irish Sea. The sun beamed in a blue sky, the wind had dropped. Childers feared he might be becalmed. If he missed the tide in Howth, he would be unable to enter harbour.

It was not mild weather that jeopardized his plans.

At midnight a north-west wind sprang up. He was alerted by a clap of canvas and a jerk of the boom. He looked at the glass. Dirty weather on the way. He checked the sidelights and noted the compass-bearing. He double-lashed everything in readiness for the concussions to come.

The air turned sulphurous; stars came and went under ragged clouds. Childers had the impression of a moon galloping in the sky. After an initial sparrow-like tweet, the wind hummed, then cracked like a whip before ushering in the worst storm on the Irish Sea in thirty-two years.

Molly lay in the cabin, holding on to a metal stanchion, thinking of her sons soon to be orphaned. Mary Spring-Rice crouched green-gilled in the cockpit, for the first time terrified.

Childers was obliged to stay on deck all night and fight every inch of the way. He was tired to begin with. It had not been easy sleeping, with the cargo taking up most of the air-space; and his limbs ached from being cooped up. Now he was to be tested to the limits.

Waves, black, mountainous, snow-capped, broke all around him, fizzing like champagne.

He grasped the tiny wheel, entwining his knees in the spokes, determined to die rather than let go. Rising and falling, his temples bursting, he thought not of God, life, death, wife, children; only of rifles, rifles, rifles.

The darkness was now absolute. His head seemed stuck in a bag. The yacht rolled as though wanting to breast the sea, detaching objects and hurling them like projectiles across the deck. Somewhere, a plank crumbled and sprinkled him with chips of wood.

A sudden gust whipped off his sou'wester so that rain plastered his hair to his head like a scab. The gale's huge hand pressed against his mouth. Water, now fresh, now salt, splashed his eyes, jammed his ears, dribbled into his mouth, streamed up his nostrils; it blinded,

18

deafened and choked him. In spite of his sea-boots and oilskins, he was soaked to the skin. His clothing was heavier than armour and his brittle limbs shivered from the cold.

The wind was his worst enemy. It turned him inside out. It left him drunk, almost senseless, tempting him to sleep, to surrender himself to a deep and lasting aqueous peace.

Now when the *Asgard* pitched, it dropped like a stone over a precipice. Then, with all hope gone, it lifted and soared like a bird.

At the height of the storm, too weak a sound to be heard above the tumult but felt by Childers like an earthquake, the tackle broke. He roused himself from a kind of coma. Having lashed the helm, he crawled tremblingly on all-fours, grabbing every ring-bolt, groping till he found the mainmast. The sky cleared momentarily, revealing an ermine-coloured sea.

Taking a huge breath, he, a tiny, shapeless, clumsy mass, began to climb. Step by step he ascended the rigging, expecting every second to be ripped off by an indifferent animal-like wind and sent spiralling afar into the sea. Spluttering and blowing amid a tangle of ropes, he was keen to finish his task, with thick, pneumatic fingers, before the boat broke up.

He hugged the drunk and heaving mast in the pitch dark. Squally rain nettled his eyes. A howling wind tore at his hair, anaesthetized his teeth, forced its way through compressed lips and barred teeth to fill his mouth fuller than wine, roughened his sinuses, scoured his lungs like pumice, made his clothes cling to him like an extra layer of skin. Never had he needed his remarkable strength and will-power more. His hands chafed, blistered and froze so that he could not feel them as slowly, surely, he lashed the tackle down.

When he regained the deck his legs felt boneless and he was almost spent; but he continued his solitary vigil, barnacled to the helm, until the wild seas calmed.

It had been a close call.

At daylight, when Molly came on deck, he was crouched over the wheel so still she wondered at first if he were alive. His face was a Russian winter. His hair and eyebrows were salt-white turning him into a grizzled old man. She kissed him tenderly and put a drink to his lips.

Though his body ached, he had the boat in position. Ten miles south-east of Howth he hove to.

It was a chill fresh morning, pearly-grey like the inside of a sea-shell, with sharp showers.

___ ran up the flag of the local Cruising Club in preparation for sailing into Howth the next day. Then he went below to sleep.

On shore, young Bulmer Hobson, as innocent to look at as he was ruthless within, had made preparations for the landing. An Ulsterman himself, he admired the efficiency with which Carson's men had run Ulster's arms into Larne at night and spread them through the province by trucks, cars, and even Rolls Royces. He wanted to go one better.

The arms on the *Asgard* did not match Ulster's in number or quality. But what he could do was bring them ashore *in broad daylight*. That would fire the imagination of Home Rulers everywhere.

Sunday 26 July broke, calm and peaceful. The British gun-boat, which had been blockading Dublin Bay, had gone south on a wild-goose chase inspired by Hobson.

From Dublin, several hundred Irish Volunteers set out under a smart young officer, Ned Daly, on an apparently normal route march with broom-handles for rifles. Most of them had no idea what to expect in Howth.

Hobson was pleased to note that the Royal Irish Constabulary was having the day off. Only a few children joined them occasionally to jeer.

At 10 a.m., the *Asgard* lay behind Lambay Island in a heavy swell. Darrell Figgis was to come out in a motor boat. That was the signal for the yacht to enter harbour.

Childers checked with Molly. 'Figgis did say the boat would be here by 10 if all was well?'

She nodded.

Another hour passed. Were the RIC on to them? If they sailed into harbour – and time was running out – would they fall into a trap?

The truth was more prosaic. Figgis had chartered a motor boat from the coastal town of Bray. It had made its way north up the coast for fifteen miles in rough seas. The boat's owners had had enough for one day.

Figgis was crouched on the pier, cajoling, cursing as only an Irish man knows how, offering bribes the pilot in Hamburg would have given an arm for. No use.

Gordon Shephard, next to Figgis, caught occasional glimpses of

the *Asgard* at the edge of the island. 'She's there, I tell yc
'The bloody boat's there.'

Childers had his orders: 'If there's a hitch at Howth, ... around
Ireland to the Shannon. You will be able to unload in the west
in safety.' There *was* a hitch; but his crew had been at sea for
twenty-three days with only five on shore. They were spent.

Michael O'Rahilly, called The O'Rahilly because he was the head
of his clan, arrived on the pier. Nearly forty, he was married to
a Philadelphian, Nancie Browne. A devout Catholic from Kerry,
he spoke Irish loudly and abominably with broad gestures to his
children on top of the Dalkey tram. He often entered a café and
addressed everyone in this murdered Irish, to ensure that the old
language of the Gael was heard sometimes even in Dublin.

Next to him was a small man with a back like a ramrod. Charlie
Burgess had changed his name to its Irish equivalent: Cathal Brugha.
He had a fluffy moustache, flint-grey eyes and a firm jaw. A com-
mercial traveller by trade, he was a fine athlete and gymnast.

The two of them had brought a party of twenty to unload. Provided
the *Asgard* appeared. They checked their watches for the tenth time.
They put their glasses on the sea. Nothing. It looked to them like
another Irish foul-up.

Behind them in town, several taxis drew up. Inside were young
men with their girls in summer dresses, seemingly on a day's outing
to Howth with its harbour and verdant hills.

The taxis were, in fact, for transporting the ammunition boxes
into Dublin. Hobson thought the Volunteers were not yet disciplined
enough to be given live rounds; they might start a private war at once.
The boxes were to be entrusted to the Fianna, the Irish Boy Scouts,
whom he trusted because he had trained them himself.

The young men helped their girl-friends out of the taxis and went
into the dining-room of the hotel overlooking the harbour. They
asked for menus and ordered lunch.

In Philadelphia it was early morning. Sir Roger Casement was
staying with an Irish-born business man, Joseph McGarrity. Joe,
tall, oval-faced, was a leading light in the Clan na Gael, the chief
Irish separatist movement in the States.

Casement, just over from Dublin, had helped finance and organize
the arms-running. Too on edge to sleep, he had steeled his heart

against failure. Soon, he felt, he would be receiving a telegram, Picnic prevented or broken up.

'Go on, Childers,' he urged, tugging on his black beard. 'Go *on*.'

Childers was still wrestling with his lonely decision.

Molly eyed her husband pityingly. One mistake and the whole glorious enterprise would be ruined. If captured, Erskine would also be in for a heavy fine, perhaps imprisonment.

He suddenly jumped to. 'Well, what are we waiting for?'

Molly grabbed the helm. Mary Spring-Rice stood up in the bows in a bright red skirt, the signal that all was well. The three-man crew manned the halyards as the *Asgard* surged in on the tide.

The O'Rahilly saw the white yacht first and yelled, 'Look, the harbinger of liberty.'

In the hotel young men startled their girl-friends by pushing their meals aside and rushing out of the main door towards the harbour.

Molly luffed; down came the main, followed in moments by the jib and the mizzen.

'Jesus Christ!' gasped Childers. They were heading straight for the wall of the east pier. For one nasty moment he thought the boat would founder and, irony of ironies, discharge her precious cargo in Howth harbour.

Alongside the quay twenty Volunteers appeared. Mary called out with delight, 'I can see Gordon and Figgis.' At the head of the pier someone caught the rope and made the *Asgard* fast. It was 12.45 p.m.

Now hundreds of Volunteers converged on the yacht. That was when Childers knew he had succeeded against all the odds.

Hobson put a guard at the entrance to the harbour as his men, with a wild cheer, tossed their broom-handles in the sea. There was a scramble for the rifles until Childers demanded, 'Who's in charge here?'

Up stepped Cathal Brugha. 'Me.' As soon as he took over, order was restored.

From the western breakwater customs officials made for the *Asgard* in a motor launch. When a few unloaded rifles were pointed their way they turned back. Four against a thousand were not decent odds. They put through a telephone call to Dublin Castle instead.

In the Castle, the seat of British administration, Assistant Commissioner of Police David Harrell took the call. He alerted the

British Under-Secretary at his lodge in the Phoenix Park, west of the city.

Sir James Brown Dougherty, Ireland's top civil servant, said, 'Put the Metropolitan Police on the alert.'

Harrell obeyed but on his own initiative he phoned the military for help. If the Irish Volunteers now had rifles, his men, who were not armed, would be mown down.

A detachment of a hundred of the King's Own Scottish Borderers under Captain Cobden left barracks and joined Harrell's police patrol. They headed for Howth on hastily requisitioned trams.

In 77 Amiens Street lived a man named Clarke, the owner of a tobacconist and newsagent shop in the centre of Dublin which was scarcely bigger than a prison cell. Over the shop, in Gaelic letters, was the name 'T. S. O'Clerigh'. Everyone knew him as the Old Chap or plain Old Tom Clarke.

For Dublin Castle this frail-looking jug-eared tobacconist with hair like a half-blown dandelion was Enemy Number One. The biggest file in the Castle, red for very dangerous, had on its cover: 'Clarke, T.'

Clarke had been a member of the secret and banned Irish Republican Brotherhood since 1878. No one had been more faithful to the oath he took: 'Our duty is to nerve and strengthen ourselves to wrest by the sword our political rights from England.'

At twenty-five he had learned to blow up rocks on Staten Island in New York. From there he was sent to England to blow up London Bridge or the Houses of Parliament. Caught at once with a case containing liquid explosives, he was tried at the Old Bailey in 1883. In a careless moment he had corrected a remark made by the State Prosecutor about the type of bombs used in the campaign. It cost him penal servitude for life. He vowed never again to use one more word than was needed. On 21 September 1898 he was let out of Pentonville Prison after serving fifteen and a half years.

He went at once to visit his old jail mate John Daly, now Mayor of Limerick. There he fell in love with the third of Daly's eight nieces, Kathleen. He had gone on vacation with them to County Clare by the shores of the Atlantic. He and Kattie had risen at five and climbed a hill to see the sunrise. Soon after he went ahead to America to get a job, married Kattie in New York, and settled in Brooklyn where their first son was born in 1900.

John Devoy, an Irish-American who had himself been in a British prison, took him under his wing. Devoy was head of the Irish Republican movement, its chief organization being the secret Clan na Gael.

Clarke became a naturalized American. Then it struck him that if England went to war with Germany the Irish at home might not be ready to rebel.

In 1907 he returned to Dublin to find the Brotherhood as organized as cows in a field. He knocked them into shape. He became the contact with the Clan in the States. His letters to Devoy, sent by courier, began 'Dear Uncle' and were signed 'T. James'. From the Clan he received funding for any Irish venture that might hasten the day of independence. The Castle was right to class him as Enemy Number One.

Now fifty-seven years old, Clarke was wiry and narrow-waisted. Grey eyes glinted behind metal-framed spectacles. His footsteps, short and crisp, expressed the determination that nerved his entire being. In a Brotherhood recently filled with young recruits, he, the treasurer, remained the drummer; they marched to his beat.

On this Sunday afternoon Clarke had a visit from his best friend. Sean McDermott, just over thirty, had a relaxed cheery manner but he would stop at nothing to win freedom for Ireland. Three years before, polio had badly affected his spine; he walked now with the aid of a stick. Not that it stopped him touring the country, signing on Irish Volunteers while he appointed members of the IRB as their senior officers.

'The arms are on their way,' McDermott said.

Clark's eyes lit up. 'Didn't I always say, Sean, there's no way to get the foreigner out of here except at the point of a gun.'

They had been speaking for only five minutes when two trams went by in the direction of Howth, crammed with police and armed soldiers.

'They're on to us,' Old Tom said.

Sean jumped up. 'I'll hire a taxi and we'll go and see.'

In the harbour, Gordon Shephard and Figgis leaped on board to lend Childers a hand. The two ladies stepped ashore to be greeted by a charming, sandy-haired man with a handle-bar moustache and a smile that revealed a sunny nature.

'Sorry Professor MacNeill could not be here,' The O'Rahilly said. MacNeill was the Chairman of the Irish Volunteers. He gallantly kissed the ladies' hands and told Molly in a broad Kerry accent, 'You're the greatest soldier, ma'am, indeed y'are.'

To Molly's American ears there came repeatedly what sounded like 'Tremendjus', 'These ladies are just after doing somet'ing tremendjus for Oirland.'

Ammunition was rushed off by taxi to hiding-places all over the city, and the rifles were handed to the Volunteers.

In their eagerness to help, some of them tore one of the *Asgard*'s sails. After instant repairs, Gordon and Mary Spring-Rice, together with The O'Rahilly, waved the *Asgard* farewell as the Childers sailed back to England to the cheers of Volunteers lining the quay.

A Force 6 wind was blowing but Childers, with one last glance back at the now almost deserted pier, was content. He was proud to have made his contribution to Home Rule.

If only he had know that Professor MacNeill was only nominally in charge of the Volunteers; that the arms he had risked his life for were now in the hands of extremists like Clarke and McDermott, who had no time for Home Rule but were set on establishing a Republic by force.

The Volunteers headed back to Dublin, chatting noisily, their heads held high. For the first time, a thousand Irishmen in the south were in arms – even if they were not yet to be trusted with ammunition.

Ahead of them and in their direct path, two trams with eighty police and a hundred armed troops aboard halted at Clontarf. The Crown forces alighted in utter silence and took up positions across the street.

As soon as the Volunteers saw their way was barred they swung right into the Malahide Road.

Harrell's men wheeled to head them off. Once more the Volunteers, without ammunition, found themselves facing a double line of kilted soldiers with rifles and fixed bayonets. Armed police, all of them giants, stood on either side of the troops at right angles.

Captain Cobden gave the order, 'Load.' A pause. 'Aim.'

As the Volunteers shuddered to a halt, Harrell instructed his constables, 'Seize their arms.'

Most of them, not knowing the Volunteers had no live rounds, refused to budge. Those who stepped forward were cracked on the head with oak batons. The few members of the Royal Irish Constabulary present countered with rifle butts. In the scuffle, pistol-shots from the Volunteers grazed a couple of foreheads.

The two forces disengaged and Hobson, who had driven up, advanced to parley with the Assistant Commissioner.

'Our weapons,' he said, 'are not loaded. But any more trouble and they soon will be.'

Hobson was joined by Darrell Figgis and Thomas MacDonagh, a university lecturer. Either of them could have talked the hind leg off a horse. MacDonagh, in particular, was a stocky, sharp-nosed whirlwind of speech and action.

In his quick staccato voice, he addressed Harrell. 'Begad, man, I ask you, what in heaven's name are you up to?'

Harrell seemed mesmerized, enabling Hobson to go back and make sure that Ned Daly was withdrawing his men through the nearest roadside hedge. That done, he phoned colleagues in Dublin to send every available vehicle for transporting the rifles into the city. Out of sight, Clarke and McDermott were already piling them into their taxi.

With the soldiers stood at ease, MacDonagh and Figgis demanded to know of Harrell by what authority he was breaking the law. Then there was a planned distraction. A local celebrity known as Pope Flanagan rode up with a clatter on an enormous old nag and added his considerable voice to the discussion.

In the general mêlée, a pint-sized Volunteer did his bit by grabbing the rifle of an RIC man, a giant who swung the rifle round with the titch hanging on for dear life.

When Harrell managed to get a word in, he said the Volunteers had imported arms into Ireland against the 1913 Act.

'Ah,' said Figgis, 'is that it?' He insisted that the Volunteers had done no such thing. They simply took charge of them after they had been imported.

'Then who did bring them in?' asked Harrell, sardonically.

'T'was me entirely, sir.' Figgis held out his hands, asking to be handcuffed.

Before Harrell could take up the offer, Chief Inspector Dunne signalled him madly. There was not a Volunteer in sight.

Harrell, red-faced, told Captain Cobden he could stand his men down and return to barracks.

'Into the trams, men,' the Captain ordered, only to find that the trams, too, had mysteriously disappeared.

It was a long march back to Dublin. News of the arms landing had spread. For two hours, along the way, the Scottish soldiers were ragged about their kilts and what mysteries were or were not hidden under them. In full gear, on a mid-summer's day, they were at the end of their tether.

Crowds had pelted them with sticks, stones and bottles. Some of the soldiers' heads were streaming with blood. In addition, an astonishing number of hearses had whizzed past them on their way into the city. Citizens in the know removed their hats and signed themselves out of respect.

A senior officer, Major Haigh, hearing what was going on, left barracks to take charge. Disgusted with the crowd, he ordered his men to make feinting movements with fixed bayonets to force them to keep their distance.

The screaming and the stone-throwing went on.

At 6.30 p.m., the troops reached the quay on the Liffey just west of O'Connell Street known as Bachelor's Walk. The tram terminal was packed as usual on a Sunday evening. With the situation getting uglier by the minute Haigh halted his squad and ordered them, 'About turn.'

A handful knelt and aimed at onlookers who were still yelling abuse. The major had no idea that Cobden had made his men load at Clontarf. When he held up his hand for silence, one tired and frightened soldier took it as a signal to open fire. He pulled the trigger and twenty others followed suit, some firing twice.

A stunned silence ensued as three people fell dead and thirty were wounded, one fatally. One of the dead – she was bayoneted as well as shot – was the mother of a soldier serving in the British army.

Augustine Birrell, Chief Secretary for Ireland, a witty and humane man, was dining alone in his London home when he was informed of the arms landing and the tragedy in Bachelor's Walk. He was deeply upset at the loss of life. Extremist Republicans, especially in America, were bound to make a meal of that. But there were more serious long-term consequences.

There were now in Ireland two militant citizens' forces deeply divided on the Home Rule issue. The Irish Volunteers had been bound to buy weapons once Carson had imported arms on a massive scale into Ulster.

Birrell took a big dose of bicarbonate of soda for his dyspepsia. He was never without it. Once, when things were really bad, he had gone to a chemist's shop and laid on the counter enough money to buy a pillar-box full.

He went to the Irish Office. In the morning, a few Cabinet colleagues and several generals in the War Office would demand that he disarm the Volunteers. They knew nothing about Ireland, nor about the difficulty of trying to disarm civilian armies in cities full of sympathizers. It would lead to civil war.

It was not until midnight eastern time that McGarrity found out that Howth had been a success. He ran upstairs to tell Casement. A day of agony and apprehension was over.

An excited Devoy telephone, from New York. 'I wanna tell you this is the greatest deed done in Ireland in a hundred years.'

Casement knew that Devoy had not really trusted him before. He thought of him as a lackey who had for years served British interests as a consul. Well, he was a liability no more.

McGarrity spoke of him as Wolfe Tone, an eighteenth-century patriot, reincarnate. Calls kept coming in through the night. Irish-Americans were delirious with pride, hope, joy. Newpapers kept asking for interviews.

'Just think, Rory,' McGarrity said, when the phone was momentarily silent, 'there's now a thousand of us armed and ready to fight for our independence!'

Next day, in Dublin, Hobson received the first cable from the States pledging £1,000 'in recognition of splendid gunrunning into Howth'. For the first time in that generation Irish-Americans believed that the Irish back home were willing and able to help themselves. Soon American money was overflowing the Volunteers' treasury. The O'Rahilly said, laughingly, 'I can scarcely count the filthy stuff.'

Hobson was keen to make propaganda out of what had happened on the quays. 'The Bachelor's Walk Massacre' sounded fine. He had that special Irish talent for turning funerals into political demonstrations.

The coffins of the victims were followed by Volunteers marching through Dublin with reversed arms to the music of 'The Dead March'. A British soldier was photographed weeping as he accompanied the coffin of his mother. One banner in the procession read: 'Killed by the King's Own Scottish Murderers'.

Masses were said and memorial services held all over Ireland.

There was a lesson in this, but Birrell suspected politicians and generals were not capable of learning it. In the light of British atrocities century after century, the Irish, one of the most peace-loving races on earth, hated *nothing* more than the British gunning down their fellow Irishmen.

28

But the troubles in Ireland were soon to be overshadowed by much bigger ones in Europe.

Germany had been under Kaiser Wilhelm II for twenty-six years. The eldest grandson of Queen Victoria thirsted for popularity and power. He had a belligerent manner and a bull's-horn moustache which seemed to defy the law of gravity and which he put each night in a *Schnurrbartbinde*, a moustache-bandage. A Court Circular once described his participation in a Sunday service as 'the All-Highest paying his respects to the Highest'. If court preachers were to be believed, he and God were virtually indistinguishable.

Wilhelm had colonial ambitions which required the build-up of a huge fleet to match Britain's.

Britain, naturally, assumed that the high seas, trade and colonial expansion were best left in her hands. To counter German expansion, she entered into a defensive alliance with Russia and France.

And yet, in mid-1914, the European situation seemed tranquil enough. Towards the end of June, British vessels were on a friendly visit to Kiel. For the first time in years British and German ships moored side by side. There had been races, banquets, speeches, with the Kaiser presiding.

Then on Sunday 28 June, like lightning in the night, Archduke Franz Ferdinand, nephew of the Austrian Emperor and heir to the Austro-Hungarian throne, was murdered in the streets of Sarajevo.

At Kiel, Winston Churchill, the young cherubic-looking First Lord of the Admiralty, saw Kaiser Wilhelm come ashore from the white Imperial Yacht *Hohenzollern* with its ensign '*Gott mit Uns*' and jump into a bright yellow Mercedes. The Great War Lord was enjoying the theatricality of the moment.

To the man-in-the-street, an assassination by Serbian fanatics in, of all places, the Balkans, was a little local difficulty. The King of Italy in 1900 and the American President McKinley in 1901 had been struck down without it ending in war.

Only the astutest politicians grasped that the Archduke's death might be the spark to set the world alight. The Germans felt strong enough to fulfil their expansionist ambitions: Admiral Tirpitz had created their navy; Krupp would provide them with arms. They were more likely to act, believing that both Russia and Britain were menaced by civil war.

Yet Germany drifted into war not from malice but from ineptitude; not because it wanted war but because it did not want peace enough.

Hence it allowed its protégé Austria to make outrageous demands on Serbia without rebuke, even with secret encouragement.

Winston Churchill believed that war in Europe was now more imminent than in Ireland, with Germany, France, Russia inevitably sucked in, and, with luck, Great Britain, too. He was soon proved correct.

On the last day of July, Prime Minister Asquith was dining at Downing Street with Churchill and his Foreign Secretary, Sir Edward Grey. They were discussing Russia's threat to mobilize her forces when an official from Grey's department came in with an urgent message from the British Embassy in Berlin. If the Russian mobilization was held up, it said, the Kaiser might be willing to restrain his ally, Austria.

It was a slim chance but worth taking. Asquith decided to go at once to the Palace. He quickly wrote out a telegram.

With no official car available, a secretary telephoned for a taxi. A cab-driver, suspecting that this was a leg-pull, stopped outside Number 10.

Out stepped a familiar figure dressed formally in black.

'Where to, Guv?' the cabbie gulped.

'Buckingham Palace,' said Mr Asquith.

The King had been asleep only forty minutes when his personal aide, Rear-Admiral Sir Colin Keppel, entered the royal bedroom and shook him awake. 'The Prime Minister to see you, sir.'

In the Audience Room, Asquith, his big face lined and tired, felt that this was the weirdest moment of his premiership as His Majesty appeared, only half awake, with a dressing-gown over his night-shirt.

He would be obliged, he said, if the King would consent to send a telegram to Tzar Nicholas II, Emperor of all the Russias, in his own name. He held out the piece of paper. 'If you'd care to look through it, sir?'

'Can't,' said the King, who could only read big type. 'Read it to me, if you would.'

Asquith did so.

The King said, hesitantly, that it would need one or two modifications.

Asquith was perturbed. It was unlike His Majesty to meddle in diplomacy. 'Changes, sir?'

'Yes. Begin it thus: "My dear Nickie" and end it "Georgie".'
A relieved Asquith made a note of the changes and left.
It was 1.40 a.m. on Saturday 1 August.

From his beautiful lakeside home where he was breakfasting, Count von Bernstorff, the German Ambassador to Washington, could hear the beat of drums across the Starnberger See. Patriotic crowds a few miles away in Munich were singing *Deutschland über Alles*, among them a twenty-five-year-old failed painter and architect named Adolf Hitler.

The telephone rang. Artur Zimmermann, the Under-Secretary at the Foreign Office, apologized for interrupting his vacation but he would have to return to the United States at once. First, though, he was wanted in Berlin for a briefing.

'Owing to troop movements, Excellency, the journey might take longer than usual.'

At 5 o'clock that evening of 1 August, Germany took the initiative and declared war on Russia. The German Foreign Office was, therefore, pleased to receive a telegram from their Ambassador in London. For some time, Count Lichnowsky had been telling them that 'the old Gentleman' (Asquith) had no intention of going to war. Now, he said, Sir Edward Grey had assured him that if Germany did not violate French territory, Britain would remain neutral.

When the Kaiser and the Chancellor heard this they were delighted. Wilhelm, above all, in spite of his bellicose talk, did not want a war in which his battleships would be sunk; they were to frighten off potential aggressors, not for use. He immediately caused Moltke, his Chief of Staff, great consternation by telling him he was wiring his cousin, George V, that if England guaranteed French neutrality, the Germans promised not to cross the Belgian frontier before 7 p.m. on 3 August.

Kaiser Wilhelm was in a deep sleep in his Berlin Schloss when his man-servant, Schulz, woke him up. There was a telegram from George V. Ambassador Lichnowsky had misunderstood Grey's words.

The Chief of Staff was immediately summoned and his Imperial Majesty, clad only in his pyjamas and moustache-bandage, barked, 'Mobilization has to be speeded up.'

As Moltke left, the Kaiser was muttering, 'To think that Georgie and Nickie should have deceived me. If grandmother had been alive, she would not have allowed it.'

Though Monday 3 August was a Bank Holiday in England, the Commons reassembled at Westminster. The long green benches were crammed. Extra chairs were placed on the stretch of floor between the Bar and the Despatch table, usually neutral territory.

When the Foreign Secretary rose to speak, he already knew that John Redmond, the leader of the Irish Nationalist MPs, had had a quiet word in Asquith's ear.

Grey had clean-cut, handsome features with a high smooth forehead and craggy nose. His manners and appearance were those of a quiet country gentleman.

Germany, he declared, had tried to buy Britain off. It would be easy for that country if Britain remained neutral. But could she afford to be? Germany had demanded of the Belgians the right to pass through their territory. 'The essence of the matter, is that Belgium must not be violated.'

Members leaped to their feet in agreement, cheering and waving their order papers.

With a hurried glance at Redmond, Sir Edward Grey went on: 'The one bright spot in the very dreadful situation is that Ireland – and this I should like to be clearly understood abroad – is not a consideration among the things we have to take into account now.'

Edward Carson looked at the Government front bench and saw tears running down Churchill's cheeks.

Few listened more attentively to the Foreign Secretary than Augustine Birrell, Britain's Chief Secretary in Dublin. No one knew better than he the old maxim of Irish rebels: 'England's difficulty is Ireland's opportunity.' For days he had been asking himself how war would affect Ireland. If things went badly, Britain might need to keep a standing army there of 60,000 men.

Grey's brief reference to the situation in Ireland set the stage for Redmond. Taking a deep breath, he rose from his corner seat below the gangway. This was the Mother of Parliaments and he was proud to be a House of Commons man. A fine orator, he looked the part with his neat greying hair, grey brows over slightly bulbous eyes and grey moustache. His rich, Celtic voice rang through the Chamber.

The Germans, he said, could not rely on civil disturbance anywhere in the United Kingdom. The Home Rule issue had changed the

Empire's view of Ireland and her view of Empire. There were in Ireland two large bodies of Volunteers.

'I say to the Government that they may tomorrow withdraw every one of their troops from Ireland.' To loud murmurs of approval, he went on: 'I say that the coast of Ireland will be defended from foreign invasion by her armed sons, and for this purpose armed Nationalist Catholics in the South will be only too glad to join arms with the armed Protestant Ulstermen in the North.'

The unthinkable happened: Unionists stood to cheer Redmond. Apart from Carson. He remained seated and silent.

Redmond, his watery eyes glistening, was delighted at his triumph and not a little puzzled. He had not pledged a single Irishman for the front. He had simply said Irishmen would defend Ireland – provided, that is, they were given the arms. But his contribution was interpreted as a war speech and, on reflection, he was content with that. Especially if the Ulster Unionists now dropped their objections to Home Rule.

When the chimes of Big Ben struck 11 p.m. on 4 August 1914, King George V, Queen Mary and the Prince of Wales went with heavy hearts on to the balcony of Buckingham Palace, to wave to a country at war.

Hearing the cheers, Prime Minister Asquith remembered the remark of a predecessor, Sir Robert Walpole: 'Now they are ringing bells; in a few weeks they'll be wringing their hands.'

Churchill, having sent an Admiralty signal to all ships: 'Commence hostilities at once with Germans,' scurried across to Number 10. It was a warm evening. His broad white forehead was beaded with sweat as he entered the Cabinet room, a big cigar in his mouth and a puckish smile on his face.

'The Fleet is under war orders.' Try as he would, he could not hide his indecent elation.

Sir Edward Grey, more circumspect, returned to his office on the second floor of the Foreign Office and peered through the tall window into the deepening gloom of London.

'The lamps,' he said, 'are going out all over Europe; we shall not see them lit again in our lifetime.'

In the Irish Office, Augustine Birrell took out his bicarbonate of soda. He would need a lot more of the stuff before the war was over. The Ulster Volunteers had nearly 40,000 rifles and the Irish Volunteers after Howth had at least a couple of thousand. As he swallowed his bitter medicine, he knew that, across Ireland, glasses were being raised with far more palatable brews.

In his run-down house at Glenalina Terrace, at the head of the Catholic Falls Road, Belfast, sat round-faced, bow-legged James Connolly. Aged forty-six, he was exceptionally well-read for someone who had left school at eleven. A devout Marxist, his present job was organizer for the Irish Transport and General Workers Union.

While he was musing at an open window, his nineteen-year-old daughter came in. He felt in his bones that now, *now* was the time to throw out the British.

'What's on your mind, Daddy?'

'Ah, Nora. I was thinking of what that madman Redmond said recently in Parliament. He's not like an Irishman at all. He said we should protect our Irish shores against the foreign enemy.'

'When England is the chief foreign enemy.'

Connolly grinned. His eldest daughter was an apt pupil.

'But you always said Germany is as capitalist as England.'

'True, but at least it hasn't ruined Ireland as the Brigand Empire has for centuries. Anyway, if Irishmen have to die, it's better they die in their own land, fighting for their own freedom and not being slaughtered abroad for the sake of English capitalists. Now, if you'd leave me for a minute.'

No sooner had Nora gone from the room than Connolly picked up the phone and got in touch with the Irish Republican Brotherhood in Belfast.

In Dublin, Tom Clarke, Sean McDermott, Clarke's wife Kattie and her brother, Ned Daly, were hugging each other. England was involved in a European war for the first time since 1815.

They were all teetotal, otherwise they would have toasted 'England's war, Ireland's opportunity.'

Casement in his New York hotel was also celebrating in convivial company.

On his first night in the States, to cheer himself up in a strange city, he had waited until it was dark before slipping into more casual gear. He left the hotel by a rear exit and wandered the streets, past picture houses with movies starring Charlie Chaplin and William S. Hart.

A profoundly lonely man, he was missing the opportunities for

34

making friends with adult males and mature boys whom he had encountered on his consular travels. In his voluminous diaries, he had recorded, in addition to his great work for the downtrodden natives in places like the Belgian Congo and the Putamayo region of Brazil, his mostly one-night stands. He had devised a schoolboy's code to describe their superb black limbs and flowering genitalia, and how much they had cost him.

Homosexuality he considered to be a serious malady, like diabetes or heart-trouble. The victim had to live with it as best he could; and he knew how exhausting it could be. It meant a double life. He was sad to have to deceive his nearest and dearest. Like his County Antrim cousin, Gertrude Bannister. Like his London confidante, Mrs Alice Green.

He had sometimes been aware of fathers warning their sons about him. But no one close to him had ever had the slightest suspicion. He knew that if once he made a false move he would lose not only his honour but his credibility as a reformer. Since he was preparing to do what all Englishmen and many Irishmen considered treachery, he resolved to be doubly wary.

On that first night, to make sure he was not being followed, he suddenly jumped on a trolley and got off a couple of stops down the line. He then doubled back to Broadway where he ran into a plump six-footer in his mid-twenties with blond hair and a gap in his front teeth. The stranger identified himself in thick broken English.

'Adler Christensen, sir. Norwegian.'

He was down on his luck, he said. Having run away from home to go to sea, he was stranded and starving in New York. They had struck up an instant friendship and, after dining, Casement had invited him back to his hotel. He did not realize the profound effect that this young man was going to have upon his life and work.

Now, in the first flush of war, Casement raised his glass. 'Adler, to a swift German victory.'

In his office of the *Gaelic American* in William Street, Lower Manhattan, surrounded by typewriters and scattered copy, sat John Devoy.

He was in a collarless shirt, with sleeve garters; in spite of the heat, the windows were shut. Short, silver-haired, grizzled, growing deaf, Devoy laughed about once a year. His one consuming passion was Ireland.

Born there in 1842, he had joined the Foreign Legion at nineteen

35

for the military experience and deserted after two years. Back in Ireland, he joined the Fenians, a violent separatist movement. He was captured and sentenced to fifteen years. He served five until an amnesty in 1871 allowed him to leave for the States.

In America he brought unity to the Irish-American scene. Now he was without a peer.

A bachelor wed only to his work, snappy as a New York cab-driver, tough as a cop, wily as a Philadelphia lawyer, he lived in a seedy hotel on 14th Street. He had no friends, only allies. As the years passed, he became ever more autocratic and scurrilous. His stock reply to the query, 'Why?' was a papal, 'Goddammit, cos I say so,' his favourite expletive was, 'Whoreson!' and when he got annoyed he threw down his hat and stamped on it till he felt better.

His entire working day from sunrise to beyond sunset was spent in the dusty offices of the *Gaelic American*, next to a noisy railroad, writing letters, articles, checking copy, stoking in every conceivable way his hatred for England. Everything that reminded him of England stuck in his craw.

Thirty years before he had prophesied in a speech in Holyoke, Massachusetts: 'Ireland's opportunity will come when England is engaged in a desperate struggle with some great European power or European combination.' He had prayed night and day for this blessed event to happen before he died.

His gnarled hand, never more than a few inches from the telephone, grabbed it. A normally taciturn man, Devoy was as excited as a rooster. He started calling his allies in the Clan, Judge Dan Cohalan of New York, Joe McGarrity in Philadelphia. Each said, 'Early days yet, John,' but he knew in his old bones that it was Ireland's time for a burst of glory.

He got through to Casement in his hotel room. 'You were right, sir. Germany and Britain are at war. Congratulations!'

Casement, gagging the phone and gesturing to Adler to stop giggling, felt as if he had been canonized.

Afterwards old Devoy, the most unsentimental of men, went back over his boyhood days, remembered the ravishing green of old Ireland which he had not seen in over forty years.

One day, yes-*sir*, he would return like the salmon – when Ireland was free, of course.

In the Old World, German troops, as planned seven years before, were massing on the Belgian border. Their Chancellor, the tall, stooped, crew-cut, chain-smoking Bethmann-Hollweg, was appalled that things had gone so far.

He had been convinced of two things. Firstly, that Britain, fearing a civil war in Ireland, was not willing to go to war. Carson's posturings in Belfast had significantly influenced his judgement. Secondly, that Britain's 1839 treaty with Belgium was a mere scrap of paper.

But the British, too, were prepared.

Before dawn on 5 August, a British cable ship, the *Teleconia*, moved through the North Sea. A few miles off Emden, where the Dutch coast joins the German, Royal Navy engineers used giant grapnels to cut Germany's slime- and seaweed-covered cables connecting it to France, Spain, Tenerife and the two cables to New York via the Azores.

The Secret Service was no less active. The Head of counter-espionage, MI5, was Vernon Kell. Known as 'K', he was a gaunt-faced man who invariably wore dark glasses. He got on the phone to Basil Thomson, Head of the Special Branch. Thomson was in Scotland Yard off Whitehall awaiting Kell's call.

Their conversation was brief, the matter had been discussed fully in advance.

Before midday on the first morning of the war, the CID rounded up the entire German spy ring in the United Kingdom, from Brighton to Newcastle, including twenty-two top-secret agents. Within hours, the German General Staff learned that they had been virtually deprived of intelligence in mainland Britain. When they tried to use their transatlantic cables, they found they were not functioning. If they had been cut, all news reaching the States from the theatre of war would be tinged with a British bias. Maybe America, too, would cease being neutral. The difficulty was compounded in that the wireless station at Sayville on Long Island was not yet finished.

The Foreign Office ordered all Zeppelin crews to stand by. They told the Admiralty to contact the High Seas Fleet and torpedo-boat flotillas. Over the wireless station at Nauen, just outside Berlin, the message went out: 'War with England.'

All ships belonging to the enemy in German ports were seized, including a British steamer, the *Castro*, stuck in the Kiel canal.

Herr Meyer, a Foreign Office official, was asking, 'If we use Nauen, surely the enemy will be able to pluck our messages out of the air?'

'Maybe so,' was the response of Artur Zimmermann, the big, bluff

Under-Secretary, 'but fortunately, the British will never be able to crack our codes.'

With the war only thirty-six hours old, there was a meeting in the Speaker's Library of the Commons between Edward Carson, John Redmond and the Speaker, Lowther.

At fifty-seven, Redmond had been for fourteen years Chairman of the Irish Nationalist Party. His life-long aim was to achieve Home Rule for Ireland within the British Empire with himself, naturally, as Irish Prime Minister. Few Parliamentarians were prouder of the Empire and the Irish contribution to it in places like Australia and Canada. Squat, with a slightly round face, hawkish in profile, he wore a bow-tie and a flower in his buttonhole. He feared that the war would delay Home Rule.

Edward Carson was both politically and physically the opposite of Redmond. Tall, lean and reserved, he was hoping that the war would not only delay Home Rule but bury it.

Redmond stressed that after his pledge of the Irish Volunteers to defend Ireland from German aggressors, the Home Rule Bill had to be put on the statute book, war or no war.

Carson said bluntly, 'Ulster will refuse to be part of it.'

The Speaker heard them out. Then: 'I assure you both that the Prime Minister intends to go ahead with the Bill.'

'You mean,' Carson said, his voice rising, 'Mr Asquith intends to betray Ulster when we can do nothing about it because of the emergency?'

Afterwards, Redmond, still apprehensive, wrote to Asquith, 'The Liberal Party has the greatest opportunity that has ever occurred in the history of Ireland to win the Irish people to loyalty to the Empire.' He feared that without Home Rule his constitutional approach would give way to violence.

A few days later, in a Dublin house safe from prying eyes, the men of violence met in the shape of the Supreme Council of the Irish Republican Brotherhood. In their eyes, *they* were the legitimate government of Ireland. In quiet times, they were a moral force, encouraging disaffection, but when the crisis came, as now, they were to await the decision of the Irish people for rebellion.

'Before this war ends,' said Tom Clarke, 'we will rise in Dublin and establish a Republic.'

All eleven around the table nodded.

He went on, 'The Clan in the States has promised us military aid. Uncle will also use all his diplomacy to ensure that a rising will give us, like Belgium, the status of belligerents at a final peace conference.'

They all murmured their approval.

'Is it your wish, gentlemen, that I tell Uncle of our decision?'

It was agreed unanimously.

In fact, Clarke's letter to New York was already on its way by courier.

After that August meeting of the Brotherhood, McDermott walked back with Clarke to his tobacconist's shop in Great Britain Street. They felt they had been given a mandate to organize a rising in their own time, in their own way. As two of the three core men of the Executive, they were in a position to dominate the IRB and, through it, top-ranking officers in the Volunteer movement in Dublin and elsewhere.

Utterly without scruples, they co-opted anyone useful to the cause, dispensing with the interlocking circles by which the Brotherhood normally functioned.

'Remember,' Clarke said, 'there never yet was an Irish rising that was not betrayed by informers.'

Even as they spoke, an event 1,500 miles away was destined to prove more useful to the British than any spy had ever been.

On 20 August, in the Gulf of Finland, there was an engagement between Russian and German ships. In thick fog, a German cruiser, the *Magdeburg*, became isolated from the rest of the German fleet and went aground on the red granite island of Odenholm. As the fog began to clear and the Russian fleet closed in, the captain of the *Magdeburg* saw he was doomed.

He ordered a radio officer to row out and drop the Navy's codes into deep water. Having seen him leave, he signalled in code to his command ship that all ciphers had been destroyed.

But the radio officer's dinghy capsized and he was drowned. Once in range, the Russian fleet hit the *Magdeburg* with heavy broadsides. Afterwards, seeing many bodies floating in the shallows, the Russian skipper ordered his crew to bury them. Among the corpses washed up was the radio officer's. In his arms were lead bindings which an astute Russian sailor recognized as belonging to code-books.

The skipper sent down divers for the books themselves. To his surprise, they were successful. Even more surprisingly, within days, a decision was made by the Russian Admiralty in St Petersburg to offer them to the British.

In the States, John Redmond's pledge of support for the British in the war proved popular among Irish-Americans. It reduced Casement's chances of raising funds for the Irish Volunteers. Radical elements said, 'Why fork out to arm *them* when they intend to do Britain's dirty work for her?'

Casement, therefore, told Devoy that he was going to Berlin to ask for military aid.

Devoy's grey eyes narrowed. 'What d'you have in mind?'

'Forming an Irish Brigade from among their prisoners.'

'Like in South Africa?' Devoy knew that Major MacBride had formed such a Brigade in the Boer War.

Devoy gave it plenty of thought. Personally, he didn't give a damn about the Germans, and when he heard Casement saying, 'Poor Kaiser, poor Kaiser', he frankly wrote it off as bull-shit.

Casement was right about one thing, though: the Hun might, just *might* come in useful.

The German Ambassador, Count von Bernstorff, Berlin's top man in the western hemisphere, was just back in the States.

In a final briefing at his Foreign Office in Berlin, he was told that his best policy in the Anglophile atmosphere of America was to avoid all appearance of aggression towards England. Besides, Berlin was hoping to come to an early understanding with Great Britain.

As soon as Devoy heard from Clarke that the IRB intended to rebel some time during the war, he asked Bernstorff to meet the Clan na Gael in New York. Bernstorff agreed. From his favourite New York hotel, the Ritz-Carlton on Madison Avenue, where he kept a regal suite, he was chauffeured to the German Club on 59th Street.

Devoy, flanked by his top aides, blasted off right away. 'Mr Ambassador, friends in Ireland assure me they're gonna use this war to try and win their independence.'

Bernstorff nodded, giving nothing away.

'They will need,' Devoy continued, in his rasping voice, 'arms and trained officers, not money. We'll provide that. I think you'll agree there might be mutual benefit in this.'

The Ambassador, as though his face were carved in wood, did not so much as blink.

Devoy's features, in contrast, were all screwed up. 'A rising in

Ireland, well-organized and equipped, would divert British forces from Europe. Might even immobilize their fleet.'

Bernstorff was an intellectual, with a broad high forehead, topped by hair slicked into a wave, and a Kaiser-like moustache. His wing-collar and his tie, kept in place by a diamond-studded pin, gave him an old-world appearance.

'Very interesting,' he kept repeating, in a perfect English accent like Casement's that grated on Devoy's ear.

Though he received the Clan courteously enough, Bernstorff had to tread warily in view of Berlin's instructions. Besides, he was a diplomat; subterfuge and military matters were best left to his young military attaché, Captain Franz von Papen.

After the meeting, Bernstorff wirelessed his despatch to Berlin at once. It was very cool.

As he saw it, the squabbling Irish in the British Parliament had closed ranks and agreed to fight for the Empire. A big disappointment to Berlin, he knew.

Secondly, as he looked at the large table in his drawing-room with its campaign map of Europe, he was convinced that Paris would fall in days and Britain would back off.

Finally, he admired the English. They were of the same race and creed as the Germans, with the same love of beer and tobacco. Born in London himself, he had spent his first ten years there. He had even proposed to his wife in Hampton Court Palace.

Devoy assumed the meeting was a success. It tickled him that, through the Ambassador, the Brotherhood in Dublin would have a reliable means of communicating with Germany. That was one in the eye for the damned English.

Casement wrote an Address to the Kaiser. Millions of Irish-Americans, he said, had a feeling of 'sympathy and admiration for the heroic people of Germany. We draw Your Majesty's attention to the part that Ireland necessarily, if not openly, must play in this conflict. So long as Britain is allowed to exploit and misappropriate Ireland and her resources, she will dominate the seas. Ireland must be freed from British control.'

Devoy got the Clan Executive to sign it and Bernstorff forwarded it to Berlin in the diplomatic pouch.

To be doubly sure, Devoy sent a courier, John Kenny, to Berlin with the Clan's programme. Kenny handed it in person to the Chancellor. From Berlin he went on to Dublin, where he briefed Clarke and told him how Uncle would send on all his letters to Berlin.

41

That night, when McDermott entered Clarke's shop, he saw this black little figure perched on a stool behind the counter, gazing into space.

'Sean,' he said, his soft voice throbbing, 'we can now plan the rising in earnest.'

That planning was to take months and depend on factors beyond Clarke's control.

In the first place, Carson decided that he did not like the Kaiser after all. Assured by Lord Kitchener, the new Minister for War, that Ulster could have a regiment of its own, he turned loyalist again.

'England's difficulty is *not* Ulster's opportunity,' he had said to a cheering crowd in Belfast's Ulster Hall. 'England's difficulty is our difficulty, and England's sorrows have always been and always will be our sorrows. We do not seek to purchase terms by selling our patriotism.'

Then the Home Rule Bill was put on the statute book, though its implementation was to be delayed until the end of the war. It envisaged the possibility of at least part of Ulster being excluded.

John Redmond accepted this. He was a realist; he knew in his heart that, war or no war, Ulster would fight rather than be forced into a Union with Dublin. But the Bill enabled him to return to Ireland as a conquering hero. He made his way to Parnell's old shooting lodge of Aghavannagh, County Wicklow, on the slopes of Lugnaquilla. The nearest station was three hours from Dublin on a branch line, and he still had to travel another seven miles. His 'home' was a symbol of his remoteness from Irish life. Of the real Ireland, he now knew little.

He loved Aghavannagh. It is Synge country, with herons crying over black lakes, haunted by grouse and owls, thrushes and larks in their season, with the gorse a burnished gold in spring. He enjoyed shooting, the long rambles in the blue-toned hills past the occasional cottage over which drifted the blue smoke of turf fires. He relished the peace, the twice daily swim, in cool mountain pools, the chance to catch up with home news from old friends, and sometimes just watching the peak of Lugnaquilla breasting a soft and feathery sky.

On his way home, on Sunday 20 September, he chanced to hear of a parade of Volunteers at Woodenbridge. He paused to give them a short impromptu address. For all his famed diplomacy, he was a deeply emotional man.

With Home Rule already assured, he said, it would be a tragedy 'if young Ireland confined her efforts to remain at home to defend her shores from an unlikely invasion, and shrank from the duty of proving on the field of battle that gallantry and courage which has distinguished our race all through its history.'

This speech caused twenty on the Executive Committee to resign, including John MacNeill and The O'Rahilly. Redmond was encouraging their men to serve not Ireland but England.

In the *Irish Volunteer*, MacNeill pointed out that so far Redmond had only got a *promise* of Home Rule, with a threat of partition, at that. How, then, could he offer Irish blood?

The Nationalist movement split. 150,000 followed Redmond, calling themselves National Volunteers. 13,500 stayed with their founder, John MacNeill, to be known as the Irish Volunteers and, in some quarters, as Sinn Feiners, meaning All-Aloners, those who wanted no part with Britain.

Tom Clarke saw that he had to target MacNeill's more compact and independent group. If the Brotherhood could infiltrate them, they would have a disciplined army when the time was ripe. He and McDermott began to choose their key men.

First, Patrick Pearse, headmaster of St Enda's Irish-speaking school. He was already on the Supreme Council of the Brotherhood.

True, Pearse cast two shadows. He admired Napoleon and acted like Don Quixote. He wept over the death of a kitten while being convinced that Ireland would only gain her freedom through a blood sacrifice. But as he rose in the Volunteer ranks he was likely to prove very useful in a rising.

Then there was Joe Plunkett, a round-faced, short-sighted man in his mid-twenties with a sickly pallor in his cheeks. His chief hobbies were poetry and the strategy of war.

Next was Eamonn Kent, a tall, handsome man who loved all things Irish, the language, the music, the dance. The little he said came through clenched teeth but he had a will of iron.

Clarke also admired Thomas MacDonagh, the ebullient university lecturer who had intervened with Harrell over the arms landed at Howth, and Eamon de Valera, a mathematics teacher who, born in New York, was Irish from the soles of his feet.

Old Tom chose these men because, unlike MacNeill and The O'Rahilly, they would never be satisfied with Home Rule. They wanted an Irish Republic *and* were prepared to fight for it.

In the States, Bernstorff was becoming more and more impressed by

Devoy and Casement and their idea of forming a Brigade from Irish prisoners.

He telegraphed their proposal to Berlin, adding that if it came to a life and death struggle with England, 'I recommend falling in with Irish wishes.'

This message was intercepted and passed on to the British Admiralty in London. It came out of the tube in its cylinder and dropped with a twang into the metal basket.

Alfred Ewing, a Scot, had been appointed by Admiral Oliver as chief cryptographer. He and his staff of five, sensing this might be important, worked on it for hours without success. As Herr Zimmermann had said, the code was beyond them.

They put the telegraph on file.

On 1 October, Asquith gave Birrell a new Under-Secretary.

Sir Matthew Nathan, aged fifty-two, was extremely able yet relaxed. He was squarely built, with a fine head and strong jaw. His dark, handsome face, bristly moustache, and masterful voice made him popular with the ladies.

In London, Birrell briefed him in advance.

'The first thing you have to know, my dear fellow, is this: though the large and imperious Lady Aberdeen, wife of the Viceroy, believes she rules Ireland, and is the real Lord Lieutenant, it is in reality neither herself nor her bearded diminutive husband. It is I, the Chief Secretary, and now you, my deputy, who rule them.'

Nathan looked up from his note-taking, not sure whether to laugh or not.

'The Viceroy,' Birrell continued, 'is nothing but bright buttons and silk stockings, for ceremonial occasions, *vous comprenez?* The less told him the better for British administration in Ireland. Her ladyship will complain bitterly. Having learned a few words in the vernacular, which is more than most locals have, she thinks she is an expert in all matters Irish.'

Nathan's blue-grey eyes twinkled. He was beginning to warm to his new chief.

'The Viceroy himself plainly means well, which makes things so much worse.'

Birrell told him in confidence that he was asking the PM to get rid of the Aberdeens as soon as possible.

Birrell not only liked Nathan, he trusted his judgement. The admiration was mutual. Both were Liberals which, Birrell warned him, would not endear him to most Irish civil servants who were Tories and Unionists. 'They won't bless you for speeding the advent of Home Rule, my dear chap. But that's what we're here for. I don't know if the Irish can govern themselves but one thing's certain: no one else can.'

These two were the best team Ireland had had in years. Birrell had already seen over fifty Irish Bills through Parliament dealing with matters like land-purchase and the National University. While he was obliged, as a member of the War Cabinet, to spend most of his time in London, there was a private wire from the Irish Office to Dublin Castle.

Nathan was so able and so nice, he had a relatively easy introduction to the most bewildering country in the Empire.

He worked from 9.30 a.m. to 7 p.m. He saw his top civil servants, army and police chiefs every day. Detectives gave him a run-down on all subversives, like Clarke, Pearse and MacBride; and on places like the HQ of the Irish Volunteers and Liberty Hall, a building by the Liffey which was the home of the Transport Union.

In October, the Union leader, Jim Larkin, the greatest outdoor speaker of his time, sailed for the States to raise funds. He left James Connolly in charge of the Union.

Scottish-born, short and stout, Connolly looked like a farmer. He never drank or smoked. A slight speech impediment caused him to say, 'I'm a so'alist and proud of it.'

When Connolly called his first Union meeting, he could see the members thinking, This poor bastard is no substitute for Big Jim.

Larkin was a giant, Connolly was small. Larkin was lean and mean, Connolly was round and chubby. Larkin had a voice like a storm, and, well, who could match *that*?

One of his audience was Michael Mallin, a former drummer in the British army. Another was Robert Monteith, a former British NCO. During the strike of 1913, he had seen a patrol of mostly drunk policemen baton a man to death on the quays. Later, his fourteen-year-old step-daughter Florrie was carried in unconscious, her golden hair matted with blood. She had been clubbed by a policeman. Monteith had seen to it personally that the culprit was repaid in kind.

Another fervent admirer of Larkin's there that evening was Constance Countess Markievicz. Big Jim's fiery eloquence had converted this former socialite to socialism.

They were all sharing the general apprehension when, without warning, Connolly burst into life.

'I'm of the workers, comrades. We work hard. But don't the capitalist bosses have their anxieties, too? Course they do. They're never quite sure, poor things, where to take their holidays.'

The Countess cackled loudly and one or two of the men sniggered.

'I mean,' Connolly went on, 'did you have the problem of knowing where to go this summer? To the sunny Riviera, perhaps. Or the vine-clad slopes of France. Or the lakes and fjords of Norway. Or maybe sailing up the Rhine to toast bewitching German *fräuleins* in frothy German beer.'

Now everyone was grinning. This wasn't at all bad.

'Or did you take the easy way out, comrades, by staying in bed to save a meal and telling the wife not to worry about what to buy with the pennies you gave her?

'And while you squandered your substance thus on riotous living, on drunken debauches, on saturnalia of domestic vice, did you ever stop to think of your master, poor, dear, overworked, tired master? No, you insensitive lot. Yet if it was tough on you knowing how to spend your pennies and what to do with your one-day vacation, how about that poor rich fat sod whose life is one long holiday?'

Hard-bitten Dubliners actually stamped their feet and clapped their agreement.

Connolly's voice went on a mountain climb. 'We, comrades in poverty and sorrow, we who toil from dawn to dusk from January to December, from when we're ten till old age at forty, what do we know of troubles, except the landlord, the fear of losing our jobs, the perils of sickness or accident, the lack of necessities, the dampness of our homes, the insolence of our superiors, the awful future in the poorhouse?

'With these trifling exceptions, comrades, we have nothing to bother us. Whereas our poor tormented bosses are working hard in their mansions with their feet up. Working with their brains. Poor bosses! Mighty brains! Using those big bosses' brains to enslave people like us. But, you know, as a so'alist, I don't much care for a system where the boss has more power than God Almighty.

'One word of warning. People talk about a Republic. But the new lot won't be any different from the old. We'll still be a bit of the capitalist Empire. The party evicting us from our slums will wear green uniforms and the Harp instead of the Crown; the warrant turning us out on the roadside will be stamped with 'Irish Republic'. Capitalists, brothers, are stinking capitalists the world over. Which is why I intend to spread this' – he began to unfold a huge banner in front of them – 'over the face of the Hall.'

When the Countess took the other end of the banner, they all read: 'We serve neither King nor Kaiser but Ireland.'

13 October was a red-letter day for the British. Four German destroyers were sunk and a fast Russian cruiser, specially commissioned by the Admiralty in St Petersburg, arrived in England.

Admiral Henry Oliver and Sir Alfred Ewing were summoned to the Russian Embassy where they were handed a compact, heavy, sea-stained package. Back at the Admiralty, they opened it to find they had been given the German naval codes, lined in lead, from the *Magdeburg*.

It contained the work-columns on which the codes were based, plus the key to the cipher system by which the codes had maximum variability. It could be changed from hour to hour. It was brilliant. But was it still in operation?

Ewing tried it on that day's intercepts. Splendid. His team could decode them with little difficulty.

He grew very excited. The Germans, with their transatlantic cables cut, were forced to use telegraphic messages.

He suddenly remembered he had on file Bernstorff's telegraph to Berlin of 27 September. His team could hardly believe what it revealed.

Sir Roger Casement, former British consul, was hoping to raise an Irish Brigade in Germany and travel with it to Ireland for a rebellion.

Casement was then in New York, shaving off his beard for his mission. Afterwards, fingering his smooth chin in embarrassment, he had a final word with Devoy, Cohalan and McGarrity.

Devoy could not catch all that was being said. He asked repeatedly in a loud voice what the hell was going on and people yelled top secrets back at him.

One thing he failed to hear: Casement was taking a servant named Christensen with him because he spoke German.

They checked his passport and ticket to Christiania (Oslo). A Clan member, James Landy, came in. He gave Casement his identity papers and a 'Sons of Veterans' badge. He also handed him his spare glasses and some letters addressed to himself, including one from the Assistant Secretary of State.

Cohalan and McGarrity gave Casement a last run-through.

'Name?' said Cohalan.

'James Landy, without an e.'

'Subject of which country?' asked McGarrity.

'American citizen.' Casement's cultured English accent made his two interrogators wince.

'Mother's name?' said McGarrity.

'O'Mara.'

'Wrong,' snapped the Judge. 'That's your wife's maiden name. Your mother's name was . . . ?'

'It's on the tip of my tongue. It's . . . Sorry.'

'Joyce.'

'Of course.'

It was plain that Casement was going to make a hell of a rotten spy, with that accent and his bad memory for details. Devoy hoped that if he survived the next twenty-four hours things might just work out.

As a red herring, a room had been booked for Casement in a Chicago hotel while in New York he went through his papers again and practised an American accent, without much success.

He looked in the mirror. It was obvious he had shaved off his beard because of the whiteness of his chin. He sent out for buttermilk and washed the rest of his face in it to try and tone down his complexion.

After a restless night, he went on board a small Danish steamer, *Oskar II*, with Landy. In the cabin they switched roles. Adler Christensen was already installed next door.

A British agent on the quay picked up the phone and got through to British Intelligence with the news that Sir Roger Casement was on board *Oskar II*. The message was flashed to the Atlantic Fleet with the order, 'Take all necessary measures to apprehend him.'

As soon as it was in British territorial waters, the ship was intercepted by a British cruiser, the *Hibernia*, and ordered to proceed to Stornoway.

Casement felt he had been twigged, but how? He thanked his lucky stars he had Adler with him. He unlocked a case, threw some diaries and papers through a porthole and handed Adler some important official letters.

'Make sure,' he said, 'they do not fall into the wrong hands.'

Christensen crossed his heart and went at once to his cabin where he steamed them open. Realizing he had struck gold, he started making copies.

At Stornoway, half a dozen Germans were removed from the *Oskar II*, one of them the ship's bandmaster. Casement's lack of a beard saved him from detection.

Adler returned his letters and Casement, suspecting nothing, locked them up again.

It was foggy when they arrived at Christiania at midnight on 28 October and booked into the Grand Hotel. Next morning, Casement went to the German Legation to present his credentials to the Minister von Oberndorff, then back to his hotel to await instructions on how to proceed to Berlin.

In the afternoon, Christensen took a stroll. Making sure he was not being followed, he made his way to the British Legation. A reluctant porter admitted him when he whispered, 'I have precious information for the Minister.'

The Minister was out, so he had to make do with a junior official, Francis Lindley.

Christensen spoke English with a Norwegian accent spiced with American. He had come, he said, from the United States with an English nobleman who had been decorated by the King.

'This Englishman and myself, sir, I must admit it, are doing, how shall I say, certain terrible things.'

Lindley, young and inexperienced, suspected this was a confession of homosexual practices but he was not sure. The reference might be to espionage.

Christensen spoke of letters that had come by chance into his possession.

'These letters,' said Lindley, 'are from—?'

'The German Legation in Washington. They contain ciphers. I make a copy.' He waved a piece of paper in front of Lindley but refused to hand it over.

'You don't happen to know,' said Lindley, 'the name of this man?'

Christensen refused to say more except that he was travelling to Germany to stir up trouble in Ireland.

'I wonder, Mr Christensen, if you would be good enough to come back tomorrow morning.'

When Adler returned to the hotel, Casement said, 'Where have you been? I've been so worried about you.'

Christensen went on about how he had been waylaid in the lobby. 'An Englishman shoved me into a chauffeured limousine and we drove a long way to a big building.'

'The address, Adler. This is important.'

Adler thought deeply and came up with 79 Drammensveien. He had been asked about his employer, he said. 'I didn't give you away.'

'Of course not, my dear boy, I never dreamed you would. But did they mention me at all?'

Christensen shook his head.

Casement looked up the British Legation in the phone book. As he suspected, it was at 79 Drammensveien.

He was so trusting, he failed to see the obvious flaws in Christensen's account. How was he forced into a car in a crowded lobby? Was his assailant armed? Had he gone quietly, this muscular six-foot twenty-five-year old?

What Christensen said fitted Casement's presuppositions. He was a marked man. The British would stop at nothing to silence him.

Casement was also deceived because of his infatuation.

In the British Legation, lights burned into the night. Wires to and from New York brought the information that Christensen was listed in police files as 'a dangerous type of Norwegian-American criminal'.

Officials were puzzled. If the companion really was Sir Roger Casement, why was he employing a crook with a record?

Next morning, Christensen slipped back to the Legation where he was questioned by the Minister himself. Mansfeldt Findlay found him exactly as New York had given him to expect, fleshy and dissipated. Could he rely on the word of a criminal?

Christensen produced an article written by his master and a pamphlet, *The Elsewhere Empire*. Findlay glanced at them. They were pro-Irish, anti-British diatribes, meant obviously for American consumption.

'But you still haven't named this English gentleman.'

After a long hesitation: 'Roger Casement, sir.'

Findlay counted out, very slowly, twenty-five kroner.

Christensen was shaken by such stinginess but the Minister assured him, 'That is the normal fee. We pay better for some sorts of information.'

Christensen objected that what he had told him so far was important enough.

50

'Hardly,' the Minister said. 'We knew that already, you see.' He winked conspiratorially. 'If, on the other hand, you let us know what happens when you both reach Berlin, that' – he wagged a finger – 'might be worth considerably more.'

Seeing he was willing to co-operate, the Minister produced from his drawer a simple code for keeping in touch. Then: 'Mr Lindley tells me you have some sort of cipher.'

'Not on me.'

Christensen returned, out of breath, to tell Casement, 'I was on my way to breakfast when I was jumped again and told I would be paid well if I made another visit to that place.'

This time, he said, he was met by a very tall man, clean-shaven except for a very thin greyish moustache. He introduced himself as Mr Findlay. He looked unmistakably English in his tweed suit and with an accent very like Casement's own. He already knew their identities.

Casement blinked in surprise. 'What else?'

'He said that as you are travelling incognito, no one would notice if you simply, well, disappeared.'

'He said *that*?'

Adler dredged his memory. 'His actual words were, "If someone knocked him on the head, and dropped him in a convenient fjord, that sort of thing, you would not need to work for the rest of your life. And who would be the wiser?"'

As Casement tried to take this in, Christensen said that Findlay had given him a code to communicate with him. He showed it to a fascinated Casement.

Finally, he said, Findlay had given him twenty-five kroner for his cab fare home. 'If I'm interested in a bigger reward, I'm to return this afternoon.'

Casement was in a rage. All his old antipathy towards the British at the way they had delayed his reports on atrocities in the Belgian Congo and South America bubbled over. He went to the German Legation to see Oberndorff.

'Might it not be advisable, Minister, if I am whisked off to Germany at once?'

Oberndorff made arrangements for that evening.

Back at the hotel, Casement told Christensen to return to the British Legation and pretend to be interested in whatever plot they were hatching. Meanwhile, he himself would openly make arrangements to travel to Denmark.

When Christensen saw Findlay that afternoon, he showed him both the cipher and a sample of Casement's handwriting. It included a letter in which Casement had written of his servant: 'I am glad I brought him, he is a treasure.'

'And so you are,' Findlay crowed, 'a treasure.'

Christensen asked for $100 but settled for 100 kroner.

'And is your *master* intending to stay long?'

Christensen told him that Casement was pretending to travel to Denmark.

'What a deceitful fellow he is,' said Findlay, archly.

No sooner had Christensen left than Findlay pressed a buzzer. 'You heard? Come in at once, please.' He could not stomach Casement's un-British behaviour.

'Listen,' he told his young naval attaché, 'I want you to board Casement's train as it's about to leave. There's a King's Messenger travelling to Denmark in the same wagon-lit. Tell him these two men are dangerous.'

Christensen returned to give Casement a graphic account of blowing smoke from his cigar in the Minister's eyes.

'I also used very foul language many times.'

'What did he offer you?'

'$5,000 if I lured you where you could be kidnapped. He also promised to pay me handsomely for any information I smuggle out of Germany. As an advance, he gave me these—' he held up the 100 kroner.

Casement hugged him in delight. 'Adler, you are such a treasure.'

Oberndorff made arrangements for Casement to travel with a German Foreign Office official, Richard Meyer.

At the station, Casement had just bought *The Times* and the *Daily News* when Christensen hissed, 'I think we are being followed by a Britisher.'

The King's Messenger was, in fact, easily identified by the cut of his suit.

Casement congratulated him on his powers of observation.

In the middle of the night they left the wagon-lit and switched to another part of the train. Eluding their watchers, they crossed by ferry to Sweden and reached the German frontier at Sassnitz without mishap. On the last day of the month they booked into Berlin's Continental Hotel, with Casement signing himself in as Mr Hammond of New York.

On Monday 2 November, he went to see the Under-Secretary at the Foreign Office on the Wilhelmstrasse.

The porter showed him into a large waiting-room, a fine salon with oil paintings of former Emperors with medalled uniforms and bristling moustaches. Seated in an immense armchair of faded black leather, he brought his diary up to date.

The reason for his trip was nothing less than national resurrection, 'a free Ireland, a world nation after centuries of slavery, a people lost in the Middle Ages refound and returned to Europe.'

Artur Zimmermann came in. Aged fifty-six, he was a big, jolly man with blue eyes, bushy moustache and receding reddish yellow hair. On one cheek was a duelling scar. He thought nothing of drinking four pints of moselle at a meal.

'So sorry, Sir Roger, for the delay.'

He pleased Casement by reacting to his account of Findlay's attempt to kidnap him with, 'How perfectly dastardly'.

'Yes, sir, they stick at nothing.'

After a brief chat, Zimmermann took him to meet the Head of the English Department. Count Georg von Wedel was of upright build, with brown eyes and an impeccable English accent.

'You think you can raise a Brigade from Irish prisoners of war?' asked Zimmermann.

Casement, with his experience of recruiting for the Irish Volunteers, said, 'Scores, hundreds even, will join.'

Wedel wrote a favourable report to the Chancellor. He suggested that the General Headquarters should put all Irish PoWs in one camp to allow Sir Roger Casement to try and influence them in Germany's favour.

That afternoon, seated under a portrait of King George V in his ornate Castle office, Sir Matthew Nathan was reading copies of telegrams from the Minister in Christiania. Birrell had forwarded them from London with a covering note.

'It seems,' he wrote, in his best pantomime manner, 'that Roger Casement is drumming up German support for an invasion of Ireland. But are the Germans so much more unwise than the Romans that they want to come to Galway?'

With the Irish enlisting in the British army in their thousands, Nathan did not believe they would rise in support of the Germans. In any case, if there was even a hint of an invasion, the Admiralty would surely keep him posted.

*

Henry Oliver of the Admiralty had been promoted. His replacement as Director of Naval Intelligence (DNI) was Captain Reginald Hall.

Now forty-four years of age, Hall had the most penetrating eyes and a facial tick that earned him the nickname of Blinker. His broad jutting chin tried to link up with a long sharp nose and he had a voice that barked like a machine-gun. Within days, his subordinates felt they had been hit by a hurricane.

His job, he recognized, was the most important in the country. Luck had put his team in the position of being able to read German messages without them being aware of it. He could, if he wished, telegraph messages of his own to their agents and make them do his will. He might even order German ships and submarines into waters where they could be picked off by the British navy.

He began to recruit the best team available even against the traditions of the Senior Service. He took on board civilians, City brokers and merchants, bright sparks from Oxbridge colleges. In his team were a Director of the Bank of England, an art expert, and a Roman Catholic priest complete with pipe and dog-collar. Some were young, some long past their prime. What they had in common was a working knowledge of German and a love of puzzles of all sorts.

All German messages intercepted by wireless hacks found their way into Hall's offices which had been moved out of the main building into the old to become known as Room 40 OB (Old Building). With the aid of the *Magdeburg* codes and German military codes recently provided by the French, there was little that Hall's team could not unravel.

Behind the 'No Admittance' sign, long dark corridors now hummed with activity. Unused rooms without a lick of paint on the walls were taken over. They were seldom aired and no charladies were allowed to poke their noses inside them.

In one smoke-filled room there might be four or five experts around a table, trying to work out an intercept. Like a Quaker meeting, it might go on for eight hours without one word being spoken. Until someone said, 'Is this it?' Or, 'Are we being led up the garden here?'

Hall enrolled one or two dilettante types belonging to gentlemen's clubs such as St James's. Their sole purpose was, while dining, to shoot their mouths off in the company of foreign diplomats who could be relied on to transmit the false information they were fed.

Hall even took on women as cipher experts and typists. They became known as 'Blinker's Beauty Chorus'.

Though he demanded and received absolute loyalty, he was no respecter of regulations. Britannia not only ruled the waves; in wartime she was entitled to waive the rules. His intelligence service had the edge over MI5 in that he had no scruples about employing agents abroad. He was even using Captain Guy Gaunt, the naval attaché in America, who was abusing diplomatic privilege as flagrantly as Bernstorff.

If a thing needed doing, Hall cut through red tape to do it and many a time licensed his agents to kill.

Casement was only three weeks in Germany when, on 20 November, the German Chancellor authorized a statement which Casement had drafted. It admitted that the well-known Irish Nationalist, Sir Roger Casement, was in Berlin and had been received by the German Foreign Office.

> Should the fortune of this great war ever bring in its course German troops to the shores of Ireland, they would land there, not as an army of invaders to pillage and destroy, but as the forces of a government that is inspired by goodwill towards a country and a people for whom Germany desires only *national prosperity* and *national freedom*.

Devoy read this and was thrilled. He sent a message on behalf of the Clan to Casement through the German Embassy in Washington, assuring him that the Statement had made an excellent impression.

That was to be Casement's one and only success.

Christensen, now code-named The Informer by the British, was giving Findlay letters written by Casement to his friends in America and England. Some confirmed that he was trying to organize an invasion of Ireland with German help. The British Foreign Office took the matter very seriously and forwarded them to Birrell.

The Foreign Office in Berlin disagreed completely with their British counterpart over the value of Christensen. Ever since they had learned of his meetings with Findlay, they had judged him a charlatan without one redeeming feature. He wore make-up, he had expensive habits and a big lying mouth.

Herr Zimmermann thought his story was a fabrication from beginning to end and Casement was a fool for believing him.

Casement's real test came when he tried to fulfil his obligations to the Germans and form an Irish Brigade. Two pro-Nationalist priests, Fr O'Gorman and Fr Crotty, had been sent from the Irish College in Rome to assist him.

The Irish PoWs were brought together in Limburg, thirty miles north-west of Frankfurt. On 3 December, Casement addressed them for the first time. Only success here would convince the Germans that he was genuine and effective.

He was in a foul mood, because he had been politely told by the German Foreign Office that his manservant was a scoundrel and had a wife in America, which he refused to believe.

He introduced himself to the PoWs and briefly explained that he was recruiting for an Irish Brigade, so called after the Brigade of 300 Irishmen who fought against the British in the Boer War. His brief address ended with handing out copies of the *Gaelic American* and putting up a poster calling for volunteers.

The PoWs read it in angry amazement: if they were willing to fight against England for their own country under its own flag, they would be treated as guests of the German government.

Having drawn a blank the first day, Casement tried again.

Many of the PoWs were campaigners with ten years' service; comrades of theirs had been killed or wounded at Mons. He was jeered at and jostled, and boos went all along the line.

He perceived that this was no temporary set-back. His mission was doomed to failure. This, together with growing doubts about Adler's loyalty, began to affect his health.

On the day Casement took to his bed a General Council of the Irish Volunteers met in Dublin. They formalized the break with Redmond's National Volunteers and chose their own HQ personnel.

MacNeill became Chief-of-Staff; Patrick Pearse was Director of Organization; Joe Plunkett was Director of Military Organization; Thomas MacDonagh was Director of Training; The O'Rahilly was Treasurer; Hobson was Quartermaster-General.

From then on it became even clearer to Tom Clarke that this was the group to target for use in the rising.

Already Pearse was proposing to the new HQ staff that the Volunteers should fight back if the British imposed conscription on Ireland or tried to disarm them. Even MacNeill agreed with him on that.

Under Clarke's guidance, the Brotherhood began making plans for a rising in the guise of self-defence.

Clarke was particularly pleased with Pearse. He was becoming very important, and not just as an orator. That frank face of his would deceive an angel. He had the slyness of innocence; he was a dove with a serpent's tooth. He was now wholeheartedly committed to bloodshed in Ireland's cause.

'Too many rebels,' Tom told Sean McDermott, 'funk the ultimate test. Pearse ain't one of them. Under that schoolmasterly exterior, I reckon, is a spine of steel.'

In Room 40, Hall chanced to hear that a British trawler had recently hooked an iron-bound sea-chest in its nets. He investigated and found that it contained a book of codes which he believed had come from one of the four German destroyers sunk on the day the Russians handed them the *Magdeburg* codes.

He had a hunch that it was Berlin's code for communicating with naval attachés abroad. There was great excitement in Room 40 when his hunch proved to be correct.

His team was growing all the time in wireless operators and cryptographers. Part of their job was intercepting Bernstorff's messages to the Wilhelmstrasse.

From them they learned that Cohalan in the States had advised against publicizing the Findlay affair until there was full proof. Also that Devoy was sending a priest from Philadelphia, John T. Nicholson, to recruit for the Brigade. 'He is in every way qualified. Speaks Irish well. Has visited Germany and is full of sympathy with the work we want done. Born in Ireland but is an American citizen.'

In Ireland, Redmond, in contrast to Casement, was at the height of his popularity. On Saturday 19 December, he held a rally at Limerick Racecourse. It was a biting, wintry day with the grass already sere, but over 10,000 Volunteers turned out to greet him.

The entire country was at fever-pitch. At mass meetings in Kilkenny, Waterford and Derry, the Irish had been wildly enthusiastic at the prospect of Home Rule.

Redmond was overcome with emotion as he stood on the platform at Limerick. Home Rule, he told them, was their form of nationalism.

It would make them full members of the Empire. The Bill was already law, only suspended for the duration. Yes, this war would not last long, not with Irishmen fighting the Germans.

There were more prolonged cheers.

Just before Christmas, Birrell told Nathan that a new viceroy was to be announced on New Year's Day. Lord Wimborne, formerly Sir Ivor Churchill Guest, was Winston's cousin.

In Birrell's view, he was a crude young man without any fine strands of character. 'But if he manages to keep his temper, with that charming wife of his, he might not do too badly. He might even do really well.'

Two days after Christmas, Casement met with Herr Zimmermann to sign a treaty.

By its terms, Irish PoWs who volunteered for the Brigade would be fed and equipped at German expense; they would fight under the Irish flag and be led by Irish officers. The Germans agreed to send the Brigade 'to Ireland with efficient military support, and with an ample supply of arms and ammunition for the Volunteers in an attempt to recover Irish freedom by force of arms.'

The treaty was not to be published until Casement had conscripted a large enough expeditionary force.

Already realizing his prospects were nil, he made plans to return to Limburg and go through the motions.

On 28 December, Birrell passed on to Nathan a flimsy from the Foreign Office. He summed up Casement as having 'a strain of madness and vanity'. In Germany, he was in touch with Burke Cochrane, an influential American lawyer gone wrong, and in New York with the old Fenian, John Devoy. He seemed to be getting at Irish PoWs in Germany.

Birrell wrote: 'It is all very *vague* about numbers and *nationalities*. Are they coming as open *enemies* – to storm our coasts, and seize our Irish castles – or as *secret* agents of the Kaiser? However, we must be ready for either dread contingency! The weather will upset their stomachs if not their plans!'

Nathan did not take things so lightly. He cancelled his vacation in England. He also met with General Friend, Army Commander in Ireland, and Chamberlain, Inspector-General of the Royal Irish Constabulary, who both assured him their men were on their toes.

He asked for increased surveillance of old IRB men in Limerick and Belfast. He brought his list of potential rebels up to date and tightened postal censorship.

In particular, he kept a close watch on MacNeill, Chairman of the Volunteers, especially after they intercepted a letter from Casement asking him what arms he required from Germany.

After the loneliest Christmas of his life, Casement left Berlin on Wednesday 30 December on the night train for Limburg. By the time he arrived the next evening, he was exhausted and suffering from a bad cold. He went straight to bed where he saw the New Year in.

'My God,' he moaned, as he heard the clock chime, 'will the whole of 1915 be like this?'

On 2 January, in overcoat and muffler, he drove up the steep hill to the camp. Seeing him, Irish PoWs muttered, 'Here comes the bloody Boer,' and, 'The fecking Fenian's been let loose again.'

He climbed on to a table to address eighty out of the 2,400 prisoners in the camp. Sniffing, his voice hoarse, his legs shaky, he explained the purpose of the Brigade.

'If you decide to join, men, you will be guests of the German government. You will be switched to another camp near Berlin where there is better food and accommodation.'

'Champagne and caviare, eh?' one of the Munsters said in a mock upper-crust English accent.

'If Germany defeats the British on the seas—'

'Some bloody *if*,' a Dublin Fusilier chipped in, as the PoWs edged closer and closer.

'In that case,' Casement continued nervously, 'I will see to it you are landed in Ireland where our fellow countrymen will help you drive the British out of our land.'

'And if Germany gets its come-uppance?' a Ranger yelled.

'Then you will be sent to America on a free passage with money in your pockets to begin a new life.'

With the soldiers now only inches away, an angry cry went up, 'How much is Germany paying you, mate?'

With the table starting to rock, Casement jumped to the ground where he was jostled and elbowed. He swung his umbrella around to defend himself until German guards rushed to form a wall around him.

Back at his hotel, the desk clerk said, 'A letter for you, sir.'

A sour look spread over Casement's face as he read it. It was from Devoy, complimenting him on his splendid work in Germany.

His only hope was that Adler was getting useful information from the British Minister in Christiania.

'I have now more details about Sir Roger's return to Ireland.' Findlay, in his swivel chair, gestured for Christensen to continue. 'He has already booked his passage.'

'On?'

'The *Mjolnir*. I could go and meet it at Gothenburg before it sails to Christiansand. If the money is right.'

Findlay stroked his perfectly smooth cheek. 'I will certainly think about it.'

'Think!' Adler roared, moving to the door. 'What's there to think about? I'm going to tell Casement about you.' He left the room, slamming the door behind him.

Moments later, the door opened quietly and he returned.

Findlay had not budged. He opened a drawer, drew out a bank roll and, as Adler's tongue licked his upper lip, counted out 2,000 kroner.

'By the way,' Findlay said, pleasantly, 'there's another whopping amount for you if you help us capture our fugitive.'

'I would need that in writing.'

'Come, come—'

'In writing,' Christensen insisted, 'or no deal.'

Findlay shrugged. This was wartime and, as a minister of the Crown, he was simply putting a price on a traitor's head. 'Very well.'

'On official notepaper,' Christensen said.

After the briefest of pauses to take in the nerve of the man: 'Why ever not, my dear fellow?'

He wrote out, on British Legation notepaper, a pledge of £5,000 reward and signed it with a flourish.

Only afterwards did he ask London's permission. Nicolson gave it but warned him not to put anything in writing.

A few days later, the *Mjolnir* arrived in Christiania.

Findlay's naval attaché reported, 'He was not on board, sir.'

'Jesus!'

There was a scratching on the door. It was Christensen.

'This mess,' he said, 'is probably due to faulty German intelligence. If I had been able to contact Casement in Berlin I would have forewarned you.'

60

'I'm sure you would have, my dear chap.'

When Christensen left, Findlay sat brooding for a long time. The truth had finally dawned on him; the man was a double-agent.

He wrote to London admitting that he had not the requisite talent for probing the mind of such an immoral and loathsome beast.

Christensen returned to Berlin with Findlay's letter. He now knew it would not bring him £5,000 but it might at least improve his standing with the German authorities. With Casement out of town, he handed it in to the Foreign Office.

Wedel read it once, twice, with incredulity. A British Minister could not possibly be so naïve. Christensen must have pilfered a sheet of legation notepaper and written it himself. He decided to check with their man in Christiania.

Within days, Oberndorff sent him on a hand-written letter of condolence he had received from Findlay a few years before. The writing matched that of the letter brought by Christensen.

Wedel wrote to Oberndorff saying that the British Minister was incriminated in an attempt to snatch Casement but he was to have no further dealings with The Informer.

To Wedel, the affair was a distraction. He simply put the two Findlay letters in his file.

On 23 January, Casement returned to Berlin, tormented by doubts about Adler's loyalty. He had his suspicions but could not forget his tender care on the journey into exile.

He was at a very low point when Herr Meyer happened to mention Findlay's letter. This was marvellous news. It proved two things: Adler was no liar and Findlay was vicious and unprincipled. He could use this letter to discredit not just him but the British FO and government, as well.

Except Wedel refused even to let him see it.

He created a scene but Wedel would not yield. Casement, therefore, wrote an open letter to Sir Edward Grey about the whole affair and arranged for it to be typed. Since the German Foreign Office refused to back him, he would take it to Norway himself. He and Adler would confront Findlay together. If this meant the end of an Irish Brigade, so be it.

Sunday 31 January found him and Adler at the Sassnitz ferry, facing one of the bleakest outlooks in the world. Only then did it finally hit him that his plan was crazy.

61

His body went rigid, his eyes glazed over. The long-expected collapse was upon him. He held out his arm and allowed Adler to grip it and lead him, like a tired old man, to the hotel to await the train back to Berlin.

On the last weekend of January, a more relaxed Nathan was vacationing in England where he talked with Birrell and lunched with Wimborne, the Viceroy-elect.

No sooner was he back in Dublin than he discussed with General Friend the problems arising from the arming of the Volunteers. He spoke with Hamilton Norway, Head of the Post Office, assuring him that the IRB, once 40,000 strong, now numbered at most a thousand.

Chamberlain of the Royal Irish Constabulary told Nathan of a series of lectures at the Dublin Headquarters of MacNeill's Volunteers. The chief instructors were James Connolly, the Union leader, and Thomas MacDonagh, the Brigade Commander.

'What are they teaching, Chamberlain?'

'The art of warfare in towns, sir, with emphasis on communications, mapping, street-fighting.'

He handed over a verbatim report of a lecture by Connolly.

Nathan, an ex-soldier himself, saw at once that he knew a thing or two. Connolly's thesis was that a street is like a mountain defile. Forces moving through a street are easy targets for snipers posted at windows or on roofs. Barricades across streets which cannot be attacked by artillery are impregnable to frontal assault. The best way to control a street is to take one house and create a tunnel inside it to other houses.

Nathan read aloud, 'Every difficulty that exists for the operation of regular troops in mountains is multiplied a hundredfold in a city.'

Chamberlain said, 'MacNeill, their Chief of Staff, says all this talk of street-fighting is purely in the event of an emergency, say, should conscription be imposed on Ireland or arms be confiscated by the Government.'

'I understand,' Nathan said thoughtfully. 'Thank you.'

Casement booked himself into a sanatorium in the Grünewald where he had a private room. Months of depression and paranoia were to follow, during which the Irish Brigade made no progress.

In the Wilhelmstrasse, a censor stopped a letter home of a Dublin PoW, Private Smythe: 'Dear Mother, I am very pleased to receive your letter yesterday. They are hoping to form an Irish Brigade here, but we will die first – Johnnie.'

In New York, Devoy was furious with Casement for allowing himself to be side-tracked by a peripheral matter like Findlay's letter. He was only now hearing of his ham-handed way of recruiting. Instead of speaking to each man privately, he had addressed men in large groups, Catholics and Orangemen.

Worst of all, he heard that Casement was offering the Irish Brigade to the Germans to help liberate Egypt. He was plainly off his rocker. The Clan had told him all along that the only place for the Irish to fight was Ireland.

'Liberate Egypt, for Chrissake!'

He decided to confide in Casement no more.

In Dublin, with the new Viceroy due, Birrell told his Private Secretary, Sam Power, to impress on him that he could be as ornamental as was possible in wartime.

'But do explain to this bear, Sam, that he must not dance on my platform.'

'Do my best,' Power said, with a grin.

'If he gets notions, suggest to him the usual grand tour. Above all, make sure he tells everyone that he is merely the prelude to Home Rule and not Viceroy for ever and ever, Amen.'

Birrell was facing a more personal problem. His wife, Eleanor, was dying. The inoperable brain tumour, diagnosed a couple of years before, was now much worse. He visited her often in hospital. She did not recognize him, living uncomprehendingly in an imaginary world where there was no pain. He sat for hours at her bedside, holding her hand, the tears running down his cheeks. Ireland and Home Rule and Roger Casement were very far from his mind.

She died on 10 March, leaving him free to go to Dublin.

On 10 March, Pearse, Plunkett, Hobson and The O'Rahilly were made commandants on the HQ staff of the Irish Volunteers.

Officers of the Dublin city battalions were also appointed. Ned Daly was to be in charge of No 1, Thomas MacDonagh of No 2, Eamon de Valera of No 3 and Eamonn Kent of No 4. All but de Valera and The O'Rahilly were members of the Brotherhood.

Three days later, Pearse addressed the four commandants.

'Gentlemen,' he said, solemnly, 'I have information for your ears only.' They watched him closely. 'A rising is planned for this September.'

He outlined the general strategy and the areas to be controlled.

'Each battalion will be responsible for blocking the roads connecting the military barracks with the city centre. They must be neutralized at all costs.'

The four young commandants had no illusions as to the size of their task. The Dublin Barracks were gigantic.

'Build up your strength with men from your own area. Choose your HQ, keeping in mind that you will need access to food and supplies. You will receive notification of the rising on grey notepaper. The messenger will say, 'Howth'. Pick your own code-word so that HQ knows the message has been received and understood.'

De Valera immediately chose 'Bruree', the name of the place where he was bred.

McDermott reported Pearse's briefing to Tom Clarke at his shop in Britain Street.

Clarke said, 'I'll put Uncle in the picture right away, though I'll stress the final date may depend on the Germans.'

Clarke also thought it a good idea to send someone to Berlin to update Casement on events back home and find out how the Irish Brigade was shaping up.

'Plunkett's your man,' McDermott said. 'He has permission to travel to Switzerland to try and cure his consumption.'

A few miles west of Clarke's shop, in the Viceroy's Lodge in the lush setting of the Phoenix Park, Wimborne had begun entertaining on a lavish scale.

Lady Wimborne, already nicknamed 'Queen Alice', was a dimpled delight. Next to her bed, quite safe from her husband's prying eyes, was a large framed picture of her Spanish lover.

As to Wimborne himself, known to the ladies as 'His Ex', he was, after thirteen boring years of marriage, a fairly frank brandy-swilling bounder. He was stagy, with a tendency to express himself with wide gestures of his arms. He flapped his eyelids at attractive women and sometimes borrowed their earrings to adorn his own tyre-sized ears.

His secretary was Lord Basil Blackwood. Three years older than the Viceroy, he had a reputation, not altogether justified, for being a womanizer in his own right. One guest was even heard to say, 'If Basil ever gets to heaven, they had better lock up the Virgin Mary.'

From Wimborne's point of view, Blackwood had a less amiable side. His Ex needed him to take down his letters and refill his glass, yet he kept asking to join the Grenadier Guards in France.

'God,' Wimborne moaned to the ladies, 'dear Basil has no will to live.'

Against the background of a city plotting rebellion, the Viceroy passed his days and his nights in Castle balls and private revels. And Nathan hoped it would long continue so; it kept his Lordship out of Irish affairs which he lacked the diplomatic skills to cope with.

In Berlin, Casement, with typical generosity, decided to send Adler to New York. He wrote to the Clan asking for their help.

Devoy thought Christensen might prove useful at some time. He organized a well-paid job for him and replied: 'We will welcome our Norwegian friend and do all we can for him.'

In mid-April, Casement was visited in Munich by Joe Plunkett who travelled under the alias of James Malcolm.

'In my view,' he told Joe, over and over, 'a rising in Dublin in 1915 would be criminal stupidity.'

When Plunkett met with the Irish Brigade in Limburg, he recognized it for the flop it was. Recruited by Irish priests, they had their own quarters and their own uniform, green with shamrock and harp, which Casement had designed. Only fifty showed the remotest interest in fighting for Ireland, though they were very willing to attack Germans in their immediate vicinity, especially those foolish enough to call them 'English'.

He was received at the Foreign Office and discussed arms for Ireland with the Chancellor. Tubercular, foppish, he did not exactly impress Bethmann-Hollweg.

A rising in Ireland combined with a German push on the western front, Joe told him, would rock the British. He added, free of charge, advice on how to win the war.

At the General Staff, he asked for 50,000 rifles with ammunition for the Volunteers. He was told bluntly that the millions of Irish-Americans in the States should provide them.

Before he left Berlin, Casement warned him not to rely on the Germans for anything. They had no moral sense.

*

At midday on 7 May at Buckingham Palace, King George V gave an interview to President Wilson's roving adviser, Colonel Ed House. They discussed in particular the activity of German submarines in British waters.

His Majesty said, 'Suppose they sink the *Lusitania*, Colonel, with American passengers aboard?'

The Colonel replied, 'America would be outraged enough, sir, in such an eventuality, to enter the war.'

'Torpedoes cleared.'

Kapitänleutnant Schwieger of the U-20, his eye screwed to the periscope, acknowledged. In his sights, just off the Old Head of Kinsale in southern Ireland, was a four-stacker identified by its gold lettering: *Lusitania*.

The 32,000-ton liner had left Pier 54 in New York for Liverpool on 1 May, the day on which Bernstorff had placed a notice in American papers warning American citizens not to travel across the Atlantic on British ships in wartime.

Thirty-two-year-old Walther Schwieger, in command of the U-20 for the first time, estimated that the liner was 700 metres distant and travelling at 18 knots.

'Torpedoes ready, Herr Kapitän.'

'Up . . . Down,' he commanded. 'Up a little. One degree right. . . . Meet it. Fire!'

The submarine rocked slightly as its 21 1/2-foot, one-ton torpedo was released with a hiss of air from the forward tube. There was silence below, apart from the yapping of a Dachshund, as the torpedo homed in at a cutting angle of 90 degrees on the starboard side of the *Lusitania*. It was 2.10 p.m. on 7 May.

Between 8 and 11 that night, boat after boat put in at Queenstown Harbour with survivors and the dead. There were piles of corpses, from babies to the very old, among the paint drums and coils of rope on the old wharves. Later, the bloated and, in some cases, naked bodies were transferred to a shed. Queenstown seemed nothing but a huge charnel house.

Of the 1,200 drowned, 118 were Americans.

Walter Hines Page, the American Ambassador in London sent off a wire virtually urging the President to cast neutrality aside in favour of Britain.

Judge James Gerard, the American Ambassador in Berlin, also felt that President Wilson would now come off the fence and recall him. He went to the Foreign Office and handed in a note to Herr Zimmermann. It pledged that America would do what was necessary to safeguard its citizens on the high seas.

Zimmermann, puffing on a huge cigar, started to yell, 'You would not dare do anything against us. We have 500,000 German reservists in America who will rise in arms against your Government if it takes action against us.'

Gerard, his glasses steaming with indignation at the thought of naturalized Americans siding with Germany against their own country, replied quietly, 'We, sir, have 501,000 lampposts in America to hang them from.'

The American Press was so outraged that Devoy was afraid that America would enter the war on Britain's side and brand his work for Irish independence as treachery. He never did trust President Wilson, anyway, that teetotal, non-smoking Presbyterian with his lop-sided idea of neutrality, providing the damned English with all the arms they needed.

Wilson was furious but Ed House and the American Ambassadors were wrong. After his usual White House breakfast of two eggs in orange juice, he merely typed the first of his notes demanding freedom of navigation for merchant shipping. He remained committed to the idea of a peace without victory between the European combatants. He did, however, order Secretary McAdoo of the Treasury to watch personnel in the Austrian and German Embassies suspected of plotting on American soil.

When the Head of the Secret Service, William J. Flynn, tapped the phones of the German Embassy in Washington he was surprised to overhear conversations between Bernstorff and certain ladies who found it hard to take no for an answer.

In New York, the tapping was done by Police Commissioner Arthur Woods, while the Bomb Squad of the Department of Justice tailed German diplomats.

Meanwhile, the U-20 returned to Wilhelmshaven where Schwieger received a hero's welcome and countless offers of marriage from patriotic *fräuleins*.

In England, due to a stalemate in the war, pressures were building up for a Coalition Government. Birrell's was the only post no one wanted, least of all himself.

Redmond was offered a Cabinet post but no Irish Nationalist could accept preferment in advance of Home Rule. He telegraphed Asquith:

'In view of the fact that it is impossible for me to join, I think most strongly Carson should not be included.'

This hardly needed spelling out. Before the war, Carson, in the name of Ulster, had described Home Rule as a mere piece of paper and had threatened to oppose the Army and Parliament with brute force.

In fact, six members of the new Cabinet were committed to resist Home Rule, including Carson.

Birrell agreed with the Nationalist who said that Mr Asquith had betrayed a previously hidden sense of humour.

In Dublin, the Supreme Council of the IRB, realizing a Unionist-filled Cabinet would alter the mood in Ireland, appointed a Military Committee. Its task was to prepare in detail for a rising.

Pearse was a natural, being the Volunteers' Director of Operations. Joe Plunkett was chosen as strategist. The third was Eamonn Kent, a man of steel and a tremendous fighter.

On the last day of May, one of the greatest fighters of all, a small, red-bearded man, was on his soap-box outside Liberty Hall attacking conscription. Francis Sheehy-Skeffington, known as Skeffy, was a Dublin legend.

In 1903, he had married Hanna Sheehy and, to express their equality, they called themselves Sheehy-Skeffington.

Skeffy was thirty-six years old. His handshake was brisk, his voice somewhat shrill, and he was transparently sincere in each of his many unpopular causes – pacifism, socialism, nationalism, feminism, teetotalism, vegetarianism. Almost everyone in Dublin was proud to say he or she had hit Skeffy at some time, either with a fist or a missile.

He was easily recognizable in his long stockings, boots, tweed cap, and the saucer-sized button in his lapel, 'Votes for Women'. He was often seen hanging from a lamppost, with a policeman tugging on his knickerbockers to bring him down, while he squeaked in his broad Cavan accent, 'One last point before I go.'

Whenever he was accused of being a crank, he bowed and said, 'Correct. A crank is a small instrument that makes revolutions.'

On this particular occasion, this fighting pacifist was saying, 'There is no such thing as a war to end war, my friends. Each war is a prelude to the next,' when he was pulled off his soap-box and arrested under the Defence of the Realm Act for opposing recruitment.

Sentenced to six months, he found himself in Mountjoy Jail alongside Sean McDermott, who had been convicted for the same offence. Hanna brought their six-year-old son, Owen, to see him. This was his second visit. He had been there aged three to visit his mother when she was in for breaking windows in the Castle while campaigning for women's rights.

Skeffy went on hunger strike. After six days, he refused drink. Four days later, he was released under what was called the Government's cat-and-mouse legislation. He was allowed out until he was fit enough to be imprisoned again.

When he returned home, Owen saw him through the window. He hardly recognized this pale skinny spectre as his father.

Skeffy's voice was so thin he could barely give him his usual greeting, 'Hello, laddie.'

Plunkett returned to Ireland on 25 June and immediately reported to Clarke, Pearse and Kent.

'Jolly depressing news, I'm afraid. There is no Irish Brigade and so, precious little hope of German assistance.'

Clarke refused to be downhearted. 'Redmond's Volunteers are drying up whereas ours are growing daily.'

Pearse said, 'Redmond is still preaching that a Home Rule Parliament is as certain as the rising of tomorrow's sun. If he believes that he's the only one in Ireland.'

'Right,' Kent said firmly. 'He's finished.'

Old Tom exhaled the smoke from his cheroot. 'The future lies with us, all right. What we need now is one big gesture to find out if the people are for us or not. You guys must have heard of Jeremiah O'Donovan Rossa.'

They smiled. Who hadn't heard of Rossa?

An early member of the IRB in 1858, he had been captured in 1860. At his trial, he defied the Judge. Jailed he defied the prison authorities.

One morning, the Head Warder called out, 'Atten-*tion*. Salute the Governor.'

The Governor was peering through the bars when Rossa threw the contents of his slop-pail over him, hitting him full in the face.

'That,' said Rossa, fed up with all the false salaams, 'is my salute to you.' He grabbed the timber doors and shook them until the whole building seemed to quaver.

Rossa was never to forget the Head Warder crying in a whiny voice, 'Oh, sir, 'tis clean water.'

He was given thirty-five days solitary with his hands behind his back. His food he had to lap up like a dog. He spent his time reading D'Aubigny's *History of the Reformation*, turning the pages with his teeth.

Released in 1871, he went to the States with John Devoy. An enthusiast, he was given to crazy schemes which annoyed the hard-headed Devoy, who once accused him of being a drunkard and an embezzler.

Clarke had known Rossa well in America. They had knelt together at the graves of dead Fenians and prayed for their souls. Not in English, Rossa said, a language God never listens to. They had filled cemeteries with the roar of prayers in Irish for the Irish dead. It was Rossa who had inspired Clarke to take part in the dynamite campaign in London which brought him fifteen years in jail.

'Old Rossa's been fading for a couple of years,' Clarke said. 'And his wife, Molly, has agreed with me that when he dies, she's gonna send him home.'

Devoy had been visiting him in St Vincent's Hospital on Staten Island. By this time Rossa imagined he was still in an English prison, and nurses had to use force to stop him jumping out of the window.

Devoy, knowing one dead Fenian was worth a thousand German rifles, told McGarrity, 'An excellent idea of Clarke's. Why not send the old bugger home?'

Rossa died on 29 June 1915. He had a solemn High Mass on Staten Island before being shipped to Ireland where the body was given a grand reception.

Clarke never doubted who would deliver the panegyric at the graveside in Glasnevin.

Patrick Pearse prepared it in his little Connemara cottage at Rosmuc, County Galway, the 'Connacht of the bogs and lakes'. It was ten miles from the nearest railway station and half a mile along a winding lane from the main road. To his romantic soul this was the real Ireland.

The three-roomed cottage, lime-white, thatched, with a green door, was surrounded by bogland and heather slopes under an ever-changing sky. It faced north towards the everlasting mountains, the Twelve Pins of Joyce country. To complete the picturesque setting, beside it was a fifty-acre lake over whose clear waters herons hovered.

He loved this country, knew every hill and stream by name. When he travelled it he spoke only Irish and exchanged blessings with the people after their own fashion.

Though peaceful by nature, Pearse believed that a man with a loaded rifle is entitled to a certain respect. In his view, if there was one thing more ludicrous than a Loyalist with a gun it was a Nationalist without one.

Preparing his panegyric, he was inspired. He had always loved histrionics; his friend and fellow teacher at St Enda's, Thomas MacDonagh, used to say that he only became a headmaster so he could speechify whenever he liked. This was *the* great occasion of his life. When he was a little boy, his mother and his Great-Aunt Margaret had sung him rebel songs figuring the musical name of Jeremiah O'Donovan Rossa.

He had written to Clarke, 'How far can I go?' On his desk was Old Tom's reply: 'As far as you can. Make it as hot as hell, throw all discretion to the winds.'

Sean McGarry, who was editing a souvenir programme for the funeral, asked James Connolly to contribute an article.

'No,' Connolly said brusquely. He had been banking on a rising in September and there was no smell of one as yet. 'When are you tin-pot revolutionaries going to stop blethering about *dead* Fenians and get a few *vertical* ones for a change?'

When McGarry reported back to Clarke, he smiled and said, 'Guess I'll have a word with him myself.'

He met Connolly in his office in Liberty Hall.

'You were asking about dead Fenians, Seamus,' he said. 'I wanna tell you there's no such thing. And something else. This funeral's gonna be the best possible way of balloting the people.'

Connolly, face to face with a vertical Fenian, one of the greatest, not only wrote an article, he promised that his trade union soldiers, the Citizen Army, would parade in force.

Most towns displayed big posters advertising the funeral. Special trains were chartered at reduced fares.

A worried Nathan wrote to Birrell that 14,000 rail-passengers were expected. 'I have an uncomfortable feeling that the Nationalists are losing ground to the Sinn Feiners [the Irish Volunteers] and that this demonstration is hastening the movement.'

His prophecy proved correct. On Sunday 1 August, packed trains brought mourners from all over Ireland.

In the City Hall, that afternoon, Mary O'Donovan Rossa gave Tom Clarke the honour of removing the tricolour and replacing the cover on the casket.

There was an air of tremendous excitement on the streets as the hearse, drawn by two plumed black horses, was preceded by a group of priests: seculars, Dominicans, Benedictines, and four tall Capuchins with brown habits and sandalled feet. They were followed by kilted scouts of the Fianna, Gaelic Leaguers, Transport Union workers with their banners, mayors and members of corporations from all over Ireland, many carriages and several pipe bands. An armed escort of the Irish Volunteers and the Citizen Army marched alongside the hearse.

Thousands, bare-headed, processed around Dublin before heading for Glasnevin to the strains of the Dead March. The heavy rain of morning had given way to unblemished skies.

In his cell in Mountjoy, Sean McDermott was straining to hear. He felt proud to be an Irish felon on a day like this.

Above the whir of trams on the North Circular Road and the hooting of railway engines, he caught the strains of the pipers' bands and the tramp of thousands of feet. He stood and bowed his head.

The procession stopped in silence outside the prison, a mark of respect for Rossa who had been inside it fifty years before. When it continued, Sean did not move for over an hour till the sounds had died away.

Dominating Glasnevin cemetery was an Irish round tower, 160 feet high and topped by an eight-foot cross weighing two tons. Under it slept Daniel O'Connell, the Liberator. Buried nearby was the great Parnell, dead at forty-five, who said, 'No man has a right to fix the boundary to the march of a nation. No man has a right to say to his country: thus far shalt thou progress and no further.'

For Irish Catholics, graveyards were powerful places and funerals acts of defiance. Protestants had always had their cemeteries and funeral rites. But until 1825 Catholics had to bring clay from the grave, place it in the coffin at the house of their deceased and pray for him there.

On this day, in Glasnevin, sunlight was reflected off stone, the air was fragrant with the odours of drying earth, the children watched in wonder the drift of dandelion fluff.

After the funeral rite in Irish, an expectant hush settled on the crowd.

Clad in the grey-green uniform of the Irish Volunteers, Patrick Pearse stepped forward and removed his cap. Now his broad white brow was visible and the clear grey eyes. Out of his left pocket, he took four pages of foolscap with his bold clear writing on it. Behind him was the burly Major John MacBride and to his left, beyond Darrell Figgis, was Tom Clarke, who stood sideways on to get a better view.

With his right hand in his belt, Pearse spoke a few words in Irish before switching to English. His phrases moved on, slow and austere. His emotion was the more impressive for being under perfect control as his voice echoed round the natural amphitheatre.

He spoke, he said, in place of the grey-haired fighters for Ireland's freedom, because he represented a new generation re-baptized in the Fenian faith.

> We stand at Rossa's grave not in sadness but rather in exultation of spirit. O'Donovan Rossa was splendid in the proud manhood of him, splendid in the heroic grace of him, splendid in the Gaelic strength and clarity and truth of him. In a closer spiritual communion with him now than ever before, we pledge to Ireland our love, and we pledge to English rule in Ireland our hate.

There were stirrings all around him. Clarke's eyes widened behind his glasses; if only McDermott could hear this.

'Hate' was not a word much used at funerals. But it struck a chord: forgiving wrongdoers is good, forgiving wrongdoing is unforgivable.

Pearse's eyes were closed now, as though his speech came from the very depths of his being.

> This is a place of peace sacred to the dead, where men should speak with all charity and with all restraint; but I hold it a Christian thing, as O'Donovan Rossa held it, to hate evil, to hate untruth, to hate oppression, and hating them, to strive to overthrow them ... Life springs from

73

death; and from the graves of patriot men and women spring living nations.

At this, even grey-haired warriors strove to check their tears.

> The Defenders of this Realm have worked well in secret and in the open. They think that they have pacified Ireland. They think that they have purchased half of us and intimidated the other half. They think that they have foreseen everything and provided against everything – here Pearse threw back his head, like a blackbird in full-throated song – but the fools, the fools, the fools! – they have left us our Fenian dead, and while Ireland holds these graves, Ireland unfree shall never be at peace.

After a deep silence came a new sound in an Irish cemetery: round after round of applause. They cheered O'Donovan Rossa and O'Mahoney, Stephens and O'Leary; they cheered all the Irish rebels that had ever been.

Finally, came the command to the escort. 'Load, aim, fire!' A volley rang out over the grave, followed by the Last Post played by Bugler William Oman of the Irish Citizen Army.

Clarke kept his eyes skinned, hoping that Crown forces would try to disarm the escort, thus precipitating a conflict.

Nothing happened. Not even an RIC stenographer was present. Birrell and Nathan, damn them, were obviously playing a waiting game. No matter, a fool could see the Volunteers had the country behind them.

The crowd dispersed.

Pearse walked the long way home alone and sat quietly in his study at St Enda's. He was now in the forefront of the movement. From that day on, there was no turning back.

Nathan's report on the funeral reached an unimpressed Birrell on the 3rd. In reply, he said of Rossa, 'I do not suppose anybody in the whole concourse cared anything for the old fellow, who never cared for anything at any time.'

It was one more sign that Redmond's constitutional Home Rule stance was less and less popular. Birrell, therefore, agreed with Clarke on one thing: Republicans and the forces of revolution were in the ascendant.

Next day, Tom Clarke went west to Limerick to visit his old prison mate.

John Daly still ran his bakery from his wheelchair. Though he was old now, completely bald and with a huge straggly beard, he still had a glorious twinkle in his eyes and a brain as sharp as ever.

Clarke gave him a glowing report of the funeral.

'What about the September rising, then, Tom?'

'Delayed. Without German arms, we should have to confine the fighting to Dublin which would be a pity. If only we could get someone in there to give Casement a hand.'

'Well, Tom,' Daly said, 'we both know the right man.'

They sent for Bob Monteith, whom Nathan had banished to Limerick and who was helping to train the local Volunteers.

Without hesitation he said, 'I'll go, provided my wife and kids are taken care of.'

Clarke assured him, 'There's no question about that.'

First, Monteith had to travel to the States. He had no difficulty obtaining an exit permit. Nathan was pleased to get rid of him.

A few days before his departure, he went to Dublin to say goodbye to his family.

His thirty-four-year-old wife, Mollie, was a remarkable woman, beautiful and intelligent.

'I'll soon make arrangements,' he said, stroking her auburn hair, 'and you can follow me across.'

He embraced all his children warmly, but he could not hide a special fondness for Pat and little Vie.

He landed in New York on the morning of 9 September. On Ellis Island, an immigration official asked, 'Where's the Atlantic Ocean?'

'I'm glad to say,' he replied, 'it lies between here and England.'

His first call was on John Devoy at his office in Lower Manhattan.

Having prepared a home for his family at 137th Street in the Bronx, he concentrated on getting to Germany. An American passport was out of the question in view of his anti-British record.

He had long talks with Devoy and did not take to him. His value to the cause was beyond dispute but did he have to be so autocratic?

Something else annoyed him: Devoy seemed to have no respect for Sir Roger Casement.

*

75

Casement was at Ammer See, vacationing with the family of Dr Charles Curran, an Irish-American whom he had met in Munich.

He glanced at the calendar. It was 13 September. The date meant something to him. Why? Then he remembered.

It was on 13 September 1848 that John Mitchel, a Protestant, an Irishman and an eternal diarist like himself, wrote a memorable passage in his diary.

Mitchel was in exile in Bermuda, under endlessly azure skies, no rain for weeks, with white moon-blinding rocks about him, and thinking, as was Casement now, of the misty mountains and rain-drenched grass of Ireland.

He hunted out his slim volume of Mitchel's *Jail Journal*, almost as precious to him as À Kempis's *Imitation of Christ* which he kept by his bed. He opened it and read:

> This thirteenth of September is a calm, clear, autumnal day in Ireland, and in green glens there, and on many a mountain side, beech leaves begin to redden, and the heather-bell has grown brown and sere: the corn-fields are nearly all stripped bare by this time; the flush of summer grows pale; the notes of the singing-birds have lost that joyous thrilling *abandon* inspired by June days, when every little singer in his drunken rapture will gush forth his very soul in melody, but he will utter the unutterable joy.

Casement paused. The beauty of Mitchel's words, the intensity of the images he conjured up, were too much for him. Tears streamed down his cheeks and moistened his grey-tinged beard as he remembered Ireland.

In Ireland, Pearse was now using his cover as the Volunteers' Director of Operations to extend plans for the rising beyond Dublin.

He visited Austin Stack in Tralee. Knowing Stack's family history and his reputation as a leader, he appointed him Brigadier of the big Kerry division.

'And, by the way, Austin, you'll need extra arms.'

A few days later, Kerrymen went *en masse* to Dublin for the All-Ireland Final. Stack had arranged for rifles and ammunition to be picked up at The O'Rahilly's place, 40 Herbert Park, Dublin.

After the match, supporters packed the arms into beer crates and covered them with Kerry scarves and favours. When the train reached

Tralee, 'drunks' were detailed to distract the RIC; a few mascot-dogs played their part by barking at their heels. The jostling, singing supporters provided cover to get the arms to a safe place.

Soon after this, Pearse sent Dermot Lynch, one of the Brotherhood, to Kerry. He asked various IRB men where was the best place to land and distribute arms in the west. Limerick was fine but, they all agreed, the best harbour was Fenit in Tralee Bay.

Lynch reported back to Pearse and McDermott who had just been released from Mountjoy Prison.

Now that Tralee had assumed major importance in IRB thinking, Pearse summoned Stack for a long interview at St Enda's. He told him in the almost bashful way he had that the IRB had now scheduled a rising for Easter 1916.

'Hopefully, Austin, the Germans will provide us with arms. If so, they are likely to come ashore in Tralee Bay. In which case, your job will be to land and distribute them.'

'May we have more details, sir?'

'Unfortunately, I cannot give them as yet.'

Stack asked, 'Are you hoping the Volunteers will rise all over Ireland?' Pearse nodded. 'Beginning here?'

'Correct. We shall seize Dublin and declare a Republic.'

Pearse's matter-of-fact tone completely underplayed the audacity of the enterprise.

'Once the north, south and west have consolidated, all Volunteers will head for Dublin where British fire-power is bound to be concentrated. One final warning. It is vital to keep this secret *until the very last minute*. If you have to confide in others, give the least information to the least number of people.'

A distant bell sounded. Pearse struggled into his gown.

'And now, if you'll excuse me, I have to take my boys for a history lesson.'

Monteith, happy that his family had joined him in New York, now concluded that the only way to get to Berlin was the oldest.

Devoy had reached the same conclusion. Amid the usual welter of papers in his unaired office, he said, 'Being a stowaway is damned dangerous, Bob. If you want out, that's fine by me.'

'Hell, no!'

'I thought you'd say that,' said Devoy, with a twisted grin. 'That's why I asked someone over to talk us through it.'

He pressed a buzzer and in walked Adler Christensen.

After introductions, Christensen started telling Monteith in his strongly accented American what a great man Casement was.

'That's enough,' Devoy butted in, scratching his grizzled chin. 'Just tell us how we get Bob here to Germany.'

'First, sir, I book a cabin on a neutral ship to Copenhagen. This gentleman can hide under my bunk.'

'And if someone sees me, the steward, say?'

Christensen rubbed a greasy forefinger over his greasy palm. 'Never fails.'

Devoy's cold eyes shone. If this worked, it would open up a whole new channel for Irish-Americans to join the Brigade.

'Right,' said Monteith, the most practical of men, 'you've got me on the boat. How do you propose to get me off?'

'You won't need a passport because we'll choose a ship that only puts into neutral ports.'

In spite of considerable doubts, Monteith and Devoy had no choice but to trust him.

The 29th was Pat's second birthday. Monteith took Mollie and his two girls to a 3rd Avenue photographer. In the studio, Mollie, in a long dress and broad feathered hat, was seated. The girls in linen caps stood next to her, Pat on a small round table on Mollie's right, Vie on her left.

When Monteith went to pick up the pictures, he kissed them and put them in his wallet. When he left the States, he wondered, would he ever see his loved ones again?

September came and went, and in Ireland nothing stirred. Connolly had set his heart on an autumn rising. He had several reasons to be depressed, as he told Bill O'Brien and the Countess Markievicz, in whose house he lodged.

In the first place, international socialism had failed. Everywhere in Europe, socialists were fighting the capitalists' war against their fellow socialists.

Second, he despised the Irish Volunteers.

'They have absolutely no idea what they want a rising for,' he fumed, his seal-like eyes blazing. 'They empty out a barrel of rotten apples and fill it with rotten pears. All they're good at is sermons over the dead. No guts for a fight.'

His companions were used to this. They let him go on.

'Take MacNeill. He wants every shoe-string in place before he sanctions a rising.'

'You've hit it on the chin, old bean,' the Countess said, in her squawky voice.

'There's only two places where such revolutionists exist.' The Countess joined him in saying, in a sing-song fashion, 'On the stage of comic operas or the stage of Irish politics.'

Bill O'Brien put in tentatively, 'We have to be better prepared, wouldn't you say?'

'Nonsense,' Connolly snorted. 'You need a leap in the dark for an insurrection. If MacNeill's old fogies won't take that leap, by God, the Citizen Army will.'

Countess Markievicz clapped her hands in support.

'Time for manoeuvres,' Connolly snapped.

His idea of soldiering was in the best Gilbert and Sullivan tradition. He, his Chief of Staff, Michael Mallin, and the Countess Markievicz called out the Citizen Army at short notice.

When the Countess asked Connolly what the target was, he replied: 'The Castle.'

'I say,' she said, 'how absolutely spiffing.'

The Castle meant different things to different people.

To the Anglo-Irish, it meant the rule of law, the defence of their long-held lands and privileges.

Not long ago, the Countess and her giant Ukrainian husband, Casimir, had been automatic invitees to the big Castle occasions like the St Patrick's Day Ball. Dressed in ermine and silk, dripping with diamonds, she had been borne in gilt carriages to banquets where she flirted with generals and politicians.

Now she saw the Castle as the embodiment of seven centuries of British tyranny, a machine for governing Ireland against her will.

Connolly, whose background was the antithesis of the Countess's, was the first man she had come across who believed implicitly in the equality of women. He had commissioned her in the Citizen Army. With her usual enthusiasm, she had told the youngsters, 'Now, my old darlings, pawn your shirts, if need be, and buy yourself a *gun.*'

'Yes, Madame,' they said, quite used to her weird way of talking.

Madame herself took pains to look the part in her immaculate dark green uniform and a slouch hat pinned on one side with the Red Hand badge of Labour. She wore riding breeches, though she covered them with a long dress, and carried a rifle as she marched that early October night through a gas-lit Dublin to do what no Irish rebel had yet succeeded in doing: take Dublin Castle.

James O'Brien of the DMP, a constable with greying hair and

kindly face, stood at the Gate of the Upper Yard. He peered through the fog and, recognizing his attackers, held up his hands in mock surrender. He was used to civilians parading with arms now that the Volunteers had promised to defend Ireland against German invasion.

'Don't shoot, Count-*ess*,' he pleaded.

The Citizen Army accepted his surrender and retired to Emmet Hall in Inchicore, followed by the Castle's secret police. The G-men stayed outside all night in a downpour, while the Citizen Army celebrated their historic victory with tea and buns and sang blood-thirsty songs the Countess had composed, the favourite being, 'The Germans are winning the war, me boys.'

The day before he left for Germany, Monteith lunched with Devoy who lectured him on what happened to men who let Ireland down.

'All found dead,' he said, in his dry, hollow voice. 'One whoreson failed through drink, another cos of a woman, another cos of a bribe.'

Monteith beckoned the wine waiter, saying to Devoy as he did so, 'I love a drink, myself.' To the waiter: 'A bottle of Chablis.' Back to Devoy again. 'And, to be honest, this whoreson loves all women. But none of them enough to make me sell out my native land.'

The waiter returned and filled his glass, then tried to do the same for Devoy but he put a wrinkled hand over the top.

Monteith raised his glass, 'To wine, women and – old Ireland.' That put a stop to Devoy's warnings.

They went through the schedule for the last time.

Monteith was to sail from Hoboken, New Jersey, to Copenhagen. The ship was scheduled to call only at the neutral ports of Christiansand and Christiania.

The next evening, 6 November, Monteith said goodbye to his children at their home on 137th Street.

His own two girls were too small to understand but to Florrie, now sixteen, he whispered, 'I want you to stay with your mother until I come back.'

'How long will that be, Daddy?'

For a long moment, he stroked her shoulder-length blond hair. 'Maybe soon, Florrie, maybe never.'

After a last hug of the children, he left with Mollie. They took in a Broadway theatre followed by supper but were too sad to enjoy it.

Monteith was a perfectionist who reduced his risks to a minimum.

British agents might be tailing him even now. At Hoboken, as rehearsed, he shook Mollie's hand casually and spoke to her in a cool voice to stop himself breaking down, 'Goodbye. Be seeing you.' Without a backward glance, he went to his hotel.

In the morning, he met Christensen on the quay and, carrying his suitcases for him, went on board the *SS United States*. The cabin was tiny. He slipped under the low bunk and pulled the cases around him.

At about 1.30 in the afternoon, he heard someone inspecting the cabins. An official peeped in and locked the door after him. So far so good, except there was a lot of dust under a bunk not swept in years. He was dying to sneeze.

Half an hour later, it was anchor's aweigh. He crawled out, stretched his limbs and looked through the porthole at the Statue of Liberty, as the boat manoeuvred in the river.

The sea was rough and he was soon sick. He kept his heaving to a minimum so as not to make a noise. When a steward popped in to make up up the bunk, he saw two boat-like boots a few inches from his nose and prayed he wouldn't throw up all over them. What annoyed him most in those first few days was the sound of endless tangos being danced on deck.

On the eighth night, around 11 p.m., Christensen burst in and whispered hoarsely, 'A British cruiser. Taken us in charge.'

In spite of their neutrality, the British sent a prize crew on board and escorted them through Scottish waters into Kirkwall in the Orkneys.

A shaky Christensen wanted Monteith out. He distracted the searchers, sometimes with come-hither winks, before signalling 'All Clear' and Monteith tiptoed to a cabin already checked. He quickly memorized where everything was and unscrewed the bulb so that anyone inspecting the place would be in pitch darkness.

Christensen supplied him with sandwiches and water and left him to slide under another dusty bunk.

At Kirkwall, passengers and crew disembarked for questioning. Mail bags were seized, letters read, phonographs played.

One night, a voluble drunk came into the cabin, lurched into the bunk and started snoring gustily. The bunk's wires practically touched Monteith's twitchy nose. Worse, as the night cooled, the ship's steam heat was turned on. Wedged up against scalding pipes, his clothes scorched and blisters formed on the entire right side of his body.

His hell only ended after a couple of hours when someone came in and woke the snorer up. He turned out to be an officer of the watch who was wanted on deck.

At about 7 in the morning, hearing further searches being carried out, he switched cabins. Children had returned to the ship to play. Their ball dropped through the skylight and rolled right up against his body. Kids started yelling for someone to go and get it back.

He flicked the ball away and pulled a floor covering over himself just as the door opened and an adult voice said, 'Got it.'

It was another five days before the boat was allowed to continue. Christensen, when he finally found him, told Monteith, 'The British have taken into custody four or five men. German citizens, spies, so they say.'

The band played tangos again. Back to abnormality.

Two days after that, on 19 November, they were sailing up the breathtaking fjord to Christiania.

Monteith had barely recovered his peace of mind when Christensen jolted him again. He claimed to have heard another sea-search was planned before Copenhagen.

'Better get off here, I reckon, and go on to Copenhagen by train?'

Adler's one motive for coming on the trip was to visit his parents in Christiania.

Over the loudspeaker, a voice said: 'Passengers disembarking have passports and landing papers ready, please.'

Monteith gripped Adler by the shoulder. 'I thought you said – What the hell are we going to do?'

'What are *you* going to do?' Christensen retorted, brandishing his passport.

'I don't know a word of your lingo,' Monteith grinded out, their faces almost touching. 'You'll have to interpret for me.'

'What is there to say?' Christensen spat through the gap in his teeth as he freed himself. 'You knew the risks.' Seeing Monteith getting very angry, he added, 'Don't *worry*. There's always friends, family, luggage-handlers coming on board. Just grab some bags, carry them down the gangway and mix with the third-class passengers.'

Monteith went warily on deck to find both gangways were manned by police: at the top, in the middle and on the quay.

He picked up a stray suitcase and joined a line of passengers. With a sinking feeling, he had started down the gangway, when he stumbled.

That gave him an idea.

He lurched, bumping against passengers. He cannonaded against a policeman at the top of the gangway who stretched out a hand.

'Steady there, sir.'

He got to the middle, humming crazily to himself, belching and moving sideways like a crab. His spell on board ship in a confined space really had made him unsteady on his pins. The embarrassed gendarme in the middle of the gangway let him pass without a glance.

One last hurdle: the gendarmes on the quay. He tripped and fell a dead weight into the arms of one of them who tossed him aside, with a disgusted look at his companion. In spite of Adler, Monteith had made it safely ashore.

They booked into the Grand Hotel in the centre of town. Monteith signed 'Jack Murray' in the book.

'Identification papers?' the clerk said.

He fumbled in his pocket, pointed to his bag.

'Later,' the clerk said.

But no sooner was Monteith in his room than the manager, who had lately been booked for not reporting an illegal immigrant, went to the police.

'A foreigner's just checked into the Grand,' he said.

'Suspicious?'

'Could be.'

'Keep an eye on him,' the duty officer said, 'and we'll drop in and see him by and by.'

Monteith had eaten and was asleep for a bare thirty minutes when Christensen, who had taken a walk and heard rumours, shook him.

'Wake up, man. The cops are on to us.'

It was still only 6 a.m. when the two of them squeezed through a back window and went to Adler's home. There they managed to get some sleep.

Adler's father helped out by booking two tickets on the night train to Copenhagen plus two for a local journey.

When the fugitives approached the station, they saw armed police at the entrance to the main platform, checking on passengers. Adler's father with a friend went through the check-point while they went on to the unguarded platform for the local train. They then crossed over to where Adler's father handed them punched tickets for Copenhagen.

The train left at 8.30 a.m. On board, they posed as brothers, with

Monteith pretending to be blotto. They sprinkled whiskey over the sleeping compartment and Adler pressed a few kroner on the Swedish customs official to ensure privacy.

Officials at the Danish border made Adler fill in forms for the two of them. Having placed them in a crammed folder, they left for the dining-room. Adler removed the forms, tore them up and tossed them out of the window.

'There,' he grinned. 'We no longer exist.'

Arriving at Copenhagen at 7.30 in the morning, they went to the German Legation. There was no passport for Monteith but a spectacled frosty-looking secretary assured them, 'The German frontier guards know you are coming.'

They left Copenhagen at 10 a.m. No sooner were they at sea than passengers at the rails shrieked, *'Unterseeboot.'* A British submarine, nosing around between Denmark and the German port, surfaced 300 yards away.

'Jesus,' Monteith muttered, 'now I'm for it.'

To his relief, it soon submerged again. Three German destroyers were heading towards it at a rate of 30 knots.

It was 5 in the evening when they arrived at the port of Warnemunde. The Customs let them in with a nod and they took the 6 o'clock train for Berlin where they arrived, without incident, just before midnight.

Monteith tried two hotels given him by Christensen but Casement had gone to Munich. He was non-plussed. Munich was a long way from Berlin and even further from Lübeck.

Next day, 23 November, after getting his ID, he caught the night train for Munich, arriving at Casement's hotel at 9 a.m. Entering his room, he felt this was the proudest moment of his life. He knew Casement by repute as a crusader for the dispossessed in the Congo and the Putamayo and Ireland.

'Everyone here accepts,' Casement explained, 'that it's only a matter of time before America allies itself with Britain.'

A German naval victory was out of the question and without that they had no hope of victory.

While he was talking, Monteith was noting his height – about 6 feet 2 inches – his arrow-straight back, the way he moved like a panther, the black hair and beard tinged with silver, the expressive eyes. In Berlin, Haughwitz of the German General Staff had told him Casement was not well. It was not immediately obvious except that his hands quivered a lot.

'All of which, my dear Monteith, has rather put a damper on my efforts to raise an Irish Brigade.'

'My orders, sir,' Monteith said, 'were to press on and that's what I intend to do.'

The presence of an ally seemed to revive Casement. They caught the train to Berlin at 7 that night and went on on the 26th to Zossen, seventeen miles south of the capital where the Brigade was now stationed. Fifty Irishmen were in a camp with a quarter of a million Germans. Monteith was impressed by Casement's concern for each of his men. The men themselves he found shifty-eyed and undisciplined.

Casement introduced him.

'The Lieutenant has come from the home country. He is in command here until a more senior officer can be sent from the United States.'

Monteith's first job was to recruit more men so, after a few days' rest in Berlin, he met with his two chief aides, Sergeants O'Toole and Beverley, caught the train to Limburg and booked into the Alte Post Hotel.

Next morning – it was a Monday – still in civvies, he began at 9 prompt. He planned to interview fifty men a day individually. He applied no pressure and offered no bribes. He admitted his own mistake in fighting for the British long ago.

They listened with, at best, indifference, as if to say, Who the hell is he?

Within the first hour, he knew he was in for a hard slog.

A fortnight later, a rejuvenated Casement wrote to Joe McGarrity, asking him to try and get some Irish-Americans into Berlin. 'If we can get twenty privates and two officers, we have a chance.'

The message was forwarded to Devoy. It was his best news from Casement in many a long day. Christensen had proved it *was* possible to get men into Germany.

As soon as Christensen was back from Berlin, Devoy contacted him, told him what he had in mind and started handing him bundles of dollar bills.

Birrell was becoming increasingly worried about Ireland. First, there was his Government's indifference. When Carson had resigned from the Cabinet, Asquith had simply replaced him with another Unionist, the notable barrister F. E. Smith.

Next, the Commons, backed by generals like Sir John French, now in charge of Home Forces, wanted to conscript even Irishmen. For that, Birrell felt, the army would have to enter villages and cart off Micks and Pats at bayonet-point. It would utterly destroy John Redmond and his Party, which, presumably, was what Unionists wanted.

Only loyalty to the Prime Minister, to John Redmond and to Ireland stopped him resigning. With the war dragging on beyond all expectations, the cry 'Home Rule is on the statute book' had faded to the point of inaudibility.

Across the stormy sea, the Sinn Feiners were growing stronger all the time.

At St Enda's School, Pearse never stopped. In addition to his many burdens – giving lessons, organizing the Volunteers throughout the country, trying to pay his bills – he went on writing.

As darkness fell, he was at his desk, reading over his new one-act play, *The Singer*. Largely autobiographical, it expressed his mystical ideas about the need for a rising to throw the British out of Ireland. He set it in the west, in wild hill country.

Its hero is Macdara, a young man who is very silent, until he stands up to talk to the people. Then he has the voice of a silver trumpet and words so beautiful they make people cry. And there is a terrible anger in him, for all that he is shrinking and shy.

Macdara admits that when he came home and his mother stretched out her arms to him, it was as though she were the Virgin meeting her Son on the way to the cross. Human love was not for him, only a cold, chaste hardening of the heart before he meets inevitable death in front of a jeering crowd.

He is not content to be a poet. He is a teacher and a fosterer.

'The true teacher must break bread to the people: he must go into Gethsemane and toil up the steep of Golgotha.' For he knows God's Name is suffering and loneliness and rejection.

His young brother dies for his people and Macdara decides to follow him, wishing that he and he alone could sacrifice himself for all like Christ.

Macdara, his mother says, is 'the Singer that has quickened the dead years and all the quiet dust.'

Accused by the elderly of embarking on a foolish thing, he replies, 'And so it is. Do you want us to do the wise?'

He goes to meet the Gall (the foreigner), pulling off his clothes to be naked like Christ, saying, 'One man can free a people as one Man redeemed the world. I will take no pike, I will go into battle with bare hands. I will stand up before the Gall as Christ hung naked before men on the tree!'

Pearse knew he could not stage this play, not with the rising so near. But he was happy to have written it. It was an expression of his faith.

An unwise thing had to be done because the wisest things had not won Ireland an inch of freedom. The way of the cross was the paradigm of all unwise deeds that can make the dead dust dance at the sound of the voice of a Singer who loves enough. If only he, Patrick Pearse, could die alone as Christ did, and by dying save his peers.

That, he knew, was impossible. Many would have to die for the foolish yet necessary thing that he and his colleagues in the Brotherhood at home and abroad had set their hearts on.

He went on his knees beside his desk and prayed for all of them in Ireland, and America, and Germany.

That same evening, Devoy wrote to the German Foreign Office, saying of Casement, 'He has full authority to speak for me and represent the Irish Revolutionary Party in Ireland and America.'

Devoy had discovered that Christensen was claiming maintenance for his wife, who turned out to be a kept girl-friend whom he had brought with him from Berlin.

A bachelor-prude, Devoy did not like the idea of him living with a slut in New Jersey at his expense.

'That bastard, that whoreson,' he muttered over and over, now convinced that he was in the pay of the British.

Unable to replace Casement, he had no choice but to back him.

He wondered how the request for submarines to transport arms and ammunition to the Kerry coast was being received in Berlin. They were certainly taking their time about it.

On 5 November, the German Admiral Staff finally replied to the General Staff that their High Sea command thought Tralee Bay was not deep enough for submarines. If attacked, they would be detected and sunk.

That same day, a solitary Irish-American, McGooey, arrived in Berlin. Casement was hoping for a couple of hundred. He prayed things were going better in Ireland.

*

From the point of view of the Administration, Ireland was moving towards crisis.

From the Castle, Nathan told Birrell that, in his view, the Nationalist Party had lost control of the country. Redmond confirmed that the Sinn Fein Volunteers were growing in strength. But Birrell was in a dilemma. If he did not repress the Sinn Feiners, they would grow; if he did, they would grow even faster.

Even Wimborne knew what would happen if conscription were enforced in Ireland. If he failed to enlist soon, say, 10,000 Irishmen, the Cabinet might impose conscription. In which case, support for the Sinn Feiners would be overwhelming.

The German War Office finally made Monteith a lieutenant. He arrived back in Zossen in uniform at 2.30 in the morning of 28 November to find it under two feet of snow. In his absence, the men had been chafing under Teutonic discipline. They were without overcoats, had been granted no leave and were deprived of weapons because they could not hold their drink. He moved into the officers' quarters. His job was virtually impossible but he would give it all he had.

He called Casement in his hospiz, suggesting that a break in Zossen would do him good. He himself had never felt lonelier in his life.

On the last day of November, at midday New York time, he was remembering Mollie. He had made a compact with her that they would think of each other at this time every day.

'Mollie Darling,' he wrote, 'I forgot to take one of your curls with me when leaving America. Send me one at once, then I shall feel that I have you with me, and will feel safe no matter what or how great the danger may be.'

Three days later, to his surprise, Casement turned up. Monteith booked him into a fine old inn, the Golden Lion, half a mile from the camp. He looked well and joined the men on route marches north to Mittenwalde and bought everyone beer.

In his African days, Casement had thought nothing of walking fifty miles a day on mud roads and in intense heat. He could still manage five miles an hour. The two of them were so deep in conversation they were soon a mile ahead of the column. They turned round to wait for the short stout Sergeant-Major. He eventually puffed up, complaining, 'Sir Roger, you're killing us all, sir.'

Those long walks imprinted themselves indelibly on Monteith's brain: the long white roads without any turnings, the smell of fallen leaves decaying in the crisp air, the wind sighing through the gaunt naked branches of the trees.

Mile after mile they walked, part of a platoon yet strangely solitary, alone under the moon and stars, walking through shadows. And Casement talked of his terrible experiences in the jungles and swamps of Africa and by the banks of the Amazon and into Putamayo.

But most of all, as they crunched snow under their boots, they remembered the greenness of Ireland, the softness of its rain; and wondered what were the chances of a rising against the British.

In mid-December, Casement was bucked by a flattering letter from Christensen in Jersey City. A couple of days later, came a note from Devoy exposing him for what he was.

So nothing Adler had said, nothing in their relationship had been genuine. The wretched Germans, who thought him a double-agent, had been right all along.

For a sensitive man like Casement, this was the final humiliation. His one consolation was that he had done his best for someone he had thought of as a friend.

What had he left now, except his love for Ireland?

Would Ireland, too, reject him?

At this time, an unsigned article, 'Peace and the Gael', appeared in the Dublin magazine, the *Spark*. The author was Patrick Pearse. He wrote of the heroism of the war.

'It is good for the world that such things should be done. The old heart of the earth needed to be warmed with the red wine of the battlefield. Such august homage was never before offered to God as this, the homage of millions of lives given gladly for love of country.'

When Connolly read it, he nearly had a fit. He said to Bill O'Brien: 'Listen to this. For love of country? Whose country? Lives given gladly. What utter bilge! Our poor sods enlisted out of need and died because of incompetence. Irishmen should only fight for Ireland, Bill. Their place to die is here and now, not far off on someone else's battlefield that will leave this country as enslaved as ever.'

He wrote a counterblast in his own *Workers Republic*.

'No, we do not think that the old heart of the earth needs to be warmed with the red wine of millions of lives. We think anyone who does is a blithering idiot.'

John MacNeill sensed a growing restlessness among his men. He tried to calm things down in his own publication, the *Irish Volunteer*, calling for patience and discipline.

Connolly read that with equal contempt.

Patience! After seven centuries of oppression! Quiet well-paid academics in their ivory towers were still calling for patience! Parasite capitalists were killing off the workers in factories and on the battlefield for a few pence extra profit and MacNeill was pleading for patience!

'My God, Bill,' he exclaimed. 'In future, we're going our own way, you hear me? That bourgeois lot will never do *anything* for Ireland.'

Neither MacNeill nor Connolly knew that the IRB was at that very moment intent on doing something great for Ireland. In Clontarf Town Hall, in a room set aside for them by the Republican caretaker, they met to elect a new chairman of the eleven-man Supreme Council.

Denis McCullough said to McDermott, 'I'm going to propose Pearse.'

'For the love of God,' Sean hissed, 'don't be daft.'

'He's a grand chap. Why not?'

'Because,' said McDermott, through clenched teeth, 'we can't control him, that's why not. Leave it to Tom and me.'

McDermott proposed McCullough himself. As he lived in Belfast, the two ringleaders felt he would be out of their way.

The motion was carried. McCullough said, 'Just send me a wire any time you want me.'

'We won't be sending any wires,' Clarke muttered for only McDermott to hear. Then, in his slow, impressive voice: 'Gentlemen, I propose a rising for Easter 1916.'

McDermott seconded it with a voice of thunder and Pearse was not far behind. The only member to object was McCartan. 'How can we rise when the people are not with us?'

Old Tom said, at his most persuasive, 'Didn't the Rossa funeral tell us what Ireland really wants, Paddy?'

Next, Clarke and McDermott manoeuvred the Council into adding their names to the Military Committee. With Pearse, Plunkett and Kent already on it, the extended group of five was to be known as the Military Council.

There were now 2,000 IRB men in leading Volunteer posts

throughout the country. At Easter, Clarke and McDermott were convinced, they would answer to *them* and not to MacNeill.

Their plan was to keep other top Volunteers in the dark, too, such as Hobson, the Secretary, and O'Rahilly, the Treasurer, who, like MacNeill, favoured defensive action only. This was a terrific gamble, but Clarke and McDermott felt they had no choice. Every single Irish rising had been ruined by informers. Theirs would be the exception.

More than ever they now depended on Pearse's leadership to bring over the entire Volunteer movement when they gave the word.

From this time on, Clarke developed still closer links with the States. It was now imperative for Devoy to persuade the Germans to send them aid.

With Christmas near, Casement was deeply depressed and not merely by life at Zossen. He had come to see the war less as Ireland's opportunity than as a disaster for mankind. All those beautiful lives being lost, to no purpose. He could not forget seeing hundreds of poor on the streets of Berlin, unable to afford the official casualty sheet, waiting until lists were posted on hoardings.

One couple stood for them all in his memory: a shawled white-haired lady and her weeping husband with his long-stemmed pipe, coming away from the list, shaking their heads in bewilderment and saying, '*Todt, todt, todt.*' Their son was dead. It was now plain to Casement that Death was the only victor.

He accepted Monteith's advice to get away for Christmas. In Munich he could be hospitalized again and meet with his old friend, St John Gaffney, the American Consul.

Casement was not the only one feeling the strain.

In Dublin Castle, on Christmas Eve, Nathan noted in his diary: 'Feeling rather seedy, the result of the wartime running down and fifteen months of over-pressure.'

He was an approachable man, with a kind word for everyone. At the end of a long day, he often went out with members of the Society of St Vincent de Paul to visit the Dublin slums. He helped the SVP provide night shelters for the homeless. Though a Jew, he felt that Christmas Eve was a particularly appropriate time to help the poor, of which there were so many.

Monteith spent most of Christmas Day at Zossen, breaking up

drunken squabbles. Late at night, he settled down to write to Mollie:

Dear old Pet,
No letter from you yet. I am so lonely today. You remember last year in 8 Hartstonge Street, with the little ones running around wild.
Why do you grip me so much, and why are my thoughts so centred around you? Mollie, write me. I do so want your sympathy. My work is so hard, and difficulties so many, but of course if I had you here to tell all my worries to, things would run smoothly.
I can't write more now. Fondest love. Kiss them all for me. Yours ever, Ça ira.

Britain's mood at the year's end was also dark. Allied losses were appalling and the retreat from the Dardanelles had been a crushing blow to morale. Everyone was talking of something the English hated: conscription. The Coalition Cabinet was divided on its application to Ireland. Birrell knew Ireland's future hung in the balance.

Only the Military Council in Dublin felt any optimism; the Republican star was rising.

Old Tom said, 'If only the Germans supply us with arms.'

When in the New Year conscription was introduced into the United Kingdom, Birrell, Nathan and Wimborne breathed a joint sigh of relief. Ireland was excluded.

The Chief Secretary, however, was still pressurized by prominent Unionists like the Earl of Midleton to proscribe the Volunteers and some of their clerical supporters. The Anglo-Irish, Birrell thought, understood Ireland least of all. Didn't Midleton realize that his proposals would bring about a bloody rebellion? That a sure-fire way to arouse the nation's wrath was to imprison a priest for sedition?

Casement returned to Zossen in early January. He seemed well enough, but a week later Monteith received an emergency call to visit him at the Golden Lion.

He knocked on the door. No answer. He edged it open to find the room dark and airless. He threw back the curtains to find that Casement had suffered a complete breakdown. His bronzed face had turned ashen, his cheeks were pinched and his breathing was scarcely perceptible.

Monteith felt first his forehead, it was freezing; then his hand and it burned.

'How do you feel, Sir Roger?'

The reply was like the mewing of a kitten. 'I am dying,' he managed to say. 'Not long to go.'

'I'm sending for a doctor.'

'No, no, no. Please, no.'

He struggled out of bed and pulled on his dressing-gown. When he tried to walk he stumbled, and Monteith caught him just before he fell. Monteith felt he was witnessing a tragic and monumental sorrow.

'You know what I tried to do?' Monteith nodded. 'It's important ... someone ... knows.' On his desk were documents and a letter file. 'Read these ... please.'

As he began to read, Casement said, in words glued together, 'The Americans, not wanting to send more money. Say we're wasting thousands dollars. But I can't take money from Germans. Our struggle, not theirs. Devoy writing to the German Foreign Office ... telling them I'm no good.'

He turned his face to the wall and wept like a child. Monteith looked on his Chief with infinite compassion. In living for others, he had eliminated himself. In between gulps for air, Casement explained that he felt more than ever in a false position.

'Think of my guilt in all this. I have got my fellow Irishmen to give up allegiance to the British in favour of the Germans who are no better.'

Monteith said he saw things in much the same light.

Casement swallowed painfully. 'I refuse to let my boys risk their lives. Pointless venture. In Ireland, I mean. They would be tried, shot as traitors. Couldn't bear that.'

Monteith gave him a sedative and sent for the elderly Dominican priest, Fr Crotty. He also called in a specialist. Dr Oppenheim confirmed that Casement's condition was serious and booked him in to a sanatorium in Bavaria.

'By the end of the month,' he said, 'I'll have him well enough to travel.'

Monteith was left to shoulder all the burdens.

Back at Zossen, he found a fresh crisis had blown up. Twenty-four of the thirty-eight who had volunteered for Egypt withdrew.

Monteith cursed them inwardly. How could the Germans trust such a rabble? Captain Nadolny, the most cynical member of the General Staff, who had developed a loathing for Casement and all he stood for, was furious. 'I'll send them all to the Western Front,' he roared.

'You will do no such thing,' replied Monteith, assuming the mantle of his Chief.

In the end, it was German officers who objected to Irishmen being given arms when they could not even hold their beer. Monteith was relieved. From then on, he was able to direct all his efforts to preparing the Brigade for the rising.

As the rising drew nearer, Pearse met with Stack and other Volunteer leaders in Cork, Galway and Limerick. He told them there were to be manoeuvres at Easter.

With things moving along nicely, Clarke's chief worry was Connolly. When members of the Military Council next met, he admitted, 'That guy's getting me down.'

'He seems to think,' McDermott said angrily, 'that all except his Citizen Army have gone soft.'

'He's getting anxious,' Pearse pointed out. 'We are sixteen months into the war, and nothing has happened.'

McDermott snorted. 'What can he do with his pitiful little force of a couple of hundred?'

'The trouble is, Sean,' Old Tom said, 'if he goes it alone, the Administration will try and disarm the Volunteers. MacNeill will respond with a token gesture of defiance, and goodbye to a real rising, maybe for years.'

Eamonn Kent, the most silent member of the Military Council, said, 'His mouth is likely to dig all our graves.'

Pearse said he would get MacNeill to have a word with him. 'He can be pretty persuasive.'

'If Connolly's not stopped, sir,' Pearse said artfully, 'the Government might try to disarm us as well as the Citizen Army. Then we'd have no choice but to fight back.'

MacNeill nodded. 'I'm so pleased, Mr Pearse, that you and I both see that a rebellion now would be counter-productive. Ireland will get its freedom in stages, beginning with Home Rule. You agree?'

'How could I disagree with that?' said Pearse.

Connolly was invited to the Volunteer HQ in Dawson Street.

MacNeill was late, causing Connolly to say sarcastically to Pearse, 'Just what you'd expect from an academic.'

MacNeill arrived in a puff and began, 'Maybe a little more, shall we say, caution is called for?'

'Listen, *Professor*,' Connolly said, an edge to his voice, 'I intend to start a rising in Dublin. If your lot want to join in, they'll be welcome.'

'And you listen to me, Mr Connolly,' replied MacNeill, flushed to his high cheek-bones. 'Do not expect any support from me.'

'You've missed my point,' Connolly returned sharply. 'I've stopped expecting anything from the likes of you.'

'You can't see over the tops of the houses. The British will squash you in ten minutes.'

Connolly had stamped to the door. 'Then, Professor,' he yelled back, 'we shall have the glory of dying for Ireland while you, *you* will one day give wonderful lectures on it.'

Pearse realized things were worse than he had imagined. If Connolly did not ruin things by a premature rising, MacNeill would do *his* best to stop the real thing at Easter.

When he reported back to the Council, Old Tom asked, 'Does this Connolly guy have a bodyguard?'

Pearse shook his head.

Sean McDermott smiled at this further proof of Connolly's *naïveté*. 'Good,' he said, 'that'll make things a lot easier.'

On 19 January, Connolly was persuaded at gun-point to meet with Pearse, Kent and McDermott in a safe house in the Dublin suburb of Lucan.

'We'd be grateful,' McDermott said, 'if you heard us out.'

'Why should I?' roared an utterly fearless Connolly. 'What have I in common with you fancy nationalists?'

Pearse said, 'Our aims are the same.'

'Never!' Connolly roared. 'You want to substitute Irish capitalists for British. The noses of Connemara peasants will be ground just as flat.' His round grey eyes were watering with indignation. 'You bourgeois rebels blether a lot and do damn all. Molly Maguires changed into Molly Coddles.'

Pearse listened patiently. Then: 'You are quite wrong about us.'

'Prove it.'

Pearse cast a glance at McDermott who nodded.

'We are planning a rising.'

'Before Doomsday?'

'Soon.' Connolly sat bolt upright in his chair. 'You are the only one outside the IRB Executive to know this.'

'The IRB!' exploded Connolly, who hated secret societies. 'Does MacNeill know it?' Pearse shook his head. 'You mean the Volunteers' Chief of Staff doesn't *know*?'

Receiving no answer, he stomped to the door.

'Won't you hear us out?'

'He's your boss. Why *not* MacNeill?'

'He might try and stop it.'

Connolly was intrigued. He had never heard anything so crazy.

'MacNeill,' Pearse went on, 'is our front-man. We needed his prestige, his reputation as a moderate.'

Connolly nodded. 'But how will you get his Volunteers to rebel when he is dead against it?'

At Liberty Hall, Mallin was worried. Connolly's orders were, that if he disappeared without word for three days, they were to presume the British had snatched him and mobilize the Irish Citizen Army.

The Countess Markievicz said, 'There's something bally odd about this, Michael. I'm for taking the lads out right away.'

Mallin restrained her. 'Going out now would be suicide.'

At Lucan, the IRB pointed out to Connolly that his Citizen Army had no links outside Dublin. What could *they* do?

'Any gesture,' Connolly retorted, 'is better than none. Besides, can't you see the British are just waiting to pounce and disarm us?'

They told him their plans were better than his, broader, more developed.

'Details,' he demanded, 'places.'

McDermott said these matters were secret, they had to be. Too many Irish rebellions had failed because of informers, even a slip of the tongue. 'Take our word for it.'

'*Your* word,' snorted Connolly. 'I'm a so'alist, I only trust the working man.'

'Won't you *listen*?' pleaded Kent.

'You listen to me,' said Connolly. 'If I don't turn up at the Hall in a couple of days, my lot will presume the British have lifted me. They'll take the Citizen Army out regardless.'

'It's bilge like that,' said Kent, fuming, 'that makes it impossible to do business with you.'

96

McDermott asked, 'What could a force like yours achieve?'

'A child may stick a pin into a giant's heart,' said Connolly. 'And Britain's heart is here, in Ireland.'

'Except,' Pearse said, coaxingly, 'the bigger the child with the pin the more likely he is to succeed.'

The Brotherhood went apart to discuss their predicament.

Kent was adamant. 'The man's too pig-headed and impulsive. He couldn't keep his mouth shut under water.'

McDermott added, 'He's likely to put ads in that paper of his, "A Rising at Easter" or fly a flag over the Hall.'

Not one of them was happy with cutting Connolly in, but did they have a choice?

Pearse said, 'He has guts,' and all agreed he had a sound knowledge of guerilla warfare.

'I'd rather have him in than out,' Pearse said.

In the end, he won them all round.

'Grand. Let's tell him right away.'

They went back and began to expound their strategy: to take over major buildings in the centre of Dublin. HQ would be the General Post Office in O'Connell Street.

Plunkett brought out the maps. 'Our first aim is to neutralize the British Barracks.' He took time to explain the positions to be adopted by the four Volunteer battalions.

Connolly said, without thinking, 'The British will send troops to Kingsbridge from the Curragh and Athlone.'

'Correct,' Pearse said, encouraged. 'If we can't stop them detraining there, Ned Daly will do his best to make sure they don't attack the GPO from the west. The 4th Battalion will be under Eamonn Kent.' He nodded to Kent to continue.

'My job will be to control the area south-west of the river around the breweries and the North Dublin Union.'

Pearse looked hard at Connolly. 'Well?'

'Looks all right on paper,' Connolly conceded. 'The British'll never shell Dublin. The capitalist property-owners will never allow it.'

McDermott, with an effort, let this piece of socialist clap-trap pass.

'How many Volunteers can you field?'

'In Dublin,' said Kent, who liked to stress their superiority over the Citizen Army, 'we hope to have 3,000. Outside Dublin, another 13,000.'

Connolly blinked. 'The provinces are in on this?'

Pearse nodded. 'We're also hoping for massive help in matériel from Germany.'

'Fantastic,' whistled Connolly.

By the time they got down to details, Connolly was already voicing the possibility of his own Union members organizing trains to transport German arms.

At Liberty Hall, many of his members were backing the Countess's demand for instant action.

'Listen,' Mallin said, 'the boss can't have been picked up by the British. Otherwise they would've lifted the Volunteer leaders, too, and there's no sign of that.'

'Then who *has* jolly-well lifted him?' asked the Countess.

'I think I know,' Mallin said.

He put out the word on the streets that he wanted to speak with McDermott as a matter of urgency. Within the hour, he received a phone call. He was given the number of a house in the north of the city. 'Be there in fifteen minutes.'

He met with McDermott, Pearse and Kent.

'I reckon,' he said, 'you've snatched Connolly. I warn you I can't keep the Citizen Army back much longer.'

'And what,' Kent said sarcastically, 'would your little lot achieve?'

'Die, my friend, to our eternal glory and your shame.'

Pearse said warmly, 'By God, you're right about that.' He held out his hand and Mallin clasped it. 'Take my word,' Pearse said, in that hypnotic voice of his, 'Connolly is not under duress and he will be back soon.'

At the safe house, Connolly was slowly, painfully, exhaustingly, getting the proof he needed.

He began to contribute more and more. The Citizen Army could at least subdue the Castle, pin them down. And why not occupy Stephen's Green? With all its important approach roads, it was well placed to prevent the movement of Crown forces to the GPO.

As the hours passed in feverish discussion, Pearse noted with satisfaction his vocabulary change from what *you* to what *we* are going to do. They did not even know what day of the week it was when, finally, Connolly grabbed Pearse's hand and said hoarsely, 'God grant, Pearse, that you're right!'

Pearse, equally shattered, whispered, 'I hope so, too.'

*

On 22 January, before breakfast, Connolly reappeared at the Countess's place, Surrey House in Rathmines. He had been promised a regular update on the rising. Having been sworn to secrecy, he refused even to say where he had been.

The Countess said, 'From now on, you are going to have a bodyguard, old chum, like it or not.' She handed him a whistle. 'Just blow on that and the lads will come running.'

He put it to his lips but only a chick-like peep came out.

She helped him upstairs.

'I feel I've just walked forty miles,' he said, as she heaved him on to his bed.

By the time she took off his shoes, he was asleep.

Pearse, his right leg twitching as it always did when he lied or dissembled, was telling MacNeill that he had won Connolly over. He had solemnly promised to talk no more nonsense about taking on the British on his own.

'Glad to hear it,' MacNeill said.

Lord Wimborne, into his fourth month of recruiting in Ireland, was not pleased with the results. Ulster was providing more men than the other three provinces together.

Soirées at his lodge provided His Ex with relaxation. Among the guests were Lady Cynthia Asquith, the Prime Minister's daughter-in-law, and Churchill's cousin, Lady Gwendoline, and Nathan, who had acquired the reputation of a famous charmer.

Birrell, too, was there on one of his periodic visits, looking, as Lady Cynthia thought, like a mellow old Thackeray. He was relaxed and flirting with the ladies. His conversation, centring on royal bastards, was smutty and amusing.

When Lady Cynthia enquired about his lumbago, he replied, 'Painful, my dear, but alas not mortal.' When Wimborne asked him, 'Would you care to visit a shell factory with me?' he replied, 'Sorry, never did have much interest in fossils.'

During an amateur performance of *The Rape of the Lock*, Lady Cynthia cut a silver curl from the head of the Chief Secretary of Ireland.

Once in Ireland, he was reluctant, because of that damned sea, to leave.

Early in February, the Military Council met with Connolly again in Kent's house near the Phoenix Park.

'I'm still concerned,' he said, 'that MacNeill knows nothing of what you – I mean, we – are up to.'

Joe Plunkett said, 'I do have a little scheme to get him on our side.'

He gave an outline and Connolly smacked his lips. 'I like it.'

Afterwards, Clarke said, 'We promised to tell you the latest developments, Seamus. Well, we've sent a courier to New York to inform Uncle of the precise date of the rising.'

'Which is?'

'The twenty-third of April.'

'St George's Day. That's one in the eye for the damned English.' Then Connolly calculated. 'But ... but that's Easter Sunday.' A smile lit up his face. 'Rising,' he murmured. 'Resurrection?'

Those whom MacNeill trusted also met at this time. In his group were Hobson, J. J. O'Connell, and Sean Fitzgibbon.

'I take it,' MacNeill said, 'we are all opposed to the idea of an unprovoked rising.'

They nodded.

He distributed copies of a memorandum. 'I have drawn this up because I am completely opposed to the idea that a rising is compulsory just because there is a war on.'

They all murmured agreement.

'I also object, gentlemen, to the romantic notion of some sort of blood sacrifice for Irish nationality.'

'So do I,' affirmed Hobson.

'We hold our arms in readiness, naturally, but only for use if there is conscription or we are faced with suppression. Our policy is the same today as when we were formed: when the war ends, with thousands of Volunteers returning from the front, we shall constitute a single well-armed force to claim our right to Home Rule.'

The group scanned the memorandum.

'You will note, gentlemen, I simply do not believe military failure will bring anything but death and disaster. A rising with no prospect of *military* success is against my conscience and I will oppose it to the last breath in my body.'

On 5 February, Devoy was handed a message by a courier, Tommy

O'Connor, who was a steward on an Atlantic liner. When it was decoded, he read, with amazement that the Irish could not delay the rising much longer.

'We have decided to begin action on Easter Sunday. We must have your arms and munitions in Limerick between Good Friday and Easter Saturday. We expect German help immediately after beginning action. We might be compelled to begin earlier.'

'Jesus!' Devoy whistled in delight, presuming that MacNeill was behind the letter. 'He must be one helluva guy to bring the whole damned crowd out so early.'

He opened his diary and circled the dates in red. The arms had to be landed between 20 and 22 April.

Thrilled, he soon met with Dan Cohalan, Joe McGarrity and the other Clan heads at the Old Irish American Club in Philadelphia.

Cohalan said, 'We better come clean right here and now and say that our Government will not allow arms for Ireland out of an American port.'

Devoy had to agree. 'Nothing for it, then. We've gotta rely entirely on Germany. I just hope to God that guy Monteith has the Brigade ready to go.'

On 10 February, he asked the German Embassy to forward the Irish message to Berlin.

As usual, he said to the military attaché, von Papen, 'I'm sure, Captain, that you and your assistant, von Igel, will take care to keep this note far away from prying eyes.'

'It is quite safe with us,' Papen returned haughtily.

Trusting no one, Devoy wrote a supplementary letter to Mr W. Pfitzner, Esschenlaan 16, Rotterdam, Holland. He wanted to make doubly sure that the German General Staff knew about the rising and that Irish-Americans were unable to provide munitions. It was up to Germany.

The message was sent aboard the SS Sommelsdyk.

On 11 February, Joe Plunkett announced his engagement to Grace Gifford whose sister, Muriel, was married to Thomas MacDonagh.

Grace, like several of her sisters, was a nationalist and a convert to Catholicism. Whenever the girls entered a gloomy Sinn Fein room, they turned it into a flower-garden. A beautiful, broad-faced girl with a resolute chin, Grace was an artist with a special talent for caricatures.

They planned a double-wedding on Easter Sunday; Joe's sister,

Geraldine, was marrying Thomas Dillon. Neither of them had any illusions about living happily ever after. Joe would be leaving the wedding reception to take his position in the firing line. That apart, he needed an operation for glandular TB.

In a poem for his future bride, he wrote:

> *And when I leave you, lest my love*
>   *Should seal your spirit's ark with clay,*
> *Spread your bright wings, O shining dove –*
>   *But my way is the darkest way.*

On 12 February, Sir John Denton Pinkstone-French, British Commander-in-Chief Home Forces, got a note from General Friend, commanding in Ireland. It suggested that trouble was brewing in the Emerald Isle. French decided it was time for a chat with Birrell at the Irish Office.

After the pleasantries, 'Give me a run-down, will you?'

Birrell said, 'I'm not too concerned with the provinces.'

The General, straight-backed as befitted a cavalry officer, crossed to the map on the wall. 'Danger spots?'

Birrell pointed south, 'Cork,' and east, 'Dublin itself. A lot of labour agitation there back in '13. Bad for morale.'

French made as if to brush crumbs off his white moustache. 'Worrying, you reckon?'

Birrell smiled. 'They have neither the arms nor the men. I'm not worried about a rising so much as the cowardly placing of bombs, that sort of thing.'

'Thank you.' The General was putting on his cap, satisfied that the boys in khaki had a grip on things. 'Keep me posted if the Sinn Feiners get up to any hanky-panky.'

Joe Plunkett's sister, Philomena, known as Mimi, was often used by the Military Council as a courier. She arrived in New York to give Devoy more details of the rising.

He was pleased at the precision of MacNeill's plans.

Included was a code for the Germans. 'Finn' meant everything was fine. 'Brann' meant there were problems.

Devoy liked that little touch. 'Brann' was the legendary name of the Chief of the Fianna's dog who scented and warned of danger.

After Papen had evaluated the Irish request for arms and encoded it, the German Ambassador sent telegram No 675 to Berlin on 17 February.

His covering note to the German Foreign Office said: 'The Irish leader (Devoy) tells me that revolution begins Ireland Eastersunday stop requests deliver arms between Goodfriday and Eastersaturday Limerick Westcoast Ireland stop protracted waiting impossible comma desire cabled answer whether promise help from Germany. Bernstorff.'

Room 40 at the Admiralty, now with a vast staff, was currently dealing with a couple of thousand German Fleet signals and wireless communications every day.

Hall could not believe his luck. The Germans, with remarkable arrogance, were still taking it for granted that their codes were unbreakable.

Within hours of Bernstorff's message being sent, Hall found on his desk a note marked 'Urgent'.

He read it.

'Good God,' he said.

Soon after, Devoy's letter to Mr Pfitzner was also intercepted. By then, all British agents on the Continent had been told to watch out for the departure of a German arms boat. Destination: Ireland.

Devoy, with the bit between his teeth, sent off further messages to Berlin via Bernstorff. One long letter to the German General Staff was in English.

According to Dublin, he said, the British had 30,000 troops, most of them with no experience and little training, as well as 10,000 well-armed RIC.

The rebel force consisted of 40,000 trained Irish Volunteers. They possessed 10,000 Lee-Enfields with 200 rounds apiece, plus an extra 20,000 inferior rifles.

They anticipated that 50,000 of Redmond's Volunteers would join in, as would thousands of untrained civilians.

Dublin wanted Germany to send rifles, machine-guns, field artillery and a few senior officers.

Limerick was ideal for the landing. If the rebels took Limerick, all ports from Galway to South Kerry would fall in a few days, and isolated detachments of British troops would be easily rounded up. Dublin would be dislocated and British power in Ireland would lose its cohesion.

The Germans would have the benefit of submarine bases on the west coast. Heavy guns hauled up the Kerry mountains would enable them to keep British warships away from Valentia Island with its wireless station.

The rebels hoped for 100,000 rifles. They would have no trouble finding three times that number of men to use them.

Finally, Devoy, through the German Ambassador, got his dig in at Casement whose every letter lost him a night's sleep:

> Americans respectfully request that Sir Roger Casement remain in Germany as Ireland's accredited Representative until such time as the Provisional government may decide otherwise. (Signed) Graf Bernstorff.

Casement, then in a Munich sanatorium, was determined not to stay in Germany. With an imagination as excited as Devoy's, he drafted a letter to the Admiral Staff.

Still not knowing the precise date of the rising, he proposed that he should leave Germany for Ireland on, say, 18 March by submarine. He would land around Dublin with details of the German navy's part in the rising. He would link up with the Dublin Supreme Command and arrange in detail the landing and distribution of arms. A courier would bring Dublin's final plans to a U-boat waiting at an agreed point.

While Casement was working on this, the German General Staff received Bernstorff's radio telegram, No 675, dated 17 February. Now that the rising had a definite date, they once more urged the Admiral Staff to tell them, if submarines were out of the question, how to send arms to Ireland.

In one of several changes of mind, the Military Council switched back the site of the arms landing from Limerick to Fenit Harbour, Tralee, and informed Berlin.

On 23 February, Pearse visited the Tralee Volunteers. In a private session attended by Austin Stack and the Chaplain, Father Joe Breen, he repeatedly said something that would have alarmed John Devoy, who had told the Germans of a landing between Good Friday and Easter Saturday.

'We expect the arms on the night of Easter Sunday/Easter Monday. Not before, or else the British would be forewarned of the rising.'

This had not been conveyed to Berlin.

'Make sure,' Pearse went on, 'that trains are ready to transport the arms to surrounding Volunteers forces and the RIC are confined to their British Barracks.'

He spoke the next words with special emphasis.

'Remember, the rising begins in Dublin at 6.30 p.m. on Easter Sunday, so no disturbances before then.'

Afterwards, Stack went over all the details with Father Breen, with special emphasis on the landing of arms in the night of Easter Sunday/Monday.

In New York, Devoy took a call from McGarrity.

'How's things, John?'

'Still no word from Berlin.'

'Will they have time to land those arms between 20–23 April?'

'God knows, Joe. If they don't arrive, I dunno how MacNeill's gonna cope.'

The entire German General Staff laughed when they received Devoy's request for artillery and men. They might spare some rifles and maybe a few machine-guns but that was their limit.

On 28 February, the Admiralty told them the best way to get arms to Ireland was by means of two or three trawlers, preferably manned by Irish PoWs with naval experience and knowledge of Irish waters.

'An investigation as to how many rifles, machine-guns and 3.7 cm cannons can be stowed away in a trawler has been ordered to be carried out here.'

Within days, their North Sea Station reported back.

A journey of 2,700 sea-miles would need a reserve supply of coal and provisions for about twenty days.

By 1 March, Nadolny of the General Staff had co-ordinated the Admiralty's replies. He was now aware of the change of destination from Limerick to Tralee but neither Berlin nor New York knew that Dublin had also changed the date of arrival.

Nadolny presumed on the basis of Devoy's visionary letters that a huge operation had been mounted in Ireland, heavily funded by New York. Germany felt unable to contribute much; their own forces had already been stuck for a week in the mud around Verdun and, if things continued, they were likely to lose a quarter of a million men.

Nadolny got the Foreign Office's approval for this telegram B No 6080 to be encoded and sent to Washington:

> Between 20 and 23 April, in the evening, two or three trawlers will be able to deliver about 20,000 rifles and 10 machine-guns together with ammunition as well as explosives near Fenit Pier in Tralee Bay. Irish pilot boats will have to expect vessels, before dusk sets in, north of Tralee Bay and, at short intervals, to show two green lights close together. Delivery will have to be carried out in a few hours. Please wire whether through + + + + [Devoy] necessary steps can be secretly taken in Ireland. (Signed) Nadolny.

German HQ hoped that these arms would assist a revolution which, in turn, might lead to the withdrawal of many British troops from the Western Front, thus assisting a German breakthrough.

At this high point in his life, Devoy persuaded the Clan that they needed an open organization to foster the Irish cause.

On 4–5 March, 2,300 delegates from all over the States came to an Irish Race Convention at the Hotel Astor, New York. John W. Goff of the Supreme Court, Moses-like with his white hair and beard, took the Chair.

Devoy argued passionately that the Irish Volunteers were justified in resisting efforts to disband them. If force was used, their American cousins should help them fight back. On a world-scale, it looked a mere scuffle. But what if Ireland, on the basis of it, were to appeal to a Peace Conference after the war for her independence?

'I say to you, gentlemen,' he concluded, 'Ireland must take action as a belligerent, establish a national government and hold military posts.'

The Convention backed him. They formed the Friends of Irish Freedom Organisation (FOIF). It launched a fund and made this declaration signed by 350 representatives of most Irish organizations, including the Ancient Order of Hibernians and the Knights of Columbanus:

> It is to Ireland we turn in order to see the most finished results of English misgovernment and selfishness . . . We appeal to the Concert of Powers, and particularly America,

106

to recognize that Ireland is a European and not a British Island; and we demand in the name of liberty and of the small nationalities that Ireland may be cut off from England and restored to her rightful place among the nations of the earth.

In Germany, things moved swiftly.

On 7 March, Monteith returned from machine-gun practice to find a note. He was to come to the German General Staff.

He arrived in Berlin at 3 in the afternoon. Captain Nadolny told him of Devoy's message about a rising.

'This American gentleman,' he sniffed, 'has made a request for officers, artillery and machine-gunners and, obviously, the Fatherland will do its best.'

Monteith bit his tongue in remorse at the things he had recently been saying about Germany.

'We have notified our response to the gentleman in New York,' Nadolny said, screwing his monocle into his eye. 'We were intending to use three small trawlers but the Admiralty say they will not have enough capacity, so we have switched to a single steamer.'

'Not enough capacity,' Monteith echoed, his eyes widening.

'Lastly, Devoy requests that Sir Roger stays in Berlin.'

Monteith knew this was a snub but Casement was not fit to travel, anyway.

In a buoyant mood, he went for a more detailed briefing to the Admiralty. Staff Captain von Haughwitz told him the arms would be landed at Fenit Pier, Tralee from 20–23 April, at some time between 10 p.m. and dawn.

'Wonderful,' Monteith exclaimed. 'Our men will do wonders with about 100,000 rifles.'

Haughwitz blinked. 'The boat can only take 20,000.'

'What the hell is the good of that?' cried Monteith. 'Our men are fantastically brave but there are 100,000 British troops either in Ireland or less than three hours away.'

Haughwitz shrugged. 'We are already over-stretched.'

On 9 March, Devoy returned to his office from the Convention to find that Bernstorff had forwarded to him Nadolny's long-awaited telegram B No 6080. He read it with shaking fingers. In marked contrast to Monteith, he was perfectly satisfied.

'Now, Lord,' he muttered, 'dismiss your servant in peace.'

Mimi Plunkett was about to leave for home. Devoy encoded the telegram and told her to hand it to Pearse or Clarke personally.

Both Nadolny's telegram B No 6080 as well as Devoy's acceptance of its terms relayed by Bernstorff on 12 March to Berlin were intercepted by Room 40 and put on Hall's desk.

'Pretty small beer,' he murmured. 'Still, I suppose we'd better do *something*.'

A depressed Monteith went to see Casement in his Munich sanatorium and told him what Haughwitz had said.

Casement was even more appalled at the German contribution.

'A few obsolete arms and no men at all,' he said, his hands trembling badly. 'We need a force of at least 50,000.'

'Yes, sir.'

'The damned Germans prefer an unsuccessful rising to none at all. Cheap Irish blood, that's what they want.'

Having something to do at least gave Casement a new lease of life. He worked for hours with Monteith on how to get the arms ashore. He also outlined his plan of going in advance to Ireland by submarine, whatever Devoy said.

'Meanwhile, my dear chap, you stay on at Zossen. You'll have to train the machine-gunners who will travel with you on the boat.'

Monteith took the plan to Berlin.

The Admiral Staff's reply was blunt. 'We have not a single U-boat to spare.'

Monteith, increasingly agitated, went to see Nadolny at the General Staff.

He began, 'Sir Roger thinks—'

Nadolny cut across him. 'I am not the slightest bit interested in what your Sir Roger thinks.'

Monteith had to stifle a strong impulse to punch him on the nose.

'Besides why does he *want* to go to Ireland three weeks beforehand unless—'

'Are you suggesting,' Monteith growled, 'that he would betray the cause to the British?'

'I am not suggesting anything, my old china,' said Nadolny, who liked to indulge in quaint English phrases. 'New York, not I, made the decision that Sir Roger should stay in Germany. As honoured Ambassador, naturally, of a country now in the throes of rebellion.'

In Dublin, having to keep MacNeill in the dark was the one weak link in their preparations. At any moment, he might twig what was happening and take counter-measures.

Plunkett's plan, which had aroused Connolly's admiration, was now put into effect.

For weeks, Joe had been forging a document purporting to come from the Castle. The Administration, it said, intended rounding up key men among the paramilitaries, including MacNeill, Pearse and Connolly. It was also about to search buildings where arms might be hidden, such as the Volunteer HQ, St Enda's School and Liberty Hall. This type of government action was the one thing that MacNeill had sworn would lead him to resist by force.

Plunkett's ruse was clever in that there was a sound basis for such a document. The Castle *was* edgy and undoubtedly kept files on all potential troublemakers in case mass-arrests were necessary at short notice.

Plunkett started the rumour that an employee sympathetic to the Volunteers had access to plans in the Castle. He was copying and deciphering them slowly and at great personal risk.

Plunkett's assistant, Rory O'Connor, first broke the news to the Editor of *New Ireland*, Mr Patrick J. Little. He called a meeting of a few pacifists and some friends of MacNeill at the home of Dr Seamus O'Kelly on the Rathgar Road.

Skeffy was among those invited.

'Doesn't it prove,' he said, in his shrill, thin voice, 'that the Castle wants to stir things up? Wants a pretext for suppressing a rebellion which they themselves have caused?'

As the days passed, more of the document was leaked. Things went so well that Plunkett was left with only one decision: when to publish the document in its entirety. That would cause quite a stir.

Back to Ireland at this time came a character who had caused many a stir in his time.

Fifty-three-year-old Major Francis Fletcher Vane, Baronet, of the 8th Munster Fusiliers was one of the most colourful officers in the British army.

He wore at a rakish angle a peaked cap, beaten beyond all reason. His face was a glorious sunset red, his mouth heavy, almost sensual. He walked with shoulders sloping forward, his swagger stick under his arm and his hands joined behind his back. With the features of a

Silenus, he had an unerring eye for pretty women. They found him irresistible, though what his secret was no one knew.

Among his equals, he was reckoned an eccentric. In the Boer War, he had made unpatriotic protests against the internment of Boer women and children in concentration camps.

To his men, he was a hero. In battle, oblivious of bullets, he spent his time encouraging others. And his sayings were legendary. One of them was, 'Brutality, like measles, is catching.'

As soon as war broke out, he enlisted and was sent to recruit in Ireland. He had been born there and, though already a Home Ruler, command of Irish troops made him realize just how Irish he was.

He had not endeared himself to his superiors. Too often, he was a gentleman among men who only pretended to be. They often mistook his honesty for pride.

When he recruited in Cork he was amazed to find the walls plastered with Union Jacks and, underneath, 'Come and Fight for Your Flag'. He immediately pasted an Irish harp over the Union Jack.

When his CO reprimanded him for allowing his men to wear a shamrock in their caps, he was frankly puzzled. Was the Home Rule Bill on the statute book or wasn't it? Sometimes military logic was like the peace of God: it surpassed understanding.

He had recruited thousands of men; they loved his relaxed, unorthodox ways. In spite of his blimpish looks and exaggerated English public school accent, he hated bullies and had a passionate love for an underdog.

He had been in Aldershot, attached to an Irish division which he had helped to recruit, and was ready to leave for France when his Divisional Commander called him in and roasted him for encouraging his men to think of themselves as Irish instead of British. Vane had not heard such filthy language since he was an eleven-year-old at Charterhouse.

The odd thing was, on the CO's desk was a notice which Vane himself had written: 'It is cowardly to swear at your men for they cannot swear back. Besides, you will want all your big swear words for really great occasions.'

At the end of a long tirade, the General demanded his resignation.

'Terribly sorry to disappoint you, sir,' Vane said amiably. 'No member of my family in 400 years has resigned his commission in wartime.'

'Very well,' the General said darkly. 'But you will not be going with the Division to France.'

By March 1916, Vane had one thing to thank the General for: his life. Almost the entire division, including his own Irish lads, had been wiped out in France.

Vane had quite enjoyed himself since in the flesh-pots of London. He could afford it, never having been short of money. Though he had never had a settled job, apart from the Army, he was loosely attached to Lloyd's of London.

Now, with the approval of his old Chief from South African days, Sir John French, and his friend Harold Tennant, Kitchener's Under-Secretary for War, he had been given the job of recruiting in County Longford.

He was shocked to find how attitudes had changed since he was last in Ireland. It was very difficult to drum up any interest in the Army. Putting Home Rule on ice was one reason.

Another was Kitchener's distrust of the Irish.

Kitchener was not alone in questioning their loyalty. The Viceroy was becoming more and more agitated by the growing number of dissidents and Nathan's apparent indifference towards them. He demanded briefings by the DMP and General Friend. He also wanted more deportations of troublemakers, especially any with German connections. Nathan agreed to him being briefed, though he told his aides not to let him see anything sensitive.

On 16 March, an informer told Nathan that Thomas MacDonagh had said at a Volunteer parade that it would be 'sheer madness' to attempt a rising without help from Germany.

It struck Nathan as obvious. What on earth was Wimborne worried about? Without massive support from abroad, how would a tiny badly armed force dare take on the might of the British army? And, with Room 40 unwilling to risk giving their secrets away, nothing had been heard of Casement for ages.

Friday 17 March, St Patrick's Day, seemed appropriate for the German Admiral Staff to run through the expedition to Ireland.

Haughwitz explained that a steamer of 1,400 tons would depart on 8 April and arrive in Tralee Bay between Good Friday and Easter Sunday. A pilot boat would guide it in.

They studied the charts. Fenit Pier was clearly a good landing site.

As to the ship's cargo: 20,000 captured Russian rifles, a million rounds of ammunition and 400 kilograms of explosives. The Army had guaranteed delivery on time.

The Admiralty had before them another in the latest of Casement's requests to go to Ireland in advance in a U-boat. The General Staff had ordered them to turn it down, which they did only too gladly.

Casement, like Devoy, was still under the illusion that MacNeill was in charge in Ireland. Unknown even to Monteith, he now wanted a U-boat in order to get back early and try to persuade MacNeill to call the rising off.

Captain Heydell raised the question of whether the arms boat would be equipped with a radio.

'Depends,' Haughwitz replied, 'on whether the steamer has an electric plant or not. We have not selected one yet.'

'What are the rising's chances of success, Herr Kapitän?'

Haughwitz shrugged. 'Even if it flops, the effect on British morale will make this small expenditure worthwhile.'

Still hoping for a U-boat, Casement wrote in his diary:

'St Patrick's Day. In three weeks from today I shall probably be at sea in the most ill-planned enterprise that the history of Irish revolutionary efforts offers.'

One thing he could do: stop the Irish Brigade from travelling to Ireland. So scrappy was the planning and so poor the equipment, they would either be killed on landing or taken prisoner and shot as traitors.

He re-read his 'treaty' with Herr Zimmermann. It said that the Brigade would return to Ireland only if there was some prospect of success. That implied effective troop-support which the Germans were refusing to give.

Tension was high in Dublin city centre on St Patrick's Day.

The Irish Volunteers and the Citizen Army paraded with rifles and fixed bayonets. Some of them had six-foot long pikes which they stacked outside church during Mass.

The marchers held up traffic for two hours in the city centre where MacNeill took the salute on a podium. Beside him was The O'Rahilly, next to whom was Patrick Pearse who was thinking that within a month all these men and thousands like them across the country would be fighting for a Republic.

That evening, the Superintendent of the Dublin Metropolitan Police reported to Nathan.

'There were 4,555 Sinn Feiners taking part in the parade, sir, of whom only 1,817 were armed. Half had rifles, the other half shot-guns.'

Nathan was impressed at the exactness of the figures.

'How did the ordinary citizens react?'

'Jeered and complained like hell about the traffic jams.'

That evening Nathan received the RIC report on a monster turn-out of Sinn Feiners in Tralee led by a noted trouble-maker, Austin Stack.

Wimborne was furious at this open defiance of authority. When Nathan called on him at his lodge, he said, 'Can't you see that this is all brewing up into something ghastly?'

Nathan, who frankly thought him a fool, did his best to calm him. He pointed to the enormous disparity in fire-power between the Sinn Feiners and the British army as well as the reaction of decent ordinary citizens who looked on Sinn Feiners as cranks. He did promise to give serious thought to deporting troublemakers like a young man called Mellowes.

'And,' Wimborne asked, 'what about that old chap, the one who runs a tobacconist shop in Great Britain Street?'

'Clarke.'

'Yes, him. All that coming and going in his place proves he's up to no good. Why not deport him, too?'

Nathan said, guardedly, 'I'll have the Attorney-General look into it. But, as I recall, there's no record of him actually saying anything treasonable.'

Nathan, having reassured the Viceroy, now tried to reassure himself. Could this big parade possibly be the prelude to a rising?

He went over the facts and figures again before concluding, Impossible. Not even Sinn Feiners like Tom Clarke could be that stupid.

Tom Clarke, with trembling hands, received Nadolny's message which Mimi Plunkett had just brought back from the States.

Clarke had waited years for this. Those weapons would help the west to rise and not just Dublin.

In New York, John Devoy called McGarrity in Philadelphia.

'Happy St Pat's Day to you, Joe.'

'You, too, John. I just can't wait for Easter Sunday.'

'Not another word,' Devoy barked. 'You never know if this damned phone is tapped.'

McGarrity laughed. With their contacts in the German Embassy and the secret codes Papen was always boasting about, there was just no way any outsider could guess from such a remark what was happening in Ireland.

In Room 40 of the Admiralty, Hall was working late.

His team now had the German naval code, VB 718, their military code and the one for naval attachés which had been fished out of the sea. They had also obtained from Brussels the German consular or diplomatic code No 13040, one of the two used between Berlin and all German missions in the western hemisphere including Washington.

His secretary brought in the latest telegram. It was from the German General Staff to Bernstorff:

> Instead of three trawlers, a small steamer of 1,400 tons cargo will come. Lighters will have to be in readiness. Anticipated that from 8 April onwards at 12 midnight there will be sent from Nauen, as introduction to the news, the word 'Finn' as sign that expedition has started. The word 'Bran' will be given if a hitch occurs; a date after 'Bran' signifies that arrival of steamer has been postponed to this day. Wavelength 4,800 metres.

Hall read it, blinking furiously, then called Thomson at Scotland Yard.

'BT, just to let you know things are hotting up.'

──────PART TWO──────

COUNT-DOWN TO THE BATTLE
21 March–23 April 1916

And I say to my people's masters:
  Beware,
Beware of the thing that is coming,
  beware of the risen people.
                    Patrick Pearse

On 21 March, at the German naval base at Wilhelmshaven, on the northern seaboard, low grey-black clouds chased each other across a sullen sea.

Lieutenant Karl Spindler, the tall, handsome young skipper of the small outpost-boat *Polar Star* received a note from his flotilla Chief, Commander Forstmann.

'Come and see me at 5 p.m. Urgent.'

As he tramped through pelting rain, he sensed that this was important. He walked with determination. His motto was: 'What seems impossible becomes possible if you want it enough.'

'Yes, Karl, a top-secret assignment for you.'

As Spindler shook the rain off his greatcoat and cap and smoothed his brilliantined black hair, Forstmann went on:

'I want you to pick a crew of twenty-one. See that each of our six boats is represented.'

Spindler awaited an explanation but none was forthcoming.

'Choose unmarried men, preferably without any family commitments.'

Spindler's keen eyes lit up. 'You mean—'

'Sorry I can't say more at this stage.'

That night, Spindler slept little. At 5 a.m., he left on a four-day patrol. As soon as they were at sea, he told his crew of a dangerous expedition ahead.

'I'm asking for volunteers. Bachelors have preference.'

As he expected, every bachelor aboard put up his hand.

While Spindler was telling his men about a top-secret operation of which he himself knew no details, General French, at the Horse Guards, London, received in his office the Director of Military Intelligence, Major-General G. M. W. MacDonagh.

'Sir,' said MacDonagh, 'I've been told by an absolutely reliable source that there is to be a rising in Ireland.'

French arched a white eyebrow. 'Tell me more.'

'All I can say is it's near and Irish extremists are in league with Germany.'

'How near?' said French.

'Is Easter near enough?'

'And the Germans are supplying them with arms?'

'To be landed in the west of Ireland.'

'Anyone else know?'

MacDonagh said, 'Admiral Bayly at Queenstown has been told.

117

He's stepping up patrols along Irish coasts.'

'Can't see any arms boats getting through our blockade.'

'Not a chance,' said MacDonagh.

Next day, French had an appointment with a top Irish delegation that included Birrell, Wimborne and Friend. They discussed the general situation in Ireland. Wimborne was pessimistic, Birrell took the line that the Sinn Feiners were too ill-armed and disorganized to be a threat.

When the meeting ended, French touched Friend on the arm. 'Mind staying behind for a minute?'

He repeated what MacDonagh had told him.

'Interesting, sir,' Friend said. 'Aren't you going to tell Birrell?'

'Unwise, old chap. Politicians never could keep their traps shut, you know.'

'Did MacDonagh tell you his source?'

'Couldn't. Intelligence chappies have this passion for the hush-hush, you know. Anyway, worth keeping an eye open?'

The same Thursday, Countess Markievicz was as usual entertaining at Rathmines. After a childhood and youth spent in the luxury of Lissadell in County Sligo, she was now totally taken up with the Citizen Army, the women's branch of the Volunteers and the Irish Boy Scouts which she had founded.

Antique furniture had been pushed into corners, Persian rugs rolled up, oil paintings put out of harm's way. Tea was provided for a big crowd in the kitchen where Madame was cutting slices of bread an inch thick.

Connolly, who boarded there while his family continued living in Belfast, was sitting brooding by the fire. He had just had bad news. Nathan, yielding to Unionist pressure, had interned some key members of the Volunteers. They were in Arbour Hill Detention Barracks awaiting deportation.

His thoughts were interrupted by a chant, 'We want Mick. We want Mick.'

Michael Collins had come back from London to take part in the rising. Young, slim, dark-haired, he had been in the IRB for some time. He was popular with the lads, being good with his mitts, a great singer of pub songs and full of Irish devilry. Word was he was going places.

'Give us Emmet's speech from the dock, Mick.'

After not too much persuasion, Collins got to his feet. The hilarity subsided as he lost himself in the part of Emmet, a youth who knew that the next day, at noon on 20 September 1803, he was to be publicly hanged outside St Catherine's church in Thomas Street.

The Countess's eyes brimmed with tears from the start, whereas Connolly sat gazing into the fire. He did not care for histrionics.

In a Cork voice of bell-like clarity, Collins was declaiming, 'I have, gentlemen, but a few more words to say. I am going to my cold and silent grave, my lamp of life is nearly extinguished, my race is run. The grave opens to receive me and I sink into its bosom.'

Even Connolly went taut, hearing these famous lines.

Collins, his magnificent dark head on one side, continued:

> I have but one request to ask at my departure from this world, it is, *the charity of silence*. Let no man write my epitaph; for as no man who knows my motives dare now vindicate them, let not prejudice or ignorance asperse them. Let them and me rest in obscurity and peace; and my tomb remain uninscribed, and my memory in oblivion, until other times and other men can do justice to my character. When my country takes her place among the nations of the earth, *then*, and *not till then*, let my epitaph be written.

All of them semed to see the executioner lift up the severed head and cry, 'This is the head of a traitor,' and all had a single thought, 'Will Emmet's epitaph be written in our time?'

When Spindler came ashore on 25 March, after the usual dull patrol, he already knew that his new command was named the *Libau*. He immediately went aboard the leading ship in the flotilla and, with Forstmann's approval, finalized the crew.

'I don't want to seem paranoid,' Forstmann said, 'but there are spies everywhere, Karl, and this is top secret.'

'Must be,' Spindler said, 'if even I don't know what the hell it's all about.'

'You soon will,' his Chief promised.

Before noon next day, the crew, each with only a knapsack, were on an express train heading east, destination unknown. They alighted in the afternoon at Hamburg.

Spindler was aching to see his new patrol craft, maybe a secret design. Instead, in dry dock, was a boat that compared with his recent command, looked like a liner.

A second surprise: it was English, built in Hull. It had been trapped in the Kiel Canal at the outbreak of war. Its name, the *Castro*, had been blacked out but was still legible.

On the bridge, it was uncanny, as if the English crew had left but a few minutes before. Documents were scattered everywhere, drawers pulled out, instruments abandoned. But the engines and boilers had been overhauled and the living quarters refurbished.

Next morning, Spindler was told, he would begin the first stage of his mystery voyage.

'One thing, Herr Kapitän,' a tight-lipped official in a dark suit said. 'Make sure no unauthorized person comes aboard, *none*.'

In the morning, church bells were calling parishioners to Sunday service as the boat was towed by two tugs into midstream. Though his crew were in naval uniform, Spindler flew the flag of a German merchant ship.

His orders were only temporary: to report back to Wilhelmshaven. No sooner was the *Libau* there than a bigger vessel manoeuvred into position to screen it from prying eyes. Only engineers with special clearance were allowed on board. Spindler's own crew had to load the equipment in sealed boxes.

Austin Stack was summoned to Dublin to meet with the Military Council.

He gave a full account of his plans for landing arms at his home town of Tralee and distributing them in the west which they approved.

'I'd be grateful,' Pearse said, 'if you could come to town again next month.'

They checked their diaries and settled on 11 April.

Stack returned home. In case he was picked up, he told his Adjutant, Paddy Cahill, under oath that there would be a rising on the 23rd and arms would be brought into Fenit on Easter Sunday/Monday morning.

Cahill was shaken rigid. 'Is that all you can tell me?'

'It's better so, Paddy,' Stack said. 'Dublin says it's crucial that no shots are fired before the Republic is proclaimed there.'

At Wilhelmshaven, Spindler had the name *Libau* painted on the side of his new ship. He mustered his crew and told them to drop hints in town that they were headed for Libau on the Baltic coast of Latvia.

'Where *are* we headed, Herr Kapitän?' someone asked.

'You won't believe this,' Spindler replied, 'but I haven't the faintest idea.'

He was more intrigued still when one of the *Libau*'s hatches was battened down and he was not allowed to look inside. That first night, an armed guard was put on the boat.

In the morning, Spindler was at last allowed a full inspection.

Below deck, there were big iron doors. He heaved them open, only to find himself staring at a blank wall beyond.

In one of the cabins, under a sofa-bunk, he was shown a secret entrance. He clambered down it, through a series of manholes and concealed ladders, to a lower hold that stretched from one side of the ship to the other. One iron water-tight bulkhead, seemingly without an entrance, was false; inside, enclosing a big space, was a partition that could only be opened from inside.

Another hold below that was filled with a reserve of coal. It was obviously going to be a long trip in waters too dangerous to stop and refuel.

He was given a written assignment to take command. Without it, he might, if captured, be shot as a spy. It read:

'Holder of this, Lieutenant of the Reserve *Spindler* is herewith appointed to the command of auxiliary cruiser. (11.H.C.A. VII of 18.X.1907. Art. 3.)'

The document was officially stamped and signed: '*Wilhelmshaven*, 30.3.1916. von Krosigk, Admiral and Chief of the Marine Station of the North Sea.'

Impatient at the best of times, Spindler was now seething with curiosity. He had his official appointment at the highest level but still no clue as to what it might be.

As April began, he was summoned to Berlin for an Admiralty briefing. Finally he knew his assignment was to transport men and arms for a rising in Ireland. The secret hold was to be the hiding-place of fifty Irish PoWs formed into a Brigade to fight on their own soil.

He was introduced to a distinguished Irish civilian who, though not in good health, struck him as being a man of outstanding charm. His chief assistant, younger, sturdier, more military, assimilated better the details of the mission. Both were to travel with the Brigade.

The Irishman with the beard knew no German so talks were held in English. He spoke passionately about the evils of English rule in Ireland and how this mission might both help the Irish cause and bring about a swift end to the war.

121

Spindler's mind was already working on the details: departure time, best route to avoid British patrols.

He was delighted with all the arrangements until he looked at his calendar and saw against Easter the words: 'Full Moon'.

In spite of the impression he made on Spindler, Casement, sick and lonely, was in a black mood. He realized that New York and Dublin had written him off as a well-intentioned meddler, whereas he believed that he and he alone was in a position to grasp the cynicism of the Germans.

Without German personnel and submarines, with only 20,000 rifles made at the turn of the century in Orleans, France, and captured from the Russians at Tannenberg, the Irish had absolutely no chance. To cap it all, they were being given ten machine-guns that his Brigade were not trained to fire.

Not that the arms were likely to reach Ireland, anyway. The chances of a single boat beating the British blockade were minimal. That he himself was betrayed mattered less than that his men were doomed to death and the rising to failure.

One evening he asked Monteith to give him the names of the men he could rely on. Monteith listed, with difficulty, a dozen. It made no sense to send the Brigade at all.

At 3 p.m. on 3 April, they went to the German General Staff. Zimmer 178 overlooked the bank of the Spree.

A determined Casement said to the two young Captains, 'I am sorry to disappoint you, gentlemen, but your contribution to the expedition does not justify me in sending the Brigade.'

Haughwitz and Huelson were stunned.

'Sir Roger,' Haughwitz said, 'may I remind you that we have taken immense trouble with your men on the understanding that they would return to Ireland for a rising.'

'True, but that depended on your country providing adequate back-up. You have reneged.'

The discussion sea-sawed for an hour until Captain Nadolny joined them. He got the gist of the matter in seconds and was furious. The way things were going in France, his country would soon be calling up fifteen-year-olds and eating more potatoes than the Irish. He brushed Casement's objections aside.

'Your views no longer count. If our agreement of December '14 no longer holds, your part in this is finished.'

He made as if to shake Casement's hand goodbye.

Casement drew himself up to his full height. 'What are you saying, Captain?'

'Simply that you have broken a solemn treaty. That being so, those Irishmen now belong to me and I will send them wherever I please and that includes Ireland.'

'Just try it,' Casement said coldly.

'I do not need your encouragement.'

'If the agreement is dead, Captain, what may I ask is the status of the Irish at Zossen?'

'Status? Oh, deserters.'

'Who made them desert,' said Casement, 'except you? You intend sending deserters to Ireland?'

'Listen to me,' Nadolny said, red in the face. 'To land the arms, we need the Brigade to provide gunners.'

The courteous Haughwitz intervened to say, 'If you do not provide gunners, Sir Roger, why should we provide guns?'

'I will telegraph Devoy in America,' said Nadolny, 'to order the Brigade to go.'

'Do that,' Casement said, calmly. 'He will refer back to me and I refuse to budge one inch.' He pointed through the window to the river bank. 'Take me out there and shoot me if you like. But I will never agree to my young men going to a certain death.'

'I always knew you were a fool,' Nadolny snapped, 'I never thought you were a coward as well.' He went to the door, opened it wide and said, in a voice quivering with anger, 'If the Brigade is like you, there is no point in sending it, anyway.'

Casement returned to his hotel. Pleased to have saved his men from virtual suicide, he now returned to the bigger matter of trying to stop a rising doomed to failure.

He put in another request for a submarine.

In Dublin, Pearse's criterion of what constituted success differed from Casement's. Dying in a noble cause, a blood-sacrifice, was success in itself.

On the day that Casement withdrew the Brigade because a rising could not succeed, Pearse took the final decision for it to go ahead.

He got the approval of MacNeill and the Volunteer Executive for three days of manoeuvres beginning on Easter Sunday, at 6.30 p.m. in Dublin, at 7 p.m. in the provinces.

The ostensible aim was to test mobilization with full equipment. The real aim was a Republic.

123

On 8 April, he published his General Orders in the official magazine, the *Irish Volunteer*.

The Military Council had decided some time before that arms should not be landed until the rising in Dublin was off the ground. They presumed, with reason, that there would be no difficulty in conveying this change of date to the Germans.

They had, after all, agreed a signal system which implied that the arms ship could be contacted at sea. Berlin could, if necessary, radio the skipper to hold back until the night of Easter Sunday/Monday. Not that it should be necessary. They were sending two messengers, Joe Plunkett's father and sister, to make sure that the change of date was known.

Plunkett Senior was given a verbal message for Berlin. As a Papal Count, he had a pretext for visiting Rome. On the way, he would go to Berne from where the German Ambassador in Switzerland would relay the message.

At the same time, the Military Council sent his daughter Mimi back to New York with a coded message to be transmitted to Germany via their Washington Embassy.

Their minds at rest, the Council met to put the finishing touches to the plans for the rising.

Spindler was in Wilhelmshaven when he was told that he was to leave next day for the Baltic. In Lübeck, he would receive final instructions. Admiral Scheer, Commander of the Fleet, personally wished him success on his important mission.

As soon as the ship left port at two in the afternoon, two large boxes were lifted out of a hatchway, containing Norwegian gear for the crew: plain blue suits, caps and sweaters. Even the black buttons on the clothing were stamped with the name of a Norwegian firm. It was like a pantomime as huge Bavarians struggled into uniforms far too small for them.

The crew lined up for Spindler to give them their orders.

'From now on, men, strict discipline must cease. No more heel-clicking or salutes, you understand. Shaving is forbidden. I want everything aboard to be relaxed. Learn to put your hands in your pockets. Try it.'

It was not easy for well-trained men after weeks on patrol to behave like merchant seamen. They thrust their hands in their pockets, then withdrew them at once.

'Keep them there,' yelled Spindler.

He retired to his cabin where his orderly, Bruns, brought him coffee on a tray.

'From now on, your name is Henrik.'

'Yes, Herr Kapitän.'

'And I am no longer Herr Kapitän.'

'No, Herr Kapitän.'

'Listen, Henrik,' Spindler snorted, 'I don't want you carrying that tray like an English butler. Look at your left hand.'

Bruns had it smartly down the seam of his trousers. His fingers twitched as he did his best to look casual.

God in heaven, thought Spindler, he probably stands to attention at the pissoir.

They sailed down the Elbe again and passed through the Kiel Canal. Next day, they were in Lübeck. There Spindler was given his orders in great detail.

The ship was to leave so as to arrive in good time at Fenit Harbour from 20 April at the earliest to 23 April at the latest. A pilot boat would lie in wait during those days at the entrance to Tralee Bay near the Island of Inishtooskert. This vessel would make itself known as follows: by day, one of the crew would be wearing a green sweater and by night two green lanterns would flash intermittently.

Spindler was free to steer whatever course he chose and to adopt whatever measures suited him best when he reached his destination. Being without a radio, one thing he knew: once he left, he would be out of contact until he landed in Tralee Bay.

On the day of Spindler's briefing, Count Plunkett arrived in Berne. He repeated his message to the German Ambassador for transmission to Berlin. Time was short.

That afternoon, Casement went to Zossen with the Brigade confessor to say goodbye to his men. His one consolation was that he had saved them from certain death.

His face was lined and thin, and he was close to tears as he pretended to be going east to see what campaign possibilities were there.

The reality was, he was only going to Ireland with Monteith and Sergeant Beverley so as not to seem a coward. The venture was a mere piece of gun-running and beneath contempt. Was this the Germans' idea of a military campaign? A sick man who had never fired a gun in his life and a couple of soldiers disguised as sailors, each of them generously supplied with poison in case they had to take their own lives. Were they seriously expected to invade a Kingdom with 20,000 rifles and some cartridges?

The Germans, as he saw it, only wanted a diversion – for their own sake, not for Ireland's. He wrote in his diary:

'I go on – because I am fool enough, or brave enough or coward enough – I know not which – while I know it is hopeless.'

In Dublin, that 5 April, the Volunteer HQ Staff met in emergency session in MacNeill's house in Rathfarnam. The Chief of Staff was growing more and more anxious.

Hobson had told him he was suspicious about Pearse's mobilization orders for Easter. Some Volunteers, he said, were abusing their positions. MacNeill himself, on his travels around the country, had heard Easter mentioned as a deadline for some sort of action or revolt.

Those present included Pearse, The O'Rahilly, Kent, MacDonagh, Hobson and O'Connell. The numbers for and against a rising were about equal.

'Tell me, MacDonagh,' MacNeill asked his university colleague, 'is there anything at all to these whispers of a rising?'

'I honestly can't say,' replied MacDonagh, who was not a member of the Military Council.

Briefed by Hobson, MacNeill said, 'I want you each to give me a solemn promise.'

They looked at him questioningly.

'That none of you will give the Volunteers any orders outside of normal routine without checking with me personally beforehand.'

Kent and Pearse had no hesitation in promising. They were running a revolution not a Sunday school; they could not afford the luxury of a conventional conscience.

As he left the meeting, Pearse had one major concern. He trusted the Germans implicitly but it was clearly getting harder each day to keep the rising from MacNeill and the rest of his Executive.

He reported back to Clarke. Tom knew the absolute reliability of Kent and his brother-in-law, Ned Daly. As a precaution, he decided to co-opt MacDonagh on to the Military Council. It was a shrewd move. Apart from the fact that MacDonagh was an IRB man, as Brigade Commander he would be able to guarantee the unswerving support of the fourth of the commandants, Eamon de Valera.

*

126

In Tralee, Austin Stack sent Cahill to Dublin to get two green signalling lamps from McDermott for contacting the German arms vessel.

When they arrived, Stack said, 'We won't be needing them, Paddy, before Holy Saturday afternoon.'

That seemed to be a sufficient margin since the ship was not due for more than twenty-four hours after that.

The lamps were hung in the Rink, the Volunteers' drill-hall in Tralee.

Confusion in Ireland was growing.

Like MacNeill, McCullough, President of the IRB was hearing rumours of a rising and it worried him. He went from Belfast to Dublin to talk with Old Tom.

'Is there to be a rising soon or not?'

'Why are you so worried?' Clarke countered.

'Level with me, Tom.'

'I don't know where you get your information from, Denis,' Clarke replied. 'But as God is my witness, I know absolutely nothing about a rising.'

McCullough relaxed. 'You'd let me know if anything crops up. After all, I am President of the Supreme Council.'

'You'd be the first to hear,' Clarke said.

On 6 April, Count Plunkett's letter from Berne arrived in Berlin. It read:

Ashling (Secret)

Dear Sir Roger,

I am requested, as a delegate sent by the President and Supreme Council of the Irish Volunteer Army to give you this urgent message from Ireland:

(1) The Insurrection is fixed for the evening of next Easter Sunday.

(2) The large consignment of arms to be brought into Tralee Bay must arrive there not later than dawn of Easter Monday.

(3) German officers will be necessary for the Irish Volunteer Forces. This is imperative.

(4) A German submarine will be required in Dublin Harbour.

The time is very short, but it is necessarily so, for we must act of our own choice, and delays are dangerous.

Yours very sincerely,

A Friend of James Malcolm.

Someone somewhere along the line had erred. Very badly. Paragraph 2 should have read 'not *earlier* than dawn on Easter Monday.'

Nadolny read the letter and took it not as a modification but as final confirmation of plans already agreed. The Admiralty had already guaranteed that the boat would arrive no later than dawn on Easter Monday. It might even arrive earlier.

The letter was handed to Casement. That night, he discussed it with Monteith. 'It proves,' he said, 'that the Volunteers depend absolutely on German troops and arms.'

Monteith had to agree that Section 3 of the letter made that plain.

'I really hate what the Germans have done to us,' Casement said. 'For myself, I'd be glad to go to death on the scaffold or spend the rest of my days in an English jail, anything to get away from this country and these third-rate people.'

'I think I would, too, Sir Roger.'

'I only hope,' Casement said, despairingly, 'that, in time, people will see I may have been a fool to trust the Germans but not a scoundrel.'

Monteith and Beverley, a debonaire Sergeant in the Brigade with a certain artistic flair, were the only gunners now travelling with him.

He said, 'You two had both better join me at the Hotel Saxonia while we are waiting for the boat.'

At Lübeck, Spindler double-checked that he had everything he needed: adequate coal, provisions for six months, plenty of water – and the arms in containers stamped with black and red shippers' marks and labelled Genoa and Naples.

Next, he went through the Norwegian equipment: books, the latest newspapers from Christiania. His crew were even given forged letters and photos of their Norwegian girl-friends. From hot-blooded German bachelors there were catcalls and a few offers to swop pin-ups.

A routine was established.

Objects that might arouse the suspicions of a snooping British vessel were to disappear down through the sofa bunk into the hold. This became known as the Conjuror's Box. There they stored German uniforms, arms, books, charts, flags.

On board, there had to be two of most things – Norwegian and German – from sardine tins to buttons and field dressings.

In addition to their own ship's papers and charts they had phoney Norwegian equivalents, as well as letters from the supposed owners telling them to avoid waters infested by German submarines and to pick up pit-props at Christiania for Cardiff, Wales. Not one of the crew could read this material. If they were boarded by a British patrol with a Norwegian speaker they would be lost.

Once the arms were in the hold, they were camouflaged to a depth of several feet with pit-props, heavy tin baths and wooden doors. Every item bore the shippers' markings and the destination: Genoa and Naples.

With the ship now disguised as a tramp, the name *Libau* was blacked out.

Having seen to all this, Spindler returned to Berlin for last-minute instructions.

The Chief of the Admiral General Staff said, 'For the safety of your men, Herr Leutnant, keep them in the dark as long as possible about their mission.'

On Friday 7 April, Casement, with Monteith and Beverley, was summoned to the General Staff for a meeting with Nadolny, Huelson and Haughwitz. After talking them through the details of their departure, Haughwitz said all three were to return the following afternoon.

'Here, you will change into sailors' gear, then proceed to Hamburg.' He coughed apologetically. 'Might I suggest, Sir Roger, if you can bring yourself to do it, that you shave off your beard before you reach Ireland.'

Nadolny, pleased to be seeing the back of Casement, was unusually cheerful.

'I am so sorry, my dear chap,' he said, 'there's no private submarine for you. It is *ausgeschlossen*, completely out of the question. Never mind, it will all work out, I am sure.'

Back at his hotel, Casement took a surprise call from Heydell of the Admiralty. 'I would be grateful if you could come round and see us at four this afternoon.'

'About?'

'A U-boat.'

Monteith waited at the Saxonia while Casement went excitedly to the Admiralty. There he was left in a waiting-room, catching up on back numbers of English papers, for over two hours.

The Germans only had a score of U-boats but lately, under pressure from America, the Kaiser had restricted their activity to military targets. The Admiralty was now debating using one on the Irish escapade, if only to get rid of Casement who endangered the whole enterprise.

At 6.30 p.m., Heydell came in, smiling, to say, 'Good news. The submarine is on. We shall settle the details later.'

'Fine,' exclaimed Casement, 'but you will be sure to land me in good time for the fight.'

Captain Stoelzel came running upstairs to say everything had been settled in a rush. 'Yes, Sir Roger, you'll be there in good time for the scrap. Can you come back tomorrow at 1 p.m.? In the meanwhile, not a word to anyone.'

Casement went back to his hotel and told Monteith the good news.

At 7.45 p.m., Haughwitz arrived. He seemed genuinely pleased that Casement had got his submarine.

'But that poison the Navy supplied,' he cautioned, 'I'd still take it with you. You never know.'

At 8 p.m., Monteith got a call from the Foreign Office to pop round right away. When he got there, he was met by Herr Meyer.

'Sorry to plague you so late at night, Lieutenant, but I need your final assessment of your prospects.'

'That's easy,' said Monteith. 'Nil.'

'I don't suppose,' Meyer said, gloomily, 'that I could persuade you to change your mind at the last minute.'

'No, I intend to go.'

'I mean try and get the Brigade to go with you? You have a wife and children in New York. There would be quite a considerable sum in it for you – and them.'

Monteith got to his feet.

'Herr Meyer, until now you have acted as a man of honour. I'll pretend you never said that.'

Meyer said, 'I agree with you, Lieutenant. The suggestion was completely dishonourable. Sometimes one has to—'

He bowed his head.

The submarine was good news if a trifle late. Now it was a race against time. Casement naïvely hoped that the U-boat would have the edge on the steamer and get him home in time to cancel the rising. He did not grasp that the Germans were sending him by submarine simply because if he travelled by ship and it was boarded he would give the game away.

On 8 April, Spindler left Berlin for Lübeck, still without the final go-ahead. The Irish leader, he gathered, was being a nuisance. Was he accompanying the arms or not?

Not, it seemed, for he had no sooner joined his ship than he received a telegram: 'Proceed to sea.' With Count Plunkett's letter misinterpreted and with his daughter, Mimi, still in mid-Atlantic with a request to delay the arrival of the arms ship, Spindler prepared to sail without a radio.

The next day, it was Sunday 9th, Spindler left the ship, to return half an hour later with a big, old shaggy dog of questionable breed. No tramp steamer was complete without one.

'This,' he told his crew, 'is Hector.'

At 6 p.m., the ship slipped out of Lübeck. His orders: to rendez-vous off Inishtooskert between 20 and 23 April.

He was glad there was no radio aboard. A wireless mast would alert the British navy that they were more than a tramp steamer. As ordered, he told his crew only the bare essentials. He gave them each a Norwegian name and made them practise getting their tongues round it. From then on, no German names were to be used.

'First of all, men, let me introduce myself. My name is Neils Larsen.'

'Welcome aboard, Herr Kapitän,' they choroused, in good humour.

He handed round Norwegian phrase books. 'These might come in handy for the odd swear-words. At a pinch, we can switch to Low German.'

'Fine,' someone chuckled, 'who understands that?'

'Now, men, everything on board that looks new – clothes, flags, books, instruments, and especially ship's papers – they must be made old. Get to it.'

Within seconds, books were whizzing around decks and cabins until they were torn and dog-eared. Clothes were ripped and tarred. If anyone's beard was not shaggy enough, a comrade was only too pleased to rub in oil and coal dust. Dozens of chalk marks and obscene drawings were put on the walls. Old Norwegian meat tins and newspapers were strewn everywhere.

Because he looked Scandinavian, a seaman named Mathieson was given the wheel. Someone had the job of teasing Hector to make him bark very loudly when required. Never were too many sailors to be allowed on deck at a time.

Finally, they all had to learn code-words to be whispered or spoken down the voice-pipe and the engine-room telegraph. In the evening session, Spindler taught them the most important of them.

' "*Tyske*" is Norwegian for "German": that now means, "Stand by with naval ensign, uniforms and arms." The Norwegian phrase: "*Pedersen skall tom Kaptejn kim*" (Pedersen is to come to the Captain) means: "Stand by to blow up the ship! Fuse ready!" '

The crew shuffled their feet uncomfortably. Why did they need that?

'Now,' Spindler said with a grin, 'if any one has any questions . . . he had better keep them to himself.'

To avoid the British blockade, he had chosen an arrow-head path. They would sail north long and leisurely between Norway and Shetland to the edge of the Arctic Sea. At the tip of the arrow they would turn south-west between Ireland and the Faeroes towards their destination: Fenit Harbour.

On the first night out, the boat's name and markings had to be changed. A storm blew up so that the sailors, slung over the side and seeing only by the light of electric torches, received quite a buffeting. They painted in '*Aud-Norge*' in letters five feet tall. Six-foot Norwegian flags – blue, white and red – were painted fore and aft. Wet and freezing, they managed to finish, fortified by large doses of brandy.

First light found a Norwegian tramp steamer, the *Aud*, rocking on the Baltic.

Each crew member had to find a handy hiding-place – behind hawsers and pipes – for his own weapons. They might be needed in a hurry if, say, they were boarded. Cook hid a number of guns under cold ashes in a disused oven.

A last chore. They threw overboard the last reminders of the ship's original owners, including excellent English utensils.

Spindler once more assembled his exhausted crew.

'If the signal given is, "Enemy ship in sight", everything German has to be bundled into a big bag on the bridge – even sextants, telescopes, log-books, charts. You, Max,' he pointed to an athletic-looking seaman, 'will rush to the galley with it. Cook will pass it along to the Conjuror's Box where the steward will grab it and fly down the ladder. Meanwhile, the rest of you will be replacing it all with Norwegian gear. Right, men. Let's see how long it takes.'

At a signal, the *Aud* sprang to life. Amidst a whirl of activity, Max grabbed a final bundle, ran with it and it disappeared from sight.

Spindler checked his watch. 'Two minutes exactly. Not bad for a first attempt. I am sure we will be able to knock a few seconds off that with practice.'

That morning of the 10th, just before entering enemy waters, Spindler took one last precaution.

He surrounded a large quantity of TNT with a three-foot-wide cement casing to increase the explosive effect. The detonating wires led to the upper-deck where the ends were concealed. To avoid accidents, the fuses were kept in a different place.

On his last night in Berlin, 10 April, Casement was the dinner guest of beefy-faced St John Gaffney, recently dismissed from his post as American consul in Munich.

He was looking very thin and ill; his clear grey eyes expressed not just pain but a certain bewilderment, as if the world had become too chaotic for him. His main worry was lest the Irish Brigade thought he had walked out on them.

'Nothing of the sort,' Gaffney assured him. 'And I promise you, Rory, I'll take good care of them.'

But not even the best champagne could lift Casement's spirits.

The loyal Monteith, meanwhile, wrote in his diary:

> This enterprise is in my opinion a deliberate cold-blooded attempt to get rid of Sir Roger Casement and myself, under the pretext of helping our country.
>
> Without me and perhaps without Beverley the world will move along in the same way, but in Sir Roger Casement the world loses one of her best and greatest men.

It occurred to Monteith that though he might not be missed by the world at large, he would certainly be missed by his wife and children. It was all the more maddening in that he was going to die in a useless cause.

If only he could see his loved ones one last time.

*

In the Bronx, New York, it was Monday evening. Two little girls who lived on 137th Street were playing on the sidewalk.

The dark one, aged two and a half, was trying to whip a top. The older golden-haired girl was tapping an old cycle wheel and running after it.

A friendly, round-faced man with his hat on the back of his head stopped the wheel.

'Hi, Vie,' he said, like a benign uncle. 'Long time no see.' He handed her the wheel back. 'Is your pa in today?'

'No, sir.'

The man took out a bag of candy. 'There, Vie, your daddy told me to give you that.'

The girl shrank back. Her mother had warned her a hundred times not to talk to strangers.

'You can trust me. Now, where's your daddy, darling?'

Just then Mollie Monteith ran down the steps, she grabbed both her girls and hurried them into the house.

'Did you tell him anything?' The girls shook their heads. 'You're sure?'

They said, 'No.'

Mollie picked up the phone and put through a call to Devoy.

'Sorry to bother you, Mr Devoy, but those British Vigilantes have been getting at my kids again. Hadn't I better move house?'

On 11 April, the *Aud* was sailing along the Danish coast when Spindler heard the rush of a submarine's bow-wave and the ringing of its telegraph as it surfaced.

He thanked God it was a U-boat.

When the Commander hailed him from the conning tower, Spindler chuckled to himself. He had met him only a couple of days before in Kiel.

'State your port of origin and destination.'

Spindler pretended not to know any German, so they conversed in English, the lingua franca of the sea.

'We are from Danzig, Herr Kapitän,' Spindler called out. 'Heading for Christiania.'

'There is a danger of mines here,' the Commander told him. 'Follow me and I will see you safely through.'

Spindler whispered to his mate, 'Perfect gentlemen, these Germans.'

*

On 11 April, Major Price, the Intelligence Officer at Dublin Castle, sent a report to Sir John French in London.

While the Irish in general were loyal to the Crown, he said, the Sinn Fein Volunteers were practising drill, rifle-shooting, night attacks, and running officer-training camps. They seemed to have considerable funds for arms, though often they stole them.

Hundreds of home-made grenades had been seized by the police, and only two days before they had captured guns, revolvers and bayonets from Sinn Feiners on their way from Dublin to Wexford.

Price gave it as his opinion, backed by General Friend, that a rebellion was on the cards. The Sinn Feiners were only looking for an opportunity.

Sir John French found nothing substantially new in it. He remembered the boss-man Birrell saying very clearly on two recent occasions that the Sinn Feiners simply could not compete with Crown forces.

'File it away,' he said to his secretary.

On that day, Stack went to Dublin for a last meeting with the Military Council.

'I have kept those in the know to a very few whom I trust,' he said. 'But we are quite ready.'

'And,' asked Pearse, 'you will be able to keep the Army and the police in their barracks till the arms are distributed?'

'Certainly, sir.'

'You *have* stressed,' said Pearse, 'that not one shot is to be fired until the Republic is proclaimed in Dublin.'

'Absolutely,' said Stack. 'I've even warned the pilot not to go out signalling before Sunday evening.'

'The arms boat will not arrive until the morning after the rising,' Pearse said confidently.

'Then,' Clarke said, in conclusion, 'I think things are all sewn up in Tralee.'

In Berlin that evening, Casement, Monteith and Beverley were driven to the General Staff for their final briefing.

Monteith, worried about Casement, suggested that he stay behind.

'No!' Casement had a reason for going that his friend still did not suspect, 'I must go.'

Nadolny said cynically, 'Of course. After all, Sir Roger, you have your honour to think of.'

Monteith said, 'He's ill, can't you see that?' He rounded on

Nadolny. 'Why send him to certain death? England is thirsting for his blood. And *there is no point to it.*'

'Please,' Nadolny said brusquely, 'we will take the next item on the agenda.'

He handed Monteith the code for communicating with Germany in case the Irish operations were prolonged and they needed more arms. 'Sectpol' was the calling-up signal.

'Any messages with that prefix,' Nadolny said, 'will be transmitted without delay to the General Staff in Berlin.'

They were each given a berth-ticket for a separate sleeper on the train.

'Remember, gentlemen,' Haughwitz emphasized, 'if you meet in the corridor or the washroom, act as if you are complete strangers.'

Back in his hotel, Casement made the last entry in his German diary:

> The last days are all a nightmare, and I have only a confused memory of them, and some periods are quite blank in my mind, only a sense of horror and repugnance to life. But I daresay the clouds will break and brighter skies dawn, at least for Ireland.
>
> I am quite sure it is the most desperate piece of folly ever committed; but I go gladly. If those poor lads at home are to be in the fire, then my place is with them.

It was late that night when, with his companions, he caught the overnight train to Wilhelmshaven. Next morning, Wednesday, they boarded a steam cutter for the U-20 which was about half a mile out, taking on stores.

The Captain, Walther Schwieger, was checking his orders. He was to be one sea mile north-west of Inishtooskert Island just after midnight on 20 April onwards. Between 20 April and 23 April, the *Aud*, under Norwegian colours, would rendezvous at the island and take off his three Irishmen. If the U-20 was late, the steamer had orders not to wait. It would be guided in by pilot boat to Fenit and discharge its cargo. The pilot boat would then return to Inishtooskert to collect the Irishmen. If the U-boat failed to make contact with the steamer or the pilot boat, the Irishmen were to be put ashore in a rowing boat.

One thing was paramount: there was to be no landing from the U-boat prior to 20 April. If, on the other hand, they failed to make their destination by the 23rd, they were to abort the operation.

Pictures were taken of the passengers as they boarded. Casement had doom in his eyes. He shook hands with Schwieger who, single-handed, had almost brought the United States into the war by sinking the *Lusitania*.

Monteith noted that the U-20 had four torpedoes. Two were in the chutes, the others slung above. It also had a wireless.

At breakfast, which had been held up for the visitors, Casement asked casually how fast the submarine was.

'When submerged and under electrical power,' Schwieger replied, 'we can travel at 8 or 9 knots. On the surface, with heavy oil engines, at 12 knots.'

After breakfast, when the order was given to submerge, the visitors were sent centre-wise to the Captain's cabin. The majesty of silence was broken only by a little rattling noise, made by the diving fin connections, and the faint swirl of water as it rushed into the tanks, and the sharply uttered, '*Achtung*,' and, '*Jawohl, Herr Kapitän*,' as the seamen responded to commands.

Down, down, they went, slower as the water pressure increased, encased in steel, their ear-drums popping.

Casement, the eternal diarist, wrote, as an aid to memory, 'Left Wicklow [Wilhelmshaven] in Willie's yacht.'

That afternoon, among the bunch of coded wireless messages picked up on the east coast of England was one of particular interest to Room 40.

It contained the signal 'Oats'. It was an alert from British agents on the Continent. Casement had left Germany bound for Ireland. 'Hay' would have meant a hitch.

A pretty woman secretary entered Captain Hall's office. 'He's on his way, sir.'

'Thank you, Ruth.'

Putting various Intelligence reports together, Hall now knew that a submarine and an arms ship were on their way to Ireland. He also believed from various intercepts that a rising was planned for 22 April.

'Right,' Hall said, 'alert our subs to find the boat and the U-boat and keep them under surveillance.'

French's Adjutant-General had asked the Irish Office if they were still convinced no Irish rebellion was on the cards.

Nathan answered: 'Though the Volunteer element has been active

137

of late I do not believe that its leaders mean insurrection or that they have sufficient arms if they do.'

Birrell was feeling in low spirits at this time. Cabinet intrigues were getting him down. He was desperately hoping for an Easter break with his two sons in the west of Ireland where he would be able to breathe more easily.

Nathan cheered him slightly by telling him that things seemed to be improving. True, that ass Wimborne was still talking of deporting trouble-makers like Clarke and Connolly, but a number of arms finds was lifting morale in the Castle. They also had well-placed informers in the ranks of the Volunteers.

Nathan wrote: 'We are at last getting some information as to what is going on here – for the first time since I have been in the place.'

In the basement of St Enda's, Pearse, with the rising only thirteen days away, watched as two former pupils of his, Bulfin and Desmond Ryan, with other young IRB comrades, were busy manufacturing bombs and handgrenades.

The bell on the front door rang. Pearse was called up to see a visitor. It was Paddy Cahill from Tralee.

They went into the study to the right of the entrance hall. The news from Stack was encouraging. The planning was almost complete.

Pearse wanted Stack to know he was sending Sean Fitzgibbon of the Volunteer HQ to help plan the unloading of arms. He did not mention his one worry about Fitzgibbon: he was not a member of the Brotherhood. In fact, he was a MacNeill man. He hoped this would not make any difference once the rising was sprung upon the Volunteer movement. But it was another calculated risk among many, another possible avenue of failure.

The U–20 was only a day and a half at sea when it broke down.

Casement was convinced that this was a delaying tactic to make sure he did not reach Irish shores before the arms ship. In fact, the crank actuating the diving fins had snapped. The skipper had no option but to put in for repairs.

He wirelessed ahead to the German base at Heligoland.

The message was picked up, decoded and passed on to Hall.

'So,' he muttered, 'that's where the blighters are.'

He was now able to anticipate their path.

'Ingenious bastards,' he grumbled. 'They're going the long way round.'

With a thousand other more important intercepts to deal with in the main theatre of war he found it somewhat hard to take this Irish expedition seriously. Still, he owed it to colleagues in the Senior Service in Ireland to alert them. Not, of course, in such detail as to compromise his secret weapon. He was only prepared to give hints which the enemy would judge had been obtained from other, more orthodox sources.

Joe Plunkett was a patient in Miss Quinn's Private Nursing Home in Mountjoy Square, Dublin. Though pale and exhausted, his mind could not rest. The first stages of his plan to deceive MacNeill had gone well. Now for the final act.

He asked his friend O'Connor to take the forged document to Kimmage to be printed in its entirety.

'Tell them, Rory, to leave out capitals and all punctuation because they are lacking in the original.'

It was a neat touch.

O'Connor took the document to Joe's brother George and Colm O'Lochlainn at the Plunketts' family home where they had set up a small handpress.

When they ran their eyes down the page, they were staggered. Here was proof that the Castle was preparing to take over the Volunteer HQ, St Enda's, Liberty Hall and many other centres. The Administration also intended rounding up MacNeill, who was O'Lochlainn's teacher, Pearse, Connolly, Clarke and Joe Plunkett himself. They were even going to raid Archbishop's House, Drumcondra. That last was verging on the incredible. Archbishop Walsh was on record as saying repeatedly that violence against the British was a mortal sin and could not be justified.

Work was almost finished when O'Lochlainn was bothered by the fact that in the document the Archbishop's House was called Ara Coeli.

'That's the name of Cardinal Logue's House in Armagh,' he said.

He made Jack Plunkett go by motor bike to ask Joe about that. He returned within the hour.

'Joe said just change it to Archbishop's House.'

In Tralee, Stack's first choice of pilot had let him down. He asked Pat

O'Shea, a young student-member of the IRB, to meet him at his office in Dr O'Connell's law firm. Putting his finger to his lips, he led him upstairs to an empty room where he told him of the rising.

'German vessels are heading this way laden with arms for the Volunteers. I want you, Pat, to find me a pilot.'

'When for?'

'The arms'll be off Inishtooskert on the night of Easter Sunday or the morning of Easter Monday, not before.'

O'Shea said, 'Mort O'Leary of the Maharees is your man.'

'Right,' Stack said. 'Have him come to Tralee on Saturday 22 April for final instructions and pick up a couple of green signalling lamps from the Rink.'

Next day, Admiral Sir Lewis Bayly, Commander of the Western Approaches, stationed in Queenstown, County Cork, received an intriguing piece of information from Room 40. It was a combination of intercepts and information, not wholly accurate, from agents on the Continent.

'A ship left on the 12th accompanied by two German subs. Due to arrive the 21st and a rising timed for Easter Eve (22nd).'

Bayly passed this on to his army counterpart, General W. F. H. Stafford, Commander of Queenstown defences which included eight southern counties. He also alerted Galway.

On that same Friday, 14 April, Mimi Plunkett finally made it to the offices of the *Gaelic American* in Manhattan. She went to the rest room and extracted a coded message hidden in her underclothes.

Devoy was not expecting her. He had a gut-feeling that something was very wrong. For safety's sake, he took her to the offices of a colleague, some distance away.

The message, when decoded, read: 'Arms must not be landed before night of Sunday 23rd. This is vital.'

A shaken Devoy immediately called the German Embassy but it was Friday, after 5 p.m. No one answered. That night, he did not sleep a wink.

First thing in the morning, he handed in a typed copy of the message to Papen, with 'goods' substituted for 'arms'. The military attaché promised that as soon as the lines were open that evening it would be wirelessed to Berlin.

*

The U-20 arrived at Heligoland, the Gibraltar of the North Sea, at 3.30 in the morning. Engineers said repairs would take time.

Two hours later the Irish party transferred to the U-19. A twin of the U-20, it was commanded by twenty-nine-year-old chunky, cheerful Lieutenant Raimund Weisbach.

Schwieger, having memorized his orders, had burned them as a precaution. Weisbach, therefore, received only a verbal briefing.

While Casement fumed at the delay, Monteith made use of it. Knowing they might have to go ashore on a small boat, he practised stopping and starting the outboard motor in Heligoland harbour. On one start, the engine backfired and sprained his wrist. It was very painful and began to swell at once.

To Casement, this was just one more bad omen. 'How will you be able to handle a machine-gun?'

'I'll manage,' Monteith said, through gritted teeth.

The U-19, with the small boat stowed on board, was ready to set off at 1.30 p.m. Weisbach said the journey would take five days. They were to travel on the surface, except for a regulation ten miles a day below.

While he felt well, Casement did all he could for Monteith, even cutting his bread for him. He told the crew, 'If Ireland is victorious in this rising, I'll see you have sent to you the best Irish eggs and butter.' During recreation he waved a green flag and sang Irish rebel songs to a guitar accompaniment.

By the 15th, in rough, open sea, he was sea-sick and unable to eat. The black bread and ersatz coffee tasted of diesel oil. His saliva would start an engine.

The three Irishmen were with four others in a cabin meant for four. The air was foul; condensation dampened and verdigrised their clothing and bedding; the smell was indescribable. The incessant ringing of bells and the engine noises made sleep impossible.

Monteith and Beverley, in oilskins, went up the conning tower for fresh air but Casement could not manage it. He lay in his bunk, getting weaker and weaker.

While Casement was fighting nausea, Bernstorff in Washington received Dublin's note sent on by Devoy. He, too, was shaken that, at this late stage, they wanted the arms shipment delayed until Sunday 23 April.

Because this note was top secret, it was not sent from Sayville.

Hall had long been aware that Bernstorff was contacting Berlin

141

by an unknown route. He guessed it was from Argentina through Chile but exactly how he did not know. In fact, the messages were transmitted from Buenos Aires to Valparaiso and thence to Mexico City where the Swedish chargé d'affaires encoded them on the American transatlantic line. Messages on the Swedish Roundabout took about four days to reach Berlin.

Bernstorff used this route to relay Dublin's note to Berlin.

At Queenstown, Admiral Bayly planned on the basis of Devoy's telegram of 10 February. Room 40 did not communicate the precise location of the arms landing, Tralee, nor the exact date of the rising, Easter Sunday.

But, both at sea and on land, the British were on the watch in the west.

This was something that Pearse and Clarke, still thinking in terms of informers, did not even suspect.

On the *Aud*, Spindler knew that the 16th, Palm Sunday, was critical. It was the day he would have to try and break through the British line.

At 4 a.m., the entry in the log read: 'Weather: overcast, increasingly misty, occasional heavy showers, wind, south-west 4, freshening, corresponding sea.'

The ship was averaging 10 knots. With 150 nautical miles to cover, he calculated he would arrive in the middle of the enemy line at about 8 p.m. That was fine. It would be dark and at the hour of a change of watch. Also, on a Sunday, extra rum was handed out, so the watch tended to be less vigilant.

Room 40 picked up a message from a British submarine.

Ruth entered Hall's office. 'They are tailing the German steamer, sir.'

'Good,' Hall said, 'make sure they stay there till they reach the Tenth Cruiser Squadron. Just keep us in touch but no one is to get too near. It may be armed with torpedoes and there's one, possibly two U-boats in attendance.'

On Palm Sunday, at Liberty Hall, Connolly put on uniform for the first time and, flanked by Michael Mallin and a beaming Countess Markievicz, marched out into a packed Beresford Place. The occasion was a ceremony that had been planned for some time.

Molly O'Reilly, a striking redhead from the Women's Section of the Irish Citizen Army stood in the centre of the Place to receive from Connolly, a green flag, emblazoned with a harp but no crown.

'I hand you this flag,' he intoned, 'as the sacred emblem of Ireland's unconquered soul.'

The bugles rang out and the battalion presented arms. Molly carried the flag into the Hall and up to the roof from where it was flown from the flag staff. Pistols were fired in the air by trigger-happy members of the Citizen Army.

Clarke and McDermott were there and, with the rising a week away, were less than enthusiastic at this needless act of provocation.

In Dublin Castle, they had more immediate problems.

Stafford, General Officer commanding Queenstown, called Major Price, Military Intelligence Officer.

'Listen carefully, Price. I've a piece of news from Admiral Bayly. One, possibly two German subs and a vessel containing arms have left Germany for Ireland.'

Price thanked the General for the information and immediately phoned General Friend who was in London.

'Good God!' said Friend. 'What a roundabout way to get intelligence. We've had stuff like this before.'

'Do you want me to take any action, sir?'

'Just keep on the alert, Major. If there were any hard evidence, the Admiralty would have let me know direct.'

From four in the afternoon, as the *Aud* steamed south-west, it ran into heavy fog. Spindler could hardly believe his luck.

He had been delayed on the edge of the Polar Sea because of the crystal-clear sky and gentle swell of the sea. Hardly ideal weather for running a blockade. Even in peacetime, a ship emerging from that far north would have aroused suspicion.

By 6 p.m., so dense had the fog become, visibility was down to only three ships' lengths. Every available man was on the look-out, some with binoculars screwed into their eyes. The sea was rising; big white caps were breaking over the bow. Tension mounted as they approached the enemy's line.

Spindler had never known time pass so slowly. To his fifth enquiry in as many minutes, the bosun answered, 'It is 7.15 p.m., Herr Kapitän.'

That was when Spindler saw a great black-grey mass loom ahead only two cable-lengths from the *Aud*.

'Hard a-port . . . Maximum speed. Emergency stations!'

It was a 10,000 tonner of the British Tenth Cruiser Squadron, the *Orcoma*. Both ships continued parallel at 200 yards' distance. The powerful British ship reduced speed to keep alongside.

Aboard the *Aud*, emergency procedures went into operation. As many of the crew as could be spared went below. Anything with German markings was transferred to the Conjuror's Box. On the bridge, Spindler, knowing binoculars were trained on him, spat his lungs out.

'Someone get that bloody dog to bark,' he yelled.

The crew smoked like chimneys, allowing themselves only an occasional almost scornful glance at the British ship.

From the *Aud*'s chart house, the second officer reported through the window, 'More and more British sailors on deck, eyeing us. Several large guns pointed at us, fore and aft.'

'Don't tell me,' groaned Spindler.

'You were right,' the second officer said, grinning, 'about when we would meet up with them.'

'Damn it,' returned Spindler, 'do they intend escorting us to the Faroes?'

He peered at his watch. It was 7.30 p.m. For normality's sake, he ordered seven-bells to be clearly stuck. It seemed to have an effect. The number leaning over the rails of the cruiser dwindled. It was cold and wet, and nearly time for a change of watch. Perhaps they had visions of steaming grog below.

'Light masthead light and side lights,' Spindler ordered.

By now, there were only a few on the cruiser's bridge. At eight-bells, a new watch took over.

'God in heaven,' Spindler muttered, 'if only I had a torpedo.'

With the wind rising to force 5 or 6, the cruiser, having kept pace for nearly an hour, increased speed. Big waves boomed over her bows and poured in great streams out of her forward scuttles.

What now? thought Spindler.

To his surprise, the cruiser took a SSE course and disappeared into the fog.

There were whoops of delight aboard the *Aud*. They had beaten the blockade.

Spindler ordered, 'Full-speed ahead.'

James Connolly's play, *Under Which Flag*, was having its first performance that night at Liberty Hall, with Sean Connolly of the Abbey Theatre in the lead role. It was about an Irishman torn between serving in the Irish and the British army.

In between rehearsals, Connolly gave his final lecture on guerilla warfare.

'Listen, comrades,' he concluded, 'it'll be a thousand to one in the enemy's favour. But if we win, remember this: never surrender your weapons. We may need them another day to fight not only for political but for economic liberty as well.'

Less than a mile away, in Parnell Square Hall, there was a concert organized by the *Cumann na mBan* the women's branch of the Volunteers. At the last minute, Hobson was a substitute speaker.

'I'm sorry to have to tell you,' he said, 'that a minority of the Volunteers are drifting into confrontation with the rest of us.'

The audience looked at each other, shrugging.

Hobson went on, 'We really do have to perfect our organization and preserve it for a Peace Conference when this war ends. We don't want one more forlorn failure.' He said with emphasis, 'No man has the right to sacrifice others to make for himself a bloody niche in history.'

Most present were deeply disturbed. For the first time, they gathered there was some sort of rift in the leadership of their movement.

A messenger was soon on his way to Clarke and McDermott.

'Jasus,' said McDermott. 'First Connolly waving a fecking green flag at the British and now Hobson dividing the Volunteers.'

Clarke stroked his large left ear. 'We shall have to deal with Hobson, Sean. We can't have him shooting his mouth off like this with the rising only a week away.'

Under Which Flag, playing to a capacity audience, reached its climax at 11 p.m.

Sean Connolly ran the Green Flag which had been raised over the Hall that afternoon on a pole centre-stage, saying, 'Under *this* flag only will I serve. Under *this* flag, if need be, will I die.'

The curtain fell to tumultuous applause, with the Countess Markievicz and her companions, Dr Kathleen Lynn and Madeleine ffrench-Mullen, leaping to their feet in the front row.

'Bravo,' the Countess cried, clapping her big smooth hands, 'absolutely divine.'

145

Sean Connolly took several curtain calls and after calls of 'Author! Author!', Connolly appeared, as happy as a performing seal.

'The next act of the play,' he said, 'will be written by all of us together.'

In the noisier theatre of the North Sea, Spindler was grateful no destroyer was tailing them. But with each passing minute, the wind and sea were rising. Fog yielded to squally rain. The barometer was dropping like a shot bird. The *Aud*'s speed in a strong north-westerly dropped from 10 knots to 5. Then to 4.

On the Monday of Holy Week, the seven-man Military Council met at Liberty Hall and elected themselves the Provisional Government of the Irish Republic. All of them were IRB men. Pearse was voted President.

They went through the Proclamation they were to issue at the rising. Pearse had composed it but he integrated Connolly's social concerns, in particular the equality of all citizens, including women.

General Friend, still in London, wrote to Dublin Castle, asking Nathan what he thought of General Stafford's phone call to Price.

Nathan was mystified. He had not heard rumours of projected landings on the south-west coast. In fact, he was so convinced things were quiet that he had invited his sister-in-law, Estelle, to bring her two children to his lodge with young Dorothy Stepford, niece of Mrs Green, for Easter.

It was news to Birrell, too. He had been contemplating visiting Aran. He helped himself to a big dose of bicarbonate of soda.

Room 40 did not intercept the IRB message to the German authorities that arms were not to come ashore before Easter Sunday night. Even the IRB did not know that it had arrived too late to alter the *Aud*'s plans.

Admiral Bayly's command was meanwhile keeping a close look-out for a vessel carrying German arms and flying a neutral flag. Trawlers had been warned to watch the entire west coast from the Aran Islands to the Kenmare River in the south. In between were Shannon, Tralee Bay, and Dingle Bay.

Bayly ordered out the *Gloucester*, a light cruiser, and four destroyers from the Grand Fleet, as well as a few sloops. All were on red alert. But they still had no precise information where the arms were to come ashore. Bayly hoped that Stafford, in conjunction with the Royal Irish Constabulary, would help him there.

Nathan called in Chamberlain, the Inspector-General of the RIC.

'There's probably nothing in this,' he said, 'but Stafford has put the south and west on the alert. Do what you can to help out.'

He also warned Edgeworth-Johnstone, head of the DMP, to keep his eyes skinned and get what information he could from his informers in the Volunteers about a possible insurrection.

Edgeworth-Johnstone said, 'I've already asked them, sir, and they tell me there is not a single sign of one.'

'I didn't think there would be,' Nathan said.

On the 17th, as it turned south, the U-19 ran into high seas and a storm force 10. Casement was throwing up badly as the submarine corkscrewed through the water.

Around the *Aud*, too, seas were rising and the barometer falling. Spindler knew that if the cargo broke loose, it would be impossible to do anything about it. If he opened the hatches, the holds would flood instantly.

For two days, he had not been able to make a single astronomical observation. Currents around Iceland were bound to have taken him off course but he did not know by how much. To avoid having to nose into every bay on the west of Ireland to find Tralee, he would have to fix his position in the next day or two.

He decided to head for Rockall, two hundred miles west of the Scottish coast. It was a sandbank with a diameter of three miles from east to west. At the western end was a rock, the only visible portion of a terrifying reef on which dozens of ships perished each year. No scientific survey had yet been made.

Graveyard or not, Spindler had to risk an approach from the west. Even a distant sighting would enable him to set a course.

In the last hours of the 17th, the *Aud* took a battering. Winds reached force 11, there were giant hailstones and mountainous seas with darkness of biblical intensity over the deep.

A ship passed them, a 12,000-tonner. It was an unlit British cruiser on patrol. Spindler held his breath. Mercifully, due to the storm, he guessed, it missed them. Odd, though, that the entire crew were asleep on a night like that.

The winds did not abate. He would like to have lain-to but the schedule was too tight. A storm like that might last for four days. He had oil jetted on to the water to reduce the roll and make the combers break before reaching the stern.

A new day dawned, grey and wrinkly. They were heading west for Rockall and possible disaster. Seagulls would indicate the reef but, in the storm, would they see that lonely jutting rock in time?

From 8 o'clock he had men tied to the rails and heaving over the lead. There was no other way of knowing when they were closing on the sandbank's outer edge. They should, with luck, see the rock when two miles away at – he glanced at his watch – maybe 1 p.m.

10 a.m., 11 a.m., midday. Crew members, mercilessly buffeted against the rail, kept calling out, 'No bottom!' The reliable sounding-machine was not giving any signal.

Above the sea's din, Spindler called out weakly through a megaphone, 'More oil on the sea from the bow.'

Suddenly a wild shout: 'Bottom! Sixty-three fathoms!'

Spindler, his neck tense as a log, responded with an instant roar, 'Reduce speed. Sharp look-out.'

As the moments ticked by, he was horrified to find there was no consistency in the levels being called out. One minute it was 70, the next it was 28.

It seemed they were being slowly, irrevocably, drawn on to the reef like so many vessels before.

The sea crashed, the air vibrated. Visibility was less than a thousand yards. To starboard, the *Aud* had to weather enormous breakers, foam-topped like boiling milk.

'Hard a-port!' he yelled, his tattered voice no louder than a whisper in the wind. 'Hard over!'

Waves house-high, with blinding spray, broke over the gallant ship and the sea gushed up as from a geyser. Water squeezed in through every crack with hose-like pressure.

Detecting breakers and the direction of the reef in conditions like this was impossible. Spindler half-expected the deck to collapse or a hatch to cave in. Would the steering gear withstand the onslaught? Things were made worse by the *Aud* sloping to starboard like the roof of a Swiss chalet. He thought she would be sucked down into the deep. Each time she nosed up again, he wanted to cheer.

A couple of hundred yards to starboard, two gulls appeared. The skipper's elation was dashed by the Quartermaster yelling, 'The compass. It's gone mad.'

148

Spindler checked, only to see the card wheeling faster and faster. The compass said north, then immediately after south-west, refusing to steady. The only way he had left by which to judge direction was by watching the seas breaking over him. And still the soundsmen gave inconsistent readings.

More birds appeared, fifty, a hundred, whole flocks whirling, fluttering, veering on stiff wings, their screechings lost in the louder howl of the wind.

Nearby lay rocks and destruction.

He yelled, pointing, 'Hard a-port! Quick, man, quick!'

The words were drowned out but Mathieson had sized up the situation for himself and whipped the wheel round, just clearing the reefs. Next moment, the *Aud* was caught in the overpowering grip of a whirlpool.

Spindler felt that with the engines at full-steam they were being sucked down and down. For his men's sake, he tried to keep the terror out of his face.

Hailstones two inches in diameter rattled down on the ship as the seas rose mast-high around it. The *Aud* shuddered in every plank. The leadsmen, with life-lines around them, their oilskins streaming, kept to their posts, calling out, '28, 23, 15.'

Then came a violent shock suggesting the ship was aground. The hull shook and quivered for several seconds. Spindler expected the mast, even the funnel, to come crashing down. With engines turning at full-speed, the *Aud* was stationary.

In the engine-room, the Chief shot a glance at the telegraph clock. One second the black hand pointed to FULL, the next to STOP. At his elbow, the voice-pipe was whistling.

'Chief,' he heard Spindler call, but he was already rushing up the ladder to report, 'No water in the engine-room.'

'Thank God for that.'

As the Chief, purple-faced and perspiring, disappeared, taking the iron steps two at a time, Spindler put the boat over to port, then to starboard. It did not budge.

Glancing aft, he happened to see what the problem was. The deck was invisible. Huge green waves had come aft and poured down the well-deck, flooding it to the bulwark rail. The scuttles were jammed, the scuppers, too, blocked up. The pent-up mass of water made the ship too heavy to move!

'Anyone overboard?'

'All accounted for, sir.'

He waited for the water to clear, then tried the helm again. The *Aud* answered.

In the engine-room, the gong sounded as the black hand jumped to FULL again.

Spindler, feeling the piston-rods sliding in and out, wanted to scream in delight. He had only to hold to a north-easterly course for a few more minutes and they would clear the reef and be on their way to Tralee.

At Volunteer HQ, Pearse asked Sean Fitzgibbon to go on a mission to Stack in Tralee and to Mick Colivet in Limerick.

Fitzgibbon was so surprised to hear of German arms being landed in the west that he asked, 'Does MacNeill approve of this?'

'Would I tell you to do something the Chief of Staff disapproved of?' answered Pearse, evasively.

Fitzgibbon shrugged. His instinct was to check with MacNeill before leaving but he had a train to catch if the orders were to reach the west in time.

Wimborne, back from England on the 17th, heard from Nathan the next day of Stafford's communiqué.

'What's his source?'

Nathan had to admit he did not know.

'None of this makes sense,' the Viceroy said. 'A rising on Easter Eve? That's a mere four days away. There are Volunteer manoeuvres planned for Easter *Sunday*. Anything from those informers in their ranks?'

'Nothing,' said Nathan. 'It sounds like a terrible mix-up. Someone somewhere has heard of the manoeuvres and confused them with a real rising.'

'And what's all this,' Wimborne went on, 'about an arms ship? Where's it supposed to be coming from?' Getting no reaction from Nathan. 'Can only be America.'

They called in the Inspector-General of the RIC and all three concluded that these were nothing but rumours. If the source was Stafford, how on earth would he know more than RIC under-cover agents who had infiltrated the Volunteers?

'It can't be important,' Wimborne said. 'If it were, surely the War Office in London would have informed you directly. Incidentally, where is our Commander-in-Chief?'

'In London,' said Nathan.

'There you are, then,' said Wimborne. 'If this were serious, wouldn't Sir John French send Friend back at once?'

They called in Major Price. He was usually the most suspicious of all personnel in the Castle, yet even he felt it advisable in the circumstances to adopt a softly-softly approach to the trouble-makers.

After clearing the reef, the *Aud* still had a two-hour battle with the storm.

There were times when Spindler thought the cargo was shifting and they would all be drowned. But they made it. As if to confirm their escape, the compass started acting normally. It was like seeing Lazarus rising from the dead.

By 5.30 on that Tuesday evening, they were clear of the eastern edge of the bank and he was able to lay a course normal for a tramp steamer, SSE. They were on schedule. Next stop, Ireland.

As soon as he arrived in Limerick, Sean Fitzgibbon passed on his instructions. Colivet was amazed. So far, Pearse had told him he was to hold the line of the Shannon in the event of hostilities. These new orders were not in the least hypothetical.

'Don't you agree, Sean, that this sounds like a rising?'

Worried even more, Fitzgibbon said, 'I haven't the faintest idea.'

'If it is, I'm telling you, we're not ready. If arms are landed, I don't even have the men with the skills to fire them.'

Fitzgibbon now strongly suspected that MacNeill was having the wool pulled over his eyes.

'If I were you, Mick,' he said, 'I'd go to Dublin tomorrow and ask Pearse straight out.'

Tuesday 18 April began as normal in the advertising agency run by Wolf von Igel, an attaché at the German Consulate in New York. The offices were on the top floor of a skyscraper. There was no security in spite of Devoy's constant nagging.

But Igel had at last got the message. He was under suspicion for complicity in attempting to blow up the Welland Canal connecting Lake Ontario and Lake Erie, west of Niagara Falls. If his involvement were proven, he was liable to prosecution for infringing American neutrality.

In the States, there was much ill will towards the Germans for allowing their submarines to sink neutral shipping. Captain Hall decided it was a good moment to try and influence the President. He gave the Americans a tip-off.

Igel was in his office, removing papers from the safe for a more secure hiding-place when half a dozen burly, neatly dressed men appeared outside. Their chief asked briskly of a male assistant for Igel's office. He had pointed before he realized something was wrong. They pushed past him.

Igel, a strapping former Lieutenant in the German army, was standing next to the open safe. The table was littered with dossiers marked 'Top Secret'. Before he could move, two men pinioned his arms while the rest gathered up the documents.

'Crooks!' von Igel screamed, kicking out.

Von Skal, an elderly assistant at the German Consulate, rushed in from his office and there was a scuffle.

Momentarily, Igel managed to wrench free and slam the safe door shut. Skal picked up the phone and was trying to call the operator when one of the men broke the connection.

'I'm an American citizen,' yelled Skal. 'I am going downstairs to phone.'

The Chief took out a gun and levelled it. 'Try it, sir, and it'll be the last thing you do.'

'Shoot and be damned,' Skal said defiantly.

The pistol was lowered. 'We are acting on the orders of Mr Marshall, the United States District Attorney.'

'You mean,' gasped Igel, 'you are Secret Service?'

The Chief did not answer. He merely motioned towards Skal. 'Let him go. We're almost through here.'

As Skal went to alert his Embassy, the agent left.

Back at base, they found among the documents the message just received in code from Dublin on the 15th and wirelessed to Berlin via Buenos Aires and Stockholm. They had no difficulty in reading it because attached to it were a copy of Devoy's covering message and a code-book.

The Military Council in Dublin requested that the goods, obviously arms, should not be landed on the Kerry coast until the night of Easter Sunday/Easter Monday, five days hence.

When Marshall, the DA, read this, he whistled, 'This is most peculiar.' There was a prima-facie case for thinking that this in itself was proof that the Germans had infringed President Wilson's Proclamation of Neutrality. He thanked his lucky stars. It was no small thing to risk infringing any country's diplomatic immunity.

The State Department passed this information on to the New York *World* whose editor was an Anglophile. He, in turn, handed it to a British Embassy official who put it on the desk of his Ambassador, Sir Cecil Spring-Rice.

From the British point of view, the jigsaw lacked only one piece. They did not know that the *Aud* had no wireless and, therefore, never would receive the message. Thus they had no more idea than Clarke or Pearse that the boat was likely to turn up at Tralee days before anyone was ready for it.

In Berlin, Bernstorff's 15 April telegram No 435, sent on from Stockholm, arrived at 1.25 on the morning of Wednesday 19 April.

It read: 'Delivery of arms must occur precisely on Sunday 23 April in the evening.'

Captain Nadolny read it with a certain detachment. For ten days the *Aud* had been out of contact with land, somewhere on that immense sea. His detestation of Casement came out as a general condemnation of 'Those damned stupid Irish.'

The Admiralty coolly informed Devoy that the arms ship had no radio and there was nothing more they could do. The *Aud*'s Captain had his orders and would abide by them.

Devoy was left fuming that in this emergency he had no simple code for communicating to Dublin the mess they were in.

In Dublin, Pearse and his colleagues on the Military Council went on with their preparations. They did not know that Casement was on his way in a submarine, hoping to call the rising off. Nor that the arms ship was being tracked all the way.

They expected the ship or ships to appear off Inishtooskert on Sunday night, after the rising had begun. The arms would be unloaded at Fenit and distributed early Monday throughout Cork, Tipperary, Limerick and the west. By then 3,000 well-armed Volunteers would have risen in Dublin. Thousands more, many with German arms, would rise in the provinces and pin the British down so they could not relieve Dublin. It would be the most impressive rising in Irish history.

'Our security's been so damn tight,' Tom Clarke said, 'I really believe the English haven't caught a smell of the rising.'

Joe Plunkett was not present; he was recovering from major surgery. But he had made plans to send three specialists to Kerry to set up their own transmitter in a remote spot near Tralee. This

153

would enable them to communicate with the arms ship as it sailed down the west coast.

The Council were so sure Berlin had received their change of plans that Pearse did not bother to tell Stack to keep watch from Good Friday, just in case.

Stack himself had known the precise date of the arms landing for a month. He took it for granted that the Germans knew. Curiously, though he lived in the west of Ireland where even trains from Dublin rarely ran on time, he expected a boat coming from Germany in wartime with British patrols everywhere to be dead on schedule.

In Dublin, Clarke at last gave the order for MacNeill to be handed a complete copy of the Castle document.

He read with horror that General Friend was planning to arrest Volunteer leaders and confiscate their arms. He let it be known, to Pearse's satisfaction, that if the British tried anything of the kind, his men were ready to resist unto blood.

At 11 a.m. Pearse met Michael Colivet, Commandant of the Limerick Brigade in the lounge of the North Star Hotel near Amiens Street Station.

'Now, Michael, what is on your mind?'

'These instructions which Sean Fitzgibbon gave me, Mr Pearse. It seems the arms from Fenit will arrive at Abbeyfeale.' Pearse nodded. 'I'm to take charge of my share and send the rest on to Galway.'

'Correct,' said Pearse, and sniffed to indicate that a waiter was within earshot.

'Well, then,' said Colivet, raising his quacky Limerick voice, 'I may just be a plain farmer from the west but I know when I'm being diddled over the price for my wheat.'

' 'Tis a perfectly fair price I'm offering you, Mr Ryan,' said Pearse, in an agricultural accent that did not suit him.

When the waiter took the order and left, Colivet whispered, 'After the distribution of arms, the outlying battalions are to march on to Limerick City and then east to Dublin.'

'Indeed,' Pearse said. 'Where is the obscurity in that?'

'None. It is plain as a pikestaff that you and MacNeill mean Sunday's manoeuvres to be a rising.'

Pearse said, 'A Republic is to be proclaimed, yes. So make sure there is no clash with police or troops before then.'

For the moment, Colivet was lost for words. Then: 'I take it the Germans are coming in force.'

'I am not in a position to answer that.'

'So they *are* coming,' Colivet said triumphantly.

'Please,' implored Pearse, whose right foot tapped the floor, 'I am not in a position to say that.'

'No need, sir. Tell Mr MacNeill we'll do our best.'

They stood up, shook hands and left just as the waiter was bringing coffee.

Colivet walked alone in O'Connell Street. He took in the trams, the people passing to and fro in their day-to-day activities and fell to wondering what it would be like on Sunday. There was no time for day-dreaming. He had to plan a rising in Limerick and there were only four days to go.

While Colivet was at Kingsbridge Station waiting for a train home, Dublin was buzzing with activity.

At a meeting of the Dublin Corporation, a Sinn Fein alderman, Tom Kelly, was reading the Castle document to his colleagues. They were furious. It seemed to them the British were hell-bent on provoking the Volunteers.

'They want bloodshed on the streets of the capital,' Kelly said, 'to prove that we Irish are a rebellious lot and not worthy to govern ourselves. As if the Volunteers would be so daft as to take on the British army!'

Meanwhile, in the next street, a corporation employee handed Sean Connolly, the Abbey actor, a duplicate key to the City Hall, which overlooked Dublin Castle.

In another part of the city, Pearse gave de Valera of the Volunteers' Third Battalion details of the rising for the first time.

James Connolly and MacDonagh made a thorough inspection of all the buildings they intended to seize on Sunday.

Afterwards, MacDonagh addressed B Company of his 2nd Battalion.

'That Castle document, men, must be taken very seriously. It may mean that when we go out on manoeuvres on Sunday, some of us might not be coming back.'

John Dillon, in his home north of O'Connell Street, was picking up all sorts of rumours. He was sure, he wrote to Redmond in London, that elements in the separatist movement were planning some devilish business.

The excitement was even getting to John MacNeill, the most unflappable of men. He called a meeting of the Volunteer Executive at his house that evening to discuss the document.

'If the authorities try to disarm us, gentlemen, I want you to take the necessary counter-measures. We must preserve our arms and our organization at all costs.'

'We will, sir,' Pearse assured him.

The O'Rahilly chipped in with, 'You do mean us to take only defensive measures?'

'Naturally,' MacNeill said. 'It would be madness for an amateur force like ours to take on a regular army.'

In spite of this reservation, Pearse was pleased. His last major problem seemed to have been solved. The manoeuvres now had the full backing of the Chief of Staff and would be taken very seriously by all the men. Within the hour, the newly alerted Volunteers were buying up food and supplies, and oiling their rifles.

Back at St Enda's, Pearse went to a room where Liam Mellowes was hiding. Nora, Connolly's daughter, had recently been to England where Mellowes had been deported and helped smuggle him back, disguised as a priest.

'It looks to me, Liam,' Pearse said, 'that nothing can stop us now, not even MacNeill. In a couple of days, you will be in Galway, leading the rising there.'

Not everyone in MacNeill's Executive was taken in.

Back at Volunteer HQ, Bulmer Hobson and Captain J. J. O'Connell went through the Castle document with a fine-tooth comb.

'I don't like it one bit, J. J.,' Hobson kept muttering.

Raiding Archbishop Walsh's House in Drumcondra was particularly suspicious; the British knew that would raise a riot. Further, a swoop on the scale envisaged in the document would mean blood flowing in the streets.

Hobson looked at O'Connell. 'It makes no sense,' he concluded. 'Not the slightest.'

'If it's mere scaremongering,' asked O'Connell, 'who's responsible for it and who stands to gain?'

'I detect in this the hand of Joe Plunkett and his cronies.'

They drove back to MacNeill's place.

'Are you saying,' he asked them, 'that I'm the victim of some plot?'

He dredged his mind for clues he might have missed. He had recently been on tour in Tralee and Stack's officers there seemed surprised that he knew less about some of Pearse's orders than they did. But Pearse was so honourable.

MacDonagh? But Thomas was his colleague at the University. A more upright and conscientious man he had never come across.

'You have been used,' insisted Hobson, 'as a pawn in a wicked conspiracy.'

O'Connell chipped in with, 'There may be more to those Sunday manoeuvres than any of us realized.'

MacNeill sat back in his chair. Whether the Castle document was a forgery or not, and on that he suspended judgement, he had a premonition that something terrible was about to happen.

That evening at Liberty Hall, the Citizen Army was drilling when Connolly invited three officers, McCormack, Doyle and Frank Robbins, to join him and Mallin in his room.

'Listen, lads,' he began, 'the rising is fixed for Sunday at 6.30 p.m., 7 p.m. in the provinces.' Seeing their enthusiasm, he went on: 'Our main job is to take and hold St Stephen's Green.'

Mallin put a map on an easel.

'Our first aim,' he said, 'is to check any advance of the military from Portobello Barracks. The Green covers several main streets' – he pointed – 'Grafton, Harcourt, Leeson, Kildare, Dawson and so on. To hold on to the Green, we'll have to take over some of the buildings on the north side, like the Shelbourne Hotel, and build barricades across the main approaches.'

Connolly pointed at Doyle.

'You, Joe, with sixteen men will take Davy's pub, here, at Portobello Bridge. When troops from the Barracks get in range, let 'em have it.'

Doyle's eyes gleamed. He was a bartender in Davy's pub and he had one or two scores to settle with the landlord.

Nathan was working late in his office when he was told that the informer in MacDonagh's B Company was outside.

'Show him in.'

The skinny, shifty-eyed fellow, running his cap through his hands, said that MacDonagh had told them they were going out on Sunday and some might not come back.

After dismissing him, Nathan put the police on increased alert.

157

He also issued an official denial that the Castle had any intention of disarming the Volunteers. He had the impression that someone or some group was trying to stir up trouble.

In London, Birrell finally had to call off his trip to the west of Ireland, the only place he felt he would find peace. John Redmond was threatening fire and brimstone over the appointment of a Protestant and a Unionist as Attorney-General.

Birrell consoled himself with the thought of curling up in his flat in St James's Street and reading a new romance about the French Revolution. There was nothing like history to take the mind off the gloom and doom of Anglo-Irish politics.

That night at St Enda's, Pearse found his mother so sad, he put his arms around her.

'Something's bothering you?'

She admitted to thinking he would perhaps be killed.

'Is that so bad, little Mother?' he said, smiling.

'If Willie is left behind, yes.'

'That would be terrible for him,' he had to agree.

'Do you think, Pat,' she said, in a sobbing voice, 'you could write something for me, a kind of souvenir, if you get the time?'

'Of course,' he said, 'if ever I get the time.'

At sea, it had been a day of splendid spring weather. In the course of the evening, the *Aud* had sighted two more cruisers. Neither of them took the least notice of her.

Spindler felt his luck was uncanny; he was like a punter in a dream picking the winner in every race.

He began saying to himself, What if the English know we are coming? If so, they don't need to engage us at sea, merely wait for us to go ashore and trap us on terra firma.

Spindler was on the watch when a third cruiser loomed out of the darkness 300 yards off with its lights screened. No more substantial than a silhouette, it gave no sign of recognition. Thinking this was the last cruiser of the line from the Hebrides chain, he turned in at midnight.

Three hours later, he was woken up by a shrill whistle in the voice-pipe next to his bunk. 'Another auxiliary cruiser, Herr Kapitän, five miles to port.'

He was no sooner up on deck than it, too, veered off.

They were due at the rendezvous in two days' time. Puffy-eyed, he measured the chart. At their present rate, they would arrive a day early, incredible in view of what they had been through. He ordered reduced speed in a south-easterly direction.

Battermann called out, '*Another* cruiser, Herr Kapitän. Three miles to starboard.'

It was emergency stations once again, with everything pouring into the Conjuror's Box while Hector barked furiously. All these swift changes were becoming tedious.

The ship was a 6,000 tonner of the Royal Mail Steam Packet Company with two guns pointed in their direction. Her crew took a good look at the *Aud*'s starboard side, crossed to her stern, then veered off eastwards.

Spindler was more baffled than ever. Enemy ships kept looking; but not once, as the law of the sea demanded, had they asked where the *Aud* came from and was headed.

One thing reassured him: there was just no way the British could have known about the arms landing in Tralee. He himself had been told at the last minute and his crew had still not been given a single detail.

In view of the behaviour of the British, Spindler felt the best thing to do was to disguise the *Aud*.

In the course of Wednesday night, his crew built a wood and canvas casing, six-feet high, around the funnel. When morning came, they would paint Spanish signs and flags over the Norwegian.

Not for the first time he wished he had a wireless to contact Tralee.

'I only hope,' he joked with his first mate, 'the Irish haven't started the rebellion already. That'll only make the British twice as vigilant.'

So certain was he becoming of success that he made plans for their getaway after the gun-running. He would mount four dummy 10.5 cm guns and raid British vessels below 3,000 tons. How would they know the *Aud* had only one machine-gun aboard?

He was laughing to himself when a cry rent the air, 'Submarine ahoy,' and all his certainties vanished.

The periscope turned out to be a floating meat tin.

Early on Maundy Thursday morning, the *Aud* was near its destination, at the front-end of the time-span allowed. Better early than late, he thought. That should please the Irish.

159

The wind had died in the night; it was a fresh, still morning. Though the crew were tired after hours of putting the casing around the funnel, he could not let them rest. All hands were needed to open the hatches and remove the cargo camouflaging the arms.

The upper deck soon looked like the packing department of a big store, piled high with window-frames, door-frames, tinware, zinc buckets and piles of tin baths. Packing cases and straw were thrown into the ship's furnace, the rest heaved over the side. It was half an hour before Spindler noticed that the *Aud* was trailing flotsam – baths, coffee cans, pails – to the horizon.

An armed British motor launch, passing within six miles, took in the extraordinary scene and sailed on.

That, too, struck Spindler as distinctly odd.

The U-19 had also experienced calmer seas once it turned south down the west coast. Casement, though still weak, was feeling slightly better. In the night hours he had discussed with Monteith the various expeditions that had landed or attempted to land in Ireland over four centuries. All had met with shipwreck or disaster. And theirs was the smallest of all.

'The hardest part,' Casement said, 'is we have absolutely no idea how things stand at home or what the plans are. We do not even know how dependent the Volunteers are on German arms.'

On the *Aud*, eight-bells signalled it was noon. According to Spindler's calculations, they were only forty-five miles from Tralee, 52 N 11 W. If there were no hitches, they should arrive at Fenit in four hours.

He ordered full-speed ahead. They had taken so long to jettison their cargo, there was no time to change to Spanish markings after all. Yet he was happy. He had, he remembered, only one more enemy to beat that night: the full moon.

Two more hours of feverish activity followed. Steam winches and unloading tackle were readied. Hatches were opened; in the holds, the topmost cases were put in slings ready for hoisting ashore. Small bags were packed with pocket torches and tools for ripping open the cases in order to make weapons immediately available to the Irish rebels.

While this was going on, Spindler took his chief officers aside.

'I presume the Irish will deal with the harbour authorities, but if not and they come aboard to inspect our papers,' Spindler winked, 'I'm sure you know what to do.'

His men made chopping motions with their hands.

'It'll take seven to eight hours to load,' he said, 'Fenit is a mere seven miles from Tralee with a connecting railway. If the alarm is raised, the British could be on to us within half an hour.'

His officers gasped. They were sailors not soldiers; they had no experience of fighting trained troops.

'Now you understand why we have to unload the machine-guns first. The rebels will be waiting on shore. I hope to God they are, anyway.'

He asked someone to see that their naval ensign was ready to be unfurled. He checked personally that the explosives were in place.

'I want two more large charges placed foward,' he said, 'just in case we have to scuttle the ship.' Then: 'Hands wash and into clean No 2s.'

The crew went below to clean up and put on their uniforms, except for their caps which they stuffed in their pockets. They wore a dagger and pistol in their belts. Finally, they pulled on their old Norwegian overalls.

At the Volunteer HQ, Hobson and O'Connell were visited by Liam Manahan, a Commandant from the Limerick Brigade.

'When,' he asked Hobson, 'is the crisis expected?'

Hobson's eyes narrowed. 'Crisis, what crisis?'

'There's a lot of talk in our area.'

'It must be because of the Castle document,' O'Connell said, non-committally.

On his way out, Manahan ran into MacDonagh.

'What on earth are you doing here, Liam? You should be home on full alert.'

' 'Twas just that I heard rumours of a crisis. But Hobson assures me 'tis nothing at all.'

'Listen to me,' MacDonagh hissed, 'there is a danger of immediate raids and arrests.'

Manahan's eyes widened. 'That's not what Hobson said.'

'He and his ilk are not in it.'

'In what?'

MacDonagh grabbed his arm. 'For God's sake, Liam, take it from me, things are as serious as can be.'

MacDonagh was disturbed by all the talk flying about. Hobson was astute; if he grasped what was going on he would tell MacNeill. Then there would be trouble.

*

Shortly after 1 p.m., the *Aud* was alone on the sea. On the horizon, there were what seemed to be long, low bluish clouds that slowly crystallized into a land bathed in sunshine.

Spindler mustered his entire crew.

'You guessed we were not headed for Libau.' They smiled, nudging one another. 'That there is Ireland.'

They cheered. Some sniffed the air. *Ja*, that lovely fresh smell was Ireland.

'Set your watches, men, by Greenwich Mean Time. Which makes it now ten minutes after twelve.' As they put their watches back, he went on: 'I warn you, if we are captured, our uniforms might not save us from being shot. Are you with me?'

They roared, 'Yes!'

He went meticulously through each man's task.

'Engineers: We may have to move up the shallow channel to Fenit. Be ready to pump out the water-tanks to lighten ship.'

'*Ja*, Herr Kapitän.'

'Ship's doctor. Where are you? Good man. I want you to hand round surgical dressings.' He nodded. 'The rest of you remember, if there is an emergency, there will be a big medicine chest in the mess-room. Clear?'

No one had any questions.

'Very well. Every man to his post. And good luck.' And, he murmured to himself, 'God knows we'll need it.'

The coastline, for all its rich and varying hues, was the most inhospitable he had ever seen. The mountains were steep, high and bald; they were seamed with clefts and gullies and protected by overhanging cliffs.

As the boat came closer, he picked out numerous islands and jagged rocks and reefs. It would need all his seamanship to bring the *Aud* through safely. At least the steepness of the cliffs was a guarantee of deep water – or so the manuals said.

For the one and only time the U-19 spotted the *Aud*. It was two miles on the starboard beam.

Lieutenant Weisbach did not try to make contact; he had no orders to do so, nor did he offer any explanation to his passengers. It made Casement more suspicious than ever.

As the submarine passed the mouth of the Shannon, about five miles off the coast, the light from Loop Head was just visible on the port side.

Weisbach warned that from there to the Inishtooskert Island, they would have to be doubly vigilant in case they ran into a British patrol craft.

On the *Aud*, Spindler, not the best of navigators, focused his glasses on shore, looking for signs of life, a house, perhaps, or a lighthouse. Nothing but rocks.

'Where in hell's name,' he murmured, as he edged nearer shore, 'is the entrance to Tralee Bay?'

Many inlets looked like it. After fifteen minutes, he saw what he took to be a small three-pointed rock in Smerwick harbour, known as 'Three Sisters'. Beyond, would be Tralee Bay.

The look-out on the port bow called out, 'Sail ahoy.'

Spindler felt an indescribably joy. He picked out the triangular shape of a white sail. The pilot cutter, what else could it be?

He soon found out. He was nowhere near as far south as he thought; in fact, he was at the Shannon estuary. On its north side was a small island on which stood the Loop Head Lighthouse with its signalling station. Owing to a trick of light, the sail was the Lighthouse itself. He had no doubts that British soldiers were occupying it. He had always intended giving it a wide berth since it was bound to be bristling with machine-guns.

He cursed himself for being such a damned fool.

He slowly switched to starboard, and with his glasses scanned every hill, cliff, gully, as well as the water ahead.

By 3 p.m., Loop Head was very close with its signal station and a few small attendant buildings. On the cliff, a wireless mast rose 200 feet. There was nothing else. Except on either side of the mast a dozen black muzzles poking out of concrete gun-emplacements, all pointed his way. British marines or coastal guards were watching their every move.

Casually, Spindler ordered below all men not needed on deck. The rest strolled around nonchalantly, pulling on briar pipes, spitting overboard. He himself, like an old salt, tramped the bridge: six paces to port, six to starboard.

From the Lighthouse there was no warning shot, no signal of any kind. Yet British indifference was worrying Spindler more and more. Did it mean things were going well or had already gone irreparably wrong?

The enemy's unconcern was not as complete as he thought. The Commander of the signal station relayed that a foreign steamer, the

163

Aud, was acting suspiciously. In Naval HQ at Queenstown, Admiral Bayly promptly sent two destroyers to intercept. The noose around Spindler's neck on sea and land was tightening.

Unaware of this, he steered the *Aud* away from Loop Head, flying a green flag. Ahead were the Seven Hogs or Magharee Islands, while on the south and east sides of the Bay were a few fishermen's huts outside Fenit.

The nearest of the Hogs or Hags was their rendezvous point, Inishtooskert.

In Tralee, Austin Stack was briefing the pilot, Mort O'Leary.

'The arms boat is arriving in three days,' he said, 'on the night of 23/24.'

'When do you want me, Austin?'

'On Holy Saturday night. In the Rink there's a couple of green lights. When you go out in the Bay, show them from the sea-side and pilot the boats in. Provided they manage to beat the blockade.'

At 4.15 p.m., the *Aud* was one mile from the small, low-lying, uninhabited island in the north-west corner of Tralee Bay. The green flag had no effect. Neither Casement's submarine nor the pilot cutter with a green flag at the masthead and a man in a green jersey in the bows was to be seen.

This was the bitterest disappointment of Spindler's life. They had survived tempests and British patrols and now this. The entire crew were peering into the distance, some with glasses. The whole place seemed dead. Since there was scarcely any current, Spindler ordered, 'Cut engines.'

The resulting quietness and sense of foreboding were over-whelming.

In Tralee, Mort O'Leary left Stack and, on his trip across the Bay, saw a two-masted vessel lying off Inishtooskert where the arms boat was due in a few days. It struck him as an odd place for a ship to be. Why didn't it come into harbour? It was too big to fit Stack's description.

Supposing it to be a British decoy ship – there were lots of them around – he continued his journey home.

On the *Aud*, the minutes ticked by. Ten, fifteen, thirty. Spindler scanned the shore with his glasses. Nothing. Were the damned Irish all having a nap? To refresh his memory, he reread his orders. He was at the right spot at the right time; if nothing happened in half an hour, and no communication seemed likely, his orders were, 'Use your own judgement whether to go in or turn back.'

'Turn back?' he muttered. 'Never!'

But if he went in in daylight, he might just as well signal to the British, 'Here are some arms, take them as a present from your admirers in Germany.'

'Herr Kapitän!'

His mate was pointing in alarm towards Kerry Head. The northern buttress of Tralee Bay was ablaze. Orange flame and thick swirling smoke rose into the spring sky.

'Warning? Might this be a warning from the rebels,' he said, hoarsely, 'telling us to go home?'

How was a German sea captain to know that this was the Irish farmer's perennial way of clearing stubble and furze bushes from the hills? He mustered his entire company on the bridge.

'I want to level with you,' he said. 'We seem to be on our own. The British may be on to us. Say the word, and we'll get the hell out of here.'

'*Nein!*' they yelled back.

Brimming with pride, Spindler said, 'Thank you,' and sent them back to their posts.

He tried to work out what had gone wrong. A code-word was to be put in news broadcasts from their Nauen transmitter. This should have been picked up by rebel receivers on the Irish coast. Maybe the word had been omitted. For all he knew, without a wireless, the west had started a scrap of its own, resulting in martial law. That would also explain why the British seemed to know all about them.

His chief worry was Casement. Was he already in Ireland? Had he been arrested? Had the U-boat been delayed by bad weather or engine trouble? Had the U-boat already landed Casement, in which case the pilot boat would return for the *Aud* under cover of night?

There were a hundred questions and not a single answer.

At 4.30 p.m., Con Collins arrived at 44 Mountjoy Square, Dublin, where McDermott was staying.

'Thanks for coming, Con,' said McDermott. 'I'd like you to take a message for me to Limerick and Tralee.'

165

On his way to the train, Collins sneaked a look. It read: 'All going well and according to plan.'

In Berlin, the Admiralty received a wire about the break-in in their New York office. They reacted at once.

Top priority was given to a coded wireless signal sent to all U-boats in Irish waters:

'Come in, commanders. Everything betrayed. Return immediately with *Libau*.'

The message was repeated over and over. No U-boat picked it up.

The British did.

Spindler realized that remaining at a standstill looked suspicious. He decided to explore the inner parts of the Bay with its semicircle of barren hills.

At half-speed, the *Aud* sailed along the northern shore. A few hundred yards from Fenit there was a small pier with a lighthouse. Spindler picked out a few tall masts and houses in the village. To add to his gloom, there was a flagstaff flying the British ensign; at its base was what appeared to be a British Tommy on guard with a rifle on his shoulder.

That, too, struck Spindler in his nervous state as very odd. At any time, the guard should have been interested in them, why not now with heightened tension?

He prayed that an Irish rebel would see his green flag.

At her home, Surrey House, in Rathmines, Countess Markievicz needed a green flag to fly over the General Post Office during the rising.

Among her guests was Laurence Ginnell, an Irish MP very sympathetic to the national cause. She grabbed his green bedspread and went downstairs.

She had only a small amount of gold paint and it had dried up. She opened a tin of mustard, wet it and mixed it with the paint. While four guests held the bedspread taut, she painted on it, 'Irish Republic'.

All the time her brown cocker spaniel, Poppet, jumped and barked and finally tore a strip out of it.

'Get down, dear old darling,' the Countess said.

*

At dusk, Spindler replaced the green flag with occasional green flashing lights as he pointed the *Aud* north towards the flat coast below Kerry Head. Risks he had to take. The signals became bolder, more frequent, and still there was no reply from land. So perfect was the peace, they might have been cruising on a lake in Germany.

For two hours this went on. The crew, with their sense of the sacredness of duty, could not believe that the British were either so lax or so foolish as to take them for a harmless trader. This had to be a typically subtle English trick, the kind their instructors had warned them about in training.

In fact, in Tralee they were being taken for a harmless trader.

Con Collins reached Tralee at 10 p.m. Stack met him at the station and took him to his own lodgings in Upper Rock Street. There, he read McDermott's message.

'Everything here, too,' he told Collins, 'is under control.'

In Mountjoy Square, Dublin, McDermott was briefing a team whose job was to steal equipment from a Wireless College in Cahersiveen on the Ring of Kerry. Present were Denis Daly, the leader, Charlie Monaghan, Donal Sheehan, Colm O'Lochlainn and two from Cahersiveen, Denis Healy and Con Keating, a skilled wireless operator.

'Now, boys,' said McDermott, 'for the last time. You'll be catching the train to Killarney in the morning.'

Daly said, 'You didn't tell us if we're to be armed.'

'Indeed, Denis. In case of trouble. You'll travel in separate compartments. Proceed to the rendezvous' – he pointed with his walking stick to a map – 'outside the town, here, where you'll be met by two cars from Limerick. Tom McInerney is seeing to them. You proceed to Cahersiveen.' He turned to Keating. 'You're sure, Con, that Wireless College has everything you need.'

'I know exactly where it's stored.'

'Grand. First you go to Ballygambon Cross' – he tapped the map again – 'nine miles outside Tralee. Stack is sending a party to pick the equipment up on Saturday morning. They'll transport it for you to Ballyard near Tralee. Con Collins is in Tralee already and he'll help you set it up.'

Daly said, 'That'll give us plenty of time before the arms ship arrives on Monday morning.'

Unlike Spindler, Lieutenant Weisbach had waited for the dark and deeper water.

At 11 p.m., the U-19 was abeam the Loop Head Lighthouse. The weather suddenly turned squally.

On the *Aud*, with midnight approaching, Spindler glared at the brightening sky. The moon would rise within the hour. He risked a last approach to within a mile of Fenit pier and flashed the green light. Nothing. Disappointed, he steamed back to Inishtooskert.

It was black now, so he had almost to feel his way along the west side. That would give him some shelter from the light of that great blister of a moon. In the stillness, he felt that the rattling of the *Aud*'s anchor chain must be carrying as far as that Tommy on guard at Fenit harbour.

Weisbach felt his situation had improved with the rising of the moon. The U-19 was now clear for a hasty submergence if that should be necessary.

He headed for the rendezvous. He reached the spot, one mile north-west of Inishtooskert, where he confidently hoped he would meet up with the *Aud* and the pilot boat.

The *Aud* had just left to take up anchorage for the night.

At the Volunteer HQ, Hobson was still working in his office when J. J. O'Connell and Eimer O'Duffy burst in.

'We think you should know,' O'Connell said, 'that in the country several companies have received orders to prepare for an insurrection on Easter Sunday.'

Many pieces of a puzzle suddenly formed a pattern in Hobson's brain: Managhan coming from Limerick with strange talk of an imminent crisis. That Castle document whose contents made no sense from the British point of view. Above all, his impression over many months that there was another secret and manipulative force at work within the Volunteers. And those manoeuvres only three days away.

'Jesus,' he said, clicking his fingers. 'They're planning a rising on Easter Sunday!'

'Who are?' they said together.

Hobson did not answer. He jumped up from his desk.

'We've got to get in touch with MacNeill at once.'

'My car's outside,' O'Connell said.

Weisbach waited for the *Aud*. When it failed to appear, he started to cruise round. He was not hopeful of making contact. At four miles, the *Aud* would be invisible against the mountains. Its green lights were oil-sourced, which meant they could only be seen from a mile away. Further, if the *Aud*'s skipper knew his job, the signals would be visible only from shore, not from further out to sea where the sub was.

He looked to the west for the pilot boat's green lights. Nothing.

His fear was growing for the safety of his craft.

MacNeill, a gown over his pyjamas, peered through the window of his large Victorian villa, checking to see who was visiting him at this ungodly hour. Satisfied, he opened the front door, putting his fingers to his lips to indicate that his wife and children were asleep. He ushered Hobson and O'Connell into his book-lined study.

Hobson explained briefly all his fears and suspicions, ending with, 'We have been betrayed.'

MacNeill, rubbing his eyes in tired incredulity, demanded to know who was behind this.

'Your Director of Operations,' Hobson said. 'He planned the Easter manoeuvres as a cover for the rising.'

'Pearse?'

A generally pacific man, MacNeill could be terrible in his wrath. 'We must do something. *Now*.'

'It's turned midnight,' O'Connell pointed out.

'You woke *me*, didn't you?' MacNeill thundered.

With an effort, Casement heaved himself up into the conning-tower alongside Monteith and Beverley. All three strained their eyes for the green lights of the pilot boat. They were so strung-up, they wanted to look in every direction at once.

Monteith heard the thumping of Beverley's heart and felt that the final act of their useless tragedy had begun.

Pearse cycled home after an exhausting day. It was well after midnight when his sister Margaret greeted him in the hallway.

'Did you manage to get Mass and Communion, Pat?'

'I did.' He was already on the staircase. 'I need sleep. I'm all in.'

169

He was no sooner in his room on the top floor than a car drew up outside with a squeal of tyres. He heard the slamming of the doors and angry voices which he recognized. His sister answered the bell.

'I am sorry, gentlemen, he has retired for the night.'

'It's all right, Margaret.'

Pearse was already descending the stairs. He gestured to MacNeill, Hobson and O'Connell to join him in his study.

'About these orders of yours to Volunteers in the west,' MacNeill began peremptorily. 'Attacks on barracks, seizure of railways. It can mean only one thing.'

Very quietly, Pearse said, 'A rising, yes. You were deceived but it was necessary.'

MacNeill flowing mane bristled in his rage. A rising was out of the question, he said; the odds against it were ludicrous. The British would withdraw forces from the Western Front rather than allow a Republic on their very doorstep. Outside Dublin the Volunteers were simply not armed or trained, it would be a massacre.

'What hurts me most,' he continued, 'is the lies. I always gave my enemies my word that the Volunteers' programme would always be public and explicit.'

His spectacles were steaming up.

'This is treachery, Pearse, for your own selfish and vainglorious ends. War is not a Passion play in the Abbey, you know, and civilians with rifles are not soldiers.'

Pearse was thinking, Another example of a Gaelic League professor selling out the movement. His fine-sounding phrases are camouflage for doing nothing. Irish leaders have always found some excuse for chickening out. He is talking about the waste of innocent Irish blood when 150,000 Irishmen are in the British army, shedding their blood for England. He has a Sunday-school attitude to good and evil. He has no idea that failures can be triumphs, that without deaths there can be no resurrections.

When MacNeill paused for breath, Pearse, in his mesmeric voice, said: 'You cannot stop the rising. Things have gone too far. Officers will obey me, not you.'

He turned to Hobson. 'You're an IRB man. You have a duty to obey our call.'

Hobson reacted bitterly. 'The IRB constitution says force should be used only when it has popular support.'

170

Quietly, Pearse said, 'Your logic is impeccable, Hobson. It's just that you do not understand the Irish people.'

'What you are doing,' MacNeill thundered, 'is against the teaching of the Church you claim to obey. One condition of waging a just war is that is has some prospect of success and a rising at this time has absolutely none.'

Pearse disliked MacNeill's textbook theology with its textbook God who would have condemned Jesus for going up to Jerusalem.

'You are prepared,' went on MacNeill, 'to pit a half-armed, half-trained little body of Volunteers against a professional army of a million.'

Pearse, with a little nod, accepted that those were the odds.

'Can you not see,' MacNeill said, shudderingly, 'that many of our countrymen will die, some of them mere boys? Will you tell their mothers how and why they died, *will you?* The time and circumstances are simply not right for revolutionary action. Only look around you in the streets. Most people are British sympathizers. The thousands of Irishmen in their army prove that. Multiply that by five for their families who are proud of them and depend on them for their livelihood, *that* is how loyal Ireland is to Britain at present.'

'We differ, you and I,' Pearse said, quietly, 'about what constitutes success and failure.'

'Yes, we do,' cried MacNeill. 'You think that bloodshed is victory enough.'

'It was enough in Jesus's case.'

'You are forgetting something, Pearse,' MacNeill retorted angrily. 'Jesus died, he *refused* to kill. Once you start the wheel of violence turning, who will be able to stop it?'

Pearse muttered, too softly to be heard, 'That wheel has been turning for 700 years.'

'As for me, I refuse to get involved in your guilt.'

'And you intend—'

'To do all in my power to stop you.' MacNeill stomped to the door. 'Short of calling Dublin Castle.'

Hobson and O'Connell followed him out to the car. In the courtyard outside, Pearse heard MacNeill saying, 'I want you to cancel all Volunteer activity this weekend.'

O'Connell said, 'I'll go to Cork straight away.'

Pearse, in considerable anguish, looked through his study window towards the mass of the mountains, quietly reciting lines he had composed six years before:

> *I have turned my face*
> *To this road before me,*
> *To the deed that I see*
> *And the death I shall die.*

His beautiful, doe-eyed mother came in, solicitous.

'Is there something wrong, Pat?'

He assured her it was nothing. Even if plans had to be trimmed, there was no turning back. Sheer will-power would see him through.

Mrs Pearse, seeing that her dear eldest son was preoccupied, left with, 'God love you, Patrick.'

For a long time, he sat brooding, no sounds save from a nearby waterfall and wind in tall trees. They made him lonely somehow and, suddenly, sad. He was beginning to feel the hard hand of fate upon him. MacNeill's spoiling tactics were the sort of thing that had dogged Irish rebellions throughout history.

For another hour and a half the U-19 cruised around the bay. The night had turned murky, starless. In the conning tower, without a compass, the three Irishmen did not know where to look. A smooth sea was running, water whispered on the hulk. It was, frustratingly, an ideal night for gun-running.

Monteith felt his spine hardening like cement and his body grow numb. Had the Germans planned it like this to get rid of them? With the fury of a frustrated soldier, he wanted to fight someone, to tear something to bits. He could not imagine his own people letting them down.

Yet the German officers seemed no less frustrated. If they were pretending, they were superb actors. Their language was becoming more and more colourful.

Monteith felt the submarine was nothing but a grey ghost adrift on a sea of ineptitude. It was clear to him no pilot boat was coming; they would have to row ashore.

Weisbach decided to wait no longer. In the shelter of the bay the sea was perfectly calm and lit by misty moonshine. He would look for a flat stretch of beach.

'Full-steam ahead.'

As the U-boat moved on the surface towards Tralee Bay at 14 knots, the three Irishmen went below to check their gear for landing. In their cabin, Monteith took his .37 calibre Mauser pistol out of its wooden case and loaded it. Casement, looking forlorn without

172

General Sir John Maxwell

Erskine Childers (in oilskins) unloading arms from the Asgard *at Howth*

Sir Edward Carson addressing an anti-Home Rule rally in 1913

Patrick Pearse after his oration at the funeral of O'Donovan Rossa

John Redmond

Augustine Birrell

*Sir Matthew Nathan (l.) with
Augustine Birrell*

Lord Wimborne

Admiral Sir Reginald Hall

Sir Roger Casement

Casement (without cap)
aboard the German
submarine U-19

Eoin MacNeill

The Countess Markievicz with her daughter and stepson

Sheehy-Skeffington with Captain White, a British soldier who trained the Irish Citizen Army

The O'Rahilly

his beard which he had recently shaved off, was fumbling with his equipment.

'Can you load one of these, Sir Roger?'

'I have never killed anything in my life.'

Monteith sat beside him. He showed him how to load, open and eject. He gave him a cartridge clip to practise with. After a while, Casement shook his head and gave it back.

'Will you load it for me, please?'

In spite of his bad wrist, Monteith did so. He put on the safety catch, replaced the pistol in the holster and handed it over. He caught a look of loathing on Casement's face.

Hell's bells, thought Monteith, a revolutionary who hates guns.

Casement was sure the British would capture the arms ship. No rifles for the Volunteers, the enemy alerted, the leaders of the rising seized. It was such a mess. Would they fight without German arms? Not knowing added to his anguish. For half an hour, he closed his eyes and leaned his head on a locker.

At 2.15 a.m., an officer poked his head round the door. 'Empty your pockets and destroy anything on you in writing.'

Monteith asked the skipper for the boat's outboard motor to be fitted.

'Sorry,' Weisbach said, 'it would attract attention.'

Who to? Monteith thought, but he did not voice it.

'The Lieutenant is right,' Casement said, itching to contact the rebels as soon as possible and tell them how things stood.

The chilliness of the morning hit them as soon as they reached the deck. The boat was lifted from the forward hatch. It was only 12 foot by 4 1/2 foot and a tight fit for them and their belongings. They put on their lifebelts and strapped their gear to the seats. Each had a bag with a change of underclothes, flash lamp, notebooks, a pair of Zeiss binoculars and a sheath-knife. They secured the ammunition, 1,000 rounds for each pistol, in a waterproof tin box and waited for the sub to hove to.

The Quartermaster on the watch, who admired Churchill, whispered to them, 'Should you see Winnie, tell him, "The North Sea Rats are raiding your corn bins, why not dig them out?" '

The boat was lowered to the water, where it sat like a squat tub. Monteith complained, 'Our people are running a revolution and they can't send out a pilot boat for a shipload of arms.'

'Hush,' was Casement's reply, 'it will be a much greater adventure going ashore in this cockle shell.'

After handshakes, Beverley took his place in the centre, Casement was in the stern with Monteith in the bow. They pulled away from the submarine as it drifted off in the mists like a great grey whale. They were a couple of miles off shore. The boat had no rudder, so Casement steered with a third oar. To begin with they went in circles, due to the fact that the rowing-oars were not a pair. In spite of his damaged hand, Monteith took them both and shortened his grip on one to make it match the other.

After an hour, Casement made out a line of white foam and they heard the distant thunder of waves breaking on shore. With 200 yards to go, Monteith looked over his shoulder, only to see foam-topped waves, serried like the heads of cobras, rearing over the boat. Dropping from a height of six feet, they crashed on top of them.

'Look ou-out!'

Casement was hurled against Beverley and, combined, they smashed into Monteith. They had scarcely struggled back to their seats when another wave flipped the boat over. The lifebelts saved them and with one touch Monteith righted the boat. The empty fuel tanks on the sides gave it buoyancy. Beverley and Monteith gripped the sides while Casement, gasping and spluttering, clambered in the stern. He steadied the boat while they got aboard. Fortunately, Monteith had secured the oars.

No sooner had they pulled off again than they hit a sand bank. Rollers swept over them, and the boat refused to budge. Time after time they were struck side-on by waves that threatened to shake the craft to pieces. The cold, lead-like force of the waves slamming every inch of their bodies sapped their energy further.

Monteith dug an oar into the bank and, with a monumental effort, pushed off before the oar gripped the bottom. Losing his balance, he went overboard again. He had clung to the oar so that Beverley was able to grab the end and haul him aboard.

Settled again, they waited for a big wave and levered themselves off the sand bank. Within a few minutes they made it to the beach. They had come to Banna Strand.

They crawled out of the boat, almost spent. While Monteith held the sides, Beverley untied the kit and carried it ashore before helping Casement hobble up the sandy slope.

With his knife, Monteith tried to hole the boat. His hand was swollen to pumpkin-size and every effort jarred it more. In the end, weak and shaky, he had to be content with half-submerging it. As he moved away, a big wave lifted it and dropped it on his right foot. He screeched in pain as he felt his ankle wrenched from under him.

Limping to the beach, he found Casement below high-water mark, with the sea lapping him from head to toe. In moonlight, he seemed like a sleeping child.

Monteith dragged him, seemingly unconscious, up to dry sand. Shattered by the futility of the mission and his affection for his Chief, he took out his pistol. It would be a kindness to put him out of his misery.

Casement was not unconscious but in a kind of trance. Even in the shatteringly cold water, even when trying to get a foothold in the shingle to wade ashore – was it tiredness, hunger, sickness, a stab of mysticism to which he was always prone? – he felt nothing but an overwhelming joy.

The long exile in America and Germany was over. He was in Ireland, which he thought he would never see again. He was going to his death but nothing mattered now, for he was home at last. A smile played at the corners of his lips; in spite of the misery, for the first time in years, he was happy.

Monteith removed his gun from Casement's temple and tossed it aside before dragging him to his feet. He had to get Casement's circulation going soon or he might not make it. He pummelled his legs and body, while water streamed from his hair and clothes, then walked him slowly like a horse after a race.

The sandhills, dotted with rushes and coarse grass, were full of skylarks and Casement heard them singing as they rose and fell in the starless dawn. The first sound he heard above the beat of the breakers and the shuffling of the surf was the larks over the dunes right up to an old Viking fort, the Rath of Currahane.

This was Ireland, the old, the agelessly old Ireland which he loved with every fibre of his being. He was, though sick and wet and practically lifeless, home in Ireland at a time of primroses and skylarks. When they had warmed up a little and wrung out their clothes, Monteith said, 'Well, Sir Roger, we've had the little adventure you spoke of.'

Casement patted him on the shoulder, gratefully. 'Yes, my friend, and now we are much nearer the end of the chapter.'

Monteith, hurt in hand and foot, took charge. It was his decision to try and find a car to get Casement to Dublin. They would have to hide their belongings. Guns, in these circumstances, would be a liability and they had no strength to carry them.

Having buried everything but their overcoats in the sand, they set off.

'Tonight, when it's dark,' Monteith said, 'Beverley and I can come back and dig our equipment out.'

He gazed around him at one of the most deserted spots on the west coast.

'I can't see many people coming here, not on Good Friday.'

It was a few minutes to four.

At 4 a.m., a farmer, John McCarthy, strolled on Banna Strand. Awake at 2 a.m., he did something he had never done before: to honour Good Friday, he visited a holy well.

On the way back he was looking for driftwood when he saw a dinghy a dozen yards from the shore. It was half-submerged, with three oars floating beside it. He had never seen a boat like it. Without a keel, it had a top canvas cover to keep the water out. Inside was a sheathed dagger.

Exploring further, he noticed signs of digging. Scraping the sand away, he found a big black tin tied with ropes.

Soon after 4 a.m., the *Aud* still lay-to. As each hour passed, Spindler had hoped against hope that the Irish would make contact. At dawn, he knew it was hopeless.

It would be suicide to sail to Fenit Pier and try to land arms in broad daylight in a country that was on a war-footing. If he pretended they were stranded owing to engine failure, a swarm of bureaucrats would come on board, checking. Though logic dictated he should head straight for home, he hated turning back now. His men felt the same way.

One said encouragingly, 'The Irish are bound to spot us.'

That very moment, the look-out sighted a boat clearing Kerry Head.

'Steamer on the starboard bow . . . Pilot steam-*er*.'

A relieved Spindler stood by the halyard, ready to hoist a green flag.

John McCarthy went up the strand and called on a neighbour, Pat Driscoll, who helped him drag in the dinghy.

When they opened the black tin box, they found it contained 1,000 rounds of ammunition, a case with field glasses, twenty-eight section maps of Ireland, a copy of the *Imitation of Christ*, *The Rubaiyat of*

Omar Khayyam, an electric torch, a packet of German tobacco and a green flag. Higher on the beach, Driscoll caught his seven-year-old daughter playing with three loaded Mauser revolvers. He snatched them from her before she killed herself.

McCarthy drew his attention to three sets of footprints in the sand.

'They're fresh, Pat. I'll stay here if you'll go to the Barracks at Ardfert for the police.'

The three men had walked inland for about half a mile in a south-easterly direction towards Tralee. There was a drifting coastal fog, and, with no sun or moon, visibility was reduced to thirty feet.

They came to a stretch of water, twenty yards wide and waist-deep. They waded across. It must have been a sewerage outlet for it smelled vile. Casement's overcoat was so heavy with the wet that Monteith carried it for him.

They emerged on to marshy bogland which filled their lungs with the smell of rotten vegetation. On they plodded up to their knees in mud and sludge before reaching firmer ground. Thankfully they came across a running stream where they stripped and cleaned up. By the time they were dressed their bones were aching from the cold.

As they continued, the sun pierced the haze. They came to a big farmhouse. Mary Gorman, a young woman with tousled hair who always rose at 4 a.m., was looking over the half-door and sizing up the morning when she found herself staring at three strangers.

'Damn you, girl,' Monteith hissed in alarm.

Casement touched his arm. 'Captain, never damn a fellow human being.'

A farm cart was approaching with two men on, so they hid behind a wall until it passed.

Two hundred yards from the path were the foundations of a pre-historic fort. It was circular, thirty yards in diameter, and surrounded by a trench and a thick thorn hedge. They pushed through the hedge and Casement immediately collapsed.

Monteith said, 'Sir Roger, I suggest you stay here. We'll go to Tralee for help.'

Casement agreed. His top priority was to get word to the Volunteer Executive that an arms ship was on its way and the Germans were not providing back-up. His companions went through their overcoat pockets. Monteith found a few sandwiches which he tore into strips and started to grind under foot.

Casement said, 'May I? I'm rather hungry.'

The sandwiches, made of black bread and German sausage, were soaked in salt water. Monteith handed them over, knowing they were inedible. He then stretched out on a wall to dry the sea-drenched pictures of his wife and children. Seeing the look in his eyes, Casement said, 'I'll look after them for you.'

After they had hidden their overcoats in the bushes, Monteith, thinking he was in most danger, gave Casement the code from the German General Staff.

Finally, they shook hands, not knowing if they would ever meet again. Casement waved sadly as the younger men set off on the ten-mile trek to Tralee.

Too late, Spindler realized that the trawler heading their way with its guns trained on them was hoisting the British ensign. So his luck had finally run out. He could have kicked himself for being caught off his guard. The British would be boarding in a few minutes.

He ordered, 'Batten all hatches.'

To his mate he said, 'I'm going below, Düsselmann. Don't forget our plan.'

He was no sooner in his cabin than the officer-of-the-watch warned him through the voice-pipe, 'We only had time to close Hatch No 2, Herr Kapitän. On the port side the cases are still exposed.'

'*Herrgott!*' Spindler exclaimed. The cases were inscribed '1,000 English cartridges', '2,000 Russian cartridges'.

Setter II was only twenty yards off. Through the porthole Spindler saw the skipper, short, stocky, scruffy, with a red muffler and a matching red face. With armed men on either side, he was calling through a megaphone. Düsselmann replied in English that the skipper was asleep and even as Norwegian skippers go he was a ripe bastard.

It was 5 o'clock when *Setter II* made fast to *Aud*'s stern. The skipper climbed up the boarding ladder, puffing and blowing, with a few of his men. After much hedging Düsselmann agreed to wake Spindler who swore sensationally in Low German for all the boat to hear.

'Tell the filthy fecking gutless son of a bitch,' he yelled at Düsselmann, 'that I'm getting dressed.'

This he did, but very slowly.

Pearse had spent the early hours of Good Friday wondering whether to make one last effort to get MacNeill on their side. Cancelling Sunday's manoeuvres could do untold damage to the cause. Hobson was perhaps already sending the order around the country.

When it seemed a reasonable hour, he telephoned first Sean McDermott, then MacDonagh.

Düsselmann entertained the mottle-faced skipper and half a dozen of the boarding party with a bottle of whiskey in the fo'c's'le.

Spindler, now dressed, opened the locker under his bunk and put several bottles of the hard stuff on view before flinging open his cabin door.

'About time,' the British skipper said, brandishing a rusty old pistol. His red nose was sniffing as if it had caught a whiff of paradise. Tottering into the cabin, he collapsed on the sofa. To his horror, Spindler saw that his German tunic was on the back of a chair. He quickly threw a towel over it.

'Lots of things to ask you,' the skipper drawled.

'We're from Norway. Headed for Genoa and Naples by the normal route. We're anchored here because our engine's broken down and we're putting into Tralee for repairs.'

To his relief, the skipper was not the least bit interested.

'Just want to examine your holds, old boy.'

The skipper was so relaxed, he left his gun on the cabin table while he climbed shakily up on deck. Grasping his Browning pistol already cocked in his pocket, Spindler ordered two of his crew to fling open Hatch No 2. There were no arms to be seen, only pit-props.

'Bit of a mess,' Spindler said. 'Happened during that damned storm.'

'It hit us, too,' the skipper said, sympathetically.

Spindler began shepherding him back to his cabin. 'Another drink?' It was a magic formula.

'Didn't I see . . . ?'

In seconds, pop went the cork of a whisky bottle. The skipper noticed the label. 'White bloody Horse!' he slapped Spindler on the back. 'Splendid chap.'

'Water, Captain?'

'Good God, no. We never see that sort, not White Horse. Don't want to spoil it with bloody H$_2$O.' He raised his glass. '*Prosit, cherchez la femme,* and all that.'

'Cheers. Care to see the ship's papers?'

'Suppose I should, really.'

With a huge swig to strengthen him for the ordeal, he grabbed the phoney papers, blackened and pawed all over. He merely glanced; they meant absolutely nothing to him. He took another big draught and hiccuped.

'Perfectly in order.' He took out a book. 'If you'd care to sign this.'

'Sure,' and Spindler signed 'Niels Larsen, Captain of the Norwegian steamer *Aud*, with pit-props from Christiania, for Cardiff and Genoa.'

The skipper merely noted the name and closed the book. 'Thanks, Larsen, you're a good sport.'

He poured himself another whisky without a by-your-leave. Liquor had forged a bond between them. Spindler casually tapped the Norwegian newspapers spread on his table.

'Three weeks old. I don't suppose you have any English papers you don't want?'

A grateful skipper sent his mate to get a pile out of his cabin. Meanwhile: 'These damned Germans are everywhere, Niels – may I call you Niels?'

Spindler nodded.

'Skunks and fucking bounders the lot of them.'

'Don't I know it,' said Spindler.

An English petty officer was soon back with a bundle.

'Rumours of refreshment?' he said, with a grin.

While he, too, was imbibing, Spindler ran his eye over the most recent papers.

'Niels,' the skipper said, the smoke from his pipe fouling the entire cabin, 'you don't need to keep an eye on U-boats in this area.' He shook his head. 'No, no, no. I'll watch out for you while you're undergoing repairs.'

'Oh,' said Spindler, perturbed, 'I shouldn't think there's any trouble from them swine.'

'Least I can do for your—' – tears streamed down his cheeks – 'your fantastic, hic, kindness.'

Spindler excused himself for a moment and left them in charge of Düsselmann. In the fo'c's'le he found the English sailors were blind drunk. Someone whispered that they had sent four bottles over to *Setter II* for good measure.

He returned to his cabin to find them trying to sing, 'It's a Long Way to Tipperary'. The tune was taken up by the group in the fo'c's'le. The skipper was by this time into the brandy, hiccuping his exceeding 'gradidude'. He confessed his intention of going for safe anchorage behind Kerry Head.

'Get some shut-eye there. Did you know, Niels, British war ships are not allowed to have whisky on board?'

'Ridiculous,' said Spindler, trying to put a sob in his voice. 'Have you been here long?'

'Two weeks. Orders to intercept a German steamer. Expected any time.' As a shaken Spindler plied him with bottle after bottle: 'Thought at first you might be him, Niels.'

Spindler laughed hollowly.

'Yeah, sorry about that. You Norwegians are good chaps, no harm in telling you.' He touched the side of his blue-veined nose. 'Strict secret, mind.'

'Of course.'

'Well, our naval staff, clever bloody lot, have found out that these damned German swine want ... wait for it ... they want to join the Irish in a revo—' – he twisted his head drunkenly in order to finish the word – 'lution.'

'I wondered why the harbour was so well defended.'

'Bristling with bleeding guns,' said the skipper. 'Clever bastards, those Germans, but no match for us.'

Spindler and his mate giggled their appreciation. They stuffed cigars and another half-dozen bottles of whisky in the Britons' pockets. There was a poignant farewell and, in ten minutes, the English were climbing back, with difficulty, on *Setter II*.

Spindler looked at his watch. Seven o'clock. He had lost two precious hours entertaining those nitwits. There was not the slightest hope of contacting the Irish on shore. The skipper, even in his cups, was bound to relay their engine trouble to the signal stations.

Spindler also knew that if he were to raise anchor at once, their story would ring false. There was nothing for it but to wait for the dark and then move thirty miles out into the Atlantic before the moon was up. In a day and a half they could be in Spain.

In the meantime, he gave orders to cover the arms and batten down those bloody hatches.

Pat Driscoll had alerted the Barracks.

Two armed RIC men, Sergeant Thomas Hearn and Constable Bernard Reilly, suspected that the discovery of guns meant this was important. Grabbing their carbines, they began a thorough search of the shore and the dunes.

Monteith and Beverley hugged the shore line. They were dying for a smoke but though their tobacco was dry in the pouch the matches were sodden.

On a bridge over the branch railway to Fenit Point they said, 'Good morning' to a farmer who did not bother to reply. The sun was shining, their clothes were beginning to dry. Their spirits rose. Then it started to rain. They were tired and their legs numb. Monteith was limping badly and he held his hand Napoleonically in his jacket to ease the pain.

They asked a carter if he had a match to spare. He handed over a few as though they were gems, without a word. By the time they reached Tralee, they were still soaked but smoking contentedly. The town was very quiet at seven in the morning. Not knowing the local Volunteers, they looked for a newsagent that sold the right sort of papers, without success.

They passed a huge police barracks and saw people moving churchwards for the Good Friday celebration. At the far end of the town, they brushed each other free of sand and mud before going back by a different route. This time, they came across Spicers, in Dominick Street, that sold the *Irish Volunteer*.

They went in and Monteith said, 'You sell the right sort of papers.'

The proprietor said, cautiously, 'I sell all sorts.'

'Look here,' Monteith blurted out, 'I'm in a hole and I have to trust you as an Irishman to help me out. I must see the commander of the local Volunteer corps at once.'

'Don't tell them anything, Dad.'

A pretty young woman had overheard in the kitchen.

'It's all right, Hanna.'

'I don't blame you, miss.' Monteith realized she thought him a spy. 'I just want to deliver a message.'

He touched his clothes.

'It's so urgent we had to swim here. If you don't trust us, send someone to say that a man named Murray has come with a message that can't wait.'

Hanna called her young brother downstairs and whispered, 'You heard, Georgie. Go and tell Mr Stack.'

At around 8 a.m., Pearse, MacDonagh and McDermott arrived at MacNeill's house.

After a long discussion with Hobson, MacNeill had wrestled all night with how to sort out the mess the Volunteers were in. He could not come to terms with the fact that he had been betrayed by men he thought of as his friends. He was still in bed when his wife announced that he had visitors. He refused to see Pearse but asked McDermott to come up.

'I'd better tell you at once,' he told McDermott, 'that I have issued orders through Hobson and O'Connell for all Sunday's manoeuvres to be cancelled.'

Furious inside, Sean kept cool. 'I appreciate your feelings, sir, but there is something you should know.'

MacNeill lifted his head in anticipation.

'Within a couple of days, the German Imperial Navy is landing vast quantities of arms and ammunition on the Kerry coast.'

MacNeill stirred on his pillow. Nothing on so big a scale had happened in over a hundred years. But was it true?

McDermott seized the advantage. 'Whether the Germans land these arms successfully or not, there *is* going to be a rising. Just as certainly, the British are going to disarm the Volunteers. You are on record as saying that if they do, you will resist with all your might.'

'Pearse,' he said warily, 'did not mention German arms last night.'

'Sir Roger Casement has been negotiating on our behalf with Berlin for over a year. Nothing can prevent what we hope will be the final rebellion against British rule.'

'You dare to threaten me?'

'I'm not threatening anyone,' McDermott said. 'The fact is, the flower of Irish manhood is determined to grasp their freedom on Sunday. If you interfere, they could be left with only ashes.'

MacNeill could already taste them in his mouth. After reflecting a long time, he said, still dazed, 'It seems a fight is inevitable and we are all in it. It's not my idea.' He scraped his dry hands together. 'I leave it to you who planned it.'

'Thank you, sir,' McDermott said, doing his best to hide the contempt he felt.

MacNeill gestured irritably to the door. 'If you would kindly wait downstairs, I will dress and join you and the other two . . . gentlemen for breakfast.'

McDermott went to the dining-room exultant. He intimated that MacNeill had resigned.

'Washed his hands of the whole thing and none too soon.'

183

'Splendid,' said MacDonagh. 'With Pearse here as Chief of Staff, things will run smoothly from now on.'

MacNeill came down with a note already written. 'Government action for the suppression of the Volunteers is now inevitable and may begin at any moment; preparations are going on for that purpose. We are compelled to be on our guard until our safety is assured. All government statements through the press or otherwise are in the circumstances worthless.'

Pearse read it. MacNeill was still not committed to anything positive but he would stay out of the way for a while.

McDermott said, 'We'll need a note for Hobson telling him to do nothing.'

MacNeill hastily scribbled one. 'Here, take it.'

After a courteous but strained breakfast, Pearse went back to St Enda's where he issued mobilization orders for 4 p.m. on Sunday outside their temporary HQ, Liberty Hall.

McDermott sent notices that Volunteers were to stand by throughout the country to defend themselves against suppression by the Army. A close friend of his, Jim Ryan, went to Cork to make sure that J. J. O'Connell had not confused them there.

In his lodgings in Tralee, Stack was breakfasting with Con Collins when young George Spicer burst in. 'There's a stranger in my da's shop. Wants to see you, urgent.'

Stack asked George to describe him. Big, burly, black hair, military moustache.

It rang no bells. A trap, maybe?

'Tell him I'll be there in an hour or so.'

When George ran home with this message, Monteith reacted angrily. 'That's not good enough. Go back and tell him to please be here in half an hour.'

George said, 'A lady down the road serves food. I'll take you there if you like.'

'Thanks, son.' He and Beverley had not eaten for eighteen hours. 'But as soon as the commander arrives, let me know.'

They went and banged on the lady's front door. She leaned out of her upstairs bedroom. 'Down in a minute.'

For ten minutes, they shivered on the doorstep. To Monteith this was a nightmare. First no pilot boat, and now they were waiting in full view for some peeler to pick them up. At last, there were sounds of life inside. Half a dozen keys turned in locks and they were let in to an unlit draughty kitchen. Soon the lady, talking non-stop, had a fire going and put a substantial Irish breakfast on the table. It was their first square meal since Wilhelmshaven.

They gulped down their food and hurried back to the Spicers. A Volunteer called Joe Melinn called for his morning paper and Hanna told him about the two strangers. Peeping into the kitchen, he recognized Monteith at once.

He rushed in and shook him by the hand. 'Wait here, Bob,' he said. 'I'll go home and get the pair of you a change of clothes.'

When he returned he kitted Beverley out, complete with cap and overcoat. Monteith was grateful for clean underclothes but the suit was too small. The boots, too, were very tight and hurt his swollen foot. But with food inside him, with his clothes in front of the fire giving off a scorching smell and reminding him of Molly's ironing, he was content.

There was a fire, too, in the Volunteer HQ in Dublin.

In spite of his late night, Hobson was the first in and he immediately started burning correspondence and lists of names. The police were likely to raid them before the day was out. As the staff clocked in, he got them to help. The offices reeked with burning when McDermott arrived.

'Before you do anything else, Hobson,' he said, 'I reckon you ought to read this.'

Hobson snatched the note. It said: 'Take no action till I see you. Am coming in. Eoin MacNeill.' In manipulating MacNeill, he thought sourly, the conspirators had had an easy task.

All that morning he was burning papers and waiting for MacNeill who never showed up. Meanwhile McDermott reported back to Clarke. Hobson worried them. He had proved at Howth that he was second to none in grit and guile.

'We shall have to deal with that traitor,' Clarke said. 'Here's what we'll do.'

At about 10 a.m., Stack and Collins cautiously entered Spicer's.

'Good God,' said Collins, 'Bob Monteith. What the blazes is this all about?'

Stack knew nothing about Casement coming to Ireland. He wondered if Pearse knew and if so why he had not mentioned it.

Monteith said that Pearse must be told at once that Casement thought a rising in present circumstances was madness. Germany was providing no men, only antiquated rifles. He had difficulty getting through to Stack. 'Shouldn't you send a pilot out? The arms boat might be in the Bay this very minute.'

Stack muttered, 'I'd need to speak with Casement myself before changing my orders. Incidentally, where is he?'

Monteith described how they had come ashore near a church with a steeple.

'Ardfert,' Stack said. 'You must've landed on Banna Strand.'

'We left him in a fort six miles or so from here.'

Stack guessed this was the ruins of Ballymacquin Castle. 'Either that or McKenna's Fort, Currahane. We'll try both.'

While Stack was ordering a car, Monteith said to Beverley, 'I'd be grateful if you'd guide them. My face is well known to the RIC. Besides, I'm practically a cripple.'

Beverley, a quiet man, simply nodded.

As the clock was striking 11 a.m., a Model T Ford arrived, driven by Moss Moriarty. Stack, Collins and Beverley, given the name of David Mulcahy, piled in. Hanna Spicer went along to give them a party air.

Before settling down to rest Monteith asked if someone could take a message to Dublin. While he was waiting for him to come, he drifted into sleep.

In a corridor at Liberty Hall James Connolly ran into his second-in-command, Mallin, a short, dark, handsome, self-composed man.

'Have you been drinking, Michael?'

Mallin shook his head.

'Tell the truth, man,' yelled Connolly, whose tongue could raise a blister on a plank. 'Look at you, shaking all over like a dog from a stream.'

'I have not taken a drink in a long while, Seamus.'

'My God,' Connolly persisted, dropping his voice, 'we're going out in a couple of days and your job in the Green is vital to us.'

As Connolly stamped off Frank Robbins, a twenty-year-old bachelor recently appointed Sergeant in the Citizen Army, said, 'What was all that about?'

They went upstairs to a room overlooking the Liffey where Mallin, a silk-weaver by trade, kept a loom. He was in the process of weaving a bright piece of poplin. 'The boss thinks I've been drinking.'

Seeing his shaky hand, Robbins said, 'Have you?'

'I was in India, in the Army,' said Mallin. 'Contracted malaria. It comes back from time to time. Had it bad recently but I'm nearly better now.'

'Why didn't you tell *him* that?'

As he passed the shuttle through the thread, Mallin replied, 'I guess I was too proud to, Frank. I thought he might have trusted me by now after me saving him in January.'

'He's on edge, Michael, we all are.'

While Frank was filling shotgun cartridges, he pointed to the loom. 'What's that for?'

'If I go, my wife'll have nothing for the kids, y' see. I'm hoping she'll be able to sell this for about ten pounds to tide her over.'

It was a small thing but it made Dobson realize the strain the married men were under.

The Ford reached Ardfert at 11.30 a.m. and from there headed north towards Banna. On the way they met a horse-drawn cart driven by a local lad, twelve-year-old Martin Collins. On the cart was a boat.

'That's ours, all right,' Beverley whispered.

Behind the cart strode an RIC constable. Further on, they came across two more RIC men, Hearn and Reilly, searching the dunes.

To add to their problems they had a blow-out. They were putting on the spare tyre when two more policemen came up and questioned them. On a Good Friday this was no routine work, yet who had alerted them?

Stack explained, with a lightheartedness he did not feel, that they were on a picnic. When the police were out of hearing, Stack said, 'Security's too tight. We shall have to go back.'

The others agreed. Even if they found Casement, they could only protect him by force, which Pearse had forbidden. Their one hope was that if the police did capture him they would not identify him.

They made a detour to get out of the danger area. Even so they were stopped twice more by RIC patrols. Finally, the car was halted by a squad of four armed police, led by a Sergeant Loftus who asked them if they had any firearms.

Collins produced a Browning pistol.

'I'll take that from you at present,' said the Sergeant. 'Anyone else?'

Stack said he had an automatic but he would not give it up to anyone.

While Collins and Beverley were invited into the Barracks, Stack stayed in the car for five minutes till he had had enough. With his gun in his pocket plainly pointed at the Sergeant, he said, 'Am I to be kept waiting much longer?'

'They'll be with you in a tick,' the Sergeant said jumpily. He gave Collins back his Browning. 'Off you go.'

They drove full-speed towards Tralee.

At one in the afternoon, District Police Inspector Frederick A. Britten of Tralee phoned General Stafford at Queenstown, telling him that three strangers had come ashore and were probably hiding on the strand. There was also a rumour that the Germans had landed.

Forewarned of this possibility by Admiral Bayly, the General told Britten to keep his men on full alert.

'I'll send you reinforcements by morning.'

Twenty minutes later, the two policemen who had been searching the dunes approached McKenna's Fort. Reilly sighted someone in the undergrowth.

'Stay where you are,' he ordered, levelling his carbine, 'or I'll shoot.'

A tall pleasant-faced gentleman rose to his feet, smiling.

'Shoot? Whatever for?'

'Step forward, sir, please, and identify yourself.'

'With pleasure. I'm a visitor to your charming countryside. My name is Richard Morten and my address is The Savoy, Denham in Buckinghamshire.' Morten was Casement's best friend in England. 'Do you mind not pointing that thing at me.'

Sheepishly, Reilly lowered his gun.

'I'm an author,' Casement went on. 'I've written a life of St Brandon.'

Reilly was observing the stranger's wet trousers and the sand on his boots. With Casement at his most plausible, the two policemen were wondering whether to take him into custody when Martin Collins beckoned to the Sergeant.

'What is it, son?'

The boy held out his hand. In it were crumpled pieces of paper. 'That tall gentleman over there, when he saw the Constable climbing over the fence, he threw them away.'

The Sergeant patted the lad on the head. On two typewritten sheets were numbers in a foreign script and phrases corresponding such as 'Await further instructions', 'Further ammunition needed', and 'Send another ship to . . .'.

They searched the fort again, this time finding three overcoats. In one was a printed slip: 'N 0113 Berlin nach Wilhelmshaven, April 11/12.' It was Casement's berth-ticket from Berlin which he had overlooked when emptying his pockets on the U-19.

'What language might this be, sir?' enquired the Sergeant.

' 'Tis not Irish, anyway,' said Reilly.

Casement's vanity was badly dented. He had dined with American Presidents, been knighted for services to the Crown, had dealt firmly with the German General Staff; and, within hours of reaching Ireland, he had let himself be outsmarted by what Devoy would have called a kid and a couple of country cops.

'Honestly, I have never seen it before.' He did not even make a convincing liar.

Finally came the clincher. Reilly found something in the dust. 'German sausage, I bet.'

The Sergeant pointed to the pony and trap.

'I'd be obliged, Martin, me boy, if you'd give us all a lift back to barracks.'

It was soon after 1 p.m. when Lieutenant W. H. A. Bee, RNR, on an armed trawler, the *Lord Heneage*, picked up a message from Loop Head.

'Suspicious vessel sighted in Tralee Bay. Investigate.'

A second message from Smerwick station followed. A foreign vessel had been seen the night before heaving things overboard.

The *Lord Heneage* was now tracking the *Aud*, its big gun on the fo'c's'le deck uncovered and ready to fire. Spindler saw it to the west through his glasses. It was bigger and faster than *Setter II*. With the capstan creaking and groaning, the anchor was weighed in double-quick time. He spat out his commands. 'Due-west, full-speed ahead.'

The hostile craft was less than nine miles away. They were not likely to have a drunken old soak examining their cargo a second time. He ordered all hands to the stokehold. His men rattled down the ladder and grabbed every available shovel.

Taking the wheel himself, he sailed as close as he dared to the shore. Black plumes from the *Aud*'s funnel rose up the cliff face and wedged into crevices of the rocks. He kept calling through the voice-pipe the shortening distance between them and their pursuer and ignored all signals to stop.

Directly ahead was their old friend, *Setter II*. It had stopped 500 yards from a shore battery. Spindler handed the wheel to his Second Mate, Strehlau. He needed to think.

There was an exchange of signals between the shore battery and the *Lord Heneage*. This time, *Setter II* was bound to be less friendly. One thing he could do.

'Strehlau,' he ordered, 'ram it.'

Setter II hoisted a flag but in the still air it hung limply. It could only be signalling 'Stop at Once'. On shore the guns were aimed and waiting for the command to fire.

Spindler yelled down the pipe, 'Prepare to light fuses and blow up the ship.' Just then, as *Setter II* turned to port, a breeze unfurled her flag. He was astonished to see the signal was 'TDL', that is, '*Bon voyage*'. He grabbed the wheel from his second mate and swung it round to port, avoiding a collision with only a ship's length to spare. He saw the red-faced skipper hanging on to the rail for dear life. Then the old soak took his cap off and waved it round his head, calling, 'Three cheers for the *Aud*.'

The commander of the shore battery was just about to yell, 'Fire!' when the cheers on *Setter II* made him hesitate. 'What the bloody hell—?' he roared.

The *Aud*'s crew added to the confusion by waving their Norwegian caps in response as Düsselmann ran up the signal, 'XOR', 'Thank you'. Spindler ordered the dipping of his flag in salute. The German command was similar to the Norwegian word that was the signal to blow up the ship. As a member of the crew stepped forward to unfurl the German ensign, the Chief Engineer lit the first fuse.

Someone screamed, 'Chief, you heard wrong!' and he put the fuse out with his bare hands.

The *Aud* was still only a mile out, well within range of the shore battery. Fortunately, *Setter II* and the *Lord Heneage* took five minutes to sort out the confusion before joining in pursuit. That breather was all Spindler needed .

The *Lord Heneage* radioed Admiral Bayly: 'Suspicious vessel sighted south of Tearaght, steering south-west.'

Stack stopped the car at 1.30 p.m. near Killaham Cross, at the home of Mickeen Jer O'Connell. He asked him to look after Beverley.

After a meal, O'Connell took him for safety to Mick Hanlon's farm at Gloundallive, a mile from Ballyduff village. It was a desolate spot.

'You'll be safe here, all right,' said O'Connell.

Spindler yelled, 'We've got to get out of here, and fast!'

Düsselmann took the wheel and Strehlau worked the telegraph. The temperature in the engine room rose well above 100 degrees. Below, the stokers, with sparks flying off their shovels, were dripping with sweat. The pressure-gauge needle was well into the danger zone, and, in a ghostly blood-red light, they went on throwing in coal like devils in hell.

Though the *Aud* could not go any faster, Spindler still urged them on. 'More steam, you blackguards, or, by all the pigs' snouts in Germany, I'll blow the ship up.'

More clanging of shovels, furnace doors opening and closing, a heavier throbbing in the heart of the ship. The chief engineer, stripped to the waist, black with coal-dust and sweating through every pore, poked his swollen face through the hatch at the top of the ladder.

'If we go on like this, Herr Kapitän,' he bleated, showing teeth and eyes of startling whiteness, 'the boilers'll burst.'

'If we don't,' Spindler replied cheerfully, 'we had better all make our wills.'

After a heave for air, the begrimed bullet-head shot below, leaving behind a thick odour of hot metal and oil. The clanging of revolving brass and steel grew louder, the water in the bilges thumped against the sides. They were travelling at an incredible 13 knots.

Soon they were out of sight of the battery and by 3.30 in the afternoon there was no sign of their pursuers. Spindler informed his crew, 'The immediate danger has passed.'

The news was greeted in the engine-room with loud cheers. The Chief took steps to lower the pressure; slowly the needle moved into the black.

'Soon we will be out of the Bay,' Spindler said, though with their pursuers alerting their command, there were bound to be problems ahead.

Once in the open sea, he had the whole Atlantic to choose from. With a brisk north wind blowing, he opted for the south. It fitted his story best; he was sailing under a neutral flag to Cardiff and Italy. A pity the weather was so damned good, especially with four hours of daylight left. If only they could hold out till dark, he would change course to due-west to avoid coastal interference.

Then Spindler had a fresh shock. Sailing towards them from the south was a steamer that looked very like the *Aud*. As the distance between them shortened, he noticed it, too, was flying the Norwegian flag.

Good God, he thought, if this is the real *Aud*, what a meeting this will be!

He did not hang around to find out.

At Ardfert Barracks, Sergeant Hearn telephoned Tralee about his captive and was told to bring him in at once in a side-car. At Tralee, Casement asked to see a priest.

Fr Francis M. Ryan, a Dominican of Holy Cross Priory, was sent for. 'I believe,' he said, putting on a purple stole as he settled in a chair, 'you wish to make your peace with God.'

The prisoner knelt beside him, and the priest blessed him in Latin. 'Now, my son, how long since your last confession?'

'This,' Casement whispered, 'is my very first, Father, and I want you, *please*, to listen very carefully.'

Apart from stiffening a little, the priest gave no sign that this was out of the ordinary. Casement identified himself, explained briefly what his mission was and begged him to warn the Volunteers not to try and rescue him.

'Tell them, Father, that the rebellion will fail if it is counting on German aid. It is not coming. Someone must convey that to Dublin.'

Fr Ryan, his hand pressed against the side of his head, said, eventually, 'I'm a priest. I cannot get involved in politics.'

'I am not asking you to. A rising is planned. It is doomed. You can stop it and avoid a lot of bloodshed.'

'The best man to contact,' the priest decided, 'is a parishioner of mine, Paddy Cahill.'

He lifted his right hand and said, 'For your penance, say three Hail Marys.'

Hobson was working hard that afternoon in his office when Sean Tobin, a leading member of the Brotherhood, popped in.

'Bulmer,' he said, affably, 'there's a meeting at Martin Conlon's house in Phibsborough.'

Hobson sensed there was something fishy about this.

'I'll be along directly.'

'It can't wait. A car's outside.'

In spite of the friendly tone, Hobson knew he had no choice. On entering Conlon's house he found himself looking down the barrel of Ned Daly's gun.

'You'll be staying here,' Daly said, 'till the rising is under way. Then you can decide if you're for us or against.'

Hobson felt only an enormous relief. He was very tired, and events were now, thankfully, outside his control.

Austin Stack was at home when Cahill arrived about 4.30 p.m.

Stack told him about Casement. 'What I want you to do, Paddy, is find out where he is now.'

Cahill left and rounded up a few scouts to scour the district for news. While he was doing this, Billy Mullins met him, with, 'Fr Ryan is wanting to see you in your office.'

'What about?'

'He wouldn't say. Only that 'tis urgent.'

'Can't be as urgent as what I'm at,' Cahill said. 'Tell him I'll be there about 6.15 p.m. after the meeting at the Rink.'

At 5 p.m., Con Collins left to visit friends while Stack went to the Rink to address the Kerry IRB centres and Volunteer officers. On Pearse's instructions, he had played his cards close to his chest. Only three officers in the whole of Kerry knew that Sunday's manoeuvres were the real thing.

He went through the Easter timetable. The men were to parade at 11 a.m. Sunday. At midday most Volunteers were to march the seven miles to Fenit Pier and the rest were to be disposed around police and army barracks in a mock attack.

'Next,' he said, as casually as he could, 'on Easter Sunday night, we'll be getting arms from a German boat.'

The men bubbled with delight as he took them through the details. Connolly had sent William Partridge to organize the railway men who would transport the arms along the west coast. Someone said the docks were some distance from the railway. 'How will we get the arms to the trains?'

Paddy Cahill had just come in. 'I have forty horse-and-carts for precisely that purpose.'

'You know, men,' Stack said, 'that only a month ago there was an exchange of fire between the Volunteers and the RIC at Tullamore.' They nodded. 'Be ready at any time to go to your Maker. I suggest you all make your Easter duties.'

At 5.30 p.m., a colleague, Michael Flynn, entered the Rink and whispered to Stack. 'Bad news. Collins has just been arrested. He's asking for you.'

Stack groaned. Collins was supposed to set up the wireless station to communicate with the arms ship. He continued with his briefing, only to be interrupted minutes later by another urgent message.

Outside, a scout told him, 'I'm just after being at Ardfert. They say an important prisoner's being held there.'

Problems were multiplying. Collins was in Tralee Barracks, and Casement, it seemed, at Ardfert. He felt he ought now to tell the officers something he had planned to keep from them till Sunday afternoon. Returning to the Rink, he said that Casement had arrived from Germany and was under arrest.

'Also, men, the Sunday manoeuvres are really the rising you have all been waiting for.'

When the pandemonium had subsided, he added:

'Rule one: not a single shot is to be fired till the Republic is declared in Dublin, not even to rescue Casement.'

Nathan was working late in Dublin Castle.

A policeman came in from the Constabulary Office with a message from District Inspector Britten of Tralee. That morning, according to Britten, a patrol from Ardfert had captured a boat landed from possibly a Dutch ship. Three men had come ashore. They had found three Mauser pistols as well as maps and papers in German. One of the three men was in custody.

Nathan thanked his informant. 'Do let me know at once if there are any developments.'

He sat briefly in silence. He would have liked Friend's view of this. He took out his pen to drop Birrell a line.

As 6 o'clock approached, Spindler sighted a smoke cloud in the south-west. It was from a large two-stacker, travelling at about 20 knots.

Two sloops, the *Zinnia* and the *Bluebell*, had been ordered by Admiral Bayly to intercept the *Aud*. Spindler had his glasses on the *Bluebell*. It was impossible to outrun her.

Once more the *Aud* prepared to scuttle. Engines were cut to half speed. On the bridge, Spindler walked with studied indifference up and down. With the craft only half a mile away, he could see several 4.5 guns and any number of machine-guns. Instead of coming within hailing distance, the auxiliary cruiser zigzagged for ten minutes.

'What next?' Spindler muttered.

To his surprise, the craft turned sharply east and sped off. The only thing he could think of was that the English skipper suspected the *Aud* had a U-boat escort.

He was right. The *Lusitania* had been sunk not far south of there.

Soon after 6 p.m., Casement was sitting over a smoky fire in the billiard room when a man in his mid-twenties, carrying a small bag, entered and introduced himself.

'Dr Michael Shanahan. The Sergeant asked me to drop in on you, sir. Is it a commercial traveller you are?'

Casement could see that the Doctor recognized him at once. His voice, however, came out very even.

'I believe, Mr Morten, you are feeling under the weather.'

He ordered the two policemen out and began his examination.

'I hope you are in sympathy with the Irish cause, Doctor,' Casement whispered.

'Your heart is in good shape, anyhow,' the Doctor said loudly, tapping his chest.

'My name is Casement. I've spent twelve nights in a U-boat. Tell the local Volunteers I've been taken.'

'Nothing wrong with you,' the Doctor said, 'as far as I can tell.'

After the examination, the Head Constable, Harry Kearney, showed Dr Shanahan a newspaper picture of Casement.

'A remarkable resemblance, don't you think?'

Shanahan put a hand over the bearded portion of the cutting. 'I really can't say. Who is he, by the way?'

He left the Barracks and went at once to tell the Volunteers that Sir Roger Casement was in custody.

Stack asked Cahill to send messengers to Dublin.

'Tell them Casement is a prisoner and the arms ship is due any time.'

'What are *you* going to do, Austin?'

'I'm off to the barracks to see Con. If I'm nabbed, there's only one man qualified to take over.'

'Bob Monteith?'

Stack nodded. He handed Cahill his gun.

'Hope to see you in an hour or so.'

When Cahill kept his appointment with Fr Ryan at 6.15 p.m., he learned that Casement was in jail.

'We know, Father. He's in Ardfert.'

'Not Ardfert, Paddy, here in Tralee.'

As soon as Stack reached Tralee Barracks, he was arrested and searched, in spite of his vigorous protests. The police found on him several letters from, among others, James Connolly, Hobson and Pearse. They asked him if he knew an unidentified tramp they were holding.

'In fact, Sir Roger Casement was just this minute asking after you.'

'He's never heard of me,' Stack said. 'Why should he?'

Shaken to realize Casement was there, he began a prayer that was to go on through the night. He promised God he would never in his life take another drink if only the Volunteers did nothing to prejudice the rising by trying to break them out.

At Spicer's, Monteith was handed the local evening paper. It ran a typical journalistic story of the arrest of an unknown man.

'Unable to speak English,' he read aloud. 'A collapsible boat and arms have been found on the beach.' He snorted. 'Collapsible, be buggered!'

Garbled as the account was, it was clear enough that their equipment had been found. The only thing in their favour was that Casement had not yet been identified.

A courier finally arrived to take his message to Dublin. The lad would not accept a verbal message. Monteith wrote that if the rising depended on German help, it was unwise to proceed.

'Make sure,' he said, 'you get this to MacNeill or Hobson or another of the leaders of the Volunteers.'

Meanwhile, Cahill was telling Billy Mullins that Collins, Casement and Stack were all arrested and what Fr Ryan had said. 'There's a seven o'clock train to Dublin via Limerick, Billy. Tell them at Liberty Hall that the Germans are sending only arms and not men.'

To make doubly sure, he asked William Partridge to return to Dublin on the 7.30 train via Mallow with the same message.

Spindler's relief at the departure of the big British cruiser was short-lived. On the starboard bow, almost invisible against the painful light of the setting sun, was another cruiser. Then astern he saw another. Then another. They were surrounded. And all the ships' guns were aimed at the *Aud*.

At about 7 p.m., *Bluebell* raised the signal, 'Stop At Once'.

Everything German had long since disappeared into the Conjuror's Box and Hector was barking dutifully on the fo'c's'le deck. Now the questions began.

'Where are you from? Where are you headed?'

A signalman, Fred Schmitz, deliberately broke the signal halyards. Spindler had to flag by hand from the bridge. There seemed no hope. Yet darkness was near and a U-boat might just come in the nick of time.

The *Bluebell* was now using her searchlights to communicate with the other ships. The crackling sound from her aerials indicated she was also in wireless contact with shore.

To Spindler's astonishment, *Bluebell* signalled, 'Proceed'.

Minutes later, *Zinnia*, the command ship, received explicit orders from Admiral Bayly. 'If the *Aud* is sighted bring her to port for examination. If she resists, sink her.'

Lieutenant-Commander G. F. Wilson, RN ordered *Bluebell* to escort the *Aud* to Queenstown.

Everything was repeated. 'We are heading for Genoa. We have nothing but pit-props aboard.'

The *Bluebell* approached to within 150 yards and lowered a cutter. Two officers and a dozen seamen, all armed, prepared to board. Spindler passed round the order, 'Guns and knives ready. When they come on deck, grab them.' If they managed to take the prize crew hostage, they might still make it under cover of dark to the open sea.

The *Aud*'s chief engineer was testing a steam winch he had just fixed. The clang of it in the bowels of the ship reached the *Bluebell* just as their diminutive commander, Lieutenant Martin Hood, saw what looked like a periscope. It was probably nothing more than an old meat tin but he was taking no chances. He megaphoned his crew back aboard.

Spindler cursed his luck. Whereas no real U-boat had come to their assistance, an imaginary one had sealed their fate.

Hood signalled, 'Follow me to Queenstown. Course, south, 63 east.'

The *Aud*'s crew climbed on to hatches and rails, yelling, 'What do you want with a neutral ship?' though one said crudely, '*Sich verpissen.*'

Spindler tried, 'Don't understand.'

There was a flash as the for'ard gun fired across their bows, making *Bluebell*'s meaning abundantly plain.

Spindler, dazed by the concussion, muttered, '*Gott strafe England.*'

When he recovered, he yelled loud enough for Hood to hear, 'Full speed ahead, south, 63 east.' Then a whispered threat to the Chief: 'Go faster than 5 knots and I'll hang you from the yardarm.'

He calculated that even at that speed they would reach Queenstown well before ten next morning.

Bluebell signalled, 'Full speed ahead', and Spindler replied with a small paraffin lamp, making the dots and dashes by shielding and withdrawing his hand. 'Engine broken down.'

The *Bluebell* took no chances, zigzagging.

Spindler saw she was prepared to keep this up all night.

Two cars were approaching Killarney from Limerick.

Tom McInerney, a garage owner, was driving a borrowed 20-horse-power Briscoe American open-tourist car. The second driver, Sam Windrum, was a taxi-driver friend. They had dawdled, stopping off in a pub for a drink. And there had been several road-blocks on the journey, which was unusual. A couple of times Sam Windrum had shown his driving licence to the RIC and twice he was told it was out of date and would he not think of getting it renewed soon.

As McInerney stopped to pull a handful of grass from a verge, Sam Windrum joked, ' 'Twas my driving licence saw us through. Who would be daft enough to carry a gun with an out-of-date licence?'

The five armed men sent by McDermott and Mick Collins had been kicking their heels for some time outside Killarney Railway Station. The cars finally arrived at 7.15 p.m.

The code was: The men from Dublin asked, 'Are you from Michael?' Tom McInerney opened his hand to reveal a clump of grass, saying, 'I am from William.'

The Dublin men piled into the cars and they drove off at speed along the Ring of Kerry towards Cahersiveen. In daylight, this was one of the most picturesque roads in the world. At night, it was spooky and dangerous. McInerney brought up the rear. In the passenger seat was Con Keating, the only man in the car who knew the way. In the back were two Dublin men, Charlie Monaghan, and Donal Sheehan.

Pointing to the car ahead, Keating told McInerney, 'Orders are to keep those lights in view.'

After only a few miles, the second car developed engine trouble. The men cursed roundly. They had already lost a couple of hours' daylight and now another delay.

'Don't worry,' McInerney said. 'I'll fix it in a jiffy.'

At 9 o'clock, Joe Melinn and a crowd of fellers came to Spicer's to fetch Monteith. Whooping it up, they took him to the Ancient Order of Hibernians' Hall where they sat him down in the middle of a group playing cards.

Melinn whispered, 'You're to stay here, Bob, till closing time.'

Minutes later, John O'Sullivan, the Hall caretaker who worked on the railroad, came in. He handed round a wire from the Station-master at Fenit. When it reached Monteith, he was stunned. It read: 'Germans landing arms at Banna Strand, reward offered for capture.'

McInerney fixed the engine but by now the lead car was way ahead on the unlit road. They passed through Killorglin, a town fifteen miles from Tralee, famous for its annual Puck or Goat Fair. On the outskirts, they were flagged down by a policeman with a torch.

'I want all you lads to step out for a minute.'

Keating had had enough of delays. He drew his revolver. 'Back off, man,' he growled, 'before I plug you.'

McInerney put his foot down and they raced on. From the back, Charlie Monaghan said, 'Did you have to do that, Con? He's bound to wireless ahead.'

Rattled, McInerney asked Keating, 'Is this the right road?'

Preoccupied with the job he had to do, Keating replied irritably, 'Indeed, it is.'

'Right,' McInerney said, putting his foot down.

Just then, the car, having left the main road, soared into space off the end of the tiny pier at Ballykissane. The huge Briscoe American, with the hood wrenched open, finished upside-down in the River Laune.

McInerney came up gasping for breath in the pitch dark. He heard Keating threshing around beside him and spluttering, 'Jesus, Mary and Joseph.'

McInerney, treading water, went on listening but heard nothing more. The rising had claimed its first victims.

He had no idea where the shore was. Overwhelmed by shock and terror, he might have swum into deeper water had not someone living nearby heard the engine roar and the splash and come with a lamp to investigate. McInerney, having crossed himself in relief, swam towards him.

Ashore, he was taken to a friendly house. He was no sooner rid of his revolver and incriminating papers than the police burst in. He bluffed them with a story about Keating visiting his relatives nearby.

Without Keating, there was no chance of getting the equipment they needed to contact the arms ship. He glanced at a clock on the dresser. It was already 10.15 p.m.

He wondered if he should try and warn Stack not to expect them that night.

Stack was in jail, still praying.

He prayed that the party from Dublin would be able to set up the wireless even without Collins. At least, Keating had the expertise to contact the arms ship.

He prayed for his own release. He doubted he would be answered. His chance to do great things for Ireland was most likely over. He did not mind that, provided his men did not try and spring him.

In St James's Street, London, Birrell received Nathan's telegrams and letters. They spoke of an unidentified prisoner being taken.

This was encouraging, especially if he turned out to be Roger Casement.

The O'Rahilly arrived at the Volunteer HQ for an appointment with Hobson. A secretary told him he had left a long while ago with a group of IRB men. Realizing at once what had happened, he drove to St Enda's and broke into Pearse's study, brandishing a revolver.

'Whoever kidnaps me,' he snapped, 'will have to be a quicker shot.'

Pearse needed all his persuasive powers to calm him down. He explained just how critical things were. German arms were on the way. MacNeill himself had agreed there was nothing for it but to go ahead. But Hobson had an independent mind and might try and go against his orders.

'I do assure you,' Pearse said, 'he is no danger.'

The O'Rahilly, who found it hard to think ill of anyone, said, 'I appreciate that. But I bitterly resent being kept in the dark.'

'Remember Howth,' Pearse said, soothingly. 'You were not told till just before the arms arrived. I myself didn't know until afterwards. In these matters, caution is surely best.'

The O'Rahilly still insisted a rising was crazy. There was no preparation outside Dublin. Taking on the British Empire was like trying to lift a mountain with a crowbar.

But, he realized, Pearse was reckless and beyond argument. The mystical element in him, his lyrical lunacy could not be reached. He probably dreamed in his dreams. He wanted to make necklaces out of dewdrops, carve statues out of clouds.

When The O'Rahilly left, Pearse and his brother said goodnight to their mother and watched her go upstairs to bed.

'God love you,' they called after her.

Though they longed for sleep, their own night was far from over. There had been scares enough in the last twenty-four hours but, thank God, they were on course once again.

When the Hall in Tralee closed its doors, the caretaker gave Monteith a room for the night. O'Sullivan's wife and sister took care of him. He soaked himself in a hot bath and after, in spite of his worries, sank into a deep sleep.

In Tralee Barracks, neither Casement nor Stack slept.

Aboard the *Bluebell*, Hood issued his orders. 'Watch them closely. There may be 150 men aboard. If they open their gunports, fire. If they drop anything into the sea, shoot at it. It could be a mine.'

After midnight, Spindler mustered his crew on the bridge.

'Men, the U-boat we are banking on has not turned up. Frankly, our chances of escape are nil.'

The men shuffled their feet uncomfortably.

'Tomorrow, we shall have to blow the ship up.' Hearing the beginnings of a protest, he hastened to add, 'We have no choice. Listen. The moon is due to rise soon. Before then, we have to burn our codes and secret papers or drop them overboard, just in case the explosion is not wholly effective.'

A throb came into his voice.

'It is no fault of yours that we failed. In fact, I am prouder of you than I can say.'

He dismissed his crew and checked that the explosives were in place. He told Düsselmann, 'We shall try and ram that cruiser. I do not want the *Aud* to be lonely down there.'

The night was a glassy calm with a sea-full of stars. All was silent save for the sounds of the escorting vessels as they circled the *Aud* like famished dogs, their bows sending streams of phosphorescence over the waves. Occasionally, the peace was rent by barked orders, the slamming of furnace doors, the rattle of shovels.

Aboard the *Aud* each man retreated inside himself, praying for a U-boat. If it did not come, they knew what had to be done at Queenstown Harbour.

On the bridge, Spindler took out his book of maps. There were charts of African and American harbours, not of Queenstown. He was obliged to study it on a general chart of Ireland. He reckoned the average depth at the outer entrance was between 20 and 25 fathoms. Fine. With luck, the *Aud* would block the harbour entrance.

At 4.30 in the morning, Mullins and Partridge reached Kingsbridge Station in Dublin. Pretending not to know each other, they walked on opposite sides of the Liffey.

At Liberty Hall, the guards told them they could not see anyone until 10 a.m. There was nothing for it but to settle down and wait.

Around 7 a.m., O'Sullivan, who had been on night-shift on the railway, burst into Monteith's bedroom to tell him a hundred soldiers had arrived by train from Queenstown.

'They're here to search for you and Beverley.'

Monteith dressed in a flash and went down to a club room.

An armed Volunteer had been posted at the door. Through the window, he saw troops and police scouring the town, all armed to the teeth. Extra police were arriving by the minute in motor cars, side-cars, traps, on cycles and on foot.

He examined the back door and a possible escape route. None too soon. Outside the front door, a sixteen-man military patrol was given the order, 'Halt! Stand at ease!'

They were about to search the premises, surely.

But after a minute's breather. 'Atten-*tion!* Qui-ick *march!*'

Melinn and two other Volunteers came in to conduct Monteith to the Rink. They gave him a greasy cap and smeared soot from the chimney over his face and hands.

'You've been promoted,' said John O'Sullivan, 'to engine cleaner on the railroad.'

They went to the Rink, inside which was a guard of about a dozen men, including Paddy Cahill. Monteith gripped his hand.

'Now that Austin's arrested,' he said, 'you will have to take command tomorrow.'

'Not at all,' said Cahill, reddening. 'I'm only secretary here, I know nothing about fighting.'

'Then who *will* take charge?'

'You,' said Cahill.

'But,' Monteith spluttered, 'I don't know the men and they don't know me. Besides, I have no idea of Stack's strategy.'

'Those are orders,' Cahill said peremptorily.

'Where are the plans then?'

Cahill shrugged, 'They were never written down.'

'You mean they only exist inside Stack's head?'

Monteith was quickly getting the impression that the rebel leaders had avoided being betrayed by informers by the simple device of not communicating with anyone.

Cahill said, 'We were meant to take the military and police barracks, the telegraph office and the railway station.'

Monteith sighed as if to say, Tell me something new.

'But no details?'

'None that I know of. But after that, we're to march to Fenit, unload the German ship when it arrives and put the arms on trains for Killarney, Limerick and Galway.'

'When were you last in touch with those places?'

Cahill shrugged again.

'All right, how many men will I have under me?'

One of the Volunteers said, 'Three hundred, maybe. Not all armed, mind. But two hundred would be. Probably.'

'Right,' Monteith said. 'We have to send out a pilot at once and, if the arms ship's around, bring it in.'

'Not possible,' Cahill said, in a hollow voice. 'Y'see, all boatmen are being watched so Mort O'Leary's da would never let him go out. Anyway, there's two British boats out in the Bay. No arms ship would ever get by them.'

Monteith conceded the point. 'We'll have to fight without German arms. Someone hand me a map of Tralee.'

The men bowed their heads. Their looks suggested that Cahill was wrong to entrust their fate to this inquisitive and overbearing stranger.

'Y'mean,' snapped Monteith, 'no one has a map of Tralee?'

Someone pointed out, 'We know it, y'see,' and Cahill said airily, 'There is one somewhere, if someone will oblige.'

Minutes later, a lad returned with a map thirty years out of date. Monteith blew the dust off it, examined it briefly and returned it without a word. Had he left his beautiful family in America, worked his guts out for a year in Germany, for *this*?

'What arrangements have been made to cut telephone and telegraph wires?' Before anyone could reply, he added sarcastically, 'Stack would know, of course. Has anyone thought of having warnings printed against looting?'

Someone said, indignantly, 'There are no thieves here,' at the same time as Cahill said, with perfect vagueness, 'They *are* around, I know that.'

Monteith's hand was so badly swollen he dictated slowly, for Paddy Cahill to write down his next day's instructions.

'You can get copies printed, I presume?'

'Naturally,' said Cahill, as if nothing was beyond him.

Monteith sighed with relief. 'I want all the men to parade tomorrow, Sunday, at 8 a.m.'

Cahill put down his pencil. 'That's no good.'

'And why not?'

'Because they already know they have to be there for 10 a.m. Confusing 'em would mess up our plans entirely.'

Someone said the scouts would be on hand from 7 a.m.

'Right,' said Monteith, 'tell them to be here in plain clothes.'

Left alone, he thought the only hope of taking the police barracks would be if half the peelers went to church. Failing that, at the time of their midday meal. Men tended to drowse at that time, especially if they were allowed a whiskey or two for the feast-day.

The task overwhelmed him. He was expected to lead half-trained men, boys in some cases, against a military machine, against well-trained and well-armed men shielded by thick, high walls and machine-guns. He lay down on a bench and pulled a blanket over him. The dawn was nigh.

No sooner had he drifted off than there was a terrible bang. A Volunteer had approached the hall and not given the password. The bullet had missed him but he stood in the doorway petrified with three bayonets pressed against his chest.

More than ever convinced he was dealing with professional amateurs, Monteith gave up any idea of sleep. He examined their weapons and found they were of three types. One: the Howth rifle, a Mauser single-loader. Two: the Lee-Enfield, with a magazine. Three: the Martini Enfield, a single-loader carbine. The ammunition was all Mark VII .303, only suitable for the Lee. It tended to overheat the Martini and cause a bulge in the barrel.

He cursed even harder. His men were not only untrained, they had not heeded a warning he had given previously about the unsuitability of their ammunition.

He sent scouts to Fenit Point where the arms ship was due to berth, others to Ardfert and the rest to patrol Tralee.

He also sent a car to Killarney to try and establish contact with the Volunteers there and find out what they planned to do. Having wished the driver God-speed, he never saw him again.

The sun was up as the *Aud* approached Queenstown Harbour. It was a glorious spring morning. At other times, Spindler would have appreciated the hills, the meadows of shining green.

A signalman, Batterman, said, 'We can celebrate Easter Sunday here, Herr Kapitän.'

'Yes.'

Lately, he had been so busy he had lost track of time.

With the dawn, the destroyers exchanged signals with *Bluebell* and left. There were far too many warships in the vicinity for the *Aud* to try any tricks, yet still the *Bluebell* tracked her, never too close, now port side, now starboard.

Spindler saw the Galley Lighthouse below the Harbour entrance and soon the Daunt Rock Lightship in mid-channel. There was no traffic in the west half of the channel. He guessed, correctly, that it was mined.

'Fifteen minutes to docking time,' he mumbled to his first mate.

To himself, he added: And to destruction.

On shore, Admiral Bayly was breakfasting at Admiralty House with his niece when he was informed of the *Aud*'s imminent arrival. He invited her on to the verandah.

'It will be something to remember, my dear.'

The quays were buzzing with warships of every shape and size. On deck, crews were stretching in the early sun, watching the foreign tramp steamer with curiosity.

Spindler summoned his Chief Engineer.

'I want the condenser smashed before we blow the ship up.'

He grinned. 'You don't think I'd forget, Herr Kapitän.'

Soon, the pressure dropped so low that the *Aud* was crawling. The escort was not bothered. For the last hour, the crews had been busy getting into harbour-trim so as to have longer shore-leave. Guns were polished and covered with tarpaulin, ropes were coiled, decks scrubbed. Men appeared from below, blinking, brushing down their civilian clothes ready to go ashore.

Spindler's anxiety was growing. The cargo was deadly. The explosion that ripped the *Aud* open might blow his crew to bits.

To save as many as possible, he asked for four volunteers to stay behind, to help him scuttle the ship and hoist the flag while the rest took to boats.

The cry went up, 'No, sir, we're all staying.'

He signalled *Bluebell*, 'Where are we to anchor?'

'Await further orders.'

Three quarters of a mile from the lightship, a British cargo-steamer was closing at top speed on the *Aud*'s port side.

'About 8,000 tons?' Spindler muttered to his mate.

'*Ja*, Herr Kapitän. In ballast. See her height out of the water.'

'I'm going to ram her and take her down with us.'

His eyes betrayed his concentration.

'Port ... 10 ... 15. Ease her a little. Steady. Keep her at that.'

The *Aud*, with the condenser battered, was scarcely able to answer the helm.

He spat out the orders: 'All hands to quarters! Ready with fuses and incendiary bombs! Stand by to run up the ensign!'

Every man was tense and waiting.

It was touch-and-go because the signalman on the bridge of the *Bluebell* was semaphoring the cargo-steamer to keep clear.

When only 800 yards off, she put her helm hard a-starboard, passing the *Aud* and the *Bluebell* in a majestic sweep. Spindler again tasted failure on his tongue.

On shore, Bayly patted his niece's arm. 'I think we can relax, my dear.'

Spindler called out, 'Only 200 yards to the lightship ... 150 ... 100.'

One final scan of the surface for a friendly periscope. Disappointment.

'All ready?'

'Ready!' came from the engine-room.

Men lay on deck on their stomachs, surreptitiously raising the boats out of their chocks and lowering them to the height of the rail. From the engine-room came sounds of heavy hammers finishing off the condenser.

'Hard a-starboard.'

The telegraph in the engine-room rang three times.

'Stop!'

The *Aud* swung across the channel. A rating ran up the German ensign. Jackets and greatcoats were peeled off and flung overboard, revealing uniforms underneath.

The First Mate called out, 'Three cheers for the Kaiser,' and was answered by the crew's Hurrahs.

The Chief Engineer found a moment to call, 'Here, Hector.' The dog bounded to him trustingly. With his arm round its neck, he put a revolver to its temple. 'Sorry, old fellow. If only we could take you with us.'

He pulled the trigger just as there was an explosion that shook the boat from stem to stern. Beams and splinters shot aloft with clouds of dirty-grey smoke. Flames leaped from the saloon, the charthouse, ventilators and fo'c's'le.

From the Admiralty verandah, Bayly gave a grim little smile of appreciation. The *Aud* was German, all right; and her skipper was doing what he would have done.

A cry went up aboard, 'All hands to the boats.'

In seconds the cargo would explode. The port boat had left as the starboard boat was being lowered. In the second were the Chief, Second Mate, helmsman, and, last of all, Spindler.

'All away,' he called.

With an axe, he sliced through the painter and the boat splashed into the sea, menacingly just below where the explosives were stored in the *Aud*.

The stern was already low in the water when, to his horror, he saw a stoker was still on board. He came running along the rail with a gramophone under his arm.

'Wait,' the lad called.

As he jumped into the boat, he lost his grip on the gramophone and it fell into the sea.

'*Blöder Kerl!*' yelled Spindler.

They rowed desperately to get clear of the suction area of the *Aud*. There were several minor bangs, followed by clouds of thick sulphurous smoke. The munitions in the hold were catching fire.

'Pull,' urged Spindler, 'before she blows up round our ears.'

The *Bluebell* fired a shot, far too late. Ships were steaming futilely towards them from the docks.

Spindler had ordered a white flag to be shown as soon as the boats were launched. When he was clear round his sinking ship he was relieved to find the other boat was safe. At last he was free to look back upon his gallant little English ship that, after braving tempests and sandbanks, had met death at his hands. He stood to salute her. Her bow was rising higher and higher, wreckage was strewn everywhere, including the body of Hector.

For a while, there was silence on the *Aud*; the sea must have rushed in and soaked most of the fuses.

Five minutes after the first explosion there was a dull rumbling noise aboard. The cargo and bunkers were shifting.

There was a second violent explosion amidships. A column of steam and smoke rose in the air. Masts tottered. The blazing bows rose sheer up from the water then, next moment, she plunged like a horse with a loud hiss into the sea.

Clarke had spent the night at home in Fairview. This morning, he walked with Kattie into town. He tried to think of it as a dawn ramble, like when they were courting in the hills of the west. At the corner of Britain Street they said goodbye. He was not sleeping at home the night before the rising in case of a last-minute arrest.

'We shall be victorious, Kattie,' he said. 'But I myself expect to go down in the first rush.'

She squeezed his hand, unable to speak.

'Love to the boys. And don't forget to open the shop tomorrow morning and close it at 2.30 in the afternoon as usual.'

She promised, feeling that, without him, things would have no meaning any more.

With small firm steps, he walked down O'Connell Street and then turned left along the Liffey to Liberty Hall.

*

208

It was just before 10 a.m. when the Police Inspector at Tralee decided to send the prisoner under escort to London.

Casement was given breakfast and told he was being put on the next train.

'May I ask where, Inspector?'

'Dublin, first, then London.'

Security was so lax that the police did not put him in a black Maria. He was handcuffed and three men walked him down a street crowded with people doing their Easter shopping. Several Volunteers with pistols in their pockets watched him go by to the station, sad they had been forbidden to spring him. Nothing could have been easier.

Stack and Collins were taken before a Resident Magistrate. They were charged under the Defence of the Realm Act with conspiracy to import arms into the country.

When they were returned to the Barracks, Fr Joe Breen got permission to visit Stack to hear his confession.

'They've put Casement on a train,' Breen said.

'Thanks, Father. Have Cahill move Beverley to the safest possible place.'

At 10 a.m., the Military Council opened its meeting at Liberty Hall. They read the messages brought by Mullins and Partridge.

The situation in the west looked very grim without Stack to lead the Volunteers or Collins to contact the arms boat on Easter Sunday night.

At the Castle, Nathan was receiving a string of telegrams from Inspector Britten in Tralee.

He was now able to correct the imperfect reports of the previous day. No Dutch vessel was involved. Stack and Collins had been taken into custody on a charge of conspiracy to land arms.

By 10 o'clock he had heard from Stafford of the scuttling of a German arms ship, disguised as Norwegian. The twenty-two-man crew was safe aboard the flagship in Queenstown Harbour. Divers were being sent down to inspect the hold.

Richard Morten would arrive in Kingsbridge at 5.30 p.m. and be sent on with the German papers in his possession to England. An obvious case for Scotland Yard.

There was also a strange incident involving Sinn Feiners in which a car had driven into the sea at Killorglin.

The suspicion was growing that Morten was Casement. The military agreed that, in any case, he was ring-leader of the entire operation which had been nipped in the bud.

Nathan was cock-a-hoop. He would have liked to swoop on the Plunkett home at Kimmage and Father Matthew Park where the Sinn Feiners stored arms, but he needed more information if he was to get a conviction. Besides, why hurry? They were now in a position to pick up the rebels whenever they chose.

His musings were interrupted by a call from the Viceregal Lodge. Wimborne had been fed the same information as himself.

'What do you think?' Wimborne asked, rhetorically. 'We should charge the Sinn Feiners with hostile association with the enemy. At once. A clear breach of Defence Regulations.'

He was put out by Nathan recommending caution.

'It's not a matter of *caution*,' said Wimborne, the veins in his neck showing. 'We'll never have a better chance of putting the rebels behind bars.'

'I feel,' said Nathan, irritated with the Viceroy for trespassing on his patch, 'there is no need for –' he just avoided the word 'panic' – 'precipitate action.'

'My advice is to get Birrell over here right away.'

Nathan explained that Birrell was obliged to stay in London because of a Cabinet crisis. Unless it were resolved, the Government might fall. That was one thing Wimborne understood. It was to his advantage that the Government remained in office.

Afterwards, Nathan wrote to Birrell, bringing him up to date with events so far. They would soon know if Morten was Casement. As to rumours of the Volunteers taking action on Easter Sunday, 'I see no signs of a "rising".'

He called in Major Price.

'Tell the evening papers to draw a blanket over the sinking of the arms boat, will you? At least till the Admiralty issue an official communique.'

Some time after 10 a.m., General Friend paid a courtesy call to the HQ of the Home Forces in Horse Guards, London. He was no sooner there than the news came in about the *Aud*.

'Well, bless me,' he chuckled. 'I heard last night as I was stepping on the boat that she was taken in tow. If the Sinn Feiners were planning a little prank on the basis of a German arms delivery they *have* come a cropper.'

A fellow officer asked, 'Not thinking of rushing back, then?'
'Gracious,' Friend said, 'what on earth for?'

After hearing from Mullins and Partridge, Pearse went with McDermott to brief MacNeill about the three arrests in Tralee. They then returned to the Hall for an all-day session.

MacNeill smarted more than ever at the shabby way he had been treated. This latest development merely increased the probability of the British swooping on the Volunteers. It was, sadly, a case of rise or be crushed.

Was there *no* way to stop this senseless slaughter?

Mid-morning, the Dublin-bound train was approaching Killarney.

Casement had not uttered a word until he said, to his guard, Sergeant Butler, 'I don't suppose I could buy a newspaper.'

As they pulled into the station, the local Head Constable, recognizing his colleague, poked his head through the carriage window.

'Did you hear,' he said, 'what happened to the two lads in Puck?'

Butler shook his head.

'Their car ran into the sea and they drowned.'

Casement presumed that the drowned men were Monteith and Beverley. And Monteith had a young family. He broke down.

'Where is Puck, please?'

'That,' the Sergeant explained, 'is the local name for Killorglin.'

In between sobs, Casement said, 'Forgive me. I'm so sorry for them. They only came because of me. Two very gallant Irishmen.'

At 1 p.m., Father Breen gave Cahill Stack's order to move Beverley somewhere safe. It came too late.

Beverley had slept overnight at Hanlon's but in the morning had had a terrible row with him and been thrown out. He was on his way back to O'Connell's place when he was picked up by Constable Carter of the RIC.

'Hello, stranger,' the Constable said. 'And who might you be?'

'David Mulcahy.'

'Well, Mulcahy, I'd be much obliged if you'd accompany me to police barracks.'

Before long, the Constable was able to tell his District Inspector that he had picked up the second of the men who came ashore on Banna Strand.

211

That afternoon, Mort O'Leary and O'Shea left the Maharees for Tralee.

At the Rink, O'Leary said to the caretaker, 'Stack has a couple of green lights for us.'

When he heard where Stack was, he scratched his ear.

'But am I or amn't I to go out?'

'There's been some confusion, all right,' the caretaker said. 'The arms boat must have come and gone.'

Only then did it dawn on O'Leary that it was the two-master he had seen in the bay on Thursday night.

The train from Tralee drew into Kingsbridge Station at 5.30 p.m. Casement, feeling dirty in his salt-encrusted suit, was driven to Arbour Hill Detention Centre.

'I don't suppose I could have a bed, Sergeant?' he said. 'I haven't slept for twelve nights.'

'I'm sorry, sir,' Butler said, kindly. 'I just heard you are to be put on the 8 o'clock boat for England.'

Casement drew the lapels of his jacket up to his ears. That huge, cold place reminded him of death.

He was shown into a cell.

Minutes later, two soldiers entered. One said, 'You can get undressed now, sir.'

A delighted Casement said, 'I'm sleeping here, after all?'

'I mean, you can strip.'

Casement's heart sank. It was not simply that he hated the idea of strangers inspecting every inch of his body. He feared they might find the curare sewn into his jacket. That would be the final horror. For he had already made up his mind to kill himself.

At 6 p.m., Eamonn Kent finally broke the news to his wife. There was to be an insurrection. There were rumours of the British suing for peace.

'We couldn't let this opportunity pass without striking a blow while England is still at war, could we?'

Aine shook her head.

'We would be a disgrace to our generation.'

After writing to Birrell, Nathan motored to the Viceregal Lodge. In

212

the grand drawing-room Wimborne tried again to persuade him to arrest the Sinn Fein leaders at once.

'They are such a dispirited lot, no one will try and rescue them.'

'Dispirited, yes,' said Nathan. 'They have lost the arms they were relying on. They can't be in any mood for a rising.'

Wimborne conceded the point.

'We are witnessing,' he said, 'the end of the Sinn Fein movement.'

On that upbeat note, Nathan left for his own lodge before His Excellency changed his volatile mind.

In the late afternoon, young Colm O'Lochlainn returned to Dublin from Killarney, upset by the death of his friends and the failure of his mission. To add to his depression, in Mallow, north of Cork, he had got wind of the sinking of the *Aud* and Casement's capture.

He called on Sean Fitzgibbon and they went to Hobson's place. Getting no reply, they went to see The O'Rahilly. He had not been able to sleep after seeing Pearse the night before. There was, he believed, a suicidal strain in the man that was little short of self-indulgence. He wanted to be *important*. How many innocent men could die as a result?

He told his two visitors that Hobson had been kidnapped.

At 6.15 p.m., The O'Rahilly drove them to see MacNeill. For over two hours he had been checking proofs of a new book and taking tea with a friend. He was horrified when he heard of the loss of life. He was also staggered to learn that there would be no German arms, after all.

'Hobson won't be coming,' The O'Rahilly said. 'Pearse has had him kidnapped.'

'The wonder is,' MacNeill snorted, 'they didn't kidnap me. That would have put me out of all this misery.'

'They didn't need to,' said The O'Rahilly bluntly, 'since they now think they have you eating out of their hand.'

Fitzgibbon told him of Pearse sending him to the west.

'He made it sound as if he had your backing.'

'Another absolute lie,' said MacNeill.

O'Lochlainn explained how the Castle document seemed to originate with Plunkett. MacNeill saw very clearly that if it *was* bogus, that put an entirely different complexion on the attitude of the Administration. Even so, he felt trapped.

Probing, he asked, 'An insurrection cannot be averted, not at this stage, can it?'

They told him that it could and should be.

The O'Rahilly stressed the one rock-like fact. 'The country's not ready. The west, in particular, is in no state to take on the British army.'

'But,' MacNeill objected, 'now the British know about the German arms, they are bound to classify us all as traitors and disarm us anyway.'

They assured him this was not necessarily so. If the Castle document was a forgery and, therefore, the British were *not* preparing to swoop, an official denial that the Volunteers wanted any part in a rising would prove their good faith.

'Do you really think,' MacNeill asked, 'that the British would believe me?'

'Yes,' The O'Rahilly said confidently, 'especially if you send messengers all over Ireland cancelling the manoeuvres. No Chief of Staff would do that if he intended a rebellion.'

MacNeill was excited. 'It's really worth discussing.'

They drove to St Enda's where Pearse became very agitated at what they told him.

'We have used your name and influence for what they are worth,' he admitted to MacNeill, 'but we have done with you now. It is no use trying to stop us. Our plans are made and will be carried out.'

'Your plans,' MacNeill returned, 'are so well laid that the police in Tralee have upset them already. In any case, I am Chief of Staff and I will forbid tomorrow's manoeuvres.'

'Our men will not obey you,' Pearse said, his eyes blazing.

'If they do not, the responsibility for it and all that ensues lies entirely with you. If you want to see me again, I will be in Dr O'Kelly's house in Rathgar at 9 o'clock tonight.'

Once more, Pearse's heart sank. When they left, he put through a call to tell MacDonagh the state of the game.

In the Metropole Hotel, next to the General Post Office in O'Connell Street, Joseph Plunkett was in his suite with Grace Gifford. He had gone there directly from the nursing home. As he held her in his weak arms, he said, 'This time tomorrow, my precious darling, you will be my wife.'

They talked about the double wedding and the joint reception afterwards. There was to be no honeymoon. At 6.30 p.m., Joe would be in the Post Office.

Even if he survived the battle, he was finished. The surgery

214

had not been successful. He preferred to die like Nelson, who stood on his Pillar a few yards from the Hotel, rather than like Keats.

He poured a glass of wine and gave a toast. 'To us, my darling.'

Before they put the loving-cup to their lips, the phone rang.

'Hello, my future brother-in-law,' he said cheerily.

He gagged the phone.

'It's MacDonagh.'

Down the mouthpiece, he said, 'As usual, you've interrupted something very important.'

What he heard dampened his spirits considerably.

Afterwards he said, 'Grace, my pet, I'm so sorry to have to leave you. MacNeill is making a nuisance of himself and I have to attend a meeting in the Rathgar Road.'

That night, throughout Ireland, churches were packed, prayers said extra carefully and confessionals kept busy. Many penitents were in Volunteer uniform. Not a few, thinking they might soon be dead, played safe by wiping their chins for the last time and pledging life-long abstinence from drink.

They knew of the Castle document and its implications. They had emptied the shops of food and equipment. Those manoeuvres on Sunday could turn out to be something big. They had to be prepared both for this world and the next.

In such a climate, nothing was more consoling than the words of a priest, '*Ego te absolvo a peccatis tuis . . .*'

In Rathgar, MacNeill had gathered an odd group together to discuss the crisis which had deepened with the latest news that the German arms boat had ended in the sea. Several were distinguished men with no connection whatsoever with the Volunteer movement.

Arthur Griffith was there, as were Sean Fitzgibbon, Liam O'Briain, Joe Plunkett and MacDonagh. No one doubted either Arthur Griffith's integrity or his grasp of Irish affairs. Cold, humourless, lonely, his well-argued opposition to violence had a strong impact on MacNeill. The general feeing was that they had no hope of winning in the west.

'In my book,' MacNeill said, 'any war that is destined in advance to fail is immoral.'

Griffith, standing behind MacNeill's chair with his back to the fire, agreed. 'Humbug wrapped in green is as despicable as humbug wrapped in ermine and labelled law by the British.'

215

Joe Plunkett and MacDonagh were on their own.

After a long, one-sided debate, MacNeill announced: 'Gentlemen, to stop this useless slaughter, I am cancelling tomorrow's manoeuvres.'

MacDonagh gasped in incredulity.

'Messengers will take this order to all key commandants throughout the country.'

'Our men would never trust us again,' said MacDonagh.

'In any case,' Plunkett added, in a thin, sickly voice, 'the rising is going to take place, regardless. If you confuse our men by cancelling the manoeuvres, you will not stop the slaughter, you will only add to it.'

'My mind is made up,' affirmed MacNeill.

His two critics got to their feet. MacDonagh, his big, grey eyes uncharacteristically sombre, gestured around him. 'These gentlemen are not my colleagues.'

MacNeill asked him what he was going to do.

'I will consult with colleagues and either return or send a message.'

The O'Rahilly said, 'Pearse is a zealot. In his vanity, he wants to be remembered.'

'Zealot, maybe,' Griffith said shrewdly, 'but he is too proud to be vain.'

MacNeill drafted a note and read it out: 'Volunteers completely deceived. All orders for Sunday cancelled.'

The group approved of it.

'I will add,' MacNeill said, 'a personal letter to the commandants in major areas like Cork, Limerick, Belfast.'

He drafted it at once. It read:

'Every influence should be used immediately and throughout the day to secure the faithful execution of this order, as any failure to obey may result in a very grave catastrophe.'

It was late when The O'Rahilly drove west to Limerick.

O'Lochlainn went north to Dundalk and Coalisland.

Jim Ryan, who had just returned from Cork, telling them the rising was on, was sent back to say it was cancelled, after all.

In Tralee, Monteith received an answer to the message he had sent to MacNeill but which had been handed to Connolly.

'Go ahead,' was his reply, 'everything is all right.'

'Go ahead with *what*?' gasped Monteith.

He had no information and attempts to get co-operation from the locals aroused only animosity. His one consolation was that Dublin knew the score and still wanted the west to fight.

Very well, he would make sure they fought all right.

Beverley was exhausted. He had only joined the Brigade to get out of Germany. He had no stomach for this or any other fight. He had not even liked Casement.

He admitted everything to the constable who had arrested him. His real name was Daniel Julian Bailey. He had come on a submarine with two others, Robert Monteith and Sir Roger Casement. They were in league with a German arms vessel disguised as a Norwegian tramp.

With a trembling hand, the Constable picked up the phone to tell the District Inspector of Tralee that the prisoner had turned King's Evidence.

Britten commended him.

So the third man *was* the notorious Sir Roger Casement.

Lord Wimborne had changed his mind. The Sinn Feiners might not be deterred after all. He called Nathan again and a tired Under-Secretary walked over to see him.

'It seems to me, on reflection,' the Viceroy said, 'that revolutionaries do not act according to reason. Desperate men resort to desperate measures. I put it to you once again that we should arrest the Sinn Fein leaders straight away.'

'What did you have in mind?' Nathan enquired.

'Swoop on Liberty Hall for a start. It's a nest of rebels. The DMP have reported strange goings-on there for weeks.'

'You are not suggesting that a few Volunteers with outdated rifles and pikes are a match for our army?'

Wimborne had seen military service. He had to admit the rebels had no chance against professionals. Nathan promised that first thing in the morning he would cable Birrell and talk the matter over with the military.

In Scotland Yard, London, the Head of the CID, Basil Thomson, stood in his office with his binoculars to his eyes, scanning the foggy night sky over the Thames. It was his turn for Zeppelin duty.

The LZ 90s with their 5,000-pound loads of incendiaries had been warned by the Kaiser to keep well clear of his cousin in Buckingham Palace and of other important sites like St Paul's and Westminster Abbey. They were, however, proving to be a menace in the dock area of London. It was not easy for searchlights to pick them out at around 8,000 feet so that gunners could engage them with the new blue-sparking phosphorus shells.

At 10.30 p.m., the telephone rang. 'Yes?'

The caller said, 'BT, that stranger who arrived in a boat at Currahane. Do you know who he is?'

Thomson recognized the voice. Of late, they had been in almost constant contact, though he had never once asked him for his sources or visited Room 40.

'You're joking,' he gasped.

Captain Hall, pleased to have surprised his unflappable colleague, said, 'He'll be over early tomorrow evening.'

MacDonagh and Plunkett were not too concerned about MacNeill's countermand. In a conflict of loyalties they thought that most Volunteer officers, being IRB men, would obey the Military Council. They overlooked the fact that few were aware of a split between MacNeill and the Brotherhood. Further, the order was bound to confuse the rank and file, especially as it was in some cases borne by IRB men, like Jim Ryan.

They went from Rathgar to 27 Hardwicke Street, where McDermott was spending the night.

'Once again the Irish are betrayed,' he said chokingly, tearing his pyjama jacket in his hurry to get dressed.

He thought the Military Council should meet at once and discuss this new development. They contacted Pearse but failed to reach Connolly, Clarke and Kent.

The rising had to go on, of course, but with three important colleagues missing they decided at this late hour to leave messages at their hide-outs suggesting the full Military Council meet at the Hall for breakfast.

MacNeill had smoked many a pipe waiting for MacDonagh, his Brigade Commander, to return or send a message. This seemed to him one more item added to a long list of treachery.

He might at least be able to influence MacDonagh's immediate subordinate, his ADC, Eamon de Valera, who was a serious-minded young man. He wrote him a message:

As Chief of Staff, I have ordered and hereby order that
no movement whatsoever of the Irish Volunteers is to be

made today. You will carry out this order in your own command and make it known to other commands. Eoin MacNeill.

Then he hit on an idea that would have worried the Military Council far more than his message to provincial commandants. At midnight he cycled into town to the offices of the best-selling Irish paper, the *Sunday Independent*.

He told Cogley, the sub-editor, that he wanted a notice in the morning's edition. 'In bold type, please.'

'Certainly, sir. You're just in time.'

He took down at MacNeill's dictation:

> Owing to the very critical position, all orders given to the Irish Volunteers for tomorrow, Easter Sunday, are hereby rescinded, and no parades, marches, or other movements of the Irish Volunteers will take place. Each individual Volunteer will obey this order strictly in every particular.

Nora Connolly was in Coalisland, County Tyrone. She had been drafted there for Red Cross work. It was an assignment that pleased her. When the Ulstermen of the Irish Volunteers went to Dublin for the rising she would go too.

Her father would be proud of them, she thought. They were fifty men, good and true, well-equipped with modern weapons.

When Colm O'Lochlainn arrived at their HQ, a large hut lit by hurricane lamps, Nora was overjoyed. He had surely come to give them their marching orders.

'The Chief of Staff,' he said, 'has cancelled manoeuvres.'

She was stunned. It was impossible.

All around her, men were mumbling, 'Nothing for it. Might as well go back to Belfast.'

Nora gathered round her a handful of Red Cross girls.

With characteristic fire, she said, 'I'm catching the morning mail train to Dublin. Are you coming with me?'

'Yes,' they said.

Eamonn Kent arrived home from his battalion HQ at 3 in the morning, all keyed up after issuing his men with final orders for manoeuvres next day.

219

On his door was a note from Cathal Brugha telling him of MacNeill's notice in the *Sunday Independent*.

He woke up his wife.

'MacNeill,' he groaned, 'has ruined us, he's stopped the rising.'

Without bidding Aine goodbye, he immediately sped along the river to Liberty Hall where guards barred his way.

'I must see Connolly at once.'

They told him it was impossible. He had just gone to bed after an exhausting day.

Kent walked up to the Metropole. The night clerk said, 'Mr Plunkett gave strict orders not to be woken up till nine.'

When he trudged back home, bitter and full of foreboding, his wife said, 'You must get to bed, darling.'

'If I went to bed now,' he retorted, 'I would sleep on dynamite.'

Within minutes he fell fast asleep, exhausted.

Late Saturday night in New York, early Easter in Ireland, Dan Cohalan phoned McGarrity.

He had received a message from Valentia Island, somewhat premature: 'Tom successfully operated today.' It was signed 'O'Sullivan'.

'It's started, Joe.'

'Thank God.'

McGarrity found his large mansion too small to contain his joy. He went out to walk the streets of Philadelphia alone.

The phone rang beside Nathan's bed. 'What in the name of—?'

He looked at his alarm clock. It showed 6 a.m. And this was Easter Sunday! 'What is it?'

His sleepiness vanished instantly. The second of the castaways had been picked up and was singing beautifully.

Nathan was quivering with excitement. Something criminal *had* been planned but he was never more certain of anything in his whole life than that there would be no rebellion *this* Easter.

Still, he was a lucky man.

The ship bearing arms for the rising was at the bottom of the sea. And Roger Casement, the leader of it, was already – he glanced again at his clock – out of harm's way in England.

The mail train to London stopped at Willesden Junction. Casement was in a reserved compartment, handcuffed to Major Moul. He had spent another sleepless night and was still not over his seasickness.

220

In Arbour Hill, they had taken away his collar, tie and laces in case he tried to take his life. Fortunately, they had missed the more deadly instrument hidden in his jacket.

Into the carriage at Willesden stepped Chief Inspector Joseph Sandercock of New Scotland Yard, a burly man with a kindly soul.

'Sir Roger, pleased to meet you, sir.'

They shook hands.

'You are now in my charge.'

The signalman waved a flag and, to the sound of church bells summoning Catholics to the first Mass of Easter, the train proceeded to Euston Station.

The Belfast mail train pulled into Amiens Street Station, Dublin. Before it shunted to a halt Nora Connolly and her friends jumped out and ran the few hundred yards to Liberty Hall.

'Sorry, girls, you can't come in.'

Fortunately, an aide behind the armed guard recognized Nora.

' 'Tis so, lass,' he said, 'your da got to bed after 3.'

'D'you think,' Nora said, out of breath, 'I'd want to wake him if it were not an emergency?'

'Wait here and I'll go see.'

Connolly was just getting up when Nora burst in on him. He was in a suit with an open collar. She told him of MacNeill's countermand.

'Daddy, does this mean there won't be a rising?'

She started to cry and, to her surprise, for she had never witnessed the like before, she saw two big tears run down his cheeks.

'If there isn't one, Nora, we'd better pray God to send an earthquake or a tidal wave to bury us under the sea.' His voice grew strong. 'It would disgrace our generation.'

'In Tyrone,' she said, 'they are fifty men waiting.'

'But I heard tell, Nora, there wouldn't be fifty in all Ulster to join us as things stand.'

'You are wrong,' she insisted. 'Ask the other girls.'

He had them brought in and they confirmed her story.

'Thanks, girls,' he said, 'leave me. I have a job for you in a few minutes.'

As he scribbled addresses on different pieces of paper, he called to an aide. 'Get me six of our lads, one for each girl. They are to repeat what they told me to the Military Council and ask them all to join me here at the double.'

Nora went to McDermott's place. He had been sleeping in his clothes like her father, with armed guards keeping watch. He heard her out. Then he gave her a hug.

'Tell your dad I'll be along soon.'

When Nora returned to her father's office, she found him in a smart new uniform.

'The first time you've seen it, eh?' he said, with a grin.

He put on his sword-belt and as she went to buckle it for him, he put his hand on her shoulder.

'You should be doing this for a young man and not an oldster like me.'

He was bubbling with joy, as if things were going to turn out well after all. In spite of the lack of sleep, his grey eyes were twinkling and he was singing in his tuneless voice,

We've got another saviour now,
That saviour is the sword.

Pearse and Willie had been staying at the home of Sean T. O'Kelly. They had risen early for Easter Mass and Communion. In a church reeking of incense the purple drapes had been removed from the statues, there were lilies on the altars, the Paschal candle was lit, the bells rang out again after the Lenten silence. They prayed for the success of the rising, that Ireland, like Jesus crucified, would rise again.

In good spirits, they went back to O'Kelly's place for breakfast. There Pearse received his summons to Liberty Hall.

Monteith woke to bad news. An outlying corps of the Tralee Volunteers had concluded that, without German arms, the rising could not succeed; they refused to take part.

Minutes later, someone reported to him the Killorglin tragedy in which two Volunteers had been drowned.

He was at a low ebb when, at 8.30 a.m., two boys came in utterly exhausted. They had walked thirty miles through most of the night. Their message was the first hopeful sign: the men of Dingle were on their way and would arrive about 11 a.m.

Monteith gave the two brave lads a few shillings and told them to buy themselves breakfast in town.

Things improved a little more, when the local *Cumann na mBan*, the women's branch of the Irish Volunteers, arrived to prepare his own breakfast.

By 9 a.m., the Military Council started arriving at Liberty Hall. Clarke was first, with McDermott a close second. Nora cooked them bacon and eggs in the cavernous kitchen below stairs.

Before he left the Metropole Joe Plunkett, knowing his wedding was off, drew up his will on the first scrap of paper that came to hand and asked his brothers to witness it. He bequeathed everything he possessed to Grace Gifford. He thrust it in his pocket and, buttoning his tunic high to mask his surgical wound, went as fast as weak legs would carry him to the Hall.

At table, Connolly was handed a copy of the *Sunday Independent*. He read out MacNeill's statement in his gruff voice. After an incredulous silence, they all started talking at once. The greatest Irish rising in centuries had been cancelled by the Chief of Staff through a notice in a Sunday paper. Clarke was incensed that MacNeill had chosen to put it in a capitalist rag that he himself refused even to sell in his shop.

This notice would seem official even to members of the IRB. They had had a hard enough job telling their men that the manoeuvres were the rising; how could they convince them that *officially cancelled* manoeuvres were the rising?

Words like 'humiliation', 'absurdity', 'fiasco' filled the air. This seemed to be the fate of every Irish rising against the British.

Pearse alone suggested that MacNeill was acting out of principle not pique. 'Besides,' he said, 'who are we to complain if he acts without consulting us?'

Nathan scanned his *Sunday Independent* at breakfast.

Any lingering doubt about the wisdom of waiting on official approval from London before suppressing the Sinn Feiners was dispelled. Their Chief of Staff had cancelled 'manoeuvres', doubtless because of the loss of German arms.

'Anything wrong, Matthew?' his sister-in-law, Estelle, said over the marmalade.

'*Au contraire*, my dear. Everything is very right.'

Across the land many Volunteers, reading the *Sunday Independent*, smashed their rifles on walls in disgust. Some of the more perceptive realized that what had happened in Tralee would force the Administration to round them up. Why, then, call off a scrap that was now inevitable?

Others, of a more philosophical frame of mind, began marking their cards for next day's Grand National at Fairyhouse in County Meath.

The Military Council had barely begun their deliberations upstairs when an aide came in to say the police were surrounding the place. He explained it was due to the fact that 250 pounds of gelignite had been stolen from a quarry in Tallaght.

'They followed it here.'

Connolly went to make sure his men were on the alert. He came back to find Tom Clarke arguing that this police presence was an earnest of things to come.

'Do you guys reckon the Castle is gonna leave us alone now they know we've links with Germany, now they know we were all set to take 'em on?'

Nathan turned up at the Castle at 9.30 a.m.

The views of his military advisers coincided with his own. The notice in the *Sunday Independent* had clinched matters. Not that Nathan was one to take the opposition lightly. When the DMP told him of the haul of gelignite he said, 'It would not surprise me if Liberty Hall is a bomb-making factory.'

From Euston Station Casement was whisked off under heavy guard to Scotland Yard. He was led through the courtyard, up a huge curved staircase and along broad corridors. An order came from on high: he was not to be permitted to wash or shave. By 10 a.m., feeling thoroughly sick and humiliated, he was seated in Thomson's office overlooking the Thames.

His two interrogators had longed for many months to interview him. In the clever dirty business of counter-espionage none came cleverer or dirtier.

Basil Thomson was Assistant Commissioner of Police at the Yard and boss of both the CID and the Special Branch which specialized in political subversion. Suave, with neat hair and moustache, he wore a dark tie under a wing-collar. Reginald Hall was in smart naval uniform. Short, rosy-cheeked and bald apart from tufts of greying hair, he was often excitable. They had interrogated many suspects together, including, lately, the beautiful Marguerite Zeller, known as Mata Hari.

With Thomson calculating and Hall acting from impulse, they had acquired an almost telepathic rapport. Each knew when to let the other speak, when to jump in himself. Sometimes they both remained stonily silent, waiting for the suspect to offer them some crumb of information, anything to break the intolerable silence of two such powerful personalities.

Outside the office, Hall said, 'Right, BT, let's go and sort this traitor out,' and Thomson added, wrinkling his nose, 'I'm scared of contaminating myself but it has to be done, I suppose.'

'How do you *do*,' Thomson said, affably, as he entered. 'Please sit down, won't you, while we all get acquainted.'

Casement was thin and cadaverous, his thick black hair greying, his forehead a network of wrinkles. The mahogany-coloured hands holding up his trousers twitched with suppressed anxiety.

In one satisfied glance, Hall saw an exhausted and broken man. His rumpled appearance, from stubbly face to laceless boots, contrasted starkly with their own immaculate turn-out.

'First,' Thomson said, touching his horn-rimmed glasses, 'your name, please.'

'Surely you know it.'

Thomson smiled suavely. 'I have to guard against the possibility of impersonation.'

'Very well.' He joined his hands, with the finger-tips touching. 'I am Sir Roger Casement.'

'So your comrades informed us.'

Casement looked startled. 'I thought—'

'You thought,' Thomson said, with a light chuckle, 'that Monteith and Bailey, that's his real name, is it not, would be faithful to you?'

'I thought—'

Casement broke off, a small smile brightening his lips. They were alive, then, since someone must have identified Beverley. He did not believe they had betrayed him. Certainly not Monteith.

'We are keeping them in Ireland, Tralee to be precise, for the time being. With a man named Stack and others.'

Hall judged that Casement was too vain to be afraid of them or of anyone. *That* was the weak point he would home in on: his vanity. But something *was* bothering the prisoner, of that he was certain.

'I am not endeavouring to shield myself at all,' Casement said. 'I did go to Germany. All I ask is that you believe I have done nothing treacherous to *my* country.'

Thomson, a former prisoner governor, was an expert on the

criminal mind. In his view, Casement was pleased to be the centre of attraction *because* his crime was so hideous and his execution so certain. It was always harder to break a man who had nothing to lose.

He would need great guile to get the information he needed.

A stenographer, Sergeant Gill, was writing everything down. Thomson guessed that part of Casement's stiffness and reticence was due to that, so he soon gave Gill a break for coffee.

As the young stenographer left, he brushed past Casement and whispered, for only him to hear, '*Greater love than this no man hath.*'

'At last,' Thomson said, with a sigh, as the door closed, 'now we can talk more freely, old man. What would you say to a brandy?'

Clarke, who presided over the meeting of the Military Council, was not his usual cool self.

'Time's running out,' he said in a rush. 'Put off the rising and the men'll get confused. Go ahead and the rest of the country'll take it that MacNeill's notice is a hoax or a Castle trick.'

As so often in the past, Old Tom looked in McDermott's direction. For the very first time, Sean shook his head.

The rest also said No. For most Volunteers, even for many IRB men, they argued, MacNeill was the voice of the movement and they would obey the cancellation.

'Only till they see Dublin rise,' Clarke urged.

Once more, McDermott shook his head.

'All right,' said Clarke, gritting his teeth, 'what'll we do?'

The consensus was they needed a delay. Not so long that the authorities would have a chance to round them up. A botched rising was preferable to giving in without a shot being fired. That would end any chance of a rebellion for generations.

'But,' Sean said, 'we need time to sort out the mess.'

'How long?' asked Clarke.

Pearse suggested, 'Tomorrow at noon.'

Six hands were raised around the table.

Slowly, Clarke raised his, making the critical decision unanimous.

They would send MacNeill a note to say they had cancelled manoeuvres. That would keep him quiet and convince him he had quashed the rising. It would also stop the provinces rising before the main Dublin operation was under way.

'Sounds fine so far,' said Clarke. 'Go on.'

226

McDermott said, 'We simply add that manoeuvres have been put back by twenty-four hours.'

'That way,' Plunkett put in, 'we will still seem to have MacNeill's authority.'

MacNeill's intervention was bound to mean a lower turn-out. But once the rising began, those with stomach for a fight would join in.

McDonagh pointed out that Monday had certain advantages over Sunday, at least as far as Dublin was concerned.

'Most British soldiers will be at the Races. We should have the city to ourselves.'

As Brigade Commander he drafted a letter, dated 24 April, for mobilizing the Dublin Brigade at 10 a.m. the next day. After that the Military Council returned to the next day's tactics. They were angry that, after months of planning, they were having to improvise.

The German Admiral Staff received two telegrams in quick succession around 10 o'clock.

The first, sent via Rotterdam, read:

'London stop Nordisk steamer *Aud* sunk today off Daunts Rock stop Crew will arrive here stop.'

The second was from Christiania:

'According Lloyds Norwegian steamer *Aud* sunk off Daunts Rock twenty-second of fourth stop Hails Bergen 1100 tons built 1907 stop.'

Only now did Berlin grasp that no U-boat had picked up the message transmitted from Nauen. The Irish expedition had failed.

The Kaiser was informed.

The Press was told to play down what was an insignificant episode of the war. But both the Admiralty and the General Staff knew that if the plan had succeeded, giving them U-boat facilities on Irish coasts, the war might have been that much nearer a satisfactory conclusion.

Nathan took a stroll from the Castle to the Viceregal Lodge, arriving at 10.30 a.m. He was in the cheeriest of moods.

'You saw the notice in the *Sunday Independent*, I take it?'

'I did,' Wimborne replied.

'So there is no need for any precipitate action now.'

'I do not agree,' Wimborne rasped. 'Did you not hear those rabid socialists have stolen 250 pounds of gelignite? Not to make fireworks, I presume.'

'I don't deny they were planning something.'

'*Were*,' retorted Wimborne, his face flushed. 'It would not surprise me if the ring-leaders are even now sitting in conclave conspiring against us.'

'In the circumstances,' said Nathan, smiling palely, 'that would be a most unreasonable thing to do.'

'You talk,' Wimborne said, 'as if they are Englishmen. If they had one grain of common sense they would be grateful to stay British for ever.'

'Even they know they cannot succeed.'

Once again Wimborne bridled. 'What if they know that and decide to act *because* of that?'

Nathan's tidy mind was baffled. 'Explain, please.'

'Has it not occurred to you that this scum, this riff-raff might act unexpectedly not because they hope to succeed but simply because it is unexpected? Suppose their only wish is to surprise us, even if only by their own romantic stupidity?'

'They have only to think about—'

'They don't *think*. Irishmen, as far as England is concerned, are incapable of thinking.'

'I'll ponder,' said a bemused Nathan.

'I insist you round the ring-leaders up at once,' Wimborne stormed. 'Strengthen the Castle guard, stop all leave for the police and the Army.

Nathan bristled. 'That is not necessary at present and, in any case, *ultra vires*. I will cable Birrell for permission, Excellency.'

The use of the title was a reminder that this was an administrative act.

Wimborne glanced at the clock. 'Heavens,' he said, with a sudden switch of mood, 'it's nearly eleven. Far too late for a rising now.'

Tongue-in-cheek, a relieved Nathan agreed that the best rebellions always occurred before breakfast.

No sooner had Nathan left for the Castle than Wimborne dictated a letter to Birrell. He wanted all the rebels arrested for treachery and interned.

'I am afraid if you stir up the hornets' nest and leave the hornets we may have serious trouble.'

He concluded: 'This is in great haste for the post. I hear there is still a possibility of conscription. All the more reason for getting our suspects packed away. We shall never get a better opportunity. If you agree, do write and ginger Nathan.'

He rubbed his hands.

'Get that off at once, Basil. God only knows what those rebels are up to now.'

At Liberty Hall the seven rebels on the Military Council voted themselves as the new Provisional government.

Pearse was elected President and Commandant-General of the Irish Republic, James Connolly Vice-President and Commandant-General of the Dublin Division.

They read through the Proclamation of the Republic. Though written by Pearse, it was influenced by Connolly's passion for equality and social justice. None of them seemed to notice that it bore no date.

Clarke said, 'Mr President, if you would sign first.'

Pearse shook his head. 'You have the longest record of us all.'

With the rest agreeing, he handed Clarke the pen.

Misty-eyed, Old Tom put his name to it, feeling that all the years of imprisonment had been worthwhile. They passed the pen from one to the other like knights handling the Holy Grail.

In the chaos of events, only one thing was certain: they were all signing their death warrant.

Afterwards, Connolly took McDonagh to the machine-room and introduced him to the three compositors, Christopher Brady, Michael Molloy and Bill O'Brien. McDonagh shook the hand of each and gave Brady the text of the Proclamation.

'If you don't want to do it, we won't be worse friends for that.'

The three said it was an honour to set up such an historic document.

The men from Dingle arrived in Tralee exhausted, some having marched forty miles. They were not a little upset that they had just been jeered at and told to go home. Monteith found it odd that they had marched for hours without rations and with precious little equipment. Their guns would frighten a few crows. After the women provided them with breakfast they braved the concrete floor and went to sleep.

Within the hour, about 320 men had gathered from outlying districts, 200 of them armed. Of them 20 per cent were old men or boys of from fourteen to seventeen without so much as a walking-stick.

Monteith kept pinching himself to make sure he was not dreaming. He was risking life and limb for *this*?

229

He asked the Dingle Commandant to make sure his men bought themselves a couple of days' supply of food.

'Otherwise, I take it your men are ready.'

'Indeed, they have all made their Easter duties.'

Monteith, a Protestant, blinked.

'Now, Captain,' said the Commandant, whistling for his men to rise, 'we're off.'

'Off? Off where?'

'Why, sir, to Holy Mass, of course. 'Tis Easter Day.'

And he marched them in fours to church.

Scouts from Fenit and Ardfert reported that there were a few more police on the roads than usual, that was all. Two British warships were still in the Bay.

Monteith kitted himself out with a makeshift uniform and a ten-shot Mauser pistol similar to the one he had buried in Banna Strand. He wondered where Casement and Beverley were now.

Nathan sent a coded message to Birrell, telling him that Bailey had admitted that Casement and Monteith had led the expedition from Berlin.

'In view of definite association of Irish Volunteers with enemy now established, I agreed with Lord Lieutenant that leaders should be arrested and interned in England. Can this be proceeded with subject to concurrence of the Law Officers, Military Authorities and Home Office?'

In a hurry, he returned to his lodge to pick up Estelle for lunch at Sir Horace Plunkett's place, Kilteragh, in the leafy suburb of Foxrock.

Though Nathan's message would not arrive for twenty-four hours, Birrell was already very pleased with himself, especially after Basil Thomson had told him who the prisoner was.

His patience and guile had paid off. The Sinn Fein pig had cut its own throat. He had not needed to do anything; they, with 'the lunatic traitor' Casement, had brought disaster on themselves. He was reminded of the Irishman who, in attempting to catch a salmon with a scythe, sliced off his own head.

He wrote to Nathan, 'You may rely upon my being in Dublin by the end of the week, whatever happens I must come.'

In Tralee, the rain that started at eleven was pelting down at midday when a man in a raincoat with his collar up slipped into the Hall. Cahill immediately buttonholed him.

Monteith was fed up with all these whisperings. Either he was in charge or he wasn't. He grabbed the newcomer by the shoulder and spun him round. It was Lieutenant Whelan of the Limerick City Regiment.

'Paddy,' he gasped, 'when are you going out?'

'We're not, Bob. I've been sent to tell Stack that all operations for today are cancelled.'

Monteith, remembering Connolly's message the day before, found it hard to take in.

'Who said so?'

Whelan told him that The O'Rahilly had motored to Cork and stopped off at Limerick. He had brought a countermand by MacNeill. To spare him a journey, Whelan had come to Tralee.

'Thank God.'

Monteith, who knew The O'Rahilly well, assumed that his note to MacNeill was behind this.

Casement was right, then, the rising had depended on German support. In view of his own experiences in Tralee, no other decision was possible.

As the men came back from Mass, shaking the rain off their clothes, Monteith realized his own predicament. He was wanted by the police on more than one score; now hundreds of locals had seen him. Could he rely on them not to give him away, even through a slip of the tongue in a pub?

He took Cahill aside. 'Listen, Paddy, this alters everything. I hate to inflict my personal problems on anyone but I'm the only one around here who's in any danger. Can you find me a place to hide till this blows over?'

While Cahill tried to organize something, the Volunteers drilled and practised pitching tents in a neighbouring field.

All the time the rain bucketed down.

Sir Horace Plunkett, a rather deaf old gentleman, had been for a quarter of a century the leading light in the Co-operative movement. Small and wiry, he managed by talking very rapidly to finish his sentences inside two minutes. Lunch at his Foxrock mansion was a glittering occasion. Among the guests this Easter Day were Lord and Lady Fingal.

Nathan in a loud luncheon voice regaled them with stories of recent events, ending with, 'So I give you a categorical assurance there will be no rising.'

They all clapped and banged silver spoons on the table.

Even during luncheon Nathan's mind could not rest. He planned to spend the rest of the day conferring with Army and police chiefs. How would they get the explosives back from Liberty Hall? When Birrell gave the word, what was the best way to round up the Sinn Fein leaders?

All day, the Military Council kept in close touch with Ned Daly and de Valera, the only two battalion commanders not on the Council. They were told to hold their men in readiness for further orders.

When the meeting finally broke up, Connolly found Nora.

'We're going ahead tomorrow,' he said. 'Take the girls to the Countess's place and come back here early in the morning.'

About 3 p.m., Kathleen Clarke was at home. She was upset about the notice in the paper and wondering how this would affect the rising when in walked Tom with Sean McGarry.

'What's happened?'

'MacNeill,' he said, over-simplifying, 'betrayed us. He countermanded *his own orders* of the previous day. He could at least have told us.'

He gave her a gun. 'Don't you surrender to the police or the Army, Kattie. Better be dead than surrender.'

In mid-afternoon, Connolly and Mallin, to prove their independence, led out the Citizen Army on manoeuvres.

They marched through all the principal thoroughfares, singing with gusto their usual repertoire: 'Wrap the Green Flag Round Me', 'Ireland Over All', and the song for which the Countess had written the lyrics: 'The Germans are Winning the War, Me Boys.'

Passing the City Hall, they veered left and headed for the Upper Castle Yard. The gates were closed. The sentry on duty shouted, 'Guard, turn *out!*' and they came running, rifles pointed. Captain Sean Connolly smiled grimly to himself. Tomorrow, the march on the Castle would be for real.

James Connolly ordered the Citizen Army to march on. The soldiers in the Yard returned with relief to the guard-room.

Back at the Hall, James Connolly told his men they were confined to barracks for the night. They cheered when he said, 'From now on,

232

you are under arms and you won't lay them down till you've struck a blow for Ireland.'

Pearse wrote a note for MacNeill.

'Commandant McDonagh is to call on you this afternoon. He countermanded the Dublin parades today with my authority. I confirmed your countermand as the leading men would not have obeyed it without my confirmation.'

At 5 p.m., McDonagh took it to MacNeill's home where he spoke for a long time with him and Sean Fitzgibbon. He made clear his loyalty to Ireland but he was necessarily vague about the details. He left, saying mysteriously, 'In future, I intend to keep my own counsel.'

Only at 5 p.m. did word reach de Valera that the rising would be at noon next day. A dour young man who liked to play things by the book, he was glad to be able to obey the letter of MacNeill's notice while disobeying its obvious spirit.

To McDonagh's call for mobilization next day, he added his own signature.

By the time it was dark the Tralee Volunteers had been drilling in the rain for what seemed an eternity. They returned to the Rink where the women fed them.

Cahill had made arrangements for Monteith to go home with the Ballymacelligott corps, since they lived nearby. He was given an overcoat, a Volunteer cap, a bandolier and an old double-barrelled shot-gun.

The police were posted at the gas-lit exit to check on them as they left. But the corps waited for a downpour and then marched briskly out in fours, with a band playing noisily. It was wet as only a west of Ireland town can be. People huddled steamily on street corners and looked out of pub windows booing the Volunteers as they passed. Monteith marched painfully in boots that brought on blisters, thinking of home and wife and children far away.

Four miles out of town, the squad dismissed. Monteith went to Lieutenant Byrne's place for supper.

Back at the Castle after lunch, Nathan collected Colonel Cowan, in military command while Friend was in England, and Major Lewis, temporarily in charge of the Castle forces.

It was approaching 6 o'clock as they drove to the Viceregal Lodge. On the way, Nathan brought up the question of the stolen gelignite and the Viceroy's proposal to raid Liberty Hall, presently crammed with the Citizen Army.

'I would like you,' Nathan said, 'to work out a strategy to keep fighting to the minimum.'

Wimborne's hope of winning the military over to his point of view was soon dashed. They explained the difficulty of taking the Hall, especially when it was well-guarded.

Cowan said they would have to bring in artillery from Athlone, eighty miles away. Major Lewis added that storming a building in the city centre was not easy. They would need to consult the police, the General Staff and Major Price, the Intelligence Officer.

While Wimborne fumed at what he took to be a conspiracy against him, Nathan said, 'We shall certainly call on those experts some time.'

'What's wrong with tonight?' the Viceroy demanded in a whistle-like voice.

'It *is* Easter Sunday,' Nathan pointed out.

'*I* am not complaining.'

'Very magnanimous of you, Excellency,' Nathan said, masking his irritation. 'I'll do my best to have everyone here, then, at, shall we say, 10 o'clock?'

At 8 p.m., Tom Clarke went with Piaras Beasley, Daly's second in command, to the meeting place in North Frederick Street. Beasley had always found Clarke a dry, unemotional man. Yet he was throbbing with anger.

'Our plans were perfect,' he said, 'and now everything's spoiled. I feel as if I wanna go away in a corner and cry.'

On the way they passed the Gresham Hotel, where Sir Francis Fletcher Vane was dressing for dinner. Black trousers with a broad braid, white stiff shirt and white tie, gardenia in the buttonhole. He checked in the mirror. Passable if only his razor could reach that tuft of beard in his cleft chin.

He had come to town from Longford to address a monster meeting of young people at the Mansion House on Tuesday evening on the theme of 'Civic Responsibility'.

Never one to miss an opportunity of enjoying himself, he had invited a beautiful young thing whom he ran into in the lobby to dine with him.

Clarke was talking with McDermott at the meeting in North Frederick Street when Pearse arrived and handed out a terse note to each of the couriers.

'We start operations at noon today, Monday. Carry out your instructions. P. H. Pearse.'

Those who had furthest to travel set out at once. The rest were told to deliver the note first thing in the morning.

Thomas MacDonagh went home from seeing MacNeill to be greeted by his wife, Muriel. They went hand in hand to the children's bedrooms. MacDonagh feared this might be the last time he would ever kiss them good-night. Flesh of his flesh, living flesh of the flesh that perishes. In his heart, his wife was a widow already and his boy and girl fatherless. Yet in his children, something of himself, of *themselves* would endure.

Afterwards, with a heavy heart, he wrote for the record an account of his interview with MacNeill. This, with his will already drawn up, was to be his testament.

> *I have guarded secrets which I am bound to keep. I have,*
> *I think, acted honourably and fairly by all my associates.*
> *I have had only one motive in all my actions, namely,*
> *the good of my country.*

The high-level conference began in the drawing-room of the Viceregal Lodge on the stroke of 10 p.m. Apart from Cowan and Lewis, there were present Edgeworth-Johnstone, Chief Commissioner of the DMP, Major Price and Captain Robertson of the General Staff.

An edgy Viceroy said, 'No word yet from Birrell?'

'I do not expect to hear until after the Easter break,' Nathan said.

'Right.'

The Viceroy jabbed his index finger for emphasis.

'In addition to raiding Liberty Hall, I propose we round up sixty to a hundred leading Sinn Feiners.'

'You cannot mean tonight,' Nathan commented, dryly.

'When better? Leave it till tomorrow and their camp-followers might put up a fight. The dark's the best time for this sort of thing.'

235

Even the usually suave Nathan blinked at the absurdity of this proposal. 'I think we should act according to the book.'

'Do nothing, you mean.'

'I mean, Excellency, we have to make sure that every charge made can be sustained in law.'

'By which time the callous law-breakers may have taken over the city.'

'Hardly likely,' Nathan said, with a forced smile.

'If you haven't the stomach for it, Mr Under-Secretary, I will sign the arrest-warrants myself and get the Home Secretary's authorization later.'

Nathan thanked him for his generosity. 'I seem to remember, Excellency, everyone involved was dismissed when three or four civilians were killed at Bachelor's Walk. If you miscalculate and the Sinn Feiners riot, there could be a massacre.'

'Massacre?'

The Viceroy went quiet for a bit, then turned to Edgeworth-Johnstone. 'Chief Commissioner?'

He began diplomatically, 'I think the Viceroy is right, absolutely. It is imperative to occupy the rebels' strongholds and take their leaders into custody as soon as possible.'

'Which is precisely *when*?' Nathan demanded, archly.

'First, let me say how we should go about it. A combined police and military operation. Arrest twenty or thirty leaders in their homes simultaneously so they do not scatter.'

He cast a fawning glance in Wimborne's direction. 'I agree with His Excellency on a second score: this should be timed for about two in the morning.'

Nathan pressed him again. 'In, say, four hours' time?'

'If it were possible to do it in that time-span, I, naturally, would be all for it.'

Very quietly, Nathan asked, '*Is* it possible?'

'These leaders,' Edgeworth-Johnstone went on, as if he had not heard, 'should be put on a special boat and sent across the Channel for internment on the other side.'

'Excellent,' the Viceroy purred. 'Excellent.'

Encouraged, the Chief Commissioner went on: 'Meanwhile, occupy their strongholds in the dead of night and put pickets on them so that when the rank-and-file wake up in the morning they will realize that resistance is impossible.'

Nathan clapped noiselessly.

'Then,' Edgeworth-Johnstone said in an ailing voice, 'we institute a house-to-house search for weapons and . . . and forbid them to arm and drill . . . any more.'

'I cannot find a flaw in your strategy.' Nathan looked around the table. 'Can anyone?' They all shook their heads.

'And all this is really possible, Chief Commissioner, in' – he checked his watch – 'about three and a half hours' time?'

Wimborne, who had learned a bit of caution, said, 'May I suggest, Mr Under-Secretary, that you authorize it tonight.'

'Me?' said Nathan breezily. 'Well, if the Chief Commissioner can guarantee that all this can be done in three and a half hours.'

'I cannot.'

It was scarcely audible.

'Speak up, Mr Edgeworth-Johnstone,' urged Nathan, as the soldiers present tried to keep a straight face. 'Are you saying this *cannot* be done tonight?'

'It can . . . not, sir.'

'Really?' Nathan looked surprised. 'Then I hardly think it worth His Excellency putting his head on the block.'

The military confirmed that what the Chief Inspector had suggested would take a large force to implement. Reinforcements from the Curragh, artillery from Athlone. Even then there were problems. Troop movements would alert the Sinn Feiners. They would go into hiding or, worse, start the very rising the authorities were trying to prevent.

Nathan thanked the three officers for sharing their expertise.

'For myself, gentlemen, I cannot believe that Easter Monday, with thousands of visitors in Dublin, would be the ideal day to raid Liberty Hall. Especially with the rebels annoyed at having to abandon their fun and games at the last minute.'

The meeting broke up at 11.30 p.m. with Nathan promising that while he was unable to act without London's authorization, he would arrest the chief suspects very soon. Possibly within two or three days.

Finally, he turned to Major Price.

'Perhaps you will join me at the Castle to help me draw up a comprehensive list.'

'With pleasure, sir. When?'

Nathan eyed the Viceroy. 'Why, first thing in the morning.'

Monteith had switched to Private McEllistrim's house on the edge of

Tralee. He was treated with the utmost kindness and given a feather bed. He would have to hide out for some time, but he was beginning to feel that he might elude his pursuers after all. They might not be so vigilant, now that the rising had been called off.

On the other side of Ireland, at St Enda's, Mrs Pearse knocked and entered Patrick's study. He was at his desk.

'Don't work too late, my son. You need to conserve your strength.'

'Won't be long, Mother.' He looked up at her. 'This is to be the greatest insurrection in the history of Ireland.'

'Yes,' she said, a catch in her throat.

She blessed him and went upstairs.

Pearse took up his pen and went on from where he had left off.

'Dear Mrs Bloomer, I enclose a cheque for £5 as a further instalment. Wishing you a very happy Easter. P. H. Pearse.'

In the basement of Liberty Hall, the three compositors were steadily turning out copies of the Proclamation. They worked the night through on an ancient Wharfdale Double-Crown with cracked rollers and leaky cylinders. The type was supplied by William Henry West from Capel Street, an Englishman and a rebel.

Type was short. They had mixed founts, and many missing and battered letters. Some Es were made up of Fs and sealing wax. It meant they had to set up the type more than once. It was hard to ink it evenly and maintain a steady pressure on the rollers so that almost every copy was smudged or suffered, in parts, from barely decipherable print.

Dawn was breaking when their work was done. They had produced about 2,500 copies.

As ordered by Connolly, they handed them over to Helena Moloney for distribution in the city and, hopefully, in major towns and villages throughout Ireland, on the next and greatest day in the history of Ireland.

PART THREE

THE BATTLE
24–30 April 1916

'But where can we draw water,'
  Said Pearse to Connolly,
'When all the wells are parched away?
  O plain as plain can be
There's nothing but our own red blood
  Can make a right Rose Tree.'
                              W. B. Yeats

MONDAY

Morning presented itself as crisp and pure as the first bite of an apple. The many cyclists and pedestrians moving purposefully through Dublin were in vivid contrast to the rest of a sleeping city on this national holiday.

Two couriers, Marie Peroltz and a male companion, rang on the door of a house in Mount Street shared by two petite young women, Elizabeth O'Farrell and Julia Grenan. They were ready and opened at once. Marie Peroltz handed over two notes.

'You, Elizabeth, are to go to Athenry. Julia, your despatch is for Dundalk and Carrickmacross. When you get back, join the HQ Staff in the Post Office. Mr Connolly says you'll be needed to carry messages. Goodbye and good luck.'

In other streets, couriers were shoving out of bed men suffering from hangovers. 'Get dressed. Full uniforms.'

'What's that you say? Surely manoeuvres were cancelled.'

A piece of paper was waved in front of many a sleep-lined face. 'Can't you read? The four city battalions will parade for inspection and route march at 10 a.m. today. It's signed by MacDonagh and Pearse.'

Many did not answer the rap on the door. In the confusion of orders and counter-orders, they had gone from Dublin or were too drunk to hear.

When Nora went to say goodbye to her father at the Hall, he gave her a message from Pearse to Dr McCartan in the north.

Holding up a copy of the Proclamation, he said, 'Read it, lass. It's too risky for you to take a copy with you but try to remember it and repeat it to everyone you meet.'

It contained some of her father's most cherished beliefs. 'We declare the right of the people of Ireland to the ownership of Ireland . . . The Republic guarantees religious and civil liberty, equality and equal opportunities to all its citizens . . . cherishing all the children of the nation equally.'

It spoke of a National government to be 'elected by the suffrage of all her men and women'. If that came about, Ireland would be the first completely democratic nation in the world.

MacDonagh said, jokingly, 'Here we are starting a rebellion and all you can think of is how soon you can get out of town.'

'Take this, Nora.' Her father handed her a small nickel-plated

revolver with a box of cartridges. 'Look after the girls for me.'
He delved into his pocket and came up with money for her
journey. 'Nono,' he said, resorting to his pet-name for her, 'God
protect you.'

She clung to him, too choked to speak.

'Be proud, Nono,' he said. 'You helped save the day.'

'Goodbye, Daddy.'

'Good girl.'

He stepped back and saluted her.

Pearse had spent most of the night trying to get his accounts and
tax demands in order.

He put on his smart green Volunteer uniform, with Boer-type
slouch hat. He carried a repeating pistol, ammunition pouch, canteen
and provisions. Also a sword. Finally, he donned his greatcoat.

Mrs Pearse, proud and misty-eyed, was there to see Pat and
Willie off.

'I pinned a miraculous medal on your uniforms last night,' she
said. 'So be careful and do nothing rash.'

Pearse solemnly promised.

With his faithful brother beside him, his sword trailing behind,
the Commandant-General, Commander-in-Chief of the Army of the
Irish Republic, President-Elect of the Irish government, rode off on
his bicycle.

Mrs Pearse watched from the top step of St Enda's till they were
out of sight. She had a mother's intuition that she would never see
them again.

The five-mile journey to Liberty Hall in heavy uniform and on
a hot and humid day took its toll, especially as Pearse was a trifle
overweight.

It was approaching 8.30 a.m. when Father Aloysius, a thin, ascetic,
kind-faced Capuchin, was in the heart of Dublin walking to the
Convent in Gloucester Street to say Mass. Two cyclists, with coats
over their military uniform, passed him, puffing and blowing. He
recognized the Pearse brothers.

The holiday began with almost summer sunshine and skies of lilac-hue.
'A grand day,' said one. 'Grand, indeed, thank God,' echoed another.
It was a welcome change after a couple of weeks of typically Irish
mongrel days, part sun, part rain but chiefly rain. Spring flowers
bloomed in abundance, with papal yellow predominating.

Dublin, after London, was the greatest city in the British Empire. In eighteenth-century grandeur it excelled Edinburgh and Bath. Its railway stations, which would have passed as palaces in less-favoured cities, were crammed with holiday-makers streaming in and out of the capital.

Stephen's Green, the quarter-mile-square of rural peace in the city centre, was filling with smart bewhiskered men in bowlers or boaters. Most were up for the Royal Dublin Society Spring Show and staying in the Shelbourne Hotel. Their womenfolk walked dutifully beside them. In long sombre dresses whose ends they bunched up as they walked and topped by sturdy broad-brimmed hats, they looked like solid furniture in motion. Daughters had pony tails; small boys wheeled their hoops, their caps held on by elastic that left a red weal under their chins from ear to ear. The gaily dressed children fed crusts to ducks on the ponds or played on grass so green it seemed lit from within.

Phoenix Park on the western edge of the city also had many visitors. Most entered through Parkgate which, in best Irish tradition, was the only Park entrance without a gate. At 1,750 acres, it was bigger than several London parks put together. It had free-ranging deer and, in season, strange English pursuits such as cricket and polo, no doubt one reason why under its broad shady trees many an Irishman had plotted revolution. Maybe the heady smells of Dublin's 'black wine' from Guinness's Brewery across the River Liffey contributed to the madness.

Near the Brewery was the Royal Hospital of Kilmainham. A retirement home for Irish soldiers, it stood in 250 glorious acres snipped off the Phoenix Park.

Another British monument was the Viceregal Lodge, a low-lying two-storeyed white building in 160 acres. Walking towards it on this luminous morning were Sir Matthew Nathan and his sister-in-law. Estelle noted how grave he was as he hinted of trouble in the air. Leaving her at the main entrance, he went in to see the Viceroy. He did not stay long.

Their brief constitutional over, Nathan saw Estelle back to his own lodge before leaving for the Castle.

With Lent over, Dubliners felt free to smoke, drink – and gamble. Many were on their way north for the Grand National. Senior officials in the Administration and Army officers were driving there, too.

Many Dubliners went with their families to the east coast beaches of Killiney, Dalkey, Bray and Malahide. The open-decked trams were crowded, and terminuses, like the one at Nelson's Pillar in O'Connell Street were thronged with people in their holiday best.

Most remained in a city well stocked with spoiled priests and spoiled poets and those haggard, sad-faced men who 'drank quietly and deeply and always'.

Too few had responded to orders and were dressing militarily, preparing, as some thought, for manoeuvres, but, really, as their officers knew, for battle. Amateurs with mostly old-fashioned single-shot German rifles were preparing to take on the mightiest and best armed force in the world. A thousand men and women against an Empire.

It was 10 o'clock when Casement was brought by Inspector Sandercock to Scotland Yard from Brixton Prison, where he had spent another sleepless night.

In an ante-room, Thomson and Hall were trying to work out something that puzzled them. In the prisoner's possession when he was picked up in Tralee were a few pictures. They bore the name of a 3rd Avenue photographer. The woman in them, in a broad-brimmed hat, was very beautiful, as were her two little girls.

'Do you reckon he's gone straight, BT?'

Thomson said, 'Maybe like that Oscar Wilde chap he can manage both.'

'Odd lot, the Irish,' murmured Hall.

When the stenographer was sent out for a coffee, Casement surprised them by saying, 'May I ask a question?'

'Of course, old boy,' Thomson said, genially.

'Was there, um, a disturbance in Dublin yesterday?'

Thomson jerked his head back. 'Drunken brawl?'

'No, something more . . . more . . . .'

'Oh, you mean an armed rising?' Casement nodded. 'Nothing like that.'

Casement's eyes pleaded with him. 'You give me your word?'

'I thought we were all gentlemen here,' said an offended Thomson. 'But if it makes you feel any better, Sir Roger, I give you my solemn word, hope to die, that sort of thing.'

Hall, his eyes blinking furiously, added, 'It's perfectly quiet not only in Dublin but throughout Ireland.'

Casement sank back in his low-legged chair. 'Thank God.'

'But I thought—' Thomson began.

'I have explained already, I returned to Ireland to prevent a rising.'

'Oh?' Hall made it sound as if this were news to him.

'We had a terrible fight, the German Foreign Office and I, and I won the day. I would not let them come here. I refused to hand over my fifty boys to the hangman.'

'Hangman,' Thomson chuckled. 'A trifle romantic, old chap. Whoever mentioned hanging?'

Just after 10 a.m., at a large detached house in Ballsbridge, The O'Rahilly's wife, Nancie, shook him awake. Only the night before he had returned after driving hundreds of miles in the west, spreading MacNeill's cancellation. It had convinced him of the futility of a rising. Some Volunteer sections, as in Limerick, had about enough ammunition for a duck-shoot.

'Desmond is downstairs, says it's urgent.'

The O'Rahilly went down, stroking the pouches under his eyes, tidying his chestnut hair.

Desmond Fitzgerald said at once: 'Michael, the rising is to begin at twelve.'

'But—' Pulling himself up, The O'Rahilly glanced at his watch. 'I left the car at my sister's place. I'll have to walk over and pick it up.'

'So you are going to try and stop it?'

A wry smile passed over The O'Rahilly's face. 'If they are set on a rising, nothing on earth will stop them. I'll just get into my uniform. Go tell MacNeill what's happening.'

Nancy had a premonition of what lay ahead. As he emerged from his study, she whispered, 'Michael, O Michael.'

Having dressed, he kissed his eldest boy who was absorbed in his stamp collection. Then he folded in his arms his wife of seventeen unblemished years.

'Send the older lads to MacNeill's place,' he said, 'they'll be safer there.'

In mid-morning, Stack received a visit in Tralee Jail from Father Joe Breen and John P. O'Donnell.

They managed to whisper to him, 'On MacNeill's personal authority, the rising is off.'

'Thank God for that,' Stack said, crossing himself.

In the Department of Taxation at Crosfield, Palmerstown, County Dublin, a senior tax official had been ordered to put the squeeze on the Headmaster of St Enda's, Rathfarnam. Some sort of obscure revolutionary, he was told.

On an official form headed 'On His Majesty's Service' and in his own big sloping hand, he wrote: '24 April 1916. Dear Sir, I am advised to destrain you for all taxes due which are not paid by 29 inst. Yours faithfully, H. Harrison.'

Nathan passed through the Castle's Upper Gate at 10 o'clock to be saluted by PC James O'Brien. It was a day off for civil servants but the Constable was used to Nathan being first in and last out.

At the Viceroy's Lodge, the staff were making last-minute preparations for His Excellency's trip to Belfast. Servants were packing vast trunks under the direction of Lady Alice.

Wimborne was in the study that looked out over razored lawns and flame-shaped cypresses to the huge obelisk of the Wellington Monument. He was going over the Address he was to give at Drogheda where he intended breaking his journey. With baroque gestures, he practised in front of a mirror.

Things were more chaotic in Liberty Hall. Most of the Citizen Army had slept there overnight. Corridors and spare rooms were crammed with haversacks and equipment. Bicycles were strewn everywhere.

The Military Council met in Connolly's room to put final touches to their plans. Reports were already coming in of a sketchy turn-out. They hoped that the country would rise in sympathy, but this was less likely because of confused orders and the loss of the arms boat. Victory, never more than the barest possibility, was out of the question. Their only aim now was defensive: they would seize key buildings and hold them as long as they could, hopefully longer than any Irish rebels had managed before.

Scouts, some women, most of them lads, had been sent out to report on troop movements. Fortunately, there were none. They at least had the advantage of surprise.

The Military Council looked, for the last time as a team, at the map of Dublin. The city was shaped like an ellipse, ringed by two so-called circular roads and two canals, the Royal to the north, the

Grand to the south. Bisecting it was the River Liffey, running from west to east into Dublin Bay.

Plunkett pointed to their chief positions in a ring around the city. Two were north of the river: the GPO which was Headquarters, and the Four Courts or Justice Buildings. Four posts were to the south of the Liffey: the South Dublin Union, Jacob's Biscuit Factory, Stephen's Green and Boland's Bakery.

'Priority No 1, gentlemen,' said Plunkett in a hoarse, pained voice. 'We must cover the main British military Barracks which are sited at the four corners of the city. This is particularly necessary at the beginning to allow Headquarters to dig in at the GPO in O'Connell Street.'

At 11 a.m., Nathan was joined in his office by Major Price. In a buoyant mood, they started on their list of trouble-makers.

'Clarke' – Price began with the Castle's favourite adversary – 'McDermott, Connolly, MacNeill, Hobson and so on.'

Soon there were sixty rebels on the list.

'I can't wait to get my hands on them,' Price confessed.

With midday approaching, the four city battalions were forming across the city. Of the leaders, few had ever heard a shot fired in battle. Some of their men were not sure whether there were to be three days of manoeuvres or not. Hardly anyone knew that this was a rising.

Edward Daly was Commandant of the First Battalion. He was slight, upright, pale-faced, with a small moustache more suited to an older man, for he was only twenty-five. His command was the Four Courts and the area west of the GPO. In his district was the gigantic Royal Barracks, that would have daunted a force twenty times the size of the one he had.

His men assembled in a hall at Blackhall Place. They numbered 120; he was banking on 350.

His words were brief and to the point.

'Men, listen to me, and afterwards no applause. Today at noon, an Irish Republic will be declared. I look to every man to do his duty. The Volunteers are now part of the Irish Republican Army. In less than an hour we may be in action.'

Most were delighted, some were so shocked they started muttering that they wanted to see a priest. A few drifted away, saying,

247

'What would my mom say?' 'I'll have to tell my wife and kids about this.'

South of Daly's position, on the quays across the Liffey, was the Mendicity Institute. Once it was the most fashionable building in Dublin; now beggars came to it daily for meals. The dozen men in Daly's D Company had orders to take it over. In charge was Sean Heuston, a twenty-five-year-old Limerick man of dark features and few words. Connolly had asked him to hold the Mendicity for a few hours. They were to stop the British moving east till the rebels were dug in at the Four Courts and the GPO.

The main body of the Second Battalion, 150 men, armed with rifles, pickaxes and sledge-hammers, met in a shop near Stephen's Green.

In his ebullient way, Thomas MacDonagh said, 'This, my dear lads, is the task before us: to hold the mighty, the impregnable fortress of Jacob's, manufactory of the most delicious biscuits in the world.

'I have been all over it with James Connolly. It has two tall towers from which we shall have views of Dublin worth a shilling a look. We'll be able to see spectacular Dublin Castle to the north and Portobello Barracks to the south.

'And if that were not delight enough, we shall be able to supply other battalions with tons of cream puffs and chocolate biscuits.'

The Third Battalion was led by the much dourer Eamon de Valera. His job was to defend the eastern approaches to the city. British reinforcements were bound to come some time along the road from the Harbour at Kingstown (Dun Laoghaire). He also had to defend the last two miles of railway from Kingstown to Dublin, including Westland Row Station and the railway workshops. If that were not enough, he was to hold bridges over the canal and Boland's Bakery on Grand Canal Street.

To cover the enormous ground, he needed over 500 men. In the event, the companies from Kingstown and Blackrock who knew best the route the British soldiers would take from the harbour, did not muster. He was left with only 130.

Not a single woman appeared to help with the Red Cross or the commissariat. That was de Valera's own fault. He had put them off by his insistence that women were not to carry arms.

Seeing the size of the task ahead and the poverty of his forces, a terrible fear gripped his heart.

*

248

Eamonn Kent of the Fourth Battalion had an equally monumental task. He was to take over the South Dublin Union, a kind of small town of poor and elderly on fifty acres, with lodgings, kitchens and nursing facilities for over three thousand inmates. It was close to Kingsbridge Station in the west, the terminus for reinforcements that would soon be streaming in from British camps at the Curragh and Athlone. It was also adjacent to Richmond Barracks and the British military HQ in the Royal Hospital.

Kent had already established outposts in James's Street, Marrowbone Lane and put Con Colbert, a drill instructor and leading light in the Scout movement, in charge of Watkin's Brewery. Then he went to Emerald Square near Dolphin's Barn where the Fourth was due to muster.

Of 1,000 men on the roll, only 130 appeared.

'Men,' he said, with the brevity they were accustomed to, 'this is the real thing.'

The Fifth Battalion, led by Thomas Ashe, was to operate outside the city in the North County Dublin. They and the second section of MacDonagh's Battalion were the Post Office's only defences on the north of the city, leaving Headquarters in the GPO very vulnerable.

The rest of the rebels had been assembling at Liberty Hall since 10 o'clock.

At 11.45 a.m., William Oman sounded the bugle and 200 of the Citizen Army army fell in. Poorly equipped, untidily dressed, they were eager but ill-disciplined.

Tommy Keenan, a Boy Scout, was clutching his bag of food; he was twelve years old but looked younger. Others as small were checking items which their mothers had packed for them, from water bottles to bootlaces. Sewn inside their coats were field dressings. Some lads had turned up because they had no money to go anywhere else.

Inside, of the leaders, only Pearse, Connolly and Plunkett were left. Their one aim was not to disgrace Ireland. The success they were seeking was moral not military. They solemnly shook hands and walked out into the sun.

The Citizen Army divided into three. The section leaders had strict orders from Connolly not to shoot unarmed men. Since the DMP went unarmed, this meant they were not to shoot policemen.

Pat Fox, a widower, went up to Sergeant Robbins. He was

holding his only child, aged sixteen, by the hand. The lad was wearing his father's uniform, and it was too big for him. He also had his father's rifle.

'Frank,' Pat said, 'I'm too old for this. This here is me lad. Take him with you, please and rear him for me?'

'Sure.' Robbins was on the point of leaving with Mallin's crowd for the Green. 'What's your name, son?'

'Jimmy, sir.'

'Right y'are, Jimmy.'

Jimmy called out, 'Goodbye, Da.'

Sean Connolly, soon to head for the Castle, shook hands with a friend, saying, only half-jokingly, 'I'll be dead within the hour.'

William Partridge whispered to Bill O'Brien, 'Bob Monteith told me Casement thinks the rising should be called off.'

Partridge then joined the main body of the Citizen Army, numbering about 100. Mallin marched them to Stephen's Green. He took Jimmy Fox under his protection. He had planned to take the Shelbourne Hotel from where he would have been able to control the whole area. But not enough turned up. He put Jimmy with a squad digging trenches in the Green.

Back at the Hall, a second contingent of twenty-five, including nine women, were ready to leave for the Castle under Sean Connolly. His orders were not to take it, for it was a Red Cross Hospital, but to seal it up so its troops could not attack the GPO. James Connolly gave Helena Moloney a revolver before she marched off to the usual children's catcalls: 'There go the toy-soldiers.'

Some of the Castle contingent under Michael King had orders to seize the Telephone Exchange in Crown Alley. Others were to cut the wires from the Castle through the manhole in Dame Street in front of Lower Castle Yard.

The last group of the Citizen Army, with about seventy Volunteers, stayed outside the Hall. These made up the Headquarters Battalion. Pearse and Connolly now reviewed them.

Moving along the line, Connolly glanced anxiously at his own fifteen-year-old Roddy, his only son, as he stood to attention.

The one woman on parade was Connolly's sturdy no-nonsense secretary Winifred Carney. Bright sunshine filled the Square, shadowed only by the Loop Line railway bridge. Gulls squawked and soared on still wings above the malt-brown yeast-smelling Liffey.

Some of the Citizen Army had not been able to afford the dark-green uniform. They managed to give themselves a military air by putting a bandolier over the right shoulder and wearing a soft-brimmed hat. Some of them carried two rifles, the single-shot 1870 Mausers brought into Howth. Some had shotguns that had murdered many a crow. Some had pikes. A few had seven-pound sledge-hammers stolen from places of work like the docks.

Connolly was cheered when he told them that from now on there was no Irish Citizen Army and no Volunteers. They were the Irish Republican Army.

When Bill O'Brien repeated to Connolly what Partridge had said, he whispered back, 'We are going out to be slaughtered.'

'Is there no hope at all?'

'None whatever.'

Arthur Hamilton Norway, Secretary of the Post Office, had had a leisurely morning. After breakfasting in his Dawson Street hotel with his wife and his student son, Nevil, he went on to his club in O'Connell Street where he read the newspapers.

He was now in his elegant office in the GPO, handling a sword. The year before, he had lost his elder soldier son, Fred, near Armentières. He kept the boy's sword and colt automatic and a few souvenirs sent on by his regiment in his office safe. Two days before, Nevil had cleaned and oiled the Colt for him and charged the magazine with four extra clips. 'Keep it on you, Dad,' he said. 'These are dangerous times.'

In the last few months, from their hotel window they had witnessed Sinn Féiners parading and singing German war songs. Norway thought that Nathan listened far too much to Dillon, who sympathized with the rebels. In Nathan's last report there was a reference to the IRB being 'probably dormant'. Had he lived in the city centre and not in the peace of Phoenix Park, he might have thought differently.

Norway put the sword back in the safe and began a letter. At 11.50 a.m., there was a call from the Under-Secretary.

'Would you mind coming round? ... Yes, now. Urgent matter to attend to.'

Norway locked the safe and his office door. In the lobby, he handed his keys to the porter with, 'I'll be back in half an hour or so.'

As he went towards the exit, he felt very proud of this place, whose centenary renovations had been completed only six weeks ago. It had been a shambles when he took over. He glanced about him, admiring the large glass dome in the roof and the elaborate plaster-work, the mosaic floor, the counters all of red teak, the bright brass fittings.

He stepped out through the beautiful white pillars of the portico into the sunlight. His stroll to the Castle was brief and pleasant. Not a breath of wind ruffled the Liffey. Dame Street was a picture of peace.

No sooner was he in Nathan's office than he confirmed that the prisoner taken in Tralee had been identified as Casement.

'When he passed through here on Saturday night *en route* for London, there was no attempt to rescue him. There are rebels in the city, Norway, but they are a spent force.'

'I'm pleased to hear it.' Norway sounded sceptical.

'Naturally, we have the usual 400 soldiers on picket duty. Should be enough for the holiday, you think?' Norway nodded. 'Still, must act against the chief trouble-makers and soon.'

'Indeed, sir.' Norway's enthusiasm showed.

'That's why I asked you over. Need your help to restrict postal services to regions where the arrests will be made.'

Norway demurred. 'In a matter like this, sir, I would need written authorization.'

'Then, my dear fellow, you shall have it. Use my secretary's office. Write out whatever you think appropriate and I will sign it.'

The HQ Battalion was about to march off when The O'Rahilly drove up in his green dust-covered touring car. Pearse had not seen him since Good Friday when they had had their angry confrontation.

Seeing how young some of the soldiers were, The O'Rahilly looked on Pearse with something like loathing. And what were they going to use for bullets, rosary beads? But this was not the time for an open clash.

He jumped out of his car, saying, 'I've helped wind up the clock. Might as well hear it strike.'

Pearse took him by the hand. 'Thank you,' he said simply.

The O'Rahilly said, 'I trained these men. How can I let them fight without me?'

With the help of willing hands, The O'Rahilly started piling equipment into his car: spare rifles and ammunition; home-made bombs, many of them made out of tobacco tins, lengths of old pipe and tea canisters.

Just when Pearse was cheering up, his young and unhealthy-looking sister, Mary Brigid, appeared. She went up close to the Commander-in-Chief and said, in a thin but carrying voice, 'Will you come home, Pat, and leave all this foolishness?'

Connolly saved the situation by ordering his men, 'Form into fours.'

He had problems of his own. Michael King had just whispered in his ear that the men he needed to take the Central Telephone Exchange had not turned up. It was a disaster. British forces within the city would have no difficulty communicating.

'Never mind, Mick,' Connolly said. 'We'll take it later.'

Pearse, hollow-eyed from lack of sleep, placed himself at the head of the column. Behind him was Connolly, squat and bandy-legged, with his highly polished leggings. Next to Connolly was Joe Plunkett, the Chief of Staff. His neck was swathed in bandages and it hurt him even to walk. But in the best romantic tradition he unsheathed his sword for the march on the GPO.

Church bells rang out the midday Angelus, causing pious drunks in pubs to push their pints to arms' length, drowning out the megaphonic cry of gulls above the Liffey.

'Qui-ick, *march*,' Connolly commanded, and the Battalion set off on its three-minute march down Middle Abbey Street and across O'Connell Street, the grandest boulevard in Dublin. A right wheel brought them to the Post Office.

Waiting for them were Clarke and McDermott, who never wore uniform or took part in manoeuvres.

O'Connell Street was dominated by a 135-foot pillar, erected in 1808. On top was a thirteen-foot Nelson, carved out of soft white Portland stone. A number of men, women and children had paid their threepence for the privilege of climbing the Pillar's 168 narrow winding steps. On the balcony they looked down on the GPO, three-storeyed, with an Ionic portico of six fluted columns and a pediment topped by statues of Hibernia, Mercury and Fidelity.

Three famous adulterers were honoured in the Street. Apart from Nelson in the centre, to the north was the monument to Charles Stewart Parnell. To the south was the black statue of Daniel O'Connell who said, 'No amount of human liberty is worth the shedding of a single drop of human blood.'

Immediately below the sightseers on the Pillar balcony were a hundred armed and fully laden men.

For the sheer hell of it, Connolly yelled, 'Charge', and his troops, with pikes, rifles and bayonets held high, galloped through the columns into the Post Office.

Children squealed with delight as a few over-excited rebels fired in the air. The more cautious flower-sellers at the base of the Pillar bundled up their wares and scuttled off.

The GPO's main concourse was crowded with customers. Brandishing his revolver, Connolly called, 'Everybody out'. Many people, mistaking the uniforms, thought they were post office employees. A loud, very English voice was heard asking, 'What is the world coming to when you cannot buy a stamp in the General Post Office?'

As warning shots brought down some of the newly stuccoed ceiling, male clerks steeplechased the counters, while girl clerks struggled into coats and pulled on their hats.

Constable Dunphy, an elderly member of the DMP, was on duty and Lieutenant A. D. Chalmers of the 14th Royal Fusiliers was sending a telegram to his wife in London. Michael Collins, Joe Plunkett's *aide-de-camp*, took them prisoners.

'Don't shoot,' pleaded the policeman.

'We don't shoot prisoners,' Collins returned.

To put the insolent, loud-mouthed Lieutenant in his place, he trussed him up with telephone wire, hoisted him on his back and dumped him in a phone booth opposite the main door.

The rebels took over houses on the corners of the approach roads to the GPO and at the southern end of O'Connell Street, on Bachelor's Walk and Eden Quay.

Norway, having finished drawing up the Post Office document, knocked and entered the Under-Secretary's office.

Just then a group of the Irish Citizen Army marched up Cork Hill to the main Castle Gate. There were many veterans in the Castle Hospital, recovering from war wounds. Hearing the tramp of feet, the able-bodied among them rushed to the windows where they saw a contingent in green uniforms.

Sean Connolly had a key to the City Hall. From the roof, he would be able to cover the Castle Gate. But a big locked iron gate prevented him reaching the Hall door. It meant a swift change of plans. With a sixteen-strong squad, he directly approached the Upper Yard, known to the locals as 'The Devil's Half-Acre'. Over the gate sat the bronze figure of Justice, her back to the city. She was holding scales, both of them holed to stop the rain forcing one pan lower than the other, thus spoiling the illusion of equity.

On guard was PC James O'Brien and a soldier with a rifle loaded with blanks. The nurses coming and going always received a smile or a salute from the tall Constable with greying hair and twinkling eyes. A nurse who had been off duty for a couple of hours said, 'Sinn Feiners are parading in town. People say they're going to attack the Castle.' The Constable winked at the Tommy beside him. 'We've heard that sort of silly talk before, miss.'

The nurse passed through the gate as Sean Connolly's squad came on the scene, brandishing their weapons. The soldier, not used to this sort of thing, levelled his rifle threateningly. The Constable, pushing it aside, held up his hand.

'Let's have no trouble, lads. Can't you go somewhere else on a nice day like this?'

Yesterday, they would have listened. Not today. This policeman was guarding a building that represented the imperial power that had ground the noses of Irish people in the dust for centuries.

Sean Connolly, a small, lean man, was on edge like the rest. His thin chin quivered, he breathed heavily through the nostrils of a prominent nose, his narrow eyes got narrower. A professional actor, he knew little or nothing about warfare. He took it for granted that the Castle was swarming with troops who would soon come rushing at them.

As PC O'Brien was pushing the gate closed, Connolly's finger trembled on the trigger of his rifle. Knowing the Constable was not armed, he gave him one last chance.

'For God's sake, man, will you get out of the way?'

Nathan's pen was poised to sign the Post Office order, when the shot rang out. The gate was only twenty-five yards from his window. 'What in the name of—?'

Even Norway, hard of hearing, jumped. 'What's that?'

Nathan grabbed a revolver out of a drawer. 'That,' he said, 'is probably the long-promised attack on the Castle.'

For James O'Brien, death was instantaneous. Half his head was blown away at short range.

'Get on in.'

Despite Sean Connolly's order, his men held back, overwhelmed with horror at what they had done.

Another policeman came round the corner to investigate.

255

Helena Moloney saved his life by firing her revolver in the air and sending him rushing for cover.

A priest who chanced to be passing knelt to give the Constable the last rites.

Countess Markievicz had arrived in Dr Kathleen Lynn's car just in time to see the Constable fall.

Dr Lynn said, 'Let's get these medical supplies into the City Hall.'

Sean Connolly had to open the Hall and organize other outposts. He left the Castle to Lieutenant Tom Kain. With only half a dozen men, all Kain could hope to do was try and prevent soldiers leaving the Castle precinct. Stepping round the Constable's body, he made for the guard-room where the soldier had run for cover.

'Stand aside,' he called out to his men, as he threw a home-made grenade into the room. Though it failed to explode, they charged in to find six soldiers who surrendered without a fight. The rebels tied them up with their own puttees and grabbed the key to the Upper Yard Gate.

Nathan was rapidly trying to assess the situation. General Friend was in London. Next in seniority in the Irish Command was Brigadier-General Lowe, and he was at the Curragh. Substituting was Colonel Cowan.

The CO of the Castle garrison, Colonel Kennard, was also absent. Deputizing was his Adjutant, Major Lewis.

Not only was the top brass missing. The Ship Street garrison nearby, because of the holiday, had barely two officers and twenty-five men. It hit Nathan like a blow that Dublin Castle was at the mercy of the Sinn Feiners.

With Norway standing gaping, Nathan left the room, while Price leaped to the window, emptied his revolver at the rebels and yelled a few orders before following Nathan at the double.

Norway made his way downstairs to where the Castle messengers were huddled, trembling. They had seen Constable O'Brien lying by the Gate in a pool of blood.

Price returned to Nathan's office and telephoned the Ship Street Barracks for reinforcements. He was relieved to find that the telephone worked. It suggested that the rebels were not too well organized.

He tried the telephone to Irish Command HQ at Parkgate. It was dead. Now he was not so sure.

The main force of the Citizen Army under Sean Connolly finally gained entry to the City Hall. Others took over the offices of two newspapers, the *Daily Express* and the *Evening Mail*. From these heights, their snipers had commanding views of the Castle area, including Nathan's department.

The troops left the Ship Street Barracks at the double. Some paused to shut the solid iron Castle Gate behind them and manned the peep-holes. Outside, there were no armed rebels, only a few small ragged children, staring at them open-mouthed.

The rest of the force ran into the Upper Yard where they were met by a withering hail of fire from the surrounding buildings. One group of soldiers went to the Lower Gate and shot dead a man in civvies. He happened to be one of their own, a Sergeant-Major on leave from Donegal.

In the State Rooms overlooking the Upper Yard, nurses were tending the sixty-seven wounded veterans. They saw puffs of smoke as snipers on nearby roofs fired on soldiers who were trying to recover the body of the Constable. They eventually picked him up and carried him into the hallway where his helmet fell off. There were two holes in his head, the exit wound being particularly large as though he had been hit with a dum-dum bullet.

Wandering around, Norway found Nathan with the store-keeper breaking into the armoury to get weapons for the DMP. There were a few revolvers but no cartridges.

In his office near Nathan's, the Chief Superintendent of the DMP sent out an alert. 'I want every available man, also cars and ammunition, to get here at the double.'

The defence of the Castle now rested on Major Lewis. He was rapidly doing his sums. In Dublin there were about 2,500 troops. Each of the Barracks kept a picket of 100 on permanent standby to assist the DMP in a crisis.

One thing worried him. Most of the troops, indeed all the infantry, were Irish. Would they fire on their fellow-countrymen? Ulstermen wouldn't. But even if they remained loyal, would 2,500 troops be enough? He had as yet no idea of the enemy's strength. It was prudent to call out reserves from the four main Dublin Barracks.

Nearest the Castle was Richmond Barracks at Kilmainham.

'Send all your men to the Castle at once,' he told the CO, 'fully armed.'

The CO had scarcely put the telephone down when he had a second call: 'Sinn Feiners have seized the Post Office.'

Though a picket left Richmond within half an hour, for reasons beyond its control it did not reach the Castle until 9.35 that night.

It was early morning in New York when Mrs McGowan, Devoy's secretary-cum-housekeeper, ran excitedly into his office. 'It's come, sir.'

'It' was a message sent the previous day by Tim Ring, the telegraphist on Valentia Island: 'To Mrs McGowan: Mother operated on successfully today. Signed, Kathleen.'

Devoy immediately reached for the telephone to tell others in the Clan that the rising had begun.

By a quirk of fate, the Americans and the Germans heard of the rising just before the British with their extraordinary intelligence network.

Sean Heuston and his men broke into the Mendicity Institute. Having chased out staff and beggars, they secured doors and windows. Heuston posted his best marksmen at the windows from where they had a splendid view of the quays and across the Liffey to the Royal Barracks. Next, he supervised the building of a barricade on the quayside.

As yet, the Royal Barracks showed no signs of life. Heuston prayed that they had not been seen breaking in.

Even so, he had no doubts that the next few hours would be the busiest in his short life.

Not far away to the east, Eamonn Kent, with forty of his men stationed in outposts, set about taking the South Dublin Union and defending it against potentially massive opposition.

At a bridge over the Liffey, he and his small party were heartened to run into the Volunteers from the Plunkett family home at Kimmage. With their pikes and blunderbusses, they commandeered a tram. George Plunkett ordered the driver at gun-point to take them non-stop into the city.

He put aside his gun to get at his wallet. 'Fifty-two tuppenny tickets, please.'

Kent's men entered the Union from two directions and met up at the front gate. The complex not only housed sick and elderly; it had six dormitories for the insane as well as several maternity wards. They chose as their HQ a three-storey stone building, the Nurses' Home, on the west side of the Union.

From Richmond Barracks came the strains of the military band.

'They don't know we're here yet,' Cathal Brugha said.

The music died in the middle of a phrase.

'They know now,' Kent muttered.

In the Four Courts area, Daly posted a few men around Church Street where the Capuchins had a Hall. The fathers agreed to let them use it as a hospital.

He posted snipers everywhere, especially in North King Street which ran east-west across the top of Church Street. He had trams overturned to make barricades and broken glass spread in the roads to prevent a cavalry charge.

He sent twenty men under Joe McGuinness to take the Four Courts next to the Liffey. Under its giant dome were the law courts. Four men broke into the Lord Chancellor's Chambers, smashed the tall picture windows overlooking the Liffey and barricaded them with big legal tomes.

British law had some use, after all.

MacDonagh marched his Second Battalion from the Green to Jacob's biscuit factory. On the way, they passed a group of Mallin's men under Jim MacCormack who were about to take over Harcourt Street Station. MacDonagh called out, 'Make sure, Captain, that you avoid unnecessary bloodshed.'

Outside Jacob's, they took over a couple of pubs in a warren of streets and backstreets, then demolished the factory's main gate in Bishop's Street with axes and hammers. A ladder was chained to a lamppost and swung in an arc to break the windows for easy entrance. A couple of policemen came running to investigate but ran away even faster when half a dozen rifles were pointed at them.

Inside the huge triangular building, some employees thought it was a joke until a few shots convinced them otherwise. Still in their white overalls, they rushed headlong for home.

Burly John MacBride, who chanced to be passing, recognized the sacred sounds of battle. He went in to find Volunteers barricading windows with flour-bags. Men in grey-green uniforms were in the tall towers surveying the area through field-glasses.

MacDonagh said, 'You heard about the rising, then, Major?'

259

MacBride shook his head. 'Can't you see I'm dressed up for a wedding?'

'Shame,' said MacDonagh.

'Shame be buggered,' yelled MacBride, tugging off his jacket.

Thirty-five-year-old James Joyce, a private in the Citizen Army, with ten others approached the public house near the Portobello Bridge. The pub commanded the approaches to the military barracks. Joyce was in a good mood. He worked an eighty-four hour week for Davy, the landlord. He kicked in the front door to find the boss himself behind the bar pouring a pint for a customer.

Davy looked sourly at his watch. 'You're late. I'm giving you a week's notice.'

Joyce levelled his rifle at his head. 'And I'm giving you, you ould buzzard, just a few seconds.'

Davy dropped the glass with a crash and headed for the door as the rebels fired at all the bottles on the shelves.

At Boland's, a mill complex on the side of a stagnant canal, Eamon de Valera set up his HQ in a small dispensary next to the Bakery and posted his men around.

'Be sure,' he said, 'and feed the horses.'

A dozen of his B Company were in Westland Row Station. Deaf to the protests of the top-hatted Station-Master, they cut wires, erected barricades and put a guard on the entrance. When a number of priests tried to get on the train to Kingstown, they were stopped by Volunteers who levelled shaky rifles at them. The youngsters were more used to being threatened by gentlemen of the cloth. One priest argued that to risk the lives of innocent people was a grave sin. Soon Volunteers were kneeling in a line on the platform, gripping their rifles and confessing to all their sins save that of fighting the British Empire.

One of de Valera's squads removed parts from Ringsend electricity supply station, bringing city trams to a halt.

He posted fourteen men around Mount Street Bridge over the Grand Canal.

'In the next couple of days, hundreds of British troops will land in Kingstown and come along this road,' he said. 'Keep them out at all costs.'

In Trinity College, just south of O'Connell Street, eight members of the University Officers Training Corps were on duty. Hearing of the rising, they slammed shut the main oak doors and sent for reinforcements.

They even asked passers-by in their polished garrison accents to come in and fight for King and country.

'Rifles, my dear fellows, will be provided.'

A group of thirty men and lads had arrived by tram and bicycle in the Phoenix Park, by the Islandbridge Gate. Nearby, on the brow of a hill, was the Magazine Fort. A squat stone building, it was surrounded by barbed wire and surmounted by a castellated terrace.

They played soccer in view of the sentry on guard at the Fort's open gate but were careful how they ran. In their pockets or under their armpits were loaded revolvers.

In London, just after midday, Birrell finally received Nathan's message of the night before. He sent it over at once to Downing Street to be deciphered.

He opened his Cabinet pouch and read an odd report, passed on by the Foreign Office. The British Ambassador in Washington said that the FBI had raided a German office in New York and found details of gun-running for a rising in Ireland on 23 April.

He was puzzled. The so-called gun-running had taken place on Good Friday, the 21st. As to a rising planned for some time on Easter Sunday, that, he thought, smiling, must have come and gone yesterday without anyone noticing.

At 12.10 p.m., Colonel Cowan received a call at Military HQ, Irish Command. The DMP told him the Castle had been attacked and warned him there might be outbreaks elsewhere in the country.

Cowan promptly took steps to reinforce the Castle and the Vice-regal Lodge. It struck him that he ought also to put an extra guard on the Magazine Fort in Phoenix Park.

The soccer players had been kicking the ball around for some time when Paddy Daly saw Tim Roche arrive in a jaunting car.

'Christ Almighty,' Daly exclaimed. 'He was meant to bring a motor car.'

Roche *had* stolen a motor car for a quick get-away, only to drive it straight into a lamppost. He had then hailed the vehicle in which he was now sitting next to the jarvey.

Daly signalled his pal, Garry Holohan. With his good right boot, Holohan kicked the ball through the Fort Gate. The sentry's grin as the players raced over to retrieve it vanished when they jumped him and relieved him of his rifle. They trussed him up and gagged him.

The raiders caught the young soldiers in the guard-room unprepared, only to be themselves surprised by the sentry on the four-foot high parapet above. He was too shaken to fire.

'Surrender,' yelled Holohan.

When the sentry raised his rifle, Holohan fired twice and badly wounded him. As he stood over him, the sentry whispered, with blood streaming from his thigh, 'Don't kill me. I'm Irish myself. Five kids.'

Holohan assured him they would let his pals know.

Paddy Daly, the explosives expert, had been told the keys to the storeroom with TNT would be on a board in the guard-room. They were not there.

Most of the Playfairs, the CO's family, were in the Fort.

'Where,' Holohan demanded of Mrs Isabel Playfair, 'are the fecking keys?'

'At the Races,' she said, shaking all over. 'My husband put them in his pocket.'

They tried breaking down the door but it would not give. They piled up boxes of small arms ammunition in several rooms, smothered them with five bags of gelignite and set the fuses. They hoped the blast would trigger off the explosives inside.

The guards, with the Playfairs, were released and told to run like hell.

The rebels dispersed. Some, with captured rifles, jumped into the jaunting car and made for the south-eastern gate of the Park. Holohan on a bicycle covered their rear.

It was he who noticed the Playfair lad, aged about seventeen, running out of the Park, to raise the alarm at the Barracks. He pedalled madly, calling after him to stop, but he took no notice. He came level with the lad as he arrived at the soldiers' billets and was banging on a door.

A woman opened up as the lad turned to face Holohan. They were both heaving for breath. Their eyes met, full of fear.

Not wanting this to hurt, Holohan took careful aim and shot him three times.

*

Not far away, outside the Viceregal Lodge, His Lordship's party was about to step into the limousines.

Wimborne heard the small arms ammunition exploding in the Fort and thought it was a car backfiring until an aide rushed out of the house with the news.

'A *what*? A rising?' The Viceroy's narrow moustache bristled yet he was not displeased. This proved beyond doubt that he was the one man in Ireland who saw things clearly, chiefly because, on principle, he despised all Irishmen.

His self-righteousness was somewhat dented when an officer said, 'May I suggest, Excellency, that you take cover.'

'Cover?'

Lord Blackwood pointed out that the lodge's only defence was a sunken ditch curving around the long low fence. There was no military guard and, with the Races on, reinforcements might take time.

Just then a shell landed nearby. They were not to know that it came not from rebels but from excited soldiers, firing at random. With Wimborne in the lead, they all ran inside for cover. His Excellency poured himself the stiffest of brandies. He wanted to be proven right, but not posthumously. Having emptied his glass, he knew exactly what he had to do. He poured himself another.

The rebels in the GPO had grown to 200 as news of the rising spread.

Connolly was trying to organize them. Pearse was walking up and down, looking very impressive, with Willie, his long-haired, pale-faced brother, shadowing him. Joe Plunkett was lying down on a mattress in front of the counter trying to conserve his strength. Seeing him there in his immaculate uniform and with a white silk scarf draped round his neck, young Connolly nudged his father and grinned. Connolly took his son aside and muttered, 'That man, Roddy, has more courage in his little finger than all the other leaders combined.'

The O'Rahilly, still hurt by Pearse's distrust, pointed out that they ought to occupy the upstairs offices. Pearse told Michael Staines to see to it.

With half a dozen men armed with revolvers and automatics, Staines crept up the stairs just as telegraph girls were streaming down.

One of the girls called out, 'Hello, Michael! That's the stuff to give 'em!'

He halted his men on the landing opposite the Telegraph Office, the nerve centre of the GPO system. It was bound to be well guarded. There were stealthy movements inside. The guard must have heard noises below and locked themselves in.

Staines gestured to his men to fire through the door. Immediately, voices called out, 'We surrender.'

The rebels rushed in to find themselves looking down the rifle barrels of seven servicemen. These promptly dropped their weapons on the floor where their sergeant was lying with a head wound.

Staines was appalled at their cowardice until a British NCO said, 'We've no ammo for our rifles.'

The guard on the Central Telegraph Office had not one live round between them.

They got the Sergeant, a Scot, to his feet. A bullet had grazed his forehead.

Staines said, 'Take him to Jervis Street Hospital.'

'I'm no' going,' the Sergeant said, with a strong burr.

'Indeed, you are,' Staines insisted.

'Listen, mon,' the Sergeant said, blood pouring down his cheek, 'I've been told to guard this place till 18.00 hours and, by God, tha's what I intend to do.'

'If I give you my word,' Staines said, 'that I'll let you back, will you go and get treatment?'

They shook on it.

The manageress of the Telegraph Office was also a Scot.

'Wha'ever happens, I'm no' goin',' she growled.

Daunted by her tone, Staines warned her not to touch any instrument. He did not want her alerting the enemy.

She held up a batch of telegrams. 'Might I at least send these off? Announcements of deaths.'

'Our own people will do it.'

'Very well,' she said in a huff, 'if tha's your attitude, I'm off.'

On the roof, pigeons were disturbed as the Union Jack was hauled down. The Countess's green bedspread with its gold and mustard lettering and its edges mauled by Poppet, was hoisted instead. The tricolour, green, white and yellow, was also flown.

This was Ireland now.

Around the stone balustrade, snipers were posted, youngsters for the most part. They waved to comrades across the street in the

Imperial Hotel, owned by William Martin Murphy, the most hated capitalist in the land. On the Imperial's roof, the Irish Citizen Army were raising their flag of the Plough and the Stars, slight revenge for all they had suffered at Murphy's hands in the strike of 1913.

There were more waves to fellow snipers manning houses at street corners opposite, before the rebels went on their knees to say the first of an unending line of rosaries.

In the lobby below, Connolly's voice boomed out. 'Shut and bar the doors. Smash those windows and barricade 'em with typewriters, furniture, mailbags, whatever's handy.'

His orders were punctuated by shots from guns that went off by accident and cries from women in the street, 'Glory be to God, they're murdering our new Post Office.'

Through the Prince's Street gate, The O'Rahilly finished unloading his second batch of supplies in the covered courtyard. As he entered the lobby, many wondered what he was doing there. Word was he had done his best to stop the rising. Sensing their disapproval, Pearse went and shook his hand. There was still a coolness between them; but at last they were on the same side.

With the rebels inside the guard-room to the right of the Gate, an eerie silence settled on the Castle. Kain, peering through the window, could not understand why the enemy were not trying to flush them out. He did not realize that for the first time since the thirteenth century the Castle was a plum for the taking.

In the end, convinced that the British were hatching a deadly plot against them, he withdrew.

Soon, firing from the City Hall and the newspaper offices was returned by the military. Volleys swept Cork Hill.

When Dr Kathleen Lynn's car was unloaded, the Countess Markievicz drove it from the City Hall to Stephen's Green. As a staff officer, her job was to liaise between Mallin and the GPO.

She left the Castle area as Skeffy arrived. He saw a British officer, Captain Pinfield, fall wounded just inside the Castle Gate. Without a thought for himself, Skeffy ran to help. He saw at once that the Captain was badly hurt. He hurried to a nearby chemist and, in his high-pitched voice, urged, 'Come. We can't leave a man to bleed to death.'

With bullets striking the cobbles all round them, they reached the

Gate just as soldiers were dragging the Captain inside. The two of them turned tail and fled for cover.

In the Green, Mallin, having emptied the Park of courting couples and mothers wheeling babies in prams, closed the eight gates.

Some of his men were forcing carters to uncouple the horses which had been busily munching in their nose bags and form the carts into barricades across the road. Others were digging trenches in the flower beds.

Mallin's orders were to stop all traffic coming up the approach roads. Unfortunately, in the trenches, they made a perfect target from the tall buildings around them. Lacking the men to occupy the Shelbourne on the north side, the best they could do was to post snipers in houses at street corners leading to the Green.

The only policeman on duty was twenty-eight-year-old Michael Lahiff. He peered through the railings at what Dubliners called the Traitors' Gate, an arch erected in honour of Irishmen who had fought for Britain during the Boer War. Rebels inside the Green told him to go away.

'What do you think you're up to?' he wanted to know.

When he took no notice of a second warning, they shot him three times. He was taken to the nearby Meath Hospital where he died soon after admission.

When the Countess drove up with medical supplies, Mallin told her that owing to shortage of personnel he wanted her to take charge of digging trenches and barricading the Green.

'I'll need you as a sniper, too,' he said. 'I'm short of marksmen.'

'Suits me, old bean,' and the Countess joined in, hijacking any vehicle that came her way and taking over a couple of abandoned trams for barricades.

A commissariat and a Red Cross post were set up in the Green's summer house. Nellie Gifford and the Countess's friend, Madeleine ffrench-Mullen, were in charge. They set out delicate cakes and fine-cut sandwiches on silver salvers and, when Madam had her first breather, offered her tea in a cup and saucer of bone-china.

'How positively *egregious*,' she said.

When Birrell was handed Nathan's message of the day before, now decoded, he murmured, 'Splendid idea. Couldn't be a better time to round all the rebels up.'

He was keen to continue with his novel of the French Revolution – life was *so* exciting in those days – but first things first.

Having wired Nathan permission to imprison the Sinn Feiners and take over their strongholds, he went to the Home Office to inform Sir Edward Troup, the Permanent Secretary. From there, he went across to Scotland Yard for an update on the interrogation of Sir Roger Casement.

'It's pouring out of him,' Basil Thomson said.

Augustine Birrell could not remember a time when Irish affairs had given him so much pleasure.

When Colonel Cowan at HQ Ireland Command placed a call to the Curragh at 12.30 p.m., he was surprised to find the line still open.

The Curragh was only thirty miles away. On standby, in case of a German invasion, there was a 1,600-strong mobile column. He told the CO to prepare the 3rd Cavalry Brigade at once. Kingsbridge Station was sending trains to transport them to Dublin.

Cowan's luck held. He got through to Athlone, eighty miles from Dublin, with a request for artillery. They said the 4th Battery Royal Fusiliers from Templemore would make ready at once. A final call summoned troops from Belfast.

MacNeill had not believed The O'Rahilly's message about a rising. He cycled to Dr O'Kelly's in Rathgar.

'Seamus,' he was saying, 'I feel really grieved that a clique should try and use my movement for their own violent ends,' when in burst Sean Fitzgibbon.

'The rising. It's started.'

'But . . .,' MacNeill began. 'But that's not possible. It must be a few trigger-happy Volunteers who failed to see my notice in the *Sunday Independent*.'

Another guest was a colleague of MacNeill's, a lecturer in French. Liam O'Briain had spent the day before spreading the countermand. 'I'll go and see,' he offered.

Meanwhile, MacNeill sat down as though he were in a trance, stroking his grey-tinged beard.

O'Briain cycled along the Grand Canal to Portobello Barracks. Troops were hiding behind the canal wall as they fired on Davy's pub with rifles and a Maxim gun. The noise of battle was coming from every quarter of the city.

He cycled back to report.

For five minutes, MacNeill sat sucking his dead pipe. Then, in a choky voice: 'I'll just have to go home and get my uniform, won't I? My friends, my comrades are fighting and dying. I have to join them.'

Having said that, he remained motionless in his chair. It was simply against his conscience to join in a rebellion he held to be sinful. He cycled back home.

'What's up, darling?'

MacNeill knelt beside his wife's chair and put his head in her lap. For the first time, she saw him weeping.

'Everything, Eileen,' he sobbed, 'everything is ruined.'

It was 12.45 p.m. when Pearse walked out of the GPO to read the Proclamation of the Republic.

Joe Plunkett stood by a window to watch. Across the street, in the Imperial Hotel, he picked out the slim figure of his fiancée, Grace Gifford, in her brightest clothes; and his heart went out to her. She was one of a party come to celebrate Geraldine Plunkett's marriage to Thomas Dillon the day before. He waved and Grace waved back.

Flanked by Clarke and Connolly, Pearse went, loam-footed, to the middle of the boulevard, with his back to Admiral Lord Nelson. This was the high-point of his life, a moment to put even his oration over the grave of O'Donovan Rossa in the shade. But he read in an out-of-character mumble.

Magnificent words floated lifeless in the air.

> In the name of God and of the dead generations ...
> Ireland, through us, summons her children to her flag and
> strikes for her freedom ... We hereby proclaim the Irish
> Republic as a sovereign state ... The Republic guarantees
> religious and civil liberty, equal rights and opportunities to
> all its citizens ... cherishing all the children of the nation
> equally.

The first citizens of the new Republic greeted it with cheers and hoots as if this were a Christmas pantomime. But Tom Clarke was trembly and misty-eyed; and James Connolly was pumping Pearse's hand, saying, 'Thanks be to God that we've lived to see this day.'

As to Pearse himself, he knew it was hard to arouse patriotism for a country that had not existed for seven hundred years. The action-play they were staging was perfect. Though this generation might give it bad reviews, posterity would not.

One witness of the birth of the Republic was a journalist and classical scholar with a shock of blue-black hair and brooding eyes. Stephen MacKenna, in his mid-forties, had been a freedom fighter in foreign lands. He was mesmerized; could this great thing be happening at home, in dear old Dublin? Feeble and arthritic, he stood resting on his stick in that same place hour after hour. 'At last,' he kept muttering. 'At last.'

Copies of the Proclamation were pasted on the base of Nelson's Pillar, outside the GPO and inside the lobby where the rebels cheered. It was official: they were a Republic.

Soldiers of the Republican Army started ripping off recruitment posters and replacing them with the Proclamation.

'In future,' they cried, 'Irishmen will only fight for Ireland.'

Birrell was scarcely back from Scotland Yard when into the Irish Office burst Sir John Denton Pinkstone-French, fingering his white moustache in annoyance. A junior officer in civvies had cycled from Dublin to Kingstown with a message that was relayed by wireless from a naval vessel in the harbour.

In his best I-told-you-so voice, French said: 'There has been a rising in Dublin at 12.00 hours.'

Birrell listened dumb-founded. It was bad enough in itself but coming from the Commander-in-Chief who had repeatedly questioned his political judgement it was doubly galling. Only on 12 February, he had assured him categorically that there was no chance of a rising.

This was one of those rare moments when a man's life makes a complete somersault, when, in an instant, he knows his world can never be the same again. Into his mind flashed an old saying: 'In Ireland, the unexpected *always* happens, the inevitable *never*.' He wondered what the PM, out of town for the Easter weekend, would make of his miscalculation. That cable from the British Ambassador in Washington did not seem so odd now.

French did not wait for explanations. He was making arrangements for two infantry brigades of the 59th Division to be sent over the Irish Sea, post-haste.

Birrell tried to telegraph Nathan but, ominously, the line to Dublin was out of order. The only incoming messages were over the Government wire from the Viceregal Lodge.

He wrote to Nathan for detailed information. He then phoned

Redmond but there was no reply. He sent him a wire, instead, a kind of SOS. 'Bad news from Dublin – a serious *insurrection*. It looks bad, though as the troops are coming in from the Curragh it can have, I suppose, but one ending.'

In Scotland Yard, Casement was seated in an uncomfortable armchair with tiny legs. Thomson liked towering over suspects. He used to watch them pathetically try to raise themselves to his level, realize their inferiority was more than physical, subside and then answer all his questions.

Not that Casement was likely to be cowed. Thomson and Hall, knowing his heroic history, were aware that he fitted none of their usual categories.

The phone rang. Thomson answered it with, 'Yes? . . . Yes . . . I see.'

Afterwards, the mood of the interrogation became blacker, though Casement had no clue as to why.

In the GPO, The O'Rahilly was cheered by the arrival of Desmond Fitzgerald. He, too, had been opposed to the rising.

The O'Rahilly took charge of the upper floors, chiefly to distance himself from the other leaders. Pearse was trying to be friendly but Clarke and McDermott stayed cool. Fitzgerald was put in charge of stores. He sent youngsters out to forage for food, medicines and bedding.

'Give a receipt,' The O'Rahilly said, 'and promise them the new Republic will pay them later.'

The youngsters went for bedding to the Metropole next door where the manager greeted their promises of compensation with uglier, more realistic promises of his own.

In the Post Office lobby, the policeman taken prisoner had been put out of action by the removal of his boots. He sat in a corner clutching a bottle of Guinness, embarrassed because those brightly polished boots had hidden a pair of dirty grey socks full of holes. Next to him, Lieutenant Chalmers, released from the telephone booth, was rapidly consuming a bottle of brandy to calm his fears. When it was empty, with tears in his eyes, he asked for another.

A burly workman pushed up to Fitzgerald. 'I'm one of Jim Larkin's men,' he said in a boozy voice. 'Is there no drink for one of Jim Larkin's men?'

Fitzgerald told a girl to fetch him a glass of water. Jim Larkin's man promptly withdrew his support for the revolution.

The Scottish Sergeant returned with his head bandaged, only to be locked up in the basement with his men.

An elderly man came into the foyer and called out a girl's name. 'Your mammy wants you, darlin'. Will ye come home this instant like a good girl.'

Outside, a number of priests in cassocks and stove-pipe hats linked hands across O'Connell Street. Moving like a black tide up and down, they tried to persuade the crowd to disperse. Even threats of eternal damnation had no effect.

'Dear God,' one of them sighed, 'even St Pat with a belt of his crozier could not knock a splinter of sense into 'em.'

At the river end of O'Connell Street, a fifty-strong party of Lancers passed by, escorting five ammunition trucks from the North Wall to Marlborough Barracks. The outposts of the GPO on the quays were itching to fire on them but, since their own defences were not yet complete, they let them pass.

The Lancers rode blithely on along the Liffey towards the Four Courts. At Ormond Quay they ran into Ned Daly's men who were building a barricade. They opened fire, bringing down eight Lancers whose horses, a lather of blood and sweat, panicked in the narrow streets. The rest galloped for cover and locked themselves in buildings in Charles Street.

A couple of Lancers, separated from the main party, went wild and let off their carbines, killing a little girl before being shot themselves.

A rebel grabbed the lance of one of them and, at the end of North King Street, wedged it in a manhole with the tricolour flying from it.

Colonel Kennard, Commander of the Dublin garrison, arrived at Portobello round about 1 o'clock, fresh from his vacation. The picket that might have escorted him to the Castle had just left and was pinned down around Davy's pub.

The Barracks were in chaos. Few of the men had been under fire before and they were being sniped at from the north, from the towers in Jacob's biscuit factory.

Unable to move, Kennard contacted Lewis, his adjutant, by phone and was relieved that the Castle had not fallen.

A woman in a shawl and long skirt appeared in the Barracks and the CO, Major Rosborough, said to a corporal, 'Get her out of here.'

Throwing her shawl aside, she said, in a most unwomanly voice, 'Sergeant MacAdam reporting for duty, sir.'

He had been visiting friends near the Green and been forced to come in disguise.

Minutes later, a second company of Lancers appeared at the top of O'Connell Street on perfectly groomed and caparisoned steeds. Their orders from Colonel Cowan were to flush out the rebels in the GPO.

They formed up near the Parnell Monument, carbines in their holsters, ceremonial lances at the ready. Their CO, Colonel Hammond, was not taking this too seriously. He saw pedestrians on the parapet of O'Connell Bridge and hanging from lampposts, waiting for the show to commence; and there were those preposterous flags flying from the GPO.

He ordered his men to fan out across the 154-foot boulevard. Then, with his raised sword aglow with the sun, 'For-*ward*.' This was a parade-ground exercise. No damned Irishmen would have the cheek to fire on his lads.

The troop, upright in their saddles, lances at the ready, nut-brown leather shining, gleaming spurs a-jangle, cantered southwards, before breaking into a gallop.

In the GPO the Republicans waited dry-mouthed for their first taste of battle.

'Hold your fire,' barked Connolly in the lobby, as his men peered through the windows over the sandbags.

'Hold your fire,' called out The O'Rahilly to the sharp-shooters on the top-floor and the roof.

Tom Clarke could hardly contain his excitement. The Irish were actually going to fire on British cavalry! He had dreamed of this in prison days.

The newly arrived Rathfarnam Volunteers chose this moment to rush across O'Connell Street to the side door of the Post Office, only to find it locked. Some of them smashed windows and hauled themselves in, gashing themselves badly. A stray bullet from a rebel sniper dropped a sixteen-year-old and, in the scramble, a Volunteer shot himself in the belly.

With horses' hooves thundering on the cobbles and sparks rising off four sets of tramlines, discipline in the GPO broke down. The

Lancers were level with the Pillar when ragged rifle fire broke out from the upper windows. Four of them fell spectacularly.

The Colonel, waving his sword, yelled, 'Back! Get back, men.'

With a couple of riderless horses, they wheeled and galloped back to the Monument.

'The Leopardstown Races,' one wit called out.

The troop left four of their dead on the ground and a dead horse. Another horse was nuzzling his rider on the ground. There was another burst of firing and the great glossy beast collapsed like a broken spring with a ribbon of blood trickling from each nostril, dead beside its dead master.

The rebels were jubilant, with Clarke calling out, 'Whoopee!' but Connolly was furious that they had lost a golden opportunity of bringing down the entire troop. But at least the British knew they could not be dislodged by tactics that had failed even in the Crimea.

Even Connolly failed to realize that all the attack proved was how vulnerable HQ was from the north.

As Red Cross and St John Ambulance workers took away the dead, the Lancers at the Parnell Monument were surrounded by a crowd who stroked the restive mounts and said, 'What a terrible thing for them madmen to shoot at our brave soldiers.'

A group of black-shawled women from the slums, their bad teeth looking like mouth organs, approached the GPO. They were utterly fearless, having nothing to lose but their lives.

'Would you be moidering them poor men?' they screamed, shaking shiny fists at rebels who were grateful for their barricades. 'Dear God in heaven, is it you are not Christians at all, shooting them darlin', feckin' horses?'

From an upper window of the Mendicity Institute, Heuston's men saw an entire regiment of the Royal Dublin Fusiliers leave the Royal Barracks and march four-abreast eastwards along the quays towards the Four Courts.

'Looks interesting,' said Heuston. 'Wait for it.'

The troops on the other side of the Liffey were opposite the Institute when Heuston gave the order, 'Now!'

The British, most of them raw recruits, panicked and ran for cover, leaving a large number dead or wounded. Some hid behind the quay walls and inside an abandoned tramcar. Others rushed for side streets, unsure where the firing was coming from.

*

273

Further to the west, Lieutenant-Colonel R. L. Owens, the Battalion Commander from Richmond Barracks, was in charge of about 200 men. Ahead of him was his infantry picket under Major Holmes who was moving slowly and circumspectly to relieve the Castle.

Holmes knew the GPO had been taken. Seeing uniformed men behind the wall of the South Dublin Union, he halted and sent Lieutenant Malone with twenty men to flush them out.

Kent's men fired on them, wounding three, but Malone made it into the buildings opposite the Union and returned fire.

Owens reinforced the picket with another hundred men.

With the British beginning to encircle the Union, Kent already knew he had a real scrap on his hands when, 300 yards away, from the top of the Royal Hospital a machine-gun opened up sending his men bellying for cover. Some fled into iron sheds which bullets pierced like cheese, others into dormitories for the insane.

The rebels gave as good as they got.

A British officer, trying to scale the wall on the canal side, fell back shot through the head. Another, screened by a telegraph pole, felt it splintering in front of him from bullet after bullet till he finally copped it. Falling with a salmon-like curve, he thumped into the canal bank before splashing into the water.

The Portobello picket proved too strong for the rebels in Davy's public house. As planned, they fell back to their base in Stephen's Green.

Major Rosborough strengthened the picket to bring their number up to 200. The troops then pushed on north towards the Castle. They immediately ran into withering fire from MacDonagh's outposts and the towers of Jacob's which lay in their path.

Major Sir Francis Vane was in Bray, lunching with a former fellow officer of the Munster Regiment, Major Arthur Maunsell, when a toffee-nosed, white-gloved butler interrupted them.

'Sorry to disturb you, sirs, but it seems that Dublin has been taken over by Sinn Feiners.'

'Dammit,' Vane exclaimed, 'I left my gear at the Gresham.'

'How utterly beastly,' Maunsell said.

Vane drained his glass and jumped up. 'Awfully sorry, old man, but would you mind if I said cheerio?'

Within minutes, he was at Bray station, where he ordered a train as if it were a taxi to take him fifteen miles north to the city.

At 1.30 p.m., British troops attacked the Mendicity Institute with a machine-gun. Bullets rattled against the walls, providing cover for soldiers to cross the bridge. Some of those who made it surrounded the Institute. The rest, numbering 130, pushed on to the Castle, arriving just before 2 o'clock.

Almost at once they were joined by fifty of the Portobello picket. These had avoided Jacob's Factory by moving round by the South Circular Road. The rebels were already paying the penalty for immobility.

The outlook was now bleak for Sean Connolly and his men in the City Hall and other buildings overlooking the Castle.

At Portobello Barracks, Kennard realized how critically important was the Telephone Exchange in Crown Alley, just south of the Halfpenny Bridge. He asked Major Rosborough to send a detachment of twenty-five Royal Irish Riflemen to reinforce the guard on the Exchange. They left at precisely 1.45 p.m.

Liam O'Briain, after leaving MacNeill, met with a Volunteer friend, an Ulster Protestant named Harry Nichols. They were passing the Green when a burly Citizen Army man carrying a gun called out, in broad Dublinese, 'If yer any bleddy use come in and foight for Oirland.'

It was too good an offer to miss.

As they scrambled over the high railings, the Citizen Army man introduced himself. 'Oim Bob de Coeur. Me da was French, so ya see, revolution runs in me blood.'

The next voice they heard was in marked contrast.

'Absolutely spiffing, chaps, but all you'll get for your pains is a rope or a bullet.' It was the Countess Markievicz. 'Hold on a tick.' She had sighted someone in khaki at the window of the University Club. She took aim and fired.

'Good lord!'

She rarely missed but this time, fortunately, she did. Her target was Irish and not a soldier at all.

A scout came into the GPO to say the Castle had fallen. Tremendously excited, Pearse said, 'We are the first revolutionary group ever to do this.'

He asked Fitzgerald's wife to take a Republican flag to fly over it. Minutes later, she was about to hand it in through the Gate when she noticed the guards were in khaki. She sped back to the GPO.

Pearse took it as one more proof that they were undermanned. He and Connolly kept saying that they would have achieved so much more if only MacNeill had not interfered.

The Castle was already feeling secure with the extra pickets when, at 2.15 p.m., there was a call from Kingsbridge Station: the first reinforcements from the Curragh Training Camp had arrived. It was a mobile column under Colonel Portal, with another 1,500 to follow.

Their promptness suggested to Major Lewis that the rebellion was restricted to the city, otherwise the railway lines would have been up.

He ordered some of Portal's men straight on to the Castle.

British professionalism was not matched inside the GPO, where Red Cross personnel were bandaging up self-inflicted cuts and gun-shot wounds.

Lieutenant Clarke was examining a home-made bomb when it went off in his face. A pal, who wiped the blood off for him, seemed disappointed.

'If your head wasn't blown off, Liam, the damned things don't work.'

Some tested a few bombs on Nelson's Pillar. Apart from being a hated obstruction, it was a landmark for enemy fire. Attempts to blow it up ended in nothing but noise and smoke. The Lord Admiral, leaning calmly on his sword, did not even shudder. To wipe the smile off his face, a marksman on the roof interrupted his saying of the rosary to take potshots at him. He succeeded in chipping the big white nose before The O'Rahilly forbade him to waste any more ammunition.

In the lobby, a couple of Scandinavian sailors, with almost no English, conveyed to Connolly their desire to fight for Ireland until their boat left on Thursday. He sent them up to the roof – 'Up there. Good place. Bang-bang' – where The O'Rahilly issued them with rifles.

Helena Moloney came from City Hall with a message from Sean Connolly. 'The Castle is being reinforced, we are desperate for more men.'

'Sorry,' James Connolly said, 'I can't give you any at present. Do your best.'

276

In Dame Street, on the way back to City Hall, Helena ran into Skeffy. He told her he found the whole thing horrifying.

Having seen rebels smashing the GPO, hordes of Dubliners decided anything went. They were encouraged by rumours that the police had been ordered off the streets.

They had gathered in their thousands in O'Connell Street in 1913 when Jim Larkin had spoken to them briefly from a balcony of the Imperial Hotel. The police had retaliated by mowing down men, women and children with their truncheons. Hospitals, that night, had been full of people with broken bones.

The poor had long memories; it was time to take revenge. Anyway, with the Sinn Fein bastards holding the GPO, women were not able to collect their 'separation money'. They had tried and a Volunteer had thrown a bomb at them. They were not to know the fuse had been ignited by a radiator and the lad had only tossed it out the window to get rid of it.

'What are we to live on, then? How feed our bleddy kids?'

With sticks and iron bars, the destitute began to emerge from their hovels.

From the splendour of the Viceregal Lodge, Wimborne had issued his own Proclamation and troops had pasted it round the city. A reckless few in Dublin, he said, had started an insurrection.

> Now, we, Ivor Churchill, Baron Wimborne, Lord-Lieutenant General and Governor-General of Ireland, do hereby warn all His Majesty's subjects that the sternest measures are being, and will be taken for the prompt suppression of the existing disturbances, and the restoration of order. Given under our Seal, on the 24th day of April, 1916, WIMBORNE.

A rebel soldier pulled a copy off the wall and brought it to O'Connell Street where he read it to his comrades on the Post Office roof.

Their response was, 'Bloody grand, all right, Seamus. Will you be now sending us up some more of them bloody bombs?'

The Bray train got only as far as the city outskirts. Vane had to walk the last couple of miles to the nearest Barracks.

Portobello's main force was a 300-strong unit of the Royal Irish

Rifles, an Ulster Regiment. Vane's rank and years of service made him automatically second in command.

The Barracks were big enough to house two battalions. Soldiers and civilians were presently streaming into it, many in a state of panic. Vane's priority was to reduce the perimeter to defendable proportions. Next, he headed a task-force which went through the houses at the rear to make sure they were not harbouring snipers. He entered each house to apologize personally. 'Frightfully sorry,' he said, touching his battered peaked cap, 'for the inconvenience.'

The clock in the Castle Tower struck 3.15 p.m. as two Army marksmen managed to get up there unseen. On the balcony circling the dome of the City Hall, Sean Connolly was hoisting the green flag that he had used in the play on Palm Sunday. At that range, they could hardly miss.

Sean fell with the flag falling and billowing around him. The first rebel to kill, he was the first to be killed. The bloody hole in the centre of his forehead gave him the look of a unicorn whose horn has been wrenched out. His premonition of dying in the first hour was wrong, but not by much.

Kathleen Lynn, a captain in the Volunteers and one of the few women doctors in Dublin, was sent for. The green flag was reddened with Sean's blood. She had seen him perform in the play *Under Which Flag?* and remembered his final speech, 'Under this flag only will I serve. Under this flag, if need be, I will die.' It was a case of Death imitating Art.

For form's sake, she whispered an act of contrition in his ear. Her glasses and black hair parted in the middle would have made her seem severe but for her kindly face. She straightened his body and covered him with the flag of Ireland reborn. Further along the roof, Sean's fourteen-year-old brother Matthew was fighting back his tears.

The doctor went down and found John O'Reilly, a spindly giant of a man.

'Sean's dead,' she whispered. 'You're in charge now.'

Inside the Castle, nurses were removing beds from the Throne Room and Picture Gallery to the safety of St Patrick's Hall.

The hospital's theatres were crammed with doctors and nurses waiting to operate.

Some old soldiers, their nerves in tatters, were screaming, others, blinded and spitting up chunks of lungs ruined by mustard gas, were being led to safety.

Two of the witnesses to the looting in O'Connell Street were socialists, but of a different stamp.

Sean O'Casey, once secretary of the Citizen Army, was a scarecrow, with shoes he could put his feet in from several directions. He was short-sighted, long-nosed and shaky on his long thin pins after surgery for a tubercular growth on his neck; the wound still oozed with pus.

A militant, he thought the Irish Citizen Army had gone soft in allying itself with the bourgeois Volunteers.

'James Connolly,' he muttered, 'the finest Marxist ever, gone wrong.' As to the looters, 'These are the only true bloody socialists in Dublin today.'

Skeffy, now in the city centre, was no less a socialist than O'Casey. But he found the looters' behaviour a blot on the city's honour.

The rebels had set up barricades across Lower Abbey Street. Into them went a couple of trams on their sides, as well as hundreds of bicycles, tyres, wheels, motor cycles and side-cars, all wired together. In Talbot Street, the twelve-foot barricade was made up mostly of furniture and bedding taken from nearby houses. No sooner was a barricade in place than opportunists raided it, carrying bits and pieces home.

One rebel soldier was to spend hours chasing looters away with a woman's umbrella and whacking them with it whenever they came within range. The wonder was, someone remarked, not that Ireland was at war but that the umbrella wasn't broken.

At Stephen's Green, under the Countess's direction, barricades were more substantial.

Into one of them went two motor cars, a laundry van whose contents – shirts, dresses, underclothes – were strewn all over the road, and a big dray, with the horse that had pulled it lying dead on the cobbles.

One barricade was composed exclusively of cars. It was added to when a luxury model, driven along the east side, was stopped by Republicans who ordered the passengers out. Seeing one was a Roman Catholic bishop, the rebel leader opened the door for him, with a bow.

'Sorry, me Lord, but out with ye,' as he tried to kiss his ring.

When the driver of another car tried reversing to get away, they shot his tyres to shreds. An elderly gentleman on the pavement, in a fury, boasted, 'If they had shot the driver I'd have shot *them*.' He had a miniature revolver up his sleeve.

Guests in the Shelbourne watched through the dining-room windows, wondering aloud, 'What in heaven's name is the world coming to?'

After the troops from the Royal Barracks bypassed the Mendicity Institute, Heuston and his men were jubilant. They believed they had forced them back to Barracks.

Heuston sent Sean MacLoughlain to the GPO, to say that if they had extra men they could hold out not just for a few hours but indefinitely.

Connolly promised to send help if and when it became available, possibly that night.

In the South Dublin Union, Kent's men came under still heavier pressure. The machine-gun on top of the Royal Hospital covered British troops as they broke into the grounds and took over a few principal buildings. They ran through echoing corridors and dormitories firing as they went, causing patients to go into hysterics. Nurse Keogh turned a corner and was shot by British soldiers before they realized who it was.

In the grounds, the elderly were tottering in all directions, while nurses risked their lives trying to herd them to safety.

By 3.30 p.m., HQ was fortified enough for Connolly to bring the rest of his food and home-made bombs from Liberty Hall. For the next hour and a half the street was full of the rumbling of fifteen lorries and the cries of men unloading heavy crates.

The city buzzed with rumours. Two policemen shot dead by the rebels grew in the telling to fifty. Dubliners adored soldiers; they were their own, providing them with allowances and widows' pensions and medals on mantle shelves. But the DMP and the RIC were baton-swinging swine, spies who would sell their own mothers for a pound. One passer-by expressed the popular wish that the rebels would 'do the city a favour and shoot all the bastards'.

In the general chaos, from hovels behind majestic civic buildings, a ragged army poured into O'Connell Street.

Dublin led Europe in drunkenness and prostitution; in disease, it led the world. Dubliners rented rooms in once gorgeous Georgian houses turned into slum tenements. For them, this was a chance in a lifetime.

In full view of the Government of the new Republic founded on equal opportunity for all, a giant of a man grabbed a rifle from a rebel's hand and tossed it through a store window. A few more bricks turned Dublin's most fashionable street into an open-air market where everything was gratis.

The rich had their races at Fairyhouse; surely the destitute were entitled to their entertainments, too?

Urchins broke the huge plate-glass window of Noblett's, the sweet shop on the corner of Earl Street, and gushed in, one on top of the other. The wonder was no one was killed.

Their next choice was Lemon's, by the Liffey. They stuffed their mouths, pockets and every available bag with chocolates, bonbons, turkish delight, acid drops and toffees. For some of them, the only memory that would survive 1916 was having their fill of sweets for free.

Other chisellers broke into Dunne's, the gentleman's outfitter, to put on boaters and glossy bowler hats. Some black-faced kids, who had never had or hoped to have new clothes, built a pyramid of hats on their heads. Some flicked Donegal tweed caps through open windows to their pals like playing cards. A gang of toddlers put on silk top hats which reached down to their shoulders so they cut slits in them for eyes.

From other stores, people emerged with umbrellas and tambourines. One enterprising group, their mouths busied with toffees, wheeled out a gleaming upright piano. It was last seen disappearing down a side street, with a thin little boy, his head shaven and coated with iodine to cure his ringworm, sitting on top for the ride.

A two-year-old, his face black with dirt and lice, crouching on the kerb, was squalling at being abandoned amid glass fragments ankle-high. A big sister, her uplifted skirt crammed with pickings, tried a sharp, 'Shurrup or I'll brain yer' and a thump and, when that failed, stuffed his mouth with liqueur chocolates till he threw up.

One lad appeared in Lower Abbey Street with a golf club and a pair of high-powered binoculars around his neck. He put down a tennis ball and, after several swipes, managed to drive it down the street. He then put the binoculars to his eyes to try and trace it.

A man backed his donkey and cart up to a store and shovelled in whatever took his fancy.

Women, like flocks of spitting black geese, snatched and fought over fur coats, digging each other with elbows sharp as flint, tearing out each other's hair. Layer after layer of silk undergarments were put on over outdoor clothes.

One, less puritanical, climbed into a tram near the Pillar that advertised 'Brooks Sanitary Appliances' and 'Emu Laundry' on its sides. She stripped to the skin so as to provide herself with an entirely new outfit.

'Jasus,' one woman croaked, laden down with stolen goods, 'look at that whoor, naked as a broom stick, nothin' on her but her mortal sins.' Murder was bad enough but nudity was the sin against the Holy Ghost. She shook a balled fist. 'Isn't she a panic? God strike the hussy dead this instant. I'd call the fecking polis after her if they was about, so I would.'

In minutes, the underdressed became the overdressed. Till then, the only new clothes they had were the old ones turned inside-out. 'Amn't I the most gargeous in the world, bar none?' one demanded.

The more prescient filled baby's prams and handcarts with whatever they could lay hands on. Only book shops were left untouched.

A drunken old woman sat, more comfortably than on a sofa, on the broad brown flank of a dead horse. With bullets whistling around her, she lustily sang,

> Boys in Khaki, Boys in Blue,
>   Here's the best of Jolly Good Luck to You.

One very pregnant lady, with breasts that would fill a pail, accompanied by a large progeny, went into shop after shop like a duck with ducklings. Occasionally, she administered a hefty clout to stop them squabbling. 'No need fer that, me darlin's. There's lashings an' leavings for all of yez.'

An old crone was offering diamond rings and gold watches for sixpence. Another, hunchbacked, vulture-shaped, emerged with a sackful of shoes, none of which matched. She left them by the Pillar to look for a complete pair. When she returned in a squeaky pair of new boots, she found her precious pile was gone.

'Glory be to God, could y'ever believe there was such fecking thievery in Oirland?'

Sean McDermott came down from the second floor of the GPO,

where he and Clarke had taken over Norway's office. He went out, his blue eyes blazing, and waved his stick at the looters, 'Get off, yez blackguards!' In his fury, he almost tripped on rolls of ribbons and silks.

One woman had heaved a big box of tea out of a store, only to have it taken from her when she wasn't looking. She complained to McDermott, 'Didn't someone steal me last pinch of tay, mister?'

Another with a top hat on was covering herself from head to heel with chains and watches. Gold and diamond-set rings disappeared down her bloomers and stockings, after which she strode up and down defiantly, yelling, 'Fire away, ye divils, fire away!'

Outside the GPO, young starry-eyed Volunteers with Lee-Enfield rifles were telling the crowd, 'The whole country is rising with us. Kerry and Cork and Limerick and Galway. They're all set to march on Dublin.'

It only made the looters anxious to clean up before they arrived.

'The Germans are coming,' a young rebel said, to which the response was, 'Them fecking thieves, is it?'

Sean T. O'Kelly, a small man in civilian clothes, walked to the Pillar, where he tried to explain what a glorious thing the new Republic was.

'Isn't Clery's broken into yet?' one elderly woman demanded. 'Hivins, 'tis a great pity Clery's isn't smashed.'

Inside a less prestigious store, men were trying on caps, shirts, shoes, and one very peculiar item: pyjamas. Who would get dolled up to go to bed? One old fellow, too impatient to remove his boots before trying on a pair of pants, was tottering this way and that, complaining noisily, 'Jasus, Mary and Joseph, haven't I gone an' handcuffed me own legs.'

A bare-footed boy, with an armful of very fashionable shoes, was met by a priest in Parnell Square.

'Where'd you get those lad?'

'Earl Street, Father,' the lad called back over his shoulder, 'but be quick or they'll be all gone.'

To the south, a woman was wheeling a pram full of stolen goods along the quays when she saw a priest approaching. She immediately tipped all the contents into the Liffey.

'Afternoon, Fairther,' she grinned, 'noice day.'

In the Green, the Countess, now formally appointed by Mallin as his second in charge, was deciding what to do with prisoners.

One British officer had given his 'parole' that he would not try and escape but, after noting where their defences were, he climbed the fence and disappeared. The next prisoner so obviously lied, the Countess had him put in custody. A third was taken.

'What do you do for a living?' she asked him.

'I'm a clerk in Guinness's brewery.'

'Tell me, please, your religion and politics.'

'Protestant and Unionist,' he said, 'and proud of it.'

'Let him go,' she told her men. 'Had he lied to me I would have locked the bounder up.'

Having settled that, she pointed out to Mallin that, without control of the Shelbourne Hotel, they were sitting ducks. She suggested seizing the College of Surgeons, a kind of three-storeyed limestone fort on the west side of the Green.

Mallin ordered a few men under Frank Robbins to take it. The Countess went, too. At the front door, the caretaker, a Carsonite, was seeing off a beggar with too much drink on board. Seeing the rebel uniforms, he tried to shut them out, firing his gun and missing Robbins by inches.

Frank, his big boot in the door, his revolver round it, persuaded the caretaker to open up. His men were so angry, they wanted to shoot him on the spot.

'Waste of a bally bullet,' the Countess said. 'Now, *you*, there's an Officers' Training Corps here. Where's their armoury?'

'First I've heard of it,' replied the caretaker.

On the wall above his head was his signed and framed copy of the Ulster Covenant. 'Mind telling me what this is?'

'Never seen it before,' he said, in a palsied voice.

She ordered him to his bedroom where a rebel noticed an orange sash of the Orange Order. 'Can't think who that belongs to,' he mimicked. The caretaker was relieved when the Countess locked him in with his wife and family.

The rebels went on to the roof, raised the tricolour and took up sniping positions. For the rest of the day, they fortified and stocked the College. MacDonagh's men in Jacob's provided them with ammunition, gelignite and lethal quantities of biscuits.

As in all their strongholds, they filled every container with water in case supplies were turned off. That done, they used seven-pound hammers to break through into neighbouring buildings. They might need to leave in a hurry.

*

Nathan was talking with Hamilton Norway, when a copy of the Proclamation of the Republic was brought in.

Norway relished reading aloud the opening section, 'Having organized and trained her manhood through her secret revolutionary organization, the Irish Republican Brotherhood'. He could not resist adding, 'So, sir, the IRB was not so dormant, after all.'

Nathan smiled rawly. They were not the only words of his that would be pointed at him like a loaded gun in days to come.

Major Price entered, an apologetic look on his face. 'Would you mind us taking over this office, sir?'

'Of course. Where would you like to put me?'

'We've made nice arrangements for you in the stables.'

Norway was thinking, What a pity Birrell can't join him so the ox and the ass can be together.

In O'Connell Street, looters were into pubs and liquor stores. Some smashed the necks of bottles on walls in their hurry to submerge their back teeth. One sly old chap with a face like a red cabbage emerged from a pub, holding a jar of whiskey as reverently as a priest would a monstrance containing the Blessed Sacrament, when a bullet smashed it in his hand.

'Jasus,' he shrieked, indifferent to danger, 'the wasteful bastards.'

A crony sympathized with him. 'Why can't them bleddy bullets mind where they're going?'

Women in black, built like galleons, moving like mice, burst upon the scene, rolling their sleeves up to reveal red arms, trailing concentrated odours of carbolic soap. They even stripped the dead horses of their stirrups and saddles.

Sean O'Casey, watching out of weak, watery eyes from a doorway, saw this as pure theatre. He pushed his cap even further sideways and upwards in the Dublin fashion as he saw small bare-footed girls become Cinderellas for a day. How he relished Connolly's description of the poor as 'the incorruptible inheritors of the fight for freedom in Ireland.' As for himself, he knew these ragged illiterates were walking encyclopaedias of want, their faces prematurely old, their ferrety bodies undernourished and tubercular, their souls starved of light. They worked for five shillings a week, enough to rent slummy rooms mostly owned by City Aldermen who received tax rebates on houses unfit for human habitation.

The splendid fanlights over the front doors had no glass in them, walls were buttressed by wormy wooden beams and so thin a nail knocked in one side sometimes went in someone's head on the other, drains were permanently blocked. In most houses, the only means of cooking was an open fire. Few had running water. The outdoor toilets were shared by from twenty to forty people. One toilet served eighty.

In such conditions lived 23,000 families, some of them very 'long', that is, with over eighteen children. They slept, made love and died in one dark and dingy room with water dripping all year round, except when the pipes froze in winter, and with perennial mushrooms on the ceiling. Even prostitutes had no room of their own and had to entertain behind a curtain.

Their chairs were orange boxes; they used ginger-beer bottles for candlesticks. Their underclothes were made from flour sacks, their washtub was a barrel sawn in half. The brightest thing in the place was a gaudy picture of the Sacred Heart. They slept six in a steaming bed, bitten by mice and lice.

Even in death they were overcrowded, being buried in earthy bunks, one on top of the other, symbol of an everlasting thrift.

O'Casey believed that these 'thieves' who never missed Mass on Sundays and Holy Days were acting within their rights.

Skeffy, on the contrary, was quivering with indignation. No believer in the sanctity of private property, he disapproved of this smash-and-grab approach to goods that belonged equally to everyone. He ran like a terrier into the crowd. 'I beg of you, do not give Dublin a bad name.' When this failed, he sat down in the street and started on some posters. 'Do Not Touch', and 'Please Respect Property That Is Not Your Own'. These were instantly torn down, so he resolved to start a Peace Patrol, men with white armbands who would try and restore order now that the police were off the streets.

In the GPO, Skeffy's friend, James Connolly, was no less horrified. Though in his paper he had once deplored the fact that a starving man was sent to prison for stealing a loaf of bread and a rich man sent to the House of Lords for stealing a nation's liberty, this was too much.

'Surely,' he moaned, quoting what a Spaniard said of the Irish after the battle of Kinsale, 'surely Christ never died for *this* people!'

Someone suggested they had no choice but to shoot a few looters. Connolly was tempted. Yet over Murphy's Hotel flew the flag of the Irish Citizen Army: a yellow plough encrusted with silver stars on a green background. It reminded him of flailing batons during the strike of '13. Could he kill the very people whom the Citizen Army was formed to protect from police brutality?

'Fire a few rounds over their heads,' he said.

When the mob realized it was bluff they looted with renewed zeal. But some shots strayed, all the same.

A gentleman in a frock coat and top hat was taking cover between two pillars of Gilbey's wine shop. Suddenly he sagged, stiffened and went down on his knees, a bullet through his heart. He was to remain kneeling there, hands joined, like a figure on a sarcophagus, turning sepia, then herring-coloured, for two whole days.

Pearse also quitted his seat to the left of the main door to look on the looters with his tragic face.

A Volunteer asked him, 'Are they to be shot, sir?'

'Most certainly,' he replied, irresolutely.

An aide went out and brought one in. The man, shabby, hungry-looking, was mumbling, 'But you lot started it.'

Pearse knew that he and his like came from homes whose staple food was dry bread and black tea, where two large families lived in a room and yet took in lodgers to be able to afford a fire in winter. Slaves for so long, they saw freedom only as the right to rob others.

He touched his holster nervously, never having fired a gun. 'Ah, poor man, just keep him with the other prisoners.'

By now, Pearse was receiving intelligence from women of *Cumann na mBan*, who were cycling round the city. All four battalions had taken up their main positions and were covering the British Barracks. They had taken some railway stations, though the more strategically important ones, Amiens Street and Kingsbridge, remained in British hands. Still, not a bad start.

He asked some of the women to stay on in the GPO as nurses and assistants to Fitzgerald in the Commissary. One was young Louise Gavan Duffy. She thought the rising was a waste of lives but, like The O'Rahilly and Fitzgerald, now it had begun, she was prepared to give her all.

Apart from looting, Pearse received reports of women pelting his men with bricks and saying, 'The Tommies'll tan the arse from your bloody Sinn Fein britches, so they will.'

Dubliners resented having their holiday ruined by a bunch of crackpots playing soldiers. It was getting hard to buy even a loaf of bread. Jacob's and Boland's were not baking and who would make deliveries, anyway, in streets full of flying lead?

Church-going ladies were cursing the rebels for their sinful ways. Old people who, for the first time, were receiving pensions every Friday morning, regular as sunrise, kept calling out, 'The English give us ten shillings a week, is that not so?' while old soldiers said, 'God save the British army that gave me a medal and me service pension.'

The severest critics were the 'shawlies', women who had sons and husbands fighting for England in the trenches and were paid a separation allowance.

'If only me Johnny was back from the front,' one yelled, 'you'd be running with your tiny tails between your legs.'

Many came from houses where they had keened sons and husbands, killed in recent great offensives overseas. One of them screeched, 'You dirty bowsies, wait till the Tommies bate yer bloody heads off.'

Train after packed train rolled into Kingsbridge Station. Tommies went on by the Loop Line to the North Wall and the docks, others marched to the Castle.

In the Castle Yard, machine-guns were in place and the troops on full alert when strange metallic noises were heard near the main gate. In the intense silence, every soldier fingered his trigger nervously.

In the upper gallery were forty or so veterans, visible proof of the tragedy of war. One, with his head swathed in bandages, looked like a ghost. Some had not yet recoverd from major surgery. Some lacked an arm or leg. Most were victims of chronic rheumatism after lying days and nights in mud and water in the trenches. They dragged themselves to the windows; a blind soldier gave a piggy-back to a comrade without a leg. Their faces went white with horror as recent experiences crowded in on them, comrades blown to smithereens or lying face-down in the dirt. All ears strained to listen to that awful, penetrating sound.

A milkman appeared, rolling a big milk churn. And everyone cheered with relief.

Soon after five, James Stephens, slight of build, admired for his books and lyrical poetry, closed his office at the National Gallery where he was Registrar and walked up Merrion Street towards Stephen's Green.

He stopped near the Shelbourne Hotel where a crowd had gathered. In the Green nothing stirred. Stretched across the road was a barricade of cars and carts.

When a man stepped off the footpath and tried to extricate his cart, the Green erupted. Armed rebels jumped from behind trees to the railings, shouting and gesturing to him to clear off. He continued tugging on his cart.

Three shots rang out. It was only a warning.

He dropped the shafts and walked slowly over to the railings where ten rebels were cursing him. He lifted his right hand, attempting to explain.

Someone said, 'Leave that be, or you're a dead man.'

He did not budge.

'Go, y'hear, before I count four: One, two, three, four.'

A single rifle shot rang out and, in two undulating, squirrel-like movements, he sank to the ground.

A woman gave out a long, loud wail as Stephens and others ran to help. There was an ugly hole in the top of the man's head and blood clotted his hair. They picked him up and carried him to the hospital next to the Arts Club on the Green, yelling, 'We'll be coming back for you, damn you.'

The woman fell to her knees in the road, screeching, calling God to witness the crime that had just been committed.

In that moment, the rebels were hated.

By 5.20 p.m., the entire column from the Curragh had arrived at Kingsbridge. The organization was superb; munitions were neatly stacked and guarded. By a round-about route, a strong force reached the Castle in half an hour.

Since the military still had no idea of the strength of the enemy nor whether they were supported by German auxiliaries, Colonel Portal asked the Curragh for another thousand men.

Joe Plunkett was lying down studying maps in the lobby when he decided the outside world ought to know of the rising. He told Fergus O'Kelly to take a six-man squad across the street to a long abandoned wireless school of telegraphy. The receiver was kaput, but Kelly was hoping to get a 1 1/2 kilowatt transmitter to work.

To provide cover from British snipers, Connolly put marksmen in the DBC (Dublin Bread Company), a tall, glass-domed building nearby. They would have to wait till nightfall before hoisting the antenna on to the roof.

At Archbishop's House, His Grace William Walsh was in his study.

He was small, with a massive head and thick shaggy eyebrows. Solitary by temperament, a four-year nervous disorder had made him even more reclusive.

Still formidable to look at, he was proud to have met Dan O'Connell seventy-four years ago and been enrolled as a repealer when he was nine months old.

He had played a major part in the downfall of Parnell a generation earlier. Of course the Catholic Church was the real Government of Ireland. It had irked him that an adulterous Protestant had more authority over the Irish people than he.

His Grace had spent this pleasant spring afternoon assessing news items borne on the superb clerical grapevine. Everything he heard angered him more. His permission had not been asked for a rebellion and, to his professorial mind, it was a mortal sin. In a theological nutshell: the British were not alien rulers; a rising had no hope of success; the innocent would be slaughtered and to no purpose.

He kept repeating to his secretary, 'Hell is not hot enough for them, hell is not long enough for them.'

This solemn incantation was disturbed by a ring on the door. James O'Connor, the Solicitor-General, had arrived under military escort. He had been at the Races when he was informed of the rising and told to drop in on His Grace.

When he was shown in, the Archbishop was soothing himself at his Steinway grand piano, playing with shaky fingers a Chopin *Prelude*. He continued with a few more bars before rising slowly to face his visitor. He stuck his left thumb in his purple cummerbund, his right hand he stretched out, rock-like, for the Solicitor-General, a Catholic, to kiss his ring.

Their relative roles were thus clearly established. His Grace was the representative of an Empire older and greater by far than the British.

Before O'Connor was upright from his bow, Dr Walsh, in a rich baritone, with the hint of a lisp, asked, 'What can I do for you?'

'Your Grace, we were wondering—'

'We?'

'The Castle has asked me to ask you if you will use your authority, Your Grace.'

'For?'

'To try and stop this rising getting out of hand.'

The Archbishop's eyes froze behind his glasses. As he thought, the Government was wanting to use him as a cat's paw. The rising could not succeed, that he knew, but no word of his would bring it to an end. If he had his way, the Government would resign for dereliction of duty.

'The Castle,' he growled, 'did not use its authority to prevent a rising, and now they expect me to use my spiritual "weapons" to stop the shedding of blood, is that it?'

He went to the door and flung it open. 'Good day to you, sir.'

Stephen MacKenna had been over five hours outside the GPO mumbling, 'At last. Ah, yes, at last.'

With the aid of his stick, he walked into the foyer. Just inside the door was Pearse.

'I was wondering, Padraig, might I do something for you?'

'Indeed, sir. Go home to bed.'

'Seriously, now.'

Pearse looked him over, saw the shaky hands, the lined face, the bent back. He pointed upstairs. 'I'll sit you in an armchair and when the British charge, you can light the fuses of the bombs and drop them on their heads.'

MacKenna shook him warmly by the hand and went home to bed.

Just north of O'Connell Street, barricaded in his tall, stately family house in Great North George's Street, was John Dillon. Aged sixty-five, tall, slender, with dark eyes burning behind his pince-nez, he had a white pointed beard and white hair.

Warning his family to take cover, he peered through an upper window. Lines of women looters were passing below. He saw one of them pushing a pram filled with nothing but boots. What impressed him most was their silence, as if they were absorbed in a deep philosophical exercise.

He had no hope of contacting Redmond in London. Firing was far too fierce for him to venture out.

He had a presentiment that his life's work was in ruins.

The sun went down in glory as though it had been dynamited, leaving a grape-purple glow in the sky. The air cooled. Smoke began to ascend from thousands of chimneys, mingling its sooty smell with the odours of leaking gas and open sewers in the overcrowded tenements. Behind Palladian facades, the poor were gloating over their booty in the bedlam of their own homes.

On the streets, lamplighters poked their long rods through the hinges of the lampheads, lighting gas burners that hissed and bit blue circles out of the dusk, causing moths and winged shelled creatures of the night to ping and plop against the glass.

Affluent citizens were returning from a day at the sea or the Races into the yellow glare of the city. They were surprised and annoyed to be regularly stopped at Army or rebel checkpoints and told, 'Hands up. Who won the last race?'

Many, without trams, could not get home at all. Since, in Ireland, everyone is related to everyone else, they spent the night with family in the suburbs.

A car approached from the west. Its two occupants had hired it at Mullingar, fifty miles west of Dublin, when they learned the train line had been pulled up to prevent the movement of artillery from Athlone. One was Oliver St John Gogarty, who had once invited a budding author, James Joyce, to share the Martello Tower at Sandycove for the summer. The other was middle-aged with a tall top hat and grey beard. He was keen to be at the House of Commons next day for an emergency session behind closed doors. This was Laurence Ginnell, Westmeath MP, whose green bedspread was even then flying over the GPO, claiming Ireland for the Irish.

At Cabra, the car's windscreen was shattered by a bullet. They pulled up as a sixteen-year-old with a rifle stepped out in front of them. He approached with menace, but, seeing they were civilians, he apologized.

'Sorry, sirs. I was told to shoot at all military cars, and I thought yours was one 'cos of its blazing headlights.'

'But you could have killed us,' fumed Gogarty.

'Like I said,' the lad returned, 'I thought you might be British, so I gave you the benefit of the doubt.'

On the other side of the city, approaching Beggar's Bush Barracks, was a detachment of middle-aged, middle-class Irish reservists in the British defence force. They wore no uniforms, only armbands with GR on, standing for *Georgius Rex*. They were fondly known as the Gorgeous Wrecks, or God's Rejects, or the Methuseliers. They were returning from manoeuvres in Kingstown, ignorant of the day's events. They had rifles but no live rounds.

On Northumberland Road, near the Barracks, they were fired on by de Valera's men, Malone and Grace, hidden in No 25 opposite. Five were killed and a number wounded.

Ninety survivors made a dash for the Barracks and locked themselves in. They were surprised to find it was empty.

When James O'Connor, still smarting from his episcopal rebuff, reached the Castle at about 7 p.m., he found all the lights dowsed.

Hamilton Norway whispered that troops with fixed bayonets were in the Lower Yard. They were about to go through the Upper Gate and flush out the rebels in the City Hall.

There was a terrific din as machine-guns and rifles opened up, accompanied by exploding grenades.

Inside the Hall, Helena Moloney was amusing her comrades by telling them she had taken a Tommy prisoner. They all went flat as toothpaste on a brush. Bullets streamed in like driven hail. Plaster fell from the ceiling and splinters from walls flew in all directions. Clouds of dust rose so thick they lost sight of one another.

As she lay on the floor, Helena felt a small damp hand placed in hers. She just made out a fifteen-year-old girl employee from Liberty Hall, whose name she could not remember. She must have slipped in without anyone seeing her.

'What do you think, Miss Moloney?' she asked in a calm, thin, high-pitched voice. 'We cannot give in, can we, Miss Moloney? Mr Connolly said we wasn't to give in.'

Helena gave her hand a squeeze. 'No, my dear, we won't give in.'

On the Hall roof, the rebels returned fire so fast their rifles over-heated and they had to wrap their handkerchiefs around the barrels to prevent blisters.

As the sounds of battle waxed and waned, Norway and O'Connor in the Lower Yard saw women supporters of the rebellion being brought in and examined by torchlight. They had been caught carrying ammunition for the rebels. They were kicking and screeching like Kilkenny cats.

Norway, a Unionist, said, 'This seems to be the death knell of Home Rule.'

O'Connor, a Nationalist said, 'To be honest, I don't know we are fit for it.'

In the Castle's hospital wing, wounds were being stitched, haemorrhages being stopped. Soldiers were lying on mackintoshes waiting for surgery, with blood pouring out of gaping wounds.

In the gallery, the wounded veterans, after hours of watching at the window, were still mesmerized by the sights, sounds and smells of battle. Nurses moved among them.

'Back to bed,' they urged, 'and I'll tuck you in,' a promise old soldiers found irresistible.

At 8.45 p.m., there was a ring on the door of the presbytery of the Pro-Cathedral, a stone's throw from the GPO.

A lad said, 'They want Father John O'Flanagan in the Post Office.'

'Who does?' asked an irate elder priest.

'The Commander-in-Chief of the Republic.'

Pearse had learned that quite a few of his men had not made their Easter duties.

The priest was about to slam the door when a handsome young curate with twinkling eyes, wavy hair and a ready smile to which his wide Roman collar gave an added brightness, touched him on the shoulder. 'I'll go, Father.'

In the GPO, he was shown into an office behind the lobby. A long line of rebels was waiting to confess.

There was light relief when rebels who had been tunnelling nearby brought back two distinguished prisoners.

Confessions were interrupted as the men threw everything they could lay hands on at King George V and General Lord Kitchener, found hiding, for some reason, in the Waxworks in Henry Street.

In London, Sir John French was hosting a quiet dinner for a few brother-officers. They were discussing the little spot of bother in Dublin when, at 9.15 p.m., an aide entered with a note.

The C-in-C read it aloud. 'Six Zeppelins reported forty miles north-east of Cromer.'

He looked around the table.

'You don't suppose the Huns are planning to invade Norfolk, what?'

In the South Dublin Union, the rebels had withstood constant fierce attacks. They had their first meal of the day and knelt to say the rosary.

Kent was pleased to have achieved his main objective: he had stopped Richmond Barracks from sending troops to challenge the GPO.

Some of Colonel Holmes's picket had managed to get through to the Castle. Eighty-six of the Royal Irish Regiment arrived by the Ship

Street Barracks entrance at 9.35 p.m. They had taken nine hours to cover half a mile.

Colonel Kennard, the Dublin garrison commander, had linked up with them. He found he had over 300 men. Barring accidents, the Castle was safe.

In St Patrick's Hall, the veterans had been persuaded to go to bed. The nurses moved among them, tucking them in. One had lost a leg and had shrapnel splinters all over him.

'Well, nurse,' he said, 'if they break in, I won't be running away.'

Another had a shell splinter in his left eye, twice the size of a pinhead. He had to be restrained from going out to fight the rebels.

A young soldier with a thin white face said, 'I'd like to torture every bloody one of them Sinn Feiners, then turn the machine-guns on them.'

Empty beds were now being filled with victims of the day's fighting. One was a sergeant in King Edward's Horse. His eyes were like coins in a pond and his body was marble white; he seemed to be dying. He had led the charge on City Hall, when a youngster behind him, carrying his bayonet too low, had thrust it into his hip. In a barely audible whisper, he told a young nurse, 'Don't worry, it's nothing.'

She gave him a sip of water and saw it was the best gift he had received in his life.

When the beds in the Hall were filled, they made up others in the corridors.

Finally, word went round that the troops were to cease firing until next morning at first light.

In the Yard, two large watch-fires, fifteen yards apart, were lit, with soldiers stretching out and warming their hands.

Soon after 10 p.m., a midget of a man arrived at a house in Cabra Park. He had brought a note scribbled on a page of a diary: 'Sean T. O'Kelly to release Bulmer Hobson. (Signed) Sean McDermott.' After a bitter argument, The O'Rahilly had persuaded Clarke to order his release.

Hobson had gathered from whispers among his captors that something had gone wrong on Friday, delaying the rising. Now Martin Conlan said, 'It's started, Bulmer. Are you joining us or not?'

He did not answer. They untied his hands and opened the front door. He left without a backward glance.

In O'Connell Street, he saw guards outside the GPO being cursed by the shawlies, dead horses, overturned trams and – he could not hide a sardonic smile – the locust-like looters. These were Pearse's splendid people of Ireland who would rise up and fight for the Republic.

He remembered Connolly saying, 'Hobson, the situation in Ireland is a revolutionary one; it'll only take a spark to ignite it,' and he had replied, 'Ireland is a wet bog that'd extinguish not just a flaming torch but even a barrel of gunpowder.'

If ever he had thought of joining the rebellion, this put paid to it.

He went through streets reminiscent of the French Revolution to his office in D'Olier Street, there to rest for the night. Time enough to look for MacNeill in the morning.

To the east of the city, Eamon de Valera was tired, after spending the day rushing from one post to another. His two Vice-Commandants and his Adjutant had failed to turn up. He had promoted Captain Joseph O'Connor as Vice-Commandant in case anything happened to him but O'Connor had to stay with A Company since there was no one else.

De Valera was inspecting his outposts when he heard a murmur of voices on the railroad. He listened. Fine, they were saying the rosary. A devout man, he stayed for a decade on the edge in the gloom, praying with them.

Moving on to inspect the sentries, he gave the password. No answer. He went back to the prayer-group, only to find the sentries on their knees with the rest.

'I am sorry to interrupt,' he said, tight-lipped, 'but sentries must not leave their posts, even for the rosary.'

In the Four Courts, the rebels discovered the best-stocked wine cellar in Dublin but, licking their lips, left it alone.

They broke into the Judges' Chambers. One put on a wig and condemned all his comrades to sleep, after which, wrapping themselves round with ermine and sable robes, they gladly served their sentence.

In the Green, the rebels were convinced that, as the Countess said, 'The whole of Arland is behind us, chaps.' Kerry, Wexford, Galway, they were all in it.

When the day-long insect-sizzle was silent at last and shadows had tiptoed across the grass, and the dark finally reached and blotted out the sky, Bob de Coeur, Liam O'Briain and the rest stretched out in grave-like trenches, smelling the sweetness of dew-fall and turned earth.

'God's going to water the gardens tonight,' de Coeur said.

The women slept in the summer house, except for the Countess who curled up in Dr Lynn's car, intending to stay there for only an hour or two.

In the GPO, now without electricity, Father O'Flanagan was busy with candle-lit confessions until 11.30 p.m.

Pearse himself opened the door to let him out. As the priest went home, he buried his neck in the cape of his soutane. The weather was turning cold.

On the top floor, The O'Rahilly finished off a letter to his wife. Then he confessed to Desmond Fitzgerald that he was surprised they had lasted so long.

'Tomorrow, they're bound to come for us. I only hope the rest of the country hasn't risen, or they'll be massacred.'

Below, Pearse asked Tom Clarke how he felt. 'Grand. Haven't I lived to see the greatest day in Irish history?' And Pearse said, 'To think Emmet's revolt only lasted a couple of hours.'

'I wonder,' Old Tom said, 'how they're getting on in Galway and Limerick and Tralee.'

'Very well, I'm sure,' Pearse replied, without conviction. He was simply pleased *they* had done something. How could he have lived another week, let alone the rest of his life, if they had done nothing?

Stretched out on the floor near Joe Plunkett, Michael Collins was not happy. Proud of being now the only man in the GPO who had not made his Easter duties, he disliked the talismanic wearing of holy medals and rosaries round the neck and Pearse talking theology to justify something as plain and right as sunrise. He would have plenty of time to pray when he was dead. What concerned him was the thought that the rebellion was a shambles. He particularly hated the idea of being holed up like a dog in a kennel. Why give the enemy the initiative?

The men, too excited to lie down, were in good voice. They sang a full repertoire of rebel songs, the favourite being 'The Soldier's Song':

Soldiers are we, whose lives are pledged to Ireland,
  Some have come from a land beyond the wave,
Sworn to be free, no more an ancient sireland
  Shall shelter the despot or the slave.
Tonight we man the 'bearna baoghail' (Gap of Death)
  In Erin's cause come woe or weal,
Mid cannon's roar and rifle's peal,
  We'll chant a soldier's song.

Someone cried, 'Why not make that the anthem of the Republic?'

Collins turned over, angered at their stupidity in not grabbing sleep while it was for the taking.

Finally, they made an effort to settle. Except for Pearse. Pleased to have caught the British on the hop, he inspected the sentries at the windows and spoke an encouraging word.

It looked like being a quiet night. The moon in the clouds was like a poacher in the thickets. From time to time, a rifle barked as a sniper on the roof saw or thought he saw a soldier in khaki.

As silence descended on the Castle, Hamilton Norway persuaded the guard to open the rear gate to let him out.

Feeling he had a bull's-eye in between his shoulder blades, he ran all the way home to his hotel in Dawson Street.

Nathan had accepted the offer of accommodation with Kelly, an employee who lived with his family within the Castle walls. Without undressing, he lay on the sofa. Sleep did not come easily on this the worst night of his life.

Outside Tralee, Monteith had spent a marvellous day. He had slept in late, then breakfasted in front of a turf fire. His hosts assured him there was no police activity in the area. He had gone on a long afternoon walk, admired the scenery and the pipping of birds in the hedgerows.

About midnight, he turned in on his featherbed. Already, the past few days and months seemed like a nightmare finally over, for him if not for Casement.

As he drifted off, he was puzzled as to why MacNeill had cancelled the rising so soon after Connolly had said all was well.

The British Prime Minister had decided to leave the house party at his picturesque Thameside home at Abingdon and travel back to Downing Street. There was a crowd at The Wharf, not the best people, either. To Margot's dismay, he kept slipping away to read Quiller-Couch's lectures on 'The Art of Writing'.

At 10.30 p.m., in a cheery mood, he began his two-hour journey back to London with Hankey, the Cabinet Secretary. He was no sooner through the door of No 10 than a secretary met him.

'Message from Sir John French, sir. There has been a rebellion in Dublin at midday.'

The Prime Minister paused, stroking his wavy hair. A clock chimed 12.30 a.m. More than half a day had passed since the rising began.

Ireland, where, he liked to say, even the scenery looks in need of repair, was being troublesome again. If only it could be submerged in the Atlantic for, say, ten years.

'Well, that's something,' he murmured, and without another word, went upstairs to bed.

In Dublin, the British forces did not sleep.

Their request for help from England was being answered. Four battalions of Sherwood Foresters were on their way to Liverpool whence they would cross to Kingstown.

Closer to home, troops from Athlone had joined those from the Curragh. 150 men had arrived from Belfast, proving that the rail link from the north was still intact. Incoming troops were feted as liberators by housewives at street corners.

The military had performed a classical holding operation in the face of an as yet unknown enemy. They had secured the Castle and the docks at the North Wall. They had encircled Kingstown Harbour to ensure that reinforcements from England could land there in thirty-six hours' time. They had strengthened the Telephone Exchange in Crown Alley. By holding on to Amiens Street Station, they had even re-established telegraphic contact with London because the cables went under the Station. Inexplicably, the rebels had done little damage to railway lines into the city, nor had they blown up any bridges. They seemed not to grasp the overriding importance of communications in war.

When Kennard in the Castle contacted Cowan at General Command, they both found it hard to know why the rebels had put their HQ north of the city where it was mercilessly exposed. Why, for instance, had they not taken over Trinity College which, like the Castle, was originally at their mercy and was crammed with rifles and ammunition? They had lost their chance since it was now manned by a sizeable force.

There had been virtually no rebel activity outside Dublin, and further German help was surely a figment of the rebels' imagination. The Royal Navy had absolute mastery of the seas.

The feeling was dawning on the military that they were dealing with a bunch of amateurs.

'They can't win,' Kennard said, 'but they might be the very devil to dislodge.'

Cowan agreed. Defenders always had the advantage, especially when they were on home ground.

During the night, the military took control of the Custom House next door to Liberty Hall. And, of course, they could not allow the rebels to stay in emplacements so close to the Castle. Kennard said they simply had to flush them out. And soon.

TUESDAY

Soon after 2 a.m. on a drizzling morning, a party of 100 men and a machine-gun unit left the Lower Yard of the Castle for Stephen's Green.

One machine-gun nest was stationed on top of the Shelbourne Hotel, another on the roof of the United Services Club. At many windows overlooking the Green, men in khaki had their rifles at the ready.

At 3.45 a.m., the tall, slim, handsome Brigadier-General Lowe arrived at Kingsbridge Station with the advance of the extra thousand men called up from the Curragh. Since General Friend was an administrator, Lowe took over operations.

Kennard soon brought him up to date.

'The Sinn Feiners have taken up purely defensive positions, sir, with their HQ in the GPO.'

'Are they on both sides of the river?' Kennard nodded. 'Fortunate for us,' Lowe chuckled. 'It should be easy to break their lines of communications. Now this is what we'll do.'

His plan was to secure a west-east line. From Richmond Barracks, this line would extend to the Castle and thence east along Dame Street to Trinity College and still further east to the North Wall of the Liffey.

300

'We should be able,' Lowe said, 'to bypass all the rebel positions and isolate the HQ. See any flaws?'

Kennard shook his head.

Lowe ordered Colonel Owen to withdraw from the South Dublin Union. Owen had spent the previous day and much of the night fortifying his position. He could have the whole thing sewn up by nightfall. Under protest, he withdrew. He could not see his only use was as part of the cordon round the GPO. There was no need to risk casualties in the Union.

In London, the phone rang by Sir John French's bed. It was 4 a.m. That phone was never used except in emergencies.

He took a while to get his bearings. Discussion on Ireland the night before had lasted through several bottles of port.

'Sir,' an aide said, 'the German fleet is five miles off Lowestoft and bombarding the town. Quite a few casualties.'

Sir John replaced the receiver with a frown. Were the Germans contemplating an invasion and using the trouble in Ireland as a diversion? His military brain told him that an invasion was out of the question, but that same brain had told him the same about a rising in Ireland.

He got dressed and summoned his staff to see about reinforcing defences in East Anglia.

At 4.30 a.m., troops with fixed bayonets moved out of Upper Castle Yard, followed by stretcher-bearers.

Nurses in St Patrick's Hall were making final preparations to receive casualties. Beds were made, screens positioned, bandages and dressings checked, kettles put on to boil.

The Sergeant who had almost died from loss of blood sat up and took a few puffs on a cigarette, before he choked with the effort. A passing doctor said cheerily, 'He'll live.'

The veterans, their sleep disturbed, went to the canteen where troops were being fed and demanded breakfast three hours before the usual time. The half dozen nurses and auxiliaries had a hard job satisfying 700 with supplies meant for 70. It was made no easier by the fact that, with the gas switched off, there was only the stove for cooking.

'What's this, then?' the veterans wanted to know. 'Just one cup o' tea each and 'alf a slice of bleedin' bread?'

Their complaints ceased on the sound of deafening fire from the

City Hall. The chatter of machine-guns, the barking of rifles, the thud of grenades put everything into perspective.

Amid smoke and dust, the British troops burst into the City Hall through underground corridors, windows and from the roofs of neighbouring buildings. It was soon over.

What shook the assailants was finding that the whole place was defended by nine people.

Dr Kathleen Lynn, knowing John O'Reilly was dead, stepped forward. 'I'm the MO. I surrender on behalf of this group.'

'A bloody woman.' The troops wondered if this had ever happened before in the annals of the British army. Some even doubted its legitimacy.

Helena Moloney and Dr Lynn were taken to Ship Street Barracks and the men to Richmond Barracks.

The battle around the Castle was far from over. The rebels were still well dug-in in neighbouring houses and in the block that served the *Daily Express* and the *Evening Mail*.

Dubliners woke to a sultry day; low scudding clouds were grey and fat with rain.

Smoke rising from ranks of chimneys coalesced into a thick pall over crowded tenements. The tenants rubbed and peered through dusty windows, not daring to go out.

On the roofs, like weathercocks, men crouched drenched and shivering in silhouette, clutching rifles or blowing warmth into their fingers. One stood up to stretch, a rifle barked and he fell over like a slice of bread.

The streets were strangely silent. No shops opened, no cars or lorries moved. There were no deliveries of post, milk, bread. No policemen were on the beat, though some were in civvies finding out the disposition of rebel forces. Women at street corners made very willing informers.

The world outside the capital seemed to have ceased. The British controlled the Telephone Exchange. There were no English papers. The only local paper, the *Irish Times*, carried a mere three-line official statement to the effect that evilly-disposed persons had caused a minor disturbance. The rest of the country was quiet.

Dublin became a whispering gallery. Some started a rumour just to find out how soon it would catch up with them again and in what form. U-boats had landed vast quantities of arms, especially machine-guns. German troops in their thousands had joined forces with brigades of Irish-Americans armed to the teeth and led by Jim Larkin, come to free the old land from tyranny. People from Cork to Donegal had risen, and most towns and cities were in rebel hands. The Pope had committed suicide.

In the wet dawn, as soon as the machine-gunners overlooking the Green could pick out a target, they opened up.

The Countess was rudely awakened by bullets ripping into the roof of her car. 'Steady on, old chaps,' she said, as she hastily jumped out and took cover. She glanced at her watch. 'Thanks for waking me, I must've overslept.'

A Citizen Army man fell dead. Another, with narrow shoulders, was wounded at the Shelbourne gate; a bullet pierced Mallin's hat, an inch above the band, as he crawled to bring him in. There was no weight to Jimmy Fox.

The lad's war was brief. He had spent a cold, sodden night in the open, listening to the faint quack of ducks, then pigeons grumbling and threshing. On his cheeks, as yellow as laburnum blossom, tears were indistinguishable from rain. His chattering teeth were saying Da-Da-Da-Da-Da. Minutes later, on his blue lips a bubble trembled, the flimsy iridescent home of his last breath. It popped and he was dead.

Mallin looked with reverence at his face, bloodied and innocent as a newborn's. Then, clasping him to his breast, his lips pressed to his head, he prayed for his departing soul and his all-alone father and for his own sons, especially little Joseph, that they would not have to die like this.

Tommy Keanan pointed to Jimmy. 'Whatsamarrer wiv 'im?'

For answer, Mallin clapped him on the shoulder. 'Go home and tell your parents what you're up to.' He suddenly yelled, 'That's an order.'

With a last glum look at Jimmy Fox, Tommy legged it over the fence on the western side of the Green and ran home.

From trenches and behind trees that seemed to spin like tops in the mists, the rebels returned fire. Most of the sixty-two windows in the Shelbourne were hit, the bullets passing through cleanly without shattering the glass.

On the corner of Merrion Row and the Green, a horse went down whinnying, its flank gushing blood. Someone crawled out

303

of a nearby house and, in pity, cut its throat. It gurgled, throbbed briefly and, open-eyed, lay still.

Another wounded rebel huddled up, clothes steaming, his hands moving now and again for help but several snipers had their sights on him, waiting for a comrade to come to his aid. He was to remain there a long while, a shapeless mass of pain and misery under a steady fall of rain.

At 7 a.m., Mallin gave the order to withdraw to the College of Surgeons. From the roof, Michael Docherty was giving them covering fire when he was hit. He slumped over the parapet, his blood mixed with rain broadly staining the wall pink.

Through a hail of bullets, carrying supplies and their dead and injured, Mallin's squad scrambled over the railings and across the cobbles and tramlines to safety.

Inside, they barricaded windows with huge medical tomes, blocked up the main entrance with benches and heavy walnut bookcases. From the roof, the Countess, with a pang of envy, could just see the gentry taking a leisurely breakfast in the Shelbourne's dining-room.

Below, the Republicans tended their wounded, including Michael Docherty who, with fifteen bullets in him, refused to die. From the Anatomy Room they brought slabs used for dissecting bodies and placed their own dead on them. From the Examination Hall they moved benches that had come from the Irish House of Lords.

The women built fires and cooked breakfast. Others explored draughty lecture rooms that contained big glass cases filled with human remains preserved in formaldehyde.

The Countess came down from the roof into the Boardroom where she stood gazing at a life-size portrait in oil of Queen Victoria. Her mind went back to the old Queen's Golden Jubilee in 1887, the year of her own coming-out. She was nineteen years old. She had received lessons at Lissadel on how to curtsey before Her Majesty and how to retire backwards without stepping on her three-yard train. She managed it on 17 March, St Patrick's Day, when she was presented by the Countess of Errol, lady-in-waiting to the Queen.

So painful were these memories now, she suggested to her comrades that while they were pledged not to damage College property, they ought to make an exception of this.

The painting was ripped from its frame and sliced up for gaiters.

Norway and his wife, Mary Louisa, turned their hotel suite into a post office and, during the day, never left the phone.

304

Norway's Superintending Engineer, Gomersall, worked tirelessly to get external telegraph and telephone services back to normal. He and his men drove round Dublin picking up the ends of cables and leading them into Amiens Street Station through private circuits which they commandeered. The loss of the Telegraph Office in the GPO, therefore, hardly mattered. Telephone messages from Crown Alley were passed on to Amiens Street and relayed from there as telegrams.

In the GPO, a Volunteer hesitantly approached James Connolly. 'Pardon me, sir, but I have to get to my work.'

'God Almighty!' bellowed Connolly. 'Don't you know, man, we're in the middle of a revolution!'

'Yes, sir,' the Volunteer said, 'but y'see I have the key to the warehouse.'

'So?'

'Well, if I don't open up, the rest of the men will lose a day's pay.'

Connolly relaxed. It was an argument he understood only too well. 'Right, lad,' he said, with a grin. 'But when you get home and have a cup of cha, don't you forget the revolution is still on.'

Pearse was meanwhile writing a bulletin to cheer up the troops. Like much of his life, it was flavoured with fantasy.

'The Republican forces everywhere are fighting with splendid gallantry. The populace of Dublin are plainly with the Republic.'

The Republican sheet, the *Irish War News*, printed at Liberty Hall and priced one penny, carried the bulletin. It added, 'The whole centre of the city is in the hands of the Republic, whose flag flies from the GPO.'

Sean McDermott's friend, Jim Ryan, arrived in the GPO after relaying MacNeill's cancellation to the Cork Brigade. To his amazement, the rising was on, after all.

He reported to Connolly, hoping to be handed a rifle, but he said, 'I hear, Ryan, you are only two months from your medical finals. You can be far more use to us as a doctor.'

Ryan immediately sent out Joe Cripps who had worked in a pharmacy to raid all the chemists' shops in the vicinity. He then commandeered two back rooms as a first-aid centre and a dormitory for casualties.

Hanna Sheehy-Skeffington came in for a word with Connolly. Women were carrying bags of bread, Oxo and potatoes to their

305

strongholds. Connolly was giving them unobtrusive armed guard which Hanna thought unnecessary.

Just then Hanna caught sight of her eighty-year-old priest-uncle, Father Eugene Sheehy. Eamon de Valera had often served his Mass when he was little in the village of Bruree in County Limerick and sat on the alter step while Father Sheehy preached in honour of God and a free Ireland.

'My God, Hanna,' he cried, tottering towards her, 'what are you doing here?'

'Uncle Eugene, what are *you* doing here?'

'I have come to give spiritual consolation.'

'And I am bringing physical sustenance.'

Father Sheehy said, 'I hear that man of yours is doing a grand job trying to stop the looting.'

MacDonagh's wife came in to see Joe Plunkett.

'Muriel,' he said, lifting himself slightly off the floor and smiling. 'Will you do something for me?' She nodded. 'Tell Grace I'm so sorry her groom didn't turn up on Sunday.'

'She understands, Joe.'

'Tell her, I aim to marry her as soon as possible.'

Muriel, her eyes full of tears, promised.

Casement returned from Brixton Prison to Scotland Yard at 10 a.m. in the custody of Superintendent Sandercock.

'I do hope you had a good night's sleep,' the Superintendent said pleasantly.

Casement had still not had a change of clothes but he *had* slept a little the night before, convinced that the rising was off.

This time, Thomson tried shock-tactics. 'There has been a rising in Dublin.'

'Oh, *no-o!*' It came out of Casement as an agonized groan.

'It began yesterday. It cannot succeed, no one knows that better than you. A mere skirmish. Troops have been rushed there from all points of the compass.'

Casement put his hands over his stubbly face. Thomson, pressing home his advantage, pushed a secret buzzer. As arranged, Superintendent Patrick Quinn put his head round the door.

'The trunks from Sir Roger's lodgings in Ebury Street have just arrived, sir.'

They had, in fact, been at the Yard for over a year, ever since Casement was known to be in Berlin.

306

'Sir Roger, you wouldn't have the keys, I suppose?' He shook his head. 'Then,' Thomson added apologetically, 'would you mind us breaking into them?' Again, Casement shook his head in a daze. 'Thank you so much.'

Thomson turned to Quinn. 'You have Sir Roger's permission.'

'One thing you *could* do for us, old boy,' Thomson said. 'Not just for us but for your friends in Ireland, too. Is there likely to be a second consignment of German arms?'

Casement's head was reeling.

'Only if I signalled to them. I was the only one who had the code. Half of it I kept but the other half went into the sea. So the answer is no.'

'We have your word,' Hall began. 'But of course, we are all . . . yes, gentlemen.'

Minutes later, after a strained silence, Quinn returned with three notebooks and a ledger. Thomson and Hall handled them as if they had never seen them before.

Finally, Thomson said, 'How very interesting. Would you care, Sir Roger, to tell us something about—'

'My personal diaries,' Casement said uncomfortably.

Gill's pencil was racing over the paper.

'I see here,' Hall said, 'lists, very long lists of mostly small payments.' His voice turned razor-sharp. 'For what? Payments for what?'

Casement's horror was two-fold. His secret was out at last and known to his worst enemies. But what worried him more was the fact that brave Irishmen had taken on, against all odds, the might of the British Empire.

'What *for*, Sir Roger?'

'What for?' he mumbled. 'I cannot remember.'

Mid-morning found the looters, many from far afield, back in O'Connell Street. Rain, the policeman's best friend, was falling but there were no policemen in sight.

Chief attraction for the children was Lawrences' photographic and toy shop in Upper O'Connell Street. From the top floors, they were dropping picture frames, films and cameras to their friends below.

Many of the youngsters, still in glossy top hats and munching toffee, were letting off fireworks. Hundreds of them exploded like cannons. Rockets shot into the air. Roman candles oozed orange

307

flames. Bangers made stragglers in the boulevard jump and run for cover.

Snipers on the Post Office roof noticed that opposite them the Cable Boot Shop was beginning to smoulder. Soon it was ablaze. One of them said, 'Christ, them fireworks do more damage than our bloody bombs.'

The Fire Brigade was called. Meanwhile, a crowd gathered, many of them cheering.

One of the first on the scene was William Redmond-Howard, nephew of John Redmond. He was quick to spot the fact that the rooms over the shop were residential.

A man on the top floor poked his head out of the window. 'What's up with yous?'

He was told the whole place would soon be on fire. Some in the crowd tried to force an entry to alert the other residents. In minutes, everyone was out of the building, except for a woman who appeared at a top-floor window.

Someone screamed, 'Look, that one's expecting.'

The pregnant woman, in a panic, refused to budge.

By the time the Fire Brigade arrived the main staircase was burning. Two officers climbed it and returned carrying her, kicking and screaming, all the way down.

The firemen unrolled the hoses and played the jets on the flames, only to find the shoe shop next door was also ablaze. They managed to put both fires out but, owing to sniper-fire, were not able to complete the job. Anyone in uniform was likely to get a bullet. After they left in a hurry, the buildings were still smouldering, waiting only for a fresh gust of wind to flare up again.

Looters broke into a public house in Henry Street. At a side door to the GPO, a drunken woman offered the rebels a drink. When one of them put a bottle to his lips, an officer dashed it to the ground.

'From now on,' he said, 'anyone seen taking the brown out of a bottle will be shot without warning.'

Connolly detailed a squad to break into the printing stores in Lower Abbey Street. They returned rolling huge bales of newsprint which it took three men to stand upright. These strengthened their defences.

Connolly also had barbed wire stretched from the GPO across the street to keep crowds from walking across their line of vision.

In the Commissary, Fitzgerald was eking out the food. Not that the men complained. It was so bad, they said, who would want to eat it, anyway?

Connolly gathered that the rest of the country had not risen. Sean T. O'Kelly reported back with the news that the firing they had heard earlier was Crown forces taking the City Hall. The enemy could not possibly be overstretched. Their inactivity around the GPO was all the more puzzling. What were the British up to?

Apart from isolated pockets of resistance around the Castle, since 3 that afternoon, the British had bisected the rebel forces, gained control of the entire west-east corridor and virtually cut off the rebel HQ from contact with their strongholds south of the Liffey.

Colonel Portal replaced the OTC in Trinity with regular troops of the Leinsters. He also posted machine-guns there, only a few hundred yards south of the Post Office.

In the early afternoon, the cordon around the GPO was extended to the north without any trouble.

Next came news that four 18-pounder quick-firing guns were on the way from Athlone. The railway line was up from Blanchardstown but they were coming on by road. Two would reach Trinity by the evening.

As the artillery approached Dublin, they blasted everything in their path. At 3.30, they blew to bits the barricade at the North Circular Road Bridge, enabling the Royal Dublin Fusiliers to capture Broadstone Station from Daly's men.

They pressed on, tightening the noose around the GPO.

At Inchicore, just west of Kilmainham Hospital, the British were developing a secret weapon. The inventor was Colonel Allatt, a small plump man with white hair and white droopy moustache. His high complexion was due to a dicky heart.

The Railway Workshops were adapting locomotive boilers. They bored sniper holes in the sides and painted false holes on them to confuse rebel marksmen. When ready after only eight hours, they were lowered on to lorries supplied by Guinness's Brewery. A cross between a submarine and a baker's van, they would be able to transport twenty marksmen or a ton of supplies in safety anywhere in the city.

The Colonel kept hoisting himself up on the lorries to see if the work was going according to plan. More than once he nearly passed out with the strain.

That Tuesday afternoon, in the House of Commons, a Conservative, Mr Pemberton Billing, demanded an assurance of the Prime Minister that 'this traitor, Casement, will be shot forthwith.'

In spite of the cheers, the Government had not yet decided whether he should be tried for treason or face a court martial.

To placate Parliament, while the Cabinet was making up its mind, he was moved from Brixton to the Tower of London.

At around 4 p.m., in Grafton Street, Dublin, Hanna Sheehy-Skeffington met her husband for tea in Bewley's. He told her he had enlisted some men, including a few priests, in his Peace Patrol but talking to looters and putting up posters was having no effect.

'That's why I've called a meeting this evening to organize a civic police force.'

Hanna begged him to avoid streets where firing was taking place and went home to look after their seven-year-old son.

Just before 5.30 p.m., news reached the GPO from Fergus O'Kelly in the wireless school: 'Transmitter ready.'

Connolly composed a message, telling the outside world that an Irish Republic had been declared in Dublin and that a Republican army, authorized by a Republican government, was controlling the capital. It was picked up by Americans in time for the next day's papers.

Minutes later, Connolly greeted some of his men who had been compelled to withdraw from north Dublin. They brought with them five prisoners. One of them was Captain George Mahoney, a Cork man in the British army.

'I see,' Connolly said to him, 'that you are in the Medical Corps.'

The Captain nodded. He was, in fact, a doctor on convalescent leave from India where he had been injured in a fall in the Himalayas.

'You could come in useful,' Connolly said.

Just how useful, he did not know then.

Some time after 7 p.m., Skeffy, his meeting over, was walking home to Rathmines. Swinging his walking-stick, he kept to the middle of the road to show he was a harmless civilian. He was passing the Portobello Bridge when Lieutenant Morris arrested him and a few others and took them to the Barracks.

Skeffy had a reputation both as a campaigner against conscription and as a hunger-striker. It did not endear him to the military. His wife, a militant suffragette, was no better. All in all, a treacherous pair.

Skeffy was questioned. The only thing found on him was a circular advertizing a meeting of citizens against looting. The Adjutant, Lieutenant Morgan, reported the arrests to HQ. He was told to release all but Skeffington.

'There's no charge on the sheet,' the Adjutant said.

'Never mind, he supports Sinn Fein, doesn't he?'

'I believe he's a pacifist, sir.'

'They're the biggest damned nuisance of all, Lieutenant.'

When Skeffy heard they intended holding him overnight, he asked if his wife might be contacted to stop her worrying.

'Permission refused,' the Adjutant said.

Skeffy was put in the charge of the Captain of the Guard, Lieutenant Dobbin.

Most men in the Barracks were recruits who hardly knew how to load a rifle. Many had been separated from their units. Tempers rose as more and more wounded soldiers were brought in, some complaining that they had been shot by rebels without uniforms.

Every new arrival brought a fresh rumour: 600 German prisoners had escaped from detention and were marching on Dublin; an arms depot had been captured by a rebel force that was heading their way.

Rumours apart, the sniping from Jacob's Factory was real enough. The end result was that discipline in the Barracks had practically broken down.

Trying to keep some semblance of order was Major Sir Francis Vane.

Pearse walked into the street to read a communiqué to the citizens of Dublin. The crowd was slightly bigger than the day before.

Since he knew from Jim Ryan and The O'Rahilly that the main centres like Cork, Limerick and Tralee were unlikely to join the rebellion, his message was further proof that the first casualty of war is truth.

'The country is rising to Dublin's call,' he said, his right leg trembling. 'The British troops have been firing on our women and on our Red Cross. On the other hand, Irish regiments in the British army have refused to act against their fellow-countrymen. Such looting as has occurred has been done by hangers-on of the British army.'

As darkness fell in comparative tranquillity, General Lowe at Military HQ was able to look back on a successful day. His troops, all Irish, had remained loyal. The cordon was complete around the Post Office. The big guns were in place. Trinity College was heavily fortified.

Martial law had been declared in Dublin City and County. The curfew would make it difficult for rebel scouts – women mainly, he suspected – to move around. With a news black-out, the rebel HQ would lose contact with its outposts and be forced to surrender. The other outposts would follow suit, hopefully with little loss of life.

With massive troop reinforcements in Liverpool due to arrive at Kingstown in the morning, the squeeze could soon begin. There really was no need to hurry.

The Castle was quiet. Crown troops had stormed the buildings housing the *Daily Express* and the *Evening Mail*. Only a few rebel snipers remained.

Hospital beds were filling with wounded brought in from other areas. A nurse was posted in the gallery to give advance warning of ambulances or stretcher-bearers arriving in the Yard, where watch-fires had been lit again.

Many of those who had warmed themselves round last night's fires were either dead or dying.

In Boland's, de Valera was very tired. A mathematician, he had made detailed studies of angles of elevation, noted the best places to snipe from. He had breached a wall in the Bakery to give access to the railway.

With few men, he occupied places and soon abandoned them. Like the schoolmaster he was, he believed that his lads behaved themselves when there was plenty to do. But the tactic of being constantly on the move also led the enemy to think his force was several times bigger than it really was.

In the GPO, to Collins's disgust, the Republicans again sang rebel songs.

During the day, women scouts had reported that things were going well in other commands.

Outside, on a street corner, a bugler was playing national airs, which passers-by rewarded with a few coppers.

In Portobello Barracks, Captain Bowen-Colthurst appeared. His family owned Blarney Castle. He was very tall, with a pronounced stoop and an expression that made him the embodiment of the wild Irishman.

During his sixteen years in the Royal Irish Rifles he had fought in the Boer War, been in the retreat from Mons and was wounded at the Battle of the Aisne. At Mons, he had at first refused to obey the order to retreat and insisted on his right to advance on his own, regardless.

He had been out on several raiding parties since the rising began and inspired his men by his utter disregard for personal safety. Unknown to them, he was fighting his private war against Sinn Feiners, who, he believed, were trying to destroy the entire country.

Late at night, he approached the Captain of the Guard. 'Dobbins, I want the Sinn Fein prisoner. Hand him over.'

The Lieutenant, though recently out of school, knew this was illegal without written orders from the CO. The prisoner was under his care in 'the King's Peace'. Yet there was something in Colthurst's demeanour that made him obey. It was bad enough fighting the rebels without fighting a senior officer who had once been aide-de-camp to the Viceroy.

Colthurst towered over the diminutive Skeffy.

'This,' he said to Lieutenant Leslie Wilson, his second in command, poking the prisoner with his stick, 'I'm taking this with us on our raiding party.'

One of his men bound Skeffy's hands behind his back.

'Listen, Skeffington,' Colthurst said, 'if there's trouble from any-one, if we're sniped at from any quarter, I'm going to shoot *you*.'

The forty-strong party left the Barracks about 11 p.m. In nearby Rathmines Road, Colthurst got immense enjoyment out of firing at anyone who appeared at a window.

When two lads came out of Rathmines Church after a sodality meeting, Colthurst grabbed one of them, aged about seventeen, by the scruff of the neck.

'Name?'

'Coade,' the boy answered. 'J. J. Coade, sir.'

'Don't you know, Coade, that martial law has been declared? Which means I can shoot both of you like dogs.'

Skeffy knew this was a lie but he hoped it was only a bluff on the Captain's part. As Coade wriggled free, Colthurst said to a private, 'Bash him.'

313

The soldier raised the butt of his rifle and broke Coade's jaw. As the lad hit the ground, unconscious, Colthurst drew out his revolver and shot him in the head.

'Right, men, let's go,' and they moved off, leaving him lying in a pool of blood.

Skeffy found it hard to believe that there could be anything inside a human being to make him do such a thing.

'This is wicked, this is—'

'Say your prayers,' the Captain said, 'you're next.'

The party went another hundred yards to Portobello Bridge. There Colthurst handed Skeffy over to Lieutenant Wilson who ran him close in cruelty. Before leaving with twenty men, Colthurst leaned over Skeffy and prayed, eyes to heaven and in a shaky voice, 'O Lord God, if it shall please Thee to take this man's life, forgive him, for Christ's sake.' He turned to Wilson, saying, with bizarre normality, 'If anyone snipes at you, Lieutenant, shoot *this*.'

'Understood, sir,' Wilson said smartly.

Colthurst went from there on a killing spree. One of the houses he sacked and bombed belonged to Alderman James Kelly, whom he mistook for a Sinn Feiner called Tom Kelly. With the Alderman were two editors, Dickson and McIntyre, who had taken refuge with him because of the curfew.

McIntyre was burly and of medium height. Dickson was only 4 feet 6 inches tall and a cripple. He looked an incongruous figure in a black coat and a bowler hat. The writings of both men proved they were intensely loyal to the Crown.

'I'm taking all three of you back to Barracks,' Colthurst shouted, deaf to anything they said.

Norway was in bed when Nathan called, asking him to go to the Castle at once. Norway tried but failed to get a car or an ambulance. The drivers said that if they were stopped by rebels, with him inside, they would all be shot. He rang Nathan back and explained.

'Very well,' Nathan said, irritably. 'I will talk to you in French in case we are overheard.'

His conviction that only the Irish did not know French was immediately overturned.

'I'm sorry,' Norway said, 'but I don't speak it.'

'Are you having me—? Oh, very well, I'll just have to give you instructions in English.'

In Norway's opinion, what Nathan said was not helpful in any language whether to friends or foes. He went back to bed at 1 p.m. to the sound of sniper fire.

The firing came from the roof of the College of Surgeons where the Countess was keeping watch under the rain-drenched tricolour. Beside her were two lads.

One was Tommy Keanan. When he got home, his father had locked him in a bedroom but he escaped. The second was a youngster who was going blind; the Countess had taught him ballads and encouraged him to practise singing so he would earn some sort of a living. This boy had a rifle in his hands which the Countess pointed for him in the direction of the Shelbourne.

'The enemies of Arland, sonnie, are over thar, and I reckon you have as much right as anyone to take a few pot-shots at 'em.'

As the lad pulled the trigger, a smile of joy passed over his face.

Below, the rest of the Republican army, wrapped like mummies in rugs or pieces of carpet, were trying to sleep. Michael Mallin was on his knees, saying the rosary for his wife and children.

In the GPO the men were no sooner asleep than a group of over sixty Republicans, forced to retreat from the northern suburbs, came in. Pearse thought it merited a speech.

'Dublin, by rising in arms, has redeemed its honour forfeited in 1803 when it failed to support the rebellion of Robert Emmet.'

He then led them upstairs to the Commissary where they were handed big slices of cake before being divided into three groups. One went to the Hotel Metropole, one across the street to the Imperial, the third stayed in the GPO.

Before the men could settle down again, reports came in of British forces massing for a bayonet charge.

'This is it, men,' Connolly said to his exhausted army.

They took up their positions, on the roof, at the peep-holes. There they remained, without rest and in a state of alert, until the morning light.

WEDNESDAY

Back at Portobello, Colthurst threw Skeffy, his hands still bound, into a tiny cell and swore at him through the bars.

Skeffy, used to such language as a result of his soap-box oratory, took it without a word. Running out of abuse, Colthurst left to spend the rest of the night in prayer. For hours, he pored over the Bible by lamplight in the mess. Demented, his snorting breath kept coming in irregular gulps. Ever since his service in India, he had involved his men in impromptu Bible services. The Good Book, he told them, had all the answers.

At precisely three in the morning, he came upon Luke 19:27: 'But those mine enemies, which would not that I should reign over them, bring hither, and slay them before me.'

His eyes rolled in his head. This was the word he had sought from the Lord. It expressed the righteous protest of the British Empire against all loathsome beasts who refused it their loyalty. Like his three prisoners.

He dropped to his knees. 'O Lord God Almighty,' he said in a swift croaky voice, 'Thou hast called me to slay Thine enemies. I thank Thee for choosing me as Thine instrument.'

Long after dawn, passers-by or stragglers at street corners, in the democracy that rebellion brings, exchanged rumours with one another. Even reports of the war in France had dried up, though the thousands dying there had somehow cheapened life everywhere.

Most swore at the Sinn Feiners, but a few said with a hint of pride, 'They've lasted three days. It would've been awful if the English had quashed them in the first hour.'

To the west, in North Brunswick Street, Ned Daly's men were falling in before going out on patrol.

The convent of St John's bordered on the North Dublin Union. Almost alone among Dubliners, the Sisters of St Vincent de Paul, with their billowing habits and head-dresses built like French sailing boats, supported the rebels. They prayed them out and pleaded with God for their safe return. Father Albert, a saintly Capuchin, was also there to bless them.

Daly's men now knew the nuns by name. Sisters Brigid, Agnes, Patrick, Monica, Louise.

One Volunteer, Sean Cody, said, 'The Germans are on the Naas Road,' and Sister Agnes called back, 'You *will* put a grain of salt on that.'

In bright early sunshine, two 18-pounders were taken from Trinity and manhandled to the mouth of Tara Street.

The *Helga*, a small armed fisheries patrol boat, its one funnel belching out smoke, edged up the Liffey, to anchor opposite the Custom House next to a Guinness boat.

Inside the Custom House, troops were grouped by the main doors. The order came, 'Fix bayonets', and they awaited the word that would send them charging across Beresford Place to Liberty Hall.

On the Custom House roof and on the tower of the Fire Station next door, on the roofs of Trinity and of Burgh Quay Music Hall south of the river, machine-gunners peered down their sights.

The *Helga*'s skipper sighted their big gun on Liberty Hall. On the stroke of 8, he gave the order: 'Fire.'

The first shell hit the awkwardly placed Loop Line railway bridge, a structure so ugly that it was the only bridge over the Liffey not called after a person of note. It caused a clang that could be heard halfway across Dublin.

In the Custom House, the troops were told, 'Get ready to move!'

In the Pro-Cathedral, the noise interrupted the Introit of Father O'Flanagan who had just gone to the altar for Mass.

In the GPO, the rebels looked at each other wonderingly. Connolly smacked his fist into his hand, delighted that the British Empire was treating them seriously at last. He had never dreamed that artillery would be used by a capitalist army against a capitalist city.

'By God,' he roared, 'they're beaten.'

Willie Pearse said, 'The Germans must be about to land. That's why they're desperate to finish us off.'

The bridge and Guinness's boat obscured the *Helga*'s view of Liberty Hall. As her gunners raised their sights, an 18-pounder opened up from south of the river.

'Fire.'

This time the shell from the *Helga*, lobbed over the bridge, scored a direct hit on the Hall's roof.

'Fire.'

Another caused the main door to shoot outwards in a belch of dust and smoke. Through it a lone figure emerged, shading his eyes at first, and running like crazy on a zigzag course across Beresford Place. Machine-guns opened up on him from three angles. The paving sparked as bullets smacked into it, throwing up slivers of concrete. And still the runner kept his feet until he reached a doorway and safety.

Peter Ennis, the caretaker, had made it.

The machine-gunners gritted their teeth in annoyance. They took aim again. Next time, they wouldn't miss.

317

For a whole hour, the bombardment went on. The sides of the Hall were pitted and scarred, the roof blown away, the whole interior collapsed.

Fr O'Flanagan's Mass was over half an hour before the pounding ended.

The troops in the Custom House were at ease. They had long grasped that the man who, by some miracle, had eluded their batteries was the only one in the Hall.

Because of Trinity's strategic value and the numbers of troops billeted there, General Lowe chose it as military HQ in central Dublin. That morning, he was doubly confident. Reinforcements had come by steamer into Kingstown Harbour. They would strengthen his forces in the Royal Hospital and in Trinity.

He went on tightening the cordon around the rebel HQ from the Royal Canal in the north to the Liffey which was just south of the GPO. Already, his marksmen on rooftops were raking rebel positions in the vicinity of the Post Office.

Lowe was cautious. He felt he had to be. The British had no experience of house-to-house fighting since the Indian Mutiny. The scrap ahead would be quite different from trench-warfare. He thanked God that the rebels lacked artillery. They did not appear to have even a machine-gun. The troops from England would complete his massive superiority.

He checked his watch. If all went well, they should arrive in Trinity in about four hours.

At nine thirty, Connolly sent a typed message to Lieutenant Malone, Adjutant of the 3rd Battalion, who was posted on the direct route from Kingstown to Dublin. At least 2,000 troops had landed and were marching along the Blackrock Road.

De Valera had detailed only thirteen men to stop them passing over Mount Street Bridge into the city. They had had plenty of time to dig in and plan their campaign. Their only other advantages were surprise and knowledge of the terrain.

On the city side, with a perfect view of the bridge that spanned the canal, seven rebels had taken over Clanwilliam House. George Reynolds had under him Patrick Doyle, Richard Murphy, the brothers Tom and Jim Walsh, James Doyle and Willie Ronan.

North-east of the bridge, a hundred yards nearer the approaching army, were four men in the Parochial Hall, behind which de Valera's main force was stationed. Paddy Doyle was in charge of Joseph Clarke, Bill Christian and Pat McGrath.

Almost opposite the Parochial Hall, in 25 Northumberland Road, a big three-storeyed private house on the corner of Haddington Road, were two solitary snipers, Michael Malone and James Grace. Malone was worried that the two of them only had single-shot rifles. He buttoned up his smart overcoat and, carrying his umbrella, went in search of his battalion commander.

De Valera was in the dispensary next to the Bakery. When Malone explained his problem, he unbuckled his treasured Mauser pistol and handed it over with 400 rounds.

'Sorry I cannot do more for you.'

The slight, fair-haired Captain Mahoney, RAMC, captured the day before, visited the GPO infirmary. Two patients were in a bad way. One had been shot in the back. The other had been shot in the eye, the bullet travelling freakishly along his cheek and chest and lodging in his leg.

Mahoney said, 'These men must be hospitalized at once.'

'Impossible,' Fitzgerald said.

'But those wounds are bound to become infected.'

Fitzgerald, knowing his own men lacked medical skills, was relieved that the Captain's professionalism was aroused. He closed the door on him and left him to it.

On the roof, a ragged twelve-year-old Dubliner appeared and regaled the marksmen with the most colourful language some of them had ever heard. He reeled it off without thinking, like a priest saying Mass. 'Give it to the bloody shite-heads, me boyos. Plug holes in them Limey bastards.'

When a bullet ricocheted at his feet, he looked down on the spot with infinite contempt. 'Feck off,' he said.

A white-haired priest arrived in a puff and caught an earful.

'Be a good lad,' he urged, 'and go home to your mommy.'

'Bejasus,' the lad replied, spitting, 'ye must be daft.'

The men's faces were still creased with laughter as the priest gave them general absolution for their sins, 'Ego vos absolvo a peccatis vestris . . . .'

A Citizen Army man, who had been a sailor, appeared on the roof. His vile language was almost as bad as the boy's and more malicious. The others thought that if he didn't stop God might strike them all dead.

'Go to confession,' they told him.

'I haven't been in fifteen years.'

He was persuaded that that made it more imperative. So he went downstairs and confessed, his pipe still in his mouth.

He was replaced on the roof by Pearse, shadowed by his brother. The Commander-in-Chief stood loftily over his men.

'The whole of Ireland is proud of you. I know you've had no sleep since Monday. As soon as I can relieve you I will.'

Lieutenant Boland could stand the strain no longer.

'Would you mind ducking before you get your bloody head, begging your pardon, sir, blown off.'

Just before ten, Major Vane's party left Portobello to place an observation post on the top of Rathmines Town Hall.

The mood in the Barracks was very angry. That morning, the coffins of two fallen soldiers, draped with the Union Jack and flanked by armed men, had been carried in silence through the yard for burial.

A young Irish Lieutenant in the British army, Monk Gibbon, on leave from England, had joined Vane in Portobello and the Major had taken him under his wing. During his absence, Gibbon heard talk of a prisoner who was making a damned nuisance of himself. Just after ten fifteen, he went to see for himself.

Skeffy scrambled to his feet and bowed to the Lieutenant. His only offence was that he refused to eat breakfast because he was a vegetarian and there was animal fat in the food.

He struck Gibbon as being a smaller version of Bernard Shaw. He wore knickerbockers and sported a tiny reddish beard. He seemed a very gentle person, an odd mixture of dignity and absurdity.

'I wonder,' Skeffy said, 'if word might be sent to my wife. She was expecting me last night. Also, the soldiers took £8 off me. If this could be given to her it will help tide her over till I'm freed.'

Gibbon promised to do his best. 'Anything else?'

Skeffy sniffed and said, 'Yes, sir. They have taken my handkerchief away.'

Gibbon smiled. 'I'll go and get it for you right away,' he said.

Colthurst was at that moment demanding of Lieutenants Toomey, Wilson and Dobbin that they turn the three prisoners over to him. His eyes were big black craters, as though he had been made up as a villain in a melodrama. 'I intend,' he said, breathing heavily, 'to shoot the prisoners. It is *the right thing to do*.'

In a panic, Dobbin sent a soldier to alert the Orderly Room as Colthurst grabbed the keys from Sergeant Aldridge and unlocked Skeffy's cell door. 'Out!'

Skeffy had no idea what was going to happen. He walked stiffly across the yard, his hands still bound behind him. It was a small yard surrounded by a high wall.

Colthurst called up seven armed privates. Without warning, he gave the order, 'Fire!' and they shot Skeffy in the back.

The two terrified editors were marched out and shot down next to him.

Dobbin, his heart thumping madly, noticed Skeffy was moving. He nudged Sergeant Aldridge, 'That one's not dead.'

Aldridge went to tell Colthurst, who said coolly, 'Finish him off.'

Four soldiers then riddled the body with bullets.

Gibbon came running with Skeffy's handkerchief in his hand to find three men on stretchers, two with a ragged blanket over them. The third, a midget, had no blanket, only a bowler cupping his face. An icy hand gripped Gibbon in the stomach which he felt would stay there all his life.

Colthurst was already on the phone to the Castle to say three prisoners had been shot trying to escape.

The yard walls were spattered with blood. For the next two hours, prisoners heard sounds of washing and scrubbing. When Major James Rosborough appeared at 11 a.m., Colthurst repeated the story he had made up.

The Major reported to the Adjutants at both garrison HQ and the Castle, ending with, 'What am I to do?'

'Simple,' he was twice advised. 'Bury the bodies and forget it.'

Rosborough told Colthurst to write out his report. He administered no rebuke and did not relieve him of his command. Colthurst wrote that the three men had tried to escape; he had had no choice. Skeffington, he said, had on him incriminating documents which he had handed in to the Orderly Room.

When Vane was returning from the Town Hall, he and his men were met by a hostile crowd and cries of 'Murderers!' Never having had that charge thrown at him before, he was very angry, but far angrier when Gibbon told him what lay behind it. He saw Rosborough, who said dismissively, 'It's over.'

'Over, sir? Many incidents like this and we'll have the whole of Ireland against us.'

'I happen to agree with you,' the Major said. 'I'd be grateful if you lectured the men on how to behave during martial law.'

Vane went to the Officers' Mess, where he tackled Colthurst head-on.

'What the hell have you been up to?'

Colthurst observed him with cold, empty eyes. 'Are you a Sinn Feiner?'

Vane fought to keep his temper. 'I happen to sympathize with all brave men who stand up for a principle.'

'Exactly what I thought.'

'That doesn't make me fight them any the less but it does eliminate all the bitterness in the fighting and after.'

'Who's bitter, old man?' Colthurst said.

At midday, a surgeon was called to the Barracks to examine the bodies and arrange for their removal to the local morgue. Colthurst had already been through Skeffy's pockets. He was disappointed not to find anything incriminating. He would have to remedy that. He gave a soldier Skeffy's 'Votes For Women' badge as a souvenir.

Further west along the quays, Crown troops had taken over houses around the Mendicity Institute and, from the roofs, were blazing away with rifles and machine-guns.

Along the front of the Institute was a wall. Soldiers were creeping along the far side of it and hurling in grenades. Some hit the outside of the building, exploding harmlessly. Others went through the windows. Heuston's men picked these up or snatched them in mid-air and threw them out. Liam Staines caught one as it exploded. Dick Balfe, next to him, was knocked over by the blast. Their blood spattered the walls and the floor.

Heuston had to make a quick decision. There was not the slightest chance of them rejoining the 1st Battalion at the Four Courts. He had asked his men to hold out for three or four hours and they had lasted against appalling odds for two days. They had gone sleepless, with little food or drink, and their ammunition was almost spent. Now two critically injured men needed attention. He hoisted a white flag at a window. When firing ceased, he thanked his men before leading them into the yard.

The British had seen many of their comrades cut down. As soon as the rebels surrendered, they disarmed them and roughed them up.

Red-faced officers demanded to know why the others had not surrendered. Heuston said, 'There are no others.'

As his company was lining up, a single shot rang out from the direction of a brewery in Thomas Street and Peter Wilson, one of his men, dropped dead.

The 178th North Midland Division, commanded by Colonel Maconchy, CB, CIE, DSO, had come over from Liverpool in the night. Owing to haste and lack of space aboard, their Lewis guns had been left on the dockside.

Around midday, the Sherwood Foresters, known as the Robin Hoods, were heading an advance party of 800 along the road to Dublin. Youngsters for the most part, they soon forgot the rough crossing in the joy of being feted from the moment they left Kingstown at 10.30. Some thought they were in France. They greeted the ladies with *'Bonjoor, Madame and Mam'selle.'* Many were astonished to find that so many French people spoke almost English.

Once it dawned on them that they were in Ireland they refused offers of food in case it had been poisoned by Sinn Feiners. Later, seeing the natives were friendly, they accepted it gratefully. During the long march, tea and cakes helped them cope with the Mediterranean heat of the day. Officers were offered maps and binoculars.

Captain F. C. Dietrichsen, Adjutant of the 2/7th, was surprised to hear a couple of children calling out, 'Daddy, Daddy.' They were his own. His wife had sent them over without telling him to escape the Zeppelin raids in England. He gave them a big hug. 'See you later,' he said.

Two battalions branched off left for Kilmainham. They ran into no trouble, apart from the occasional sniper. The two battalions ordered to Trinity by the direct route – Merrion Road, Ballsbridge and across the bridge to Merrion Square – met a different fate.

The thirteen rebels guarding the Mount Street bridge put the finishing touches to their defences and gulped down what might be their last cup of tea. Their rifles were loaded, their ammunition within easy reach. They said their prayers.

Colonel Maconchy had remained with the column heading for Trinity. He made temporary Brigade HQ at the Royal Dublin

Society where prize bullocks, pedigree cattle and farm implements were being exhibited. Having settled in, he ordered the advance.

In charge was Lieutenant-Colonel Fane, CMG, DSO, a cavalry officer and veteran of Mons, now CO of 2/7. Maconchy told Fane, 'According to latest intelligence, rebels have taken over a school on the right-hand side of Northumberland Road.'

The intelligence was faulty.

Monteith had sent Tommy McEllistrim to Tralee to ask Cahill what he intended doing, in view of the rising in Dublin. Cahill said, 'If we do turn out, Monteith will have to lead us.'

'That's crazy,' Monteith said heatedly. 'I'll willingly march with the rest of you and fight till I drop. But if I tried to make Tralee in daylight they'd pick me off like an apple on a tree.'

There were signs that, owing to the rising, the RIC were intensifying their search for him. McEllistrim was a Volunteer. It seemed only a question of time before they searched his place.

From the Shelbourne Hotel, a man emerged holding big brown paper bags above his head. The Countess, on the roof of the College of Surgeons, saw him through her binoculars.

'Hold your fire, chaps,' she cried.

The sniper next to her was peeved. 'What is it, madame?'

'If you ask me,' she said, 'some generous soul is wanting to give grub to the bally birds.'

She lowered the flag to show she agreed.

From then on the Park Keeper, James Kearney, was allowed, under truce, to cross the road and enter the Green twice a day to feed the ducks.

A stone's throw away from the Shelbourne, Maurice Headlam was returning to his lodgings after a vacation. He was Treasury Remembrancer at the Castle; he looked after the salaries and pensions of Government employees. Aged forty-three, balding with dark eyebrows and pert nose, he was a pernickety, pipe-smoking, rather small-minded man.

A dead Sinn Feiner was lying beside the railings and a few young men were debating whether to bury him. An old hag was screaming, 'Let the carrion rot. Haven't they brought shame on the fair name of Ireland?'

'Hear, hear,' Headlam muttered.

After he had unpacked and freshened up, he hurried to the Castle along silent streets, reeking with the smell of cordite. In the Lower Yard, he found soldiers sunning themselves and smoking cigarettes, while bullets from Jacob's flew overhead. In a couple of days, the youngsters had acquired a kind of detachment in the face of death.

His office-keeper was less philosophical. 'I'm glad you've come, sir,' he said. 'There's a Sinn Feiner on the roof, shot dead, and my kids are scared out of their wits.'

Headlam went for a word with Edgeworth-Johnstone, Head of the DMP, whose office was next to his own, but that flushed, stout gentleman with a boyish face was marooned on the telephone.

When his office-keeper told him where the Under-Secretary was, Headlam thought it poetic justice. Nathan, at that moment, was in his stable deep in conversation with another arch critic, Norway.

Sir Matthew was in an untypically foul mood. Firstly, he knew Norway disapproved of official policies. Secondly, with the tightening of the military cordon around the city, food was scarce. Thirdly, he was not sleeping; the sofa was lumpy and the covers did not keep him warm. This had led, fourthly, to his catching a cold made more irritating by the motes of straw in the air, and, fifthly, he had only tiny women's handkerchiefs to deal with it. Hence the redness of his nose above the walrus-like moustache. Finally and climactically, his career, till now a series of ascending triumphs, was at an abrupt end.

'What I want to know, Norway,' he was saying, 'is, can you restore postal deliveries to parts of Dublin.'

'Which parts, sir?'

'That is for you to tell me.'

'On the contrary,' Norway said, with the truculence of one who knew he was dealing with a man on the way down, 'that is for *you* to tell *me*. All I know is that anyone in uniform is immediately fired upon.'

'You are exaggerating, Norway.'

'Perhaps, then, sir, you will tell me the districts which you guarantee are safe.'

Nathan disliked his tone. 'I want your answer by 4 this afternoon,' he said. 'In writing.'

As Norway left, he ran into Headlam who said, 'Funny business, Hamilton.'

Norway winked. 'We knew it, didn't we, Maurice?'

Headlam knocked on the stable door and waited for, 'Come in, please,' before entering with a sneer that made Nathan bristle. 'Anything I can do, sir?'

'Nothing.' Nathan wiped his runny nose. The wretched little hankie was a symbol of his new pinched circumstances. 'There'll be no salaries, sniff, dispensed for some time.'

When he had got rid of Headlam, he phoned Estelle at his lodge.

'Don't *worry*,' she told him. 'My two are fine. So is Dorothy. When the firing gets very hot, I just get out good old Conan Doyle and read them another tale of Sherlock Holmes.'

It was 12.30 p.m. when Fane's company passed the Royal Dublin Show, completely empty save for a few members of staff looking after the pedigree cattle. At the beginning of Northumberland Road, they were still 300 yards from Mount Street Bridge.

Fane peered ahead down the leafy, sun-dappled avenue of middle-class suburbia. It was mellow and scented as an apple-orchard, quiet as a railway tunnel. Too quiet. It reeked of the menace of man-made silence. He sniffed. It was there, stronger-smelling than a galloped horse, some *thing* that would turn that street into a battle field.

He decided to play it by the book. He waved his men on in Indian file on both footpaths with fixed bayonets, followed closely by troops four abreast.

They were expecting the threat to be on their right, that is, to the north, where the school was supposed to be occupied and behind which was the rebel stronghold of Boland's Mill.

In fact, it came suddenly from their left. Malone from a bathroom window and Grace on the top floor opened up.

Ten of Fane's men fell, the rest scrambled for cover in front gardens and behind trees. The Colonel kept his wits about him, noting that firing had come from No 25.

Round one to the rebels.

Fane's men had no experience of street warfare. Without machine-guns, field-guns, even grenades, against a dug-in force, numbers unknown, attacking from unexpected quarters, he knew his task was formidable.

Even he failed to notice that some of the firing had come from the Parochial Hall to the right and that snipers were posted in a house straight ahead across the bridge. As he marshalled his men to bayonet-charge No 25, the rebels in Clanwilliam House set their sights.

326

He blew his whistle, junior officers waved their swords as though they were in Flanders' fields and, 'Forwa-*a-ard*.'

Man after man fell to sustained volleys. The British replied but though hundreds of shots were fired at Grace and Malone, neither was hit.

Some Tommies reached the bolted front door and tried to force an entry with their rifle butts, only to be shot with revolvers at close range.

The main force passed on towards the bridge without neutralizing No 25 or the Parochial Hall. Their officers arrogantly insisted on keeping to the direct route to Trinity across the bridge, regardless of how many men were lost. Owing to faulty intelligence, they failed to realize that this was the one bridge in all Dublin dominated by the rebels. Soon the barrels of the four Volunteers on the first floor of Clanwilliam House and the four snipers in the Parochial Hall were red-hot as the British were caught in a murderous cross-fire.

In an attempt to outflank the rebels along the canal, Fane sent C Company left up Haddington Road to Baggot Street Bridge. The result was that the company came under fire from a new position, the railway line spanning the canal further down. Their officers, easily identified by their Sam Browne belts, were all killed or wounded.

When the first soldier to reach the bridge fell, a young woman emerged from a nearby house, carrying a blue enamel jug. She ran on to the bridge but bullets forced her down the grassy slope to the canal bank.

Next, a girl in a servant's apron ran on to the bridge and lifted both hands high in the air until the firing stopped. The first girl came up from the bank and joined her. They picked the soldier up and carried him to where a crowd was sheltering, including Red Cross personnel. They cheered the girls and took the wounded man to Patrick Dun's Hospital nearby.

When the firing resumed, several more soldiers fell on the bridge. Once more the girl in the apron ran out and stopped the firing. Eight men she helped in this way. The last of them was badly wounded in the back and thigh. She took off her apron and stuffed it down his trousers to try and staunch the blood. Drenched in blood herself, she was crying all the time.

The fighting had developed into a battle of wills; it went on for an hour, then another hour.

Six machine-guns had been playing for some time on Kelly's, a shop

327

that sold fishing tackle, a rebel outpost at the corner of Bachelor's Walk. At 2.30 p.m., an 18-pounder, just north of Trinity College, joined in.

With the first round from the big gun, windows in all the nearby houses shattered and the College quaked. The wham of the shell into Kelly's could be heard across the city. The three sharp-shooters on the parapet held on for dear life as the building rocked like a ship in a storm.

Crowds sat on the Liffey wall like spectators in a theatre. After a couple of days of glorious looting, they were now treated to this fireworks display.

Splinters of red brick flew and dust clouds rose in the air. Machine-guns joined in, and their fire, till now venomous, seemed strangely muted in comparison with the artillery.

The shells were incendiaries. Kelly's caught fire as petrol burst into flame and spread.

'They're all dead,' the spectators agreed, flinging their caps in the air. The inside of Kelly's collapsed, as had Liberty Hall in the morning, leaving it as empty as a dog kennel.

But the snipers survived. They had prepared their get-away by tunnelling into adjoining houses. They made it to the Metropole Hotel where Pearse sent them a commendation for bravery.

As for Connolly, he was ecstatic. 'I never knew they'd knock down buildings. They're really rattled. It proves, doesn't it, that our reinforcements are on the way?'

From the Parnell Monument, a drunk was seen zigzagging in the centre of O'Connell Street towards the Liffey. A respectable drunk, too, in bowler hat, striped trousers and with rolled umbrella. Machine-gun bullets splintered the pavings before and after him. His unstable gait was his salvation. He travelled the whole length of the street before he fell into the arms of cheering spectators and threw up.

At four in the afternoon, Norway also braved bullets to hand in his report to the Castle.

After Nathan had asked him to restart postal services, he had received the same request from Wimborne and the Irish Office in London. They were wanting to assure Parliament that all was well in Dublin when it was in a mess. He had contacted a mail contractor who had said the chances of mail deliveries were zero.

328

Nathan read Norway's report and was furious. 'You refuse to open up the postal districts.'

'I don't refuse, sir. It is just not possible.'

'You are being obstructive, Norway.'

'I am thinking of my men, sir, and not my reputation.'

After two hours of bloody and fruitless battle, Colonel Fane asked Maconchy at the Royal Dublin Society for gun-cotton and grenades. When they arrived from a nearby bombing school, he was finally in a position to blast the door off No 25.

Malone and Grace, knowing they had little time left, had made a pact: when the final assault came, they would come together and fight it out on the stairhead. But Fane's men, having blasted the house with grenades, unexpectedly entered by the middle floor, roaring and screaming.

Malone was upstairs and Grace in the unlit kitchen below, dowsing his hot rifle barrel in water. Between them were a dozen Tommies. Malone yelled, 'I'm coming down, Seamus,' just as he fell, shaking epileptically, riddled with bullets.

Grace remained absolutely still in the kitchen, hiding behind a gas cooker.

The Tommies searched every room except the kitchen, though they fired several shots into it and tossed a couple of grenades through a bomb-hole in the floor.

Grace assumed no one dared to venture into a dark place where rebels might be lurking who had proved they seldom missed.

The soldiers left, and Grace waited and waited. His sweaty hand gripped a revolver with only four cartridges left. When at last the house went quiet, he dismantled the barricade to the kitchen door, crept out and hid in the garden shed amid spades and mowers. Troops were still nosing around. He heard a soldier say, 'No one could have survived in there.'

Meanwhile, Fane's men were bellying along the gutters, then across the bridge, past dead and dying comrades. Some of them, goggle-eyed, spluttering, legs jerking, tongues stiffening, slithered in agony in all directions like hooked fishes on a bank. Shot down at close range by marksmen in Clanwilliam House and the Parochial Hall, one was squeezing his leg to stop himself bleeding to death from a torn artery, one was spouting blood from both sides of his neck through which a bullet had passed. Some had their entrails hanging out, giving off a bluish vapour like burning brandy, others' brains were exposed. Flies sizzled in thick dark gore in the burning heat. The blood of one mingled with that of another and the stench of it was overwhelming.

On came another wave.

More dead, more wounded, signing themselves, crying for their mothers. Between the crack and whine of bullets, the injured croaked for water like birds on a refuse tip or tried to put their bottles to their lips.

A solitary gull dipped down and soared aloft with bloodied beak. In a grotesque imitation of the soldiers, sleek brown rats edged up from the banks of the stagnant canal.

A couple of white-coated doctors, their hands held high, moved forward, with nurses and a priest in close attendance. In Clanwilliam House, Reynolds ordered his men to cease firing and yelled to the relief workers, 'Go ahead.' A pattern was established: fighting was followed by a pause to allow Red Cross workers to remove the casualties.

Colonel Fane was himself hit badly in the left arm. He had it bandaged and put in a sling and rejoined his men.

Reinforcements from other companies were sent in an encircling movement, B to the left, A to the right. They too were stopped by heavy fire, as were D Company.

British snipers ascended the belfry of Haddington Road church and fired from the parapet. It did no good.

Fane lost still more men outside the school opposite the end of Percy Lane, which he still mistakenly thought was occupied, and in the approaches to the bridge.

The GPO had no radio or telephone link-up even with its outposts across the street.

Captain Brennan Whitmore on the east side threw a ball of twine across the boulevard. A can was fixed on the twine to carry messages. It was on its third journey across when a volunteer Aussie marksman in Trinity scored a direct hit on it.

From then on, the rebels simply sent over pieces of paper, some of which arrived with perforations.

Mr Coade, father of the lad whom Colthurst had killed outside Rathmines church, went that Wednesday afternoon to the mortuary. He was heart-broken to see his son's fractured jaw and what the bullet, fired at close range, had done to his head.

330

He saw other corpses as well, including that of Skeffy. A priest with him also identified Skeffy's corpse.

In the billiard room of Portobello Barracks, Major Vane was lecturing the men on their duties under martial law.

'I want to make one thing plain. No one, repeat, *no one* is entitled to shoot a person down in cold blood. If I hear any of you doing that I'll see to it personally you are prosecuted under the common law. Is that understood?'

Colthurst was, meanwhile, on the rampage.

Just north of the Barracks in Camden Street, his squad was flushing out rebels from the outposts of Jacob's Factory. From one house a man emerged into the yard with his hands above his head. He was a labour leader, Councillor Richard O'Carroll.

Colthurst stood over him. 'Are you a Sinn Feiner?'

'From the backbone out!' the Councillor replied.

Without another word, Colthurst shot him in the chest, piercing his lung.

A worried soldier said, 'Are you sure he's dead, sir?'

'Never you mind,' Colthurst barked, 'he'll die when he's ready. Just drag him into the street.'

It was hours before O'Carroll was picked up by a bread van and taken to Portobello Barracks.

Soon after the shooting, Colthurst fastened on to a lad he accused of being a Sinn Feiner.

'Tell me, sonny, where are the Sinn Fein snipers?'

'I don't know, sir.'

'What a pity,' Colthurst tutted. 'Kneel down there.'

When the boy knelt, instinctively signing himself, Colthurst shot him in the back of the head.

Hanna Sheehy-Skeffington, having heard rumours, left home to look for her husband but found no trace of him. This was most unusual. Skeffy was so voluble, so distinctive in every way, even children used to point, saying, 'He went that way, missis.'

It was as if he had disappeared off the face of the earth.

About 5 p.m., the gunning of Kelly's ceased. The artillery switched to firing at Hopkins & Hopkins, the jewellers on the quay to the east of O'Connell Street. Rebel activity within had long since ceased, so they did not waste their shells.

Not far away, the improvised armoured lorries made their first appearance. Already exposed on its northern flank, the GPO was now threatened from the west where these lorries cut communication with Daly's Battalion in the Four Courts area. The British had also installed a machine-gun nest on top of Jervis Street Hospital which raked the roof of the GPO.

It dawned on Connolly that they might have to move their HQ. He made his men work harder at tunnelling into adjoining buildings. Still convinced the British would try to finish them off with a bayonet charge, he also strengthened the barricades inside the foyer.

General Lowe, in fact, never for one moment considered a frontal assault. His problem was that neither from north or south could he get a direct line of fire on the GPO with his 18-pounders.

Otherwise, he would have flattened it in minutes.

At 5.30 p.m., as the light was fading, General Maconchy telephoned Lowe from the Royal Dublin Society. 'My men are having some difficulty reaching Trinity by the direct route.'

Lowe was in no need of immediate relief. In any case, those troops could have crossed the canal by one of several bridges and still reached Trinity within half an hour. For some reason, he repeated, 'The advance to Trinity is to continue at all costs.'

The costs were soaring. Captain Dietrichsen never did meet up with his children again, for he died in 26 Northumberland Road.

From their vantage point in Clanwilliam House, the rebels made almost every shot count. Dead and dying were heaped on the canal bridge.

Any spare moment he had, Reynolds put his arm in a sling to ease the pain of blood poisoning. It seemed not to affect his aim, even though bullets from rifles and machine-guns rattled against the walls and grenades came through the windows, bursting with a roar.

The delicate ornamentation on the outside of the building was shot to bits. Inside, ceilings collapsed, pipes were pierced, causing water to cascade on to the floors below. Some bullets set furnishings alight so that poisonous fumes swept through the house.

Spluttering, their eyes red and raw, the rebels went on firing.

In the GPO, Connolly called his son to him. 'Listen, Roddy, I want

332

you to take this suitcase for me to Bill O'Brien. It contains important papers.'

'I don't know where he lives, Dad.'

'At 43 Belvedere Place.' Connolly called to a Volunteer. 'Here, Paddy, I want you to show my boy where Bill O'Brien lives. He's on an important mission.'

As Connolly took his son by the shoulder to say goodbye, Roddy saw tears in his eyes.

'It's all right, Dad,' he said in his piping voice, 'I'll be all right. Back soon.'

'No, lad,' Connolly said sharply. 'Bill is doing important Union work while we're in here. You can help him.'

It was only when Roddy reached Belvedere Place that he realized fully that the Volunteer could have brought the suitcase, there was no need for the two of them to go. His father was sending his only son away for his own safety.

Tears suddenly raced down Roddy's cheeks and he had a premonition that he had seen his father for the last time.

In the GPO, against a background of heavy gunfire, Pearse wrote his mother a letter.

'We are all safe here up to the present. The St Enda's boys have been on duty on the roof ever since we came in. They are all in good spirits, though very sleepy. We have plenty of food, all our meals being as good as if served in a hotel.'

Willie added a postscript: 'Don't worry. I saw a priest again (confession) and was talking to Fr Bowden also.'

As London's gas-lamps were being lit, John Redmond called on Sir John French and tried to explain the difference between the four armed paramilitary bodies in Ireland. The General admitted to finding it somewhat confusing.

'It is, indeed, General,' Redmond said, 'for anyone who is not Irish. I simply want to assure you that all the Volunteers are loyal except for the Sinn Feiners, the leave-us-aloners.'

'And what sort of support would *they* expect to have?'

'Almost none. Most decent Irish folk are against them.'

'Good,' French said, dubiously.

'May I suggest that the military authorities exercise caution. If many innocent bystanders get hurt, it might turn the popular feeling in favour of the rebels, you see.'

333

'I see,' French said, in an exasperated tone, as if he were expected to hit the rebels with bubbles instead of bullets.

At 6 o'clock, Maconchy ordered Colonel Oates and the 2/8th Battalion to reinforce the 2/7th.

By then, the Tommies had commandeered houses opposite the two rebel strongholds and were sniping continuously from windows and roofs.

In Clanwilliam House, a tailor's dummy, dressed in tunic and cap, kept rocking back and forth as bullets pounded into it, and an open piano gave out a tuneless sound each time it was hit. The carpets were burning and water stored in containers was needed to damp them down.

At about 7 p.m., the men in the Hall realized it was time to fall back. Leaving by the back way through an alley they ran smack into the enemy.

Joe Clarke was seized and put up against the door of a house and searched. A soldier found a revolver in his pocket and fired it at him, the bullet going through the door just as it was opened by a doctor in a white coat. He cursed him roundly. From the yard behind him came the moans of wounded soldiers whom he was treating.

The Tommies apologized, tied Clarke's hands with a rifle pull-through and led him away.

For the first time, a squad of soldiers managed to cross the canal and take cover behind an advertizing hoarding. They got close enough to lob grenades into Clanwilliam House, which burst into flames around 8 o'clock.

Inside, Jim Doyle's rifle was shot out of his hand.

Dick Murphy was at a window on the middle floor, leaning on a chair to get a steadier aim, when he was shot dead.

A sofa caught fire. Someone grabbed a soda syphon to try and put it out and a bullet shattered it in his hand.

At another window, Patrick Doyle was one second firing and yelling encouragement, absolutely silent the next. The Walsh brothers shook him and he fell to the floor, dead.

By now the dust-filled house reeked of cordite and the acrid smell of burning furniture. The roof caught fire and there was a stupendous roar as the blaze ate up everything in its path. Still the rebels fired away, the boom of the Mauser in counterpoint with the sharp retort of the Martinis.

A British soldier advanced, his hand raised to throw a grenade,

334

when Tom Walsh shot him and saw him explode in a flash of light.

The time came when the surviving rebels went for their ammunition and found it was almost spent. Reynolds went from one to another, handing the last ten rounds apiece.

'There'll be reinforcements along soon,' he promised.

They did not believe him. De Valera, though only a hundred yards away, had made no move to contact them in two days and was unlikely to do so now.

Reynolds, returning to his post, took a last proud look at the bridge. It proved fatal. When the lads fired the last of their rounds and descended the stairs, his body blocked the landing.

They had no time to spend mourning him; the stairs were giving way and dense fumes were everywhere. They rushed down to the basement. Once there, they remembered that the back door was blockaded from the outside. They had planned an emergency exit through the roof but it was blazing out of control.

In the street, they could hear soldiers cheering wildly as they advanced for the kill. A captain tried to toss a bomb through a window; it hit a sill and dropped on top of him, nearly blowing his head off.

Covering their mouths against poisonous fumes, the rebels dashed into a back room and, smashing the small barred window, crawled through it into the garden. They jumped over the end wall, then over wall after wall until they found refuge in the grounds of a convent school. Hidden in the shrubbery, they heard girls' piping voices singing, 'Hail, Glorious St Patrick.'

Three died and four survived from Clanwilliam House, one died in 25 Northumberland Road.

Colonel Maconchy, informed that the battle was over at last, rode his horse down Northumberland Road. Though Clanwilliam House was now ablaze and crowds cheered him on either side of the bridge, he was furious. Two hundred and thirty of all ranks had been killed or wounded. In the light of such senseless slaughter, he did not send his men on to Trinity. Instead he billeted them around the area where so many had fallen and where local people were keen to show their gratitude.

That night, as if in mourning, the bombardment in the city ceased.

The silence was the loudest sound of battle so far.

Tralee was also quiet. The Captain and Lieutenant of the Volunteers

335

came to Monteith with an extra bicycle. They wanted to transfer him to the home of a man who was not a Volunteer but a sympathizer.

It was curfew hour and pitch dark. There were no lights in the houses or on the bumpy country lanes. The Captain rode in front, the Lieutenant behind.

Monteith's saddle was too high and, with his bad hand and aching foot, it was hard going. Several times he nearly had his eye poked out by branches overhanging the lane. Once, he rode into a pile of stones and hit the ground with a thud. A mile further on, he went headlong into a muddy pool from which cattle fed. It was one more in a line of cold dowsings.

Finally, on a steep downhill, his brakes did not work and he had no idea where the road was. When he picked himself out of a thorn hedge, he said, 'I intend walking the rest of the way, even if it takes all night.'

A couple of miles further on, they came to the home of a Mr Lenihan. The gnarled old farmer took Monteith by the hand. 'Mr Murray,' he said, 'I don't know you or why you're in your present predicament, but I do know your cause. Anything I have in this house, sir, is at your disposal.'

In No 10, the Prime Minister asked his Minister of War to send someone to Ireland to sort things out, as a matter of urgency.

Kitchener took it for granted it had to be a soldier. Politicians had made an incredible mess of things. The most famous finger in the Empire ran down a list of possibles and came to rest against the name of 'Maxwell, General Sir John.'

'Good,' Kitchener muttered, 'just the man.'

He knew Maxwell from the past since both of them had specialized in Arabia. Good pedigree, Scottish parentage. Well thought of at Sandhurst. 42nd Highlanders, damn good crowd. He was cheerful, had good horse sense, was witty without wounding, never seemed to hurry but got things done.

Kitchener enquired of an aide if Maxwell had a clean bill of health. It seemed so. He had emerged only six days before from a ten-day check-up in a nursing home. Suspicion of the stone, but it proved negative. The Egyptians were sad to see him go. A political move, must have been. He had been adored in Cairo. His hand was unsparing in meting out right and redressing wrong.

Absolutely the right man for the job, Kitchener thought. Not much difference between Cairo and Dublin, apart from the climate.

336

Though this was a political appointment, he checked with Sir John French by telephone because of its military implications. French also knew Maxwell well and called him at once.

'Maxwell, my dear chap, would you mind popping over to see me first thing in the morning, say, 10.30?'

Within the hour, French received official notice from Kitchener's secretary of Maxwell's appointment as GOC in Ireland from the 27th of the month.

'His Majesty's government desire that in this capacity Sir John Maxwell will take all such measures as may in his opinion be necessary for the prompt suppression of insurrection in Ireland, and be accorded a free hand in regard to the movement of all troops now in Ireland or which may be placed under his command hereafter, and also in regard to such measures as may seem to him advisable under the proclamation dated 26 April issued under the Defence of the Realm Act.'

When Asquith asked Kitchener about Maxwell, he said, 'He has impeccable judgement, Prime Minister.'

In the Green, Mallin was persuaded to allow a young girl from Scotland, Margaret Skinnider, to go with William Partridge and seventeen-year-old Fred Ryan to try and set fire to buildings next to the Shelbourne Hotel.

They were all set to toss bombs with eight-second fuses through a window when an alert sniper shot Ryan dead and hit Margaret, too. Partridge carried her back to base.

The Countess held her hand as Madeleine ffrench-Mullen dug out the bullets from her right arm, right side and back. She did not utter a sound but the tender-hearted Mallin, who stood over her, was saying, 'I'll never forgive myself for this as long as I live.'

The Countess slipped out of the College and when she returned a few minutes later, she said, 'Don't worry, Margaret, me dear, I got the wretched blighter for you.'

In Boland's Mill, de Valera was worried by the scarcity of food. The neighing of hungry horses was also getting on his nerves. He let them out, and, with their heavy clatter intensified by the stillness of night, they went along the streets in search of fodder. It was a poor district without front gardens. But there were a few hedges and they would find grass further along on the banks of the canal near where his men had performed so bravely that day.

337

When de Valera heard that no one was feeding the cats and dogs in the pound, he ordered them to be released, too.

Large numbers of domestic animals now roamed the city, scavenging sometimes on corpses in the streets.

Over in the west, Daly's men had set fire to the old Linenhall Barracks. Soon they wished they hadn't.

The fire threatened the entire area and they were forced to fight the blaze with the British sniping at them as they were etched against the light.

A drunk rolled past the GPO singing, 'Two lovely black eyes,' and calling for 'Three cheers for John Redmond.'

Connolly, woken by a boy who had crept in to tell him his family were starving, found the men all expecting a bayonet assault. To encourage them, he began roaring a verse from the Soldier's Song which they all took up:

> *We'll sing a song, a soldier's song,*
> *With cheering rousing chorus,*
> *As round our blazing fires we throng,*
> *The starry heavens o'er us.*
> *Impatient for the coming fight,*
> *And as we wait the morning light,*
> *Here in the silence of the night*
> *We'll sing a soldier's song.*

Pearse and his former pupil, Desmond Ryan, did not join in. They were seated on upturned barrels, chatting like old friends around a fire. Pearse was proud that they had held out for longer than any other rising since 1789. He surprised Ryan by saying, 'It *was* the right thing to do, was it not?'

'Yes!' returned Ryan at once.

Pearse spoke as one who had turned the problem over in his head hundreds of times without resolving it. 'If we fail, it means the end of the Volunteers, Ireland – everything.'

'I suppose so.'

'When we are all wiped out, people will blame us for everything. But without this protest, the war would have ended and nothing done. In a few years they will understand.'

Ryan remembered how, at school, he had taught them about the young boy Cuchulain who had donned armour for the first time. A Druid warned him that whoever took up arms that day would have a short life but a glorious one. Pearse had put Cuchulain's response in old Irish on the wall: 'I care not if my life have only the span of a night and a day if my deeds be spoken of by the men of Ireland.'

In his eyes, that pagan hero was baptized in the persons of his pupils. Why had he founded St Enda's and fostered the good in them except to give Cuchulains to Ireland? His students, now on the roof of the GPO, were his only memorials; and no teacher, Ryan felt, had better ones.

Pearse rose and walked up and down a few times, as if wanting to believe with his whole heart but not quite managing it.

'Dublin's name will be glorious for ever.' He spoke with deep feeling. 'Men will speak of her as one of the splendid cities, as they now speak of Paris.'

Not far away, Tom Clarke was telling the young medic, Jim Ryan, about the lead-up to the rising and what their aims and motives were. Ryan was Red Cross; unlike the signatories of the Proclamation, he might emerge alive. If so, he would be the witness of what they had tried to do for Ireland.

Clarke was in the middle of his exposition when, in Portobello Barracks, Skeffy's body was being stuffed into a sack. The sack was sewn up and buried in quicklime in the Barracks yard.

THURSDAY

At dawn on a golden Thursday, all hell seemed to break loose.

The GPO was fired on from all directions. Rebels at the windows and on the roof returned it with relish.

The noise was unabated when the British destroyer *Dove* tied up at the Custom House Wharf at 6 a.m. Aboard was the Chief Secretary. A bad sailor, Birrell had not slept a wink. On deck, in a black top coat and top hat, he did not know that his replacement had already been named.

Cocking his ear, he heard firing on either side of the Liffey. High above, he detected nests of machine-guns on almost every building round about. Liberty Hall was pocked with shells. And the smell . . . .

He was whipped away to the Viceregal Lodge through deserted streets, past shuttered shops and buildings with all the clocks stopped.

Ironically, the only sign of life was a hearse followed, as the authorities had decreed, by a single mourner. Many had buried their dead in back gardens. One night, in the Castle, seventy had been interred.

At the lodge, he shook hands with Wimborne and General Friend. The food situation, he was told, was desperate and leading to violence. Some of Wimborne's aides had joined in the looting. They had gone in civvies into the city and stolen a wheelbarrow which they piled high with potatoes, cauliflowers and tinned fruit. Without it, there would have been nothing for the worthies to eat.

Once His Excellency had realized on Tuesday that he was in no danger, he displayed a theatrical talent that would have earned him many an encore at the Abbey. Hour after hour, he had dictated minutes to his secretary and given orders down the phone, 'It is His Excellency's *command*', disregarding the inconvenient fact that they were impossible to carry out.

Was he not the one blameless man in the entire country, the only one who had got things right? He marched up and down in front of Blackwood and, in between prodigious face-flushing gulps of brandy, shouted, 'I shall hang MacNeill! – I'll let the others off, but I shall hang MacNeill.'

Then came a telegram. A General Maxwell was coming over to take charge. At once he had changed his tune.

Hitherto, Ireland was fraught with danger but Britain could sleep in peace at nights because Wimborne was in control. Now, the situation had miraculously righted itself; there was no need of outside interference.

He had sent the irreplaceable Basil, who really thought Wimborne had acted all week like the Emperor of Asses, to London to tell the Prime Minister that, fortunately, His Excellency's judgement had been flawless all along and he was even now on the point of forcing the rebels to surrender.

Birrell was upset to learn on arriving at the lodge that he had been superseded. What he did not know was that Sir Henry Wilson of the Imperial General Staff, an opponent of Liberal policy in Ireland, was even then urging Maxwell to have him arrested, tried and shot.

Friend was able to tell him that the Army had the GPO in a vice. 'Troops are moving down all the surrounding streets and the whole of Sackville (O'Connell) Street is covered by machine-gun fire. We have nests on top of the Gresham and most buildings down to the Liffey. Soon, artillery will be in place.'

Birrell shuddered at the thought of artillery being used in a city of which he was very fond.

In his lodgings, Birrell's critic, the fastidious Maurice Headlam, could no longer stand the sight and smell of that horse mouldering practically on his doorstep.

He had a brainwave. He telephoned the Zoo.

'Headlam here, Treasury Remembrancer, ringing from the Green. I was wondering how you are managing with the animals.'

'Not well, sir,' the Head of the Zoo replied. 'Unless we can get food for the lions, they're likely to go on the rampage.'

'Exactly what I thought. There's a dead horse, shot, you understand, still beautifully fresh, right outside my place.'

'What's it like there?'

Headlam put his lips right up to the mouthpiece to muffle the sounds of gun-fire. 'Very quiet, really.'

'That's grand. I'll have a truck pick it up right away.'

At ten, a shell landed on the *Irish Times* printing office setting the big rolls of paper alight.

Half an hour later, Tom Clarke asked young Lesley Price to go to the Pro-Cathedral and bring back a priest. She was terrified but agreed to go.

Leaving by the side door, she hugged the walls until she reached Marlborough Street. From behind railings, people were screaming at her, 'Go back, you stupid girl, you'll get yourself killed.' They pointed to the Education Office. 'The British. In there.'

Taking no notice, she went up the stone steps and knocked on the red presbytery door. There was no reply. Shivering with fright, she took a shoe off and banged the door even harder with the heel till the paint cracked.

At last, an elderly priest edged the door open. It had been kept shut for two days.

'Come in, girl,' he hissed, 'we're in the cellars.'

When she told him why she had come, he said, 'Don't you realize they're a bunch of Communists in the GPO? Isn't Connolly there? Sure to God none of his crowd wants to see a priest.'

Fr O'Flanagan overheard. He decided that if a young lady had risked her life, he couldn't very well say no. He gathered up his priestly gear and put on his stove-pipe hat for identification.

'Not by the front door,' he said. 'Safer out the back.'

341

In Moore Street, the priest was greeting an old friend when the man fell shot. Fr O'Flanagan knelt to anoint him but it was plain he was done for. Some brave lads took him in a handcart to Jervis Street Hospital.

Lesley led the priest into a shop in Henry Street, then through gaps in the walls into the GPO. The rebels gave him a rousing welcome. He had expected to be ministering to the dying and was annoyed at first. But soon he was glad he had come; he had never seen a more cheerful crowd in his life.

They told him they were an army and wasn't an army entitled to a chaplain?

In the College of Surgeons, the Countess finally came across the OTC's armoury. It consisted of 89 rifles as well as 24,000 rounds of .303 and .22 ammunition.

William Partridge grabbed a new rifle and went up on to the roof to try it out. The trap door fell on his head and he had to be treated for cuts and concussion.

Chris Caffrey, a pretty young woman, was carrying messages between the College and the GPO. Mallin gave her a despatch for Connolly, telling him about the arms find.

Chris, like many couriers, was dressed as a war widow. She wore a black dress, a wedding-ring on her finger and a badge of red, white and blue. It enabled her to pass through the streets without hindrance. On her journeys, she picked up quite a bit of information from elderly women who had carried chairs on to the pavement to have a knit and a natter.

About 11 a.m., she slipped out of the side door in York Street. She left just as a group of men with lifting tackle were hoisting a dead horse on to a lorry marked 'Dublin Zoo'. She was seen leaving by a local busy-body who followed her down Grafton Street into Dame Street. There her shadow called out to soldiers on guard at Trinity College, 'This hussy's a spy.'

When she explained how she knew, Chris was ushered into Trinity. She stuffed Mallin's message into her mouth.

'What's that?' an NCO asked.

'A sweet,' Chris said, swallowing painfully. She held out a paper bag. 'Want one?'

She was taken into a room. Two officers entered and locked the door.

One said, 'We're holding you on suspicion of being a spy.'

'A spy,' said Chris, 'when my husband gave his life for King and country in the retreat from Mons, died in the thick mud, he did, gasping his love for me and England.'

'Strip, please,' an officer said, with a smirk.

'What?'

'Either you strip or we'll do it for you.'

Chris said, 'I want a woman with me.'

'Sorry, girl. Off with those clothes. Everything.'

'My husband gave his life for the Empire,' Chris wailed.

'Is that so, then your sacrifice will be as great as his, won't it?'

She spat in their faces before beginning to unbutton her blouse.

The rebels in Boland's and on the railway were already under continuous fire from houses in Mount Street when the British opened up from the roof of Sir Patrick Dun's Hospital.

De Valera summoned the young British army cadet who was his prisoner, G. F. Mackay.

'I'm sending a message,' he said, 'to the British CO in this area. If his snipers don't stop using the hospital to fire on my men, I will execute you.' He gripped the lad's shoulder. 'I want you to know without any shadow of doubt that, whatever happens, you will be safe here with us.'

De Valera had given orders to stop all food entering the city. A request came for an exception to be made to allow milkmen to deliver to the hospitals.

'This is wartime,' he spluttered. 'Regardless of our feelings, it's our solemn duty to see the milk gets through.'

Without sleep for days, he was looking gaunt and his behaviour was becoming erratic, sometimes manic. He hit on a bright idea to engage the enemy, and when his men were keyed up and ready to go, he decided it was not practicable after all.

Father O'Flanagan was hearing confessions at midday when there was a new sound: the thud of an 18-pounder opening up from the Parnell Monument fifty yards away. The first of many shells fell next door on the Metropole.

'Jasus,' the kneeling penitent yelped, 'them bastards, begging your pardon, Fairther, have started bombarding us.'

He rejoined his hands and continued his confession.

'I jest cursed and swore, Fairther.'

*

343

The shelling began on Boland's a few minutes later. A 1-pounder gun had been detached from the *Helga* and transported by lorry to the corner of Percy Lane. The *Helga* joined in from the Liffey.

The rebels felt threatened, especially as the Bakery roof was mainly of glass; but de Valera had a plan.

Nearby was a distillery with a tall tower. A group commanded by Captain Cullen went up the steel ladder on the outside. With brick-splinters spattering them, they managed to fix on the top a pike, adorned with a green flag with a gold harp in the middle. This, they hoped, would draw fire away from the Bakery.

In fact, shells from the gun in Percy Lane landed near the *Helga* on the Liffey, drenching the crew. The skipper, thinking he was being fired on by the rebels, replied in kind. De Valera took a schoolboy's delight in the thought of one of *Helga*'s guns firing on the other.

Shells shook the tower and burst a water tank but failed to dislodge the flag.

Below, a handful of soaked Volunteers believed they had been ordered to stay put. Simon Donnelly and George A. Lyons tried to tell them over the cannon-roar that they were to evacuate the building. Deafened and shell-shocked, they had to be dragged to safety.

In O'Connell Street, the British gunners were still having difficulty targeting the GPO. Solid old buildings nearby continued to be hit and to burn. With firemen off the streets, the fires were getting out of control.

Connolly's obsession with the notion of a final bayonet charge forced him to take counter-measures. With the British occupying all the surrounding streets, it was vital to get a few small outposts into, say, the premises of the *Irish Independent* and in Henry Street where an armoured lorry was patrolling.

He was out organizing a barricade in Prince's Street, part of which was The O'Rahilly's green Ford, when a stray bullet wounded him in the left arm. He hurried back into the GPO and asked Jim Ryan to draw a screen around him.

He rolled up his sleeve. 'Just a nick, Jim. No need to tell the others.'

After medical attention, he picked thirty men in the foyer and put them in the charge of fifteen-year-old Sean MacLoughlain who had been for a time with Heuston in the Mendicity Institute and had shown astonishing powers of leadership.

Connolly saw them into Prince's Street and through an alley into

Middle Abbey Street. Stepping into the open, he urged them on. 'Go!' As they followed MacLoughlain at the double, he edged out to check that they had made it to the offices of the *Irish Independent*. He was turning back when a sniper's bullet ricocheted off the pavement, smashing his left ankle. He fell heavily.

When he came to, he was shuddering all over; perspiration broke out of every pore. He tried to focus his eyes, to get his bearings, then crawled, an inch at a time, leaving a snail-like trail of blood, the hundred yards to Prince's Street.

In the GPO, they were wondering what was keeping him. As soon as he turned the corner, they rushed to pick him up.

The British doctor, Captain George Mahoney, applied a tourniquet. Connolly had suffered a compound fracture of the shin-bone. Once the flow of blood was stemmed, a bed was brought in and Connolly lowered on to it. The ends of shattered bones were protruding through the skin.

Mahoney whispered to Jim Ryan, 'Quick with the anaesthetic.'

All Ryan could find was a weak concentration of chloroform.

Mahoney whispered again, 'We'll need a lakeful of that stuff to have any effect.'

While the search for a stronger anaesthetic was on, another injured man was brought in. He was so badly hurt, Fr O'Flanagan anointed him.

Ryan gave Connolly more painkillers as Mahoney released the tourniquet. He picked out fragments of shattered bone and ligatured the small blood vessels. He put on a make-shift splint and, after a long search, was able to give him an injection of morphia.

In Coalisland, Tyrone, Nora Connolly was becoming increasingly frustrated.

After delivering her father's messages, she had holed out with the Volunteers for a couple of days in a big barn lit by a smelly oil lamp. With her were men awaiting the word to rise.

Once, someone put his head round the barn door. 'Where are the first-aiders?'

Her arm shot up. She went to a nearby hotel to attend a rebel who had shot himself in the thumb. It was easy to deal with, but afterwards someone clapped her on the shoulder. 'You're the one for us.'

'Fine,' she said, 'but how'd you know I wouldn't prefer making holes to plugging them?'

By now it had become clear to her that something was wrong. She felt a strong urge to join her father.

Something told her *he needed her.*

At 3 o'clock, the flagstaff over the Henry Street corner of the GPO was shot away. Soon after, a shell struck the corner of the Metropole Hotel, followed a minute later by one that brought down part of the Post Office balustrade. There were several more close misses.

The O'Rahilly put his sixteen prisoners in an inner room as a precaution.

'Whatever happens to us,' he told the guards, 'these men must be protected.'

The British bombardment of the GPO from Lower Abbey Street was being frustrated. Any obstacle over twelve feet high got in the way of their incendiary shells. A fire that began on one side of Lower Abbey Street spread via the barricades to the other. Cars, carts, furniture blazed like bonfires on St John's Day. Within the hour, it was like a forest fire. It spread south to the Liffey and north to the Imperial Hotel opposite the GPO. There had never been anything like it in a British city even in wartime.

In the Fire Brigade tower, Chief Purcell fumed at his helplessness.

In the Post Office, the rebel leaders looked on, wondering if this was an alternative to a bayonet attack.

Tommies turned out to evacuate houses along Eden Quay.

'Get out,' they called through megaphones. 'For your own safety, leave your homes and move along the river beyond the Custom House.'

In a crowded House of Commons, Sir Edward Carson was speaking on the Irish situation. He had been prepared to resist Home Rule in Ulster, even if it meant fighting the British army. Yet, without any sense of irony, he said: 'Gentlemen, we should be ready to put down these rebels now and for evermore.'

John Redmond was not to be outdone in loyalty to the Crown. With high colour in his cheeks, he hastened to express the feeling of detestation and horror with which he and his Nationalist colleagues heard of events in Dublin. It was a feeling shared by the vast majority of the people in Ireland.

'Is the insanity of a few to turn all her marvellous victories of the last few years into irreparable defeat?'

After the battle of Mount Street Bridge, the Sherwood Foresters were replaced by the 2/8th Battalion South Staffordshire Regiment, part of the 176th recently arrived. Their orders were to proceed that afternoon under Colonel Oates to the Royal Hospital, guarding a convoy of ammunition.

They were nearly there, at the Rialto Bridge, when they ran into heavy fire from Kent's men in Marrowbone Lane Distillery and the South Dublin Union. Not wanting a repeat of the day before, Colonel Maconchy asked Portobello Barracks for help.

Major Vane gathered together fifty men with experience under fire, including six officers. On arrival, he found Oates's unit was under pressure in front and on both flanks. Taking charge, he advanced with his own men and two companies of the 2/8th.

Fighting was fierce as they entered the South Dublin Union. They broke into the main buildings, running through maternity wards and causing some pregnant women to go into premature labour.

On the ground floor of the Nurses' Home, half a company of Crown forces clashed with twenty-seven rebels. At point blank range, they fired on each other with rifles and revolvers, and the troops tossed grenades.

As the assault began, Kent gave orders for the sixteen-strong James's Street garrison to be withdrawn in order to help. Most of his men in the Union were half-dead from lack of sleep. In the din of battle, they thought he meant they were to evacuate their HQ in the Nurses' Home. The result was, both garrisons started to withdraw at the same time. They met in a ground-floor dormitory between their positions at about 4 p.m.

Fortunately, one man remained in the Nurses' Home. Cathal Brugha was behind a barricade in the hallway just as British troops entered it via a tunnel. He exchanged fire with them before they tried to flush him out with grenades.

He was hit by five bullets and several large bomb splinters but managed to drag himself through the open door of the kitchen into a small yard at the rear. There he had a view of the back door as well as the door to the kitchen.

He had an automatic pistol fitted with a wooden stock. He sat on the ground, propped himself up against the wall and refused to allow the British to cross the barricade.

The rebels had heard the tremendous barrage and took it for granted that Brugha was dead.

Kent grouped his forty or so men and posted two snipers in the only places where they could see the enemy approaching. Believing that they would soon all be wiped out, he thanked them for their loyalty. They shared their last cigarettes and then recited a decade of the rosary. Now they were prepared for the final British assault.

It did not come. They were trying to work out why not when they heard someone singing:

God save Ireland, say we proudly
God save Ireland, say we all,
Whether on the scaffold high
Or the battlefield we die.

That voice, though weak, was unmistakable: it was Brugha's.

A scout, sent back to reconnoitre, peeped through the tunnel into the yard. There he was, his gun at the ready, his blood around him in an ever-widening circle. He paused from time to time in his singing to fire another round to warn the British off.

'Come on out,' he called pipingly. 'Let's see if there's a British officer to match an officer of the Irish Volunteers!'

The British had already left. Brugha had held the pass for two hours.

The scout went back to tell Kent. For the first and only time, the Commandant showed emotion. He went and knelt speechless beside his comrade whose eyes were clouding over from exhaustion and loss of blood.

Brugha had just enough strength to ask his comrades to join with him in singing before he died '*God save Ireland*', then, he said, 'Go back to fighting the British for me.'

Before the song was over, he collapsed. When his comrades cut his clothing away, they found he was wounded in twenty-five places. Some of the bullets had severed arteries. They gave him emergency treatment until they were able to move him to the Union Hospital.

'It's obvious,' Kent sighed, as they retrieved their HQ in the Nurses' Home, 'he's not going to make it.'

It was not obvious to Brugha.

In line with Lowe's strategy, a large body of soldiers met up at the Castle intending to cross the Liffey by Grattan Bridge and move east to put a further squeeze on the GPO.

Daly's men were on the drum beneath the great dome of the Four

348

Patrick Pearse surrendering to General Lowe

The Countess Markievicz (second from r.) after her surrender

Eamon de Valera under prisoner's escort

Father John O'Flanagan

Willie (l.) and Patrick Pearse

Tom Clarke

Joseph Plunkett

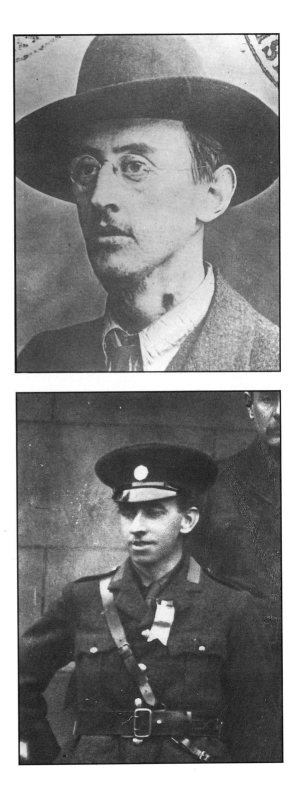

Thomas MacDonagh

Edward Daly

John (Sean) MacBride

Eamonn Kent

Cornelius Colbert

Sean McDermott

James Connolly

Courts. They fired on the Crown troops but could not prevent them crossing the river and erecting more barricades in Upper Abbey Street.

That left the GPO even more isolated, especially as the armoured lorries were now transporting men and sandbags for barricades and towing field-guns into position more or less at will.

In Boland's, de Valera, with his outposts overrun, knew he could not hold out much longer.

He sent a message to MacDonagh in Jacob's, saying that he had food but little ammunition left and a frontal attack was expected soon.

MacDonagh sent fifteen men armed with Howth Mausers on bicycles to try and relieve the pressure at Merrion Square. On the west side of the Green, one of the fifteen, John O'Grady, was hit in the stomach and flew over the handlebars. His comrades picked him up, put him on the saddle and wheeled him back to base.

'Easy, John,' someone said, 'we'll have you back at HQ in no time.' But they all knew he was dying.

When this relief effort failed, de Valera discussed with his Vice-Commandant the possibility of retreating to the Dublin mountains. Failing that, they would have to choose where to make their last stand.

The best place seemed to be Guinness's granary which had its back to the canal and was that much easier to defend.

Hamilton Norway and his wife were in their sitting-room, which overlooked Grafton Street, when the looting began there.

One very fat old lady had an orange box under one arm and her clothes so weighed down with pickings she could scarcely move. A big bundle kept slipping under her shawl, so she had to stop and hitch it up. Finally, it escaped and numerous cans of fruit went rolling away from her.

'God and all His holy angels help me,' she screamed, as black-faced boys, more like little devils, rushed to help themselves.

Mrs Norway saw a woman dropping clothes from an upstairs window when a shot rang out from the direction of Trinity College.

The woman froze before falling head-first to the pavement below.

At 6.50 p.m., the GPO Battalion heard a loud bang as a shell hit the Imperial Hotel above Clery's store.

It caught fire at once. Flames spouted through every window. The noise was deafening. Glass shattered in the heat, beams crashed down, walls rumbled and collapsed. The five rebels inside had no choice but to leave and cross the boulevard to the Post Office.

In the red air, they ran like bats out of hell across the broad stretch of O'Connell Street with machine-guns threshing away at them from every tall building around.

Four made it, one fell.

The rebels were all praying for his soul when he jumped to his feet and sped on to the GPO.

'Didn't I slip on pieces of glass?' he puffed.

At 9.30 p.m., Hopkins & Hopkins, the jewellers on the quays, set alight half an hour before, finally surrendered to the flames in an ear-splitting roar.

At 10, Hoyte's oil works burst into flame. Soon there was an explosion that rocked the Post Office walls. Hundreds of oil drums rose in the air and rained down fiery emulsion on the street. The air changed from red to an unbearable diamond-white that blistered the eyes. The heat hit the men in the GPO like a whip. The smoke swirling across the road nearly choked them.

Urged on by Clarke and McDermott, they tried to cool everything down with hoses.

Even Joe Plunkett rose from his sickbed, a bizarre figure, with creased uniform, rings on his fingers, a bangle on his wrist, a spur on one boot. Forgetting Paris in 1871, he mumbled, in between coughs, 'This is the first time a capital city has burned since Moscow in 1814.'

Night turned to day. Buildings over several acres were ablaze. Burning timber crackled before collapsing in huge waterfalls of fire. Flames leaped one hundred feet high and sparks soared like stars shooting up to a pumpkin-coloured moon.

On his Pillar, Nelson surveyed it all serenely, as though he were lit up by a thousand lamps.

Everyone saw the holocaust.

On the top floor of the Post Office, The O'Rahilly said to a youngster, 'Know why the British are doing this?'

Jimmy O'Byrne replied, 'So they can get a good pot-shot at us, I suppose.'

'No. It's to show us exactly what they think of poor old Ireland.'

350

In the foyer, even in his pain, Connolly was pleased. This was the guarantee that the Easter Rising would never be forgotten.

The Countess on the roof of the College of Surgeons pinched herself in disbelief. This was not Rome but Dublin burning.

In the Viceregal Lodge, Birrell, seeing the distant orange glow, yielded to despair at this final symbol of the failure of his life's work.

In the suburbs, as far as the hill of Killiney on Sea nine miles away, people gaped incredulously at the great fire and pointed out to their children, Nelson, whom they had never before seen at night, not even under a full moon.

The rebels' situation was becoming ever more critical.

The GPO outposts were all abandoned, save for the Metropole next door. Daly's 1st Battalion at the Four Courts, their nearest allies, was still fighting the fire at Linenhall Barracks that rivalled anything in O'Connell Street.

Inside HQ, the fumes were suffocating, mingling with the stench of dead horse flesh to make an odour worse than potato blight. A river of molten glass moved towards them across the street like lava from a volcano.

The sacking on the barricades was beginning to singe; as they hosed it down the water turned to steam.

Pearse ordered all explosives to be taken down to the cellars. 'Hurry before we are blown sky-high.'

They were sweating, their faces tanned by the heat. Their hair and eyebrows curled up, their eyes were blood-shot and their tongues parched.

Things were so desperate, Pearse ordered a group to try and tunnel under Henry Street. They struggled manfully, only to have to give it up as a lost cause.

Michael Collins felt they were paying the penalty for being holed up without emergency plans.

The leaders conferred and decided they would have to make a break for it next day.

That night, though the big guns were silent, Connolly could not sleep for the pain, the stench, the heat. Once, he peeped over the edge of his bed. Captain Mahoney was lying on a mattress below.

'Do y'know,' Connolly said, 'you're the best thing we've captured this week.'

Pearse asked Jim Ryan for a sleeping draught. 'I haven't slept a wink since we came in here.'

Ryan was astonished. They were into their fourth day.

Drugged, Pearse settled down to sleep. He was just dozing off when the fire alarm rang and he was as wide awake as ever. Restless, he rose during the night and looked out of the window. He judged from the slant of the flames that the wind had changed direction. It was blowing from the mountains to the south-east. The immediate danger had passed.

He heard Connolly twisting and turning and occasionally groaning, 'Oh, God, did ever a man suffer more for his country?'

FRIDAY

At 2 a.m. on Friday, General Sir John Grenfell Maxwell sailed up the Liffey.

The fifty-six-year-old Commander-in-Chief was on deck, peering through tadpole eyes into the chalky distance. Muffled up against the cold of an Irish spring morning, he saw what looked like an entire city ablaze.

On his right was General Hutchinson, his Chief Staff-Officer, and on his left, Prince Alexander of Battenberg, his ADC. They liked working with him; he was relaxed, did not get things out of proportion.

Maxwell did not relish the job. To start with, his wife was about to undergo major surgery. Then he felt he deserved better of petty politicians who seemed bent on humbling him. He had worked wonders, he thought, in Egypt, checking the advance of the Turks. And they loved their 'Maxaweel', as they called him, and followed him blindly.

If Kitchener hadn't picked him personally, he might have turned this job down. But it was his only chance of getting back east, provided he brought the rebellion to a speedy end with a minimum of casualties to his own boys.

He knew Dublin, which made his task easier. Fourteen years before, he had been Chief Staff-Officer to the Duke of Connaught, C-in-C in Ireland. A brief posting, thank an Anglo-Saxon God.

He lit another cigarette from the one in his mouth. He had fought a long, hard campaign against nicotine and been routed. His moustache, teeth, fingers, were yellow, and his eyes were creased perpetually against cigarette smoke. Coughing was almost a full-time occupation and he had to clear his throat whenever he wanted to speak. Still, cigarettes kept him off food. If only they did the same for the drink.

From the North Wall on, he took in the fact that Sackville Street was burning. Not as bad as it looked a few miles out to sea. Still, bad enough.

Bullets were flying. His big nose, which had earned him the nickname of Conky, sniffed the most wonderful smell in all the world: cordite, with the added aroma of yeast from the many breweries of this most liquid of cities.

When he disembarked, three cars whisked him and his staff to his HQ at Kilmainham. Within minutes, they approached the imposing Royal Hospital, temporary billet of over two thousand troops added to the usual hundred or so Irish veterans.

As they went up the drive towards the famous tower, he felt not the slightest pang of nostalgia. It was not in his nature. Besides, he preferred hot sun to belting rain, and browns to greens.

As soon as he was settled in his quarters, he had himself briefed by Friend and Lowe. He was appalled at the mess the politicians had landed the Army in. He could hardly believe reports of the Administration allowing para-military parades with rifles, bayonets and live ammunition.

That the Irish were capable of vile things he did not doubt. His mind went back to 1884 when he was a mere subaltern of twenty-five. In Cairo, it had been his privilege to see General Gordon on his way to meet his destiny in Khartoum. He rememberd those curiously detached eyes and the way he bit on his words like bullets before expelling them. Later, when Lord Wolsely sent Colonel Stewart to rescue Gordon, the entire party was massacred by a Monasir Sheikh. When Wolsely heard, he uttered a lament that Maxwell was never to forget:

'If only Stewart had died in battle instead of being murdered like an Irish landlord by a cowardly sulking reptile such as this country and Ireland produce in large numbers.'

Maxwell was told he had 12,000 men under his command. He promptly approved Lowe's strategy of strangling the rebels' HQ. In fact, the battle was almost over, he saw; this would be a mere mopping up operation, though it might be bloody.

He confirmed Lowe as head of Dublin Command and, within hours, set his personal stamp upon the campaign.

Firstly, he had a Proclamation posted throughout the city. He threatened to destroy all buildings within any area occupied by the rebels. Firmness, yes. Threats, intimidation, no question about it. He did not intend shilly-shallying with the bloody Irish. Rebels, that's what he was dealing with, not soldiers of a so-called Republic.

Secondly, he ordered a pit to be dug in Arbour Hill Detention Centre, big enough for a hundred corpses. It measured 29 feet by 9 feet. On the edge of the pit was a mound of quicklime. Not one fragment of any so-called patriot's corpse would remain for veneration.

He knew just enough of Ireland to realize that the body of an Irish felon constituted a danger to the Empire.

Dawn came to the GPO after a night of swirling smoke and sounds of walls crashing across the street. An ambulance was picking up an old man stretched out dead on O'Connell Bridge.

Already, The O'Rahilly had sent spare bombs and grenades from the top floors to a place of safety below. Each night, Fitzgerald had pulled his leg about the battle lasting longer than he anticipated, but now the end was undeniably near.

With first light, firing recommenced. Two 18-pounders opened up on the GPO but intermittently, suggesting the artillery had still not solved their problems. Machine-gun fire never stopped.

Connolly insisted on being put on a bed with castors so he could be wheeled to action-stations to encourage the men. Satisfied that they were prepared, he dictated the day's orders to Winifred Carney who typed them on her battered old typewriter. That done, he tried to read a detective story.

'A book,' he said, through gritted teeth, 'plenty of rest and an insurrection all at the same time. Not bad, eh?'

In Coalisland, Nora Connolly was tired of waiting. She had heard that her sister Ina was just north in Clogher. When she enquired how far it was, she was told, 'Just a gentle stroll.'

She would collect Ina and they'd travel to Dublin together.

Unfortunately, the path to Clogher was empty and mountainy; and there were no signposts.

Birrell went by car through heavy firing – the first he had ever experienced – to Dublin Castle. Nathan met him with a long, sad handshake and told him the Cabinet had extended martial law throughout the land.

Birrell sat down and wrote to Asquith. All his work for Ireland had been smashed by 'a supreme act of criminal folly'. The rising, he said, was little more than a street brawl stirred up by a handful of violent men, Connolly's socialists and hot-heads from the National University which he himself had fathered on the Irish people.

'Of course, all this shatters *me*. The Thing that has happened swallows up the things that might have happened had I otherwise acted.'

He suggested that martial law over all Ireland would only increase antagonism towards the military. But he knew his advice was unlikely to be heeded, especially as his other forecasts had turned out so disastrously wrong.

Later, Maxwell interviewed him and Wimborne. His Excellency kept muttering, 'I did my best to convince them but they paid no heed. *They* knew best.'

The General judged the one a total incompetent and the other a windbag. He heard them out without listening. Only he, an outsider, a professional soldier, could be objective. At least he could not possibly foul things up as they had done.

He told them he welcomed their co-operation in clearing Sinn Feiners first out of Dublin, then out of the rest of the country which was presently quiet. Meanwhile troops were infiltrating the warren of streets around the GPO and building barricades.

'I'm going to get them,' he promised. 'Every one.'

Connolly asked his secretary to take another dictation.

'To Soldiers' was a heady account of the way things were progressing, contrary to all known facts. There were risings in Galway, Wexford, Wicklow, Cork and Kerry. Vague references were thrown in to German allies and the USA straining every nerve to help them.

'For the first time in 700 years the flag of a free Ireland floats triumphantly in Dublin City.

'The British army are afraid to storm any positions held by our forces. The slaughter they suffered in the first few days has totally unnerved them.

'Courage, boys, we are winning, and in the hour of our victory let us not forget the splendid women who have everywhere stood by us and cheered us on. Never had man or woman a grander cause, never was a cause more grandly served.'

His rosy face was aglow and Winifred Carney could hardly see

355

through her tears. She went away to type copies and brought them back for him to sign.

Connolly asked The O'Rahilly to read it to the men in the foyer, which he did in ringing tones.

Pearse was more candid than Connolly in his despatch. He admitted that communications with outlying posts had ceased. Enemy snipers were growing more numerous.

'I desire now to pay homage to the gallantry of the soldiers of Irish freedom who have during the past four days been writing with fire and steel the most glorious chapter in the later history of Ireland.

'If I were to mention the names of individuals, my list would be a long one.'

He happened to glance at where Connolly was trying to inspire his men from his bed, and his heart missed a beat.

'I will name only that of Commandant-General James Connolly, commanding the Dublin Division. He lies wounded but is still the guiding brain of our resistance.

'I am satisfied that we should have accomplished the task of enthroning, as well as proclaiming the Irish Republic as a Sovereign State, had our arrangements for a simultaneous rising of the whole country, with a combined plan as sound as the Dublin plan has proved to be, been allowed to go through on Easter Sunday.'

He paused, pondering on what might have been. If only MacNeill . . . . He wanted to be fair to the man who had fostered the Volunteer movement and who would be needed in the years ahead. Besides, the loss of German arms on which the rebellion in the provinces had depended was not MacNeill's fault.

'Of the fatal countermanding order which prevented these plans being carried out, I shall not speak further. Both Eoin MacNeill and we have acted in the best interests of Ireland.

'For my part, as to anything I have done in this, I am not afraid to face the judgement of God, or the judgement of posterity.'

In Lower Abbey Street, Mr Whelan and his slight, handsome, sixteen-year-old son Christy, looked from afar at their place of work, Eason's in O'Connell Street. They saw all its windows were gone and a flag was flying over the GPO. It was impossible to go on. Bullets were flying and soldiers were urging everyone to keep off the streets.

Back home at Drumcondra, Christy told his stepmother he was tired. None of them had slept much since Monday.

'Go to bed, my dear,' she said.

After reading for a while, he went to sleep with his right hand outside the sheet. He awoke screaming in pain. His mother rushed in to find a bullet had gone through his wrist. She closed the window and bandaged his wound.

Hearing soldiers outside, his father picked him up and carried him for safety to his own bedroom. He had no sooner laid him on the bed than he felt a bullet graze his cheek. Others followed, hitting Christy several times in the head.

His father, with blood streaming down his cheek, went across to his only son and tenderly picked him up. 'Christy,' he moaned. 'Christy.'

Soldiers burst into the house through doors and windows. They grabbed the still warm lad and tossed him on the floor. Pinioning the father's arms, they took him to nearby Mountjoy Jail.

Indicating the boy, an irate NCO said to Mrs Whelan, 'That's what happens, missis, to bleedin' snipers.'

In mid-morning, the two 18-pounders intensified their bombardment of the GPO. The first incendiary shell landed on the roof about noon, but did little damage.

The O'Rahilly, still concerned for the prisoners, fed them and removed them to the cellar.

'I give you my word,' he told them, 'you will get out of here with your lives.'

The snipers on the roof were under fire from the Gresham Hotel and several had been hit by shrapnel. The men in outposts which they could no longer hold were retreating to Headquarters.

Pearse and Connolly decided that, apart from a few Red Cross nurses, the twenty girls had to leave.

When they were assembled, Pearse told them:

'When the history of this week is written, the highest honours will be paid you. You have taken part in the greatest armed attempt at liberating Ireland since 1798. You obeyed the order to come here. Now I ask you to obey a more difficult order . . . .'

'No, sir,' the girls cried.

One said, 'What was all that stuff about equality?'

Pearse held up his hand for silence. 'I am not asking you but telling you to leave. It won't be easy. Some of you may be shot. But you showed your readiness for that when you came here. Now go, and God go with you.'

McDermott went up to Pearse and hissed, 'It's a mistake, man. You might be sending them to their deaths.'

Fitzgerald's voice rose above the girls' objections. 'You heard the order,' and Pearse, firm-lipped, confirmed it.

They finally agreed, believing they might be in the way if the men had to leave the GPO in a hurry.

Winifred Carney told Connolly that she was staying whatever happened.

He grinned. 'You surprise me.'

With one of them waving aloft a Red Cross flag, the girls left. Everyone remaining, including Julia Grenan and Elizabeth More O'Farrell, held their breath until the firing in the street ceased.

'Now,' Fitzgerald said to Louise Gavan Duffy, 'we shall serve a chicken lunch.'

One of the men turned sharply from the window, where he had just brought down a British sniper.

'Chicken?' He was horrified. 'But 'tis Friday.'

When it was served in the messroom, no one would eat it.

'Wait'll we see what Father does,' whispered young Tommy Murphy.

There was a solemn silence as he put a plate of chicken before Fr O'Flanagan. The priest eyed it keenly for a moment, before spearing a piece with his fork and putting it into his mouth.

There was a tremendous cheer and all the men began to eat.

Hanna Sheehy-Skeffington's two sisters, Mrs Kettle and Mrs Culpane, went to Portobello Barracks to ask about Skeffy. The Captain of the Guard had them arrested on a charge of talking to Sinn Feiners, meaning Hanna and Skeffy.

When Colthurst heard, he conducted a mock trial to scare them.

'Guilty as charged,' he said. 'In this Barracks, we have never had anything to do with that traitor, Skeffington. This time, I'll be lenient. The sooner you two bitches get out, the better for you. And not one word till you're outside.'

Their visit, nonetheless, had disturbed him. Something had to be done about this business before it got out of hand.

By 4 in the afternoon, the fire had spread north up O'Connell Street from the Liffey as far as the Tramway Company Offices in Cathedral Street. Behind, all the houses were burning.

On the GPO side, the Metropole was now in flames, as was

358

Middle Abbey Street, including the *Freeman's Journal*, the offices of the *Evening Telegraph* and Eason's.

Howitzers in the Rotunda were finally getting the range of the Post Office. The first incendiary to cause alarm half-penetrated the roof above the portico. Some of the men threw their rifles aside and grabbed extinguishers. Others, kneeling to avoid being shot, formed a chain to provide buckets of water.

More and more incendiary shells rained on the building causing fires everywhere. Hoses were hauled up to the roof but most were old and rotten and some had been pierced by bullets. The top floor and the roof flooded and the sheer weight of water threatened their collapse.

Captain Michael O'Reilly edged his way along the steel struts of the glass dome to direct a hose on to the fire, but water only seemed to feed the flames.

Pearse went up on the roof and twice a bullet missed his head by inches. With him and Plunkett screaming orders ineffectually, The O'Rahilly took over. His main concern was to keep flames away from the ventilation shaft. If he failed, the whoosh of air would drive the fire down the centre of the building to the cellars where explosives were stored.

In the lobby, marksmen, kneeling in a black ooze of water, still manned the windows with plaster from the ceiling falling on their heads. From his bed, Connolly shouted that the British were at last about to make their frontal assault.

McDermott and Clarke helped organize the hoses as men slithered around in the filth.

Jim Ryan and Father O'Flanagan were attending the wounded.

The women who had stayed were told to take refuge in the crypt or at the back of the building in a ferro-concrete room.

The O'Rahilly soon saw it was pointless fighting the fire from above. When he and Michael Collins had cleared the roof and top storey, they made the floors as safe as possible by putting sand at the edges and cracks in the doors and then hosing them down.

In the lobby, The O'Rahilly found total confusion. It took all his voice and moral strength to make the men see that the shaft was more important than any of the small fires that kept breaking out. All hoses were directed up the shaft.

By six thirty, it was plain that the GPO was doomed. Fire had taken a grip in the lift shaft and the draught of its rampant flames sounded like a tornado as it whistled down into the heart of the building.

Still the incendiary shells kept coming.

The O'Rahilly and Liam Cullen had spent time at the rear under the glass roof, playing large hoses. Others had used smaller hoses or formed chains with buckets of water. At best, this was a holding operation.

The O'Rahilly, with frizzled hair and scorched eyebrows, interrupted his work to confer with the other leaders around Connolly's bed in the hall. All their faces were black as coal miners'. The ceiling was smouldering and fiery fragments kept falling off. Pillars groaned and threatened to collapse.

Short of raising the white flag, which Clarke and McDermott would not hear of, their only chance was to break out. At this ludicrously late hour, men were sent down to the sewers to look for a way out. They returned, fetid and filthy, shaking their heads. They would have to leave by the street.

But where to head for?

On Great Britain Street there was a soap and sweet factory built like a fortress called Williams and Wood. To reach it, though, they would have to break through the British barricades at the end of Moore Street.

The O'Rahilly said, almost casually, 'Let me know when you want to start and I'll lead the first wave out of here,' and went back to fighting the fire.

With sparks flying down the ventilation shaft, the ammunition in the cellar was no longer safe. It had to be brought up and put in the concrete room at the back.

The O'Rahilly asked for twenty volunteers. Under Dermot Lynch, they manhandled the explosives up narrow winding steps lit by naked candles. Sean MacLoughlain had just picked up an armful of bombs when The O'Rahilly lost momentary control of the hose and the youngster was hit full in the chest. Fortunately, he fell on his back, cushioning the explosives on his chest.

By now, nowhere was safe. Not the cellar, and certainly not the hall. The water pressure dipped, the stream got weaker, dribbled and stopped altogether. The O'Rahilly tossed his hose away in disgust.

Most of the men gathered in the large rear sorting-rooms and the covered courtyard whose glass cracked and sent down splinters and molten streams.

The retreat had to be well organized, for there were now 400 men in the GPO. Beams were burning and ceilings collapsing in blinding, choking smoke and showers of sparks. There was the constant zip-zipping of machine-guns and their own abandoned small-arms ammunition was going off like fire-crackers on the upper floors.

McDermott told Jim Ryan and his women assistants to prepare the wounded for transfer to Jervis Street Hospital. Mattresses and blankets would serve as stretchers. Louise Gavan Duffy, who had scarcely been off her feet during the entire week, was put in charge of the women.

Captain Mahoney, who was going with the wounded, said to Connolly, 'I'll just prepare you for the journey.'

'I am not leaving with the wounded, Captain.'

'If you don't get hospital treatment soon,' Mahoney warned, 'gangrene will set in and you'll be no damn use to anyone.'

Connolly was not in a listening mood.

Winifred Carney was not leaving her boss and Elizabeth O'Farrell and Julia Grenan were staying with the main party to nurse any fresh casualties in the retreat.

Jim Ryan stood with Father O'Flanagan and the few women aux-iliaries next to the stretcher cases, comforting them, offering them cigarettes, readying them to go as soon as Pearse gave the word.

It was almost 7 o'clock when the 2nd Battalion of the 6th South Staffords approached North King Street to the west of the GPO. They had left Trinity with orders to proceed to the Four Courts area to neutralize rebel snipers.

Mrs Hickey, a store-keeper who lived at No 168, had just crossed to the dairy when one of Daly's men came running.

'Get off the street.'

She rushed into the nearest house which was opposite her own.

'Stay here, dear,' the Corcorans said, 'till it quietens down.'

Her husband, Tom, was still at home, chatting with a neighbour Pete Connolly, the father of eight. Hickey pointed to a couple of mirrors. 'Help me shift those, will you?'

Suddenly objects in the houses began to rock and tremble at the tramp of soldiers.

Hanna Sheehy-Skeffington was in a daze. A doctor had given her Mr Coade's address and, that afternoon, she had paid him a call.

'Yes, Ma'am,' he said brokenly, 'I did see your man in the mortuary and several others.'

'You're certain it was—?'

He nodded. 'I heard him on his soap-box many a time.'

At last Hanna had confirmation that her darling, fearless, talkative man had been silenced for ever. She had walked home, determined to be brave for the boy's sake, and immersed herself in household chores.

Around 7 p.m., as the maid was getting little Owen into his green pyjamas, a fresh nightmare began. The girl saw soldiers lining up in the street. To protect the boy, she grabbed him, and dashed out the back door. Hanna, realizing soldiers would be out there, too, rushed to a window and screamed, 'Come back, you'll both be shot.'

She ran downstairs just as rifle fire shattered the windows. Next moment, soldiers were smashing their way in with rifle butts, forty of them screaming like wild wounded animals.

In command was Colonel Allatt. With him were a junior officer, Lieutenant Brown, and Captain Colthurst.

Some soldiers thundered upstairs and up on to the roof.

Colthurst, commanding a squad with fixed bayonets, stood over Hanna, Owen and the maid, and shouted, 'Hands up.'

As Owen pressed up against her, Hanna put her arms around him, saying, 'Don't worry, my son, *these* are the defenders of women and children.'

The O'Rahilly kept his promise. He brought the prisoners up from the cellars where they had spent three hours thinking the building would collapse on top of them any minute or they would roast alive.

He shook the hands of each. 'We shall probably never meet again. Goodbye and good luck.'

He gave their leader, Lieutenant Chalmers, a big white flag.

From the Henry Street exit, they made their way to Moore Lane where they ran into fire from their own Sherwood Foresters at the barricade. One man fell with a bullet in the head, Chalmers was hit in the thigh. A sergeant helped him over a wall and into the safety of a cellar.

Above the roar of the fire, McDermott managed to yell in The O'Rahilly's ear the plan of escape. They were to head for the factory in Great Britain Street. Once dug in there, they would try to link up with Daly's Four Courts Battalion. Combining, they might be able to break out of the city to the north.

The O'Rahilly gathered his advance party of thirty or so men around him. 'So, boys,' he said, ' 'twill either be a glorious victory or a glorious death.'

Louise Gavan Duffy had piled the food in the centre of the foyer. Men kept taking evasive action from falling timber as they filled their knapsacks with tea, cakes, sugar, hams. There was enough food for a month. Desmond Fitzgerald, having put them on economy rations for days, found this abundance embarrassing.

In the mêlée, two men carrying hair-trigger shot-guns shot themselves in the foot. Fitzgerald cut their shoes off and bandaged their feet and Pearse ordered them to unload.

The O'Rahilly went for a last word with Fitzgerald, who was to stay with the wounded. He was still hurt that comrades like Pearse and Plunkett had not trusted him. Not that he bore them any malice.

'Goodbye, Desmond. This is the end for certain now.'

'It seems so, Michael.'

'I thought we'd only hold out a day. The only thing that grieves me,' he said, with that ringing laugh of his, 'is that so many of my lads are good Gaelic speakers.' He put his haversack on his back. 'Never mind, when it comes to the end I'll say, "English-speakers to the fore, Irish-speakers to the rear. Charge!" '

Fitzgerald knew this was untrue. When the charge came, Michael Joseph O'Rahilly himself would be in front with nothing between him and enemy bullets save the mercy of God.

'Wouldn't it be odd,' was his friend's parting quip, 'if I had missed this and then caught my death of cold running for a train?'

Having embraced Fitzgerald, he paused for a last word with Fr O'Flanagan. He went on his knees and, with head bowed, asked for a last absolution and blessing.

He rose, saying, 'Father, we shall never meet again in this world.'

The rebels remaining prayed frantically as The O'Rahilly took his place at the head of his men at the Henry Street gate.

'Fix bayonets.' He took out his Mauser pistol and included everyone in a big round 'Cheerio'.

Pearse gave him a final meaningful handshake before shouting, 'Now!' and The O'Rahilly's men went out with Sean McDermott roaring them on.

They went from Henry Street up Henry Lane. In Moore Street, they came to their own barricade and gingerly parted it. Directly ahead was the enemy barricade. Though the entire street was eerily silent, they knew the British were peering at them down the barrels of their guns.

The O'Rahilly divided his men into two. He was to head one party up the left side of the street.

After a great gulp of air, 'This is it, lads,' and with a yell he led off, running.

In narrow streets devoid of cover, the fire from the British rifles was deafening. Of the thirty rebels, twenty-one fell.

The O'Rahilly was hit in the stomach.

He felt the bullet less as an implosion than as some vital organ exploding in a bloody flux. He dropped to one knee, doubled up in pain.

Comrades had fallen around him. The few who were unhurt joined him. Hugging the side of the street, one hand to his wound, the other grasping his Mauser, he led a second assault.

To draw fire from his men, he went on a zigzag course across the street. He was not hit again until he was near the barricade at the corner of Sackville Place. He barely had strength to pitch himself round the corner and drag himself into a doorway.

He knew he was done for. With an effort, he drew from his breast pocket a note from his son Aodghan. It had a bullet through it. On the back, in the fierce light from the burning GPO, he pencilled a few words with a remarkably steady hand.

He told his wife he had been wounded leading a charge. 'I got more than one bullet, I think.' A few words of love. He folded the paper and wrote, 'Please deliver this to Nancie O'Rahilly, 40 Herbert Park.'

With the last of this strength, he replaced the note in his pocket.

In the GPO, the Red Cross party was about to leave. It was not easy getting the makeshift stretchers through the holes in the walls, and some men were in a serious condition.

Tom Clarke took Lesley Price by the hand.

'If you happen to see my wife—' He blinked. 'Tell her the men were wonderful to the—'

It took half an hour for Fitzgerald to get the wounded through the walls of intervening houses, across a roof, up a ladder and into the bar of the Coliseum Theatre. Jim Ryan went behind the bar and said, for a joke, 'Last drinks, gentlemen.'

The priest was impressed that, with oceans of liquor at their disposal, no one touched a drop.

Captain Mahoney was called back to the GPO to fix the cage over Connolly's leg which someone had tripped over. By then the place was a complete inferno. The two men eyed each other as Connolly squeezed his hand in gratitude.

Mahoney returned to the Coliseum to find the wounded had been laid on a thick-pile carpet. The electricity was off so they had only lamps to see by.

They wanted to run up a Red Cross flag from the pole on the roof but, by the rules of war, they had to get rid of their arms and ammunition first. Fitzgerald and Fr O'Flanagan offered to take them back through the tunnels and dump them.

On the way, they ran into a sea of fire. To avoid being cremated, they climbed down into a yard and up on to the next roof. The priest failed to see an overhead telegraph wire and nearly decapitated himself.

Back in the Coliseum, they hoisted the Red Cross flag. But it was now clear that the wall tunnels had turned into channels of fire. It was only a matter of time before the Coliseum met the fate of the GPO.

They kept quiet about this and persuaded everyone to try and sleep. It was not possible to lower the safety-curtain since it operated electrically, but they all settled down in the plushest seats in the Dress Circle.

Colthurst was not only concerned about Hanna's sisters. Major Vane, too, was proving to be a damned nuisance.

It was vital to get some evidence against Skeffy. This house, he was sure, would provide plenty of that.

Hanna, Owen and the maid were taken to a front room where soldiers with fixed bayonets watched over them.

'If they move,' Colthurst ordered, 'shoot them.'

With the key he had taken from Skeffy's body he unlocked the study. Over the desk was a picture of the Kaiser. Colthurst took it down. A promising start.

He went through Skeffy's papers. There were masses of articles, manuscripts of plays, innumerable rejection slips from publishers. Also his love-letters to his wife before they were married, tied in blue ribbon.

Hanna felt their whole world was in that study and this monster was taking it apart. She heard him reading aloud from their letters in what sounded an obscene parody of love.

A soldier came down the stairs, triumphantly waving a sheet of paper. It was Owen's drawing of a Zeppelin pasted on his bedroom wall.

By 8.30, not knowing how the advance party had fared, the first of the three main waves prepared to leave the GPO. They could not wait to escape the inferno.

Michael Collins was in charge. He had made up his mind that if he got out of this alive, never again would he be a duck in a British duck-shoot.

Once in the open, they ran single-file. They, too, came under heavy fire in Moore Street. Those who survived fled into alley ways or burst into houses and barricaded themselves in.

The second group followed the same route and met the same fate.

Pearse, like the skipper of a ship, toured the GPO to make sure no one was left behind. He came back, covered with grime, his iodine-coloured eyes swollen with the heat.

With pride, he took a last look round. They had lasted far longer than he had dared to hope.

Connolly was in the final party. It moved him to see one of his stretcher-bearers, a mere lad, shielding him with his body.

As they tried to break into a stable, one man shot himself. Connolly grabbed the rifle from Richard Grogan and said, 'Help him.'

Inside, they found a family that had been trapped there for the whole week. They were half-crazy with hunger and with fear of the fire that was moving relentlessly in their direction.

'For God's sake,' Connolly yelled, 'get me out of this hole.'

Elizabeth O'Farrell and Julia Grenan were in McDermott's group. Some rebels had taken refuge in a house in Henry Place and McDermott yelled for them to move out and Joe Plunkett, waving his sword, cried weakly, 'Come out, ye cowardly curs!'

With bullets whizzing from every side, they rushed into Moore Lane. Elizabeth stumbled and fell. Sean McGarry rushed out of a house and picked her up and took her into the parlour of Cogan's on the corner of Henry Lane and Moore Street.

It was mere chance that the Provisional government came together in one spot. They were joined by Jim Ryan who had made his way back from the Coliseum over the rooftops. He had no medicines though several had just been wound-ed.

366

Behind Cogan's was the yard of a small workman's cottage belonging to the McKane family. The parents and their fourteen children had been holed up for two days without food, saying their rosary. Desperate to get in, a rebel broke the glass panel on the door. As he did so, his gun went off.

Tom McKane, about to open the door, fell, a bawling baby clutched in his arms. The bullet had passed through his shoulder and hit his sixteen-year-old daughter Bridget in the right temple.

The party burst in as Mrs McKane screamed, 'O God, where's Daddy?'

Ryan saw that the girl was dead but he might be able to save the father.

He ordered, 'Get me all the linen you have.'

The wife, in shock, was crying, 'O me darlin' man is dying. I must fetch a priest.'

'He'll be fine,' Ryan said, 'just get me an old sheet for bandages.'

Mrs McKane, wrapping her shawl around her, was soon at the door, with a sheet for a flag.

Someone pleaded, 'Don't go, missis, it's rainin' bullets out there.'

She took no notice and, remarkably, returned in a few minutes with a Fr McInerney who anointed her husband and several others of the wounded.

Connolly had arrived with his secretary and was being served beef tea. He called out to Mrs McKane, 'You are a very brave woman, ma'am.'

Elizabeth O'Farrell asked him how he felt.

His gruff reply was, 'Bad. The soldier who plugged me did a good day's work for the British.'

On Moore Street, Sean MacLoughlain was now in charge of building a barricade across the street.

George Plunkett heard an Irishman crying out for water in a side street. He zigzagged his way across Moore Lane, only to find the man was in khaki. He lifted him on his shoulder and ran back across the road. The British, realizing this was an act of mercy, held their fire. The wounded man was taken to Cogan's where he spent the night in rebel company.

The injured were made comfortable on mattresses at the front of the McKane cottage and Elizabeth spent the night nursing them. It was very noisy as Pearse had ordered the able-bodied men to start burrowing from house to house towards the top of Moore Street.

With The O'Rahilly gone, Connolly proposed that MacLoughlain should take over. 'Let him have my rank.'

Thus the rising ended with a fifteen-year-old as Commandant of the Dublin Division.

Pearse and Willie went upstairs and lay side by side on a table. But sleep still eluded Pearse. After twisting and turning for an hour, he went down to see how the tunnelling was progressing.

On the way, he passed men who were snoring and others who were quietly saying the rosary.

Not far away, in a deserted lane, Michael O'Rahilly, the man who had opposed the rising, was stretched out, gasping for water. A woman in a cottage heard him and tried to help but British bullets drove her back.

He was mumbling in Irish, 'Holy Mary, Mother of God, pray for us sinners, now and at the hour of our death.'

Hanna clasped her little boy to her breast. She was afraid that this day would remain in his memory like an immovable stone all his life.

In three hours, the soldiers tore the house to bits. They removed books, pictures, toys, linen and household goods. As they opened the drawers upstairs and found Hanna's underclothes, she could hear them jeering.

One of the soldiers guarding them, muttered in a Belfast accent, 'I didn't enlist for this. They're taking the whole bloomin' house with them.'

Outside, they commandeered a car and ordered the women in it to take the confiscated goods to the Barracks. They followed at a distance in case of snipers, leaving an armed guard on the house all night.

Colthurst was very pleased with how things had gone.

Back at Portobello, he filed some of Skeffy's papers which he classified as incriminating and which he booked in as having been found on him when he was captured.

Major Vane had been making every effort to have Colthurst put under arrest. When the new CO at Portobello, Lieutenant-Colonel McCammond, refused to do anything, he went to the Castle. General Friend and Colonel Kennard told him to be a sensible chap and not make a fuss.

Major Price said, 'Some of us think it was a good thing Sheehy-Skeffington was put out of the way, anyhow.'

Nora Connolly had finally made it to Clogher. It was late; she was frustrated and utterly exhausted after covering more than twenty miles.

Ina said, 'We can't go on tonight. Better wait till the morning, then we'll head for Dundalk.'

By 10.30 p.m., the Red Cross party realized they had to leave the Coliseum before it went up in flames.

When they tried the doors, they found them all padlocked. Luckily, they were able to force one. It gave access to a passage leading into Prince's Street from where they got into Middle Abbey Street.

So bright were the flames, British troops saw the Red Cross flag and held their fire. But they suspected a trap. It was five minutes before a Captain Orr called out: 'Two men advance and be recognized.'

Father O'Flanagan went with Captain Mahoney. Still the troops were not convinced. Both had brogues; they might be rebels in disguise.

The priest said, 'Please, we are trying to get the wounded to Jervis Street Hospital.'

A monocled Major fetched a couple of medical students from Jervis Street who vouched for Father O'Flanagan. The rebel group was then allowed to proceed to the hospital where nurses and nuns gave them a warm welcome.

Led by Louise Gavan Duffy, the girls were marched to Broadstone Station for questioning. On the way, Louise told them to say they were students from the nursing school; they had been walking down O'Connell Street when they were forced into the Post Office.

'I believe you,' the interrogating officer said. 'Might I suggest you go straight back to school.'

It was now dark in North King Street, with only the occasional blue flare lighting up the night. The South Staffs had expected this to be a routine mopping-up operation. But they had met with withering fire.

Where was it coming from? Not only from a pub a couple of hundred yards to the west. Every roof, every window seemed to be harbouring a sniper. When they tried to dismantle the barricades they were picked off one by one. Had they been without armoured lorries to drop men off in houses along the street, they would have been massacred. Rebel bullets pinged against the armour-plating of the lorries, deafening the troops inside.

Owing to the incessant firing, Mrs Hickey had not been able to cross the road home. The Corcorans invited her to spend the night with them.

Opposite, her husband, Tom, persuaded Pete Connolly to stay on. Also in the house were the Hickeys' son, Christy, and Mrs Kate Kelly, their maid. Tom and Christy were to sleep on a mattress on the floor while Kate Kelly took over the bedroom next door.

All that night, while the rebels were tunnelling through the houses in Moore Street, frightened Staffordshires under their small pompous CO, Lieutenant-Colonel Henry Taylor, were doing the same not far away in North King Street.

It had taken them hours to travel a few hundred yards, and at a cost. Before daylight, eleven NCOs and men were dead. Thirty-three men were wounded, including five officers. Of the rest, some went berserk.

For the inhabitants of North King Street, it was to become a night of terror.

SATURDAY

No 172 North King Street was the home of Mick and Sally Hughes. On the top floor lived a blind old man named Davis.

Among the refugees they were hosting were a young couple, John and Nellie Walsh, as well as several women and children. They were all trying to sleep in the ground-floor drawing-room at the rear of the house against a background of street fighting and an armoured car growling nearby.

About 2 a.m., there was a banging on the front door.

Mick Hughes hissed, 'Don't open it, Sal, they'll kill us.' But the banging got so loud, Sally shrugged and went to unlock it.

Several soldiers burst in, one yelling, 'Bloody idiot, we were just gonna blow you up.'

Another demanded, 'Any men in this house?'

Angry and panic-stricken, they searched the place and took away two twenty-year-old men.

In the drawing-room, not one word was spoken. Mick Hughes and John Walsh stood motionless and even the four small children were shocked into silence as the soldiers thrust bayonets into the sofas in the search for arms.

370

Mick said, 'I swear to God there's been no firing from this house.'

'That so?' The corporal pointed with a shaky finger to a rip in his hat. 'Look what a bloody bullet did. Nearly finished me off.' He turned to his men. 'Search 'em.'

They went through the men's pockets. Besides a penknife, Walsh had on him a cylindrical metal case, like a cartridge.

'Aha,' the corporal said, 'what have we here?'

He opened it to find a miniature statue of St Anthony.

From Hughes's pockets they took two watches, a gold bracelet and some articles belonging to his wife. The soldiers kept them, as well as seven gold rings belonging to Sally which they found in a drawer.

After locking the women and children in the downstairs kitchen, they left young Walsh in the drawing-room while they took Hughes up to the top floor.

Walsh was heard crying out, 'What are you doing that for? Don't put that on me,' as if he were being blindfolded.

Above the drawing-room old Davis had his ear to the floor. He heard Walsh say, in a soft voice, 'O Nellie, Nellie, jewel.' Then there was a thud like furniture falling.

Minutes later, a soldier was carried into the house and down to the kitchen.

'Sergeant Banks,' an NCO said, 'he's copped it.'

Sally Hughes, a kind-hearted soul, did her best for him. 'Poor man,' she said over and over.

An Army doctor came and gave him an anaesthetic while the ladies made them tea.

Afterwards, Sally tore down curtains for bandages. 'There's sheets upstairs,' she said. 'And a nice sofa for the Sergeant. I'll get them if you like.'

'Stay where you are, missis,' the NCO said, 'we'll get them ourselves.'

In Hickeys' place, No 168, the maid, Kate Kelly, was sleeping by herself. At 6 in the morning, she heard picks being used to force an entry through the wall.

She screamed, 'Someone's breaking into the house.'

Tom Hickey got up from his mattress just in time to see the wall cave in and soldiers pushing into the room. Tired and tense, they carried bayonets, crowbars and pickaxes.

One of them yelled, 'Hands up.'

Tom Hickey, his son, Christy and Pete Connolly raised them high.

A sergeant poked a frenzied-looking head through the hole. His eyes were bloodshot, veins stood out like blue rope on his forehead and neck. 'How many?' he asked in a strange, grating voice.

'Three men, sir.'

'Keep an eye on 'em till I get back.'

Tom and Pete tried to explain that they had nothing to do with the Volunteers. The soldiers listened with a bored expression on their faces.

In No 174, Michael Noonan, a quiet thirty-four-year-old bachelor was part-owner of a newsagent and tobacconist shop. He lived in and rented out the rooms over the store.

First floor up lived an elderly bird-fancier, Michael Smith.

On the second floor, one room was occupied by George Ennis, a fifty-three-year-old carriage maker, and his wife, Kate. An old maiden lady, Anne Fennell, had the next room.

Smith was in his room, the rest were on the ground floor in the back parlour when, at 7 a.m., there was a wallop on the door. Before Noonan could open up, about thirty soldiers burst in, smashing the door and windows, and yelling 'Hands up.'

Seeing it was a quiet household, the same frenzied Sergeant asked, 'How many men here?'

When Mrs Ennis told them, a dozen soldiers escorted Miss Fennell upstairs. They searched her room and made sure there was no one else in hiding. They no sooner led her down than they started to shove Ennis and Noonan upstairs.

Mrs Ennis clung fiercely to her husband. 'I want to go up with my George.'

A soldier pulled her screaming away and pressed his bayonet up to her ear, 'Shut *up!*'

'You wouldn't kill a woman?' she gasped.

'Keep quiet, you bloody bitch. We're keeping 'em prisoners, that's all.'

The women were locked in the parlour and warned, 'Move and you're dead.'

After the men were bundled upstairs, the women heard soldiers running amok, ripping up beds with their bayonets, knocking over furniture, emptying drawers and cupboards. Noises inside coalesced with noises in the street. Then, as suddenly as they came, the soldiers left.

Mrs Ennis and Miss Fennell looked tearfully at each other. There might be a guard on the door. They sat in dread, not daring to move.

An hour or so later, they jumped at the sound of someone falling down the stairs and crashing into the parlour door with such force that it gave in.

Staggering towards Kate was her husband, George, dripping blood, his eyes rolling. Before he dropped at her feet, she saw the wound.

'I'm shot, Kate.'

'Who did it?'

'Soldiers. Shot me through the heart, as I asked them.'

'And us?' Miss Fennell shrieked.

Ennis said, 'They won't touch you.' As they bent over him, he murmured, 'Someone go for a priest.'

Knowing this was impossible, they knelt and said prayers for the dying.

He whispered, 'They killed poor Noonan, too. I stayed with him as long as I could.' With his last breath, George said, 'Forgive them, Kate.'

In Cogan's, the Provisional government breakfasted to a background of gun-fire.

The sun shone brightly after a long and weary night. The McKane children had not stopped sobbing over their injured father and their sister lying under a stained sheet in the corner. The wounded were groaning; one of them had a bullet in the lung and was coughing interminably. Without medicines, disinfectant, washing facilities, the place reeked of blood.

After eating, the leaders crawled through tunnels dug in the night to a more central HQ in 16 Moore Street. It was Hanlon's, a fish-market.

Connolly was carried there in a blanket and made comfortable in a back room with a few more of the injured, including the British soldier picked up the night before. There, the leaders held a council of war, with the three nurses coming in from time to time to assist.

Trapped between the GPO and the cordon in the north, their one hope was to go west and link up with Ned Daly at the Four Courts. For this, they would need to create a diversion.

While Sean MacLoughlain crawled through the various houses

asking for twenty volunteers, Pearse went to say thank you to Mrs Cogan. Big in the charity of love, she bore no grudges. Seeing this, Pearse pointed to her eldest son, Tommy. 'Why not grab a rifle and join us, lad?'

Mrs Cogan's face clouded over, so that he apologized for his insensitivity. In his mind, he was offering the lad a chance of glory.

MacLoughlain found his volunteers in minutes and drew them up in a yard next to Sackville Place, only yards from the British barricade at the top of Moore Street.

When he and McDermott went to reconnoitre, they saw The O'Rahilly. He was on his back, his brown hair tilted back off his forehead.

The bell was tolling for the 10 o'clock Mass when the Sergeant returned to the Hickeys', 168 North King Street.

With four of his men, he led all the civilians through the hole in the wall. No 169 was a tobacconist's over which a Mrs Connolly lived and where a Mr and Mrs Carroll and their daughter had a room. These, too, were taken through the next wall to the vacant No 170.

Hickey said to Mrs Carroll, 'Isn't it terrible? So often the innocent have to suffer with the guilty.'

Inside the echoing room of the empty house, Kate Kelly, the maid, called out, 'I hope they're not going to kill us.'

A soldier laughed roughly, 'You're a bally woman, you're all right.'

The three women were left there while the three men were taken to another room at the back. The women heard Christy pleading, 'Please don't kill my da.'

Shots rang out and Kate threw herself on her knees, crying, 'O, my God!' and her lips added in swift silent prayer, 'Mother of God, pray for us sinners . . . .'

It was 10.30 a.m. when Mrs Hickey, having spent a sleepless night over at the Corcorans, said she would like to go home.

Mr Corcoran peeped round his front door to ask a British NCO if she could. Around the Hickeys' house, a dozen soldiers were sheltering from fierce gun-fire.

'You can if you like, missis,' the NCO said, 'but there's a few stiff 'uns lying about.'

This so terrified her, she went back inside the Corcorans', only glancing through the window now and again, hoping to catch a glimpse of Tom and Christy.

While the Provisional government discussed options, the injured British soldier was gazing at Pearse as if he were reminded of someone dear to him. He asked Elizabeth O'Farrell if Pearse would have a word with him.

Pearse said, 'Certainly,' and knelt beside him.

'Would you lift me up a little, sir.'

He did so.

The soldier put his arms around his neck and Pearse held him for a few moments. Then, without a word being said, he gently laid him down again.

When McDermott returned and whispered in Pearse's ear that The O'Rahilly was dead, he simply nodded.

There was a sudden clatter in the street as horses, released from a burning stable, went charging by.

Minutes later, Pearse saw a publican with his wife and daughter, clutching white flags, flash past the window. Their home had caught fire. From the top of Moore Street, a volley rang out and all three fell dead.

Pearse stood looking vacantly for a full minute, then began to pass the word from house to house: 'No more firing until further notice.

The Provisional government discussed what to do next.

Tom Clarke was in favour of a fight to the death.

Though Pearse found it attractive, the heart of the President of the Republic was full of compassion for his people; they had suffered more than enough. He turned to MacLoughlain. 'If your volunteers assault the British barricade, they will all die, right?'

MacLoughlain nodded.

Pearse glanced at the wall where there was a picture of Robert Emmet standing in the dock. It seemed to give him courage for a painful decision.

Taking a deep breath, he pointed to where the family of three lay dead in the street.

'For the sake of our fellow citizens and our comrades across this city who are likely to be shot or burned to death, I propose . . . we surrender.'

Clarke, who had not shed a tear in fifteen years in prison, turned to the wall and his thin shoulders heaved. Winifred Carney and Julia

Grenan went to comfort him, but sobbed themselves. He pulled himself together and put his arms around them.

McDermott said to Elizabeth, 'Get a white flag, please.'

He borrowed a white handkerchief and put it on a stick. Michael O'Reilly opened the door and thrust it outside. A volley caused him to withdraw it. Moments later, he tried again. This time, silence.

Realizing what Elizabeth was being asked to do, Julia started to sob, 'You'll be shot, shot.' Too many had been gunned down already waving white flags.

Pearse rehearsed with Elizabeth his message to the military.

In a last hug, the two young women prayed together, then, taking a deep breath, Elizabeth went through the door Pearse held open for her. The pavement of Moore Street echoed with her brisk, bold step. She held the white flag aloft. It was 12.45 p.m.

In the back room, Connolly stared coldly straight ahead. There were alien tears in McDermott's eyes. Winifred Carney was weeping and could not stop.

The silence held.

Julia let out a little screech, 'She'll be all right.'

Elizabeth was now almost up to the barricade. Without turning her head, she saw at the corner of Sackville Lane The O'Rahilly's hat and his revolver on the ground.

'That's hopeful,' she thought.

At the barricade, she called out, 'The Commandant-General of the Irish Republican Army wishes to treat with the Commander of the British Forces in Ireland.'

A Colonel named Hodgson said, 'How many girls are down there?'

She did not answer.

'Take my advice, go back and bring the others out at once.' Then he changed his mind. 'You'd better wait, I'll have to report this.'

He deputed an NCO to accompany her to the Parnell Monument. There, Colonel Portal, the area commander, emerged from a house and Elizabeth repeated her message.

'The Irish Republican Army?' Portal echoed scornfully. 'Sinn Feiners, you mean.'

'They call themselves the Irish Republican Army, sir, and I think it's a very good name.'

He sniffed. 'Can Pearse be moved on a stretcher?'

'Commandant Pearse does not need a stretcher.'

Portal had read a military communique which said Pearse had a fractured thigh and Connolly was dead.

He turned angrily to a junior officer. 'Take that red cross off her, she's a spy.'

The officer cut the crosses off Elizabeth's sleeve and apron. He led her to a branch of the National Bank and searched her. She had on her scissors, sweets, bread, cake. She did not seem a great threat to the Empire.

She was taken to Clarke's shop, 75A Great Britain Street, and held there for an hour while someone telephoned the Castle and the Castle contacted General Lowe at Trinity.

Joe Plunkett, stretched out in Hanlons', wrote a letter. He headed it: '6th Day of the Irish Republic.'

> My darling Grace,
> This is just a little note to say I love you and to tell you that I did everything I could to arrange for us to meet and get married but that it was impossible.
> Except for that I have no regrets.
> Give my love to my people and friends.
> Darling, darling child, I wish we were together. Love me always as I love you. For the rest all you do will please me.
> I told a few people that I wish you to have everything that belongs to me. This is my last wish so please see to it.
> Love XXXX Joe.

In front of his signature, he drew a circle with a tiny Celtic cross inside.

The effort seemed to take a lot out of him. He asked Winifred Carney to look after the letter and give it to Grace.

'That is, if you are not taken prisoner.'

General Lowe entered Clarke's shop. With him was Captain de Courcy Wheeler, the son of a Dublin surgeon, also tall and slender.

Lowe apologized to Elizabeth for the bad manners of his subordinates and asked her to repeat the message.

Afterwards, he ordered a cease-fire in the area. He had Colonel Portal put his reply to Pearse in writing and signed it.

A woman has come in and tells me you wish to negotiate with me. I am prepared to receive you in Great Britain Street at the North End of Moore Street provided that you surrender unconditionally.

You will proceed up Moore Street accompanied by the woman who brings you this note, under a white flag.

W. N. C. Lowe, Brigadier-General.

Lowe warned Elizabeth that if there was no reply within half an hour, hostilities would recommence. He drove her to the top of Moore Street.

'Notice the time, please, it's important. 2.25 p.m.'

Walking back, she saw to her left, a few yards down Sackville Lane, the body of The O'Rahilly. He lay in a pool of blood, his head on a curbstone, his feet in the doorway of the first house.

White and shaken, she ran to the house, crying, 'The O'Rahilly, he's dead.' She could tell they already knew. Michael Joseph O'Rahilly, the reluctant rebel, was the only one of the top officers to die in the rising. The irony of it made surrender even more unpalatable.

The leaders thanked her, then went into private session. Pearse read out Lowe's message and they drafted their reply which they asked Elizabeth to take back.

When she reached the top of Moore Lane, not daring to look again at The O'Rahilly's corpse, General Lowe told her she was lucky not to be shot. She was one minute late.

'Not by my watch, sir,' she said coolly.

Lowe read the reply and said, his displeasure showing, 'This is no use. You'll have to go back with my ultimatum.'

He wrote Pearse a second note:

I have received your letter. Nothing can be considered until you surrender unconditionally.

On your surrender to me I will take steps to give everyone acting under your orders sufficient time to surrender before I recommence hostilities which I have temporarily suspended. You will carry out instructions contained in my last letter as regards approaching me.

378

He told Elizabeth he would allow another half an hour, not one minute longer.

This time, they synchronized their watches.

The leaders held a short council. Afterwards, Pearse, sadly and without a word, shook hands with everyone in the house. All but his brother and Sean McDermott broke down and wept.

Pearse looked down on Elizabeth. 'Shall we go?'

Just before 3.30 p.m., kindly Sally Hughes remembered old Davis in the attic and made him a cup of tea. As she went up, she could not resist peering through the keyhole of the drawing-room.

She was shocked to see a man lying on the floor near the fireplace. She only had time to notice his socks when a soldier appeared.

'What are *you* up to, missis?'

'Who is it?' she gasped.

'Nothing for you to worry about. A Sinn Feiner from round about. Now down to your kitchen.'

Struggling to stop herself from shaking, she went back and said to Nellie Walsh, as calmly as she could, 'What colour socks is your husband wearing, my dear?'

Nellie blinked. 'Why do you ask?'

'Nothing.'

Both sat down, terrified.

When another soldier appeared, Nellie asked, politely, 'Where is my husband, please?'

'Don't *worry*, girl. They've both been taken to the Detention Barracks.'

It was 3.30 p.m. when the two opposed commanders finally met face to face at the top of Moore Street. To Pearse's right was the Parnell Monument.

He was a strange figure in his greatcoat and slouch hat with its leather strap under his chin. By his own mystical criterion, this was not defeat but victory. He handed Lowe his sword, romantically, on upturned palms. When an NCO searched him, he drew gingerly out of Pearse's pocket a round object. It turned out to be an onion.

Lowe said, 'I would like this young lady to stay in military custody so she can take the surrender notice to other outposts. Then, of course, she'll be set free.'

Pearse said to Elizabeth, 'Do you agree?'

379

'Whatever you wish, sir.'

He shook her by the hand. 'I do wish it. Thank you.'

She was put under the protection of a Lieutenant Royall and was taken for tea to Tom Clarke's shop.

Pearse stepped in a car with Lowe's tall, handsome son, John, and Captain Wheeler to be driven for a meeting with General Maxwell.

At Parkgate, Pearse proudly admitted everything.

The General hardly gave him a glance. Wheeler whispered something in Maxwell's ear.

'What's that you say? An onion?'

The sheer banality of this so-called rebel appalled him. If this object, this thing were not giving himself a mock-post in a mock-Republic, he would probably have made a tolerable errand-boy. He had seen dozens like him in Egypt and the Sudan, selling matches in bazaars.

Pearse, on the other hand, took Maxwell very seriously. He sensed that he would enable him to achieve his destiny.

'Sit down.'

The scorn was evident in the soldier's voice.

'Now pick up that pen and write an order telling your men to lay down their arms. Nothing fancy, mind.'

Pearse wrote: 'In order to prevent the further slaughter of Dublin citizens, and in the hope of saving the lives of our followers now surrounded and hopelessly outnumbered—'

'I don't want a treatise,' Maxwell interrupted him.

Pearse continued calmly: ' – the members of the Provisional government present at HQ have agreed to an unconditional surrender, and the Commandants of the various districts in the City and the Country will order their commands to lay down arms. P. H. Pearse, 29 April 3.45 p.m, 1916.'

Maxwell grabbed the sheet of paper and read it through a smoke-screen of his cigarette. He sniffed at the pretentiousness of phrases like 'Provisional government' – fractious bloody tribesmen always used that sort of pompous bloody language – then, without a word, left the room.

Silence had descended on the house in Moore Street.

McDermott and Clarke felt that Connolly needed medical treatment as soon as possible. There was something ironic in their choice of hospital.

380

Seamus Devoy was sent under a white flag to the Moore Street barricade. 'James Connolly, Commandant-General of the Dublin Division,' he said, 'is badly wounded and we intend taking him to Dublin Castle.'

The officer in charge was too shaken to reply.

'Please open your barricade to let us through.'

The gaping officer nodded.

Six stretcher-bearers under Captain Dermot Lynch picked Connolly up.

As he said goodbye to each of the other leaders, he was thinking they weren't such a bad lot, after all. He had a special word with his secretary. 'For everything, Winnie, thank you.'

The bearers halted first outside Clarke's shop where Connolly spoke briefly with General Lowe. They then back-tracked, with an escort of thirty armed guards, to Capel Street, walked south to the Liffey, crossed the Grattan Bridge and up Parliament Street.

Straight ahead loomed Dublin Castle.

From the Castle, Nathan rang Norway to say the rebels had surrendered unconditionally.

Mrs Norway was delighted; yet, with the tension lifted, she grieved more than ever for her Freddie. In the first quiet moment in days she found a case containing his letters. In it, there were three tiny hankies embroidered with her name. One of the last things he did was to send them from Armentières.

She wept uncontrollably.

Nathan's next call was to his lodge to bid Estelle goodbye. 'I am so sorry it had to end like this.'

'Don't say that. We enjoyed the excitement, *really*.'

He asked if she had slept the night before.

'Not a wink. The noise of guns was frightful.'

'Anyway, Estelle, the good news is, the rebels have surrendered.'

'Wonderful! Just as we're leaving.'

'Nothing for it, then, except to wish you *bon voyage*.'

Estelle and the three girls piled into a car. There was chaos on the streets. Never had she seen so many mules, some of them pulling gun-carriages. They had two blow-outs on the way caused by shrapnel and broken glass. But they made it in time to the mail boat, then home to England and sanity.

At Parkgate, Pearse gave the impression of a man at peace, as though he felt the future would be merciful. Though held at gun-point, a smile never left his lips and there was a beyond-the-stars look in his eyes.

He signed copies of the surrender as they were typed.

Captain Wheeler had been in charge of Pearse for only fifteen minutes when Lowe phoned, asking him to bring copies to Great Britain Street at once.

'I want you and Miss O'Farrell to take one to the rebel HQ in Moore Street. After that, maybe you'd go to the Castle and get Connolly's endorsement for his crowd in the Green.'

Connolly's arrival in the Castle Yard caused quite a stir.

He was set down on the spot where PC O'Brien had been shot, three Republicans standing to attention on each side of him, with an outer circle of armed soldiers.

For ten minutes, the authorities discussed what to do with the prisoner. It was vital to put him where he could not be snatched by rebels still at large. They settled on a room in the Officers' Quarters which Royalty had once used as a bedchamber.

When Elizabeth and Captain Wheeler arrived at Moore Street with Pearse's order to surrender, some of the men were furious. One slammed the butt of his rifle against the wall and threw ammunition down the stair-well to the basement.

'May I remind you,' Clarke said, gently but firmly, 'that I spent the best years of my life battling for Irish freedom. If I'm satisfied, why aren't you?'

Sean McDermott backed him up. 'We surrendered not to save ourselves but other people and the city from destruction.'

Someone snapped, 'We would've fought on.'

'Of course you would,' McDermott said. 'I'm proud of you. You put up a *great* fight. It's not your fault that we haven't yet won a Republic. The other side had more men, better arms, that's all.' There was pride in his voice as he added, 'Believe me, your work will tell some day. There will come a time when Irish people will look back on this Easter week and you, each one of you will be honoured.'

They knelt in the back room, rosaries in their left hands, rifles in their right. Tears ran down many a cheek and the responses came out chokingly.

*

Captain Wheeler was conducted up the Grand Staircase to Connolly's bedroom. It was a State Room, rectangular in shape, with two large windows and beautiful decor, complete with chandelier.

A white-haired surgeon named Tobin was looking after the patient. Wheeler waited by the bed until his wounds were dressed. Then: 'If you feel up to it, perhaps you would be good enough to read this.'

Connolly read Pearse's order of surrender and said he would to add his own coda. He dictated it: 'I agree to these conditions for the men under my own command in the Moore Street district and for the men in the Stephen's Green Command.'

Shakily he added an 'only' to make it read 'for the men only under my command,' and signed his name and the date: 'April 29/16.'

To speed things up, General Lowe asked Elizabeth O'Farrell to take a copy of the surrender to the Four Courts area. On her way, she was stopped several times at barricades before she ran into the Capuchin, Father Columbus. Taking the white flag, he went with her. They eventually found Ned Daly in a house at the corner of Church Street, on the quays. It was close on 6 o'clock.

Daly went to the Four Courts to tell his men, with tears in his eyes, of the Provisional government's decision.

'Fight it out,' his men cried.

'I'd like to,' he said, 'but a soldier must obey.'

In the Castle, Birrell was writing to give Asquith the latest news. He told him the Four Courts was about to surrender. It contained the Great Seal and 'all the historical records of Ireland since the day Henry the Second was foolish enough to do what the Romans never did, cross the Irish Sea.'

Reflecting on the rising, he said, 'The horrible thing proves how deep in Irish hearts lies this passion for insurrection.'

Finally: 'Let me know what you expect me to do.'

When, soon after 6 p.m., the soldiers returned to 174 North King Street to release Mrs Ennis and Miss Fennell, they were surprised to find them praying over Ennis's body.

The women now took courage and went upstairs together. Noonan was in a room on the second floor. He had been shot through the head and bayoneted.

*

Daly marched his men to St John's Convent in North Brunswick Street. The nuns who had stood every morning on the front lawn and prayed with shining faces for their safe return now filed out to say goodbye.

Sister Agnes called out to Sean Cody, 'Don't forget the Germans are on the Naas Road.'

Sean whipped out his revolver and handed it to Sister Louise Moore. 'Keep that for me, Sister.'

As it disappeared up her broad sleeves, Sister Louise said, 'Even my guardian angel won't know it's there.'

The rest handed their revolvers over to Sisters Brigid, Patrick, Monica, Agnes and even Reverend Mother. As they left, never to return, the Sisters went on their knees to say the rosary.

Lowe was waiting in O'Connell Street when the 1st Battalion arrived.

'Tell them,' he said to Wheeler, 'to lay down their arms.'

Wheeler and Daly smartly saluted each other.

'God,' groaned Lowe. 'Saluting a rebel!'

He asked officers who had accompanied the rebels on the last stage of their march: 'Who's in charge of these men?'

Daly, fearless of the implications, said, 'I am.'

There was a moment in Moore Street when Old Tom fingered a revolver, wondering whether to make an end of himself. Seeing him, his friend Sean slowly shook his head.

'I guess you're right,' Clarke said. 'I'll let the British do me the honour.'

They had delayed, savouring freedom for as long as possible, but now it was the HQ's turn to surrender.

Sean MacLoughlain, flanked by Willie Pearse and Joe Plunkett, led the way under a cloudless sky, all three waving white flags like symbols of victory. Four abreast the men marched, proudly, arms at the slope.

Down shuttered streets where the dead still lay in doorways they came to Nelson's Pillar. Above the shell of the GPO they saw their flag. The letters 'Irish Republic' were scorched and the pole it hung from was at a crazy angle but it was still flying.

On the other side of the street were their comrades from the Four Courts. They crossed to the Gresham Hotel where the military were waiting and laid down arms. Some Tommies, disciplined until the rebels disarmed, started calling them 'vicious Irish bastards'.

384

In contrast, as they were giving their names and addresses, a British officer walked behind them, saying quietly, 'If you have on you any incriminating papers, tear them up quick and drop 'em in the gutter behind you.'

Among the four hundred who surrendered were Winifred Carney and Julia Grenan. All were marched to the grassy forecourt of the Rotunda Hospital.

Joe Plunkett was almost out on his feet. A Tommy shoved and cursed him, threatening to bayonet him if he didn't get a move on. An NCO took the private by the arm. 'Do your duty, soldier, and leave it at that.'

One lad, Sean Harling, had been selling race cards for the Fairyhouse Races outside Broadstone Station when the rising started. This had been the grandest week of his life.

A British officer clipped him on the ear and grunted, 'Get the hell out of here, lad.'

'Wha's a-marrer,' complained Sean, 'amn't I a prisoner?'

He was given a friendly push, 'Go home to your mommy.'

At the Rotunda, Captain Lee Wilson noticed McDermott leaning on his stick.

'So,' he said, with a sneer, 'you have cripples in your army.'

McDermott replied, with dignity, 'You have your place, sir, and I mine. Hadn't you better mind your place?'

At which the Captain, young, thin-faced, caddish-looking, came out with a string of obscenities. He ordered machine-guns to be trained on the prisoners.

'If any of this bunch move, shoot 'em like the rats they are.'

His Majesty King George V had invited Sir John French to Windsor where he was vacationing to brief him on Ireland.

'Tell me, General,' he asked, in a comfortable room off the Long Gallery, 'how *are* things over there?'

'Going very well, Your Majesty.'

The King was concerned about his Irish subjects. 'Tell me more.'

Sir John drew out a piece of paper.

'A wire just received from General Maxwell, sir. He says, "There are strong indications of a collapse of the whole rebellion."'

'Thank God,' the King said. 'I was hoping it was a storm in a teacup.'

At 10 o'clock, when an NCO came to No 172, Sally Hughes pressed him to let her go to the top of the house. In the end he said, 'If you promise not to kick up a row I'll take you up. But first, I'll need hot water and a towel.'

At which she and Nellie Walsh burst into tears.

As he went upstairs with the basin, he called over his shoulder to a drunken sentry in the hallway, 'If there's any more bawling down there, blow their bloody brains out.'

The women waited in silent agony for half an hour until he came down, carrying a candle. He pointed to Mrs Hughes. 'You can come up.'

Sally followed him. In spite of her resolve, she shrieked when she saw her husband lying dead on the floor, riddled with bullets. His cap was over his face, his clothes were drenched with blood and water.

Lowe sent Pearse to Arbour Hill Detention Barracks. The rest spent the night in the open at the Rotunda. It was cramped. There was no food or drink. Some had not had so much as a cup of water for over thirty hours. The weather was cold and damp but there were no blankets, nor any toilet facilities. The women were treated like the men.

During the night, Captain Wilson came on duty from Mooney's pub where he had been drinking steadily. Bad before, he now seemed a demon in human form.

'What shall we do with these Sinn Feiners, boys?' His drunken drawl echoed eerily in the deserted street. 'Shoot the swine?'

'Aye, sir,' his men replied, without enthusiasm.

He went right up to one prisoner after another, holding a match to his face. 'Anyone care to see the animals?'

He was particularly hard on Tom Clarke. 'This old bastard, boys, is the Commander-in-Chief, would you believe! Keeps a tobacco shop across the street. A fine fucking general for a fine fucking army.'

He grabbed Sean McDermott's walking-stick and snapped it in half. 'Bloody cripple. Can't even walk straight let alone shoot straight.'

Seeing the red cross on Jim Ryan's sleeve, he hacked it off with a bayonet and stamped on it. 'I don't recognize *you* as Red Cross.'

Having victimized individuals, he now turned to them as a group. 'No smoking, you bastards, and lie down. If you want to shit, do it in your pants like you've been doing all week.'

Seeing he was looking for a pretext to shoot them, McDermott passed the word that they were to keep cool.

For some, that was the most wretched night of their lives. They

386

were forced to relieve themselves where they lay, even in the presence of the opposite sex.

Some huddled up to keep warm. During the night, Jim Ryan woke up to find his head resting on Clarke's shoulder.

Clarke whispered, 'You awake, young feller?'

'Yes.'

'Good, I just wanna turn over.'

Ryan was touched by his consideration.

There was surprise in the College of Surgeons. O'Connell Street, deafening the day before, was silent.

Mallin had checked that the Republican flag was still flying over Jacob's. What, then, was going on? He discussed with the Countess the possibility of breaking out if they were cornered. His preference had always been for fighting a guerilla war in the Dublin mountains.

The living prayed over the dead. The Countess, being a Protestant, was not able to join in. But that night she experienced a somersault quite as complete and unexpected as Birrell's when he heard of the rising.

Religion had so far meant little to her. In her world, it was the preserve of a rich and exclusive minority. At this, the most critical moment of her life, she felt confronted by the ancient faith of Ireland, the faith that people of her breed had tried for centuries by cruel means to eliminate.

She resolved that if God spared her, just as she had shared her comrades' political and social ambitions, she would one day share their faith.

Her family would not approve, but when had they liked anything she did?

The Connolly girls had walked to Coalisland, then thumbed a lift to Dundalk where they found all trains were reserved for the military. Nora, in particular, was footsore, having walked a long way to find Ina in the first place. Yet there was nothing for it but to walk the fifty miles to Dublin.

Thirty miles along the main Belfast-Dublin road, they stopped for the night in a field at Balbriggan within sound of the sea. They took off their shoes and stockings and pushed their blistered feet into the soft smooth earth.

Their pleasure did not last. Mists came in off the sea. It turned cold, then very cold. They gathered their clothes about them, trying to sleep, but they did not succeed.

SUNDAY

In the early hours, Frank Henderson, a young prisoner on the Rotunda lawn, knelt to relieve himself. Captain Lee Wilson noticed. He snatched a rifle from a Tommy and yelling, 'Filthy bastard,' struck him with the butt, knocking him unconscious.

With first light, the DMP and the G-men, the political division of the Dublin Metropolitan Police, woke the prisoners and armed soldiers circled them. It was time to identify the chief troubler-makers. Among the first to be hauled out were Clarke, McDermott and Ned Daly. They took a while to straighten up after that long cold night in the open.

They were marched round the corner to the Rotunda Rink and strip-searched. Clarke had damaged his elbow in the escape from the GPO. When he did not remove his jacket quickly enough, Wilson cruelly straightened his arm and tugged the jacket off.

The prisoners were still refused permission to go to the toilet.

Elizabeth O'Farrell had spent the night at the National Bank. Lieutenant Royall had stayed outside her room, dozing in a chair. When she awoke at 6 a.m., she saw through the window piles of arms next to the Parnell Monument and, among the prisoners, Winifred Carney and Julia Grenan.

No sooner was she dressed than Captain Wheeler said he would like her to take orders to other commandants.

This was to prove the most dangerous day of her life.

That Sunday morning, a calm had descended on North King Street.

Mrs Hickey looked out of the Corcorans' where she had spent the last day and a half. Everything seemed so normal. Church bells were ringing across the city; parishioners were coming back from first Mass. Of everyone passing the door she asked, with rising dread, 'Has anyone seen my man?' and they shook their heads.

She left the house and started scouring the city for her husband and son.

'The soldiers,' she told friends and neighbours, 'must have taken them somewhere.'

Wheeler told Elizabeth he would like her to deliver the surrender order first to the College of Surgeons. He drove her to Grafton Street. Some shops had been looted, a few gutted.

The car was waved through military check-points until it halted halfway. Wheeler gave her a copy of the surrender and Connolly's addition. 'Good luck, miss.'

Holding a white flag, she turned right into a silent Green. She was let into the College by a side entrance and taken to see the Countess.

'Commandant Mallin is asleep,' she said. 'Can I help?'

'It's surrender,' Elizabeth said.

The Countess, feeling a strange compulsion to sign herself like a Catholic, immediately aroused Mallin. Elizabeth, having handed him the orders, returned to the car.

'Well,' Wheeler said, 'what did they say?'

'I saw Commandant Mallin and he didn't say anything.'

Wheeler said irritably, 'You should have brought a yes or a no.'

The car took them back to Trinity where Wheeler phoned Lowe. He returned to say he would like her to take the order of surrender next to Boland's Mill.

They had to make a detour, ending up at Butt Bridge. Wheeler was apologetic. 'Sorry I can't get you any nearer. When you're back, perhaps you'd join me in Merrion Square.'

In place after place, Elizabeth asked the military if they knew where the Volunteers were. They shook their heads and warned her there was a lot of sniping in the area. She risked her life several times as she tried this street or barricade, then the next. Finally, someone told her where de Valera was.

Her heart was already thumping as she crossed the Grand Canal Street Bridge when a man within feet of her was shot. She called pleadingly to people in nearby houses and they carried him to Sir Patrick Dun's Hospital.

At the Dispensary, a guard sent her round the back where she was lifted in through a window into a small room. The Commandant, long, lean, smooth-shaven for the first time that week, was ready to drop. She handed him Pearse's message.

De Valera stretched his long neck like an angry goose. This was a trick, surely. He had just made his troops clean their weapons and have target practice. He said, in his usual dry way, 'I'm sorry, miss. I can only lay down my arms on the orders of my immediate superior, Brigadier MacDonagh.'

389

When Elizabeth left, de Valera talked it over with his second in command, Joseph O'Connor. It did not take him long to grasp they really had no choice. He took Cadet Mackay with him and crossed the road to Sir Patrick Dun's Hospital to negotiate with the British. On the way, he handed Mackay his Browning automatic.

'I'd be grateful to you if you would give this to my eldest boy, Vivion, to remind him of his father.'

Two Capuchins from Church Street, Fathers Augustine and Aloysius, turned up at the Castle asking for General Lowe. Sensing they might be useful, he saw them at once.

They had heard rumours of surrender and of a truce in their area. There were still rebels around who would not give in unless they actually saw Pearse's order. The General assured them it was genuine, all right, though, for the moment, he was out of copies.

'But,' he said, 'James Connolly is a prisoner here. Care to have a word with him?'

Neither priest had met Connolly before. They felt at once that they were in the presence of tremendous goodness. He confirmed he had added his signature to Pearse's.

He was in such pain, they did not stay long.

'Satisfied, Fathers?' Lowe said. 'Or perhaps you'd also like to see Pearse in Arbour Hill.'

Once they had Pearse's word as well, Father Augustine told Lowe, 'We'll do all we can to avoid unnecessary bloodshed.'

He thanked them, gave them a freshly typed copy of Pearse's surrender and put a chauffeur-driven car at their disposal.

Elizabeth told Captain Wheeler of de Valera's reaction.

'I understand, miss. Would you mind, then, going to see MacDonagh at Jacob's?'

He stopped the car in Bride Street and wished her luck as once again she walked alone through the firing line. At Jacob's, she hammered on the gate. A guard blindfolded her and led her for what seemed like ages until she heard MacDonagh say: 'Take it off.'

Like de Valera, MacDonagh and MacBride greeted the news with scepticism.

'Why should we surrender?' MacDonagh asked. 'We haven't once been attacked.'

Within minutes, Fathers Augustine and Aloysius arrived. MacDonagh took them aside for a quiet word. How, he asked, could

390

he be sure the surrender was not made under duress? With Pearse and Connolly arrested, he was in charge and, in his view, Jacob's could hold out for a considerable time. He had heard there was soon to be an international peace conference and the British were keen for them to fold so they would have no case.

'If anyone is going to negotiate with the British, Fathers,' he concluded, 'it has to be me. And I will only deal with General Lowe himself.'

The priests drove back to the Castle where Lowe consulted Maxwell by phone before telling them, 'I'm prepared to meet him at the north-east corner of St Patrick's Park at midday.'

He wrote out a safe conduct pass for MacDonagh so that if nothing came of their discussions, he would be free to return to his Headquarters.

At 11 a.m., after fifteen hours at the Rotunda, the prisoners were marched to Richmond Barracks.

Joe Plunkett was close to collapse. McDermott, without his stick, could not keep up, and a soldier was detailed to go with him at his pace. He took forty-five minutes longer than the rest to cover the two miles.

On the way, crowds came out of the slums around Christchurch Cathedral. The rebels had not expected a brass band, but had hoped for a certain respect. But these rude gestures, this hatred as though they had turned bread into stones, this blizzard of abuse! Dublin was well and truly Mitchel's city of bellowing slaves. They came out to pelt them with filth and rotten vegetables. From upper rooms, some contributed the contents of their chamber pots.

The crowds were most hostile in Thomas Street where Robert Emmet had been executed. 'Death,' they yelled, 'to the bloody Shinners.'

The rebels, marching now like old men into a wind, began to suspect that Captain Wilson had echoed the general feeling.

The people disowned them. The rising had failed utterly.

At precisely midday, Fathers Augustine and Aloysius walked with Lowe from the car to meet MacDonagh at St Patrick's Park. The General and the Commandant shook hands, then returned to the car to negotiate.

It took only ten minutes for Lowe to convince MacDonagh that the surrender was unforced. Too many had died already and the city had suffered enough.

They agreed on an armistice until 3 p.m. when MacDonagh said he hoped that his men and Kent's would give themselves up together.

Lowe offered him the use of his car. MacDonagh beckoned to the priests and they went back with him to Jacob's. There, Father Aloysius stayed in the car. The driver was so nervous at being in an area controlled by rebels, the friar made him a white flag out of a broom handle and a baker's apron.

Father Augustine was by MacDonagh's side as he addressed his men. He spoke calmly until he came to the word, 'Surrender', then he broke down.

'I have to tell you,' he said, when he recovered, 'that Father Augustine here advises me there is no other way.'

To the priest's astonishment, he added, 'And now Father will say a few words to you.'

The big, bearded Capuchin prayed for divine assistance. His first words proved whose side he was on. 'Everywhere, our men fought a brave fight.' His powerful voice filled the building. 'According to Commandant Pearse, our first duty is to save civilian lives. As good soldiers, you will obey your Commander-in-Chief and lay down your arms.'

'But they'll shoot us, Father,' cried one of the lads.

'You're wrong, my son. Nothing of the kind.'

After answering their fears for several minutes, he promised to return before they gave themselves up.

'Meanwhile, my sons, go on with your prayers.'

When the main party reached Richmond Barracks, they were halted on the parade ground, searched and robbed. Still without toilet facilities, a few fainted. Some handed over their watches for a cup of water. Only after they were processed in fours were their basic needs attended to.

In the gymnasium, the chief suspects were scrutinized by the G-men. They picked out the ring-leaders with, 'Ah, delighted to see you. Won't you come out here and sit with your friends along this wall?'

After that, forty were packed in one big room and given a dustbin for a lavatory. This raised a hollow cheer. When they had used it, it was removed, emptied and returned full of water. They gladly drank it.

Plunkett lay on the floor in a corner, attended by his brothers, George and John. On Tom Clarke's face, like frozen lightning, was that same suspicion of a smile; he was well satisfied with himself and the world.

When McDermott finally arrived and saw the appalling conditions, he banged furiously on the door until it was opened. 'Get rid of this cess bucket,' he roared, 'and bring these men clean water.'

The surprising thing was, the soldiers did as they were told.

Mallin's men trickled into the College of Surgeons, making their way down from the roof and from outposts through many a tunnel. Not a few had cut hands and brick dust in their hair.

They had caught rumours in flight, wild talk about the surrender of some commands. They themselves had not yielded an inch. Yesterday had been so quiet they had been able to get vast stores of food from Jacob's. The only noise in the night was the occasional rifle barking like a dog on a hill farm. Ammunition was plentiful. Mallin had been talking of breaking out into the mountains.

He appeared in the Long Room with the Countess, William Partridge and the other officers. He looked particularly sombre as he sat at the head of a long table. His handsome face was lined, his thick dark hair had lost its lustre, his triangular moustache was whitened by brick dust.

His voice faltered for the first time that week. 'I have sad news, comrades. Our leaders have decided to . . . give up.'

Everyone gasped and not a few, leaning on their rifles, murmured, 'Impossible.'

'We are . . . giving up for only one reason. Because of the number of civilians being killed.'

'It's a trick,' someone bellowed. 'We're in no danger.'

Mallin read them Pearse's order with Connolly's confirmation for the Irish Citizen Army.

The Countess said, 'It's Connolly's signature, all right, and I trust him absolutely,' and Partridge added, 'The messenger is one of our own.'

Most of the women began to cry. One of the men said, 'We should fight to the death,' and another, 'When could we trust the British, anyway? They'll shoot the lot of us.'

Mallin raised his hand for silence.

'We came here as loyal soldiers, comrades, and that is how we shall leave.' He looked around him slowly. 'I want to thank you

393

all. I did not think any group of men and women could be so loyal as you have been this week. It has been such a great honour to lead you that . . . that—'

He bowed his head over the table.

After a moment: 'Some of you with family commitments can slip away. We won't think the worse of you for that.'

A few took the hint and left.

The rest yelled back, 'We've worked and fought together, if it comes to it we'll die together.'

'That won't be necessary, I'm sure,' Mallin said. 'As for me, the worst that can happen is to be shot by the British. I expected that all along. I only hope I go to meet it as an Irishman should.'

He went up to the roof and lowered the tricolour. From a British outpost, there was a single rifle shot, the signal that the College had surrendered. It was 2 p.m.

As Mallin lowered the flag, de Valera, sombre-faced with black pouches under strange staring eyes, was at the head of his men. In front of him marched a Red Cross official with a white flag, and he was flanked by armed guards.

They crossed Mount Street Bridge where so many soldiers had been gunned down by his men, along Northumberland Road where a handful of rebels had for hours held a whole army at bay.

It hurt de Valera to see women offering British troops tea and sandwiches. Did they not realize that Ireland had as much right to freedom as Belgium?

He called out, in a tired, croaky voice, 'If only you had come out with knives and forks.'

At the Royal Dublin Society, his 117 men were herded into horse-boxes. He himself was treated as an officer and locked in the Weights and Measures Office at the Town Hall.

From a top-floor window of the Shelbourne, the British CO pointed to the bare flag-pole over the College of Surgeons.

Captain Wheeler said, 'Tell the United Services Club to hold their fire while I accept the surrender.'

Mallin and the Countess came out of the side door of the College and saluted. He had no gun, only a walking-stick which he gave up. She handed over her automatic.

'Have your men lay down their arms inside,' Wheeler said, 'then form up out here. How many are you, by the way?'

394

Mallin said, 'Apart from us two, 109 men and 10 women.'

Wheeler inspected the building and said, 'Everything seems to be in order.' He bowed to the Countess, who was a distant relative of his. 'If you'd care to travel in my car, ma'am?'

'No offence, old feller,' she said, 'but I much prefer to tag along with my own.'

Under heavy guard, the Citizen Army marched down Grafton Street to Trinity. An elderly College servant came out and shrieked, 'Shoot every one of the bastards.'

The glimpse they had of O'Connell Street amazed them. It seemed as if only the Pillar and O'Connell's monument were standing.

As they wheeled left along Dame Street to the Castle they were in for an even worse surprise. Crowds lined the way, pelting them with everything they could find. They were hungry, they had been without work for a week, some had lost family or friends, many of their houses had been destroyed.

Mallin was in uniform but with a trilby in place of the cap which a bullet had pierced. The Countess was in a slouch hat topped by an ostrich feather, green Irish Citizen Army tunic and riding breeches.

She was mocked unmercifully.

'Who does she think she is, Joan of Arc?'

'Is it a man or a woman?'

'No wonder the rebellion was such a mess when it was run by women in trousers.'

The rebels had never seen such venom. Dubliners hated them far more than they had ever hated the British. They were even waving Union Jacks in their faces. If the soldiers had not kept them at bayonet-point, they would have torn Mallin's men limb from limb.

The rebels had fought and died for these people but they had not won their hearts.

As MacDonagh went with the priests to the other garrisons, they corrected an illusion he had been under all week.

'Outside Dublin,' Father Aloysius said gently, 'there has hardly been any fighting at all. Some in Galway, I believe, and in Wexford.'

MacDonagh sat back, knowing that all their efforts had been wasted and he himself was doomed.

Near Basin Lane, the car came to a halt at a barricade. They walked from there to the South Dublin Union. A shot rang out, narrowly missing them. The priests dropped to their knees in fright; MacDonagh did not flinch.

A British officer ran up to apologize. 'The soldier who fired that shot is under arrest.'

'What shot?' asked MacDonagh.

Dick Mulcahy, who had been fighting in north County Dublin, was permitted to see Pearse in Arbour Hill to check on the surrender.

He was led down a grim corridor to the third cell on the right. Pearse was lying on a trestle. Beside him was a glass of water and a few biscuits.

Mulcahy saluted and stood to attention. 'I've come about your orders, sir.'

'All our forces, Mr Mulcahy, must surrender.'

'Nothing else, sir?'

Pearse sadly shook his head.

Mulcahy tried to say, *'Beannacht De agat*, God bless you,' but the words died in his throat. He saluted and left.

Later, two Volunteers came from Enniscorthy where they had taken over the town and ambushed the RIC barracks. Pearse wrote a special note of surrender for the Wexford men. As he handed it over, he whispered, 'Make sure you hide your arms. There will come another time.'

From the Castle, Mallin and the women were transported to Kilmainham Jail. The Countess was the only one of seventy women to be put in solitary. She knew what that meant.

The rest of the Stephen's Green contingent were transferred to Richmond Barracks where they joined their other comrades.

McDermott greeted Liam O'Briain and, noticing he had brought an old quilt, said, 'That'd be grand for Joe, he's in a bad way.' Sean folded it a few times and placed it under Plunkett's head as he lay cold and quivering on the bare boards. Major surgery, the week's rising, followed by a night in the open had almost finished him off.

Clarke, thinking this might be his last chance before he was executed, pencilled a letter to his wife.

> Dear K,
> I am in better health and more satisfied than for many a day – all will be well eventually – but this is goodbye and now you are ever before me to cheer me – God bless

you and the boys. Let them be proud to follow the same path – Sean is with me and McGarry, all well – they are heroes. I'm full of pride, my love. Yours, Tom.

On the back of it, McDermott added:

> Dear Caty,
> I never felt so proud of the boys. 'Tis worth a life of suffering to be with them for one hour. God bless you all, Sean.

Clarke unfastened his watch and gave it to a soldier. 'If you can get this note delivered to my wife, this is for you.'

The Tommy took it. 'Do my best, mate.'

Kattie did get the letter but only after three weeks. And much was to happen before then.

In the Viceregal Lodge, Birrell was penning his last letter to the Prime Minister. At 3 p.m., he was able to report that all the rebels had surrendered, bar the Jacob's contingent, and they were surrounded. Only a thousand or so rebels had taken part; outside Dublin, there had been almost no trouble.

He wrote:

> It is not an *Irish* Rebellion – it would be a pity if *ex post facto* it became one, and was added to the long and melancholy list of Irish Rebellions.
> You will I am sure *let me know* as quickly as possible what you wish me to *do* in the general interest of the country. I *fully appreciate my own position*, but I am not in the least frightened of the House of Commons and can put up (for myself) a good fight – tho' I daresay the general verdict will be adverse, and of course I can't go on . . . .

His final comment, the fruit of bitter experience, was: 'No one can govern Ireland from England save in a state of siege.'

As Birrell completed that letter, in 172 North King Street, discipline among the troops reached rock-bottom. There had been goings and comings all day; many drunk and excited soldiers had grabbed what they could.

Young Nellie Walsh finally found the courage to venture upstairs. Sick with impending horror, she edged open the drawing-room door. Her heart seemed to expand like a balloon as she saw her husband lying face down across the fireplace, his mouth and nose pressed on the hearth. She knelt and tried to turn him over but lacked the strength.

Shaking all over, gasping madly for breath, she went downstairs for a while to rest.

When she climbed up again, she saw soldiers had placed a rug, stolen from the butcher's next door, over her husband's corpse and were using it as a card table. She stood there for a few moments in disbelief. They were eating bully beef, drinking, laughing and jeering at whoever came in the door.

She went to tell her father, Mr O'Neill, who lived nearby. He hugged her and heard her out before saying there was more bad news, about her seventeen-year-old brother.

'Yesterday morning, Willie was in the street, Nell, when he came across a dead man. A bullet had gone through his eye and come out the back of his head. Thinking it might be me, he knelt to make sure and ... and he was shot by a soldier.'

The father held his daughter tight and they sobbed on each other's shoulder.

'He took five minutes to die, Nell. His last words were, "O, Mother, Mother." '

Drying his eyes, Mr O'Neill asked three men to help him carry his son-in-law on a stretcher, then, in a fury, he burst into No 172 and raced upstairs.

'That man under the carpet,' he roared, 'served for ten years in the British army like yourselves. I have one son serving in France and another just back minus an arm.'

Drunk as they were, the soldiers hung their heads in shame. They removed the carpet from the corpse and slunk away.

Nelly said she couldn't bear the thought of her man and Sally Hughes's being taken away, anonymously.

'They have to be buried properly, Dad, from this house.'

She and Sally went to the coffin-maker's shop and knocked and knocked until he opened the door. They chose and paid for two coffins which the men carried home.

At St Patrick's Park, MacDonagh, Brigade Commander, formally handed General Lowe an order of unconditional surrender. It was 3.15 p.m.

Bareheaded and tired-looking, he went on by car with Fathers Augustine and Aloysius to arrange the details with Kent's men.

In the South Dublin Union and the Marrowbone Lane Distillery, MacDonagh had the sad job of informing the rebels. Once more, Father Augustine confirmed what he said.

On the return to Jacob's, they passed the spot in Thomas Street where Robert Emmet had been hanged and beheaded. Father Augustine could almost hear MacDonagh's thoughts. He knew that he, too, would soon be executed and that his epitaph would not be written in his generation.

At Jacob's, the men gathered around Father Augustine, asking him to take messages to their folks. He filled his capacious pockets with notes, mostly to parents, which he promised to see delivered the next day.

Seeing a fourteen-year-old among the prisoners, Father Augustine winked at him and drew him aside. 'What's your name, lad?'

'Vincent Byrne, Father.'

'Follow me, Vinnie.'

The front door was barred so he led the boy to the first floor and indicated the window. The boy jumped on to the sill and the priest lowered him by his extended arms until he was able to drop to safety.

'Goodbye, Vinnie Byrne,' he called after him. 'You'll live to fight for Ireland another day.'

In Father Augustine's absence, many were giving money to Elizabeth O'Farrell. Michael O'Hanrahan, the Volunteers' Quartermaster and MacDonagh's second in charge, gave her three pounds for his mother. She then left for Bride Street, where MacDonagh's Battalion was due to surrender.

At 5 p.m., the Republican flag was hauled down.

During the short march to Bride Street, some of MacDonagh's younger lads melted into the crowd and went home. The rest laid down their arms and gave their names and addresses. All this time a solitary sniper was firing.

'Bloody British,' a Volunteer said.

In fact, it was one of their own, high up in Jacob's, who had not heard of the surrender.

In Portobello Barracks, Lieutenant Monk Gibbon came across

Skeffy's belongings in the billiard room. Soldiers were coming in, joking and grabbing souvenirs. Gibbon had no intention of taking anything until he saw a letter from George Bernard Shaw. In it, GBS apologized for being unable to give an interview on his next trip to Dublin.

Monk's ambition to be a writer proved too strong for him. As he pocketed the letter, he heard Colthurst's shrill tones. 'No, no, *no*, Sergeant, you have to say, "The prisoners were trying to escape." '

Hamilton Norway, too, was looking for souvenirs. He returned to the GPO, hoping to find his son's belongings.

The elegant building which he had lately redecorated to the highest standards was a mere bullet-ridden facade. His office was a part of space. The smouldering remains meant little to him. But he could have wept over the loss of his son's few effects.

Freddie now seemed somehow doubly dead.

Soon after 5 p.m., Mrs Hickey returned home, exhausted from her fruitless, day-long search. Two soldiers outside her shop barred her way.

'This is *my* house,' she said.

'Sorry, missis, but you can't come in. You'd better go and see an officer first.'

Apprehensive, she went to Mrs Carroll at No 170. Her neighbour said, 'I must speak to you, my dear.' Unable to check herself, she moaned, 'Oh, poor Christy.'

In that moment, Mrs Hickey knew she had lost both her men. She ran back home, barged in and flew upstairs, with the soldiers in hot pursuit yelling, 'You can't go up there, d'you hear?'

One floor up, she opened the door. 'Christy!'

He was lying on the floor, his face black, his two hands raised in the air as if in silent supplication. 'O, my poor angel, my darling son.'

She gently kissed his cold face, put his cap under his head for a pillow and joined his hands for death. Standing up, she saw her Tom also stretched on the floor. 'O Jesus, my Lord!'

Pete Connolly was there, too, with great bayonet gashes about the neck and head. The sight was too much for her. She reeled and fainted. The next she knew, she was in the street with soldiers looking after her.

Stories spread rapidly that in one night fifteen civilians had been brutally murdered. For the first time, many Dubliners began to wonder, timidly at first, who was right and who wrong in the matter of the rebellion.

At 6 o'clock, Kent's men at the Union, having linked up with the Marrowbone Lane garrison and members of *Cumann na mBan*, finally arrived in Basin Street and surrendered their arms.

Father Augustine, seeing the tall, manly Kent, felt immensely proud of him as the representative of a brave body of men and women.

Kent had given up his gun and belt to an English officer, when the friar saw they intended to strip him of his uniform. He went and shook Kent's hand with, 'Goodbye and God bless you, Eamonn,' as if to show these Englishmen the respect they, as Irishmen, had for the prisoners. The two Capuchins then glared at the soldiers before going home to Church Street after a long and tiring day.

Kent appreciated the gesture. This was the very first intimation any of the prisoners had that maybe the rising was not entirely wasted.

The arms which the Volunteers had paid for with hard-earned cash were collected in handcarts and put in lorries. The prisoners, with Kent at their head, were marched off to Richmond Barracks.

Nora Connolly's right foot was very bad, so that she and Ina made slow progress. They had been given a lift by a man searching for bread but that had still left them six miles north of Clontarf. As they reached the outskirts of Dublin, their faces were bright red from the sun. They were suffering not just from blistered feet but from dehydration and hunger, too.

At Swords, they ran into a troop of British soldiers going north and their hearts leaped with joy.

'Are they retreating?' Ina said. 'Do you think we've won?'

The nearer the city the more British troops there were, their manner showing they were the victors.

Devastation was on a colossal scale; smoke was rising on all sides and a smell of burning was in the air. Worst of all, Nora and Ina did not meet one person with a good word for the rebels. 'Thank God those crazy people have surrendered,' was the general verdict.

In Drumcondra, they went to Clonliffe Road. Their friends, the Ryan girls, told them, 'They're all surrendering.'

'Our father?' asked Nora, apprehensively.

'Wounded,' Mary said.

'Dying,' said Phyllis.

401

The Connolly sisters sat without another word.

Their mother had come down from Belfast on Good Friday and was staying at the Countess's cottage, Three Rock, on the edge of the Dublin mountains. They were keen to see her and the rest of their family but they were exhausted and, besides, it was nearly curfew hour.

'Stay with us for the night,' Mary and Phyllis said kindly, 'please.'

From Richmond Barracks, the first batch of prisoners was paraded in the square before being marched to the North Wall. They went in twos with two English soldiers on either side.

On the way, they ran into more abuse, screamed from windows.

'Shoot the traitors,' and 'Good old Staffs, go to it, bayonet the bastards.'

The men were exhausted. They had been searched, first at the Castle, then at the Barracks. Now there was this long march across a burning city. To lift their spirits, they sang lustily, led by Bob de Coeur. Threatened with reprisals if they didn't stop singing they whistled, instead.

At the North Wall, soldiers were embarking. They made way for the rebels who were packed like sardines into the North Western Railway Boat.

Only the Tommies were given life-belts.

An NCO said, 'If we're torpedoed, at least a few hundred fucking Irish rebels'll end up feeding the fishes, eh?'

The rebels were given no drinking water. Without toilet facilities, they had to make do in a very confined space among smelly, frightened cattle. They consoled themselves by reciting the rosary, many of them praying that a U-boat would sink them and put them out of their misery. When the sea was at its roughest they, one by one, lifted their heads as Jack O'Reilly, a Tralee man with a fine baritone voice, sang 'Galway Bay'.

After a twelve-hour voyage many were in bad shape by the time they reached Holyhead. From the Welsh port they were packed in a train for jails in the north of England. For thirty hours, they were to have no food, not even a cup of water.

Back in Richmond Barracks, their leaders were brought individually before a court of preliminary enquiry. British officers held in the GPO were called to witness that the prisoners had been in the GPO and in possession of guns.

That night, Clarke sat with his back to the wall, with McDermott beside him and O'Briain next to McDermott.

Sean was insistent that the Germans were coming to help.

'We haven't failed,' he said. 'The only real failure in Ireland is the failure to strike.'

In response to a call from Major Price at Parkgate, a party of Royal Engineers left the Castle in the dead of night.

At Portobello Barracks, they repaired the damage to the wall against which Skeffy and the two editors had been shot.

That night, John Dillon, in his house north of O'Connell Street, wrote to John Redmond in London, giving him a solemn warning:

> You should strongly urge on the Government the *extreme* unwisdom of any wholesale shooting of prisoners. The wisest course is to execute *no one* for the present.
>
> If there were shootings of prisoners on a large scale the effect on public opinion might be disastrous in the extreme.
>
> *So far* feeling of the population in Dublin is *against* the Sinn Feiners. But a reaction might very easily be created.

————PART FOUR————

AFTER THE BATTLE
1–12 May 1916

Be green upon their graves,
  O happy Spring!
For they were young and eager
  who are dead!
Of all things that are young,
  and quivering
With eager life,
  be they rememberéd.
                              James Stephens

May Day. At Kilmainham Hospital, General Maxwell stuck a cigarette in his mouth to give him strength to get up. But he was in good heart as his toe gingerly felt for the wooden floor. He had not put a foot wrong since he came to Ireland. He was only there twenty-four hours and the rebellion folded. After three days, it was all over, barring a few snipers.

Even the casualty report on his breakfast table did not dampen his spirits. He read with approval the editorial in the *Irish Times* calling for the utmost severity towards the trouble-makers. After taking coffee, he called in his aides, demanding they round up all potential trouble-makers.

'So get to it, gentlemen.'

He aimed to destroy the Sinn Fein movement root and branch. He was not going to make the same mistake as Birrell and Nathan. Which reminded him. He had asked the Under-Secretary to pop in that very morning.

Nathan's visit to Military House was his first outing since the rebellion began. It was brief enough. Maxwell really despised him for his lax approach and felt he had nothing to contribute.

The Under-Secretary returned to the Castle knowing that the military were in charge and that things, however bad, were likely to get worse.

Major Vane had no sooner marched back with his detail through cheering crowds to Portobello than he was summoned to the Orderly Room. He was in an upbeat mood, being especially proud of what his men had done at the South Dublin Union.

Colonel McCammond's face suggested this was not to be a congratulatory session.

'Sit down, Vane, please. Just to let you know I've taken over officially from Rosborough. He's had a tough time, lately. All of you have. Better if we have a clean sweep, don't you agree?'

'If you say so, sir.'

'By the way, Vane. Rivalry in the armed forces really cannot be countenanced.'

Vane wondered if he had heard correctly. 'Sorry?'

'Is there really any need to blacken a fellow-officer, even besmirch the honour of a regiment, out of vanity?'

Vane was speechless.

'In justice,' the Colonel went on, 'I'm obliged to replace you as second in charge with Captain Colthurst.'

'*Who?*'

'That's *enough*, Major,' the CO said in a steely voice. 'You may go.'

When he had cleared his head, Vane went to Parkgate, hoping to talk with Maxwell about Skeffy's murder. Major Price met him with, 'The General's not free. Can I help?'

Vane explained that he had come about Skeffy. 'He was murdered by one of our own officers.'

Price's head rocked back. 'This is war, old chap.'

'War is no excuse for murder.'

'In my humble opinion, men like that are best out of the way.'

'Thank you,' Vane said, peremptorily.

He went to the office of the Adjutant General, an old man with rheumy eyes who had known him since his youth.

He heard him out on Skeffy. Then: 'They're going to act even more stupidly, Francis. Execute the rebels.'

Vane said, almost casually, 'I'd like eight days' leave in England, sir, if I may.'

'Good man. You need a break. A great job you did at the South Union. I've sent in a commendation on your behalf.'

Vane did not say what his real motives were as he left to book a place on that night's mail boat to England.

Nora and Ina hobbled across the city. In O'Connell Street, they saw the Irish flag still flying over the hollow GPO and they smelt the horrible stench of dead horses and burning buildings. It hurt them immensely to hear everyone cursing 'them rebel bastards' who had brought this on the city.

They hurried on to Rathmines where they saw a poster of the *Daily Sketch*. Looking out at them was the face of their father with the caption, 'The Dead Rebel Leader'.

From outside Three Rock, they heard their mother wailing and the little ones joining in. The first thing they noticed when they went in was a copy of the *Sketch*.

It's not true, Mommy,' Nora rushed to say. 'They've confused Daddy with *Sean* Connolly. He's wounded but not dead.'

'Oh, my darlings,' she said, showering them with her tears. 'I thought I'd lost everyone, you and Daddy and Roddy.'

Wanting to be in the city near their father, they packed a few things and went to the home of his colleague, Bill O'Brien. There another shock awaited them. Both Bill and Roddy had been picked up by the police and taken to Richmond Barracks.

Bill O'Brien's parents readily offered to put all the Connollys up in their small terraced house. The guests were unable to contribute anything since they had no savings of any kind.

In Kilmainham Jail, the Countess presumed she would be shot. It was strange being alone after the comradeship and excitement of the previous week. She worried lest her sister went frantic about her. Eva was a pacifist and a vegetarian whereas she herself believed that only through fighting could Ireland become free.

Used to the spacious grounds and large house at Lissadell in sight of Ben Bulben, County Sligo, she hated being cooped up. Nor, though she mixed with the poor, had she lost her love of beautiful things, carpets, paintings, vases, first editions of illuminated books.

No matter, she had done what she was born to do.

Under the threat of death, she thought of Surrey House in Rathmines, and the mess it must be in. And her cocker spaniel, would Poppet have forgotten her? And Mrs Connolly and Mrs Mallin and their families, were they all right?

There was one benefit of living in prison. For a change she would not exceed her quarterly allowance.

In Arbour Hill Pearse wrote a long letter to his mother, explaining how he understood the rising. Then, with his usual artful innocence, knowing that the letter would be read, he added a postscript. 'I understand that the German expedition which I was counting on actually set sail but was defeated by the British.'

Next he wrote a couple of poems: 'To My Mother' and 'To My Brother'.

The first was a lament for his reserve which he had never been able to overcome.

> ... O Mother (for you know me)
>   You must have known, when I was silent,
> That some strange thing within me kept me dumb,
>   Some strange deep thing, when I should shout my love?
> ... and yet, it may be
>   That I have brought you something else beside –
> The memory of my deed and of my name,
>   A splendid thing which shall not pass away ....

409

In his poem to his brother, Willie, he wrote:

You only have been my familiar friend,
Nor needed I another.

He gave careful instructions about his literary effects and about unpaid bills. It was as if his only regret in dying was that he was prevented from paying his debts.

At noon, the Clarkes' home was raided. Fortunately, Kattie had sent their three boys to the country for safety.

For over two hours, twenty soldiers went through the house. They found nothing. Tom had learned in his prison stint that a single scrap of paper can incriminate a man. All the same, Kattie was taken to Dublin Castle for interrogation.

In his State Room, James Connolly sent for the young Capuchin, Father Aloysius, and discussed with him his idea of Christian Marxism.

The British, fearing the friar might be used to smuggle out political documents, were not keen to leave them alone. But Father Aloysius said: 'You have my word, gentlemen, that I will not bring in or take out of this room anything without your permission.'

When they withdrew, the friar drew a chair up to the bed, draped a small purple stole round his neck and said, 'Now, my son, let us begin.'

Father Aloysius was very content with his visit. He had reconciled a sinner who had been years away from the Church and promised to return with Holy Communion next morning. He left the Castle as Kattie Clarke was being driven in.

The military found her quite as stubborn as her husband. After a wasted hour, they led her to a store room in the Ship Street Barracks behind the Castle. She had to share with five other women.

In the long and lonely hours, she worried about her husband, her brother and her three little boys. There was no self-pity in her but how she missed her sisters. It was never easy being married to a hero of the stature of Tom Clarke.

✻

410

At 3 in the afternoon, Sir John French arrived in Downing Street to brief the Prime Minister on Ireland.

Asquith was beaming with delight at the speed with which Maxwell had sorted things out.

'Be sure to send him my congratulations, General, and tell him it's entirely up to him now.'

Nathan was in the Viceregal Lodge when Birrell received Asquith's telegram accepting his resignation to be made public in the House on Wednesday.

'I'd better leave tomorrow, then,' Birrell said sadly.

Later that day, after dining alone at his lodge, Nathan brought his diary up to date. Having written down the numbers of dead and wounded, it struck him that the chief casualties were Augustine Birrell and Matthew Nathan. And John Redmond and Home Rule. And the future peace and prosperity of Ireland.

Even then, at Kilmainham Hospital, Maxwell had decided with General Hutchinson and Prince Alexander of Battenberg that hanging was too good for the prisoners; they were to be tried by court martial and shot.

Later, at the whiskey stage, an aide brought in a bunch of papers. 'Letters written by the prisoner P. H. Pearse, sir. He requests you to send them on for him.'

Maxwell read out the postscript that sealed Pearse's fate, as it was meant to do.

Hutchinson grinned. 'Anything else?'

'Only a lot of sentimental, revolutionary twaddle. But, wait a sec. In this poem to his brother, yes, yes, yes, he clearly implicates him in all his proceedings.' Maxwell read aloud, ' "*In direst peril true to me.*" '

'A plain reference to the rebellion,' Hutchinson said.

Maxwell nodded and continued, ' "*Leaving all things for me, spending yourself / In the hard service that I taught to you.*" Rotten poetry but clear evidence of collusion, wouldn't you say?'

Hutchinson and Prince Alexander agreed.

'Pearse, gentlemen, has just booked himself and his brother for the bullet.'

When, later, the aide asked Maxwell if he wished him to send on the letters to Mrs Pearse, he replied, 'Certainly not. Court martials begin tomorrow.'

In Richmond Barracks, the prisoners in A. Cell were feeling better after a meal of bully beef and biscuits.

Joe Plunkett was lying in a corner with O'Briain's quilt under his head, tossing restlessly and muttering, 'Nothing was overlooked, nothing forgotten.'

Ned Daly, to keep their spirits up, sang, a love song from Gilbert and Sullivan.

There was a great spirit among them. The greatest of friendships in ordinary times do not begin to compare with friendships forged in the heat of battle.

Liam O'Briain said to Clarke, who was seated against the wall, 'Want a present, Tom?'

'Depends what it is,' Tom said, in his American drawl.

O'Briain held out his last cigar.

'Oh, gee,' Tom gasped, putting it to his nose to savour it.

He lit up, took a heave and passed it on to Sean McDermott. He puffed ecstatically and handed it on to Sean McGarry. The circle passed it around like naughty schoolboys smoking out of sight in the corner of a school yard.

When finally, they settled down for the night, McDermott went to sleep on Clarke's lap, and Willie Pearse stretched out beside O'Briain's bunk.

Willie went to sleep immediately, but he was all the time crying fitfully, 'Fire! Fire!'

As if McDermott could hear him, he responded in an agonizing voice, 'Fire! Got to get the men out! Fire!' and Old Tom stroked his head, saying, 'It's all right, Sean, we're prisoners, in the Barracks.'

Major Vane jumped off the early boat train at Euston and took a taxi to the War Office. He was at once admitted to see his old friend Harold Arthur Tennant.

The Under-Secretary for War listened in silence. Then: 'You are quite sure of your facts?'

Vane nodded vigorously.

'You see, only yesterday, Francis, I gave the Commons my absolute assurance that no man would be shot in Dublin except after a fair trial.' He pondered a moment. 'I think the Prime Minister should know about this.'

After making a couple of calls, he said, 'We should hear from the PM by midday.'

In the Viceregal Lodge, Birrell and Nathan met to say goodbye.

Always fond of one another, recent trials had brought them even closer together. One thing they shared that few of their predecessors ever had: an affection for Ireland and the Irish.

Birrell knew his Westminster colleagues looked on the rebellion in Dublin as they would one in Liverpool. How to make them understand that, for many Irishmen, England was a foreign country, a hostile one that had imposed its will on them for century after century?

He and Nathan had tried to make Ireland for the first time England's friend and a willing part of Empire for ever. What made their failure so galling was that they had very nearly brought off the impossible.

When a policy fails, it is assumed that some other would have succeeded. But, as they saw it, in spite of their failure, theirs was the best and only way. Once Carson had armed Ulster and the south followed suit, to have disarmed them by force would have plunged the whole of Ireland into bloodshed – and this during a world war.

Their only mistake was in not anticipating the rising. But both suspected that quite a few who took part in it had not foreseen it either.

The Cabinet Minister and the civil servant held each other in an uncharacteristically emotional embrace. Both were doomed politically. Neither would even have a peerage for their pains.

'Never mind, Matthew,' Birrell said, his eyes twinkling momentarily, 'there are some people I'd prefer to sink with than go with to the House of Lords.'

Birrell was driven by Basil Blackwood to the boat. He could hardly bear to see the city in ruins. If only he had done the obvious and used force. No politician is blamed for disasters, provided he does what Parliament and Press assure him is the *obvious* thing.

Now, homeward bound to feed the wolves, he found consolation in the thought that Eleanor was dead and did not have to share his shame.

As he stood at the rail, he lifted his gaze above the city to the hills, to the Ireland of bogs and furze and tumbledown thatched cabins, Ireland romantic and rheumatic, a land older than the alphabet and yet without a yesterday, a land he loved in spite of what it had done to him.

As the boat drew away, he remembered his first three discoveries about Ireland: Nothing there is explained. Everything of unimportance is known. So small is it, a whisper carries across the land.

The last of the three had turned out to be a lie.

Prince Alexander burst into Maxwell's room. 'Trouble down in Cork, sir.'

'Jesus Christ,' Maxwell exploded. Cork had been quiet throughout the rebellion. 'Tell me more.'

At four that morning a force of the RIC, led by Head Constable Rowe, had approached Bawnawd House, Castlelyons. It was the home of the Kents, a dissident family whose opposition to authority went back to the days of the Land League. Inside were four brothers, Tom, David, Richard and William, as well as their eighty-four-year-old mother.

'The old lady,' the ADC said, 'loaded rifles and shotguns while her sons blazed away. Rowe was shot dead.'

'Shit!'

Even after military reinforcements came from Fermoy, four miles away, the Kents resisted for three hours till they ran out of ammunition and the house was a wreck. All five came out with their hands above their heads. Richard Kent, in trying to escape, was shot and critically wounded.

'The Irish really are a bunch of murdering bastards,' Maxwell said. 'I'm going to have to take them in hand.'

Midday arrived without a message from the PM, so Vane left the War Office and walked to the Commons. He shocked Redmond with his story about Skeffy. He had no sooner reached his club than a call came for him to go to Downing Street.

At No 10, instead of seeing Asquith, he was shown into the presence of Lord Kitchener.

After hearing him out, the dark-skinned General said, 'I simply don't believe it.'

'I assure you it's true, sir,' said Vane.

'Sure. It's just I don't believe it! Why isn't Colthurst under arrest?'

Vane was not quite sure what was going on in Kitchener's head in view of his poker-face.

'I came across to find out.'

Kitchener called in Asquith's secretary, Bonham Carter.

414

'Take a telegram, if you would. To HQ Ireland. "I order Captain Bowen-Colthurst to be placed under arrest pending his trial by court martial." '

He touched his moustache. 'I am Secretary for War. Why was this atrocity not communicated to me?'

Bonham Carter stifled a grin. The PM had said, 'Kitchener generally finds things out sooner or later – as a rule, later,' and Margot Asquith had contributed the catty remark, 'As a General, Kitchener makes a great poster.'

As Vane was on the point of leaving, the General said, 'We'll have to see that this officer is shot.'

With his hand on the door handle, Vane said, gallantly, 'You would not shoot a madman, sir, and, in my view, the man is completely mad.'

Mrs O'Carroll, the wife of the Councillor whom Colthurst had shot on the previous Wednesday, was summoned to Portobello Barracks. She had had no idea where her husband was, and had heard only rumours that he had been shot. In fact, he had lain in agony for six days with a bullet in his lung.

She found him white, close to death. Shivering in her anguish, she said, 'Tell me what happened, my darling.'

He managed to whisper, 'Shot. Man called . . . Colt-hur—'

'Again,' she said, 'tell me his name again,' but her husband was dead in her arms.

That afternoon, Pearse was taken from Arbour Hill to Richmond Barracks to be court martialled with Clarke and MacDonagh.

The Court was comprised of three army officers with General Blackadder presiding. The judges, all elderly, had no special knowledge of Ireland. There was no stenographer present so they had to take everything down in longhand. This was not only slow, it prevented subsequent checks on facts and procedures.

The men were called individually into a small room, crammed with witnesses, detectives, three officers of the Court and the prosecutor. The proceedings were long on courtesy but short on justice. Two military witnesses identified each prisoner as having taken part in the rebellion and possessing firearms. The G-men gave evidence of their known sedition over a long period. The defendants were refused counsel or time to prepare their own defence or call witnesses.

One prosecution witness would not testify.

Captain Mahoney, who had tended Connolly in the GPO, told the Court: 'My job was to care for the British and the Volunteer wounded, impartially. That I did. I know nothing about combatants.'

Clarke was first to come before the Court. Dressed in black civilian clothes, he looked like an undertaker.

The President asked him, 'How do you plead?'

Clarke, looking into the middle distance, did not deign to answer. His silence seemed to be saying, Why are you bothering me at a time like this?

'Prisoner, do you plead guilty or not-guilty?'

Clarke felt that to plead not-guilty to trying to free his homeland from foreign tyranny was as nonsensical as pleading not-guilty to keeping the ten commandments. In his view, the judges represented British law not justice.

With his continuing silence, the elderly, mild-eyed officers of the Court shrugged and whispered in one another's ears. This was unusual, to say the least. It was like watching while a gale blew on a summer oak without disturbing a single leaf.

Blackadder said to his colleagues, 'Enter a plea of not-guilty. Now let us proceed with the first witness.'

When the witnesses had testified, the President asked, 'Prisoner, is there anything you wish to say in your defence?'

The question was greeted with the same stony silence.

The officers once more whispered among themselves before Blackadder said, 'The prisoner is found guilty.'

Still without speaking or taking notice of any of his accusers, Clarke rose and left the room.

Pearse was next. In the indictment, he was described as 'headmaster and barrister'. Though he was as single-minded as Clarke, he wanted his words on record for the history books.

In a quiet voice whose sincerity could not be questioned, he said:

> From my earliest youth I have regarded the connection between Ireland and Great Britain as the curse of the Irish nation, and felt convinced that while it lasted, this country could never be free or happy.
>
> When I was a child of ten I went down on my bare knees by my bedside one night and promised God that I should devote my life to an effort to free my country.

416

He spoke the next words solemnly.

'I have kept that promise.'

The room was stuffy. One judge had dozed off and came to with a rasping snort to hear:

> We seem to have lost. We have not lost. To refuse to fight would have been to lose; to fight is to win. We have kept faith with the past, and handed on a tradition to the future.
>
> I repudiate the assertion that I sought to aid and abet England's enemy. Germany is no more to me than England is. My aim was to win Irish freedom; we struck the first blow ourselves but should have been glad of an ally's aid.
>
> I assume that I am speaking to Englishmen who value their freedom and who profess to be fighting for the freedom of Belgium and Serbia.

General Blackadder was listening intently to every word.

> Believe that we, too, love freedom and desire it. To us it is more desirable than anything in the world. If you strike us down now, we shall rise again and renew the fight.

A light flashed in Pearse's splendid eyes.

> You cannot conquer Ireland. You cannot extinguish the Irish passion for freedom. If our deed has not been sufficient to win freedom, then our children will win it by a better deed.

Without retiring, the judges whispered loudly in each other's somewhat deaf ears before giving their verdict.

'Guilty.'

The three condemned were sent to the gymnasium.

Clarke was still silent but content; his dread was not death but life-long imprisonment.

MacDonagh was his voluble self, saying he had heard about German raids on Yarmouth and Lowestoft. 'An invasion is on the way,' he insisted.

Pearse sat on the floor, composing in his head a note to Maxwell. He wanted his letters and poems to be forwarded to his mother, together with seven pounds, his watch and other effects taken from him.

General Blackadder called Maxwell at Kilmainham Hospital to report the verdicts.

'We await your decision, sir.'

'Shoot 'em,' Maxwell said.

The cell in Arbour Hill that Pearse had recently vacated had a new occupant: John MacNeill.

He had sent his eldest son Niall with a note for General Maxwell. He wanted to help to avoid further bloodshed. Besides, he was Chief of Staff of the Volunteers; and if his men were imprisoned, he had a right to share their fate.

Colonel McCammond had collected him and taken him to Arbour Hill where, at 2 p.m., he was interrogated by Major Price. He wanted MacNeill to confess that politicians like Dillon were implicated in the rising.

'Absolute nonsense,' MacNeill said.

At 4 p.m., an aide told Maxwell that John Dillon had arrived, requesting an interview. Maxwell cursed his luck. Like most soldiers, he held politicians in contempt. He had just got rid of one in the shape of Birrell; now Dillon, an Irishman with Irish sympathies, the worst of a very bad bunch, was being a nuisance.

'Show him in,' he barked, extinguishing his cigarette.

Dillon felt the country's mood was changing rapidly. The nation-wide curfew, the mass arrests of people who, in many cases, had expressly repudiated the rising, were having an effect. In the person of Pearse, the Irish had already surrendered to the English; they did not like that. They would take even less kindly to the British slaughtering their countrymen. It reminded them of how, down the centuries, the English had cut them down, starved and evicted them and forced them to emigrate.

He was reminded of an old saying, 'Ireland's history is something the English should remember and the Irish should forget.'

It was a sacrifice for Dillon even to talk to Maxwell. It reminded him of much he preferred to forget. Could he ever make him realize that the Irish would always take the part of Irishmen about to be executed by British justice *whatever they had done*? They did not really believe in their hearts that Irishmen should be punished for breaking a law not their own or for being disloyal to a monarch not their own.

The little hope Dillon had evaporated at once in the presence of this not unkind but quintessential soldier.

Straightening his silver hair, then polishing his pince-nez, the politician expressed his point of view and Maxwell his.

'Surely,' Maxwell complained, banging the report in front of him, 'you cannot expect me in the light of appalling casualties and damage to property to put on velvet gloves?'

Dillon was thinking, Is this idiot going to send the rebels to immortality with Tone and Emmet?

He said: 'In dealing with this country, General, it's wise to remember its history.'

'History,' retorted Maxwell, 'what do I know about that? My job is to keep order here and, by God, I'll do it.'

'Jail them, General, and they won't even fill a cell. Shoot them and they'll grow so big they will fill all Ireland.'

As Dillon rose to leave, the General, who had not understood a word, was brushing his nicotine-stained moustache and saying, 'I am going to do something, sir, that you Irish will never forget. I am going to ensure that there will be no treason whispered, even *whispered*, in Ireland for another hundred years.'

That Tuesday afternoon was bright and sunny when two friars visited Richmond Barracks.

Fathers Augustine and Albert, both bespectacled, the former with thick hair and fabulous beard, the latter with receding hair and trim black beard, saw a few prisoners lying on a patch of grass opposite a big building.

'What's happening?' Father Augustine asked.

'Waiting for court martial,' a prisoner answered.

Lying on the grass was a Volunteer officer, thin and tubercular. His body was sloping backwards as he rested on his hands. His eyes behind his rimless glasses were wedged closed. To the priests' experienced gaze, he looked near to death.

A British NCO emerged from the building and called, 'Next: Joseph Mary Plunkett.'

The friars saw the young man struggle to his feet and walk, shaky as an autumn fly, towards inevitable condemnation. Minutes later, he was back in the barrack room. He had been found guilty, but he had heard rumours that they were to be sent to England. He pencilled a note to Grace Gifford on the back of his will which he had kept in his pocket.

> Listen, if I live it might be possible to get the Church to marry us by proxy – but it is difficult, I am told. You know how I love you. That is all I have time to say. I know you love me and so I am very happy. Your own Joe.

He handed the letter-cum-will to a soldier who seemed sympathetic, asking if he could get it delivered.

In his New York office of the *Gaelic American*, John Devoy was going through the files. Most American papers were against the rebellion.

'Just like 'em. Whoresons! They're against failure of any sort.'

In a fury, he bared big yellow teeth and slapped the cuttings with his blue knuckles.

'What the hell do they know, those morons? Most of them are dumb enough to think Roger Casement was the leader of the enterprise, planning it through the USA. Always looking for the local angle.'

The *New York Times* called Casement 'treacherous and perfidious'.

'What d'you expect,' he muttered, 'from an administration rag?'

The *Washington Post* was more guarded. His execution would serve no useful purpose. 'Casement, as a prisoner, kept out of mischief until the end of the war, would be practically forgotten; Casement, executed in the Tower, would become a martyr, enshrined in Irish hearts.'

'Rory, my boy,' he muttered, bitterly, 'may you be executed in the Tower.'

The *Philadelphia Enquirer* wanted Casement imprisoned for life: 'That will meet the claims of justice and Irish susceptibilities.'

'Irish susceptibilities!' Devoy's marble-chip eyes shone with scorn, as he put through a call to McGarrity in Philadelphia.

'Joe,' he barked, 'can't you darned-well do something about that *Enquirer*?'

He slammed the phone down before he got an answer.

Both the *Washington Star* and the *Chicago Tribune* were sure the rising would not advance Irish freedom.

He slammed the file down on his cluttered desk. 'We shall see about *that.*'

He threw his hat on the floor and danced on it for five minutes.

In late afternoon, an officer came into the gymnasium and ordered Pearse, Clarke and MacDonagh to stand to attention.

'You are to be transferred forthwith to Kilmainham Detention Centre and shot at dawn tomorrow, Wednesday 3 May.'

Tom Clarke relaxed. 'Thank God,' he said.

They were marched to the grim prison which was only a stone's throw away. They passed through the main gate over which was a bas-relief of a serpent in chains, into the central reception area, arched like a Gothic chapel, and up iron steps to the catwalk. It was dark and windowless. Gas pipes running along the wall were out of action owing to the emergency.

Thomas MacDonagh took out the pictures of his children.

The cell was like an opened grave, its air brown and rancid from being locked up for twenty years. A fly could not breathe it.

But the pictures of his little boy and girl brightened the place up, made him feel happy – and unhappy.

Clarke had a cell opposite the stairs. He went in shivering. In the cold damp air his breath came out frosty, like old ghosts returning to haunt him. He remembered only too well how it had been when he was a young man known by his *alias* of Henry Hammond Wilson.

Sentenced to solitary confinement in Portland Jail, he got neither silence nor solitude. For six years, from morning till night and into the night, he was harassed by guards. If he managed to fall asleep, there would be a loud report as the warder deliberately slammed shut the heavy, iron trap door. He once calculated that he had been strip-searched over 350 times. The warders looked with malicious glee and sometimes perverse pleasure between his toes, inside his mouth, inside his anus where a bull's eye lamp was shone.

He was often punished with the bread-and-water, no-sleep torture in a bid to make him mad. John Daly, whose niece he was to marry, had kept him sane. They had written to each other every week for eleven years under the noses of the authorities. Clarke had provided flies for the spider which Daly was training in his cell, though they were not allowed to talk to each other or shake one another's hand.

So developed was his sense of smell, though a guard crept along, Clarke could detect his presence by his hair-oil or the beer he had been drinking or the blacking on his boots.

Clarke shivered as he remembered sounds, smells, events burned into his soul. One incident, in particular, shocked him.

He had found Albert Whitehead, prisoner J 463, in the carpenter's shop stuffing his mouth with crushed glass, saying in a cracked voice, 'A pound of this won't do you any harm.' Clarke spoke about him to the prison chaplain. 'Sorry, J 464,' the priest said, 'if I do a thing, the Governor will ask how I know this and I'll lose my job.'

From then on, Clarke, devout but none too religious, was alienated from the Church.

He was punished for thirteen days for trying to talk to other prisoners. One winter, he spent forty days in the Arctic Cell, where it was several degrees below zero, on bread and water. He had chewed rags used for cleaning his tin plate to keep himself alive, to keep alive his love of Ireland.

He had written his own Golden Rules of Conduct: 'Clinch your teeth hard and never say die. Keep your thoughts off yourself. No mooning or brown studies. Guard your self-respect – if you lose that you'd lose the backbone of your manhood. Keep your eyes wide open and don't bang your head against the wall.'

Those rules helped him keep sane – just – until he was released on 21 September 1898. He had gone in a young man of twenty-six and emerged an old forty-one.

No, he could not live any longer in prison.

For Pearse, in a cell opposite, this was his first time in prison. He enjoyed the sound of the door clanging behind him, the bolt being drawn and the key turning in the big padlock. He liked the economy of that single candle. He stretched out his hands and stroked the whitewashed walls with reverence.

His stay would be brief and he could not imagine a better place to die. God – and the British – were being kind to him. Kilmainham was the Bastille of Ireland where many great Irishmen had expiated the crime of patriotism. It was more sacred in the annals of Ireland than was Westminster Abbey to the English.

It had housed Napper Tandy who had fought as a general with the French against the English in 1798. He would have been hanged but for Napoleon, who threatened to take the life of an English prisoner of equal rank.

Robert Emmet, aged twenty-five, Pearse's hero, had been jailed there before being taken to Thomas Street and hanged. No Irish patriot fought or died so smilingly as Emmet, a dreamer and man of peace who had turned into a revolutionary. Pearse hoped against hope that one day he would be remembered like Emmet.

Others of Pearse's heroes had suffered there: John O'Leary, John Devoy whom he had met in America, Jeremiah O'Donovan Rossa at whose funeral he had preached his great panegyric. And, of course, Charles Stewart Parnell.

There was no place in the world, not even at home in St Enda's with his mother and his pupils, where Pearse would rather spend the last night of his life.

He wrote out his court martial speech, letters to his mother and brother, and a last poem, 'The Wayfarer':

> The beauty of the world hath made me sad,
>   This beauty that will pass;
> Sometimes my heart hath shaken with great joy
>   To see a leaping squirrel on a tree,
> Or a red lady-bird upon a stalk . . .
>   And then my heart hath told me:
> These will pass,
>   Will pass and change, will die and be no more,
> Things bright and green, things young and happy;
>   And I have gone upon my way
> Sorrowful.

It was true, he had always borne himself sadly, as if he had come into the world already old.

He still hoped to see his mother and his brother before he died. He had no idea that that afternoon, Willie had been court martialled with Joe Plunkett, Michael O'Hanrahan and Ned Daly.

Ned's sister, Kattie Clarke, spent that evening in the store room of the Ship Street Barracks with six other women. From time to time, soldiers came to the door, wanting to chat and flirt. Some offered cigarettes, a few passed dirty remarks.

The women refused to exchange a word.

Kattie was praying for Tom and their sons and . . . for the new little one she now knew she was carrying.

When the soldiers gave up, the women settled down for the night.

Kattie took off her blouse and skirt to hang them on a line. She was to be interrogated again next day and wanted to look her best. It was cold and the girls had only one blanket between them. They refused to ask the British for anything.

General Blackadder was a guest at a dinner given by the Countess of Fingall, who had chaperoned Countess Markievicz in London all those years ago.

'I've just performed,' the General said, 'one of the hardest tasks I ever had to do. Condemned to death one of the finest characters I ever came across.'

He sipped his wine, and continued in a melancholy tone.

'A man named Pearse. Must be something very wrong in the state of things, must there not, that makes a man like that a rebel? I'm not surprised his pupils adored him.'

There was a sharp knock on the Friary door in Church Street. The brother porter shuffled downstairs, muttering, '11 o'clock, who's calling at this hour?' He opened the door not to a parishioner but to a soldier who handed him a letter.

'From the Major commanding Kilmainham Jail.'

Pearse was wanting to see Father Aloysius.

The young friar asked Father Columbus to join him, then, trembling, gathered up all he needed for the last rites: ritual-book, candles, small white table-cloth, stole, phials of oil for anointing. Finally, opening the tabernacle, he placed hosts in a pyx inlaid with gold.

The soldier apologized for having to make a couple of extra calls. Progress was slow owing to the curfew. The vehicle was stopped at several road-blocks by armed soldiers who peered at the occupants and examined their papers.

'Sorry, Fathers,' they were told repeatedly, 'there are still snipers around.'

As if to prove the point, bullets hit the road in front of the lorry.

Their guide said, 'It's too risky to go on. We'll have to head straight for the jail.'

Only when they got there did he tell Father Aloysius that he had been detailed to collect Pearse's mother and MacDonagh's wife.

At midnight, there was a knock on the store room door and a voice said, 'Kathleen Clarke. Out here, please.'

Kattie woke feeling sick. An officer with a lantern handed her a letter from Major Kinsman, Commandant of Kilmainham, marked 'Very Urgent'. It said: 'I have to inform you that your husband is a prisoner here and wishes to see you. I am sending you a motor car.'

One of the girls asked, 'My God, Kathleen, what does this mean?'

'It means,' she gulped, 'they're going to shoot my Tom.'

Marie Peroltz said, 'No, Kattie. Oh, no.'

'Look, Marie,' Kattie said, 'do you think the British would send a car for me at midnight if my man were not going on a journey to the next world?'

Father Aloysius was kept busy, ministering in turn to Pearse and MacDonagh.

Father Columbus went to see Tom Clarke. 'Would you like me to hear your confession?' he asked, timidly.

Clarke, with reason, had never trusted prison chaplains. 'Yes, please,' he answered warily.

The Capuchin sat on the stool and put on his purple stole as Clarke knelt beside him. '*Dominus sit in corde tuo . . .*' Before completing the sign of the cross, the friar said, 'Now, my son, first admit to God you have done a great wrong.'

Tom was absolutely shaken. 'What?'

'I said—'

Tom was on his feet in a fury. This was just one more proof that prison chaplains were on the wrong side.

He went to the door and rattled it. 'Guard, get this guy out of here.'

A soldier came running, shaking out a bunch of keys.

The priest, bewildered, was on his feet. 'But I'm only doing what the Church wants me to do.'

'For your information, Father,' Tom snapped, 'I am not a bit sorry for what I did. I *glory* in it. And if that means I'm not entitled to absolution then I'll have to go into the next world without it, won't I?'

He gestured to the door. Shaking his head, the Capuchin left for the lobby. That was where Kattie Clarke found him, looking sorry for himself.

'Your husband put me out of his cell.'

'Then you must have done something to deserve it.'

425

The warder who let Kattie into Tom's cell said, 'One hour, ma'am.'

It was a tiny cell with a wooden bed but no mattress, only a blanket. There was a small table and a stool. A soldier stayed, holding a jam-jar with a candle in.

Tom said, in his usual quiet voice, 'You know what this means, Kattie?' She nodded. 'I was scared to call you, I guess, in case—'

'No need. You married a Daly, didn't you?'

'I'm to be shot at dawn. I'm glad it's a soldier's death. I feared hanging and I had enough of imprisonment.'

Kattie, to make herself strong, said, 'And you told me better be dead than surrender.' He acknowledged it. 'And you would hold out for six months.' Another nod. 'What made you give in so soon?'

'The vote went against me.'

Radiant, as though being carried by angels shoulder-high, he said, 'This was only our first blow. Ireland will get her freedom now, even if she has to go through hell first.'

Father Columbus poked his head round the cell door. He said hello to Kattie and congratulated her on having so grand and composed a husband, then tactfully withdrew.

'What did you do to *him*?' she wanted to know.

He told her what 'that damn feller' had said.

Kattie still had not made up her mind whether to mention the baby on the way. It would bring him joy to know he was father of four; but sorrow too. He would never know if it were a boy or girl. Her having an extra mouth to feed would also add to his worries. He had suffered too much already. Hatred of people sometimes brings pleasure; but his was a hatred of wrongs and it hurt.

Tom was now so ripe in his joy, so fulfilled in his life's ambition, she felt it wiser not to risk disturbing him.

He gave her a typically brief message to the Irish people: 'I and my fellow-signatories believe we have struck the first successful blow for Freedom. The next blow, which we have no doubt Ireland will strike, will win through. In this belief we die happy.'

Time was passing.

'Take care of yourself, Kattie, and give my love to Daly, Tommy and little Emmet.'

'*Every one* of your children,' she assured him, 'will be proud of their father for ever.'

*

426

Pearse, a bachelor, was trembling with the joys of existence, though on the edge of the grave.

Father Aloysius made him even happier by saying, 'This morning I gave Holy Communion to Mr Connolly.'

'Thank God. It's the one thing I was anxious about.' After a quiet interval, Pearse added, 'You know, Father, I don't really deserve this privilege of dying for my country.'

The friar said, 'I'm sorry your mother could not be here. I will go and see her first thing tomorrow.'

He put on a purple stole over his brown habit.

'Ready?'

Pearse knelt for his confession. Afterwards, the friar gave him Communion. The flickering candlelight made it seem like a scene from the catacombs when the Church was young. He was so moved he could hardly read his ritual.

After a while, he said, 'I'll just pop in and see Mr MacDonagh. I'll be back.'

MacDonagh was gazing in wonder at pictures of his children, Donagh and Barbara.

Father Aloysius gave him the sacraments and from then on divided his time between the two men. He explained they would be blindfolded at the end but they should make little aspirations and acts of contrition in their heart.

MacDonagh happened to mention that his sister was a nun in a convent nearby. The friar was so sad that a man had to die with no one of his family present, he went to the Commandant's office to ask if he could go for her. The Major was sympathetic and laid on a car.

Meanwhile, MacDonagh tried to capture in a statement his astonishment at the order to surrender.

> For myself I have no regret. The one bitterness that death
> has for me is the separation it brings from my beloved wife,
> Muriel, and my beloved children, Donagh and Barbara. My
> country will take them as wards, I hope.

His work for the cause had left him with no time to make provisions for them. Donagh, the elder, was three and a half.

He remembered with a smile how when he and Muriel were married on 3 January 1912, Pearse, who was supposed to be best man, forgot to turn up. A workman who was trimming the graveyard hedge acted as witness. When Donagh was baptized, Pearse chanced to drop in at the Rathgar church to pray. MacDonagh had rushed over to him and shook his hand, saying in his broadest Tipperary accent, 'Well, Pearse, you got here in time for the christening, anyhow.'

Whereas he had acted honourably, he felt he had been unjustly condemned. But he let that pass, for even that wrong had somehow put him in touch with the best part of himself.

'It is a great and glorious thing to die for Ireland and I can well forgive all petty annoyances in the splendour of this.'

His thoughts returned to his family.

> To my son Don. My darling little boy, remember me kindly. Take my hope and purpose with my deed.
>
> To my darling daughter Barbara. God bless you. I loved you more than ever a child has been loved.
>
> My dearest love, Muriel, thank you a million times for all you have been to me. I have only one trouble in leaving life – leaving you so. Be brave, darling, God will assist and bless you.
>
> Goodbye, kiss my darlings for me. Goodbye, my love, till we meet again in Heaven. I have a sure faith of our union there. I kiss this paper that goes to you – he touched it with his lips – but for your suffering this would be all joy and glory. Goodbye. Your loving husband. Thomas MacDonagh

In the envelope, he put the photos of his children.

Father Aloysius would see they were delivered.

The friar knocked and knocked on the Convent door of Basin Lane. The sound echoed in streets that were empty even of the usual late-night drunks. When a startled Superior appeared, Father Aloysius begged her to let Sister M. Francesca see her brother before he died. Francesca, terrified, eyes down, hands folded in her sleeves, was soon in the car heading for the jail.

The priest left her with MacDonagh and went to see Pearse, who had written two letters.

In the one to his mother, he was still concerned with his manuscripts and unpaid bills.

> I have just received Holy Communion. I am happy

except for the grief of parting from you. This is the death I should have asked for if God had given me the choice of all deaths – to die a soldier's death for Ireland and for freedom.

We have done right. People will say hard things about us now, but later on they will praise us. Do not grieve for all this, but think of it as a sacrifice which God asked of me and of you.

Goodbye again, dear, dear, Mother. May God bless you for your great love for me and for your great faith, and may He remember all that you have so bravely suffered. I hope soon to see Papa, and in a little while we shall all be together again. I will call to you in my heart at the last moment. Your son, Pat.

With the time of execution near, Father Aloysius gave him a ten-inch crucifix of brass and black wood, with an image of Our Lady of Dolours on it and a skull and cross-bones beneath the feet of Jesus crucified. Pearse took it reverently.

When Father Aloysius left and the cell door was locked, he took a last look through the peep-hole.

He saw Pearse in silhouette on his knees, with the crucifix in his hands.

Sister Francesca was told time was up.

She remembered words her brother had written which had impressed her so much. 'The national rose of Ireland is *An Roisin Dubh*, the Little Black Rose, not the tender red flower to be plucked with the joys of life.'

She was at the cell door when she turned back and placed a mother-of-pearl rosary round his neck. 'Promise you won't take it off?'

He nodded, smiling. It pleased him that his mother's rosary, the beads on which she had unceasingly prayed for them, would, like her arms, embrace him at the end. It gave a beautiful wholeness to his life: she who had given him birth was present spiritually at his death.

Sister Francesca hoped the beads would be returned to her next day. But, as he kissed them, MacDonagh whispered, 'They will be shot to bits.'

Outside the prison, as Father Aloysius was seeing her into the car, she asked if he would keep the beads for her.

'Of course,' he said. 'And God bless you, my dear, for coming.'

Kattie Clarke was in the lobby when the firing squad arrived. It made Tom's death so unbelievably real she put in an official request for the return of his body for burial.

'I am sorry, ma'am,' the Commandant said, 'it would be wrong of me to give you any assurances.'

Father Aloysius handed all the documents confided to him to Major Kinsman, who promised to see they were delivered. He was then asked to leave.

'Surely,' the friar protested, 'I can stay with members of my flock to the end.'

The Major said there was no question of that.

Deeply disappointed, Father Aloysius returned with Father Columbus to Church Street where he vested in black ready to celebrate Requiem Mass for his three brave rebel friends.

Pearse stooped as he was led through the low doorway of his cell. He had already heard, with envy, one volley, telling him the first of his comrades had fallen for Ireland.

Along the dark, dank corridor he went, feeling the sublimity of the moment and a love for Ireland most men reserve for wife and children, down steps that clanged like pistol shots. After that first volley, the very walls grew ears.

At ground level, he was blindfolded and his hands were bound behind his back.

A second volley rang out. Those around him flinched, not for him but for themselves.

With a soldier on each side, he was guided briskly out into the Stonebreakers' Yard. It had the shape of an ellipse, its high walls shielding it from prying eyes. He felt cobbles under his feet but could not see the few side-sheds where isolated criminals broke stones, nor the covered lorry at the far gate-end into which the bodies of Clarke and MacDonagh had been thrown, nor the blood, redder than holly berries, at his feet.

He walked straight, with firm proud strides, without a doubt. He was doing something that would never end; he would go through death without hurt.

So he smiled as he imagined Emmet had smiled. Few men lived their dream; fewer still died the death of their choice.

He was halted at the north-west corner, a few feet from the wall.

*

430

'Introibo ad altare Dei.'

Father Aloysius began celebrating Mass just as the sun, symbol of the risen Christ, rose, whitening the east window.

Executions and the first Mass of the day celebrating Christ's death on the cross could only take place at dawn.

Willie had been roused in Richmond Barracks. An officer had heard that Pearse's mother could not be reached. As a humanitarian gesture, he decided to allow his brother to speak with him before the end.

Not knowing this, Willie, woken from a nightmare filled with burning buildings, suspected that he was to be shot himself. An armed guard led him towards Kilmainham Jail. He had been court martialled and was expecting execution, but surely they gave notice, if only for the relatives' sakes? Was he going to his death, without a priest to give him confession and Communion? Was he to have no chance to say goodbye to Pat and his mother?

In the Stonebreakers' Yard, the twelve-man firing squad was ready, six kneeling, six aiming over their heads.

At the order, 'Aim,' one of the squad, young, tired, found his rifle too heavy for him. It dipped in his hands.

The officer in charge said, 'As you were.' Again: 'Aim.'

Pearse's triumph was delayed a few seconds – they seemed like an added eternity – to commit his loved ones, as he had promised to God, the great Deliverer.

'Fire!'

'Kyrie eleison . . . .'

Father Aloysius repeated the immemorial prayer of the Mass, begging pardon of the Holy Trinity. 'Lord have mercy, Christ have mercy, Lord have mercy.'

Willie was at Kilmainham gate when a third volley rang out. Now he was sure they were going to shoot him.

Surprisingly, his escort halted in their tracks, looking at each other.

A warder at the gate shook his head. 'Too late.'

Willie, perplexed, was led, without a word, back to his cell. No one felt authorized to tell him that he had just heard his brother being killed.

✳

In her cell opposite Pearse's, the Countess did not know who the victims were. After each volley, she heard the single-pistol shot.

This chilled her more than anything in the rising; so cold, it seemed, so unnatural. A defenceless human being waiting for a group of armed men to pour lead into him. An officer pressing a revolver to his head and pulling the trigger.

But their leaders had done one big thing for Ireland. In view of that, death was not important.

Before Father Aloysius reached the consecration of the Mass, before the city stirred beneath the first slanting crocus-coloured rays of morning, the executed were driven in a lorry, with Pearse's boots sticking through the tarpaulin at the back, to Arbour Hill.

They were tossed without priest or prayer into Maxwell's pit and covered with Maxwell's quicklime.

MacNeill had been shaken by the three disciplined volleys from across the river.

He guessed what had happened even before he heard the lorry arrive and sounds of spades and slapping earth in the prison yard.

'*Agnus Dei* . . . .'
'Lamb of God, who takest away the sins of the world, grant them eternal rest.'

Since seeing Tom, Kattie Clarke had held on to her body where his child was lodged. Wrapped round with grief like a rope, she remembered nothing of the journey back to Ship Street Barracks. Life and death filled her mind and heart. She was aware of nothing but sharp steel piercing her husband's body and hers and their child's.

She came to with a start when there was a bang on the store room door and her name was called. A policeman said, 'You are being released.' His voice was gruff because the force could not forgive the murder of their colleague, James O'Brien, at the Castle Gate on the first day of the rebellion.

Kattie was glad to get out of that cold place. She grabbed her few belongings, hugged the other girls goodbye and left with 'Good Luck' ringing in her ears.

In the Yard, an officer said, 'It's still only 6 a.m. and there's a curfew on, so you'll need this.'

It was a paper signed by the Commissioner: 'Please pass Mrs

Clarke, of 10 Richmond Avenue, North Strand, through the streets of the City and the Dublin Metropolitan Police Area.'

As if in answer to her unspoken question, a policeman said, 'No, there is no car for you. You bloody walk.'

The gate was unlocked. She passed over the faint bloodstain on the cobbles, where PC O'Brien had fallen and began the journey home. The loneliness of the smoky streets echoed the loneliness of her widow's heart.

In a blasted O'Connell Street, a burly policeman asked for her pass. She handed it over in a daze.

'Very good, ma'am,' he said kindly. 'If I were you, I wouldn't go near that' – he jerked his thumb towards the Parnell Monument – 'the soldiers there are a bit lively.'

Kattie stepped over the rubble at the corner of what was once North Earl Street, feeling the heat of the bricks through the soles of her shoes. For the rest of the journey she saw and spoke to no one.

Once home, she who, like Tom, never drank, headed for the cabinet where liquor was kept for medicinal purposes. She poured herself a big glass of port, thinking that would be enough to knock her out for the day.

She awoke within the hour, retching, aware that her miseries were real and not a bad dream, and that Tom, her brave indomitable Tom, was dead.

At her home in Ranelagh, Muriel MacDonagh had given the children breakfast when she glanced at the paper.

In the stop-press, she saw that her husband and two comrades had been executed at dawn.

With a madly thumping heart, she grabbed the children and clung to them frenziedly.

'What's the matter, Mommy?' Donagh said, the strength of her embrace beginning to hurt.

Half an hour later, at 9.30 a.m., Father Aloysius returned to the jail to ask for MacDonagh's rosary. To his surprise, it was there together with his own brass crucifix on which Pearse, in gratitude perhaps, had scratched his initials, 'P MacP'.

The friar protested to the authorities that he had not been allowed to minister the last rites.

That puzzled the Commandant. 'But we sent a car for you so you could do just that.'

Father Aloysius explained that, according to Catholic teaching, Catholics about to be executed cannot be anointed but they have a right to be anointed after they are dead.

'*After?*'

'Yes, Major, in case the soul has not left the body.'

'I see,' the Commandant said. 'You have to remember, Padre, that we are new to this game.'

He agreed that a priest could attend any future executions. That sounded ominous but the friar was pleased to have got his point across.

He went on to the Convent to return the rosary to Sister Francesca. She shuddered to see that bullets had snapped it and six beads were missing. They knelt together and said the *De Profundis*.'

The priest walked from there to MacDonagh's place. He realized at once that Muriel already knew. As the children clung uncomprehendingly to her, he pressed his hands on their heads in a silent blessing.

'Father Almighty, in Your mercy, look after these poor fatherless little mites.'

Taking Muriel aside, he repeated what an officer had told him.

'He said, my dear, "They all died well, but MacDonagh died like a prince." '

The priest's last call was to St Enda's. In the study, Pearse's accounts were still open on the desk. He told Mrs Pearse how bravely her son had died and that he had left farewell messages with the Governor.

Seeing how apprehensive she was about Willie, he said, 'They surely wouldn't execute two boys in one family.'

She shook her head. 'I believe they will put Willie to death, too, Father.' She tried to be brave. 'I can't imagine him living without Pat, anyway. They were inseparable, you see. It was lovely to see the way they bade good-night to each other every night.'

Her tears were flowing freely now.

'No, no, Willie would never be happy living without Pat.'

In London, Redmond issued a statement to the Press which showed how out of touch he was.

He denounced 'this wicked move' of men who 'have tried to make Ireland the cat's paw of Germany. Germany plotted it, Germany

434

organized it, Germany paid for it.' The men who were Germany's agents 'remained in the safe remoteness of America's cities' while 'misguided and insane young men in Ireland had risked, and some of them had lost, their lives in an insane anti-patriotic movement.'

For the rest, Ireland held firm to the choice she had made and which thousands of her soldiers had sealed with their blood. The rebels were traitors to the cause of Home Rule.

The Prime Minister was worried enough to send his secretary, Bonham Carter, to Sir John French at the War Office.

'Mr Asquith is perturbed, General, by the drastic action of shooting so many rebel leaders.'

'Is three so many?'

'He wishes, especially, to be consulted before any death-sentence is passed on a woman, say, the Countess Markievicz.'

'Understood. Bad press, what? Like when the Germans shot Nurse Cavell.'

That was only part of it. If women had the right to be shot, they might also claim the right to vote.

James Connolly's family had passed a couple of apprehensive days at Bill O'Brien's house. Roddy had just been released from Richmond Barracks in view of his youth, but they had no news of their father. The girls decided that Ina, the least known, should go and enquire.

At the Castle Gate, she whispered to the guard, 'I've come to see my father, Mr Connolly.'

The name was not liked in that place but the Constable let her in.

A nurse said, 'Yes, your father is with us. He's still very weak from loss of blood.'

She directed Ina to the hospital wing. An officer was seated behind a desk. He wrote all details in a book, including the family's current address.

'May I see him, please?'

'Sorry, miss. But I'll let him know you called. And be sure you'll get a letter when he's allowed visitors.'

A few yards away, restored to his splendid office, Nathan was opening a coded telegram. Birrell informed him with respect that the PM also was asking for his resignation.

Nathan had been expecting it but it was bitter, all the same. He immediately complied.

Dear Mr Asquith,
The attempt to keep order in Ireland during the war has failed and you will probably consider that I can no longer be usefully employed here. In acquiescing readily in this decision I would like to express my deep regret that I have not been able better to serve His Majesty's government at this critical time and also my thanks for the kindness which you have always shown me.

He was ready to accept all blame. He even went to the Viceregal Lodge and expressed regret to Wimborne at the scale of his errors. It hurt that this man whom he had judged a fool had been right when he was wrong.

The perfect civil servant, he began to clear his desk. He made arrangements to recruit a thousand more constables to watch vulnerable buildings and dispose of the dead, many of whom were still unburied. He recommended for awards men who had acted bravely, especially those in Norway's department.

A thoroughly decent man, he acted decently to the end.

Kattie Clarke had just dropped off into a fitful sleep when the doorbell rang. It was two of her sisters, Madge and Laura. Seeing them, she broke down.

'My beloved Tom's been shot.'

They fell on her neck and hugged her, explaining breathlessly how hard it was to get transport from Limerick. Uncle John was ill in bed but he sent his best wishes.

They talked about Tom and agreed that it was a relief that their brother Ned, too, would be shot and not have to rot in jail like Tom in years gone by.

They knelt and prayed for strength to see them through the terrible ordeal ahead.

That afternoon, Redmond had a meeting with Asquith in his room behind the Speaker's Chair in the Commons.

'I beg you, Prime Minister,' he said, 'to avoid wholesale executions. They would destroy our last hopes of keeping Ireland loyal to the Empire.'

'I assure you,' Asquith replied, 'that I have given the War Office orders to go slowly on this.'

'If I may make a plea on behalf of one person in particular.' The Prime Minister inclined his ear. 'Mr John MacNeill. I cannot believe he is behind this rebellion. Far too good and sound a man.'

A shaken PM promised to do his best. He was expecting his dear colleague, Augustine Birrell.

At 3 p.m., he came.

'I know it has to be, my dear old friend,' Asquith said, 'but this is the most painful moment of my political life. I receive your resignation with' – he stretched out his arms – 'infinite regret.'

Birrell, normally composed, was in a daze. He hardly heard what the PM said, merely saw him at the window, with tears running down his cheek, jingling coins in his pocket.

Time to face the Commons. Asquith, still damp-eyed, entered the Chamber. Birrell was never noted for his tidiness but, in his rumpled suit and without his usual bounce, he seemed somehow old and broken.

Laurence Ginnell immediately howled, 'The statement he's going to make isn't worth *that*.'

The snap of his finger went round the Chamber like the snap of a neck.

Asquith stood, his face a pillar-box red against the white of his hair.

'Firstly, I have to tell the House of a telegram from Military HQ in Ireland. This morning at dawn, there took place the execution, after trial and sentence, of the three chief signatories of the rebellion.'

There were cheers in the House but not from Irishmen. And Larry Ginnell bellowed, 'Huns, Huns, Huns!'

When there was a lull in the day's business, Birrell rose from his seat behind the Treasury Bench.

Ginnell had no mercy. He so heckled him that the Speaker had to demand, 'Order. Or-*der*. Let the Right Honourable Gentleman speak.'

'Sure, give him a chance,' Ginnell agreed, gleefully, relaxing. 'We've got rid of him at last.'

Birrell was far from his usual fluent, funny self. 'I rise to make a short – a very short—'

Ginnell jumped in with, 'The shorter the better.'

Thrown by the interruption, Birrell was hesitant, repetitious, his mind still clouded by events which, he admitted, he had not foreseen.

437

Since the war, his prime concern was to give to Germany a picture of unbroken unanimity. He had no choice but to skate on thin ice. To arrest and disarm Sinn Feiners would have made trouble inevitable; it would have come sooner and bloodier, that is all.

The 'disturbance', it was no more, would be put down with courage, also with humanity to the rank and file, who had been duped by their leaders.

'When yesterday morning I drove down from Phoenix Park through all the familiar streets of Dublin and viewed the smoking ruins of a great part of Sackville Street, one ray of comfort was graciously permitted to reach my heart, and that was that this was no Irish rebellion, that Irish soldiers are still earning for themselves glory in all the fields of war, that evidence is already forthcoming that over these ashes hands may be shaken and much may be done.'

After a sympathetic silence, Asquith spoke briefly of his ten years' close association with Birrell. In the whole of his public life, he had never felt a personal loss so keenly.

John Redmond was next. All members fixed their gaze on him, on the whitening waxy hair, the white eyebrows and moustache, the heavy lids, the down-turned mouth. Had Home Rule been put into effect as originally planned, this man would now have been head of the Irish Administration.

He, too, was magnanimous. He, an Irishman, and Birrell, an Englishman, whatever their differences, had been of one heart and mind over Ireland.

He, too, would not speak of rebellion, only of 'the incident' which had broken his heart and led to the Chief Secretary's resignation.

'I sorrow and grieve at the severance. I have been for several years closely associated with him, and so have my colleagues, and we all believe that during his tenure of office, he has been animated by a single-minded devotion to what he regarded as the highest interests of the country that he went to govern. We believe that he grew to love Ireland and that he has honestly done his best for her interests.'

Birrell had been in charge. But he, too, had incurred some share of the blame since he had often advised Birrell that there was no chance of an outbreak.

The Chief Secretary, he went on, had done much for Ireland, particularly in the creation of the National University and education generally.

'I can assure him that he takes with him into retirement the respect, the goodwill and the affection of large masses of the Irish people.'

438

Redmond feared that Asquith was now leaving decisions to a soldier. If a politician of Birrell's calibre had failed to understand Ireland, what chance had Maxwell? He intimated that the United States, whose support in the war Britain wanted, would not take kindly to bloody reprisals.

Having expressed his hope that the rising might even forward 'the future complete and absolute unity of this Empire', he ended with a warning.

'I beg of the Government, having put down this outbreak with firmness, to take only such action as will leave the least rankling bitterness in the minds of the Irish people, both in Ireland and elsewhere throughout the world.'

The Commons stirred as the long lean figure of Sir Edward Carson rose.

Birrell knew that in the years ahead historians would ask who was most responsible for the rebellion. Was it Pearse, or Clarke, or Connolly?

In his mind it was Carson.

Was it not Carson who first stirred up bitterness in Ireland? Who said he would put a bayonet through a Bill passed by the King, the Lords and Commons of England? Whose arming of the Ulster Volunteers made it impossible to disarm the southern Volunteers, thus allowing a dangerous situation to fester? Was it not Carson's belligerence that had brought on Asquith's case of Ulsteritis and made him defer Home Rule so that the Irish in the south finally lost confidence in British justice and made rebellion inevitable?

Birrell waited to hear what this man with bowels of iron would say now.

Carson had recently been deluged with letters from people with thoughts not unlike Birrell's. He was accused of being the first rebel, of endangering the Empire with revolutionary talk and posturings. He dismissed such nonsense, telling himself that the Dublin rising had proved once and for all the difference between a loyal Ulster and the rest of Ireland.

Still, caution was called for.

Many in the Commons that day expected from Carson, if not a gloating speech, at least a trenchant I-told-you-so. He surprised everyone. He spoke kindly of Birrell whom, admittedly, he had totally opposed on the matter of Ireland.

'I do not think that anybody who has ever had any friendship with, or any knowledge of the Right Honourable Gentleman, will

439

fail to express regret that his career in Ireland, so well-intentioned, however you might disagree with it, has terminated in such unfortunate circumstances.

'I can assure him that many of us on this side, and many of his bitterest opponents in Ireland, will recognize that this misfortune has come upon the country, and has come upon his career rather through his desire to preserve that common front to our enemies abroad than from any dereliction of duty on his part.'

The Irish conspiracy had to be repelled with courage and determination yet, as a Dubliner, Carson knew only too well the history of the separatist movement in his native land.

'It would be a mistake,' he went on, 'to suppose that any true Irishman calls for vengeance.'

Even Larry Ginnell sat up, rubbing his ears.

'It will be a matter requiring the greatest wisdom and the greatest coolness, may I say, in dealing with these men, and all I can say to the Executive is, whatever is done, let it be done not in a moment of temporary excitement but with due deliberation in regard both to the past and to the future.'

In the late afternoon, Fathers Augustine and Albert went to a house on Dublin's North Circular Road where many high-ranking officers were billeted. They asked if there were to be any more executions the next day.

The senior officer said, 'Four.' Asked for their names, he said he had already told them more than he should.

'Never mind,' Father Augustine said, 'we will be ready.'

At Church Street, he warned two more colleagues, Fathers Sebastian and Columbus, that there was a job for them that night.

Dillon was alarmed when Nathan told him he had resigned. Soon there would be no civilian rule at all in Ireland.

Nathan suggested, 'You might like to speak with Maxwell.'

Dillon said he would. He was furious at what the General had already done: turning the Irish against England, perhaps for ever.

It was after 5 p.m. when they were shown into Maxwell's smoky office at Kilmainham Hospital.

Dillon began politely enough, trying to persuade him to go easy on the prisoners.

The General cut in. 'I intend to go on punishing the ring-leaders. Four more tomorrow.'

Dillon jumped. This was madness on madness. It was a repetition of traditional British contempt for the Irish.

'If they were English,' he spat out, 'they would be tried in England by an English jury that would demand strict proof of guilt. If they were Turks, they would have a public trial with defending counsel and a chance to appeal the verdict. But these so-called rebels are mere Irishmen, are they not, a class apart, a subject people without any rights or feelings.'

Maxwell looked over his enormous nose in scorn. He resented being lectured to by a discredited civil servant and a bloody-minded politician.

'At least they have the decency to admit their guilt,' he said. 'In fact, they glory in it.'

'What guilt?'

Maxwell was slightly taken aback by the question. 'Why, um, assisting the enemy.'

'Does a small boat carrying German arms for Irishmen constitute assisting the enemy?' Dillon said.

Maxwell looked at him sardonically. 'How would you describe it?'

'They were importing arms not to defeat Germany's enemy but their own.'

'Precisely.'

'Don't you see,' roared Dillon, losing his temper, 'they were trying to gain their own freedom and independence? And even if they are guilty of assisting the enemy, as you so stupidly put it, who are *you* to deprive them of all the normal procedures of justice?'

'Normal procedures would have exactly the same outcome.'

'So *you* decide what justice is, is that it? Justice a cloak for revenge. Tyrants always act like that.'

Maxwell's moustache quivered but he disciplined his voice magnificently.

'I might remind you, sir, that I am simply doing the job I was sent to do: to put down a rebellion and see nothing like it occurs again.'

'But,' exploded Dillon, knowing he was shouting into stone ears, 'you are *guaranteeing* it will occur again.'

'I am merely putting traitors to death.'

'No! You are seeing to it that they will never die.'

Nathan suggested diplomatically that Dillon was a man whose views on Ireland were worthy of consideration. When Maxwell promised to weigh the issues carefully, Dillon handed him a list. 'To arrest these men, General, would be a manifest injustice.'

Maxwell glanced at it. 'Leave it with me.'

When they had gone, Maxwell reflected on men of his who had died because of this unprovoked rebellion, houses in which the dead had lain for five days without burial, unarmed policemen who had been shot down in cold blood. He thought of brave boys who would never walk again or see again, their wives left widowed, their children left orphaned, a whole life-long legacy of misery – and all because of the criminal action of a few hotheads demanding a Republic without any mandate from the vast majority of the Irish people.

Well, *he* had a mandate, from the Prime Minister *and* from the ordinary decent people of Ireland, to see that justice was done.

Not revenge. Simple, unadorned, God-like *justice*.

It was late in the afternoon when Grace Gifford answered the bell. The priest on the doorstep introduced himself as Fr Eugene McCarthy, chaplain of Kilmainham Jail.

Joe Plunkett was in custody there and the Governor had given permission for them to marry. In answer to her unspoken question, he bowed his head.

Grace shed tears of joy and anguish. Should she wear white or black? she wondered.

The next few hours were to seem longer to her than the rest of her life put together. She took a taxi to Stoker's, the Grafton Street jeweller. The owner who, coincidentally, had been in the GPO buying stamps when Joe Plunkett and the rest took it over, was closing for the night. He was putting tall black shutters over the windows when a woman, her face covered by a veil, asked to see a selection of wedding-rings.

As she was trying them on, she remarked, in a choking voice, 'I want the best that money can buy.'

She arrived at the jail at 6 p.m. but was obliged to walk up and down an inner courtyard for hour after hour.

Once she asked a soldier what was behind the big wall.

'Nothing, miss,' he said. 'Just a yard where prisoners break stones.'

'And' – she pointed – 'the other side?'

'That's where the cells are.'

It made it all the harder, knowing she was on one side of the wall and Joe on the other.

'You can come in now, miss.'

Grace looked at her wrist-watch, but it was too dark to see.

'It's 11.30, miss.'

She stepped into a narrow unlit corridor, up steep iron steps. In her hand, sticky with nerves, was the ring. The Catholic chapel, painted red and cream, was on the top floor and now lit by a solitary candle held by a Tommy. They entered it through a rear door.

Above the tabernacle was a big crucifix and there were two tall windows over deep embrasures. Twenty soldiers with fixed bayonets were lining the walls like statues.

It was all so cold, so gloomy, not the way she had planned her wedding. It was to have been in white on Easter Sunday, with Easter lilies.

Lately, she reflected, her life had been a catalogue of calamities. Her elder sister Muriel had been since dawn the widow of MacDonagh. He had left behind two children and no money to care for them. Then there was Kathleen Clarke with her three children. Tom, too, was gone, and Kattie had to face the prospect of her brother Ned following soon.

Grace saw that what was happening to her was part of a pattern. She had no wish to escape it.

Father McCarthy approached the altar, robed in cassock, cotta and white stole. He greeted her with a compassionate smile.

When Joe came in, under guard, through the side door he was in handcuffs. The candle flickered as he passed. Soon, she thought, he will not stir a candle-flame or a leaf on a tree.

Side by side they stood. Her eyes were used to the dark and she saw how thin he was and how his hair flopped over his round boyish face. His skin was creamy-white, like the inside of a horsechestnut burr. Never had she seen him looking so ill or so vulnerable, this man whose high spirits and boundless gaiety had won her heart.

His uniform was creased, his topboots were unpolished and charred by fire. The bandages wrapped high around his throat were soiled and dirty, and he had not shaved in days. Only the rings on his fingers were as she remembered them.

It somehow consoled her to know that his life was nearly over, anyway. Proud that he, a hero, loved her, she recalled a line in a poem he had written for her: '*But my way is the darkest way.*'

Joe's eyesight was never very good and now he was peering

owl-like through his spectacles, trying to make out her features. She smiled consolingly at him.

The priest gestured to two soldiers to act as witnesses and they moved their rifles from hand to hand during the brief ceremony.

Bride and groom both had difficulty with the words, 'till death do us part.'

When she held up the ring, a soldier unlocked Joe's handcuffs so he could put it on her finger.

'With this ring I thee wed. . . . With my body I thee worship and with all my worldly goods I thee endow.'

Afterwards, the priest asked them to sign the register. Then two soldiers of the Royal Irish Regiment signed, too.

The brief ceremony over, Grace and Joe were not allowed one minute together. For the military, this was a chore to be gone through and it was over. Joe was handcuffed again and led back to his cell.

Grace left the prison to wait in a room that Father McCarthy had booked for her in James's Street with one of his parishioners called Byrne, who worked in a bell foundry.

At the Byrnes', Father McCarthy clasped her hand.

'Wait here, my dear, for a summons from the Governor. Trust me, it will come. Then you will see Joe again.'

The Daly girls were asleep in Fairview, when, just before midnight, Kattie heard a distant lorry. Her instincts were so razor sharp that she shot up in bed, went next door and woke her sisters.

In a strangled scream: 'They're coming for Ned.'

'It's your nerves, dear,' Madge said. 'Go back to bed.'

Kattie was peering through the window. It was some while before a military truck rumbled up.

'Dear God!' she gasped, 'didn't I tell you?'

She went down and answered the door. A policeman stretched out his hand. 'A permit from Kilmainham, ma'am, for you to see your brother.'

This was the second from Major Kinsman in twenty-four hours. Kattie's eyes so ached she could hardly read it.

'I beg to inform you that your brother is a prisoner in this above prison, and would like to see you tonight. I am sending a car with an attendant to bring you here.'

Her sisters were so tearful and shaky they could hardly put their clothes on.

Kattie said, 'The permit is for one.'

'Let them try and stop us,' said young Laura, who was close to Ned and, like him, full of fire.

The Constable and two soldiers helped them into the truck. Frequent stops at road-blocks made the journey seem endless. Each time, there was a glint of bayonets as lanterns were raised.

'It says here a permit for one.'

'They're sisters,' the Constable replied. 'Their kid brother's being shot.'

'Pass.'

'Listen,' said Kattie. 'Our brother's a hero, and we're daughters and nieces of Fenians.'

They pulled themselves together and prayed to the Virgin Mary that they would have grace like hers when she stood at the foot of the Cross.

When they alighted at the jail, they walked with heads held high and gave their names at the gate in ringing tones, as though they were princesses.

In the lobby, they nearly lost their composure when a soldier called out, 'Relatives of Daly, to be shot in the morning.'

They held hands to give each other strength.

The officer of the watch was reluctant to let all three in. 'I'll compromise,' he said. 'One at a time.'

The girls started working it out: Kattie first, then Madge, then Ned's favourite, Laura.

The officer was touched by their dilemma. 'All right, you can see him together.'

Five soldiers, one with a candle, escorted them to the central block, up the stairs, and along the catwalk to Cell No 6.

One of them called out gruffly, 'Daly!'

'Yes.'

Ned's mumbly voice made the girls tremble even more.

As a Tommy turned the key, the officer said kindly, 'Whatever you say will be considered private.'

The door squeaked open and the candle showed Ned blinking, still in his Volunteer uniform. He had been on the floor asleep on a piece of sacking next to a kind of dog biscuit.

Kattie, the most experienced, momentarily barred the entrance to enable Madge to embrace Ned first; he might have a message for her before the soldiers were in earshot.

But Madge's first words were, 'Oh, Ned, why are they giving you the highest honours? Why were you chosen to stand with Emmet and Tone?'

All three girls stood with their brother in the middle of the cell, their arms entwined. There they stayed for fifteen minutes, a quiet whirlwind of affection surrounded by soldiers with bared steel. They gathered strength from one another, feeling love pass from each to each in a bond of fond childhood memories and pride in what their family had done for Ireland. Words mattered little.

Kattie said, 'Give Tom our love.'

Ned gasped. 'Has *he* gone?'

'Yes,' Kattie said, with fierce pride. 'So have Pearse and Mac-Donagh. This morning.'

'May they rest in peace,' said Ned, giving Kattie a consoling kiss. 'What a glorious reunion we'll have in Heaven, eh?' He smiled. 'Sure, Kattie, I'll give Tom your love. First thing I'll do.'

He spoke of the brave fight his men had put up. No one broke down until the order to surrender came. He didn't like it himself and big strong men cried like children.

'As for me, girls, I'm proud of what I did. Next time, we'll win. I'm only sorry I won't be there to do my bit.'

Madge said the whole family would be happy knowing England had given him the martyr's crown.

'Your name and spirit will live on, Ned. And one day we'll all be together in another world.'

He squeezed her arm, 'Yes. The thought of that makes me very happy.'

Laura chipped in. 'Uncle John – he's too ill to travel – well, Uncle John is envious. Know what he said? "Tom and Ned have stolen one on me." He thinks he's left it too late to be shot for Ireland.'

Ned gave Kattie a copy of the charge against him.

'Ridiculous,' he said, 'accusing us of assisting the enemy, when they were only trying to assist us.' The soldiers pricked up their ears when he said, 'We took a lot of English prisoners. Officers, too. We gave them the best we had.'

'Why didn't you shoot them?' Laura demanded.

'That wouldn't be playing the game,' Ned said, gaily. 'We had strict orders. Anyone we took was to be treated under the rules of civilized warfare as a prisoner of war. No exceptions allowed.'

Kattie suddenly recognized the soldier holding the candle. He had been there the night before.

'Excuse me,' she said, her voice breaking, 'but what happened to my husband?'

'Well, ma'am,' he began hesitantly, 'you'll be pleased to know he died very brave.'

Kattie had to fight to keep back her tears.

'I was in the firing-party myself. Never saw a braver, ma'am, and I know 'cos I've been in many before.'

Kattie was too overcome to say a proper thank you.

Ned gave them a last message for his mother, his aunt, his other sisters, and Uncle John.

'Tell them I did my best.'

He gave them his purse with a few small coins in, two pencils, a few buttons from his tunic as mementoes.

'Time's up,' a soldier called.

The family pressed up close as though trying to weld themselves by the fire of love into a single being. When they broke up, there was still not one sob, not one tear. Ours, they seemed to say, is a family of heroes. We don't cry for our dead.

One last glance passed between Ned and the girls before the door clanged to, leaving him in a tomb-like blackness.

As they descended the stairs, they prayed their legs would not give way. Madge felt Laura falter.

'Remember,' she said, sternly, 'you're a Daly.'

In the lobby, they ran into the O'Hanrahan sisters, both pale and anxious. They had been waiting nearly half an hour.

Eily O'Hanrahan said, 'We're pleased we persuaded our mom not to come.' She shivered. 'What a terrible place.'

After they had all embraced, Eily explained, 'We've come to see our Michael. He's going to be deported.'

'Is that what they told you?' Kattie said.

The O'Hanrahans nodded. They showed the Dalys the note handed in at their house: 'Mr O'Hanrahan, a prisoner in Kilmainham, wishes to see his mother and sisters before his deportation to England.'

Madge, very gently, said, 'Ned is to be shot at dawn.'

The younger O'Hanrahan girl put her hand to her mouth and gasped, 'Oh! Michael!'

With growing trepidation, the two sisters went up the steps with an escort. 'Tell us, *please*,' Eily said.

The soldier, unlocking the door of Cell 69, answered, 'He's to be shot at dawn, miss.'

Eily said hoarsely, 'But Mother isn't here.'

With the officer warning them, 'Be careful what you say,' the girls rushed into their brother's outstretched arms.

'You know?' he said.

'Just this second.'

'Oh, my poor sisters.'

He had been left in pitch dark, with only a slop bucket and, in the corner, a sack to lie on. The place, long in disuse, reeked of mildew, damp and urine.

He sent his love first to his mother and then the rest of his family.

Eily told him that three were dead already and Ned Daly was going with him at dawn.

'Silence,' came from the officer.

Michael said he would like to make his will. Soldiers went and returned with an old table, a chair and a broken stump of candle. He wrote a few lines, witnessed by two soldiers. He had nothing to bequeath except the copyright of his novel, *A Swordsman of the Brigade*.

When Eily asked if he had eaten, he said, 'I had some bully beef at four.'

'That was ten hours ago,' Eily gasped. 'Have you had even a drink of water since?'

He shook his head.

Eily turned in a fury on the soldiers. 'Get him a drink.'

She blinked at the speed with which they acted. They were not cruel, only thoughtless. Within seconds, one returned with a black billycan from which Michael drank deeply.

After a farewell hug, they left him. As the cell door closed, the younger sister fainted on the catwalk.

In reception, the Dalys put in a formal claim for the bodies of Ned and Tom Clarke. Kattie demanded to know where her husband's body was.

'Sorry, ma'am,' the warder said.

Kattie flared up at that. 'You not only condemn a man to death in a secret trial and without a defence lawyer, you won't even let his wife have his corpse.'

Laura offered to send coffins in so their loved ones could be identified and laid with their own. They also signed a form requesting the return of Ned's uniform.

448

No sooner were they out of earshot than one soldier said to his mate, 'They're burying 'em in quicklime, ain't they? Even their guardian angels won't know 'em after that.'

At the gate, the car taking the Dalys home was delayed. The officer of the watch invited them to wait in his office.

'You have my deepest sympathy.' He sounded sincere. 'I just don't understand how they – and you – could want to assist the enemy.'

Kattie flashed back, 'That's easy. We're Irish. For us, *you* are the enemy.'

'What would you do,' Madge added, 'if Germany won the war and invaded *you*?'

When the girls finally made it home to Fairview, they spent the night locked in each other's arms, praying until the dawn had come and gone.

The car bringing the Pearses broke down at Terenure. Mrs Pearse was terrified that, having missed Pat the night before, she might miss Willie, too. Pat could manage on his own, she knew, but Willie needed her.

Fortunately, the car was fixed and she and Margaret arrived, tremblyly, at the jail, only to have to wait half an hour in the lobby till other relatives came down.

When their turn came, three soldiers held candles in the cell when she and Margaret entered.

The mother, simple in so many ways, was a person of heroic stature. She had already given a precious gift to Ireland. But it was not easy telling Willie that Pat whom he adored was dead.

Willie received the news like a blow to the heart. When he got his breath back, he explained in his slightly sibilant voice what had happened that day at dawn.

'Never mind, my darling,' Mrs Pearse said. 'You missed him last night but you'll be with him soon. Will you give him a message from his mother?'

Willie nodded.

'Tell him I will be braver than ever and I will carry my cross.'

Margaret held Willie's shaky hand. 'I can't tell you how proud we are of you and Pat.'

Mrs Pearse looked at Willie in the candlelight, at that strangely innocent face with its dark sensitive brown eyes. She remembered him as a baby; and, in a way, he seemed never to have lost his child-like innocence. Was it possible that her gentle, lovely son was to be shot as a traitor?

She found herself thinking, instinctively, If only Pat were here to help.

She remembered an incident long ago, when her boys were in their first school run by an old dragon named Miss Murphy. She was chastising Willie, and Pat was not having it. He stood up to stop her. 'Sit *down*, Patrick,' the dragon said. Pat replied, 'I am not *tired*, Miss Murphy.'

As to Willie, he knew his death would double his mother's heartache but he could not desert Pat now. Even at his trial, when the Court was inclining to mercy, he had insisted the he was in on the rising from the beginning. In life and death, he and Pat were inseparable.

Mrs Pearse spoke of Pat's poem, called 'The Mother'. He wrote it when he expected that he and Willie would die together.

Willie spoke the lines softly now, for his mother's sake:

> *I do not grudge them: Lord, I do not grudge*
> *My two strong sons that I have seen go out*
> *To break their strength and die, they and a few*
> *In bloody protest for a glorious thing.*
> *They shall be spoken of among their people,*
> *The generations shall remember them,*
> *And call them blessed;*
> *But I will speak their names to my own heart*
> *In the long nights;*
> *The little names that were familiar once*
> *Round my dead hearth.*
> *Lord, thou art hard on mothers:*
> *We suffer in their coming and their going;*
> *And tho' I grudge them not, I weary, weary*
> *Of the long sorrow – And yet I have my joy:*
> *My sons were faithful and they fought.*

Mrs Pearse stroked her faithful second son's long soft hair, so like a girl's. Soon, very soon, as Pat had predicted, they would be together in death.

Willie told her he had asked for a priest but none had come yet, so she enquired of the attending officer, 'Is Father Aloysius on his way?'

'Yes, ma'am. That clergyman is coming, I believe.'

In spite of his prompt answer, it sounded as if it had not crossed his mind till then. He could not grasp how important priests were to Irish Catholics. They seemed to want to die anaesthetized by religion.

Mrs Pearse suspected he was not telling the truth. She ended the visit in order to check. Willie needed a priest more than he needed her.

They said a last goodbye.

Willie looked at his mother; and his long sad face was etched in her memory for ever. Then she and Margaret hurried down to the lobby where she was handed Pat's letters written to her the night before, though some others were held back.

Margaret called out to a group of officers, 'Gentlemen, will you send for a priest? There's only an hour left.'

They promised her they would send for one at once. Major Lennon said, 'Dammit, I forgot. We might have to delay the executions now.'

It was 2 a.m. and Grace had been lying down for only half an hour when there was a rap on the door. A constable handed her a letter from the Governor. Grace Plunkett was now permitted to see her husband.

The word surprised and delighted her.

'Husband.'

She whispered it over and over as the car sped through the quiet streets, and as she went through the small entrance gate, into the reception area, and up the steps to Cell No 88.

'Ten minutes, ma'am.'

On entering the jail, she had noticed the sky lightening. No dawn would ever be the same again.

But only ten minutes? And in a small cell with an NCO and several soldiers with fixed bayonets crowded round the door?

The Sergeant examined his watch as if to time a race.

The only light was a candle. Grace picked out a plank for a bed with one blanket, a tin basin with gruel but no spoon.

Joe beckoned her to sit down on the stool and he knelt over her like a penitent confessing. This was to be their only honeymoon. The newly-weds who had so much to say to each other and so little time to say it were tongue-tied.

Perplexed by this meaningless cruelty, the best Grace could do was try and fix every detail in her mind: what he looked like, said, wanted to say but left unsaid, the candlelight reflected in his eyes. She caught a whiff of wood-smoke on his clothes, in his hair.

She had to be brave for his sake. But who understands the human heart? Would it help him if she cried or make it harder? For tears are words to those in love.

Those few precious minutes seemed first like hours and then like only seconds.

The soldiers were sleepy-eyed. Most of the faces were Irish faces. Some were downy, had never shaved; they were younger even than she and Joe. Would they really break up a marriage so recent? Would they kill a dying man, not *any* dying man but her Joseph who was only twenty-nine years old?

Their uniform provided them with absolution, turned murder into mere killing. They were doing a job, like a corporation employee clearing a drain or chopping up a tree that blocked the road.

Yes, without hate they would do this hateful thing.

It was fast approaching 3 o'clock when there was a bang on the friary door in Bow Street. The soldier said, 'Hurry, sirs, there's not much time left.'

The four priests had long been ready, wondering why the summons was so late. Clutching the bags with their gear for the last rites, they were driven off into the night.

In Joe's cell, the Sergeant tensed as the second hand neared the end of its last cycle.

Sensing this, Grace took out a pencil and wrote on the wall: 'This is Joseph Plunkett's cell whence he left me for his execution. (Signed) Grace Plunkett.'

He had left her his name. She wrote it with pride. Yes, she thought, that is a fine name to have and this ghastly place is sacred now.

Joe slipped her something as the Sergeant called, 'Time's up.' The Tommies bolted to attention.

Grace kissed Joe, clung fiercely to him before hands, not rough but firm, drew them apart.

'My darling, my husband, goodbye.'

As she was led away, she turned and saw, as through a mist, his frail figure framed in the doorway. Her heart went out to him in his terrible ordeal.

Now she was free to weep. She would never bear his child, nor feel any more his hand upon her. For ever she would be alone. Except he would be with her always, day and night, in all that might have been.

She suddenly remembered the things Joe had pressed in her hands. His keys, a lock of his hair, and a piece of paper with writing on it. His final memento. Downstairs in the lobby, by candlelight, she began to read this poem of his.

> I see his blood upon the rose
>   And in the stars the glory of his eyes,
> His body gleams amid eternal snows,
>   His tears fall from the skies.
>
> I see his face in every flower;
>   The thunder and the singing of the birds
> Are but his voice – and carven by his power
>   Rocks are his written words.

The Commandant was busy issuing orders.

To Captain Kenneth O'Morchoc, he said, 'I want you to take charge of the firing party.'

The Captain hesitated. 'Something wrong?'

O'Morchoc said, 'Request permission to stand down, sir.'

'What the hell's the matter, man? Lost your nerve?'

'No, sir., Plunkett and I played together as children.'

The Commandant sighed. 'Permission granted.'

A car halted outside the prison and four friars jumped out and rushed into the lobby.

The Major called out to them, 'You do understand, gentlemen, that we are running behind schedule.'

Father Columbus went to Daly since he had attended his brother-in-law; but he had learned his lesson.

Father Albert went to O'Hanrahan, Father Sebastian to Plunkett and Father Augustine to Willie Pearse.

The cell doors were open. The prisoners' hands were already bound when the priests heard their confessions and gave them Holy Communion.

Willie had his cap on. A soldier, realizing he was unable to remove it for confession, unbound his hands. After giving him the sacraments, Father Augustine popped in to see O'Hanrahan.

453

'Father,' he said, 'would you go and see my mother and sisters for me?'

The burly friar, pressing his hands down on Michael's thick black hair, said, 'I promise you, my son.'

He could not understand this insane haste to have men killed.

Daly was already being marched to the Yard with Father Columbus. Each friar went with his assigned prisoner. After Daly, Willie Pearse was called, then O'Hanrahan, and finally Joseph Mary Plunkett.

With each deadly volley, the kindly Capuchins marvelled at the men's composure.

Joe asked Father Sebastian to give his ring to his wife and his glasses to his mother.

'Father,' he said, 'I am very happy. I'm dying for the glory of God and the honour of Ireland.'

Grace was asking herself if Joe would feel the bullets. Would he hear the roar of the rifles or did bullets travel that split-second faster than the sound of the guns?

Please God, she prayed, there would be no dying, only being dead.

At the time when she guessed her Joseph was facing the firing squad, Grace, fingering her wedding-ring, was saying to herself, 'Till death do us part.'

But she knew, even as she heard in her head the fatal volley that turned her from a young bride into a widow, that nothing in her life or death would ever part them. Even though his feet would never walk her way again and his strong heart had ceased to beat.

She read the last verse of Joe's poem.

> *All pathways by his feet are worn,*
> *His strong heart stirs the ever-beating sea,*
> *His crown of thorns is twined with every thorn*
> *His cross is every tree.*

When the O'Hanrahan sisters got home their mother asked anxiously, 'How was Michael? You gave him my love?'

'In the pink,' they said.

They had decided not to tell her that night; she would not believe them, anyway. It would come better from a priest.

Mrs Pearse and Margaret returned to St Enda's, which had been

Pat's dream and which Willie had helped him build. It seemed so empty now, as if everything – desks, easels, beds in the dormitories – had all been removed.

In Pat's study, they went on their knees and prayed until Mrs Pearse stopped biting her fingers and, sensing the falcon had flown to the falconer, said, 'They're together again.'

The priests returned to the friary and immediately began making preparations to celebrate Requiem Mass.

When, that morning, the newspapers appeared on the streets, they approved the firm action taken by the authorities.

An editorial in the *Irish Independent* said, 'No terms of denunciation that pen could indite would be too strong to apply to those responsible for the insane and criminal rising of last week.'

'Insane' was the most popular word to describe both the rising and its leaders.

In the Letters page of the London *Times*, one writer expressed a feeling of 'detestation and horror' at the very thought of rebellion against English rule. The rebels should be treated firmly. 'This is no time for amnesties and pardon; it is time for punishment, swift and stern.'

This appeared over the name not of a retired General but of 'John Dublin', the Protestant Archbishop. Many Irish people reading it concluded that anything which a Protestant Archbishop looked on with detestation and horror could not be all bad.

By 10.30 a.m., the O'Hanrahan girls were in Church Street looking for Father Augustine when they ran into him as he was leaving a house.

'Of course,' he said, 'I'd be delighted to come and see your mother. Wasn't I just on my way there, anyhow? But first come into our parlour.'

After he had calmed them a little, they walked together to the North Circular Road.

The girls stayed outside praying while the priest went in to break to Mrs O'Hanrahan the news that her brave son, Michael, had died for Ireland.

In Richmond Barracks, one of the prisoners, old Count Plunkett, had been unable to sleep on the floor. For a long time he had stood up until his comrades managed to persuade a guard to find him an orange box. There he sat hunched up for hours on end, his homburg hat on his head, his white beard poking out of the two army greatcoats with which they tried to keep him warm.

The Count was so ill, they sent for a military doctor who tactlessly asked, 'Are you the father of Joseph Plunkett who was shot this morning?'

That was how Count Plunkett learned of the death of his son.

Each afternoon, in Richmond Barracks, two to three hundred men were paraded and sent to the boat for internment in England.

On this particular afternoon, some were chosen from Cell A. Liam O'Briain was one of them and, to his utter delight, so was Sean McDermott. Though Sean was next to him, Liam did not speak for fear of drawing attention to him. The English soldiers did not know them. With luck, Sean would make the boat and escape what, otherwise, was inevitable death. 'Prisoners,' an English NCO called, 'atten-*tion*. Quick—'

'Hold it, Corporal.'

It was a Castle detective, Inspector Burton.

'I'll just run my eye over this little lot.' In seconds, he had lighted on Sean McDermott. A nod from a colleague, Dan Hoey, confirmed his suspicion. 'Well, what have we here?' He beckoned him out of the ranks. 'You didn't really think you'd get away from me, did you?'

McDermott's face darkened. 'You seem to change your mind a lot,' he said.

Michael Collins, another on parade, swore that one day he would take revenge on that Inspector.

Later that afternoon, MacBride, Mallin and Sean Heuston were to be tried.

Sean T. Kelly, who had worked in communications during the rising, was at an upstairs window when they were marched across the square. MacBride, he knew, had little chance of getting off. The authorities had not forgiven him for raising an Irish Brigade to fight the British in the Boer War.

MacBride went in first. He marched in and stood to attention, every inch a soldier.

General Blackadder seemed to read in his eyes: 'You are soldiers. So am I. You have won. I have lost. Do your worst.'

He was allowed to call a witness, Mrs Allan. No chair was provided, so MacBride jumped up and offered her his. She testified that he had not been involved in planning the rebellion, he simply chanced on it.

MacBride was found guilty, all the same.

When he emerged on to the square, Kelly raised the window. 'Been sentenced, Major?'

'Later tonight. But it's a foregone conclusion, Sean T.' MacBride pointed a finger at his heart. 'I'll get it in the morning.'

'Something might turn up.'

'Nothing will save me, Sean T. This is the second time I've sinned against them. Their chance of revenge, eh?'

MacBride clasped one hand with the other and raised them in the air as if shaking with all his friends.

'Goodbye and God be good to you, Sean T.'

It was Mallin's turn. Before going before the Court, he warmly embraced William Partridge, who had been with him in the College of Surgeons. In the cold nights since, they had huddled up together. Whenever Mallin felt especially homesick, Partridge, an older man, had comforted him.

The chief witness was de Courcy Wheeler, to whom he had surrendered.

The President said, 'Perhaps you would care to question the Captain.'

'No, sir,' Mallin replied, fingering his rosary. 'I merely wish to place on record how grateful my comrades and I are for the consideration he showed us.'

'It is so recorded,' said the President.

After the trial, the three condemned were taken to Kilmainham.

Mallin's house was only two hundred yards from the jail; the lorry had to pass it. He peered out the back, hoping to catch a last glimpse of his wife and children. He did not know that his wife had been advised to move around regularly to avoid being picked up by the military. All that Mallin saw was his pet dog, Prinie, prized because she had once saved his little daughter from a rearing horse. Prinie was sitting like a faithful guardian by the front door.

And the house, a tiny terraced house, how beautiful it seemed, so serene, so full of wonder.

'My precious darling wife,' he prayed fervently, 'come out and show yourself with little Joseph.' She never did.

Goodbye.

He felt he had lost his last chance of ever seeing his wife and baby son again.

457

It was the Countess's turn to face court martial at Richmond. She was taken there from her isolation cell in Kilmainham.

As to assisting the enemy, she pleaded not guilty.

As to causing disaffection among the population towards British rule, she pleaded, 'Guilt-ay 200 per cent and prahd of it.'

The first witness was a seventeen-year-old page boy at the University Club. He claimed to have seen the Countess fire a pistol at the Club from behind a monument in the Green.

The Countess got satisfaction out of showing his testimony was a tissue of lies. Not that it mattered since she was perfectly willing to agree with the next witness, Captain Wheeler, that she handed him her pistol when they surrendered. She also acknowledged that she was Mallin's second in command.

When the Captain stood down, the President said, 'Madam, have you anything to say?'

In a voice as English as his, she said, dismissively: 'Yes, old feller. I went out to fight for Arland's freedom and it doesn't matter a tinker's cuss what happens to me. I did what I thought was right and I stand by it.'

She was taken back to Kilmainham Jail where she expected the same fate as the rest.

Father Augustine again spent part of his afternoon at the Officers' Quarters on the North Circular Road.

'I was wondering,' he said, 'if I will be needed tomorrow morning?'

The CO winked. 'Padre, I'll send a car for you.'

At 9 that evening, Sir John French received another anxious note from the PM.

Warned by Redmond, he did not like the idea of four more leaders being shot that morning. He asked Sir John to convey to Maxwell that wholesale executions might easily cause a revulsion of feeling in England and lay up a store of future trouble in Ireland.

Sir John was irritated. Really, politicians were the limit. They asked the army to clean up their messes, then complained because a few heads got broken.

He called in his secretary. 'A wire to General Maxwell.'

Having explained the Prime Minister's worries, he made a fatal addition of his own.

'There is no intention to interfere with the freedom of action or initiative which you as C-in-C now have.'

He snapped his fingers in the direction of his secretary. 'That's all. Send it off right away.'

In Kilmainham Jail, a stone's throw away from where Maxwell was going through his list of executions, the Countess was still awake when someone quietly unlocked the padlock and eased back the bolt. It was the Tommy on duty.

He came in and offered her a cigarette. He knew she had been found guilty and felt sorry for her. She was middle-aged. A woman. An English woman. It just did not seem right to court-martial *her*.

As they smoked, he let her ask questions. He was not too careful; she was destined for the bullet soon.

'Who's been shot so far?'

He reeled off seven names. There were no surprises, except for Willie Pearse. He was merely his brother's shadow.

'Any tomorrow?' She did not really expect an answer.

'Chap name of MacBride.'

'MacBride? But he had nothing to do with the planning.'

The Tommy shrugged; he was a soldier, not a politician.

When Father Augustine entered his cell, Major MacBride's first words were, 'A pity, Padre, we had to throw in the towel, don't you think?' Before the priest could answer, he said, cheerfully, 'I asked a Tommy for water to wash in and know what he brought me? A cupful.'

Father Augustine's cathedral laugh merged with MacBride's and rolled around the tiny cell.

The prisoner handed over a pound note, silver and copper coins. 'For the poor.' He tugged his rosary out of his pocket like an earth worm. 'Give that to my mother, will you?' He removed his watch, not a tremble of the hands, from his waistcoat. 'And that.'

He had been thinking of his wife, Maud Gonne, and how, though they had fallen out, she would, at least, approve of the manner of his death.

Then there was their son, Sean, at school in Paris, how would he take the news and what would become of him?

He knelt and confessed with the simplicity of a child.

Father Augustine gave him Communion, after which they prayed together.

'I'll stay with you to the end,' the priest promised, 'and anoint you when you fall.'

'Kind of you, Padre.'

Soldiers came along the cat-walk with metallic tread, there was a knock on the door.

The Countess had spent the night waiting to hear the shots that put an end to brave MacBride. With the coming of dawn and the dread, her ears were supersensitive. She heard the tramp of soldiers below and knew that the firing squad had arrived.

Though he was in the next block, she wanted to beat on the door and call out, 'MacBride, Major MacBride, God-speed.' But that would have betrayed the kind Tommy who had confided in her. She stuffed her hands in her mouth.

MacBride was escorted downstairs to the back door.

'Would you mind,' he said, 'if I don't have my hands bound? I promise to keep perfectly still.'

But they were fastened behind him.

'Surely, soldier, I don't have to be blindfolded?'

'Sorry, sir, them's my orders.'

Hooded like a falcon, MacBride turned to the priest, and, remembering the Boer War, said, 'Padre, it's not as if I never looked down the barrels of their guns before.'

As a piece of paper was being pinned over his heart, the friar whispered in his ear: 'We are all sinners, my son. Offer up your life for any faults or sins of the past.'

'I'm glad you told me that, Father. I will.'

With Father Augustine guiding him and flanked by two armed men, he stepped out into the Yard with an almost jaunty air.

He had had a full life; married a beautiful woman, fathered a son, fought in many a battle, so that death, a soldier's death, seemed a fitting end.

He lifted his head and smelled the air. 'A fine morning, Padre.'

The big priest beside him shuddered. 'A bit chilly.'

Beneath the blindfold, walking, as the priest thought, by the light of the Angel's Lamp, the prisoner smiled as if to say the cold did not matter all that much.

Big, gentle Father Augustine was praying, '*De profundis*,' but never had he called to God out of such great depths before.

The prisoner was positioned at the wall, fifty feet from the firing squad. The escort moved to the left, near the Governor and the prison doctor.

Father Augustine was transfixed on the spot near MacBride. The officer led him gently to the right. 'This way, please.'

MacBride said, lingeringly, 'Goodbye, Padre.'

As the officer spoke a word of command, MacBride straightened his broad shoulders, drew in his stomach, and his mouth assumed the shape of a big O.

Death, however long-awaited, always came suddenly like the cork out of a champagne bottle, like a stranger from behind a tree.

The officer lowered his hand. With the volley echoing around the Yard, the prisoner collapsed like a sack of grain.

The officer held the priest back just long enough for him to put a bullet in the dead man's brain.

Father Augustine knelt to anoint the warm quivering flesh. '*Per istam sanctam unctionem . . . .*'

MacBride's brave spirit, he felt, was already winging its way to God.

'One more execu-*tion*. One more execu-*tion*.'

The Connollys heard the newsboy's cry and Lillie, nearly out of her mind, clutched the children to her as Nora ran out to buy a paper.

Trying to stop herself shuddering, Nora returned, a false smile on her face. 'It's not Daddy.'

'Who?' said several voices.

Nora's face clouded over as she told them.

To Kattie Clarke, the Major's death was another blow. First Tom, then Ned, now MacBride, the witness at her wedding in New York.

She remembered how the trunk containing her wedding dress had been missing from the boat, and MacBride had patted her arm. She had never forgotten his comforting words, 'Never mind your trousseau, girl, you're marrying a hero, aren't you?'

Around midday, in Westport, County Mayo, MacBride's home-town, a twelve-year-old boy, Tom Heavey, was standing outside Joyce's, the newsagent's, when a railwayman passed and said, 'MacBride was shot this morning.'

Mrs Joyce, biting back her tears, said, 'Get on your bike, lad, and go tell the poor one at once.'

Tom, not sure what the message meant, pedalled as fast as he could to the Quay and burst into the ship chandler's shop and up

461

the winding steps. Without knocking or removing his cap, he went into a quiet, dark room where a silver-haired old lady was seated, hands on her lap, by the window.

Honoria MacBride had been a widow for forty-eight years, since her Sean was six months old. She raised her wrinkled eyes, questioningly.

'Sorry, ma'am,' Tom got out, breathlessly, 'but it seems, well, the Major—'

There was anguish now in Honoria's face.

'Shot this morning, ma'am.'

Without a word, the old lady just bowed her head.

At Richmond Barracks, it was Kent's turn to be tried. He stood tall and straight before the court, betraying no emotion.

At 4 in the afternoon, he wrote a note to his wife.

> I expect the death sentence which better men have already suffered. I only regret that I have now no longer the opportunity of showing you how I think of you now that the chance of seeing you again is so remote. I shall die like a man for Ireland's sake.

Later, he changed the heading of the note from Richmond to Kilmainham, where he awaited execution in Joe Plunkett's cell.

His wife came unexpectedly to visit him and it had a profound effect on him. It seemed to humanize him, to make him feel things he had suppressed for years.

Afterwards, he wrote to her.

> Aine, my wife,
> In memory of me, Aine, my thousand loves, tell Ronan that I am dying for Ireland. When understanding comes to him with the years, he will understand that much. *Dulce est pro Patria mori.* This is 7th day of May 1916, E. K.

He added a note for his boy.

> To my dear poor little son, Ronan, from his father who is on the point of dying tomorrow for Ireland. Goodbye, E. K.

462

PS Take good care of your dear mother. May God help the two of you and may He give you both long life and happiness. God free Ireland.

After several attempts, de Valera's wife, Sinead, finally managed to see the American Consul, Edward L. Adams. He had been out of town during the rising and had only just returned.

She asked him to intervene on Eamon's behalf.

'Why come to me, ma'am?'

Sinead took out of her purse a copy of her husband's birth certificate. Twice, British soldiers had raided her house in search of it. Fortunately, it was kept in de Valera's family home in Munster Street.

'As you see, sir, my husband was born in New York. He is, therefore, an American citizen, surely?'

Even if this were so, the Consul had heard that de Valera had spent almost his entire life in Ireland. He had openly boasted that he was Irish not English. Nor had he at the age of twenty-one taken an oath of American citizenship.

Adams was not in a position to check all the facts, nor was he yet sure of his Government's attitude to the rebellion.

When he made representations to Major Price and Sir Matthew Nathan, he found them both sympathetic. They had no wish to embarrass the American administration.

Nathan glanced at his watch. It was 6.15 p.m. on his last day. He had packed and, the Perfect Civil Servant, was at his desk till the end.

He took a last look around his office with its tall windows and grand ceiling. He printed on his mind the spot where the policeman fell when the rising began – was it really only eleven days ago?

Accompanied by his assistant, he drove to Kingstown.

O'Farrell looked out over the cold grey bay. 'Looks like a stormy crossing, sir.'

Nathan smiled. He had feared storms on the Irish Sea. He had realized, too late, that the storms over the land were worse.

He did not know that travelling in the opposite direction was a new Post Master General, Albert Pease. Asquith had said to him, 'Do try and get Wimborne to resign without a fuss.'

In London, next morning, Nathan worked from 9.15 a.m. to 11.45 a.m. in the Irish Office. At midday, he was in No 10. Present, apart from the PM, were Birrell and Birrell's temporary successor, Sir Robert Chalmers.

The meeting lasted for two and a half hours, with Nathan giving an update. The PM quizzed him particularly on local reaction to the executions. He reported that the tide of opinion in Ireland was turning. Sympathy for the rebels was growing and changing them into patriots.

Asquith had gathered something of the sort. Not only Redmond, many others were suggesting to him that Maxwell was indulging in slow and secret vengeance, that the General's deafness to howls of protest was alienating even those who had opposed the rising.

Nathan was not in a strong position but he urged that executions should cease and martial law be withdrawn at once.

The PM thanked him for his devoted service, and no sooner had Nathan left than he got on to the War Office.

'I realize,' he told French, 'that you are going slowly, but not slowly enough, I fear.'

French told him that Maxwell, as the PM had directed, was on his way to London.

'Fine. Ask him to attend our next Cabinet Meeting.'

The Cabinet listened to what Maxwell had to say. He had been given a free hand and put down the rebellion in a couple of days. He was now busy making sure it would not happen again.

The PM could see that what required the skill of a diplomat had been left to a plain blunt soldier.

The meeting ended with Asquith formally commending the General for his success. He expressly forbade the execution of women. Maxwell had already heard from Bonham Carter on that score. The PM, however, still left to Maxwell's discretion those who would be executed.

'I am referring, naturally,' Asquith emphasized, 'only to ring-leaders and proven murderers. Even there, General, may I suggest that these executions be brought to a close as soon as possible so Ireland can return to normality.'

The Foreign Office in London received cable No 371/2851 from Sir Cecil Spring-Rice in Washington.

Cardinal Gibbons of Baltimore was urging the British to be lenient to their Irish prisoners. His Eminence felt all respectable Irishmen condemned the revolt but 'there was a danger of manufacturing martyrs with senseless executions.'

A member of the Foreign Office staff guffawed, 'It would take a vast amount of "manufacturing" to turn Casement into a martyr, eh?'

There were knowing sniggers all round.

In Kilmainham, a young officer visited the Countess Markievicz in her cell. 'I have come, ma'am, to report to you the sentence of the court.'

'Thank you,' she said, 'you *are* a darling.' She gestured to the wooden plank that served as a bed. 'Do take a seat.'

Going a bright red, he remained standing to attention. He read out the official notice: she was condemned to death. 'General Maxwell has confirmed it.'

'Jolly good.'

'But on account of the prisoner's sex—'

'Which is hardly my fault.'

'He has commuted it.'

In his embarrassment, the young man had dropped his voice.

'Would you mind repeating that, old bean.'

He coughed. 'Commuted it.'

'Gracious me,' she said. 'I took the same risks as the men, surely I'm entitled to be executed for Arland, too.'

'I don't suppose,' the officer said, hesitantly, 'that you have any rights in the matter.'

'What *will* happen to me, then?' she asked. 'I don't suppose the King'll ask me to Buckingham Palace to pin a medal on my treacherous bosom.'

'Life imprisonment, ma'am.'

'Life imprisonment? Oh, Lor'. I know it's not your bally fault, old darling,' the Countess sighed, 'but I do wish your lot had the decency to shoot me.'

In the chapel of Kilmainham Jail, Father McCarthy celebrated Sunday Mass. The women were in the gallery at the rear, the men at floor level, among them Commandants Kent and Mallin, as well as Sean Heuston and Con Colbert.

When Mass was over, the men were ordered to form up and leave first. The women stood to attention and saluted.

A Tommy yelled, 'Put those arms down.'

They did not budge.

'Put them down, y'hear!'

The women went on saluting until all their officers and men had left.

Later that morning, Pease, the new Post Master General, went to see Wimborne at the Lodge.

His Excellency told him that Maxwell was frightening everyone with his endless executions. 'In my view, a terrible mistake.'

As tactfully as possible, Pease suggested that the PM might like to see a clean sweep of the Administration.

Wimborne was incensed.

'Not *me*! If I resigned it would imply I had made mistakes.' He fluttered his furry eyelashes. 'Never! If Nathan and Birrell had accepted my advice there would not have been one rebel at large to start a rising.'

Mrs O'Hanrahan was told that Henry, her second son, was not to be executed like Michael. His sentence had been commuted to life imprisonment.

There was joy in Kimmage, too, when the execution of Joe Plunkett's brothers, George and John, was commuted to ten years.

On the streets and in the bars, people grew more hopeful.

On that peaceful Sunday afternoon, a letter was put through the letter box of Bill O'Brien's house.

'For you, Lillie.'

The message, on Castle writing paper, said, 'If Mrs Connolly will call at Dublin Castle Hospital on Monday or Tuesday at 11 o'clock she can see her husband.'

She had been awaiting a call for days. Every hour, every minute had brought fresh anxiety. Now that word had come, terror gripped her.

'They're going to shoot him, too.'

'No, *no*, Mommie,' Ina said. 'They wouldn't dare shoot a wounded man.'

'Maybe he's better,' Lillie said. 'Maybe he's well enough to shoot now.'

'Mommie,' Ina insisted, 'can't you tell things are changing. No one was shot this morning.'

'It's Sunday, a holy day.'

'Nor yesterday,' Ina insisted.

'Look at the note,' insisted Nora. 'It says you can come Monday or Tuesday. If anything had been settled, they would have given you a definite date.'

Lillie read the note three more times, trying to get at the words behind the words. 'That must be true.'

A moment later, she wailed, 'But I still don't believe it.'

In Kilmainham, Colbert, Mallin, Heuston and Kent were told individually of the sentence of the Court.

'You are to die at dawn tomorrow.'

Mallin, still upset at having seen his dog but not his wife and children, asked 'Our families. Will they be allowed to visit us?'

The officer said, 'The Commandant is drawing up papers this very minute to arrange transport for close relatives.'

Heuston was in Cell 19. He dropped a line to his brother, Michael, studying to be a Dominican priest, hoping he would be free to come.

To his teacher-sister, a Dominican nun, he wrote:

> My dearest Mary,
>
> Before this note reaches you I shall have fallen as a soldier in the cause of Irish freedom. I write to bid you a last farewell in this world.
>
> If you really love me teach the children in your class the history of their own land, and teach them that the cause of Caitlin Ni Uallachain never dies. Ireland shall be free from the centre to the sea as soon as the people of Ireland believe in the necessity for Ireland's Freedom and are prepared to make the necessary sacrifices to obtain it.

In Cell 20, Kent wrote out a statement for the public. His stern exterior was his way of hiding from outsiders his passion for Ireland and his deep feelings for his wife and son.

His view was, the Republicans were wrong to surrender. They should have fought to a finish.

> The enemy has not cherished one generous thought for those who, with little hope, with poor equipment,

and weak in numbers, withstood his forces for one glorious week.

Ireland has shown she is a Nation. This generation can claim to have raised sons as brave as any that went before. And in the years to come Ireland will honour those who risked all for *her* honour at Easter in 1916.

I bear no ill will towards those against whom I have fought. I have found the common soldiers and the higher officers human and companionable, even the English who were actually fighting against us.

I wish to record the magnificent gallantry and fearless, calm determination of the men who fought with me. All, all, were simply splendid. Even I knew no fear nor panic and shrunk from no risk even as I shrink not now from the death that faces me at daybreak.

I hope to see God's face even for a moment in the morning. His will be done. All here are very kind. My poor wife saw me yesterday and bore up – so my warder told me – even after she left my presence.

Poor Aine, poor Ronan. God is their only shield now that I am removed. And God is a better shield than I.

In Cell 17, Con Colbert, an assistant clerk in a bakery, wrote ten brief notes to his brothers, sisters and a few friends.

To one sister, Nora, he said, 'Don't blame me – perhaps God's way of saving my soul.'

He did not want even his most beloved sister Lila to come. He chose to die uncomforted rather than cause pain to those dear to him.

In Cell 18, Michael Mallin wrote to his parents:

Forgive your poor son who is set to meet his death. Dear father, forgive me all, and you, dear mother, the pain I give you now.

I tried, with others, to make Ireland a free nation and failed. Others failed before us and paid the price and so must we. Goodbye until I meet you in heaven.

Goodbye again. A kiss for you, dear mother. God bless you all.

Your loving son, Michael.

468

Mallin's four children ranged from Seamus, who was twelve, to Joseph, aged two and a half. He missed them terribly. There was another on the way.

To his wife he wrote:

> My darling Wife, Pulse of my heart,
>
> This is the end of all earthly things; sentence of Death has been passed, and a quarter to four tomorrow the sentence will be carried out by shooting and so must Irishmen pay for trying to make Ireland a free nation. God's will be done.
>
> I am prepared but, oh my darling, if only you and the little ones were coming too, if we could all reach Heaven together. My heart-strings are torn to pieces when I think of you and them, of our manly Seamus, happy-go-lucky Sean, shy warm Una, Daddy's girl, and oh, little Joseph, my little man, my little man.
>
> Wife, dear Wife, I cannot keep the tears back when I think of him. He will rest in my arms no more. To think that I have to leave you to battle through the world with them without my help.
>
> We have been married thirteen years or so and in all that time you have been a true loving wife, too good for me.
>
> You love me, my own darling. Think only of the happy times we spent together, forgive and forget all else.
>
> I do not believe our Blood has been shed in vain. I believe Ireland will come out greater and grander but she must not forget she is *Catholic*, she must keep her Faith.
>
> I find no fault with the soldiers or police. I forgive them from the bottom of my heart. Pray for all the souls who fell in this fight, Irish and English.
>
> God and his Blessed Mother take you and my dear ones under their care. A husband's blessing on your dear head, my loving wife.
>
> A father's blessing on the heads of my dear children Seamus, Sean, Una, Joseph, my little man, my little man, my little man. His name unnerves me again. All your dear faces arise before me.
>
> God bless you, God bless you, my darlings. Your loving

Husband, Michael Mallin, Commandant, Stephen's Green Command.

I enclose the buttons off my sleeve. Keep them in memory of me. Mike XXXXXX

Around midnight, military cars were despatched to bring in the relatives.

Mallin's wife, five months pregnant, was not at home. She was staying with the two youngest at Harold's Cross with Tom, her husband's brother. The eldest boy, Seamus, and young Sean were being looked after by their grandmother and Aunt Kate.

When the car came, a policeman, a family friend, handed the official note to the grandmother, saying, with tears in his eyes, 'Mick's race is run.'

She woke Seamus and Sean with, 'Get dressed, boys.'

She was not crying but her attitude conveyed that something awful was about to happen.

Heuston was visited by his mother, his sister, aunt and a first cousin, Lil. His brother Michael came in a special car from Tallaght with his Novice Master, Michael Browne. Father Browne, a tall Dominican, was in his black and white habit. He stayed in the waiting-room, while the relatives went ahead.

They found Sean in a bare unlit cell. The young Tommy who held the candle had no stomach for the task, for he was doing his best not to cry.

Seeing how weepy his relatives were, Sean begged them not to break down.

Their conversation was punctuated by NCOs putting their heads in the door to check all was well. And once, a loud voice was heard outside, saying, 'Remember, these must be got away by three.'

Con Colbert had no family visiting but a woman prisoner came to see him, the wife of Seamus O'Murchadha, a captain of the Fourth Battalion. She had cooked for them in the Marrowbone Lane Garrison.

She began breezily with, 'How are you, Con?'

'I'm one of the lucky ones.'

'You mean—?' She gulped back the rush of tears.

He gripped her hand. 'Sorry, I thought you knew.'

She shook her head.

'Better be a corpse than a coward,' he said.

'And Eamonn Kent?'

'He has drawn lucky, too.'

He asked her to keep his prayer book for his sister, Lila, and a few buttons for others dear to him.

'They left me nothing else.' She took them reverently. 'I never felt happier,' he assured her. 'I never thought I would have the honour of dying for Ireland.'

With the soldier guarding him in tears, the young woman knelt for Con's blessing.

He protested. 'I'm not a priest.'

'No,' she said, 'you're a martyr for Ireland.'

Smiling, just to please her, he made the sign of the cross over her bowed head.

The Mallin family arrived, including Michael's two brothers, Tom and Bart, and his sister Kate.

Mallin had primed Seamus to look after his wife and other children in case he were taken from them. But he was only twelve and still not fully awake. The prison with its solemn atmosphere frightened them all. They passed a cell lit by candlelight from which came the sound of the rosary being said.

In the next cell was their father.

Mallin greeted them with a small blanket around his shoulders and a rosary draped round his wrist. He had a smile on his face, but there was no joy in it.

He said, 'I am to die at dawn.'

His broken-hearted wife could not believe it. He had told her they would escape and continue the fight in the country.

As to the children, they could not grasp they would never see their daddy again.

Father Browne had been kicking his heels in the waiting-room long enough. He insisted on being allowed to see Heuston.

Sean, looking very serene, thanked him for coming.

The Dominican stayed only briefly because he heard crying next door and wanted to help.

Mallin's guard asked him for his permit. Father Browne put his finger to his ear to suggest that he listen to the weeping inside the cell.

The soldier stepped aside. 'Just walk in, sir.'

The priest in his Dominican robes momentarily silenced the family's lament.

Mallin said he was having the best wish in his life fulfilled: holding baby Joseph in his arms for the last time. To his wife, he said, 'Darling, if you go to Liberty Hall, in the room overlooking the river, you'll find a piece of poplin which—'

'The Hall's not there any more,' she said.

Comforted by his family, even this did not upset him too much.

He turned to Fr Browne. 'See this one, Father,' – he indicated Joseph – 'I want him to become a priest.'

'That's grand,' the priest said, politely.

Mallin pointed to his wife. 'Another one on the way, Father. If it's a girl, I want her baptized Mary, in honour of the Blessed Virgin.'

Little Sean tugged on his father's tunic. 'I don't like it in here, Daddy. Why don't you come home with us?'

When the relatives left, the jail settled down to an unnerving silence. A new day was beginning. It was 8 May.

A military car brought two Capuchins. Father Albert went to Mallin and Father Augustine to Kent.

After Kent had received the sacraments, he said, 'You have to make other visits?'

Father Augustine nodded.

'Would you come back' – he gestured at the paper on the table – 'when I have finished?'

As the priest rose to go, Kent took out his watch, the one thing he wanted Ronan to have. It showed 2.30 a.m. The seconds, the last of his life, ticked audibly away.

'I have an hour or so left, haven't I?'

'Yes, Eamonn.'

Kent wrote:

> My dearest wife Aine,
> Not wife but widow before these lines reach you. I am here without hope of this world and without fear, calmly awaiting the end.

In the last phase of his journey, he lost the need of a veneer of cynicism to stop his weakness overwhelming him. Now, as the final seconds beat in his brain, for the first time in a long while he seemed to become what his friend Stephen MacKenna once called him, a kind of remote, tranquil harvest moon. He recalled the sweet days of his courtship when he had a pet name for Aine.

> Dearest 'silly little Fanny'. My poor little sweetheart of – how many – years ago. Ever my comforter, God comfort you now.
>
> What can I say? I die a noble death, for Ireland's freedom. Men and women will vie with one another to shake your dear hand. Be proud of me as I am and ever was of you. My cold exterior was but a mask. It has saved me in these last days.
>
> You have a duty to me and to Ronan, that is, to live. You will be – you are, the wife of one of the Leaders of the Revolution. Sweeter still you are my little child, my dearest pet, my sweetheart of the hawthorn bushes and Summer's eves.
>
> I remember all and I banish all that I may be strong and die bravely. I have one hour to live, then God's judgement.
>
> Adieu, Eamonn.

When Father Augustine came back from seeing Mallin two cells away, he and Kent called on every Irish saint they could remember, Patrick and Brigid, Columba and Colmcille, Kevin and Enda, and a host of others.

'You will be meeting them soon,' Father Augustine said, 'so I do not want to embarrass you by letting you forget the name of any one of them.'

He gave Kent his crucifix.

'Keep this, Eamonn, and I will be with you to the last.'

It was 3.20 a.m.

Father Albert, sweat beading his high forehead, had also circulated among the condemned and was now with Heuston, listed first of the four to be shot. Sean was in his greatcoat, for it was a cold morning. The stub of a candle was burned out. He was kneeling beside a table, his rosary in his hands.

For the last fifteen minutes, he and Father Albert knelt to pray in a darkness that seemed to bind them and the world into one.

Heuston seemed not to mind that every basic kindness had been withdrawn from him and that, at twenty-five, he was about to die.

He spoke in anticipation of meeting Patrick Pearse and the other leaders who had gone before. It struck the friar forcibly that these men were aware that their deaths were not solitary events but part of a blessed brotherhood.

They repeated over and over the prayer Heuston liked best: 'Jesus, Mary and Joseph, I give you my heart and my soul. Jesus, Mary and Joseph, assist me in my last agony. Jesus, Mary and Joseph, may I breathe forth my soul in peace with you. Amen.'

There was a knock on the door. 'Heuston. It's time.'

As they went down to the open space whence the corridor ran into the Yard, Sean said, 'Remember me, Father, to all my friends in the Fianna, to Michael Staines and to all the boys in Blackhall Street.'

His hands were pinioned behind his back. He was blindfolded. A piece of paper, four inches by five, was pinned to his greatcoat above his heart. Things were moving to the end with surprising suddenness.

Out of the corner of his eye, Father Albert saw Mallin approaching, assisted by Father Augustine. He put a small cross to Heuston's lips and the young man kissed the Crucified, whispering, 'You won't forget to anoint me, Father.'

The priest squeezed his arm. 'Of course not, Sean.'

The guard held Sean's left arm, Father Albert his right.

Outside in a bluish granular dawn was the firing squad for Mallin. Some were smoking nervously, feeling a big giddy, their knuckles gleaming like knobs of ivory. Others, not wanting to be noticed, drifted off to the toilet.

In the Stonebreakers' Yard, was a second detachment, some standing, others kneeling.

Sean and Father Albert were led to the end where there was a soap box. Sean was seated on it. With perfect calmness, he said with the priest, 'My Jesus, mercy.'

The priest moved away, feeling the grandeur, unlike any other, of a man dying freely, deliberately in the spring of his years.

The volley broke into his reverie. As he stumbled on feet of iron to keep his promise to Sean, he felt not sad but exalted. He would have given anything to change places with this brave young man.

As Sean's body was dragged away, the first firing squad was replaced by the second. Father Albert waited to attend to Michael Mallin, who was murmuring the Hail Mary.

Father Augustine was at the preparation point. His left arm was entwined in Con Colbert's right as he whispered last words in the lad's ear.

A young soldier started to pin a piece of white paper rather low on Colbert's breast. Over his head, Con said, 'Wouldn't it be better to pin it up higher, nearer the heart?'

The soldier muttered, 'This'll do.' Then: 'Now give me your hand, mate.'

Colbert shrugged, and extended his left hand.

The soldier said, 'No, the other one.'

Colbert extended his right and the soldier grasped it and shook it warmly.

As the volley rang out that ended Mallin's life, the soldier blindfolded Con's eyes and pinned his hands behind his back. 'Good luck, mate,' he said.

Moments later, an NCO called out, 'Colbert.'

Father Augustine still had his arm through Con's – 'Hold tight to God's sleeve, lad,' he whispered – and now, with Father Albert arriving breathless to take the lad's left hand, they entered the corridor lit only by a lamp carried by a soldier. Though Con was shaking and his legs felt they belonged to someone else, his lips were moving in prayer as he went before the firing squad.

Father Augustine, on the treadmill of death, left his colleague to anoint the body and rushed back to find Kent being led towards him down the hall. His heart went out to embrace this gallant man. And together they walked to the Stonebreakers' Yard.

Kent, too, dry-mouthed, heart pumping, knees jerking, was made to sit on the soap box to await his view of God's face.

Only when Father Augustine rushed to anoint him did he notice that in Kent's bound hands was his crucifix. He withdrew it to find the figure on the cross was spattered with blood.

'More exe-*cut*-ions!'

The Connolly girls had been trying to get their mother to sleep when she came to with a start at the newsvendor's cry. Nora went out to learn the names of the new dead.

Lillie was in a state of exhaustion when she turned up at the Castle with little Fiona to see her husband. The Grand Staircase up which she was conducted had an armed guard on practically every step. Outside the room in the Royal Corridor, a nurse was ordered to search her.

'Pardon me,' Lillie said, 'but what are you looking for?'

'A knife or maybe poison, in case the prisoner tries to commit suicide.'

Lillie laughed thinly. 'That proves how little you know James Connolly. Otherwise you wouldn't dream of suggesting that to avoid a little pain—'

'A lot of pain,' the nurse interrupted, kindly.

'All right,' Lillie said, dampening down, 'a lot of pain. But as long as there's life in him, he'll go on fighting.'

The first thing she saw on entering was the cage that kept the bedclothes off his leg. One glance at him and she knew the nurse was not exaggerating.

He was pale, there were circles under his eyes, his mouth was strangely twisted. And she had never seen him so skinny. He tried to lift himself off his pillow but could not.

She pressed her lips to his, feeling the familiar tickle of his moustache; and he stroked her dark hair, now streaked with grey, murmuring, 'Lillie, Lillie.'

He said he was being well looked after. The civilian surgeon, Tobin, had even crossed to London to try and find a remedy for the spread of gangrene in his body.

'*And*, James?'

'Nothing has worked so far.'

Somehow, Lillie found that reassuring.

When Madge and Laura came across their sister, she was very white. Laura whispered, 'She's not at all well.'

The day before an official had handed Kattie her husband's effects: glasses' case, pencil, post office book with seven stamps in it, knife, a pound note taken from him at the Rotunda. It was like being presented with his severed limbs.

Before her sisters could speak, Kattie said, in a hollow voice, 'In the night . . . I lost . . . the baby.'

'Oh, Kattie!' Madge said, 'I'll fetch a doctor.'

'No need. I can handle it.'

They decided it was best to leave her alone.

Kattie had never felt so empty. First, her heart, and now her body, empty.

In London, Nathan received a letter from George Bernard Shaw.

'My dear Sir Matthew,' he wrote, 'I congratulate you on coming in for the best rebellion for 118 years, probably the last chance of such an experience.'

Shaw suggested that Birrell's best defence was that he could only have avoided the danger 'by impartially disarming the population. As he was not enabled to do this, he was not in a position to conclude that any section of the population could run amok like lunatics.'

Shaw had one regret.

'Why, oh why didn't the artillery knock down half Dublin whilst it had the chance? Think of the insanitary areas, the slums, the glorious chance of making a clean sweep of them! Only 179 houses and probably at least nine of them quite decent ones. I'd have laid at least 17,900 of them flat and made a decent town of it!'

Nathan chuckled. Shaw was right about one thing. Had they tried to disarm the Volunteers north or south, they would have had not a six-day but perhaps a six-months' war. As if they had failed where others might had succeeded! As if there were not problems to which no solutions exist!

Not one sign pointed to a rising on that Monday. But wasn't there talk of a rising? the critics would ask. There was never talk of anything else, that was the trouble. The peculiarity of the Easter Rising was, it was at once the most public and most secret of all rebellions. Connolly was always 'taking the Castle' in practice, then left it alone when it was at his mercy.

How could anyone predict anything as illogical as that?

A guard unlocked an isolation cell in the Tower of London in a panic. 'I need help here,' he hollered.

The prisoner was near to death. His forehead was cold and clammy, his eyes rolled in his head, his pulse was barely perceptible.

Sir Roger Casement was rushed to the hospital wing where the doctor immediately diagnosed poisoning. He pushed a tube down his throat and pumped his stomach. It went on for over an hour before the doctor said, 'He'll live.'

For days on end, Casement had been completely isolated. Even the soldiers guarding him were forbidden to utter a single word, though a Welsh corporal did whisper that the leaders of the Dublin rising were being executed.

'I don't care whether it's against orders, sir,' he said with a lilt. 'I want you to know that lots of us are very sorry about this and I 'ope you get off. We think you are a brave man, sir.'

He was never on duty again.

Before the rising, Casement had been considered a curiosity, afterwards, the worst traitor of the war.

He had not heard a word from any of his friends. The Governor said they were all too disgusted. In fact, Gertrude had been trying for days to visit him. She had been shunted from Scotland Yard to the Ministry of War to the Home Office. She had written Roger a letter, telling him how much they all loved him and were praying for him. The Governor withheld it.

She took to walking around the Tower, trying to communicate with him through the walls. Hearing rumours that he was to be shot, she had written to Asquith but he had not replied.

To ease the pain and the loneliness, to try to banish the ghosts inside his brain, Casement tried to kill himself. He tried swallowing a bent nail, then rubbing curare, used by South American Indians to poison their arrows, into his veins. Finally, he swallowed all the curare he had.

After the use of the stomach-pump, he had to bear two silent soldiers in his cell, with a third outside looking every minute through the Judas-hole. The electric light was never switched off so that he did not know the day or the hour; and he, the most private of men, could not sleep or even think.

In deep depression, he saw his suicide attempt as just one more in a long line of failures.

Gertrude finally contacted an Irish lawyer, George Gavan Duffy, who was sympathetic to Sinn Fein. He promised to take up Casement's defence. After a week of negotiation, he was allowed to visit him.

Casement's beard was only half-grown, giving him a neglected look. His blood-red eyes were blurred, his lids too heavy to fully lift, the sides of his face frozen as after a stroke, and his fingers were bunched, almost welded together. Dark thoughts were evidently serpentining his brain. His lower lip was turned out, a glossy purple.

He peered at Gavan Duffy as at a distant object. When asked questions, he paused for a long time, seeming to have to invent language. His speech was breathless, hesitant; he had a slight stammer. It was hard for him to remember names or dates.

Gavan Duffy noticed the untreated bites on his hands, face and neck. His clothes were foetid. This most fastidious of men was still in the same sea-soiled suit he wore when picked up on Banna Strand; the dried slime showed. His brittle laceless boots were draped around his ankles. With nothing to support his trousers, he kept hitching them up nervously.

'When were you last allowed out for a walk, Sir Roger?'

Casement shook his head like a dog out of a pond.

'You mean you have never been allowed out?'

Another shake of the head.

The lawyer felt desperate to scratch himself. The cell was verminous.

He promised to procure writing material. 'Write notes to refresh your memory. It will help me in your defence.'

Casement mumbled that he wanted to be treated the same as his friends in Dublin. 'Military tribunal.' Then, in a low tremulous voice: 'Can't they shoot me, too?'

Duffy went from the Tower to see Gertrude and Mrs Green. He had met Casement, he said, but he could not be sure this wreck was the same man.

Mrs Green wrote a letter at once to the PM, telling him of Casement's condition and threatening, if nothing was done at once, to send accounts of his maltreatment to American papers.

Asquith was genuinely upset. He told his secretary to phone Major Arbuthnot of the Life Guards at Whitehall. From now on, Sir Roger Casement was to be treated decently.

At 2 that Monday afternoon, de Valera went before a court martial. It was brief and to the point.

'Can you tell us where you were born?'

'New York,' he replied. 'But I do not know if my father was a Spanish subject or a naturalized American. I have always regarded myself as an Irishman and not a British subject.'

Captain Hitzen testified that de Valera was the one who surrendered in Boland's Mill and that the Sinn Feiners there regarded him as their senior officer.

Cadet Mackay said he had been well treated while he was de Valera's prisoner.

After the trial and verdict of guilty, he was conducted to the now notorious Kilmainham Jail.

John Dillon had been hearing that the conduct of the rebels during the rising was magnificent. These were no ne'er-do-wells, no criminals.

He had also received reports of a massacre of civilians in North

479

King Street. He kept saying, 'Cromwell is risen from the dead and is stalking the land again.'

Everywhere now, in streets, pubs, pulpits, people were saying, 'Didn't those men love Ireland?' 'Really, we never knew it was worth dying for!' 'Yes, they made mistakes but aren't they Irishmen, and aren't the British, as usual, murdering them without a fair trial?' 'Jasus, these brave men are not a lot of foreigners, they're our own.' 'They might have been traitors to Britain but they weren't traitors to Ireland, not by a long chalk.'

Perched on bar stools, their noses dipped in perpetual mourning, the great philosophers were saying, 'Dear Lord, rebels, hunger-strikers, traitors, once they're dying or dead, don't we rush to claim them as our own?' One Dublin waitress said, 'They don't shoot German prisoners, although they call them "Huns" and "baby-killers"; they only shoot our brave Irish boys.'

In O'Connell Street, one elderly black-shawled lady, with eyes swollen from mourning her only son, asked, 'Could the Germans have done worse?' and her companion said, 'But the English don't hate the Germans, Maura, not the way they hate us.'

Children were collecting cheap prints of the leaders of the rising.

Lady Fingall told a friend, 'It's like seeing a continuous trickle of blood coming from under a locked door.'

Already that most feared of critics, the back-street balladeer, was writing songs that were being sung the length and breadth of Ireland.

Priests were making a good living out of saying masses for dead rebels whose names were read out from pulpit after pulpit.

The Irish, by and large, hated violence, which was why most were in principle against the rising. But now a new consciousness was dawning nationwide: what the rebels did was the violence of the brave; what was being done to them was the violence of the coward. Most ominously for the future, in Limerick, Cork and Tralee, a silent rage was deepened by their sense of guilt that the men of Dublin had risen and they had not.

Dillon was furious that he had got nowhere with Maxwell. He was trying to make villains out of Irishmen by shooting them on Irish soil. He might, while he was at it, square the circle!

Stories of maltreatment were multiplying.

Even lads had been put up against a wall for refusing to inform on their leaders; the officer in charge only stopped the firing squad at the last second.

One fifteen-year-old rebel, on being told that he had only half an hour to live, said, 'Shoot away.' They blindfolded him, pressed his back to the Barrack wall. There was the click of the safety catch being lifted. 'Last chance.' '*No!*' They removed the blindfold and sent him home to his mother.

What finally made Dillon determined to take on the Administration was when he met with Hanna Sheehy-Skeffington.

She told him in detail how Skeffy had been shot in cold blood and the murderer made second in command of Portobello Barracks.

Deeply moved, Dillon said, 'My dear, I intend to see to it that the whole of Britain, the whole world knows about your husband's murder.' He adjusted his pince-nez. 'I intend to address the House of Commons.'

In the condemned cell, de Valera decided not to write to his mother or his wife until his death-sentence was confirmed.

His mind went back to Bruree, County Limerick, and his boyhood days. He was remembering his grandmother and his uncle Pat and the brook he used to follow from Drumacummer to Trinity Well at its source in Dromin. He recalled every road and bush and bird along the way.

He imagined himself on top of Knockdoha looking north towards Tory Hill, east towards Kilmallock, south to the Ballyhoura Hills, west to the mountains of Limerick.

He was a boy again, spending all day sometimes with the cows, feeding them hay and cutting buckets of turnips for them in the evening. And he was listening to Fr Eugene Sheehy preaching the boycott while he, in cassock and cotta, sat on the step beside the altar.

He thought especially of beautiful Sinead Flanagan who taught him Irish and became his wife. And even as his long face grew longer there was a shining in his eye.

He wrote to the nun in charge of the Training College where he taught, Sister Gonzaga.

> I have just been told that I am to be shot for my part in the rebellion.
>
> Just a parting line then to thank you and all the Sisters (especially Mother Attracta) for your unvarying kindness

to me in the past and to ask you to pray for my soul and for my poor wife and little children whom I leave unprovided for.

Ask the girls to remember me in their prayers.

Goodbye. I hope I'll be in heaven to meet you.

As darkness came to Richmond Barracks, in a crowded smelly cell on Block L, Row 6, prisoners were telling McDermott, 'They won't shoot *you*, Sean.'

He shook his head. 'Sean Heuston and Con Colbert were and they didn't even sign the Proclamation. Only Connolly and myself of the signatories are left.' He seemed not in the least concerned as he added, 'The British will shoot us both.'

Not long after they had settled down for the night, an officer came to the door. 'Is John McDermott here?'

Sean awoke, rose and limped to meet him. 'Yes?'

The officer handed him a slip of paper. He was being charged with taking part in an armed rebellion.

'Court martial at 11 in the morning.'

His fellow-prisoners surrounded him, noisily. 'That doesn't mean a thing, Sean.'

He refused to discuss it. 'This calls for a concert, lads.'

On the parade ground, the officer who had just delivered the notice of certain death, heard rebel songs and the harsh, unmistakable tones of Sean McDermott.

> *I am Brian Boy McGhee,*
> *My father was Owen Ban,*
> *I was awakened from happy dreams*
> *By the shouts of my startled clan.*

As dawn approached on Tuesday, 9 May, the Chaplain of Cork Military Hospital arrived at Cork Detention Barracks.

'Father John Sexton,' he said, 'to see the prisoner, Kent.'

Fifty-one-year-old, black-haired, black-bearded Tom Kent, court-martialled on the 4th for the murder of Head Constable Rowe, greeted him warmly.

'Any news of Richard, Father?'

Father Sexton lowered his eyes. 'I thought they—. Your brother died of his wounds two days after he was taken.'

Tom signed himself, saying, 'May he rest in peace.'

He handed the Chaplain his temperance badge.

' 'Tis for Father Ahearne of Castlelyons. From him I got it and I wish it to be returned untarnished to him.'

Father Sexton said, 'He will be pleased to get it, Tom.'

He handed Kent a rosary.

It was still in Kent's bound hands when the Chaplain stooped to anoint his bullet-ridden corpse.

The news of Kent's execution was communicated to Maxwell before breakfast. He telegraphed the Prime Minister that of the ring-leaders only Connolly and McDermott remained to be tried.

'If convicted they must suffer the extreme penalty. They will be the last to suffer capital punishment, as far as I can now state.'

He told his staff, 'That will be the end of the so-called Government of the Republic. I assure you, gentlemen, no more will be heard ever again of an Irish rising of 1916.'

It was rare for Sean McDermott to ask a favour of an Englishman but he begged a Tommy for the loan of a razor.

After shaving, he ran his hand over his cheek. 'I want to make a nice corpse, men.'

As the escort unbolted the door, Sean shook hands with each of his comrades.

'Pray for me at dawn.'

After his trial, he was taken to Kilmainham where he was told the Commander-in-Chief had already confirmed his sentence.

Though the Castle's medical staff strongly disapproved of Connolly's part in the rising, he was treated with professionalism and the utmost personal kindness.

That day, Surgeon Tobin whispered to a nurse, 'His leg is not responding to treatment.'

The nurse whispered back, 'He's in agony all the time.'

The surgeon nodded. 'It'll have to come off, I'm afraid.'

He went to brief a senior officer on what had to be done.

The officer said, 'That isn't necessary.'

'I assure you, sir, it is.'

'Take it from me, Mr Tobin,' the officer said, meaningfully, 'it isn't.'

At the Viceregal Lodge, someone else was for the chop.

Lord Basil Blackwood, who was not a vindictive man, entered Lord Wimborne's study.

With distinct pleasure, he said, 'Excellency, a message has just come in from the Cabinet in London.'

Wimborne smiled. 'Oh?'

'They are asking for your—'

'Not my resignation?'

An hour later, still white with fury, Wimborne dictated his reply in formal terms that stuck in his throat.

He then poured himself a brandy that was stiff even by his stern standards.

A young nurse was told, 'Prepare the prisoner, Connolly, for court martial.'

She could hardly believe it. He was so ill, and, anyway, so nice. Many a time she had heard him and Surgeon Tobin swap poems and joke together. Everyone liked him; they just could not understand what had made him a rebel.

Having eased him on to the pillow, she washed his face and combed his hair.

'What's this for, nurse?' When she did not answer, he said, 'So it's my turn.'

'I'll see if I can get you some clean pyjamas.'

In a cupboard she found a brand new pair and helped him struggle into them.

As he gritted his teeth in pain, he said, 'I have to look my best, don't I?'

Suddenly, the door was flung open and three officers burst in. One of them barked, 'Nurse, wait outside.'

The President of the Court said sharply, 'Sit up! You know what this is.'

From the horizontal, Connolly eyed him, without saying a word.

'I told you to sit up, man.'

The young RAMC officer in the corner whispered, 'The prisoner is dying, sir.'

'Well,' the officer bellowed, 'prop him up, then.'

The nurse was called back to place pillows and a mattress in position so that he could sit upright.

His ball-shaped face white with pain, Connolly made no attempt at a defence. What was the point when they had his signature to the surrender? He strongly rejected, however, allegations that he had ill-treated PoWs.

He told the Tribunal: 'We went out to break the connection between this country and the British Empire and to establish an Irish Republic. We believe that the call we then issued to the people of Ireland was a nobler call, in a holier cause, than any issued to them during this war, having any connection with this war.'

'Is this *really* necessary?' the President demanded.

Connolly took no notice.

'We succeeded in proving that Irishmen are ready to die endeavouring to win for Ireland those national rights which the British government has been asking them to die to win for Belgium. As long as that remains the case, the cause of Irish freedom is safe.'

One officer yawned loudly, another tapped his watch.

'Believing that the British government has no right in Ireland, never had any right in Ireland, and never can have any right in Ireland, the presence, in any one generation of Irishmen, of even a respectable minority, ready to die to affirm that truth, makes the Government for ever a usurpation and a crime against human progress.

'I personally thank God that I have lived to see the day when thousands of Irish men and boys, and hundreds of Irish women and girls, were ready to affirm that truth, and to attest it with their lives if need be.'

'Anything else?' demanded the President, irritably.

'Yes,' Connolly said, undaunted, 'I want to see my wife and eldest daughter.'

The President gathered up his papers. 'Granted,' he said. 'Good afternoon.'

When Nora went with her mother to the Castle, she could hardly believe her eyes. Soldiers were on guard with fixed bayonets on every step and on the Battleaxe Landing above. Were so many needed to watch over someone too ill to shift from his bed?

Before they entered, the Intelligence Officer warned them, 'You must not talk about the rising or anything that has taken place since. *Anything*, you understand?'

They nodded.

A nurse, detailed to search them, only went through the motions. 'I refuse,' she muttered, 'to be part of this.'

The RAMC officer never left Connolly's room but when the wife

485

and daughter entered, he courteously turned to the window with his back to them, reading.

Lillie hastened towards the bed, murmuring, 'How is the pain today, James?'

'Not too bad, Lillie.' Never one to keep a secret, he blurted out, 'I've just been court-martialled.'

Both women gasped, and Lillie moaned, 'Then they're—'

'Dad's a sick man,' Nora cut in.

'If they can court-martial him, why won't they kill him?'

Connolly waved speculation aside. He told them how he came by his injury and how the medics couldn't staunch the blood. He praised the bravery of the lad who shielded him with his body when they left the GPO.

'We can't fail after things like that, can we?'

His chief concern was his family. So many girls. Owing to his many activities, he had not given them much of a life.

'Listen to me, Lillie. I reckon you all ought to go back to the States.'

'Where would we get the money?'

'Get Skeffy to edit and publish my writings.'

With a sharp look towards the officer, Norah said, 'He's gone.'

'Who? Skeffy? How?'

'In Portobello Barracks.'

'That's enough,' the young officer said kindly, 'or you'll have to leave.'

Connolly was left pondering a few moments on this surprising news. In a barracks? Did they execute pacifists?

In an attempt to cheer them up, he said, 'The rising will put an end to recruiting. Irishmen will realize it's crazy fighting for the freedom of another country while we're slaves in our own.'

Nora told him about his own son. 'Rory was in prison.'

'Really?' His eyes lit up. 'Where?'

'Richmond Barracks. He was with Sean McDermott for eight days. He gave the soldiers the name Alfred Carne.'

Lillie said anxiously, 'He's under sixteen, so they would have let him go anyway.'

Connolly chuckled. 'Imagine, he's fought for his country, been in prison for his country and he's not sixteen. He's had a great start in life, hasn't he?'

Nora told him about her long and fruitless walk with Ina from Ulster.

486

'So,' she concluded, sighing, 'all I did was carry messages.'

His eyes brimmed with pride again as he squeezed her hand.

'My little woman did as much as any of us. If you hadn't come down from the North I might not have persuaded the leaders to fight.'

One thing still bothered him.

'Skeffy, dead?' He asked it voicelessly.

Nora mouthed back, 'Murdered. By a drunken officer.'

With words that escaped her, she added, 'There's only you and Sean McDermott left.'

Nothing had ever jolted Connolly so much. No one in the Castle had hinted at anything like that.'

'All of them *gone*?'

Nora nodded. More to console her mother, she said, 'But they won't shoot you, Daddy, not a wounded man.'

He racked his brain. 'During the Boer War, the British captured a prisoner wounded just like me. Name of Scheepers. In a farmhouse. They court-martialled him,' – his voice dipped – 'then they shot him in a chair.'

Lillie passed her hand over her throbbing forehead.

Connolly gestured for Nora to put her hand under the bed covers. Into it he placed a compressed piece of paper.

'My defence at my trial,' he whispered. 'See it gets out safely.'

Feeling his rough warm skin, Nora was suddenly a child again.

'Daddy mine,' she exclaimed. 'Oh, Daddy mine.'

When they left, Nora held the paper in her clenched hand while she was being searched. She would have fought the entire British army on her own to keep it.

At Kilmainham Hospital, Maxwell was composing a report to the Prime Minister.

He was far from being the stereotype of the dumb and vicious soldier. Everything in Ireland, he realized, was thirty years too late. The rebellion happened because Home Rule had been put on the long finger at Westminster. From then on, those who backed the ballot rather than the bullet were finished.

If there were an election, he predicted, Redmond's party would lose out massively to the men of violence. The Masses and the grand funerals, the badges and the banners, all pointed the way of Sinn Fein.

Moreover, there was not now the remotest possibility that Ulster would consent to be governed by a treacherous crowd in the south, nor could mainland Britain ask it of them. By demanding a Republic in blood, the rebels had signed and sealed the partition of Ireland.

Maxwell even sensed that, sooner or later, he would be blamed for the troubles ahead. Setting politics aside, he told Asquith that his policy had been not to confirm any death sentence unless he had overwhelming evidence that the prisoner was either a leader or a rebel commander who had shot down His Majesty's troops or subjects.

He answered the PM's query about Connolly and McDermott by saying that since they were ring-leaders, it would be both illogical and unjust not to execute them.

He had set the date: 11 May.

'It is hoped that these examples will be sufficient to act as a deterrent to intriguers and to bring home to them that the murder of His Majesty's subjects or other acts calculated to imperil the safety of the realm will not be tolerated.'

When Asquith read the letter, he saw that its icy logic was irrefutable. But it was the logic of a soldier.

Sometimes, unhappily, the pursuit of justice led only to more injustice, and the passion for order ended in chaos.

The London *Daily News* on 10 May set the tone for the day. It featured an article by Bernard Shaw.

Dillon read it. Redmond read it. More importantly, the PM read it.

Shaw's view was that the Irishmen who had been recently shot in cold blood after capture or surrender were prisoners of war. It was, therefore, wrong to slaughter them. Without their own national government, these men considered themselves occupied by a foreign power. They were only doing what Englishmen would do if England were overrun by Germany. Each one knew he would be killed if they were beaten.

> This danger only adds in the same measure to his glory in the eyes of his compatriots and of the disinterested admirers of patriotism throughout the world.
>
> It is absolutely impossible to slaughter a man in this position without making him a martyr and a hero, even though the day before the rising he may have been only a minor poet.

The Irish, he stressed, have a great tradition in these matters. In a prophetic vein, he went on:

> The military authorities and the English government must have known that they were canonizing their prisoners. I remain an Irishman, and am bound to contradict any implication that I can regard as a traitor any Irishman taken in a fight for Irish Independence against the British government, which was a fair fight in everything except the enormous odds my countrymen had to face.

While civil servants in the Foreign Office were digesting this, they received confirmation of its good sense in a second cable from the Washington Ambassador, Sir Cecil Spring-Rice.

Newspapers in the States, he reported, were saying the executions were incredibly stupid and were creating considerable alarm and discussion among the public.

That afternoon, the House of Commons was crammed to capacity. Even Ministers of the Crown could not get their friends tickets for the Visitors' Gallery.

The air was buzzing with excitement as word got round that Dillon, just back from Dublin, was to address the House.

The PM and the entire Cabinet were seated when he rose on an adjournment debate to make one of the most contentious speeches in the history of the Commons.

A straight, handsome man, he adjusted his spectacles and patted his white hair into place. He claimed to speak for the entire Nationalist Party that had worked for reconciliation and Home Rule, that had encouraged Irishmen to enlist in the British army, and had indeed given thousands to death in the war. His primary aim was to stop the senseless killings in Dublin.

His magnificent voice rang all the changes. It was, by turns, scolding, beseeching, sarcastic, belligerent.

'You are letting loose a river of blood, and, make no mistake about it, between two races who, after 300 years of hatred and strife, *we* had nearly succeeded in bringing together.

'It is the first rebellion that ever took place in Ireland when you had the majority on your side. It is the fruit of our life work. We had risked our lives a hundred times to bring about this result. We are held up to odium as traitors by those men who made this rebellion; and our lives have been in danger a hundred times during the last thirty years because we have endeavoured to reconcile the two things, and now you are washing out our whole life work in a sea of blood.'

When, he demanded, his grey eyes blazing, did Englishmen ever think of Ireland except as England's back yard?

To shouts of 'No' and 'Scandalous', and frantic waving of order papers, he went on like an avalanche:

'I say I am proud of their courage, and, if you were not so *dense* and so *stupid*, as some of you English people are, you could have had these men fighting for *you*, and they are men worth having. It is not murderers who are being executed: it is insurgents who have fought a clean fight, however misguided, and' – he glared up at the Gallery where many top-ranking officers were seated, foaming at the mouth – 'it would have been a *damned* good thing for you if *your* soldiers were able to put up as good a fight as did *these* men in Dublin.'

The Chamber echoed and re-echoed with roars of anger. Some shouted, 'What impossible people these Irish are!'

When he could make himself heard, an unrepentant Dillon compared Britain with America after the Civil War.

'When the insurrection there was over, I do not think Abraham Lincoln executed one single man, and by that one act of clemency he did an enormous amount of good for the whole country.'

The chance of reconciliation in Ireland had been tossed aside.

'One of the most horrible tragedies of the fighting was that brother met brother in the streets of Dublin.'

Yet even General Maxwell agreed that the soldiers, almost wholly Irish, had proved themselves utterly trustworthy.

A profound silence settled on the House as he outlined the Sheehy-Skeffington case. He had spoken with the man's wife and checked the story out. That quaint vegetarian, that gentle pacifist had been arrested and shot in the back by a British army captain. And Maxwell refused to arrest his murderer.

The silence that attended this revelation was shattered as Dillon spoke a final word of praise for the rebels.

'I admit they were wrong; I know they were wrong; but they fought a clean fight, and they fought with superb bravery and skill, and no act of savagery or act against the customs of war that I know of has been brought home to any leader or any organized body of insurgents.'

Dillon sat down and when the hubbub subsided, the Prime

490

Minister rose. He addressed himself, in particular, to the case of Sheehy-Skeffington.

'I confess I do not and cannot believe it. Does anyone suppose that Sir John Maxwell has any object in shielding officers and soldiers, if there be such, who have been guilty of such ungentlemanlike, such inhuman conduct? It is the last thing the British army would dream of!'

There were hear-hears, tapping of benches and murmurs of assent throughout the House. In the Visitors' Gallery, the top-brass and titled ladies exchanged approving glances.

The PM took Dillon's point about the bravery of the rebels: 'So far as the great body of insurgents is concerned I have no hesitation in saying in public they have conducted themselves with great humanity which contrasted very much to their advantage with some of the so-called civilized enemies which we are fighting in Europe. They were young men; often lads. They were misled, almost unconsciously, I believe, into this terrible business.'

. The PM had a surprise in store for the House. He himself was going to Dublin.

Carson and the Unionists were not pleased. It would look to the Sinn Feiners as if their rebelliousness was even more effective than the politicking of Nationalist politicians.

Asquith not only made immediate preparations to see for himself why the Irish administration had failed. He also said to Lord Kitchener, 'Tell Maxwell to hold his hand for a while.'

Kitchener said, 'What about the two executions fixed for tomorrow?'

'Tell him to delay them. This Sheehy-Skeffington case is most worrying.'

Kitchener, who had heard the story of the murder first-hand from Major Vane, could not but agree.

Vane was back in Dublin. He had caught the night boat and spent the morning resting in the Gresham Hotel. In the afternoon, he took a cab to Skeffy's home in Rathmines.

He had been in many a battle but this was the hardest thing he had ever had to do. Hanna had a great deal, perhaps too much, to forgive. The mere sight of khaki might make her furious.

It was a relief to find the little boy playing on his own in the front garden. The Major stood there a while watching him. Here, he sensed, was a great man in the making.

Eventually, Owen saw him and waved. So Colthurst's brutality had not soured or frightened him.

'Hello, sonny, my name is Vane,' he said. 'Francis. Like your father. I'm just back from London.'

In spite of his whiskers and plum-coloured face, the boy took to him; he liked his smile.

'Owen, how'd you like to go to the zoo sometime?'

'Oh, yes, sir.' Neither of them noticed that Hanna had come to the window. 'And after the zoo, how'd you like to join me for dinner at my hotel?'

'Yes, please, sir.'

'We'd better ask your mommie, hadn't we?' Vane took the lad by the hand. 'What would you say to a nice chicken meal?'

Owen stopped and looked up at the Major with a serious expression. 'I don't eat chicken, sir.'

'I'm sorry. Why ever not?'

'My daddy never ate meat.'

'I see.'

After a pause, Owen added, 'He doesn't even eat vegetables now.'

In New York, Mollie Monteith was growing more and more worried. Still no news from Bob. She had read the list of the dead and executed in Dublin. Among them were The O'Rahilly, Tom Clarke, Ned Daly. All friends of hers. Each day she expected to see Bob's name.

She took her two little girls and went to the office of the *Gaelic American*.

John Devoy, a crusty old bachelor, was not the best of comforters but he did his best.

Mollie said, 'I read of four men in a cab driving into a river in Killarney. Only three names appeared in the paper.' She touched her children. 'Maybe the fourth was their father.'

Devoy became edgy. 'Please, please, Mrs Monteith, don't let thoughts like that get to you.'

'But you have told me nothing.'

'All I know is that the German submarine put three of our people on the coast of Kerry early on Good Friday. I can only presume that your husband is being taken care of by the men who were supposed to have met him with a pilot

492

boat.' He stood up. 'Now, please go home, ma'am, with your little ones.'

'Where's Daddy, Mommy?' said five-year-old Vie.

'He's alive,' Mollie said fiercely. 'I know he's alive.'

At Kilmainham Hospital, Maxwell was writing a reply to Kitchener.

He could not stop coughing. He had spent long days and quite a few nights sifting the evidence against the accused. He could not get out of his head the fact that this revolt had occurred when the very existence of the Empire was under threat. Some rebels had fought without uniforms, dealt out death like reptiles and then slipped back among ordinary civilians. No wonder some atrocities on the British side had occurred. The surprising thing was there were so few.

But he had to be firm. Dublin was still smouldering and the blood of his brave boys was scarcely dry on the pavements.

It seemed that the Skeffington case was what bothered Westminster most.

He admitted: 'The officer, Colthurst, is apparently a hot-headed Irishman and on this occasion completely lost his head.'

He assured Kitchener he was under arrest and would be court-martialled.

Later, in conference with his aides, Maxwell was in a foul mood. The PM had asked him to finish off the executions speedily and then asked for a delay on McDermott and Connolly.

'Isn't that typical of politicians? Left to me, the whole damn thing would have ended at dawn this morning.'

His mood did not improve when aides told him that damage to Dublin City was estimated at £2½ million, a third of the total annual revenue for the entire country. The official casualty figure was 1,351 dead or seriously wounded. 100,000 people needed government assistance to avoid starvation.

In the light of this, Maxwell composed a Proclamation. Rather late in the day, he explained that he had felt compelled to execute the known organizers of the rising.

'It is hoped that these examples will be sufficient to act as a deterrent to intrigues, and to bring home to them that the murder of His Majesty's liege subjects, or other acts calculated to imperil the safety of the Realm will not be tolerated.'

Prince Alexander came in with a cable from Kitchener. It read: 'Unless you hear to the contrary from Mr Asquith you may carry out tomorrow the extreme sentence of death upon McDermott and Connolly.'

The General sighed. 'Alex, make the necessary arrangements.'

In Cell 59 at Kilmainham Jail, de Valera still had no confirmation of his sentence. He knew his prospects were not good.

He was reading the *Confessions* of St Augustine when an officer arrived. He stood to attention. He had been expecting this and had prepared himself. Only the thought of leaving his wife and children without support disturbed him.

The officer read out: 'The said Eamon de Valera is found guilty and sentenced to death.'

De Valera had vowed to himself he would not flinch, nor did he.

After fumbling in his pocket, the officer read from a second document. The sentence was commuted to penal servitude for life.

The prisoner was wrenched back from thoughts of bullets exploding in his belly to the realization that he was going to live, after all. The sharp switch nearly unnerved him. In spite of his madly thumping heart, he still did not flinch.

The officer turned and left, clanging the door behind him.

De Valera sat down on the stool, took up his book and read a passage he had underlined: 'Thou hast made us for Thyself, O God, and our hearts are restless till they rest in Thee.'

De Valera was a commandant. When news of his reprieve spread, there was a general sense of relief that the killings were over. At street-corners, people smiled again. There were only two rebel leaders left. Surely, even 'Bloody Maxwell' would not shoot a cripple and a wounded man.

In the Tower of London, Casement was looking better. Gertrude had visited him and brought him, apologetically, a suit off the peg.

He thanked her for what he now knew was her on-going concern. He was only afraid she might lose her teaching job because of him.

He had combed his growing beard, was recovering his majestically straight back, his distinguished appearance. If only he could get rid of those tiger-toothed lice in his hair.

It had been good talking to a friend after the long silence. He was pleased that a fund had been opened to pay for his defence, even though the outcome of the trial was a foregone conclusion.

Well versed in Irish history, he knew that hanging would be his final consecration in the eyes of his compatriots. He might not go to heaven from a British scaffold but he would certainly go from there, with shiny halo, straight into the pantheon of Irish demi-gods.

One thing still bothered him. He could not reconcile himself to the fact that loyal Irishmen had rebelled against MacNeill's express command.

Already, he was making notes for his trial.

'Loyalty,' he scribbled, 'is a sentiment, not a law. It rests on love, not on restraint. The Government of Ireland by England rests on restraint and not on law; and since it demands no love it can evoke no loyalty.'

He reflected on how the English for centuries had appropriated French territory but they never executed Frenchmen for fighting to recover it.

'They did not assassinate them by law. Judicial assassination today is reserved only for one race of the King's subjects, for Irishmen; for those who cannot forget their allegiance to Ireland.'

Gripping his imagination was the green sea-girt land of his birth. Never would he see her again. But at least he, like his Dublin comrades, could die for her.

> In Ireland alone in this twentieth century is loyalty held to be a crime. If we are to be indicted as criminals, to be shot as murderers, to be imprisoned as convicts because our offence is that we love Ireland more than we value our lives, then I know not what virtue resides in any offer of self-government held out to brave men on such terms.
>
> Self-government is our right, a thing born in us at birth; a thing no more doled out to us or withheld from us by another people than the right to life itself – than the right to feel the sun or smell the flowers, or to love our kind.
>
> It is only from the convict these things are withheld for crimes committed or proven – and Ireland, that has wronged no man, that has injured no land, that has sought no dominion over others – Ireland is treated today among the nations of the world as if she was a convicted criminal.
>
> If it be treason to fight against such an unnatural fate as this, then I am proud to be a rebel, and shall cling to my 'rebellion' with the last drop of my blood.

Casement's views were now part of orthodoxy in Ireland. Forgotten were the inconveniences of the brief rebellion. The man- and woman-in-the-street were only beginning to discover who these men were whom the British were secretly executing.

Pearse was a schoolmaster, and by all accounts a grand one. And Clarke, now, he was a tobacconist whom the English had put in solitary for year after year. And MacDonagh was a lecturer in the National University, a family man who had never been heard to utter an unkind word. Not the usual crowd of plotters and mischief-makers, but idealists like Emmet and Tone.

Presently, there was James Connolly. True, few Irish folk had ever heard of him except when priests cursed him from the altar but wasn't he a prisoner, for heaven's sake, in that godless hole, the Castle? And he loved the poor, they say, as much as bold Jim Larkin.

The sentiment was growing like a tide that the rebels were wrong, but not as wrong as the situation that made them rebel. And their shooting soldiers better armed and trained than themselves was nowhere near as bad as soldiers murdering them in cold blood without a fair trial and no chance to explain why they took up arms.

Late that Thursday afternoon, Father Aloysius was called to Connolly again.

He could not believe there would be any more executions. People were sick of them. Maxwell's Proclamations made it plain that court martials were practically over. There was Shaw's article. There was Dillon's speech in the Commons and the Prime Minister's courteous response. And Connolly was a wounded man.

Father Aloysius found him no better than before, though he seemed easier in his mind.

For reasons he could not fathom, the priest was disturbed. After the visit, he was walking through the Castle Gate when he turned on his heels. He had to know if Connolly was going to be shot or not.

He asked for Captain Stanley.

The kind young officer said, 'Don't upset yourself, Padre. The PM would not possibly permit executions pending the debate in the House this evening.'

The friar found this very sensible. Why, then, could he not shake off this grim sense of foreboding?

He was back at the friary at 7 p.m. He took supper with his

brethren and settled down in his room to pray for Connolly and his friend, McDermott.

In Kilmainham, Sean was told he was to be shot at dawn.
Immensely calm, he wrote to his brothers and sisters.

> By the time this reaches you, I will, with God's mercy, have joined in heaven my poor father and mother as well as my dear friends who have been shot during the week. They died like heroes and with God's help I will act throughout as heroic as they did.

He assured his family he had had priest friends constantly with him over the last twenty-four hours.

> I feel a happiness the like of which I never experienced in my life before. You ought to envy me. The cause for which I die has been re-baptized during the past week by blood of as good men as ever trod God's earth.

He asked them to contact his friends.

> Tell them that in my last hours I am the same Sean they always knew and that even now I can enjoy a laugh as good as ever.
> Goodbye, dear Brothers and Sisters, make no lament for me. Pray for my soul and feel a lasting pride in my death. I die that the Irish nation may live.
> God bless and guard you all and may He have mercy on my soul. Yours as ever, Sean.

At 9 o'clock, Father Aloysius's devotions were interrupted. A Brother knocked to say an officer was waiting downstairs.

By a curious twist, the bearer of bad news was Captain Stanley. He stood in the hallway, cap in hand, sad-looking, shuffling his feet.

'Just to say, Padre, your services will be required at two in the morning.'

'It's not—?'

'Sorry. I'm not allowed to say another word.'

There was no point in Father Aloysius trying to sleep. He had witnessed many painful things in the last few days. There were tales of

497

atrocity in North King Street worse even than anything he had seen. Connolly's death was just one more pointless addition to the litany.

Having finished his divine office, he remained kneeling on his prie-dieu in front of the crucified Christ which had been sprinkled with Pearse's blood and now bore his name.

At 11 p.m., Connolly was woken up. For a while, he could not grasp what they were doing to him.

An officer said, 'Sorry to disturb you, but—. Are you awake?'

Connolly yawned. 'Yes.'

'You are to be shot at dawn.'

With the return of the shrieking pain, Connolly's first reaction was, Bullets are better than morphine. Then, in full possession of his wits, he asked, 'My wife?'

'Don't worry. Your wife and daughter are being sent for.'

At midnight, McDermott had visitors. Phyllis and Mary Ryan had been driven from Drumcondra. They entered his cell to see a board at the end for a bed, a chair and, on the table, a yellow candle in a metal candlestick. The candle kept spluttering and flaring up.

He gave them both a big hug. 'Can you stay long?'

'Yes,' they said.

They sat down together on the board, Sean in the middle with an arm around each of them.

For the girls it was unreal. It was like old times when they had talked the night away.

At one in the morning, a motor ambulance drew up outside Bill O'Brien's house.

An officer said, 'A message from the Castle. James Connolly is unwell and wishes to see his wife and eldest daughter.'

Lillie believed it. James had lost a lot of blood. He had been weak, in pain and could not sleep without morphine.

But Nora knew.

Lillie asked, 'Are they going to shoot my man, sir?'

'I know absolutely nothing, ma'am.'

With the curfew still in force, Dublin was dark and deserted. O'Connell Street had a haunted look and still reeked of burning.

Nora refused to be reconciled to all those armed men on the stairs and outside the room where her father lay.

As the two women entered, Connolly turned his head, painfully.

498

'Well, Lillie, I suppose you know what this means?'

She had tried so hard to fool herself this was just another visit.

'Oh no, James,' she exclaimed, 'not that.'

He spoke of the irony of being woken up after his first natural sleep in nights. At which Lillie put her face on the bed and cried. He patted her head, her heaving shoulders. This man who had hardened his heart so often to do the task fate imposed on him was now overwhelmed with compassion. He remembered his lovely Lillie when they were young. She always wore black. So long was her dark hair that when she brushed it, it reached down to her hips and, ah, those fairy curls at the base of her neck.

She was better educated than he was; and he had relied on her in the beginning to correct his grammar and punctuation.

Dear Lillie, how much the labours of his life had cost her, and she never complained. The poverty, the endless grind to make ends meet; the feeling of never being settled anywhere for more than a few years; the nights when he had gone out and she wondered if he would come back alive; his belonging to the Union or the Rebellion, so that she was mostly left alone with a large family trying to cope; the long periods when they had to be apart, living separately abroad, even.

Most painful of all was something that happened early in their marriage when he had gone ahead to America. He went, so happy, to pick them up at Ellis Island. Too happy, for it was only when he counted them that he realized one was missing. His eldest daughter, Mona. 'Where is she?' he asked in a strangled voice. And Lillie, wide-eyed, said, 'Didn't you get my cable?' 'No!' The anguish was rising in him, so he almost screamed, 'Where is my Mona?' 'Dead, James.' And his joy, as so often in his life, turned to ashes.

The story took little telling.

One afternoon, Lillie had left Mona with a sister. Her clothes had caught alight and she was burned all over, except for her lovely head. She had taken twenty-four hours to die, conscious all the time. And he had blamed himself for not being there, for not being able to take her hand, or stroke her forehead, and tell her how much he loved her.

Whenever lately he had thought of his darling little Mona he did not feel the pain in his leg at all, nor the poison that was racing through his body.

Now a fresh sorrow: knowing Lillie would have to bear another death, his, without him being there to comfort her.

'Look, Lillie,' he said, in desperation, 'please don't cry, or you'll make me cry.'

'But your life, James.' Her words were muffled in the bed covers. 'Your beautiful life.'

He stroked her hair. 'Well, Lillie, hasn't it been a full life and isn't this a good end?'

Nora was crying, too. Her father saw how his daughter's fierce dark eyes were darker still with mourning. He pleaded with her, 'Don't *you* cry, there's nothing to cry about.'

'I won't cry, Papa.'

He patted her hand. 'That's my brave girl.'

The officer looked at his watch. 'Five more minutes.'

Lillie nearly passed out. Sister Sullivan brought a glass of water to revive her.

Connolly tried to clasp his wife in his arms, but he could only lift his head and shoulders a little. So the couple held hands until the officer made them jump with 'Time's up.'

Connolly said softly, 'Goodbye, Lillie,' but her head was so heavy she could not raise it off the bed. Nora tried to lift her but even she couldn't. The Sister took Lillie by the shoulder and helped her in a daze out of the room.

Nora was at the door when her father, his face screwed up with pain and longing, beckoned to her. She ran back and he put his arms round her and pulled her to him and hugged her. In her ear, as though it were a prophecy certain to be fulfilled, he whispered, 'Don't be too disappointed, Nora. We shall rise again.'

Proudly, without tears, she backed away and blew him a kiss as the officer closed the door.

For the first and only time, James Connolly, tough Union boss, rugged campaigner, military Commander of the Dublin Division of the Republican army, broke down and cried.

Outside, Lillie moaned, 'I forgot to take a lock of his hair,' and Sister Sullivan promised to send her one in the morning.

After swathing Connolly's leg with bandages to cushion it for the journey to the jail, she snipped a lock of his hair and put it in an envelope with a note.

'Dear Mrs Connolly, Enclosed you will find that which you asked me to get for you last night. I offer you my sincere sympathy in your great trouble.'

The ambulance took Lillie and Nora home through silent streets to a silent house. All the children were abed, not knowing what was happening.

The ambulance went on to Church Street where it picked up Fathers Aloysius and Sebastian and drove them to the Castle.

Father Aloysius went up, heard Connolly's confession and gave him Holy Communion.

The officer said, 'You'll have to leave now, Padre. The prisoner has to be fed.'

The friar, shattered by this paradox, joined his confrère in the Castle Yard. There was a cold wind blowing.

For three hours, Sean and the Ryan sisters had talked and laughed without stop about everything: friends and foes, those in the rising and those who were not. They were so high-spirited, the soldier on guard was puzzled.

Their revels ended when an officer put his head round the door and nodded.

Sean wanted to send his friends a small souvenir. He asked the officer if, as a last wish, he might borrow a penknife. With it, he scratched on the inside of his cigarette case, 'Sean McD 12–5–16.'

'That,' he said, 'is for my brother, Jim.'

The girls picked a few pennies from their purses. Sean scratched on them and on the buttons of his coat – 'I've no more use for them,' he laughed – his initials, 'S McD.'

'Still not enough for all my friends.'

At 3 a.m., the Chaplain, Father McCarthy, came. The girls jumped up. It suddenly hit them that in minutes, dear, irrepressible Sean would be dead. Phyllis kissed him, then Mary held him very close, trying to imprint on her mind what his body felt like, every curve and muscle of it.

His parting words were, 'We never thought it would end like this, that this would be the end.'

When the girls had gone, Father McCarthy gave him the sacraments.

At 3.30 a.m., Sean penned his last defiant letter:

> I, Sean Mac Diarmada, before paying the penalty of death for my love of Ireland, and abhorrence of her slavery, desire to make known to all my fellow-countrymen that I die, as I have lived, bearing no malice to any man, and in perfect peace with Almighty God.
>
> The principles for which I give my life are so sacred that I now walk to my death in the most calm and collected manner. I meet death for Ireland's cause as I have worked

501

for the same cause all my life. I have asked the Rev E. McCarthy who has prepared me to meet my God and who has given me courage to face the ordeal I am about to undergo, to convey this message to my fellow-countrymen. God save Ireland. Sean Mac Diarmada.

In the Castle, Connolly was carried from his room on a stretcher into the State Corridor, on to the Battleaxe Landing and down the Grand Staircase.

His swaying upturned gaze took in the beauty of murals, ceilings and chandeliers, the doric columns of the halls. It was odd that his first home was in an Edinburgh slum and his last the most regal edifice in Ireland.

In the Upper Yard, he was put in an ambulance. The two friars and his surgeon friend, Tobin, went with him.

Father Aloysius, so young and gentle, on that brief, rocky drive through the silent streets could hardly believe this cruel thing was happening.

He found himself saying, over and over, 'No, no, no, no, *no.*'

At the jail, Sean, accompanied by the Chaplain, limped his way to the Stonebreakers' Yard.

The time was 3.45 a.m.

At Bill O'Brien's house, Lillie and Nora were on their knees at a window facing east. With the first rays of the rising sun, as if even in sleep a voice spoke to them, the children filed into the room, rubbing their eyes. Ina and Roddy and Agna and Aideen and Moira and even little Fiona who was only seven.

'What's up, Mommy?' 'Why aren't you undressed?'

Lillie tried to gather them all in her arms at once.

'It's Daddy,' said Nora.

Several horrified voices said at once, 'They're not going to kill our Daddy!'

Their father's ambulance was timed with military precision to arrive as soon as McDermott's body was put on a stretcher with a blanket over him and borne away in the early light.

Connolly was the only one of the rebel leaders not to be imprisoned in Kilmainham. The ambulance bringing him backed into the yard and dipped its headlights as if in mourning. In

502

the opaline gold-edged dawn even black buildings seemed transparent.

Surgeon Tobin, his white hair ruffled by the wind, supervised as Connolly was taken out and placed in a chair. There was a tender irony in the way the bearers were solicitous for his mummified leg.

Tobin was wondering, If I had amputated, would they still have had the nerve to shoot him?

Connolly, a forlorn figure, was propped up in the chair and roped to the back to prevent him falling off. He looked neat and tidy in his new pyjamas.

As he was being blindfolded, Father Aloysius was thinking how brave and cool he was.

To save the condemned man unnecessary pain, he was to be shot near the gate where he had entered. The other rebels had been executed at the opposite end of the yard.

The firing squad was marched in and stood to attention. Some were disturbed to see the condition of the man they were about to shoot.

Father Aloysius, sympathetic even to the plight of the young soldiers, said to Connolly, 'Will you pray for these men who are about to shoot you?'

He answered, 'I will say a prayer for all brave men who do their duty.'

Father Aloysius thought that chimed in perfectly with the Lord's own prayer, 'Father, forgive them, for they know not what they do.' It reinforced his feeling that this was not an end but a consummation.

The priests took their places behind the firing squad.

The Chaplain, who had just given the last rites to McDermott, said, 'Don't worry, Father, I will do the anointing afterwards.'

His thumb was still moist with blood and holy oil.

It depressed the young friar to think that, having shot a cripple, they were about to kill a badly wounded man and a champion of God's poor.

The priests stood side by side as Connolly seemed to lift himself a little and straighten in preparation for the end.

The firing squad aimed and fired.

Connolly slumped in the chair against the ropes, his body twitching.

The officer next to the priests stepped forward, his pistol raised.

That final bullet exploding in Connolly's brain broke the last of Ireland's chains.

POSTSCRIPT

What Happened Next

IRELAND: In 1917, all the Irish prisoners held on mainland Britain were released.

Ireland was still a long way from achieving autonomy. The bitter War of Independence lasted from 1919 to 1921 with massacres on both the British and the Irish sides. This was followed by Civil War which ended in 1923.

It was not until 1949 that Dail Eireann, the Irish Parliament, finally declared Ireland to be a Republic and withdrew from the British Commonwealth.

Birrell, Augustine: In 1929, he was entertained by Nathan for his seventy-ninth birthday. That year, the Senate of the University of Ireland which he founded made him a Doctor of Literature. The Irish Sea was too rough for him, so the degree was given him *in absentia*. He died aged eighty-four.

Blackwood, Lord Basil: He got his wish and joined the Grenadier Guards. He was killed before the 3rd Battle of Ypres on 3 July 1917.

Bowen-Colthurst, Captain: Enquiry into the death of Sheehy-Skeffington led to his court martial, but, on the evidence of two Dublin doctors, he was found to be insane. He was sentenced to stay in Broadmoor 'at the King's Pleasure'. Released after twenty months, he emigrated to Canada where he received a military pension.

Brugha, Cathal: He survived the rising, only to be shot dead by fellow Irishmen in the Civil War.

Casement, Roger: During his trial, fragments of his Black Diaries were circulated as part of a smear campaign against him. News of them reached influential people, including the American President, effectively warning them not to intercede on his behalf. He was hanged in Pentonville Prison, London, on 3 August 1916. On 23 February 1965, his remains were returned to Ireland where he was given a funeral, the like of which had not been seen since that of O'Donovan Rossa. A sick and jaundiced President de Valera, aged eighty-two, insisted on attending with head uncovered, in spite of the sleet and snow, and delivered the oration.

Childers, Erskine: In the Irish Civil War, he joined the Republican Army. Captured by the Free State soldiers, he was court-martialled and executed at Beggars Bush Barracks on 24 November 1922. He first shook hands with every member of the firing squad. His son, also called Erskine, was to become President of Ireland.

Clarke, Kathleen: She lived to a great age, becoming a Senator in the Irish Parliament and twice Lord Mayor of Dublin.

Collins, Michael: In the Civil War, he was Commander-in-Chief of the Free State forces. He was killed in an ambush in County Cork on 22 September 1922.

de Valera, Eamon: He formed his own Fianna Fail party in 1926. He became Prime Minister in 1932 and President of Ireland in 1957. He died aged ninety-two in 1975.

Kilmainham Jail: in 1920, the jail housed Irish Republican Army prisoners. When Civil War broke out in 1922, women were imprisoned there, including Grace Plunkett. On 17 November, the first executions of the Civil War took place there. The last political prisoner, in 1923, was Eamon de Valera. It was finally closed in 1924. Today it is a National Museum.

MacBride, Sean: the son of Major MacBride returned to Ireland and fought on the Republican side in the Civil War. He became Ireland's Foreign Minister (1948–51) and in 1974 received the Nobel Peace Prize.

McDonagh, Muriel: Thomas's widow was drowned in a swimming accident the year after the rising.

MacNeill, John: Court-martialled by the British on 24 May 1916 and sentenced to life imprisonment, he was released in 1917. In 1919, he became Minister of Finance in the First Dail, the Irish Parliament. He retired from politics in 1927 and died in 1945.

Markievicz, Constance: Released after a year of her life term, she was often in prison. She became a Catholic. In 1918, she was the first woman to be elected to the British House of Commons, though she never took her seat. She was on the Republican side in the Civil War and later in de Valera's Cabinet. She died by choice among the poor in a public ward of Sir Patrick Dun's Hospital in Dublin in 1927. Many thousands marched with her funeral cortège to burial at Glasnevin.

Mallin, Michael: His son, Joseph, did become a priest. His unborn child was a girl and, as he had requested, was christened Maura (an Irish form of Mary).

Mellowes, Liam: He survived the Rising which he led in Galway. He was on the Republican side in the Civil War and was executed by firing squad in Mountjoy Prison in 1922.

Monteith, Robert: He remained at large after the Rising and reached America in December 1916. He died on 18 February 1956, the same day as Judge Humphreys who sentenced Casement to death. Buried with him was a small, sea-stained tricolour found on Casement when he was arrested.

Nathan, Sir Matthew: Though he never returned to Ireland, he was reinstated to become, first, Secretary of the War Pensions Department and, later, Governor of Queensland and Chancellor of its University. He was Vice-President of the Royal Geographical Society from 1929–32. He died in England in 1939.

Pearse, Margaret: Pearse's elder sister helped Mrs Pearse to continue, with difficulties, St Enda's which they bought in 1920. She became an Irish Senator, and when she died in 1932, the school was turned into a National Museum to commemorate Patrick Pearse, first President of the Republic.

Plunkett, Grace: After her brief marriage to Joe, she never remarried. She was on the Republican side during the Civil War when, ironically, she was herself imprisoned in Kilmainham Jail.

Sheehy-Skeffington, Hanna: She was asked by Asquith at 10 Downing Street if she would forego an enquiry into her husband's death, accepting £10,000 compensation instead. He said to her: 'Nothing we can do can bring your husband back; you have a boy to educate; this is wartime and the prestige of the Army must be upheld.' Relatives of others murdered with her husband accepted. Hanna refused.

Sheehy-Skeffington, Owen: Skeffy's son became a Senator and a distinguished French scholar, without any rancour towards the British.

Shephard, Gordon: In 1917, aged thirty-two, he became the youngest Brigadier-General in the British army. He won the MC, DSO, Chevalier of the Legion of Honour. He died on 19 January 1918, when his plane crashed near Bailleul.

Stack, Austin: His sentence of death was commuted to twenty years hard labour but he was released under the amnesty of 1917. He went on five hunger strikes, under the British and during the Civil War. On the fourth of them, he was elected as Dail Deputy for Kerry. He married in 1925 and four years later died, aged forty-nine, chiefly of ulcers caused by his hunger strikes.

Wimborne, Lord: After Maxwell left Ireland, he was recalled for a time as Viceroy to Dublin and dubbed by the locals 'The Rebounder'. He was forced to resign over some personal misadventure in 1918 and was replaced by Sir John French. He died in 1939.

Wilson, Captain Lee: In 1920, Michael Collins ordered his execution. It was done.

Two final footnotes:
Nelson's Pillar: At 1.32 in the morning of Tuesday 8 March 1966, the fiftieth anniversary of the rising, it was blown up by persons officially unknown but quite certainly the IRA.

The *Asgard*, which brought arms into Howth: It now rests in Kilmainham Jail next to the Stonebreakers' Yard where the leaders of the Easter Rising were shot.

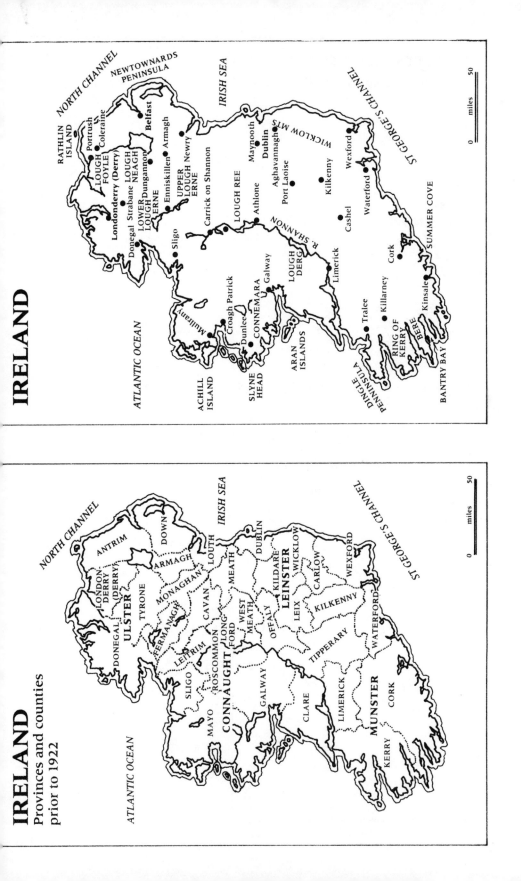

IRELAND

Provinces and counties prior to 1922

IRELAND

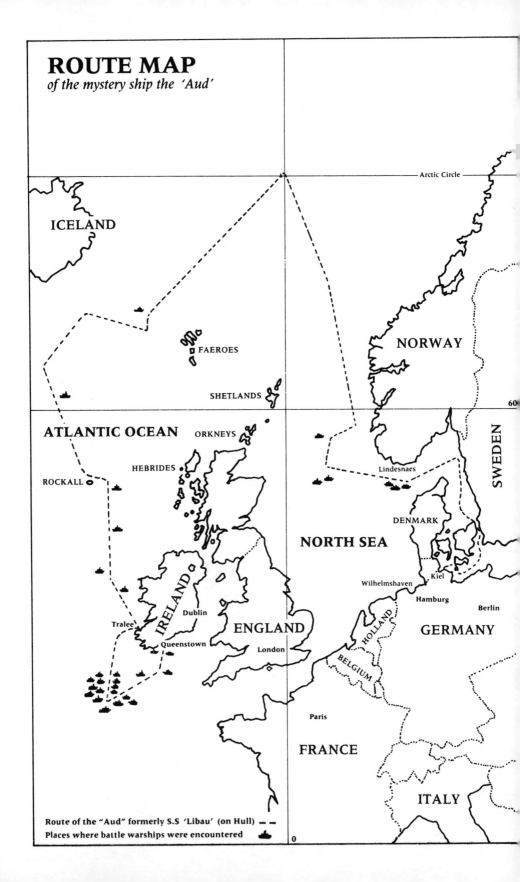

ROUTE MAP
of the mystery ship the 'Aud'

Arctic Circle

ICELAND

NORWAY

FAEROES

SHETLANDS

60

ATLANTIC OCEAN   ORKNEYS

HEBRIDES

ROCKALL

Lindesnaes

SWEDEN

DENMARK

NORTH SEA

Kiel

Wilhelmshaven

IRELAND

Dublin

Hamburg

Berlin

Tralee

ENGLAND

HOLLAND

GERMANY

Queenstown

London

BELGIUM

Paris

FRANCE

ITALY

Route of the "Aud" formerly S.S 'Libau' (on Hull) – –
Places where battle warships were encountered

0

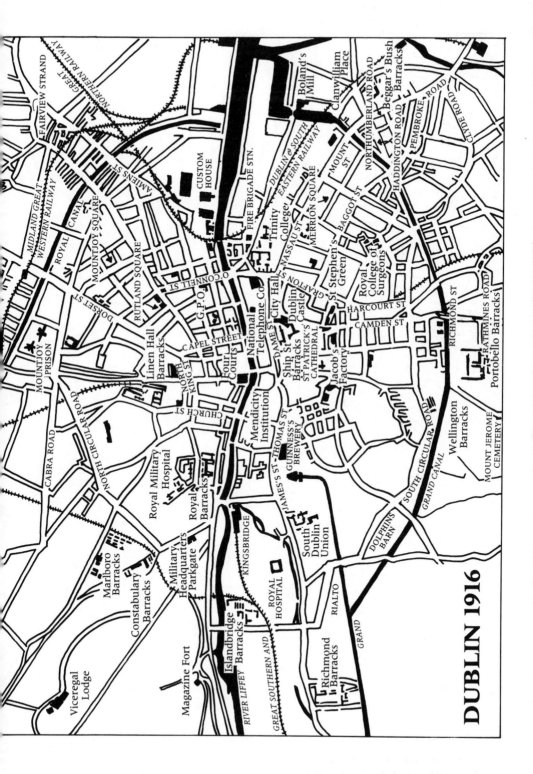

DUBLIN 1916

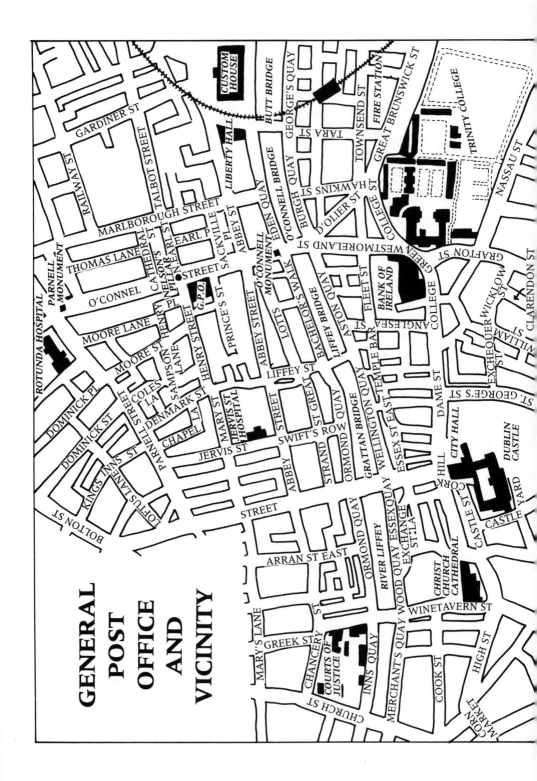

GENERAL POST OFFICE AND VICINITY

SELECT BIBLIOGRAPHY

Arthur, Sir George *The Life of Lord Kitchener*, London, 1920.
    General Sir John Maxwell, London, 1932.
Asquith, H. H. *Letters to Venetia Stanley*, Oxford, 1982.
Asquith, Margot *Autobiography*, London, 1936.
Balfour, Michael *The Kaiser and His Times*, London, 1966.
Bayly, Admiral Sir Lewis *Pull Together!*, London, 1939.
Bernstorff, Graf von *My Three Years in America*, New York, 1920.
    Memoirs, New York, 1936.
Berresford Ellis, P. (ed.) *James Connolly: Selected Writings*, London, 1973.
Bethmann-Hollweg, Theobald von *Reflections on the World War*, 2 vols., London, 1920.
Birkenhead, 1st Earl of *Contemporary Personalities*, London, 1924.
Birrell, Augustine *Things Past Redress*, London, 1937.
Bourke, Marcus *The O'Rahilly*, Tralee, 1967.
Bülow, Bernhard Fürst von *Memoirs 1910–19*, 4 vols., Boston, 1931–2.
Caulfield, Max *The Easter Rebellion*, London, 1965.
Churchill, Winston Spencer *The World Crisis*, 4 vols., London, 1960.
Clarke, Thomas J. *Glimpses of an Irish Felon's Prison Life*, Dublin, 1982.
Coffey, T. M. *Agony at Easter*, New York, 1969.
Collins, James *Life in Old Dublin*, Dublin, 1913.
Connolly, James *Labour, Nationality and Religion*, Dublin, 1910.
    Labour in Irish History, Dublin, 1910.
    The Reconquest of Ireland, Dublin, 1915.
Connolly O'Brien, Nora *The Irish Rebellion of 1916, or The Unbroken Tradition*, New York, 1918.
    Portrait of a Rebel Father, Dublin, 1935.
Craig, Maurice *Dublin 1660–1860*, Dublin, 1980.
Cronin, Sean *Young Connolly*, Dublin, 1983.
Cruise O'Brien, Conor (ed.) *The Shaping of Modern Ireland*, London, 1960.

States of Ireland, New York, 1972.

Dangerfield, George *The Damnable Question*, London, 1977.

Deacon, Richard *A History of the British Secret Service*, London, 1982.

de Beaufort, J. M. *Behind the German Veil*, London, 1917.

de Courcy Ireland, John *The Sea and the Easter Rising, 1916*, Dublin, 1966.

Desmond Williams, T. (ed.) *The Irish Struggle, 1913–26*, London, 1966.

Devoy, John *Recollections of an Irish Rebel*, New York, 1929; Dublin, 1969.

    Post Bag, vol. 2, Dublin, 1952.

Documents Relative to the Sinn Fein Movement, London, 1921.

Dubhgaill, M. *Insurrection Fires at Eastertide*, Cork, 1966.

Dudley Edwards, Ruth *Patrick Pearse: The Triumph of Failure*, New York, 1978.

Dudley Edwards, Owen *The Mind of an Activist – James Connolly*, Dublin, 1971.

Ervine, St John *Craigavon, Ulsterman*, London, 1949.

Figgis, Darrell *Recollections of the Irish War*, London, 1927.

Fingal, Countess of *Seventy Years Young*, Dublin, 1943.

Fitzgibbon, Desmond *Memoirs, 1913–16*, London, 1968.

Fitzpatrick, Samuel A. S. *Dublin, a Historical and Topographical Account of the City*, London, 1907.

Fox, R. M. *Rebel Irishwomen*, Dublin, n.d.

French, Gerald *The Life of Field-Marshal Sir John French*, London, 1931.

Fuller, J. F. C. *The Decisive Battles of the Western World*, vol. 2, London, 1975.

Gaughan, J. Anthony *Austin Stack, Portrait of a Separatist*, Dublin, 1977.

Gerard, James *My Four Years in Germany*, New York, 1917.

    Face to Face with Kaiserism, New York, 1918.

Gibbon, Monk *Inglorious Soldier*, London, 1968.

Grant, N. F. (ed.) *The Kaiser's Letters to the Tsar*, London, 1920.

Greaves, C. Desmond *The Life and Times of James Connolly*, London, 1986.

Guedalla, Philip *The Hundred Years*, London, 1939.

Gwynn, Denis *The Life and Death of Roger Casement*, London, 1931.

    The Life of John Redmond, London, 1932.

The History of Partition, 1912-25, Dublin, 1947.

Gwynn, Stephen (ed.) *The Letters and Friendships of Sir Cecil Arthur Spring-Rice*, Boston, 1929.

Hachey, T. E. *Britain and Irish Separatism, 1867–1922*, Chicago, 1977.

Headlam, J. W. *The History of Twelve Days, July 24 to August 4 1914*, London, 1915.

The German Chancellor and the Outbreak of War, London, 1917.

Headlam, Maurice *Irish Reminiscences*, London, 1947.

Healy, T. M. *Letters and Leaders of My Day*, London, 1928.

Henry, O. F. M., Cap (ed.) *The Capuchin Annual*, Dublin, 1966.

Hobson, Bulmer *A Short History of the Irish Volunteers*, Dublin, 1918.

Ireland Yesterday and Tomorrow, Tralee, 1968.

Hochlin, A. A. & M. *The Last Voyage of the Lusitania*, New York, 1956.

Holloway, Joseph *Memoirs of the Abbey Theatre*, London, 1967.

Holt, Edgar *Protest in Arms: The Irish Troubles, 1916–23*, London, 1960.

House, Colonel G. E. *Intimate Papers*, New York, 1926.

Hoy, H. C. *40 O.B. or How the War Was Won*, London, 1932.

Hyde, H. Montgomery *Roger Casement*, London, 1960.

Carson, London, 1974.

Inglis, Brian *Roger Casement*, London, 1973.

Jackson, T. A. *Ireland Her Own*, London & New York, 1971.

James, Sir William *The Eyes of the Navy*, London, 1955. Published in New York, 1956 as *The Code Breakers of Room 40*

Jenkins, Roy *Asquith*, London, 1964.

Joll, James *Europe since 1870*, London, 1973.

Jones, F. P. *History of the Sinn Fein Movement and the Irish Rebellion*, New York, 1919.

Kee, Robert *The Green Flag, Vol. 2, The Bold Fenian Men*, London, 1987.

Ireland: A History, London, 1980.

King, Clifford *The Orange and the Green*, London, 1967.

Kurenberg, Joachim von *The Kaiser* (Tr. of *War Alles Falsch?*) London, 1954.

Leask, H. G. *Dublin Castle*, Stationery Office, n.d.

Le Roux, Louis *Patrick H. Pearse*, Tr. Ryan, D. Dublin, 1932.

Tom Clarke and the Irish Freedom Movement, Tr. Ryan, D. Dublin, 1936.

Longford, Earl of, & O'Neill, T. P. *Eamon de Valera*, London, 1974.

Ludwig, Emil *The Germans*, London, 1942.

Lynch, Diamuird *The IRB and the 1916 Insurrection*, Cork, 1957.

Lynch, Florence Monteith *The Mystery Man of Banna Strand*, New York, 1959.

Lyons, F. S. L. *John Dillon: a Biography*, London, 1968.
  Ireland Since the Famine, London, 1973.

Macardle, Dorothy *The Irish Republic*, London, 1968.

McCann, John *War By the Irish*, Tralee, 1946.

McHugh, Roger (ed.) *Dublin 1916*, London, 1966.

MacLochlainn, Piaras *Last Words*, Dublin, 1971.

MacColl, Rene *Roger Casement*, London, 1956.

McDowell, R. B. *The Irish Administration, 1801–1914*, London, 1964.

Magnus, P. *Kitchener*, London, 1958.

Markievicz, Countess *Prison Letters*, London, 1987.

Marjoribanks, E. and Colvin, I. *Life of Lord Carson*, 3 vols., London, 1924.

Marreco, Anne *The Rebel Countess*, London, 1967.

Martin, F. X. (ed.) 'Eoin MacNeill on the 1916 Rising', *Irish Historical Studies*, Dublin, 12 March 1961.
  The Irish Volunteers, 1913–15, Dublin, 1963.
  (ed.) *The Howth Gun-Running, 1914*, Dublin, 1964.
  (ed.) *The Easter Rising of 1916 and University College Dublin*, Dublin, 1966.
  (ed.) *Leaders and Men of the Easter Rising: Dublin 1916*, Dublin, 1967.

Mackenna, Stephen *Journal and Letters*, (ed. Dodd, E. R.), London, 1936.

Midleton, Earl of *Ireland – Dupe or Heroine?*, London, 1932.

Mitchel, John *Jail Journal*, Dublin, 1982.

Mitchell, A. & O'Snodaigh, P. (eds.) *Irish Political Documents 1916–49*, Dublin, 1985.

Mooney, Michael M. *The Hindenburg*, London, 1972.

Monteith, Robert *Casement's Last Adventure*, Chicago, 1932; Dublin, 1953.

Moody, T. W. *The Fenian Movement*, Cork, 1968.

Morgan, Austen *James Connolly, A Political Biography*, Manchester, 1980.

Nicholson, Harold *King George the Fifth*, London, 1952.

Norman, Diana *Terrible Beauty: A Life of Constance Markievicz*, Dublin, 1987.

Norway, Mrs Hamilton *The Sinn Fein Rebellion As I Saw It*, London, 1916.

Nowlan, K. B. (ed.) *The Making of 1916*, Dublin, 1969.

O'Broin, L. *Dublin Castle & the 1916 Rising*, London, 1966.
   The Chief Secretary: Augustine Birrell in Ireland, London, 1970.

O'Casey, Sean *Autobiographies* vol. 1 & 2, London, 1980.

O'Connor, Ulick *A Terrible Beauty is Born*, London, 1985.

O'Dulaing, Donnacha *Voices of Ireland*, Dublin, 1984.

O'Faolain, Sean *Constance Markievicz*, London, 1967.

O'Kelly, J. J. *A Trinity of Martyrs*, Dublin, n.d.

O'Hegarty, P. S. *History of Ireland Under the Union, 1801–1922*, London, 1952.

O'Higgins, Brian *The Soldier's Story of Easter Week*, Dublin, 1926.

Papen, Franz von *Memoirs*, London, 1932.

Pearse, Mary Brigid *The Home Life of Padraig Pearse*, Cork, 1979.

Pearse, Patrick *Collected Works*, (ed. Desmond Ryan), Dublin, 1917–22.

Ransom, Bernard *Connolly's Marxism*, London, 1980.

Regan, John X. *What Made Ireland Sinn Fein*, Boston, 1921.

Rintelen von Kleist, Franz *The Dark Invader*, London, 1933.

Robbins, Frank *Under the Starry Plough*, Dublin, 1977.

Ryan, Desmond, *James Connolly*, London, 1924.
   The Phoenix Flame, London, 1937.
   The Rising, Dublin, 1949.
   Labour and Easterweek, Dublin, 1949.

St John Gaffney, Thomas *Breaking the Silence* , New York, 1930.

St John Gogarty, Oliver *Sackville Street and Other Stories*, London, 1988.

Sawyer, Roger *Casement, The Flawed Hero*, London, 1984.

Sellwood, A. V. *The Red-Gold Flame*, London, 1966.

Skinnider, Margaret *Doing My Bit For Ireland*, New York, 1917.

Shannon, Martin *Sixteen Roads to Golgotha*, Dublin, 1965.

Singleton-Gates, Peter *The Black Diaries*, London, 1959.

Spindler, Karl *The Mystery of the Casement Ship*, Berlin, 1931.

Stephens, James *The Insurrection in Dublin*, London, 1978.

Stewart, A. J. Q. *Edward Carson*, Dublin, 1981.

Tansil, Charles Callan *America and the Fight for Irish Freedom: 1866–1922*, New York, 1957.

Thomson, Basil *Queer People*, London, 1930.

Thomson, David *Europe Since Napoleon*, London, 1981.

Tierney, Michael *Eoin MacNeill, Scholar and Man of Action 1867–1945*, Oxford, 1980.

Tuchman, Barbara *The Zimmerman Telegram*, New York, 1958.

Vane, Sir Francis Fletcher *Agin the Governments*, London, 1929.

Van Voris, Jacqueline *Constance de Markievicz*, Massachusetts, 1916.

Wilkinson, Burke *The Zeal of the Convert*, Buckinghamshire, England, 1978.

Wilhelm II, Ex-Kaiser *My Memoirs*, London & New York, 1922.

Young, George and Kenworthy, J. M. *Freedom of the Seas*, New York, 1929.

Younger, Calton *A State of Disunion*, London, 1972.

INDEX

521

527

529

MacNeill, John *cont.*
  Easter Sunday 'manoeuvres',
    approves 123
  imprisonment 418
  IRB's manipulation of 43, 56,
    150, 151, 162, 169, 185
  Irish Volunteer 90
  Irish Volunteers, role in 24,
    25, 62, 91, 112
  'Castle document', forging of
    100, 109, 139, 168, 213
  Sunday Independent, notice
    in 219, 223, 226
  surveillance of 59
  trial 506
MacNeill, Niall 418
Maconchy, Colonel 323-4, 329,
  332, 334, 335
Magdeburg 39, 47, 54
Mahoney, Captain George 310,
  319, 345, 351, 361, 365, 369
Mallin, Michael
  Citizen Army, role in 79, 96,
    98, 142, 232
  description 45
  Easter rising, role in 250,
    259, 265, 266, 283-4, 303-4,
    315, 337, 342, 387, 389,
    393-4, 395
  execution 507
  illness 186-7
  imprisonment 396, 465,
    468-70, 471-2
  trial 456-7, 467
Malone, Michael 318, 319,
  327, 329
Manahan, Liam 161
Markievicz, Count Casimir 79
Markievicz, Countess
  Constance (Gore-Booth)
  Citizen Army, role in

  78-80, 96, 118-19, 142,
    166, 232
  Connolly, James, and 46,
    78-80, 98, 145
  Easter rising, role in 256,
    265-6, 275, 279, 283, 296-7,
    303-4, 315, 324, 337, 342,
    351, 387, 389, 393-4, 394-5
  imprisonment 396, 409, 432,
    459, 506-7
  trial 458, 465
Maunsell, Major Arthur 274
Maxwell, General Sir John
  Grenfell
  Birrell, Augustine, and 355
  Bowen-Colthurst, Captain,
    and 494, 493-4
  Cork, problems in 414
  description 352-4, 487
  despatched to Ireland
    336-7, 340
  Dillon, John, and 418,
    440-2, 480
  Easter rising, collapse of 3-4,
    8, 385, 407, 487-8
  executions, of rebels, 440-2,
    458-9, 464, 491
  Pearse, Patrick, and 380
  Wimborne, Lord, and 355
Melinn, Joe 185, 199, 203
Mellowes, Liam 113, 507
Mendicity Institute 248, 258,
  273, 275, 280, 322-3
Meyer, Richard 52, 61, 130
Military Council
  see Irish Volunteers
Mitchell, John 76, 391
Mjolnir 60
Molloy, Michael 229
Moloney, Helena 238, 256,
  276, 302